PERSONAL FINANCE

SECOND EDITION

PERSONAL FINANCE

E. Thomas Garman
Virginia Polytechnic Institute and State University

Raymond E. Forgue
University of Kentucky

HOUGHTON MIFFLIN COMPANY *Boston*

Dallas   Geneva, Illinois   Palo Alto   Princeton, New Jersey

Photography on cover, part openers, and facing title page: Martin Paul Studio, Boston, Mass.

Printed in the U.S.A.

Library of Congress Catalog Card Number: 87-80112

ISBN: 0-395-38102-9
ABCDEFGHIJ-RM-9543210-8987

Contents

CHAPTER 3

Budgeting 52

PART TWO

Money Management

CHAPTER 4

Financial Services and Cash Management 98

CHAPTER 5

Credit Use and Credit Cards 141

CHAPTER 6

Borrowing 164

CHAPTER 7

Managing Taxes 193

PART THREE

Managing Expenditures

CHAPTER 8

Some Major Expenditures 236

CHAPTER 9

The Housing Expenditure 258

CHAPTER 16

Investing in Bonds 493

CHAPTER 17

Buying and Selling Securities 515

CHAPTER 18

Mutual Funds as an Investment 561

CHAPTER 19

Investing in Real Estate 593

CHAPTER 20

High-risk Investments 616

Preface

The 1980s have brought individuals the benefits of many new savings and investment options, but making financial decisions has become more complex. It is much more difficult to manage finances today and avoid financial pitfalls than it was just ten or fifteen years ago. A solid understanding of the concepts and principles of personal finance is therefore absolutely vital. Accordingly, we believe it is essential to provide more than a simplistic approach to personal finance.

We have approached the subject from the perspective of a mature person who will apply and use many of the specific personal finance concepts and principles: in financial planning, budgeting, cash management, credit management, taxes, major expenditures, income and asset protection, investment planning, and retirement and estate planning. We present the material in a way that will encourage readers to learn more about financial planning and to learn more about how to manage finance effectively and successfully.

Two broad goals underlay our efforts in writing *Personal Finance:* to help students develop competence, and to help them develop confidence.

To develop competence in the subject of personal finance, the reader must be provided wide scope. We have worked to make this the most comprehensive textbook available, including all traditional topics and some of particular importance (such as high-risk investments and investing in real estate). In addition, virtually all data in tables and illustrations are current through the summer of 1987. To help the reader become a life-long competent manager of personal finances, we take a "how-to" approach, explaining, for example, how to manage cash, reduce income taxes, select an insurance agent, select a stockbroker, choose a mutual fund, and calculate how large a home mortgage loan can be afforded. We outline step-by-step procedures for the more complex financial activities, such as developing a total financial plan, planning and reconciling a twelve-month budget, and determining how much life insurance is needed. Moreover, we aim to help the reader plan for a successful financial future—which is an increasingly complex task in a continually evolving financial marketplace.

To develop confidence in the subject of personal finance, the reader needs to be led *through,* not simply *to,* the material. We aim to acquaint the reader with the subject matter logically and to offer no unanticipated "surprises." Assuming that most students in personal finance have little background in finance, economics, and mathematics, we have provided the underpinning knowledge when necessary. Numerical examples are always explained parenthetically, and we have endeavored to discuss the benefits and costs of different personal finance decisions. Key words and concepts—which are printed in bold, color type—are clearly and completely defined when they first occur and also in later chapters, in case the chapters are read out of sequence.

Throughout the text are over two hundred tables, charts, and illustrations, including many facsimiles of forms that are used in personal finance, such as checks, cash management account statements, credit and insurance applications, and portions of tax tables. Both beginning- and end-of-chapter pedagogical materials are designed to develop confidence in the subject of personal finance.

Major Changes in the Second Edition

We have thoroughly enjoyed the challenge of updating and revising *Personal Finance.* The first edition was popular with students because of the informal writing style, and with instructors because it was so readable that the students came to class prepared. We have again aimed to keep the narrative conversational and yet clear and concise.

Responding to the comments and suggestions of both users and nonusers, we made major revisions in topical treatment, organization and content, and pedagogy.

Topical Treatment To keep pace with changes in the financial services industry, we have added emphasis on a number of current topics, such as zero coupon bonds, universal life insurance, annuities, creative home financing, new regulations on individual retirement accounts, salary reduction retirement planning, personal financial decisions facing dual-earner households, renting vacation homes, variable-interest credit cards, home-equity credit line loans, dividend reinvestment plans, 12b-1 hidden fees on no-load mutual funds, and interest-rate-sensitive life insurance.

Organization and Content We have held close to the successful format of the first edition, with two major changes. Our new Chapter 4, "Financial Services and Cash Management," was expanded to incorporate the first-edition chapter on savings, as well as to add a great deal of new material. In addition, we resequenced the insurance chapters, so that Chapter 13, "Life Insurance," now immediately precedes the investment chapters.

Careful readers will note changes in every chapter. The following chapters underwent substantial revision:

Chapter 2, "Financial Planning and Recordkeeping"—extensive clarifications on the components of financial statements

Chapter 3, "Budgeting"—new sections illustrating financial plans and using a revolving savings fund

Chapter 4, "Financial Services and Cash Management"—descriptions of the changing financial services industry and the new providers of financial services

Chapter 7, "Managing Taxes"—completely revised and updated to reflect tax reform

Chapter 12, "Health Insurance"—a new section on disability income insurance

Chapter 13, "Life Insurance"—a special emphasis on interest-rate-sensitive life insurance

Chapter 17, "Buying and Selling Securities"—new sections on calculating a stock's potential total return and on illustrating diversified portfolios of investors

In addition, tax reform necessitated substantive changes to Chapter 19, "Investing in Real Estate," Chapter 21, "Social Security and Other Retirement Plans," and Chapter 22, "Estate Planning."

Appendix A now has over two dozen key illustrations of how to use the present and future value tables. Appendix B thoroughly explicates how to use the indexing method to calculate Social Security benefits. Appendix C offers a summary list of all the major concepts in *Personal Finance*.

Pedagogy   We have added some new learning aids and made substantial revisions to other pedagogy.

"Modern Money Management"—This new feature, a continuing case study, appears at the end of each chapter beginning with Chapter 2. In each "installment," we examine the challenging, true-to-life financial decisions faced by a young married couple, Harry and Belinda Johnson. The decisions they must make in each chapter are independent of those in earlier chapters—so that chapters can be covered out of order—but all are interrelated.

Case Problems—We have completely rewritten more than three-quarters of the end-of-chapter case problems. All require the student to apply the concepts covered in the particular chapter.

Readings—We have added a list of Suggested Readings at the end of each chapter. All are from current periodicals such as *Money* and *Changing Times*.

Glossary—The glossary has been completely revised to reflect our inclusion of new key terms.

Ancillary materials—The *Instructor's Manual* and *Study Guide* are completely new. We also now offer a computerized version of the *Study Guide* and of the test bank portion of the *Instructor's Manual* usable with IBM PC and Apple II computers.

Organization and Topical Coverage

As can be seen in the table of contents, we have approached topical coverage in a manner that provides a full explanation of the fundamentals of a topic before commencing further study. For example, chapters on fundamentals of insurance (Chapter 10) and the fundamentals of investments (Chapter 14) precede chapters on specific types of insurance and investments. In addition, each chapter has a place in an overall sequence, but each is also a complete whole. Thus the chapters can be rearranged to be read in another developmental sequence with minimal loss of comprehension.

Part One provides an introduction to financial planning. Chapter 1 lists reasons for studying personal finance, describes factors affecting income, and previews all remaining chapters. In Chapter 2, we explain the concept of financial planning and review the types of financial records and statements that are pertinent to success in personal financial management, such as tax records and documents, balance sheets, and income and expense statements. Chapter 3 presents an overview of the financial tasks, problems, and challenges over various periods of the life cycle and then illustrates a complete financial plan before examining the specifics of budgeting (goal setting, planning, decision making, implementing, controlling, and evaluating).

Part Two, comprising four chapters, discusses the specifics of managing money. Chapter 4 examines the new concept of "cash management," which involves making effective use of the changing financial services industry to earn maximum interest on your checking account, savings account, money market account, and other low-risk savings instruments. Chapter 5 discusses credit use and credit cards, including the legal protections now available, and Chapter 6 treats the subjects of non–credit card borrowing and credit overextension. In Chapter 7, we take the student through all phases of personal income taxation, including the "true" marginal tax rate, and we give advice for those who are audited. (To emphasize our view that reducing personal taxes can be crucial to obtaining funds for spending, saving, or investing—and improving one's lifestyle—we discuss taxation wherever it is appropriate to do so in other chapters.)

In Part Three, we focus on expenditure management. We cover "Some Major Expenditures" in Chapter 8, discussing ways money is wasted (and how to reduce waste), buying tips, and details on the buying process with emphasis on automobile purchases. Chapter 9 focuses on the housing expenditure, covering all aspects of buying a home as well as renting (especially since renting is sometimes the wiser choice), and information on selling a home.

Insurance is the topic of Part Four. Following Chapter 10, which covers numerous insurance fundamentals, are chapters examining property and liability insurance (emphasizing automobile and housing-related property and liability losses), health insurance (including the important topic of disability income coverage), and life insurance (including single-premium life insurance and universal life insurance).

Because the topic of investments is too complex to treat superficially, Part Five, "Investment Planning," contains seven separate chapters on investment fundamentals, stocks, bonds, buying and selling securities, mutual funds, real estate as an investment, and high-risk investments. This breakdown of the topic into numerous chapters will offer instructors more flexibility in deciding which topics to teach. In all these chapters, we provide enough details for the student to decide which investment alternatives are most suitable. Also, we provide specific guidelines on when each investment should be sold.

The text concludes with two valuable chapters on financial planning for the future: Chapter 21 examines Social Security and other retirement plans (including the new regulations on IRAs), and Chapter 22 reviews the essentials of estate planning, including wills and the importance of trusts in estate planning.

Finally, we have provided four appendixes: present and future value tables (along with two dozen illustrative problems); details of the indexing method of calculating Social Security benefits; a summary listing of the most important concepts in personal finance (perhaps to be used by instructors on the last day of teaching a class in personal finance); and how to use personal computers to aid personal financial management.

Learning Aids

This book offers a number of learning aids for each student:

Objectives beginning each chapter

Narrative introduction, giving a rationale for study and summarizing chapter contents

End-of-chapter summary to reinforce key points

"Modern Money Management" continuing case study

Lists of Key Words and Concepts accompanied by the page numbers on which each term is introduced and defined

End-of-chapter review questions

Case problems to apply concepts and mathematics to "real-life" situations

Suggested readings lists of recent articles of particular interest, from such publications as *Changing Times*, *Money*, and *Business Week*

Throughout the text, we have incorporated boxed inserts to add emphasis and stimulate interest as they illustrate additional relevant concepts, problems, and controversies that underscore the practical aspects of personal finance. Numerous headings and subheadings improve readability and reinforce the organization of the topics.

In addition, key terms and phrases are reinforced in several ways. All key terms—over 700 in all—are highlighted in boldface, color type the first time they are defined. For easy reference, the terms are repeated in a glossary at the back of the book. We have used boldface type again in the index to identify key words and the numbers of the pages on which they are defined.

Supplements to Text

Six supplements are available with the *Personal Finance* text: an *Instructor's Manual,* a student *Study Guide,* a set of professional transparencies, computerized versions of both the *Study Guide* and the test bank portion of the *Instructor's Manual,* and a top-selling computer software program.

Written by the authors, the *Instructor's Manual* has five components:

Suggested course outlines to emphasize a general personal finance, an insurance, or an investments approach to the subject

Outside research class assignments (and illustrative answers)

Answers and solutions to all end-of-chapter Modern Money Management questions, review questions, and case problems

Test bank of over 1,500 questions with both the correct answers identified and the page numbers in the textbook where the appropriate narrative responds to the question

Transparency masters for most text tables and figures as well as some boxed inserts and formulas, totaling nearly two hundred masters

A comprehensive *Study Guide,* written by the authors, has the following components:

Detailed chapter summaries of all key ideas

Lists of objectives

Lists of Key Words and Concepts

Completion exercises with correct responses printed alongside for programmed learning

True-false and multiple-choice questions to provide a self-check of learning. All key terms are covered.

Additional case problems and applications, giving students the opportunity to practice their analytical and decision-making skills utilizing personal finance concepts and principles as well as mathematical computations

Answers and solutions to *Study Guide* questions and problems

Approximately fifty professional-quality transparencies are free to adopters of fifty copies or more of *Personal Finance*. These transparencies—which include selected tables, figures, formulas, and boxed inserts from the text—illustrate the most commonly taught concepts in personal finance.

Microstudy and *Microtest* are computerized versions of the *Study Guide* and of the test bank portion of the *Instructor's Manual*. They are designed for use with IBM PC and Apple II computers.

"Managing Your Money," by Andrew Tobias, is a top-selling personal finance computer software package. This software is free to adopters of fifty copies or more of *Personal Finance*.

Acknowledgments

We realize that an instructional package of this breadth and depth could not be created without the assistance of many people.

We should, of course, mention our reviewers, who offered helpful suggestions and criticism of the first edition of the text. We especially appreciate the assistance of Jeffrey Born, University of Kentucky; Joel J. Dauten, Arizona State University; Mary Ellen Edmondson, University of Kentucky; Elizabeth Goldsmith, Florida State University; Roger P. Hill, University of North Carolina, Wilmington; Jagdish R. Kapoor, College of DuPage; Thomas R. Pope, University of Kentucky; Mary Stephenson, University of Maryland, College Park; Jerry A. Viscione, Boston College; and Grant J. Wells, Ball State University.

A survey of 1,200 personal finance instructors gave us additional insights into what teachers wanted in the overall instructional package. In-depth questionnaires were completed by a number of users and nonusers.

Then, a number of people were asked to provide detailed suggestions for the new edition. The text has been unquestionably strengthened by their contributions. We are deeply appreciative of the generous assistance given by Hal Babson, Columbus Technical Institute; Rosella Bannister, Eastern Michigan University; Robert Blatchford, Tulsa Junior College; Andrew Cao, American University; Charlotte Churaman, University of Maryland; Elizabeth Dolan, University of New Hampshire; Hilda Hall, Surry Community College; Naheel Jeries, Iowa State University; Eloise J. Law, State University of New York at Plattsburgh; Kenneth Marin, Aquinas College; Julia Marlowe, University of Georgia; Jerald W. Mason, International Association of Financial Planning; Randolph J. Mullis, University of Wisconsin (Madison); Steven J. Muck, El Camino College; Donald Neuhart, Central Missouri State University; William S. Phillips, Memphis State University; Carl H. Pollock, Jr., Portland State University; Eloise Lorch Rippie, Iowa State University; Wilmer E. Seago, Virginia Polytechnic Institute and State University; Dorothy West, Michigan State University.

We would also like to acknowledge Sidney W. Eckert for his invaluable assistance with the original development of *Personal Finance*. In addition, we wish to thank the many students who had the opportunity to read, critique, and provide research inputs for various components of the *Personal Finance* project. Some particularly helpful people were graduate students Jean A. Sturgeon, Annette Barfield, and Janet

Bissantz, and undergraduate students Lisa Weiss and Jeffrey A. McMillion.

A project of this dimension would never have been completed without the assistance in manuscript preparation, typewriting, and word processing, which often was above and beyond the call of duty. Humble thanks go to Mary R. "Flash" Rupe. And most important, we thank our friends and families for their patience, support, understanding, and sacrifices during the book's development, revision, and production. Lucy Garman has been an especially capable editor and proofreader.

Finally, we wish to thank the hundreds of instructors of personal financial management around the country who have been generous enough to share their views on what should and should not be included in a high-quality textbook with ancillary materials. We have attempted to meet those needs in every way possible not only in the text but also in the *Instructor's Manual* and the *Study Guide*. We hope we have succeeded because we share the strong bias that students need to study personal finance concepts thoroughly and learn them well so that they may apply them effectively and successfully in their personal lives.

E. Thomas Garman
Raymond E. Forgue

P.S. Dear Students: If you are going to save any of your college textbooks, be certain to save this one. The principles of lifetime financial success remain the same forever. Also, you may wish to present the book as a gift to a spouse or a parent.

PERSONAL FINANCE

PART ONE

Financial Planning

C H A P T E R   1

The Importance of Personal Finance

OBJECTIVES

After reading this chapter, the student should be able to

1. list the reasons for studying personal finance.
2. describe the goals of financial planning.
3. identify the factors that affect personal income.
4. describe the relationship between the goals and steps in the personal financial management process.

You are lucky to be reading this book because few people have the opportunity to study personal finance formally. Typically, people finish school, get a job, and start spending their earnings. And in that spending, they often make many mistakes. For example, they might choose a bank that has high costs for checking services or use credit cards that charge ridiculously high interest rates. They might finance an automobile for more in interest per year than necessary, rent an apartment that turns out to be too expensive, or buy a home in January and, because of a career change, move to another community in August, forced to sell quickly at a financial loss. Finally, they might invest in a company on the recommendation of a friend, only to find its value sharply declining, or pay an additional $400 in income taxes because they neglected to put some funds into a qualified retirement program.

You, too, will make mistakes in personal finance, because we all do. This textbook will thoroughly introduce you to the hows and whys of personal and family finance. Studying this text will help you to make fewer mistakes in personal finance and to become successful at managing the financial aspects of your life.

This chapter begins by examining reasons for studying personal finance. We then review the broad goals of personal finance so you can begin to reflect on your personal financial values and goals. In addition, we discuss the major factors that affect personal income. Finally, we provide an overview of the six major steps in personal financial management.

Reasons for Studying Personal Finance

You probably recognize that life and the living process sometimes can be difficult and will get more involved as you grow older. You will make many complex decisions throughout your life, some related to your education, your career, and your personal lifestyle, and many that affect your financial success. Although making these kinds of decisions may be accompanied by some anxious and uncomfortable moments, as you gain experience and become better educated you will be better prepared to choose wisely.

Handling your personal finances with skill will help make your life more enjoyable. Unfortunately, many people do not learn about personal finances until they become mired in financial problems. Studying personal finance will enable you to face successfully the financial challenges and responsibilities of life by helping you to (1) acquire financial knowledge, (2) develop your financial skills and learn to use financial instruments, (3) clarify your financial values and goals, and (4) identify specific needs and wants that can be satisfied with your financial resources.

Figure 1–1 shows how these four essential components of studying personal finance will result in *effective personal financial management,* which includes planning, analyzing and controlling financial resources to meet personal financial goals. The processes of personal financial management involve using financial knowledge, skills, and tools in a confident manner to take advantage of favorable financial opportunities, to solve personal financial problems, to achieve self-satisfaction, and to strive toward personal or family financial security.

Acquiring Financial Knowledge

Most of us seek a life of quality and financial security. We want to be able to make intelligent decisions about how to spend or invest our money and to eventually acquire some degree of wealth. A practical approach toward achieving these goals involves learning about the specific financial activities we will encounter: recordkeeping and budgeting, cash management, credit use, borrowing, paying taxes, making major expenditures (such as housing and an automobile), buying insurance, making investments, and making plans for retirement. In order to handle your personal finances both systematically and successfully, you must acquire knowledge about these topics.

Developing Financial Skills and Using Financial Tools

As you acquire financial knowledge, you will develop financial skills and learn to use financial tools. *Financial skills* are techniques of decision making in personal financial management. Preparing a budget, selecting investments, choosing an insurance plan, and using credit are ex-

FIGURE 1–1
Components of Studying Personal Finance

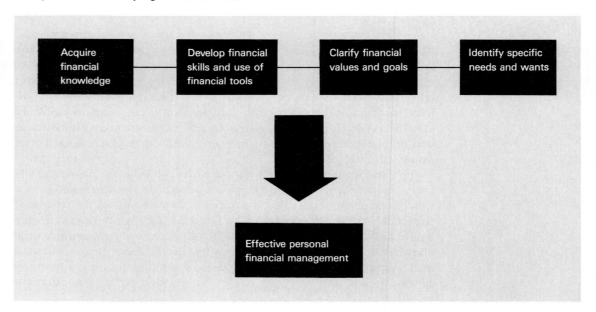

amples of financial skills. *Financial tools* are the forms, charts, and other instruments used in making personal financial management decisions. Examples of financial tools are checks, credit cards, and debit cards, an investment prospectus, and financial charts and tables.

Clarifying Financial Values and Goals

A basic understanding of how you feel about money is important to effective personal financial management. In fact, studying personal finance gives you the opportunity to clarify your financial values and goals. Do you value a dollar more for the security it represents (a conservative and traditional viewpoint), for the expected return it might provide if prudently deposited in a savings account (a more moderate viewpoint), or for the potential return it might provide if invested in the volatile commodities market (a risk-taking perspective, with greater possibility of either gain or loss of money invested)? There is no single correct choice, because different people have different financial values.

Gaining a better understanding of your financial values, which remain rather consistent throughout life, will help clarify your financial goals as well. For example, Linda Page of Prescott, Arizona, wants to own an expensive, sporty-looking automobile within five years of her graduation from college. A $16,000 Ford Mustang might fulfill her goal, or it might take a $48,000 Porsche. Linda is quite conservative in money matters, so she decides on the Mustang, for three reasons: (1) she expects a relatively low and safe return on her present investments, which would not provide much extra money to be spent on car payments; (2) she probably would never seriously consider spending as much money on a car as a Porsche costs, because she believes that is too much for transportation; and (3) she would not feel comfortable having so much money tied up in an automobile when she could invest the funds elsewhere. Linda's conservative nature wins out.

Your financial values and goals are interrelated; and you will probably need to clarify them. The chapters ahead provide several opportunities for personal values clarification.

Identifying Specific Needs and Wants

We all have many needs, and sometimes too many wants. *Needs* are those items that people find are necessary to have to survive and live in society. Examples of basic needs are food, shelter, clothing, and medical services. *Wants* are items that people would like to have to improve their comfort and satisfaction. Your individual wants will largely depend on your interests, tastes, lifestyle, and financial resources.

You will be able to satisfy more of your wants as you increase your knowledge of personal financial management. You will also learn to apply this knowledge to help you distinguish between your needs and wants and to help you set priorities. If your financial management is ineffective, you may have to spend most of your money on needs. If you become effective in handling your personal finances, however, you can acquire all your needs as well as numerous wants.

Goals of Effective Personal Financial Management

Financial success is defined by the individual or family that seeks it. For some, financial success may be a financially secure retirement. Others may want vast wealth by the age of fifty, and others may want just enough money to educate their children. A more modest objective could be to "stay ahead of the bill collectors." Each person must establish his or her own long-term personal financial objectives.

The broad goals of effective personal financial management are (1) maximizing earnings and wealth, (2) reaching financial security, (3) finding life satisfaction, (4) practicing efficient consumption, and (5) accumulating wealth for retirement and a financial estate to leave to heirs. These goals are very much related; in fact, to achieve one, you probably need to achieve the others. The following sections describe the goals of personal financial management.

Maximizing Earnings and Wealth

We think of money, property, and investments as part of wealth. In order to attain the goal of maximizing wealth, you must first seek to maximize earnings. Maximizing earnings is an ongoing process, whereas the maximizing of wealth tends to be the end result. Whether you choose to maximize earnings primarily through employment or through investments will depend on your tastes, interests, and *lifestyle* (your particular way of living). Later in this chapter we will discuss some of the factors that affect personal earnings.

Practicing Efficient Consumption

We use earnings for two purposes: consumption and savings. Since consumption spending, or buying goods and services, uses up the largest portion of income, it is important to practice it efficiently.

Practicing efficient consumption requires developing good personal financial management techniques, such as keeping sound financial records and using credit and checking accounts properly. Failure to practice efficient consumption is often the result of the careless use of money on nonessentials, abuse of credit, and/or poor judgment on purchases. As you study personal finance, you may encounter unfamiliar areas of consumption, such as buying a home. Thorough study of unfamiliar purchases can help you achieve your goal of efficient consumption.

Finding Life Satisfaction

Most people generally strive for quality in their lives. Some very important goals associated with quality of life are love, self-esteem, good health, achievement, and a general feeling of security. Many Americans find additional life satisfaction in owning material goods and enjoying investment income.

What kinds of things will give you satisfaction in your life? Having a challenging job and earning a good living? Having warm personal relationships? Achieving a sophisticated lifestyle? You may feel that accumulating many costly material goods is your best measure of quality of life. Or you may value good health more than material goods. In order to reach the life satisfaction you seek, you must make decisions related to your personal financial management, such as what to buy, how much to save, whether to invest, and where to live.

Reaching Financial Security

Financial security is the comfortable feeling that your financial resources will be enough to fulfill any needs you have. To reach financial security, first you need to prioritize your spending. For example, if you spend most or all of your earnings on recreation or entertainment, you will have little money left for purchasing necessities.

Putting money in real estate, stock investments, and insurance can help reduce feelings of financial insecurity, especially as you look toward retirement. Many good investments will increase in value beyond the rate of inflation. Also, as you buy and care for personal property, such as household goods and an automobile, future acquisition and replacement costs are not overwhelming.

Accumulating Wealth for Retirement and an Estate

People often seek to accumulate wealth to (1) provide income at retirement and (2) build a financial estate that can be passed on to their survivors upon their death. If you plan to take on the responsibility of a family, you may also wish to plan to assume some responsibility to ensure that their financial necessities will be met after your death.

Retirement is a state of life that people either look forward to or cringe from with apprehension. It is the number one reason why people save money. A popular retirement goal is having an income sufficient to live in a style that is "comfortable." Retirement and estate accumulation are essential goals to work toward during your lifetime.

Factors That Affect Personal Income

Of course, before you can even consider how to achieve your personal financial goals, you must give some thought to how you will earn a living. Personal income is affected by some factors that are controllable and some that are not. Your choices in life will make a difference in the amount of your income. Controllable factors include the career you choose, the amount of education you obtain, the geographic region in which you live, and your decision to marry or remain single. Noncontrollable factors that can affect income are sex and race, age, stage in the life cycle, and inflation.

Career

Whether you decide to become a computer programmer, medical doctor, schoolteacher, or something else depends on your interests and aptitudes. Finding areas of employment in which you are interested—

as well as good at—is a difficult but important task. Working at a job that is interesting can be enjoyable and personally rewarding. Also, having a high aptitude for a certain career will likely result in your excelling at that job, which will bring future promotions and raises.

You have probably taken "interest inventory" and aptitude tests at some point in your schooling to help you discover more about yourself and your interests. It may be helpful to review these test results with a counselor at your school. You can also choose from a wide variety of courses that might stimulate your career interests. Many college students change their majors several times. This illustrates the sampling process people go through in trying to decide which career areas best match their interests and aptitudes.

Table 1-1 illustrates both the starting salary and the salary for experienced individuals for various careers requiring a minimum of a bachelor's degree. In some fields the starting salary is close to the salary for more experienced workers, as in the case of underwriters. In other careers, such as economist or security sales, the experienced people enjoy much higher salaries. As you go about selecting a career, be aware of these differences as well as your interests and aptitudes because such factors definitely affect the amount of income you will earn.

TABLE 1-1
Careers and Income (Careers That Require a Minimum of a Bachelor's Degree)

Occupation	Average Starting Salary	Average Salary of Experienced Individuals
Accountant	$20,300	$ 33,500
Actuary	18,700	46,800
Airline pilot	16,600	83,200
Architect	15,600	29,700
Chemical engineer	28,500	42,500
Chiropractor	15,600	62,400
Economist	20,800	52,000
Geologist	23,700	43,700
Librarian	19,500	28,100
Metallurgical engineer	27,600	42,500
Physician	46,200	112,700
Professor	22,800	32,200
Public relations	12,500	26,800
Securities sales	15,000	66,600
Social worker	16,300	26,500
Teacher	16,600	25,200
Underwriter	19,200	24,600
Veterinarian	20,800	47,800

Source: U.S. Department of Labor, Bureau of Labor Statistics, *Occupational Outlook Handbook* (Washington, D.C., April 1986); authors' extrapolations to January 1988

TABLE 1–2
Education and Income (Persons Over 25)

Educational Level	Male (n = 68,229,000)	Female (n = 71,591,000)
Elementary		
Less than 8 years	$ 7,857	$ 4,615
8 years	10,818	5,415
High school		
1–3 years	12,870	5,689
4 years	18,997	8,137
College		
1–3 years	22,581	11,018
4 years	29,698	15,256
5 years or more	35,249	20,678

Source: Bureau of the Census, *Current Population Reports,* Series P.60, No. 154 (Washington, D.C., August 1986). June 1987 data obtained in telephone interview.

Education

More than one-half of today's high school graduates go on to some form of higher education. Whatever their reasons for going to college, the result is a personal investment. Table 1–2 shows that educational investment pays off in higher incomes. The higher the educational level of the head of a household, the higher both the average annual family income and the average lifetime family income.

Completion of a college bachelor's degree is a significant educational achievement. The educational attainments of the adults in the work force are as follows: 20 percent have four or more years of college, 19 percent have one to three years of college, 42 percent have four years of high school, and 19 percent have less than four years of high school. Such education and training increase people's *human capital,* the abilities, skills, and knowledge that permit them to perform work or services. Employers generally want to hire people with college degrees, as it is evidence of training in selected areas. Table 1–3 shows the average salary offered to bachelor's degree candidates, and Table 1–4 shows the starting salaries for various technical career opportunities that do not require a bachelor's degree.

Completing a four-year college degree program is not a prerequisite for many high-paying and emotionally satisfying careers. However, developing the kind of expertise through education that employers demand is clearly associated with higher incomes. It also should be noted that education yields many benefits beyond higher income, such as enjoyment of work and more understanding of people and the world in which we live. Table 1–5 shows the relationship between education and unemployment. The lower the level of formal education, the

TABLE 1–3
Average Monthly Salary Offers for Bachelor's Degree Candidates (Data Combined for Men and Women)

Occupation (by Title for All Types of Employers)	Average Salary Offer
Administrative and management occupations	
Accountants and auditors	$1,800
Business administration	1,589
Financial analysts	1,819
Management trainees	1,596
Personnel and labor relations	1,485
Computer and mathematical occupations	
Computer programmers	2,063
Computer scientists (includes systems analysts)	2,207
Mathematicians/statisticians	2,138
Marketing and sales occupations	
Advertising/marketing	1,764
Retail/wholesale sales	1,675
Technical sales	1,896
All other occupations	
Communications	1,392
Engineers	2,348
Farm and natural resources management	1,653
Health-related	1,928
Insurance and real estate	1,624
Production	1,790
Researchers—nonscientific	2,583
Researchers—scientific	2,542
Social workers and recreational workers	1,332
Transportation and distribution	1,918

Source: The College Placement Council College Salary Survey (Bethlehem, Pa.: The College Placement Council, March 1987), page 3. Used with permission.

higher the level of unemployment. Thus, those people with greater amounts of education are less likely to be unemployed, and consequently, they enjoy a more comfortable lifestyle.

Geographic Region and Community Size

Incomes are higher in the West and North than in the South, as shown in Table 1–6. This is the result of less unionization of employees in the South, lower living costs, and other factors. The growing desire of many people to live in the sunbelt states is causing more people to move to that region, bringing more industry, increased living costs, and eventually higher incomes. Employers in metropolitan areas pay higher incomes than those in more rural areas, largely because they must compete with many other employers for persons with good skills.

TABLE 1-4
Technical Careers and Income (Careers That Generally Do Not Require a Bachelor's Degree)

Occupation	Average Starting Salary	Average Salary of Experienced Individuals
Accounting clerk	$13,800	$17,100
Aircraft mechanic	16,600	22,800
Dental hygienist	12,500	16,100
Drafter	13,100	21,800
Electrocardiograph technician	13,500	25,000
Flight attendant	13,500	23,900
Regulatory inspector	15,600	23,900
Photographer	21,600	24,100
Physical therapist	20,400	25,000
Respiratory therapist	17,700	24,000
State police officer	14,600	19,200
Surveying technician	12,100	15,600

Source: U.S. Department of Labor, Bureau of Labor Statistics, *Occupational Outlook Handbook* (Washington, D.C., April 1986); authors' extrapolations to January 1988.

Sex and Race

Table 1–2 also shows income figures for both sexes. On the average, females earn only 70 percent as much as males. One reason for this discrimination in earnings is that women typically have been concentrated in many low-paying careers. They make up 90 percent or more of employed bookkeepers, bank tellers, nurses, and secretaries. These fields have been dominated by women for decades; many employers continue to label them as "female" jobs and pay low wages to those people who perform them.

Similar discrimination in earnings occurs among races; household income for Hispanic families is 73 percent of that for white families, and household income for black families is only 41 percent. Some employers also discriminate against women and minorities in opportunities for continuing education, promotions, and employment itself.

TABLE 1-5
Unemployment Rate and Education (Civilian Noninstitutionalized Population Age 16 and Older)

Educational Attainment	Percent Unemployed
4 years of college or more	2.5
1–3 years of college	5.3
4 years of high school	8.1
Less than 4 years of high school	14.4
All education levels	7.5

Source: U.S. Department of Labor, Bureau of Labor Statistics, *Current Population Survey* (Washington, D.C.: January 1986). June 1987 data obtained in telephone interview.

TABLE 1–6
Household Income by Geographic Region and Community Size
(Year-round, Full-time Workers)

	Number (thousands)	Median Income
Geographic region		
Northeast	18,562	$30,544
Midwest	21,847	27,930
South	30,311	25,077
West	17,738	29,778
Community size		
Inside metropolitan area	68,363	30,045
1 million or more	37,699	31,919
Inside central cities	16,497	25,158
Outside central cities	21,203	36,211
Under 1 million	30,664	27,934
Inside central cities	12,934	25,528
Outside central cities	17,731	29,490
Outside metropolitan areas	20,094	21,956

Source: U.S. Department of Commerce, *Current Population Reports,* Series P.60, No. 154 (Washington, D.C., August 1986). June 1987 data obtained in telephone interview.

Individuals are now helping to raise the aggregate income for women and minorities by entering fields such as business management, medicine, military service, law, and engineering—and by postponing marriage. Society gains from the rising incomes and successes of women and minorities.

Marital Status

Many, but not all, single men and women want to get married and have families; only 58 percent of all adults are married. A growing proportion of individuals are deciding to remain single. Today, approximately 69 percent of the males and 51 percent of the females between the ages of twenty and twenty-four are single.

Census Data on the Net Worth of Americans

Census data released in 1986 provided insights into the financial net worth of Americans. Net worth is the amount left when you subtract what you owe from what you own. The median net worth of white households was $39,135, Hispanic households was $4,913, and black households was $3,397.

Beyond these startling statistics categorized by race were some revealing insights about the factors related to net worth. Households headed by college graduates had a median net worth of $60,417; it slipped to $31,892 for those headed by high school graduates and to $23,447 for those headed by someone with less than a high school education. Education clearly makes a difference in net worth.

Marriage is another factor. Households headed by married couples had a net worth of $50,116; it dropped to $13,885 for households headed by unmarried females and to $9,883 for unmarried males. Staying married also makes a difference in net worth—probably because two people can earn, save, invest, and create more net worth than a single person.

TABLE 1–7
Family Income and Marital Status, Year-round, Full-time Workers

	Number (thousands)	Median Income
Married-couple families	31,132	$37,820
Wife in paid labor force	19,973	40,593
Wife not in paid labor force	11,159	32,632
Single householders		
Male householder, no wife present	1,307	29,059
Female householder, no husband present	3,946	21,822

Source: Bureau of the Census, *Current Population Reports,* Series P.60, No. 154 (Washington, D.C., August 1986). June 1987 data obtained in telephone interview.

According to census data, more than 2 million single persons have chosen to live together without a legal wedding ceremony. A far greater number of young people have decided to marry but to postpone having children. Both groups join the growing number of *dual-earner households,* in which both spouses work for income. The old adage "two can live as cheaply as one" should probably be updated to read "the income of two increases the consumption level of one." Decision making may be more difficult with two income earners, but having two incomes greatly increases the resources available for financial planning and spending, as Table 1–7 shows.

Age and Stage in the Life Cycle

Employers do not pay their youngest employees the highest wages because those employees lack experience. Table 1–8 reveals that an increasing average income is paid to workers over their lives, that is, until the age of fifty-five and older. Because many of the oldest members of the population do not have as much formal education as younger workers, they are generally not employed in the higher-paying jobs

TABLE 1–8
Income and Age of Householder

Age in Years	Number (thousands)	Median Income
15–24	3,174	$15,089
25–34	14,894	26,023
35–44	14,913	32,669
45–54	16,967	36,653
55–64	9,744	30,605
65 and over	10,067	19,162

Source: Bureau of the Census, *Current Population Reports,* Series P.60, No. 154 (Washington, D.C., August 1986). June 1987 data obtained in telephone interview.

and thus, as a group, earn less income. Age is also an income-determining factor for some types of physical labor; older workers often lack the strength of younger ones.

Inflation

Does an income of $30,000 per year sound high to you? How about $40,000? Or even $60,000? Perhaps these do sound high, but what if a steak dinner for two costs $175 and the price of an inexpensive Chevrolet is $24,000? What you earn in dollars is only as valuable as what it can buy. When prices are rising, income must also rise in order to maintain its purchasing power. *Inflation* is a condition of across-the-board increases in the prices of goods and services. It occurs when the supply of money (or credit) rises faster than the supply of goods and services available for purchases. Inflation also can be self-perpetuating. Workers will ask for higher wages thereby adding to the cost of production. Manufacturers will charge more for their products in response to the increases in the cost of labor and raw materials. Lenders will require higher interest rates to offset the lost purchasing power of the loaned funds. Consumers will lessen their resistance to price increases because they fear prices will be even higher in the future.

From an individual's point of view, the impact of inflation is significant. Consider the case of Scott Lind of Ames, Iowa, who took a job three years ago at $22,000 per year. Since that time Scott has had annual raises of $1,100, $1,200, and $1,300 but still cannot make ends meet. The reason? Suppose the inflation rate was 6 percent each year. Even though Scott received raises, his new income ($22,000 + $1,100 + $1,200 + $1,300 = $25,600) did not keep up with an annual inflation rate of 6 percent ($22,000 × 1.06 = $23,320 × 1.06 = $24,719 × 1.06 = $26,202). He lost purchasing power in the amount of $602 ($26,202 − $25,600) if his costs went up the same as the general price level.

The *consumer price index (CPI)* is a broad measure of the cost of living for consumers and is published monthly by the U.S. Bureau of Labor Statistics. More than 400 prices of various goods and services sold across the country are tracked, recorded, weighted for importance in a hypothetical budget, and totaled. The index has a base time period from which to make comparisons. If 1967 is the base year of 100 and the CPI is 350 in 1987, the cost of living has risen 250 percent since the base period. Similarly, if in 1988 the index rises from 350 to 369, the cost of living has gone up. This time the increase has been 5.4 percent over one year (369 − 350 = 19; 19 ÷ 350 = 5.4).

When prices rise, the purchasing power of the dollar declines, but not by the same percentage. It falls the reciprocal amount of the price increase. In the example above, prices rose 250 percent over twenty years and the purchasing power of the dollar declined 71.6 percent. (The base year price of 100 divided by the 1987 index of 350 equals .286; the reciprocal is .714 [100% − .286], or 71.4 percent.) Similarly, in the case above in which prices rose 5.4 percent, the purchasing power declined 5.1 percent (350 ÷ 369 = .949; the reciprocal is .051).

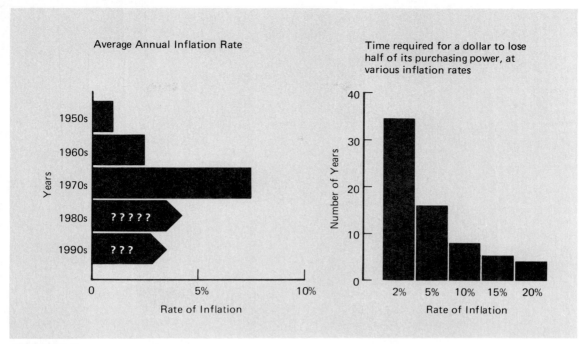

FIGURE 1-2
Inflation and the Half-life of a Dollar
Source: The Conference Board. Used with permission.

Your *real income* (income measured in constant prices relative to some base time period) is the number that is important. It reflects the buying power of the current dollars, or *money income,* that you have to spend. Figure 1–2 illustrates inflation rates of recent decades and the half-life of a dollar, or the time required to lose half of its purchasing power. If inflation in the late 1980s and 1990s continues to slow somewhat from that of the 1970s, the purchasing power of a dollar will last longer. In any event, it is important to calculate your own real income to ascertain whether or not you personally are losing the battle against inflation.

Steps in Personal Financial Management

There are six major steps toward achieving your personal financial goals. This text is divided into six parts to guide you through each of these steps: (1) financial planning, (2) money management, (3) managing expenditures, (4) income and asset protection, (5) investment planning, and (6) retirement and estate planning. Figure 1–3 shows how these steps are related to the goals discussed earlier in this chapter.

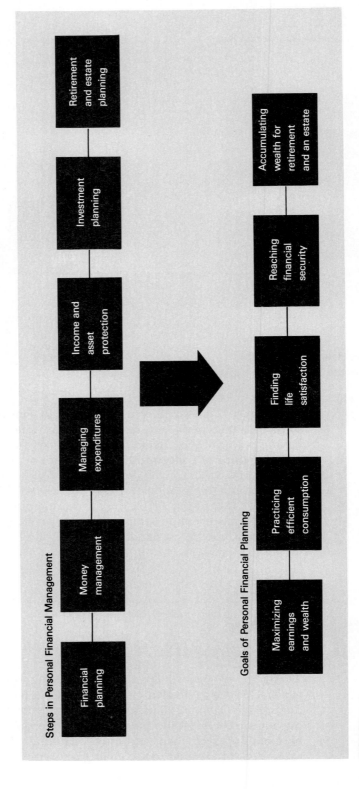

FIGURE 1–3
Steps and Goals in Personal Financial Management

Financial Planning

It is important for financial planning to be as thorough as possible and for the plan to be properly carried out. Problems can result if some aspects of your plan are neglected, as you can see in the situation described below.

John Babson of Columbus, Ohio, aspired to financial success like that of his parents, both of whom were physicians. He enjoyed an affluent lifestyle when growing up and wanted to lead a similar life of his own. He enjoyed being a liberal arts major, but it did not permit him the opportunity to take many science classes. Premed students, of course, must have a very strong background in science. Consequently, John did not score well on the national medical school entrance exam. His decision to get married during his senior year of college did not help him advance his plan either. Financial strains and increasing time constraints made it difficult for him to take the necessary science classes before he could retake the medical entrance exam. Working as a salesperson for two years enabled him to take the science courses at night, pass the medical exam, and begin his way toward medical practice and financial success.

The topics discussed in Part One of this text should help you avoid making decisions that might impede your progress toward financial goals. In addition to this chapter, they include Chapter 2, "Financial Planning and Recordkeeping"; and Chapter 3, "Budgeting."

Money Management

Another major step in personal financial management is learning efficient ways to manage money and money substitutes. Let's consider the case of Helen Daniel of LaFayette, Louisiana, to try and determine the primary reason for her dilemma in managing money.

Helen saw a beautiful living room suite displayed in a local furniture store window. She went inside the store to look it over. Then she decided to buy it. Helen used her VISA card to buy the suite, which cost $699.95, plus tax. About a month later her VISA bill came in the mail. The following statement was printed on her bill: "If you choose to pay a portion (but a minimum of $40), you may do so, but a finance charge of 1.75 percent per month will be assessed on the average daily balance. To avoid a finance charge, pay the full amount by the 25th of the month." Helen chose to pay only $40, since she also had her auto insurance payment to make and was almost broke.

Because Helen did not pay the full amount due, she had to pay a finance charge. That decision would cost her about 21 percent per year (1.75 percent × 12 months) in finance charges if she continued the payment plan of sending in $40 a month. Helen may not have practiced efficient money management with her payment choice, as she could have borrowed the money from her company credit union at 12 percent annual interest.

Analysis shows that Helen's method of payment was not the best choice to make. What appears to be an easy purchase with a credit card sometimes can turn out to be otherwise when you end up paying the extra credit charges with each payment. However, a student of personal finance can learn to reduce, if not eliminate, such problems by mastering the topics in Part Two of this text: Chapter 4, "Financial Services and Cash Management"; Chapter 5, "Credit Use and Credit Cards"; Chapter 6, "Borrowing"; and Chapter 7, "Managing Taxes."

Managing Expenditures

Managing expenditures is another step in personal financial management. This entails gathering information and making decisions about buying goods and services. Soon you will need to make important decisions related to your financial well-being, such as buying a new car, furnishing an apartment, and purchasing insurance. Thus, you must learn to make efficient decisions regularly as you deal with financial opportunities. The first financial decisions you make may not be the best, but your skill at making them will improve as you read, discuss, and practice the necessary information.

To illustrate the problem of managing expenditures, let's study the financial situation of a young couple just out of college. Ellen and Bill Frasier of St. Louis, Missouri, finished college together after being married for two years. Both decided to work, but Ellen became pregnant and had a difficult pregnancy. She had to quit working for money income. Before learning of the pregnancy, the couple had decided to buy a house rather than continue to rent for $475 per month. Living in their new home, a single-family dwelling, required paying $686 per month on a loan. The house was about twenty years old and needed some repair. During the first year, repair costs amounted to more than the Frasiers planned. Also, the baby was born, and hospital and baby bills had to be paid.

Essentially, Bill and Ellen did not clearly anticipate overall housing costs (including repairs and rising utility costs) in addition to the new baby costs. They may have made a more prudent decision—perhaps continuing to rent for another year or two—had they practiced more careful financial planning. Knowing more about home ownership and its related costs probably would have altered their purchase decision, at least until they had additional money available for the expenses.

Predicting the future is no easy task. To prepare you to make better financial decisions, Part Three includes Chapter 8, "Some Major Expenditures"; and Chapter 9, "The Housing Expenditure."

Income and Asset Protection

Individuals obtain insurance to financially protect themselves, their survivors, and things of value that they own. The following case shows some of the pitfalls of buying insurance protection.

The "hard sell" for life insurance was put on Don Mullis, of Madison, Wisconsin, as he was completing his senior year in college. A typical "insurance sales pitch" made the need for insurance protection seem enormous, and Don bought a $50,000 whole-life type of life insurance policy. It would cost him $1,096 each year, and although the insurance started immediately, the payments did not begin until one year after his graduation.

Don could have made a wiser decision on his insurance protection had he studied life insurance more carefully. His decision to buy $50,000 of coverage was unjustified; he had little need for this amount because he was single and his parents did not depend on his income. Buying whole-life insurance also seemed unwise since term life insurance may have been a better choice (whole-life policies have a savings feature that makes them much more expensive than term policies). And Don neglected to find out to what extent his future employer would pay for his insurance. Many employers provide life insurance coverage for employees at little or no cost to the employees.

To protect your automobile and other personal property from financial loss, you need to develop the skills required to buy protection through insurance. Part Four introduces you to several areas of income and asset protection: Chapter 10, "Insurance Fundamentals"; Chapter 11, "Property and Liability Insurance," Chapter 12, "Health Insurance," and Chapter 13, "Life Insurance."

Investment Planning

To achieve the goal of maximizing earnings and wealth, we must of necessity look to the future. Investing in the future in order to obtain a reasonable return on money is no small task—it requires skill and knowhow. Let's consider the case of Jane Ridnour of North Platte, Nebraska, to examine some of the decisions to be faced in investment planning.

"Should I save in a regular savings account or invest in government or corporate securities?" Jane had pondered this question ever since receiving $10,000 from the estate of her late grandfather. She knew that the regular passbook savings account would provide FDIC (Federal Deposit Insurance Corporation) protection for this $10,000. Consequently, she put the money in a regular savings account that earned her a return of 5.5 percent interest, paid quarterly.

But using a regular savings account is not the only way to put money to work and still maintain a high degree of security. If Jane had known more about saving and investing, she probably would have invested her money differently. She would have discovered, for example, that her $10,000 could have given her about an 8 percent return if she had invested in short-term government securities. It would have given her the same protection as the regular savings account, provided the same amount of *liquidity* (ease of conversion into cash), and yet given her a greater rate of return on investment.

Jane's situation is not unique, and it points up an important lesson: you must investigate before you invest. You must learn the hows, the whys, the wheres, the whens, and the whats of investing. The chapters in Part Five will provide you with the skills and tools to make intelligent investment choices: Chapter 14, "Investment Fundamentals"; Chapter 15, "Investing in Stocks"; Chapter 16, "Investing in Bonds"; Chapter 17, "Buying and Selling Securities"; Chapter 18, "Mutual Funds as an Investment"; Chapter 19, "Investing in Real Estate"; and Chapter 20, "High-Risk Investments."

Retirement and Estate Planning

Sooner or later, you must think about what to do when you retire from your regular job. If you plan intelligently, you can have a comfortable retirement income and a sound financial estate to draw upon during those years. Your estate also can be your legacy to surviving loved ones after your death. Even though retirement and estate planning seems premature to most people, it is one of the major steps in personal financial management.

Estate planning is a long process that develops throughout your life. It is not something hastily done a year or two before retirement. One disadvantage of careless estate planning is the difficulty of correcting poor decisions made years ago. This is illustrated by the following "missing link" in the estate planning of Leland Waterson of Dallas, Texas.

Leland thought he had planned everything very thoroughly as he was growing older. He had earned the highest educational degree he could, taken all the right courses, planned his finances carefully, saved and invested frugally, secured a sound insurance program, and kept a reasonable amount of money in his checking account ready for current expenditures and/or emergencies. But Leland worked almost all of his career for a small company that did not have a good retirement plan.

Leland was able to provide for his wife, Joan, and family through a limited amount of savings, stock and bond investments, and life insurance in case of his death. Fortunately, Leland and Joan were always in good health, and both came from families that lived well beyond the usual life expectancy.

For the first three years of retirement, Leland and Joan did fairly well on his Social Security income, the small company pension, limited earnings from savings, and investments. But they began to feel the pinch as these income sources could not keep up with the *personal inflation rate* (the rate of increase in prices of items purchased by a person or household). Leland used more and more money and got less and less for his dollar. Most of his retirement income was fixed at about $1,150 per month, but inflation was 6.7 percent per year. Consequently, Leland's *purchasing power* decreased. In one year, his fixed income of $1,150 per month decreased to about $1,078 in purchasing power: $100.0 \div 106.7 = .937$; reciprocal is .063; $1,150 - ($1,150 \times 0.63) = $1,077.55$, or $1,078.

Leland could have avoided this problem of decreasing purchasing power by arranging to have a greater retirement income to offset inflation. It is important that this kind of long-range planning be done carefully. The chapters in Part Six will provide you with information about how and when to make such efforts: Chapter 21, "Social Security and Other Retirement Plans"; and Chapter 22, "Estate Planning."

Summary

1. The four reasons for studying personal financial management are acquiring financial knowledge, developing skills in using financial instruments, clarifying financial values and goals, and identifying financial needs and wants that can be satisfied with financial resources.

2. There are five goals of personal financial planning. The first is to maximize earnings and wealth. The second is to practice efficient consumption. The third goal is to find satisfaction in life. The fourth is to reach financial security. The fifth goal is to accumulate wealth for retirement and an estate.

3. Financial security is highly dependent upon income levels. Factors that affect personal income can be both controllable and noncontrollable. Controllable factors include career choice, education level, place of residence, and marital status. Noncontrollable factors are sex, race, age, stage in the life cycle, and inflation.

4. The six steps in personal financial management are (1) financial planning, (2) money management, (3) managing expenditures, (4) income and asset protection, (5) investment planning, and (6) retirement and estate planning. Success in these steps is related to the specific goal(s) of personal financial management that are being sought.

Key Words and Concepts

consumer price index (CPI), 14
dual-earner households, 13
effective personal financial
    management, 4
financial skills, 4
financial tools, 5
human capital, 9
inflation, 14

lifestyle, 6
liquidity, 19
money income, 15
needs, 5
personal inflation rate, 20
purchasing power, 20
real income, 15
wants, 5

Review Questions

1. Cite reasons to study personal finance.
2. What are the four components of studying personal finance?
3. Differentiate between financial skills and financial tools.
4. Give an example of clarifying financial values and goals.

5. Differentiate between needs and wants.
6. List the five broad goals of effective personal financial management.
7. Explain how efficient consumption relates to effective personal financial management.
8. Identify controllable factors that affect personal income.
9. Explain how career selection affects personal income.
10. Describe the relationship between education and income.
11. Why do incomes vary geographically?
12. How are sex and race related to earnings? Explain.
13. What is the relationship between the unemployment rate and education?
14. How do incomes vary by community size?
15. Why does income change during the life cycle?
16. Give an example of the effect of inflation on income.
17. Differentiate between real income and money income.
18. Identify the six steps in personal financial management.

Case Problems

1. Bill Gustafson of Lubbock, Texas, is a senior in college, majoring in sociology. He anticipates getting married a year or so after graduation. He has only one elective course remaining and must choose between another advanced class in sociology and one in personal finance. As Bill's friend, you want to persuade him to take personal finance. For each of the items listed, give one example of how it might benefit him.
   a. Acquire financial knowledge.
   b. Develop financial skills and use financial tools.
   c. Clarify financial values and goals.
   d. Identify needs and wants.
2. You have been asked to give a brief speech on the goals of effective personal financial management. As you have only five minutes for the presentation, it will be impossible to discuss all five broad goals. Therefore, you have decided to simply mention the five and focus in detail on only one. Choose one of the broad goals and describe what it means to you. Be sure to show how that one goal relates to overall financial success.

Suggested Readings

Business Week Careers. July/August 1987. A special issue with eleven articles on the problems and challenges women face today and will face in the future.

"Careers: Prospects for Your Perks." *Changing Times,* January 1987, pp. 77–85. The effects of tax law changes on how people are compensated.

"The *Changing Times* Annual Survey: Jobs for New College Graduates." *Changing Times,* February 1987, pp. 43–59. Complete outlook for dozens of careers.

"Eighth Annual *Working Woman* Salary Survey." *Working Woman,* January 1987, pp. 53–64. Annual report on numerous positions grouped in useful ways.

"Finding Work Through an Employment Agency." *Consumers' Research,* February 1987, pp. 27–30. The ins and outs of paying an agency to locate a job.

"The Shape of Things to Come." *Changing Times,* January 1987, pp. 28–47. Impact of technological breakthroughs on the decade of the 1990s on job markets, careers, and the economy.

"And Some Fall by the Wayside." *Forbes,* April 6, 1987, pp. 162–166. How to avoid taking some corporate jobs that have little career future.

"Women with Promise: Who Succeeds, Who Fails?" *Working Woman,* June 1987, pp. 79–84. How to build the skills needed to move up the career ladder.

CHAPTER 2

Financial Planning and Recordkeeping

OBJECTIVES

After reading this chapter, the student should be able to

1. explain the concept of financial planning, its components, and its value.

2. describe the purposes and uses of organized and complete financial records.

3. state the purpose, value, and components of key financial statements, particularly the balance sheet and the income and expense statements.

4. provide examples of how to use financial statements in decision making.

T oday's affluent society offers a bewildering and complex array of financial alternatives in banking services, housing accommodations, investment choices, insurance coverage, savings options, tax-savings devices, credit sources, and retirement plans. Because information about these financial opportunities usually is obtained piecemeal from different sources, decision making becomes even more difficult.

For these reasons, most people need financial planning. They have the idea that they want to succeed financially but lack clear objectives and goals, which makes it difficult to choose correctly among alternatives. People generally have financial records, but too often the records are poorly organized and some cannot be located easily. Such an approach to personal finance may result in failure rather than success.

This chapter begins with an explanation of financial planning: what it is and how it can be important to you. An overview of financial recordkeeping follows, presented in enough detail perhaps to inspire you to consider reorganizing your own financial records. Throughout the remainder of the chapter we discuss financial statements and provide several examples to illustrate the personal finances of single persons, young married couples, and established families.

Financial Planning

Financial planning is the process of developing and implementing plans to achieve financial objectives. It is not a single plan; rather, it is a coordinated series of plans covering various parts of a person's overall financial affairs. Financial planning begins by recording in writing the financial objectives and goals that reflect your values, attitudes, life cycle circumstances, wants, and needs.

Financial Goals

Financial goals are the long-term objectives that your financial planning and management efforts are intended to attain. You should state explicitly your financial objectives in order to help you make choices and to serve as a rational basis for your financial actions. You should make financial plans with appropriate objectives and goals in two broad areas: (1) *plans against risks,* and (2) *plans for capital accumulation.* Figure 2–1 provides an overview of effective personal financial management.

An example of a financial goal in planning against risk is provided by Francine Mason of Radford, Virginia. Francine is a college student and has little extra money. Still she was concerned about the risk of being legally liable if she caused an accident with her automobile. After consideration of the risks and costs involved Francine decided one financial objective was to protect herself against automobile related lawsuits. Her short-term goal was to spend the least amount of money on

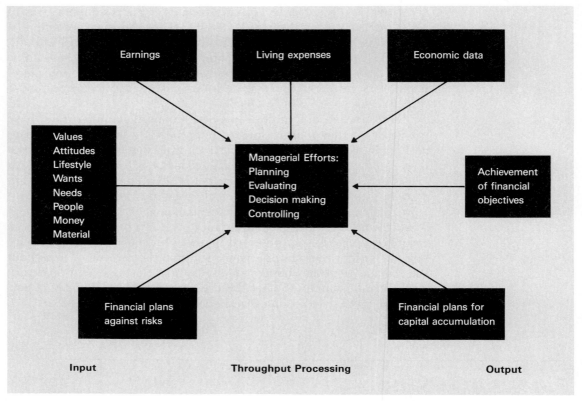

FIGURE 2–1
Overview of Effective Personal Financial Management

necessary insurance coverage. After telephoning three insurance agents to compare premium costs, Francine bought a policy with the minimum coverages allowed by Virginia law—instead of higher optional coverage available—and paid $176 annually.

Ellen Law of Plattsburgh, New York, a recent college graduate with a new job as a marketing specialist, decided that one of her financial goals was to plan for capital accumulation. She established an emergency fund equal to three months' take-home pay that she could use for unexpected medical or automobile expenses not covered by insurance and that would provide a financial cushion if she should lose her job. Accordingly, Ellen began to put $300 a month into a bank savings account.

Assumptions

Financial planning requires that you make certain assumptions about the economy before taking appropriate action. People often do this subconsciously; for instance, they may assume that inflation "will be about the same for the next few years" or "the cost of credit—interest rates—will probably remain steady for some time." People who make conscious and explicit assumptions about the economy are often re-warded with favorable financial opportunities. For example, Laurie Wesswick of Laramie, Wyoming, correctly assumed that interest rates were going to decline during the last business slump, so she put some of her funds into savings certificates of deposit before rates declined and locked in the greater return for two years.

Strategies

In order to be successful, a financial plan must have logical and consistent financial strategies to help guide the operations of the plan. For example, a conservative investor, Wilma Hall of Dobson, North Carolina, decided her strategy would be to sell any of her corporate stocks if the price rose or fell more than 20 percent of her original cost. This permitted Wilma to make respectable profits when they were available and restricted her losses.

Resources

Successful financial planning also considers the variety of resources that are available to meet a person's financial goals. One of the most important resources is the employee benefits package provided as a fringe benefit by an employer. This often provides a comprehensive range of benefits to an employee, many of which affect financial planning. Larger companies often provide: life insurance, supplemental life insurance, dependent life-insurance coverage for spouse and children, short-term disability insurance, long-term disability insurance, health care and/or insurance for individual and dependents, dental insurance, prepaid legal services, a savings plan with tax advantages and matching contributions from the employer, and a supplemental investment and retirement plan.

Table 2–1 lists thirteen areas of financial planning. Most people do not make written financial plans in all these areas. Many people ignore

---

TABLE 2–1
Thirteen Areas of Financial Planning

Plans against risks

1. Medical costs
2. Property and casualty losses
3. Liability losses
4. Premature death
5. Income loss from disability

Plans for capital accumulation

6. Tax fund
7. Revolving savings fund
8. Emergency fund
9. Education
10. Savings
11. Investments
12. Retirement
13. Estate planning

certain areas (retirement and liability losses, for example) and act with only partial knowledge in others (relying solely on employer-provided life insurance for example). Success in financial matters is a result of effective financial planning. Chapter 3, "Budgeting," provides an illustration of a financial plan. All subsequent chapters will examine personal finance topics in enough detail so that you will feel comfortable and confident with the subject to the extent that you will be able to make an effective financial plan and follow it through with effective financial management.

Financial Recordkeeping

Records and documents of all types follow us throughout our lives. For example, a birth certificate records your entry into the world, report cards show your progress through school, and employment evaluations detail your working life. The Internal Revenue Service expects people to maintain financial records for tax reporting, and banks encourage customers to keep a record of check writing. Having accessible, organized, and complete financial records is typically a prerequisite for effective financial planning. Your financial records will help determine where you are, where you have been, and something about where you are going, financially.

Original source records are formal documents that record personal financial activities. Purchase receipts, checks returned from the banking institution, stock certificates, and photocopies of filed income tax returns are all examples of original source records. If properly organized, they can be located and used when needed. You can use original financial records as backups for previous financial transactions: to prove a purchase, verify a price, or prove ownership. Thus, you can show the Internal Revenue Service, for example, that claims for a tax-deductible expenditure are justified, document the price of a product purchased, or demonstrate ownership of an automobile by displaying the title. The primary reason for keeping records of any kind is to be able to use the information for some future purpose.

TABLE 2–2
Financial Records: Categories and Contents

Category	Contents
Financial plans	Copy of written financial plans and revisions Balance sheets and income statements
Budgeting	Annual budget Annual cash flow statement Current budget control sheet Old budget control sheets List of short- and medium-term budget goals
Insurance	Life insurance policy details Calculation of life insurance needs Automobile insurance policy Health insurance booklet explaining coverage Health insurance claim forms Current medical history on family members Property, casualty, and disability insurance details Receipts for payment of premiums
Housing	Copies of legal documents (lease, mortgage, deed, title insurance, termite inspections, etc.) Receipts for home improvements
Taxes	Numerous receipts for tax deductible costs, such as medical, real estate and personal property taxes, charitable contributions, and miscellaneous expenses Copies of income tax forms filed for last three years Cancelled checks for current year Income tax estimates for next year Payroll records
Credit	Charge slips for credit transactions Monthly credit statements Credit card numbers and addresses Credit contracts Telephone numbers for lost/stolen cards
Investments	Log of all savings and investment transactions, interest, and dividends Written record of investments
Automobile	Title and ownership identification (unless required by law to be kept in the auto) Log for costs of maintenance and repairs
Warranties, operating instructions, and receipts	Warranties, operating instructions, and service contracts for expensive items (such as television, VCR, stereo, and appliances Purchase and repair receipts for same
Personal/legal	Copies of personal resume Employee policies handbook Fringe benefit and retirement information List of items placed in safe-deposit box Copy of will and letter of last instructions

Date	Description of Improvement	Who Paid	Amount	Accumulative Cost of Home
1-6-87	Purchased new condo	Brown + Smith, Builders	$88,000	$88,000
1-30-87	Carpeted bathroom	Clifton Flooring	330	88,330
2-4-88	Installed storm door	Sears	140	88,470
8-6-88	Built-in wall cabinets	ETG Remodeling	2,400	90,870

FIGURE 2–2
Housing Ownership Record

Both original and other types of financial records are useful in financial management. Table 2–2 shows some categories for all types of financial records and what contents might be included. Use whatever recordkeeping system works for you, being sure that you can easily keep it up to date.

Many people maintain written logs or records of financial activities and keep them filed with their original source records. Figures 2–2 and 2–3 illustrate two valuable records. The ***housing ownership record*** (Figure 2–2) shows the dates and amounts spent to improve (but not maintain) the home. This record is kept for tax purposes because such expenditures on improvements help reduce taxes when the home is sold. The ***tax-deductible expenditure record*** (Figure 2–3) serves as a written record of all income tax-deductible expenditures by date, amount paid and to whom, and tax classification. Such a system helps many taxpayers reduce their final tax liability because they are less likely to overlook tax-deductible items.

FIGURE 2–3
Tax-deductible Expenditure Record

Date	To Whom/For	Deductible Category					
		Medical	Taxes	Interest	Charitable	Casualty	Miscellaneous
1-10	Giles County-property tax		135.00				
1-14	Methodist church-pledge				25.00		
1-20	Giles Hospital-wrist	240.00					
1-20	ASID professional dues						100.00

Ways of Safeguarding
Financial Records

Since some effort goes into developing and maintaining records, it makes sense to keep records safe. It does little good to keep records and then run the risk they will be misplaced, stolen, or lost through fire or other causes due to faulty safeguards. Storage places can vary from a cardboard box to a file cabinet in your home to a safe-deposit box located in a bank. Methods used to safeguard records need not be elaborate or expensive. Table 2–3 shows some record-safeguarding devices in and outside the home.

Safeguarding Records in the Home

Most people maintain their own financial records someplace in their home. A desk drawer, a ring binder, a box, a portable file, an expandable paper or cardboard file, or an inexpensive paperboard file box are examples of places to maintain records. More elaborate record-safeguarding equipment, such as a fire-resistant file cabinet or a safe, can be used to ensure a higher degree of safety.

Safeguarding Records Outside the Home

People usually feel that some records are more valuable than others. Examples include investment documents, insurance policies, birth certificates, school records, marriage licenses, and other documents proving ownership. Commercial safekeeping devices are available to protect them. *Safe-deposit boxes* are secured lock boxes available for rent in banks. Safe-deposit boxes are very safe, not only from theft but also from fire and other catastrophes. By design, a box takes two keys to open—the customer has one and bank personnel hold the other. Two keys are used so that no one can open the safe-deposit box independently. Also, a signature comparison is made for each request to open a box. This almost eliminates the possibility of someone finding or stealing your key and gaining access to private documents. You can make arrangements for a safe-deposit box by requesting one from a bank official, completing the required signature cards, and paying a small annual fee ($15 to $60).

Another way to store papers or records is to use a secure spot at your place of employment. Many people keep copies of records at their workplace, since the possibility of records at home and in the office being destroyed simultaneously is slight. In any case, it is important to safeguard records, papers, or valuables either inside or outside the home since they reflect useful financial evidence. Because your records are personal, you must make decisions about how and where best to safeguard them.

TABLE 2–3
Record-safeguarding Devices

Device and Location	Record for Safeguarding
Safe-deposit box— bank	Birth certificate
	Installment contracts
	Government bonds
	Marriage license
	Divorce papers
	Military discharge papers
	Real estate documents
	Social Security card (copy)
	Stock certificates
	Insurance policies
	Passports
	Insurance policy numbers/descriptions
Fire-resistant cabinet or safe—home	Automobile title
	Bills of sale
	Important canceled checks
	Birth certificate (copy)
	Social Security earnings record
	Guarantees and warranties
	Evidence of the cost of investments
	Health records
	Financial records
	Evidence of the cost of home improvements
	Important receipts
	Insurance policies
	Tax return copies (for last 3 years)
	Copies of will and burial instructions (and note giving location of original)
	Education records
File cabinet or safe— home	Bank statements
	Current canceled checks
	Current receipts
Carried on person	Auto registration
	Driver's license
	Social Security card
	Other identification
	Credit cards
File cabinet or safe at lawyer's office	Original will
	Letter of last instructions
	Original trust information

Financial Statements

Financial statements are compilations of personal financial data designed to communicate information on money matters. They are used, often along with other financial statements, to provide indicators of the financial condition of an individual or family. The two most useful statements are (1) the balance sheet and (2) the income and expense statement.

Both statements are designed to allow a thorough review of a person's financial condition. A *balance sheet* describes an individual's or family's financial condition at a particular time, showing assets, liabilities, and net worth. The balance sheet gives a status report as of a certain date as well as a starting point for progressing financially. For example, if your balance sheet shows that you have a large cash balance, you can take action to achieve goals that require ready cash.

An *income and expense statement* relates an individual's or family's income and expenses by listing and summarizing the income and expense transactions that have taken place over a specific period of time, such as a month or a year. For example, if your weekly income were $500, an income and expense statement prepared on a monthly basis would show income of $2,000. Likewise, if weekly food costs were $80, a monthly statement would show food costs of $320.

The Balance Sheet

It is useful to determine your financial assets and liabilities at least once a year. The information on the balance sheet then can be compared to previous balance sheets to help calculate how much financial progress you are making and provide directions for future planning. If you are serious about increasing your wealth, and most people are, then you need to sit down with pencil and paper and figure out your present financial position—the sum of what you own less what you owe. Note that applications for personal loans and home mortgages will ask for the same information.

Components of the Balance Sheet

There are three parts to any balance sheet: assets, liabilities, and net worth. Your *assets* are the current dollar value of the items you own. Your *liabilities* are the dollar value of the items you owe. Your *net worth* is the dollar value left when what is owed is subtracted from what is owned, or when liabilities are subtracted from assets.

What Is Owned—Assets   As noted, the asset section identifies things that are valued at their current market prices, not amounts originally paid. It is useful to classify assets as monetary, tangible, or investment assets. *Monetary assets* are cash and near-cash items that can be readily converted to cash, as they are primarily used for living expenses, emergencies, and savings. *Tangible assets* are physical items that have fairly long life spans and could be sold to raise cash but whose primary purpose is to provide maintenance of a lifestyle. *Investment assets* are tangible and intangible items acquired for generating additional income and/or in anticipation of increases in their value. Here are some examples of each kind of asset:

Monetary Assets

Cash (including cash on hand, checking accounts, savings accounts, savings bonds, and money market funds)

Tax refunds due

Money owed to you by others

Tangible Assets

Automobiles, motorcycles, boats, bicycles

House, mobile home, condominium

Household furnishings and appliances

Personal property (jewelry, furs, tools, clothing)

Other "big-ticket" items

Investment Assets

Stocks, bonds, mutual funds, IRAs

Life insurance and annuities (cash value only)

Real estate investments

Company pension and thrift plans

What Is Owed—Liabilities The liabilities section includes any items that reflect debts owed. It would include both personal debts (money borrowed from a friend) and business debts (money owed to a store or a bank). Also, the type of debt owed could be short-term (an obligation to be paid off within one year) or long-term (perhaps a four-year debt on a car or a thirty-year debt on a home). As you construct the liabilities section of your balance sheet, be sure to include all debt obligations; otherwise your financial condition will not be accurate. Examples of items to include in the liabilities section of a balance sheet, with some suggested subheadings, are

Short-term Liabilities

Personal loans (owed to other persons)

Credit card and charge accounts (owed to stores)

Check overdraft line of credit debt outstanding

Bank credit cards (VISA, Discover, MasterCard)

Travel and entertainment credit cards (American Express, Diners Club, Carte Blanche)

Insurance premiums

Professional services (doctors, dentists, lawyers)

Utilities unpaid

Repair services unpaid

Rent unpaid

Taxes unpaid

Long-term Liabilities

Automobile or other transportation loans

Household furnishings loans

Home mortgage

Education loans

What Is Left—Net Worth   Net worth is determined mathematically, and since it must balance, this is the derivation of the term *balance sheet*. It is calculated as follows:

What is owned − what is owed = what is left

or

Assets   −   liabilities   = net worth

You may determine which terminology to use. The terms are not as important as your understanding of the purpose of each section of the balance sheet. The assumption made in determining the net worth section is that if you were to convert all assets to cash and pay all liabilities, the remaining cash would be your net worth.

Illustrated Balance Sheets

The amount of detail shown on a balance sheet depends on for whom it is prepared. Some balance sheets are more detailed than others; you must decide how much to include to accurately show your financial condition on a given date.

Tables 2–4, 2–5, and 2–6 show balance sheets reflecting the degree of detail that may be included for a college student, a young

---

TABLE 2–4
Balance Sheet for a College Student (Bill Soshnik)

Assets		
Cash on hand	$ 85.00	
Checking account	335.00	
Savings account	800.00	
Personal property[a]	1,240.00	
Automobile	3,600.00	
Total assets		$6,060.00
Liabilities		
Utilities	$ 30.00	
Telephone	70.00	
Bank loan—auto	3,100.00	
College loan	1,000.00	
Government educational loan	2,500.00	
Total liabilities		$6,700.00
Net worth		(640.00)
Total liabilities and net worth		$6,060.00

[a] Schedule includes clothes, $800; dresser, $50; television, $150; chair, $30; table, $40; desk, $120; and dishes/tableware, $50.

TABLE 2–5
Balance Sheet for a Young Married Couple (Roy and Mary Als)

Assets

Monetary assets		
Cash on hand	$ 65	
Savings account	550	
Checking account	360	
Total monetary assets		$ 975
Tangible assets		
Automobile	4,300	
Personal property	2,800	
Total tangible assets		7,100
Investment assets		
Stocks	260	
Bonds	500	
Mutual fund	1,200	
Total investment assets		1,960
Total assets		10,035

Liabilities

Short-term liabilities		
Utilities	$ 68	
Credit cards	225	
Rent due	425	
Total short-term liabilities		718
Long-term liabilities		
Education loan	2,200	
Bank personal loan	275	
Auto loan—GMAC	3,200	
Total long-term liabilities		5,675
Total liabilities		6,393
Net worth		3,642
Total liabilities and net worth		$10,035

married couple, and a couple with two children. Notice that Table 2–4 includes very few items. This is typical of single persons who have not acquired many things of value. Observe also the excess of liabilities over assets. This is not unusual for college students, for whom debts seem to rise much faster than assets. In such an example, they are technically *insolvent* because they have a negative net worth. When students graduate and take on full-time jobs, their balance sheets typically change. Tables 2–5 and 2–6 show balance sheets with greater detail and more items, reflecting the increasing financial complexity that occurs at later stages in their lives.

Sources of Information for the Balance Sheet

To construct a balance sheet you need to compile dollar values for your assets and liabilities. Your checkbook, savings account record, and receipts of various payments or investments will be good sources from which to begin. You may have to estimate approximate dollar values for

TABLE 2–6
Balance Sheet for a Couple with Two Children (Rick and Sue Hira)

Assets

Monetary assets			
Cash on hand	$ 260		
Savings accounts	1,500		
Rick's checking account	600		
Sue's checking account	700		
Tax refund due	700		
Rent receivable	660		
Total monetary assets		$ 4,420	
Tangible assets			
Home	76,000		
Personal property	9,000		
Automobile	11,500		
Total tangible assets		96,500	
Investment assets			
Fidelity mutual fund	4,500		
Scudder mutual fund	5,000		
General Motors stock	2,800		
New York 2006 bonds	1,000		
Life insurance cash value	5,400		
IRA	6,300		
Real estate investment	84,000		
Total investment assets		109,000	
Total assets			$209,920

Liabilities

Short-term liabilities			
Utilities	$ 120		
Credit cards	1,545		
Total short-term liabilities		1,665	
Long-term liabilities			
Sales finance company—auto	7,700		
Savings and loan—real estate	72,000		
Total long-term liabilities		79,700	
Total liabilities			$ 81,365
Net worth			128,555
Total liabilities and net worth			$209,920

household furnishings, jewelry, and personal belongings. Remember to value such items at their *fair market value,* or what a willing buyer would pay a willing seller. The dollar values of homes, automobiles, investments, life insurance, and other cash items will be more precise. The degree of precision used to determine the value of assets depends on the purpose and use of a balance sheet. In most cases, your judgment will suffice and detailed estimates are unnecessary. Many people find it useful to make a detailed list or schedule of items summarized on the balance sheet, as illustrated in Figure 2–4, because it helps identify the proper fair market value.

Automobiles

Description	Date of Purchase	Cost	Market Value and Date
Toyota Tercel Wagon - 1987 Model	July 1987	$12,520	$11,000 Dec.-87
Chevy Impala 4 door - 1971 Model	June 1986	$600	$500 Dec.-87

Jewelry and Art

Description	Date of Purchase	Cost	Market Value and Date
1/3 carat solitaire diamond setting	June 1986	$1,600	$1,400 Dec.-87
Remington print	March 1985	$400	$600 Dec.-87
Oriental vase - 12" blue	August 1986	$550	$650 Dec.-87
Oriental vase - 16" blue	November 1986	$900	$1,100 Dec.-87

FIGURE 2–4
Lists or Schedules of Balance Sheet Items

A list of suggested sources for providing the fair market dollar values of assets follows:

1. *Cash items:* from your personal or bank records.
2. *Home:* from the agency where your home is financed or from any real estate broker.
3. *Automobile:* from the lender who financed your automobile or from any lender.
4. *Cash value of insurance policy:* from the policy "cash surrender" table in your policy or from your insurance company.
5. *Investments:* from financial publications or from an investment broker.
6. *Other items of value:* from professional appraisers (for jewelry or collectibles such as valuable coins or stamps).

Below are some suggested sources that provide the dollar values of liabilities:

1. *Personal debts:* from those to whom the debts are owed.
2. *Charge accounts, credit card accounts, loans from banks, and other unpaid bills:* from the lenders in the form of statements or bills.

3. *Other debts:* from debt repayment record (amount of debt incurred less amount of payments made equals remaining debt).

The Income and Expense Statement

The income and expense statement is very different from a balance sheet. The balance sheet shows your financial condition at a single point in time; the income and expense statement summarizes financial transactions over a period of time, such as the previous year. The purpose of the income and expense statement is to show the total amounts that have been earned and spent over a time period. Thus, rather than having to refer to each checkbook entry to know how much you have spent on food during a month or year, you refer only to the "food" category of the income and expense statement.

The income and expense statement allows you to review how well you have done financially in the past period. It shows whether you were able to live within your income. If your expenditures were greater than your income for a given period, for example, you would need to make some spending or income adjustments.

Components of the Income and Expense Statement

An income and expense statement consists of three sections: income (total income received), expenses (total expenditures made) and net income or loss (the difference between total income and total expenses).

Income You may think that income is only what is earned from salaries or wages. However, there are many other types of income that you should include on an income and expense statement, such as the following:

> *Wages and salaries*
> *Bonuses and commissions*
> *Allowances*
> *Child support and alimony*
> *Public assistance*
> *Social Security*
> *Pensions, profit-sharing*
> *Scholarships and grants*
> *Loans*
> *Interest received* (from savings accounts, bonds, or loans to others)
> *Dividends received* (from investments)
> *Gains and/or losses* (from securities or other property)
> *Tax refunds*
> *Other items* (gifts, rent income, pensions, royalties, temporary jobs)

Expenses   All expenditures made during the period covered by the income and expense statement are included in this section. The number and type of expenses shown will vary with each individual and family. Many people separate the expenses by whether they are fixed or variable. *Fixed expenses* are expenditures usually in the same amount each time period; they are often contractual. Examples are rent payments and automobile installment loans. It is usually difficult, but not impossible, to reduce a fixed expense. *Variable expenses* are expenditures over which an individual has considerable control. Food, entertainment, and clothing are variable expenses. Note that some items, such as savings, can be listed twice, as both fixed and variable expenses. Below are several categories of expenses that you could include in a typical income and expense statement.

Fixed Expenses

Housing (rent, mortgage loan payment)

Automobile (installment payment, lease)

Insurance (life, health, liability, disability, renter's, homeowner's, auto)

Contributions (church)

Loans (appliances, furniture)

Savings (Christmas club, regular plan)

Investments (monthly investment plan)

Pension Contributions (employer's plan, IRA)

Taxes (income, real estate, and personal property)

Variable Expenses

Food (at home and away)

Utilities (electric, water, gas, telephone, cable television)

Transportation (gasoline and maintenance, licenses, registration, public transportation)

Medical (physicians, dentists, hospitals, medicines)

Child care (nursery, baby sitting, domestic help)

Clothing and accessories (jewelry, shoes, handbags, briefcases)

Cigarettes and tobacco

Lotteries and gambling

Alcohol and wine

Education (tuition, fees, books, supplies)

Household furnishings (furniture, appliances, curtains)

Personal care (beauty/barbershop, cosmetics, dry cleaner)

Entertainment and recreation (hobbies, recreational equipment, health club, records/tapes/discs, movies)

Contributions (gifts, Christmas, church, school, charity)

Vacations/long weekends

Credit cards

Savings (variable amounts)

Investments (variable amounts)

Miscellaneous (postage, books, magazines, personal allowances, membership fees)

There is no set list of categories to be used in the expense section, but you need to classify all expenditures in some way. The more specific the categories are that you select, the more specific the information that you show in the statement will be.

Net Gain (Loss)   The net gain (loss) section is an important part of the income and expense statement because it shows the amount remaining after you have itemized income and subtracted expenditures from income. The sample figures below illustrate this calculation.

Total income − total expenses = net gain (loss)
$12,500 − $11,400 = $1,100 net income
$14,900 − $15,700 = ($800) net loss

It is important to strive to have **net gain** (total income minus total expenses where income exceeds expenses) rather than **net loss** (total income minus total expenses where expenses exceed income). This shows that you are successful in managing your financial resources and do not have to use savings or borrow to make financial ends meet. When the subtraction shows a net income, that amount is then available (in your checking and savings accounts) to spend, save, and invest.

Illustrated Income and Expense Statements

Income and expense statements vary in detail and amounts depending on who is preparing the statement. Tables 2–7, 2–8, and 2–9 on the following pages show income and expense statements for a college student, a young married couple, and a couple with two children. This last statement vividly illustrates the additional income needed to rear children and shows the increased variety of expenditures that reflects the family's life-cycle changes.

It appears that the more a person earns and spends, the more detailed or involved the income and expense statement becomes. Remember, though, that regardless of the detail or length of the statement, its purpose is always the same—to summarize the income received and the expenses made during a given period of time.

TABLE 2–7
Income and Expense Statement for a College Student
(Bill Soshnik), January 1, 1988–December 31, 1988

Income

Wages (after withholding)	$4,650
Scholarship	1,750
Government grant	2,500
Government loan	2,600
Tax refund	110
Loan from parents	100

Total income	$11,710

Expenses

Room rent (includes utilities)	$1,500
Laundry	216
Food	1,346
Auto loan payments	1,392
Auto insurance	422
Books and supplies	1,032
Tuition	3,260
Telephone	282
Clothing	475
Gifts	300
Auto expenses	656
Health insurance	102
Recreation and entertainment	260
Spring break	100
Personal expenses	300

Total expenses	$11,643
Net gain (available to spend, save, and invest)	$67

Sources of Information for the Income and Expense Statement

Every check written, every receipt received, every payment made, and every earnings payment received provides a source of information to be included in the income and expense statement. Since the statement is a summary, the transaction data are taken from other sources. Some original sources from which information can be gathered include the following:

Checks received	Invoices
Pay records	Statements
Canceled checks	Bills marked paid
Receipts	Payment books or records

Of course, if you keep poor records and save few documents, it will be difficult to prepare a sufficiently detailed income and expense statement. Several helpful examples of keeping detailed and accurate income and expense information appear in the section of this chapter titled "Financial Recordkeeping."

Income

Husband's gross income	$18,500	
Wife's gross income	26,000	
Interest and dividends	300	
Total income		$44,800

Expenses

Fixed expenses			
Home rent	$ 5,100		
Renter's insurance	260		
Auto loan payments	1,975		
Auto insurance, registration,			
and taxes	876		
Life insurance	240		
Hospital loan payments	775		
Federal income taxes	11,964		
State income taxes	1,412		
Social Security taxes	2,686		
Total fixed expenses		$25,288	
Variable expenses			
Food	$ 6,132		
Utilities	2,800		
Gasoline, oil, and repairs	2,250		
Medical expenses	460		
Clothing and upkeep	2,628		
Church	300		
Gifts	340		
Personal allowances	925		
Miscellaneous	240		
Total variable expenses		$16,075	
Total expenses			$41,363
Net gain (available to spend, save, and invest)			$3,437

Ways of Affecting the Financial Statements

Financial activities can affect financial statements. First, changes in market value affect the asset and net worth sections of your balance sheet. An antique vase valued at $900 last year with a current market value of $1,100 increases net worth by $200. Similarly, an automobile valued at $12,520 last year may have depreciated to $11,000, decreasing net worth by $1,520. Second, your liabilities can increase as you acquire more debts or decrease because you make payments. Third, the net gain (or loss) from the income and expense statement reflects an increase (or decrease) in the assets and net worth on your balance sheet. You might take the net gain, for instance, and place it in a savings account, which increases net worth. Fourth, funds can be shifted among categories. For example, assume you make an auto installment payment of $300 to the finance company by using cash from your

TABLE 2–9
Income and Expense Statement for a Couple with Two Children (Rick and Sue Hira), January 1, 1988–December 31, 1988

Income

Husband's gross salary	$33,180	
Wife's salary (part time)	8,500	
Interest and dividends	1,800	
Bonus	600	
Tax refunds	200	
Rental income	7,720	
Total income		$52,000

Expenses

Fixed expenses		
Mortgage loan payments	$10,800	
Homeowner's insurance	460	
Auto loan payments	2,400	
Auto insurance and registration	891	
Life insurance	1,200	
Hospitalization insurance	680	
Savings at credit union	360	
Federal income taxes	10,200	
State income taxes	1,400	
City income taxes	220	
Social Security taxes	2,686	
Real estate and personal property taxes	950	
Total fixed expenses		$32,247
Variable expenses		
Food	$ 5,900	
Utilities	1,800	
Gasoline, oil, and repairs	1,700	
Medical expenses	1,425	
Medicines	165	
Clothing and upkeep	2,160	
Church	600	
Gifts	600	
Personal allowances	1,160	
Children's allowances	480	
Miscellaneous	270	
Total variable expenses		$16,260
Total expenses		$48,507
Net gain (available to spend, save, and invest)		$3,493

checking account. Your net worth would not change because your assets were reduced by $300 and at the same time your liability for the auto loan was reduced by the same amount. If instead the $300 was taken from your current earnings, net worth would have increased, as only the liability changed.

Using Financial Statements in Decision Making

You can use balance sheets and income and expense statements independently or together to assist in your financial decision making, as illustrated below.

The Balance Sheet

Look over the assets on the balance sheet for Rick and Sue Hira in Table 2–6. Do they have too few monetary assets compared to tangible and investment assets? Many experts recommend that at least 25 percent of your assets be monetary, higher as you near retirement. Do you have too much invested in one asset or have you diversified, as the Hiras have? Check your net worth figure to see if you are too much in debt; or, are you like the Hiras, who are in a position to afford to take on additional responsibilities? Also, have your balance sheet figures changed since last year? And, of course, are you making progress toward achieving your financial goals?

The Income and Expense Statement

Look over your income figures to see what proportion comes from labor compared to what proportion comes from investments. Like the Hiras in Table 2–9, most people desire to have a growing proportion of income from investments. Twenty percent is an achievable goal for many persons. In the expense area, it is vital to ask, "Am I spending money where I really want to?" In which categories could you reduce expenses? In which categories could you increase income? The Hiras, for example, might consider increasing their savings and investments.

Using Statements in Combination

You can also use financial statements to assist in providing answers to questions such as, "Is my consumption efficient?" "Do some expense items need justification?" "Would I have enough money if a financial emergency arose?" "Do I have too many debts in relation to assets?" "Can I take on more credit payments?" "Can I afford to buy a luxury item?" "Is there a reserve large enough to cover two or three months of expenses if I become unemployed?" "Should I save and invest more?" "Do I have enough funds to increase my investments?" "In which areas can I reduce expenses to have money for an alternative purpose?" "Is my present homeowner's or renter's insurance coverage sufficient?" "Am I achieving my financial objectives?"

Clear answers to these questions come from using financial statements; they help you assess your financial condition and achieve your financial goals. The balance sheet reports on a particular day. The income and expense statement reports on a past time period. The future is the domain of the budget, which is the subject of the next chapter.

Modern Money Management: Continuing Narratives

Throughout this textbook we will present a continuing narrative about Harry and Belinda Johnson, a fictitious young couple who illustrate many of the important concepts in personal finance. Financial details and narrative about the Johnsons will appear within each chapter when the material is first, self-explanatory, and second, useful to understanding the personal finance concept being presented. If fuller discussion is necessary, it will appear only at the end of a chapter. Therefore, we suggest you turn to the end of this chapter to "meet" the Johnsons, find out about their lifestyle, and look at their financial statements.

Summary

1. Most people need financial planning to achieve their financial objectives. Financial planning should reflect an individual's values, attitudes, and life-cycle circumstances and have appropriate objectives in two broad areas: plans against risks and plans for capital accumulation.

2. Success in financial planning requires explicitly stated financial objectives, certain assumptions made about the economy, logical and consistent financial strategies, and consideration of resources available to meet the objectives. There are thirteen areas of financial planning.

3. Having accessible, organized, and complete financial records is a prerequisite for effective financial planning. Many people also maintain written logs and records of financial activities, including their original source records. Your financial records are useful in preparing financial statements that can help you evaluate where you are, where you have been, and something about where you are going.

4. Financial records can be stored within the home and outside the home. Original items for which there are no other sources or copies could be stored in a safe-deposit box in a bank.

5. Financial statements are compilations of personal financial data designed to furnish information about how money has been used and to provide information about the financial condition of the individual or family involved.

6. The balance sheet describes an individual's or family's financial condition at a particular point in time. Its purpose is to show their present financial position.

7. The income and expense statement lists and summarizes an individual's or family's income and expense transactions that have

taken place over a specific period of time, such as the previous year. It summarizes recent financial history.

8. Financial statements, such as a balance sheet and an income and expense statement, can be used effectively independently or together to assist in financial decision making.

Modern Money Management

The Johnsons' Financial Statements

Harry Johnson graduated with a bachelor's degree in interior design last spring from a large, state-supported university in the Midwest. He attended a community college in his home town before transferring to the university. Belinda graduated last year from an excellent business program at a mid-size college near where she grew up on the west coast. She and Harry met at a conference for student leaders when they were juniors, and their relationship continued to develop, culminating in their marriage in June.

Balance Sheet for Harry and Belinda Johnson, January 31, 1988

Assets

Monetary assets
Cash on hand	$ 570		
Savings—First Federal Bank	190		
Savings—Far West Savings and Loan	70		
Savings—Smith Brokerage Credit Union	60		
Checking account—First Interstate Bank	310		
Total monetary assets		$ 1,200	

Tangible assets
Automobile—1985 Toyota Supra	11,000		
Personal property	1,200		
Furniture	800		
Total tangible assets		$13,000	
Total assets			$14,200

Liabilities

Short-term liabilities
Electricity	$ 65		
VISA credit card	390		
Sears	45		
Rent due	400		
Total short-term liabilities		$ 900	

Long-term liabilities
Education loan—Belinda	3,800		
Auto loan—First Federal Bank	8,200		
Total long-term liabilities		$12,000	
Total liabilities			$12,900

Net worth			$ 1,300
Total liabilities and net worth			$14,200

Harry and Belinda both found jobs in the same city. Harry works at a small interior design firm and earns a gross salary of $1,450 per month. He also receives $3,000 per year from a trust fund set up by his deceased father's estate, which will pay that amount until 1998. Belinda works as a salesperson for a regional stock brokerage firm; when she

---

Income and Expense Statement (First Six Months of Marriage) for Harry and Belinda Johnson, August 1, 1987–January 31, 1988

Income

Harry's gross income ($1,450 × 6)	$ 8,700	
Belinda's gross income ($1,900 × 6)	11,400	
Interest on savings accounts	15	
Harry's trust fund	3,000	
Total income		$23,115

Expenses

Fixed expenses

Rent	$ 2,400	
Renter's insurance	110	
Auto loan payments	1,200	
Auto insurance	320	
Medical insurance (withheld from salary)	390	
Student loan payments	720	
Life insurance (withheld from salary)	54	
Cable television	120	
Health club	300	
Savings (withheld from salary)	60	
Federal income taxes (withheld)	4,080	
State income taxes (withheld)	700	
Social Security (withheld)	1,400	
Auto registration	40	
Total fixed expenses		$11,894

Variable expenses

Food	$ 2,300	
Electricity	450	
Telephone	420	
Gasoline, oil, and maintenance	400	
Doctors' and dentists' bills	310	
Medicines	40	
Clothing and upkeep	1,300	
Church and charity	800	
Gifts	480	
Christmas gifts	350	
Public transportation	580	
Personal allowances	1,040	
Entertainment	780	
Vacation (Christmas)	700	
Vacation (summer)	600	
Miscellaneous	440	
Total variable expenses		$10,990
Total expenses		$22,884
Net gain (available to spend, save, and invest)		$231

finishes her training program in another month, her gross salary will increase $200 a month to $2,100. She has many job-related benefits, including life insurance, health insurance, and a credit union.

The Johnsons live in an apartment about halfway between each place of employment. Harry drives about ten minutes to his job and Belinda gets downtown to work on public transportation in about fifteen minutes. Their apartment is very nice, but small, and is furnished mostly with old furniture given to them by their families.

Soon after starting their first jobs, Harry and Belinda decided to begin their financial planning. Each had taken a college course in personal finance, so after initial discussion, they worked together for two evenings to develop the two financial statements presented here.

Key Words and Concepts

assets, 33
balance sheet, 33
fair market value, 37
financial goals, 25
financial planning, 25
financial statements, 32
fixed expenses, 40
housing ownership record, 30
income and expense
    statement, 33
insolvent, 36
investment assets, 33

liabilities, 33
monetary assets, 33
net gain, 41
net loss, 41
net worth, 33
original source records, 28
safe-deposit box, 31
tangible assets, 33
tax-deductible expenditure
    record, 30
variable expenses, 40

Review Questions

1. Why do most people need financial planning?
2. What is financial planning and in what two broad areas does it occur?
3. What three things do you need to be successful at financial planning?
4. List the thirteen areas of financial planning.
5. Of what value are financial records and how can they be used?
6. List some appropriate categories for organizing financial records.
7. Why do many people maintain additional written logs or records of financial activities?
8. Where can you maintain financial records in the home?
9. Explain how a safe-deposit box works.

10. Why are financial statements prepared?

11. How can you use a balance sheet?

12. Explain how to derive net worth.

13. Differentiate between monetary, tangible, and investment assets.

14. Explain the difference between short- and long-term liabilities.

15. Why must assets be listed on a balance sheet at their fair market value?

16. What does an income and expense statement show the person who prepares it?

17. Differentiate between fixed and variable expenses.

18. Explain what net income can be used for.

19. Identify three ways of affecting financial statements.

20. Explain and give two examples of how you can use financial statements in decision making.

Case Problems

1. Roy and Mary Als of Albany, New York, were recently married. Mary prepared a draft of their balance sheet as shown in Table 2–5. As Roy was examining their financial statement, he wondered how Mary obtained the financial information to value their fixed assets accurately. Describe how she probably determined fair market prices for each of the tangible and investment assets.

2. Rick and Sue Hira of Des Moines, Iowa, spent some time making up their first balance sheet, which is shown in Table 2–6. They are a bit confused, though, about how various financial activities can affect their net worth. Using the figures in their balance sheet, calculate *and* characterize the impact of each of the following events (which could occur over a year's time) on their net worth.
   a. Their home is appraised at $82,000, and the value of their automobile drops to $9,500.
   b. The Hiras make monthly payments on their auto loan, reducing the balance owed to $5,000.
   c. They take out a bank loan for $1,545 and pay off their debts of $1,545 on credit cards.
   d. They take $300 from their earnings and put it into their savings account.

3. Review the financial statements of Roy and Mary Als (Tables 2–5 and 2–8), and respond to the following questions:
   a. The Alses seem to have too few monetary assets compared to tangible and investment assets. What do you recommend they do over the next few years to remedy that imbalance?

b. Comment on their diversification of investment assets.

c. How does their net worth compare to their total liabilities?

d. The Alses seem to have almost all their income coming from labor versus investments. What do you recommend they do over the next few years to remedy that imbalance?

e. The Alses want to take a two-week vacation next summer, and they have only eight months to save the necessary $1,200. What reasonable changes in expenses *and* income should they consider to increase net income the needed $150 a month?

Suggested Readings

"Financial Planning That Gets Results." *Consumer Digest,* March/April 1987, pp. 49–54. Suggestions on setting realistic goals and selecting the right experts to assist.

"Fortune Forecast: Inflation Won't Come Roaring Back." *Fortune,* May 25, 1987, pp. 37–38. *Fortune's* predictions on the future of interest rates, inflation, and the economy.

"How the Wealthy Get That Way." *Fortune,* April 13, 1987, pp. 32–38. Entrepreneurship remains the road to top financial success.

"Introducing the Changing Times Prosperity Index." *Changing Times,* January 1987, pp. 67–74. A new way of looking at wealth suggests that Americans are better off than previously thought.

"Ready . . . Set . . . Go: Get Organized." *Changing Times,* January 1987, pp. 63–66. How a financial blueprint can show gaps in your financial planning.

"Sizing Up Your Finances." *U.S. News and World Report,* June 8, 1987, pp. 52–55. Details and worksheets to assess your financial status.

"Would It Pay You to Go Back to School?" *Better Homes and Gardens,* April 1987, pp. 34–36. Pros, cons, and decision-making suggestions.

CHAPTER 3

Budgeting

OBJECTIVES

After reading this chapter, the student should be able to

1. illustrate the impact of life-cycle periods and stages on the financial tasks, problems, and challenges facing people today.

2. identify the six phases of budgeting.

3. recognize the relationship between long-term and short-term goals and their importance in the financial goal-setting phase of budgeting.

4. identify the purpose of the planning phase of budgeting.

5. describe the issues to be considered and the tasks to be performed in the decision-making phase of budgeting.

6. describe the key aspects of the implementing phase of budgeting, particularly the creation of a cash flow calendar and establishment of a revolving savings fund.

7. illustrate the purposes and methods of controlling budgets.

8. explain the importance of the evaluating phase of budgeting.

" **P**lan the work and work the plan," say good organizers. Once you have taken stock of your financial position, you must take action to move toward effective financial planning.

We discussed the first step in Chapter 2—preparing the balance sheet and the income and expense statement. The second step is budgeting. A *budget* is a document or set of documents used to record estimated and actual income and expenditures for a period of time. *Budgeting* is a process of financial planning and controlling that involves using those records to set and achieve short-term goals that are in harmony with long-term goals.

We begin this chapter by presenting background information useful in developing good perspectives on budgeting. We examine life-cycle periods, stages, and pathways as well as the financial tasks, problems, and challenges confronting people today. Next, we provide some information about today's confident generation of young Americans. All of this is preparatory to a fuller understanding of the process of budgeting: establishing financial objectives and goals, planning, decision making, implementing, controlling, and evaluating.

Life-cycle Financial Activities

A *life cycle* is a description of the progress of human life along a continuous sequence of family-status periods and stages. It includes three life-cycle periods—childhood, singlehood, and couplehood—and numerous stages, as shown in Figure 3–1.

Singlehood or Couplehood?

Upon becoming adults, people enter into a time of predominate economic self-sufficiency. At that point, individuals move into either the singlehood or couplehood life-cycle periods. Then they remain in either the singlehood or couplehood period or move back and forth between the periods while going through certain stages. For example, an individual in early singlehood could follow the traditional pathway: 4, 5, 6, 7, 8, 9, and 10. (See Figure 3–1.) Or perhaps an individual could choose to follow stages 1, 2, 3, 11, and 12, the single adult's pathway.

What is important to point out is that earnings and consumption are sharply affected by an individual's changes in periods and stages in the life cycle. Numerous factors affect an individual's movement through periods of the life cycle, including values, attitudes, abilities, education, emotional makeup, jobs, careers, procreation inclinations, religion, marital stability, spouse's lifespan, life goals, opportunities, and luck. Many of these factors are controllable and, therefore, we can assume, within the destiny of the individual.

FIGURE 3–1
Life-cycle Periods, Stages, and Pathways

Source: Adapted from the original article by Ronald W. Stampfl, published in the *Journal of Home Economics*, Spring 1979, and reprinted by permission of the American Home Economics Association.

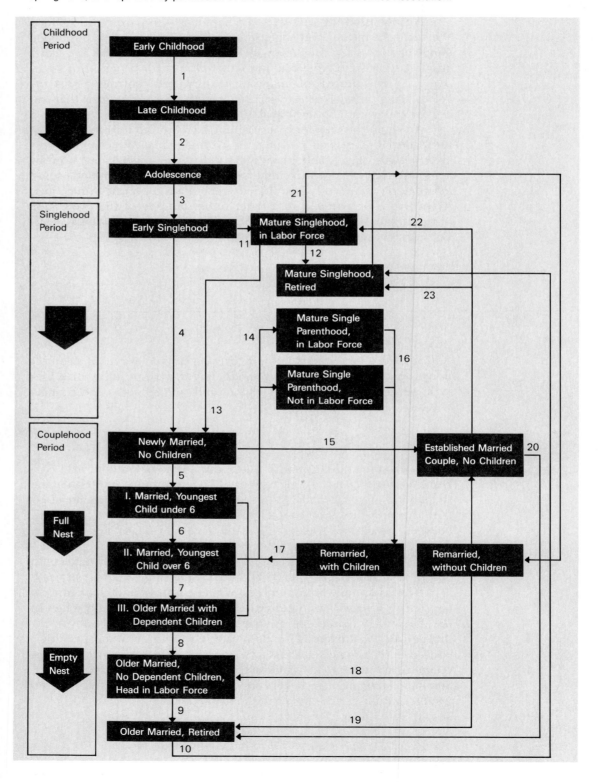

Changes in the life cycle bring about numerous financial tasks, problems, and challenges, as depicted in Table 3–1. The resources each person brings to financial management problems vary. Importantly, the remainder of this book addresses *each and every* task, problem, and challenge thus identified; therefore we hope that it becomes a valuable resource for your effective financial management.

A Confident Generation of Youth

The complexion of American society changes with each passing generation. According to U.S. Census data, today only 58 percent of the approximately 90 million households are married-couple households. Another 14 percent are single-parent families. Twenty-four percent are single-person households and the remaining 4 percent are households with two or more unrelated persons. Among this latter group are about 2 million couples living together but not married.

Of the total U.S. population of about 240 million, there are 29 million 18- to 24-year-olds, split almost evenly between males and females. More than 30 percent are in school and 75 percent are single. Young people are postponing marriage. The median marriage age is 25.5 for men and 23.3 for women. Sixty-two percent of men and 47 percent of women 18 to 24 years old still live with their parents, many because of financial reasons.

A recent *Washington Post*–ABC News poll reveals the 18–24 age group to be "optimistic, ambitious, independent, sober, competitive, pragmatic and restless but not rebellious." Many seem to have an entrepreneurial spirit and want to be in business for themselves. Seven out of ten say that they eventually will be better off financially than their parents. "Being well off financially" is reported as an essential or very important goal by 71 percent. In short, today's confident generation of young Americans appears to believe that "you can have it all."

Budgeting and Its Phases

Success in meeting life's financial tasks, problems, and challenges is likely to be greater if you have a good understanding of the process of budgeting. The purpose of budgeting is to help you achieve long- and short-term goals that are consistent with your overall financial plans. This is an *exciting* endeavor even though many people associate budgeting with words such as *tedious, nervousness, recordkeeping, time consuming, self-denial, frustrating, details,* and *failure*.

Budgeting forces you to think about what is important in your life, what things you want to own, what it will take to obtain them, and more generally, what you want to achieve in life. Budgeting gives you control

TABLE 3–1
Financial Tasks, Problems, and Challenges over Various Periods of the Life Cycle

	Singlehood, Transitional	Singlehood, Mature	Couplehood, Childless	Couplehood, Full Nest, First Stage	Couplehood, Full Nest, Second Stage
Characteristics	Views current status as transitional. May have unclear values. Highly mobile in housing and career. Possesses few assets. Income probably at lowest point, but rising.	Makes commitment to lifestyle and career. Possesses clear values and is goal oriented. Earns higher income. Enjoys quality vacations.	Makes commitment to relationship. Clarifies values and goals. Highly mobile. Possesses few assets. Both spouses earn money income.	First stage, youngest child under age 6. Decreased mobility. Some assets have been accumulated. Material needs seem to increase. Income does not rise much, may drop.	Second stage, youngest child over age six. Income continues to rise. Increased mobility. Have many assets. Both spouses may earn money income.
Financial management tasks, problems, and challenges	Use credit for the first time. Purchase first automobile, basic furniture, stereos, etc. Learn to control a budget. Establish a record-keeping system. Make a spending plan. Start a savings plan. Overspend budget. Rent an apartment.	Effectively handle increasing income. Need a more complex budget. Expand savings program. Start to make growth investments. Need financial planning. Buy a home or rent a dwelling. Purchase life and health insurance.	Discuss and resolve disagreements over money. Resolve value and lifestyle differences. Buy life insurance. Consider opportunity costs of having children. Need a more complex budget. Avoid paying too much in income taxes.	Discuss and resolve spending styles. Buy renters and/or homeowner's insurance. Additional costs of child. Need a more complex budget. Potential unemployment of one parent. Match expenses to income.	Desire to replace assets with better quality. Higher expenses for children. Increased budget demands. Income tax return audited. Purchase a second home. Increase savings for children's education.

Buy automobile insurance.
Establish financial goals and plans.
Pay income tax.
Resolve computer billing errors.
Pay medical bills.
Cover education costs.

Buy renter's and/or home owner's insurance.
Should itemize on income taxes.
Plan income tax strategies.
Write a will.
Build an emergency cash reserve.
Establish an individual retirement account (IRA).
Open a money market account.
Consider disability and liability insurance.
Consider tax-exempt investments.
Consider professional financial planning.
Develop an effective recordkeeping system.
Maintain credit standing.
Assess progress toward financial objectives.

Write a will.
Consider buying a house or condominium.
Establish an individual retirement account (IRA).
Build an emergency cash reserve.
Open a money market account.
File claims for medical insurance reimbursements.
Potential overuse of credit.

Frustrated with slow financial progress.
Revise will.
Consider estate planning.
Start an education savings plan for children.
Potential credit misuse as needs increase.
Purchase a second automobile.
Increase/change life and health insurance.
Start saving for down payment on a home.
Establish a spousal individual retirement account (IRA).
Consider life insurance for dependents.
First home purchase.
Itemization of income taxes.
Reexamine family/personal goals.

Consider debt consolidation to pay bills.
Consider disability insurance.
Consider opportunity costs of returning to school.
Have spouse return to earning money income.
Involve children in financial matters.

(continued)

TABLE 3–1
(continued)

	Couplehood, Full Nest, Third Stage	Couplehood, Empty Nest, Fourth Stage	Single Parenthood	Retirement
Characteristics	Third stage, all children have reached adolescence or left home. Values clear. Improving financial situation. Less mobile. Possess many assets. Both spouses may earn money income.	Empty nest, no children at home. Strong financial position. Values clear. Mobility possibility increases. Both spouses may earn money income.	Income limited. Reclarifying values. Mobility increases. Some assets have been accumulated.	Values clear. Financial condition sound. Less mobile. Possess many assets.
Financial management tasks, problems, and challenges	High educational costs for children. Money available for nonessential items (appliances, new furniture, boat). Tax shelter planning. Plan for retirement. Estate planning. Increasing recreational expenses. Automobile insurance for teenager.	Desire to replace assets with better quality. Children need occasional financial aid. Pay for extended travel, home improvements. Increase emergency cash reserve. Purchase other housing to accommodate changing needs.	Potential sharp drop in income. Compensate for or buy skills of a partner, such as housekeeping and day care. Income not rising much. Consider opportunity costs of returning to school. Need to acquire more assets.	Decrease in income. Living on fixed income. Concern about outliving income. Increase in medical costs. Reduce life insurance. Buy Medicare. Purchase supplemental health insurance. Update will. Consider part-time job.

Make conservative investments.
Open a money market account.
Consider disability and liability insurance.
Update home owner's insurance.
Consider tax-exempt investments.
Consider tax-free gifts and loans to children.
Consider professional financial planning.
Increased childrearing costs.
Consider changing housing after children leave home.
Evaluate dependents' future financial needs.

Set up trusts for children.
Update will.
Consider tax-free gifts for children.
Consider tax-exempt investments.
Consider professional financial planning.
Reduce life insurance.
Analyze future retirement income and sources.

Consider renter's/home owner's insurance.
Need to match expenses to income.
Frustration with slow financial progress.
Make a will.
Start education savings plan for children.
Buy life insurance.
Potential credit misuse.
Involve children in financial matters.
Cope with increasing child care costs.
Need to establish short- and long-term goals.

Use up part of investments without outliving funds.
Sell home/buy a retirement home.
Switch to lower-risk investments.
Establish trusts to reduce taxes.
Update letter of last instructions.
Finance leisure activities.

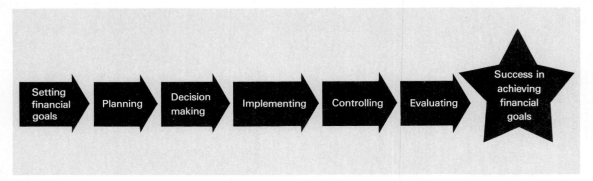

FIGURE 3–2
Phases in the Budgeting Process

over your finances by providing the necessary information and insight that cannot be obtained in any other manner. The six-phase budgeting process illustrated in Figure 3–2 can be adapted to suit your needs while giving you the competence and confidence to manage your financial affairs successfully—forever.

The Financial Goal-setting Phase of Budgeting

Written financial plans to achieve goals and objectives need to be made in two broad groups: (1) plans for protection against financial risks, and (2) plans for capital accumulation. The thirteen areas of financial planning (previously listed in Figure 2–2) are illustrated in Table 3–2 (pp. 62–63), which shows corresponding operational objectives and goals for a young couple.

The key to developing financial plans in all thirteen areas is to identify your long- and short-term goals. You can do this during the financial goal-setting phase of budgeting. *Long-term goals or objectives* are generally targets or ends that an individual or family desires to achieve using financial resources one or more years in the future. Long-term goals and objectives provide direction for overall financial planning. One long-term goal might be to save $15,000 within five years for a down payment for a home. Others could be more general, such as to have substantial shares of common stock investments that would pay dividends equivalent to 5 percent of an individual's salary income. When placing dollar values on goals up to five years in the future, it is generally fair to assume that interest earned on savings will offset inflationary increases. (Otherwise, use Appendix A1.)

Long-term goals and objectives need to be somewhat flexible given the length of time involved in achieving them. You should recognize that thinking about and writing down an overall financial plan does not mean your life's goals are set forever. As circumstances change, you will want to review and revise your overall financial plans. An annual review is appropriate. Involving all members of the family in the decision-making process gives each person a feeling of ownership as well as a sense of commitment to the overall financial plan.

Short-term goals or objectives are needs and wants requiring financial resources that can be satisfied within one year. These goals should be consistent with the general direction of long-term goals and objectives. One short-term objective might be to pay off an outstanding VISA credit card balance within six months. Another might be to save $1,200 by July so you can go to Europe on vacation. Often, short-term goals represent partial steps toward achieving long-term goals. For example, to achieve a long-term goal of saving $15,000 for a down payment for a home within five years, your first-year goal may be to save $3,000.

You should express explicitly both long- and short-term goals when possible. Figure 3–3 provides worksheet examples of how much must be saved to reach short- and long-term goals. Short-term goals in

FIGURE 3–3
Goals Worksheet for Harry and Belinda Johnson

Date worksheet prepared *January 20, 1988*

LONG-TERM GOALS WORKSHEET

1 Goals	2 Approximate Amount Needed	3 Month and Year Needed*	4 Number of Months to Save	5 Date Start Saving	6 Monthly Amount to Save (2÷4)
European vacation	$ 3,000	August 1990	30	2-88	$ 100
Down payment on new auto	5,000	October 1991	45	1-88	111
Down payment on home	15,000	January 1993	48	1-89	312

*Goals requiring more than 5 years to achieve require consideration of investment return and after-tax yield, which will be presented in later chapters.

Date worksheet prepared *January 20, 1988*

SHORT-TERM GOALS WORKSHEET

1 Goals	2 Approximate Amount Needed	3 Month and Year Needed*	4 Number of Months to Save	5 Date Start Saving	6 Monthly Amount to Save (2÷4)
Part of down payment on new auto	$ 1,332	12-88	12	1-88	$ 111
Part of European vacation	1,100	12-88	11	2-88	100
Christmas vacation	700	12-88	12	1-88	58
Summer vacation	600	8-88	6	2-88	100
Anniversary party	250	6-88	5	1-88	50

TABLE 3-2
Financial Plans, Goals, and Objectives for Harry (Age 23) and Belinda (Age 22) Johnson (Prepared in January 1988)

Financial Plan Areas	Long-term Goals and Objectives	Short-term Goals
Against risks		
1. Medical costs	Avoid large medical costs.	Maintain employer-subsidized medical insurance policy by paying $65 monthly premium.
2. Property and casualty losses	Eventually buy renter's insurance. Always have maximum automobile insurance coverage.	Make quarterly premium payments of $120 on automobile insurance policy. Comparison shop for lower rates for automobile insurance.
3. Liability losses	Eventually buy liability insurance.	Hope for the best.
4. Premature death	Have adequate life insurance coverage for both of us as well as lots of financial investments so the survivor would not have any financial worries.	Maintain employer-subsidized life insurance of $34,200 on Belinda. Buy some life insurance for Harry. Start some investments.
5. Income loss from disability	Eventually buy disability insurance or have sufficient investment income not to worry.	Hope for the best.
For capital accumulation		
6. Tax fund	Have enough money for taxes (but not too much) withheld from monthly salaries by both employers to cover eventual tax liabilities.	Reconfirm that employer withholding of taxes is sufficient. Have some extra money withheld to cover additional tax liability because of dividends on trust from deceased father.

7. Revolving savings fund	Always have sufficient cash in local accounts to meet monthly and annual anticipated budget expense needs.	Develop cash flow calendar to ascertain needs. Put money into revolving savings fund to build it up quickly to the proper balance. Keep all funds in interest-earning accounts.
8. Emergency fund	Build up monetary assets equivalent to three month's take-home pay.	Put $200 a month into emergency fund until it gets at least up to one month's take-home pay.
9. Education	Maintain educational skills and credentials to successfully compete with coworkers. Have employer assist in paying for Belinda to earn a master's in business administration (MBA) degree. Eventually have Harry complete a master of fine arts (MFA) degree and perhaps even a doctor of philosophy (Ph.D.) in interior design.	Both take one graduate class per term.
10. Savings	Always have a nice-sized savings balance. Regularly save to achieve our goals. Save some portion of any extra income or gifts. Save $15,000 for a down payment on a home to be bought within five years.	Save enough to pay cash for a good quality video cassette recorder (VCR). Pay off VISA credit card balance of $390 soon.
11. Investments	Own substantial shares of a conservative mutual fund that will pay dividends equivalent to about 10 percent of family income at age 45. Own some real estate and common stocks.	Start investing in a mutual fund before next year.
12. Retirement	Retire at age 60 or earlier on an income that is the same as the take-home pay earned just before retirement.	Establish individual retirement accounts (IRAs) for Harry and Belinda before next year. Select the best retirement benefit plan offered by employer to meet long-term needs.
13. Estate planning	Provide a substantial sum of money for surviving spouse	Each spouse makes a will.

particular must be stated clearly or you will never know when you have achieved them. "To save enough for a down payment on an automobile" is not as clear as "to save $2,400 by December of this year for a down payment on a new Honda Civic."

The Planning Phase of Budgeting

Budget planning is a developmental phase in budgeting in which personal financial planners decide on the structural and mechanical aspects appropriate for their personalized budgets. You should plan to have a positive attitude toward budgeting, maintain flexibility, plan the recording format, plan to use the cash or accrual basis of budgeting, plan to use various budgeting classifications, and plan to budget over a certain time period.

A Positive Attitude

Developing a positive attitude toward budgeting is important because effective financial planning cannot be done without it. If you enjoy recordkeeping and desire a very detailed budget then you can easily spend five hours a week on appropriate tasks. If you do not particularly enjoy numbers, accept the fact—with a smile on your face—that you need to spend one hour a week on budgeting efforts; then do it. Recognize, too, that it is your financial life that you are managing and only you will ever know what will satisfy you.

The Importance of Flexibility

Allowing for the unknown or for unexpected financial activities is part of the budgeting process. Bear in mind that budgeting is a process, a working tool, and that its use should be flexible. Do not treat a budget as if it were engraved in marble. Make and use a budget to fulfill your changing needs, wants, and goals.

For example, suppose you earmark $60 a month for medical expenses. Suddenly, you need emergency medical service to treat a severe stomach ulcer (perhaps caused by too much worry and poor eating habits). Common sense would tell you to treat the problem even though the cost exceeds the $60 allowance. Such occurrences typically mean that other expenditures will have to be reduced or eliminated. On the other hand, don't be overly flexible. To purposefully overspend on recreational activities because you feel constrained on a $100-per-month allowance may not be prudent.

Recording Format

People sometimes become frustrated with the budgeting process because of the recordkeeping it requires. For your budget to work, you must keep records and use a recording format that suits your needs. You can choose from among self-prepared, commercial, or computer budget records.

Value of Recordkeeping in Budgeting *Recordkeeping,* the process of recording the sources and amounts of dollars earned and spent, is an integral part of the budgeting process. Its primary value lies in providing detailed information as to what happened financially during any given period of time. Recording both the *estimated* and the *actual* amounts for income and expenditures will help you keep track of money flow.

If you do not record data, such as $49.22 spent for food during the week, your alternatives are to trust the amount to memory or to keep a receipt of the expenditure. You could keep receipts for all expenditures and payroll check stubs for all income received, and memorize estimates for all projected earning and spending, but such a practice would likely be inaccurate and cumbersome. Keeping track of all income and expenses may be one of the more uninteresting tasks in the budget process, but it is the only way to collect sufficient information to evaluate how close you are to achieving your financial objectives.

Self-prepared Budget Records Many people decide that commercially prepared records are inflexible, and they prefer to design a budget record suited to their own needs. Figure 3–4 shows four samples of self-prepared budget records that range in complexity. In the next section of this chapter you will learn how budget data are recorded.

Commercially Prepared Budget Records Numerous types of commercially prepared recordkeeping forms and booklets are available. They range in price from a few dollars for some forms to perhaps $100 for an elaborately prepared kit. A disadvantage of these kinds of records is that they reflect another person's ideas about how your budgetary data should be recorded. It is not essential to use an expensive format; you should simply pay for the kinds of forms that satisfy your needs.

Computer Budget Records The use of personal computers and word processors in the budgeting process is becoming commonplace. Radio Shack, Apple, IBM, Lanier, and Wang are just a few brands of electronic recordkeeping equipment that are widely used. You can either purchase computer budget programs from these companies or design your own budget programs. Electronic recordkeeping has many advantages. The data stored in a computer's memory can be displayed on a screen for analysis almost instantaneously, in most cases by the pressing of a button. In the more expensive systems, printed documents can be generated. The price of electronic recordkeeping equipment is well within reach of many individuals and families and will probably become more accessible as costs lower and home computer use expands.

(a) Simple Form for Each Budget Classification

Food Budget—$90			
Date	Activity	Amount	Balance
2-6	Groceries	$20	$70
2-9	Dinner out	8	62
2-14	Groceries	11	51

(b) More Complex Form for Each Budget Classification

Date	Activity	Amount Budgeted	Expenditures	Balance
2-1	Budget estimate	$90		$90
2-6	Groceries		$20	70
2-9	Dinner out		8	62
2-14	Groceries		11	51
2-20	Groceries		25	26
2-26	Dinner out		10	16
2-28	Groceries		9	7
2-28	February totals	90	$83	$7

(c) Simple Form for All Expense Classifications

Date	Activity	Food Bud—$90	Clothing Bud—$30	Expenditures Auto Bud—$60	Rent Bud—$275	Savings Bud—$60	Utilities Bud—$40	Total Exp. Bud—$680	Remarks
2-1	Gasoline			10				10	
2-6	Groceries	20						20	Had friends over
2-8	Gasoline			7				7	Good price
2-9	Dinner out	8						8	
2-14	Groceries	11						11	Pepsi on sale
2-15	Subtotals	/39		/17				/56	
2-16	Telephone						41	41	
2-17	Tire			64				64	Emergency

FIGURE 3–4
Budget Forms

Cash or Accrual Basis?

You can use either of two systems of financial recording in your budgeting process. **Cash basis budgeting** recognizes earnings and expenditures when money is actually received or paid out. **Accrual basis budgeting** recognizes earnings and expenditures when the money is earned and expenditures are incurred, regardless of when money is actually received or paid. Most people follow the cash basis in the budgeting process because it is easier to use.

To illustrate both practices for recording financial transactions, suppose you are paid on the twentieth of the month for work done the

(d) More Complex Form for All Income and Expenditure Classifications

			Income		Expenditures								
			Salary	Other income	Food	Cloth.	Auto Expend.	Rent	Savings	Util.	Total Expend.	Remarks
Estimates			700	40	90	30	60	275	60	40	680	
Balance forwarded (from January)			—	—	6	—	14	—	—	2	28	
Sum			700	40	96	30	74	275	60	42	708	
Date	Activity	Cash In										
2-1	Paycheck	700	700									
2-1	Texaco-gasoline						10				10	
2-6	Safeway-groceries				20						20	Had friends over
2-8	7/11 – gasoline						7				7	Good price
2-9	Dinner out-Pizza				8						8	
2-14	Giant-groceries				11						11	Pepsi on sale
2-15	Subtotals	/700			/39		/17				/56	
2-16	AT&T-telephone									41	41	
2-17	Goodyear-tire						64				64	Emergency
2-28	Totals	700	700	40	83	28	57	275	60	39	660	Good month

FIGURE 3–4
Continued

first through the fifteenth, and on the fifth for work done the sixteenth through the end of the month. Using the cash basis, you would recognize and record income on the fifth and the twentieth, when it is paid. Using the accrual basis, you would recognize and record income on the fifteenth and at the end of the month, when it is earned. Likewise, if you record a VISA card purchase at the time of the purchase, you are using the accrual basis, when the expenditure is incurred. But if you record the purchase when you actually make the VISA card payment, you are using the cash basis.

Either basis will work as long as you use it consistently. Once you decide on a basis, stick with it. Otherwise, your cash position will shift constantly and budget accuracy will be difficult to maintain.

Budgeting Classifications

People who use only a checkbook for budgeting purposes have only two broad budgeting classifications: income (deposits to the checking account) and expenditures (checks written). Although this is useful data there is much to be gained by having more detailed classifications.

Table 3–3 shows some simple as well as complex budget classifications for income and expenses. The illustrated simple budgeting classifications number only twelve expense items and that is a suitable format for many people. One danger exists: too many expenditures may be

TABLE 3–3
Sample Budgeting Classifications and Expense Guidelines

Simple	Complex	

Income

Salary
Nonsalary

Income

Salary	Capital gains
Rent	Tax refunds
Interest	Loans
Dividends	Other

Expenses[a]

Food (12%–30%)[b]
Housing and utilities (20%–45%)
Transportation (5%–20%)
Insurance (2%–10%)
Clothing (1%–10%)
Medical (2%–8%)
Entertainment/vacations (2%–5%)
Savings and investments (0%–10%)
Personal/miscellaneous (2%–5%)
Credit payments (0%–15%)
Gifts and contributions (1%–10%)
Taxes (8%–20%)

Expenses

Fixed expenses	*Variable expenses*
Home mortgage loan	Revolving budget savings fund
Life insurance	Other savings
Health insurance	Food at home
Disability insurance	Food away from home
Homeowner's insurance	Electric
Automobile insurance	Water
Church	Telephone
Other contributions	Cable television
Christmas gifts	Gasoline and oil
Other gifts	Automobile maintenance and
Automobile loan	repairs
Loan 1	Auto registration
Loan 2	Public transportation
Savings (withheld from salary)	Doctors
Federal income taxes	Dentists
State income taxes	Medicines
Real estate property taxes	Child care
Personal property taxes	Domestic help
Mutual fund investment	Clothing and accessories
Monthly investment plan	Tobacco products
Pension contributions	Alcoholic beverages
Individual retirement account	Education
	Furnishings and appliances
	Personal care
	Entertainment
	Recreation
	Vacations
	Long weekends
	Credit card 1
	Credit card 2
	Savings—other
	Investments—other
	Miscellaneous

[a] The percentages represent the range of expenses of various family units.
[b] The U.S. Department of Agriculture reports that more than half of all meals are eaten outside the home.

classified under "miscellaneous," which will take away from the information value of the classifications. Should that occur, perhaps when the miscellaneous classification amounts to more than 5 percent of the total expenditures, simply review each expenditure carefully and try to create other classifications. For example, you might need to create a new classification called "contributions" or "vices." You can break the broad

Using a computer to help you manage personal finances may be a good idea depending upon your circumstances. It is not too expensive if you already own a computer. Most commercially available software programs for personal finance cost from $150 to $250. (Popular programs include Andrew Tobias's "Managing Your Money," available from MECA, 285 Riverside Avenue, Westport, CT 06880, and "Dollars and Sense," from Monogram, 8295 S. La Cienega Blvd., Ingleside, CA 90301.) Before making a purchase, however, realize that you must have the self-discipline to input data regularly or you will have simply wasted your money on software that is not functional because your financial management data base is outdated.

Benefits of using a computer in personal finance are many: laborious calculations are reduced to a minimum, comparisons of data are simple to perform, budgets can be created easily with many revisions, income taxes can be prepared, investments can be analyzed, banking transactions can be performed, shopping can be done, financial statements can be prepared, and financial plans can be developed.

Finding a software program to fit your needs requires some investigation. After talking to friends and conducting some research on the topic, you may want to visit local libraries, schools, and colleges and try out the programs that are available. You should consider software that has data base management (an electronic filing cabinet suitable for checkbook and budgeting information) and spreadsheet capability (permits calculating the effects of a variety of transactions).

classifications into more detailed categories; many computer programs offer more than one hundred budget classifications. Should you need additional ideas, recall that Chapter 2 presented other suggestions.

It is important in planning budget classifications to note the four different ways that savings can be categorized in the budget: (1) savings withheld from income and deposited directly to a savings account, (2) savings as a fixed expenditure (paying yourself a set amount each period), (3) savings as a variable expenditure (paying yourself an undetermined amount each period, and (4) savings that may be available after all other expenditures are paid. The problem with the last two methods is that you might not save at all.

Time Periods Covered

Most people plan an annual budget to cover income and expenses for a twelve-month period. They also develop monthly budgets because they receive their paychecks on a monthly or semimonthly basis. Using a limited time frame, such as a month, enables you to identify and control your financial activities and to maintain accurate records.

The Decision-making Phase of Budgeting

The decision-making phase of budgeting focuses on the financial aspects of budgeting and the decisions about where the funds will come from as well as where they should go. Thus, the financial manager begins by examining a number of factors that affect budgeting decisions. He or she then makes realistic budget estimates for income and expenses, and continues decision making by resolving conflicting needs and wants.

Factors That Can Affect Budgeting

It would be convenient if all the data contributing to a budget were objective and automatic. But putting together a budget is not so precise. Invariably, there will be both external and internal forces that greatly influence the ultimate budget design, including inflation and economic conditions, personal spending style (as well as the influence of a partner's conflicting spending style), opportunity costs in decision making, marginal costs, and the time value of money.

Inflation and Economic Conditions

Inflation is perhaps the single most influential factor affecting budgets. The inflation rate at any given time will necessarily affect your purchasing power. For example, given a family income of $23,000 and annual inflation of 6.5 percent, what would be the effect on purchasing power? The purchasing power of $23,000 would drop in one year to $21,597 (100.0 ÷ 106.5 = .939; reciprocal is .061; $23,000 × .061 = $1,403; $23,000 − $1,403 = $21,597).

Serious unemployment in the general economy may also influence your budget. Of course, a loss of income caused by a temporary layoff from a job most certainly affects your budgeting.

A significant increase or decrease in government taxes will also alter the amount of money available to spend, save, and invest. A decrease in taxes would increase the aggregate amount of money available to spend; an increase in taxes would decrease it.

An increase in interest rates can have a serious effect upon budgeting because the amount allocated for credit purchases will need to be increased. Suppose it is June and you are planning to buy a $92,000 home with a $12,000 down payment; you will then obtain a thirty-year mortgage loan at 9 percent for the balance. By July the interest rates may have risen (or fallen). If, for some reason, you must wait until July to buy the home, you may have a monthly mortgage payment of $702 instead of $644, only because interest rates have increased by one percentage point. You must consider inflation, interest rates, and general economic conditions in your budget planning.

Personal Spending Style and Couples with Conflicting Styles

We each have our own *personal spending style*, which is influenced by our values, attitudes, emotions, and other factors shaped through the experiences of life.

Five types of personal spending styles are apparent among people. Can you recognize them? First are "tightwads," who save so much that they do so compulsively and little is left even for essentials. Second are the "givers," who are generous to a fault. Whether they have the money or not they always seem to be giving gifts or other financial kindnesses. Third are the "me-spenders," who love to spend money on themselves.

They enjoy leading the materialistic lifestyle. Fourth are the "big spenders," who simply like to spend money and enjoy it more if other people notice. They often reach for the bill when at a restaurant with a group. Buying status-symbol automobiles is common with both "me-spenders" and "big spenders." The fifth group is composed of "normal" people. They do not have a pattern of excessive spending behavior as do the previous four groups but they usually have some degree of normal spending faults.

Some couples have conflicting spending styles. If two people with sharply different spending styles commit to a relationship, some problems will probably arise. The idea of "his and her" money may come into play; whoever earns the larger or only salary may want to tell the other how to spend. During disagreements over money, one person may say or think, "I earned it and I'll spend it." For another thing, one member of the couple may try to control the relationship by controlling all the spending of money. In such situations one person usually handles all the family finances and is extremely reluctant to share responsibility. That person usually maintains power by doling out money at his or her own discretion. In addition, one person (or both people) may resort to retaliatory spending. For example, the wife might spend money on something expensive for herself. The husband then wants to do the same thing—spend money on himself—whether or not the funds are available. Finally, *impulsive buying* may cause financial stress. This is an emotional, almost reckless buying of goods and services with little regard to planning or need.

Disagreements over finances are almost always cited as the number one or two reason for divorce. Errors of various types and degrees of severity seem to slip, sometimes unnoticed, into spending behavior. Clearly, it is in the interest of all couples to talk with each other about financial matters. Early in a relationship, and later as needed, it would be wise for couples to share with each other their individual financial goals as well as financial fears. Then the spirit of open communication and compromise can contribute to successful, effective financial management.

Opportunity Costs in Decision Making   Another factor that affects budgeting is *opportunity cost*. This is the cost of giving up one option for another. Often there is only so much money available to spend and a decision must be made between two alternatives. For example, Randy Cord of Malibu, California, was three days from payday with only $20 in his pocket. His kitchen was bare, yet he wanted to take his date to the movies. Alternatively, he could pick up some items at the grocery store and make it until payday. Since he could not do both he had to consider various opportunity costs in making his decision. For example, if he decided on the movie, he would have to eat at his parents' home for a couple of days.

Most opportunity costs involve personal tastes and preferences that are difficult to quantify. Other opportunity costs include money figures and often these should be considered carefully. For example, what are the opportunity costs for taking a job versus completing a master's degree in two years? Or, what are the opportunity costs of renting an apartment versus buying a home?

Marginal Costs in Decision Making   *Marginal cost* is an aid to decision making when the additional (marginal) price or cost of something is compared to the additional (marginal) value received. Sometimes making financial decisions is difficult enough without having to consider too many variables unnecessarily. The concept of marginal costs reminds us to compare only important variables.

For example, two new automobiles were available on a dealership lot in Norfolk, Nebraska, where Curtis Douglas was trying to make a decision. Both were similar models although one was a Chrysler and the other a Ford. The Chrysler, with a sticker price of $13,100, had a moderate number of options while the Ford, with sticker price of $14,800, had numerous options. It is unnecessary for Curtis to consider all the options in comparing both vehicles. The concept of marginal costs says to compare the additional costs, $1,700 in this instance ($14,800 − $13,100), with the additional options. Curtis need only decide if all the additional options are worth $1,700.

Time Value of Money   One of the most important concepts in personal finance is the *time value of money. Present value* is the current value of an asset that is to be received in the future. *Future value* is the valuation of an asset projected to the end of a particular time period in the future. Given assumed rates of return for a number of years, these values can be calculated.

For example, Dave Hollin of Jackson, Tennessee, was interested in two investments that paid certain sums of money in the future. First, his bank was offering him a $5,000 savings certificate of deposit for three years paying 7 percent interest. Second, a friend wants to borrow the same sum for three years and pay Dave back $6,000 in a lump sum. There are four ways to determine which is the best action for Dave to take.

1. *Basic math method.* First, let's use basic mathematics for future value (*FV*). Assuming a rate of interest of 7 percent, the *FV* at the end of one year would be $5,350 [$5,000 + (0.07 × $5,000)]. The *FV* after two years would be $5,724.50 [$5,350 + (0.07 × $5,350)]. The *FV* after three years would be $6,125.22 [$5,724.50 + (0.07 × $5,724.50)]. So, Dave would earn more by not lending the money to his friend because the bank will give him $125.22 more ($6,125.22 − $6,000). This method works fine but can become cumbersome.

2. *Basic calculation method.* Using formula 3–1 results in the same answer, where *i* represents the interest rate.

$$FV = (\text{Sum of money})(i + 1.0)(i + 1.0)(i + 1.0) \ldots \quad (3\text{--}1)$$
$$FV = (\$5,000)(1.07)(1.07)(1.07)$$
$$FV = \$6,125.22$$

3. *Calculator method.* Using any type of calculator will provide the same answer using formula 3–2, where i represents the interest rate and n represents the number of years.

$$FV = (\text{sum of money})(1.0 + i)^n \quad (3\text{--}2)$$
$$FV = (\$5,000)(1.07)^3$$
$$FV = (\$5,000)(1.225043)$$
$$FV = \$6,125.22$$

4. *Table method.* Using Table 3–4 permits determination of the future dollar value of an investment. For the same illustration above use the table in the following manner. Go across the top row to the 7 percent column. Read down the 7 percent column and across the row for three years to locate the factor 1.225. Multiply by the present value of the cash asset ($5,000) to arrive at a future value ($6,125). (Note that this figure is off $.22 from the precise calculation because of rounding.) Appendix A and appropriate sections in later chapters provide a more complete explanation of the time value of money and its applications. Note that all the calculations assume that the interest earned was not withdrawn but left to be reinvested. This is known as **compound interest,** which is simply the calculation of interest on interest (because it is reinvested) *as well as* interest on the original amount invested.

An appreciation of compounding can be seen when funds are left to grow over a longer period of time. Figure 3–5 demonstrates the impact of a $5,000 investment earning 7 percent, using compound interest. The $5,000 grew to $74,850 in forty years. If instead, the interest earned each period was withdrawn and not reinvested, the procedure would be called **simple interest**. The formula for simple in-

TABLE 3–4
Future Value of $1 after a Given Number of Periods (Portion of Full Table Shown in Appendix A1)

Periods	1%	2%	3%	4%	5%	6%	7%	8%	9%	10%
1	1.010	1.020	1.030	1.040	1.050	1.060	1.070	1.080	1.090	1.100
2	1.020	1.040	1.061	1.082	1.103	1.124	1.145	1.166	1.188	1.210
3	1.030	1.061	1.093	1.125	1.158	1.191	**1.225**	1.260	1.295	1.331
4	1.041	1.082	1.126	1.170	1.216	1.262	1.311	1.360	1.412	1.464
5	1.051	1.104	1.159	1.217	1.276	1.338	1.403	1.469	1.539	1.611
6	1.062	1.126	1.194	1.265	1.340	1.419	1.501	1.587	1.677	1.772
7	1.072	1.149	1.230	1.316	1.407	1.504	1.606	1.714	1.828	1.949
8	1.083	1.172	1.267	1.369	1.477	1.594	1.718	1.851	1.993	2.144
9	1.094	1.195	1.305	1.423	1.551	1.689	1.838	1.999	2.172	2.358
10	1.105	1.219	1.344	1.480	1.629	1.791	1.967	2.159	2.367	2.594

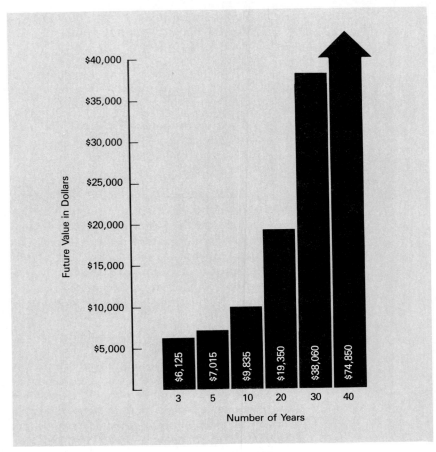

FIGURE 3–5
Future Value Illustration of $5,000 Earning 7 Percent Compound Interest

terest (*SI*) is shown in formula 3–3. For this example, the simple interest calculates to $14,000.

$$\text{Simple interest} = (\text{principal})(\text{rate})(\text{time}) \qquad (3\text{–}3)$$
$$SI = (\$5,000)(.07)(40)$$
$$SI = \$14,000$$

This $14,000 in simple interest when added to the $5,000 invested would total $19,000, which is $55,850 less than the $74,850 that compounding would yield. With compounding the asset seems to grow slowly at first and then grows dramatically; that is the power of compound interest.

Making Realistic Budget Estimates

Budget estimates are the recorded amounts in a budget that are planned and expected to be received or spent during a certain period of time.

Everyone's budget is different because people vary. Yet it is useful in planning your own budget to review how other people allocate their money. Table 3–5 (p. 76) illustrates the budget estimates for a college student, a single working person, a married couple, a married couple with two young children, and a married couple with two college-age children.

Note that in Table 3–5 the college student's budget requires monthly withdrawals of previously deposited savings to make ends meet; the budget is also quite inflexible. The single working person's budget allows for an automobile loan but not much else. The married couple's budget permits one automobile loan, an investment program, contributions to individual retirement accounts, and significant spending on food and entertainment; having two incomes helps. The budget of the married couple with two young children allows only for an inexpensive automobile loan payment; note that one spouse has a part-time job to help with the finances. The budget of the married couple with two college-age children permits a home mortgage payment, ownership of two paid-for automobiles, savings and investment programs, and a substantial contribution for college expenses. This budget has income meeting expenses because one spouse works part-time and there are monthly withdrawals of previously deposited savings.

To make realistic budget estimates of income and expenses you need reliable financial information. The more accurate the estimates, the more valuable the budget. Most people begin by making budget estimates for one pay period and then multiply by twelve to obtain annual budget figures. Note that accuracy is important, but it is much simpler to round figures to the nearest dollar.

Important record information can be obtained by following a few suggestions: For income data, look at your copies of last year's income tax forms. Review payroll stubs for gross income information as well as what amounts were withheld for taxes, insurance, and the like. Talk to your employer to obtain similar information for next year, and perhaps ask about a possible salary increase as well. Interest income probably can be estimated closely by looking at statements and passbooks from the previous year.

Fixed expenses, such as rent and automobile insurance premiums, can be recorded accurately since the information is known. The variable expenses are more difficult to estimate, particularly if you have never prepared a budget before. It should be helpful to review the sample budgets of others, as illustrated in Table 3–5, and the expense guidelines in Table 3–3. If you use a checkbook, review the checkbook register for the previous year. Perhaps you have a box or drawer where you keep receipts. Lacking any previous financial records, you might find it useful to keep a detailed log of expenses for one month and then make your initial budget estimates.

You can also make fair estimates for things you know you want to do. If you have seven Christmas gifts to buy and estimate about $50 each, it's easy to estimate $350. If you want to go out to dinner once a

TABLE 3–5
Sample Monthly Budgeted Expenses for Various Family Units

Classifications	College Student	Single Working Person	Married Couple	Married Couple with Two Young Children	Married Couple with Two College-age Children
Income					
Salary	$ 300	$1,700	$1,600	$2,000	$2,200
Salary	—	—	1,400	160	600
Interest and dividends	5	15	15	15	80
Loans/scholarships	200	—	—	—	—
Savings withdrawals	570	—	—	—	500
Total income	$1,075	$1,715	$3,015	$2,175	$3,380
Expenses—fixed					
Housing	$250	$300	$ 400	$400	$ 700
Health insurance	—	—ª	60ª	70ª	70ª
Life and disability insurance	—	—ª	10ª	15ª	15ª
Homeowner's/renter's insurance	—	—	10	10	15
Automobile insurance	—	40	60	40	60
Gifts and contributions	10	20	40	60	80
Automobile loan repayments	—	250	250	150	—
Loan 1 (TV/stereo?)	—	80	80	40	—
Loan 2 (other)	—	40	40	—	50
Savings (withheld)	—	20	20	10	100
Federal/state taxes	30	290	520	320	480
Real estate taxes	—	—	—	—	40
Personal property taxes	—	5	10	10	10
Investments	—	—	120	20	50
Pension contributions	—	80	80	100	150
Individual retirement account	—	20	240	50	165
Total fixed expenses	$290	$1,145	$1,940	$1,295	$1,985
Expenses—variable					
Revolving budget savings fund	$ —	$ 40	$ 50	$ 50	$ 45
Other savings	—	—	150	—	—
Food	210	120	280	240	200
Utilities	20	50	60	70	90
Automobile gas, oil, maintenance	—	60	60	60	100
Medical	10	30	40	70	50
Child care	—	—	—	60	—
Clothing	20	50	60	50	40
Vices	20	40	60	40	40
Education	400	—	—	—	500
Furnishings/appliances	10	10	30	20	20
Personal care	10	15	25	30	30
Entertainment	40	60	100	60	120
Vacations	15	30	40	30	60
Credit card 1	—	20	20	20	20
Credit card 2	—	—	20	20	—
Miscellaneous/personal	30	40	80	60	80
Total variable expenses	785	565	1,075	880	1,395
Total expenses	$1,075	$1,710	$3,015	$2,175	$3,380

ª Over and above amount subsidized or provided by employer.

week at $15 per meal, you might estimate $60 a month. What you want to avoid in estimating expenses is putting in unrealistically low figures: it can be very frustrating when higher expenditures do occur. Simply be fair in your estimates. The next step is to add up your total budget estimates for annual income and expenses.

Resolving Conflicting Needs and Wants by Revising Estimates

The shock for most people in budgeting comes when their estimated expenses far exceed their estimated income. Three choices are available: earn more income, cut back expenses, or try a combination of more income and less expenses.

Extra income, of course, is usually hard to find. Therefore, the immediate task is to decide what is really important in the budget. You have to reconcile conflicting needs and wants as you revise your budget until total expenses do not exceed income. This is known as *reconciling budget estimates*. Review the fixed expenditures to see if they are accurate and are all truly necessary. Look through each of the variable expenditures and change some "must haves" to "maybe next year." Perhaps keep some quality items but reduce the quantity. For example, instead of $60 for four meals out per month consider dining out twice a month at $20 for each meal. Table 3–6 illustrates the annual budget for Harry and Belinda Johnson. It reflects their efforts to revise estimates until total planned expenses were less than total planned income.

The sometimes uncomfortable process of reconciling needs and wants is healthy. It helps identify your priorities. It tells you what is important to you in life now. It suggests what you need to sacrifice to have something else. In short, the process of reconciling your financial wants and needs in making and revising budget estimates is crucial in developing what it takes to achieve your financial goals.

The Implementing Phase of Budgeting

In the implementing phase of budgeting, you proceed to put the budget into effect primarily by recording day-to-day financial activities. Specifically, you record expenditures made and income received during the budget time period, manage cash flow problems, determine totals for the time period, and prepare financial statements.

Recording Actual Income and Expenditures

An *expenditure* is an amount of money that has been spent. You may plan a budgetary expense, but when the money has been spent it is an *actual expenditure*. It is important to keep an accurate and up-to-date

TABLE 3–6
Annual Budget Estimates, 1988, for Harry and Belinda Johnson
(Prepared January 15, 1988)

	January	February	March	April	May	June
Income						
Harry's salary	$1,450	$1,450	$1,450	$1,450	$1,450	$1,450
Belinda's salary	1,900	1,900	2,100	2,100	2,100	2,100
Interest	15	20	20	30	30	35
Trust	—	—	—	—	—	—
Total income	$3,365	$3,370	$3,570	$3,580	$3,580	$3,585
Expenses—fixed						
Rent	$ 400	$ 400	$ 400	$ 400	$ 400	$ 400
Health insurance	65	65	65	65	65	65
Life insurance	9	9	9	9	9	9
Renter's insurance	—	—	—	—	—	110
Automobile insurance	—	—	—	—	—	320
Automobile loan payments	200	200	200	200	200	200
Student loan	120	120	120	120	120	120
Savings	60	60	60	60	60	60
Health club	50	50	50	50	50	50
Cable television	20	20	20	20	20	20
Expenses—variable						
Savings/investment/long-term	—	—	—	—	—	—
Revolving savings fund	220	220	220	220	220	(80)
Food	380	380	380	380	380	380
Utilities	100	100	100	100	50	50
Telephone	70	70	70	70	70	70
Automobile gas/maintenance	45	45	265	45	45	45
Medical	60	60	60	60	60	60
Clothing	210	210	210	210	210	210
Church and charity	125	125	125	125	200	125
Federal income taxes	680	680	680	680	680	680
State income taxes	117	117	117	117	117	117
Social Security taxes	233	233	233	233	233	233
Gifts	80	80	120	80	160	40
Christmas gifts	—	—	—	—	—	—
Public transportation	50	50	50	50	50	50
Personal allowances	175	175	175	175	175	175
Entertainment	130	130	130	130	130	130
Automobile license	—	—	—	—	—	40
Miscellaneous	75	75	75	75	75	75
Vacation—Christmas[a]	—	—	—	—	—	—
Vacation—summer[a]	—	—	—	—	—	250
Anniversary party[a]	—	—	—	—	—	—
Total expenses	$3,674	$3,674	$3,934	$3,674	$3,779	$4,004
Difference (available for spending, saving, and investing)	($309)	($304)	($364)	($94)	($199)	($419)

[a] Provided for in revolving savings fund.

July	August	September	October	November	December	Yearly Total	Average per Month
$1,525	$1,525	$1,525	$1,525	$1,525	$1,525	$17,850	$1,487.50
2,100	2,100	2,100	2,100	2,100	2,100	24,800	2,066.67
35	35	35	40	40	20	355	29.58
—	—	3,000	—	—	—	3,000	250.00
$3,660	$3,660	$6,660	$3,665	$3,665	$3,645	$46,005	$3,833.75
$ 425	$ 425	$ 425	$ 425	$ 425	$ 425	$ 4,950	$ 412.50
65	65	65	65	65	65	780	65.00
9	9	9	9	9	9	108	9.00
—	—	—	—	—	—	110	9.17
—	—	—	—	—	320	640	53.33
200	200	200	200	200	200	2,400	200.00
120	120	120	120	120	120	1,440	120.00
60	60	60	60	60	60	720	60.00
50	50	50	50	50	50	600	50.00
20	20	20	20	20	20	240	20.00
70	(530)	70	70	—	(700)	1,550	—
380	380	380	380	380	380	4,560	380.00
50	50	50	75	75	100	900	75.00
70	70	50	70	70	90	840	70.00
45	45	45	45	45	45	760	63.33
60	60	60	60	60	60	720	60.00
210	210	210	210	210	210	2,520	210.00
125	125	125	125	125	125	1,575	131.25
680	680	680	680	680	680	8,160	680.00
117	117	117	117	117	117	1,404	117.00
233	233	233	233	233	233	2,796	233.00
40	80	80	80	80	40	960	80.00
—	—	—	—	—	—	—	—
50	50	50	50	50	50	600	50.00
175	175	175	175	175	175	2,100	175.00
130	130	130	130	130	130	1,560	130.00
—	—	—	—	—	—	40	3.33
75	75	75	75	75	75	900	75.00
—	—	—	—	—	700	—	—
—	600	—	—	—	—	—	—
$3,459	$3,499	$3,479	$3,524	$3,454	$3,779	$43,933	$3,661.08
$201	$161	$3,181	$141	$211	($134)	$2,072	$172.67

record of expenditures. You may wish to place your budgeting records in the kitchen or family room where they are easy to locate. This will remind you to record expenditures daily. If you have a good memory, or keep a notepad in your pocket or purse for that purpose, expenditures can be recorded every few days. When recording in the "activity" column, be descriptive, such as shown in Figure 3–5, as you may need such information later. Many people also write comments in a "remarks" column in their records for the same reason, as shown in parts c and d of the figure. If you use a pencil, mistakes are easier to correct.

Cash Flow Calendar

For most people, income remains somewhat constant month after month but planned expenses can rise and fall sharply. This is a major reason why people occasionally complain that they are "broke, out of money, and hate budgeting." As you will soon see, this problem can be foreseen by the creation of a cash flow calendar and eliminated by using a revolving savings fund.

The budget estimates for monthly income and expenses in Table 3–6 have been placed in summary form in Table 3–7, providing a *cash flow calendar* for the Johnsons. This is a budgeting device upon which annual estimated income and expenses are recorded for each budgeting time period in an effort to ascertain surplus or deficit situations. As has been observed, even though the Johnsons' planned annual income exceeds expenses, they start out the year with too many expenses, resulting in deficits for six months straight. In later months, income usually exceeds expenses, resulting in a planned surplus at the end of the year.

Effective management of cash flow can involve curtailing expenses during months with financial deficits, increasing income, using savings,

TABLE 3–7
Cash Flow Calendar for Harry and Belinda Johnson

Month	1 Estimated Income	2 Estimated Expenses	3 Surplus/ Deficit (1 − 2)	4 Cumulative Surplus/Deficit
January	$ 3,365	$ 3,674	−$309	−$309
February	3,370	3,674	−304	−613
March	3,570	3,934	−364	−977
April	3,580	3,674	−94	−1,071
May	3,580	3,779	−199	−1,270
June	3,585	4,004	−419	−1,689
July	3,660	3,459	+201	−1,488
August	3,660	3,499	+161	−1,327
September	6.660	3,479	+3,181	+1,854
October	3,665	3,524	+141	+1,995
November	3,665	3,454	+211	+2,206
December	3,645	3,779	−134	+2,072
Totals	$46,005	$43,933	—	+$2,072

or borrowing. If you borrow money and have to pay finance charges the credit costs further push up monthly expenses. It is better to borrow from yourself using a revolving savings fund. The Johnsons need to increase contributions to their savings, as they budgeted only enough to pay for two vacations and an anniversary party, and nothing else.

Revolving Savings Fund

In its simplest form, a *revolving savings fund* is a variable expense classification in budgeting into which funds are allocated in an effort to create a savings amount that can be used to balance the budget so as to prohibit the individual or family from running out of money. It involves planning ahead—as a college student does who saves money all summer (creating a revolving savings fund) to draw upon during the school months. Most people need to establish a revolving savings fund to use in a planned way for two purposes: (1) to meet occasional deficits and (2) to accumulate funds for large expenses, such as automobile insurance premiums, medical costs, Christmas gifts, and vacations.

The Johnsons' revolving saving fund is shown in Table 3–8. It provides enough savings to cover expenses for their planned vacations and anniversary party. Their revolving savings fund, however, will not contain enough money to cover their frequent monthly deficits in cash flow. The revolving saving fund concept works wonderfully if enough money is in the fund to cover the largest cumulative deficit. Thus the Johnsons need $1,689, the June figure in Table 3–7. They have two alternatives: (1) to borrow money to cover deficits during the first several months of the year, or (2) to cut back on expenses enough to create surpluses during these months, or both. Note also in Table 3–7 that at the end of December the Johnsons have a planned surplus of $2,072. This should be more than enough to put in their revolving savings fund to begin the new year.

TABLE 3–8
Revolving Savings Fund for Harry and Belinda Johnson

Contributions		Withdrawals	Balance
Beginning balance			—
January	$220		$ 220
February	220		440
March	220		660
April	220		880
May	220		1,100
June	170	$250	1,020
July	70		1,090
August	70	600	560
September	70		630
October	70		700
November	—		700
December	—	700	—

Determining Totals for the Time Period

After the budgeting period has ended—usually at the beginning of a new month—add up the actual income received and expenditures made during that period. You can do this on a form for each budget classification (as shown in parts a and b of Figure 3–5) or on a form with all income and expenditure classifications (parts c and d of Figure 3–5). Such calculations indicate whether you have overspent in any of your budget classifications. If you are new at budgeting do not be too concerned about this; overspending almost always occurs in some classifications while underspending happens in others. Use such information to refine your budget estimates in the future, and in three or four months you will be able to estimate more accurately.

Preparing Financial Statements

Once all financial activities for a time period are completed and the figures recorded and totaled, it is easy to summarize them. You can use budget data to develop a balance sheet and an income and expense statement. We discussed these two comprehensive financial statements in Chapter 2.

Also, you can prepare miscellaneous financial statements for budget classifications as illustrated in Table 3–9. Sometimes such summaries can be insightful as part 2 of Table 3–9 shows. In this case, the actual expenditures for the telephone are regularly running below budget estimates (see Table 3–6), suggesting that future estimates for the Johnsons should be lowered.

TABLE 3–9
Miscellaneous Summary Statements for Harry and Belinda Johnson

1. Income and savings statement

Income

January	$3,371	
February	3,379	
March	3,590	
Total quarter income		$10,340

Savings

January	$ 520	
February	450	
March	550	
Total quarter savings		$ 1,520

2. Variable expenditure statement—housing-related items

	January	February	March	Total
Food	$360	$390	$370	$1,120
Utilities	106	111	97	314
Telephone	60	58	62	180

The Controlling Phase of Budgeting

In the controlling phase of the budgeting process, an individual or family uses various methods and techniques to help keep income and expenditures within the planned budget totals. The controlling phase occurs simultaneously with the implementing phase, since the best time to control spending is during the budget time period.

Purposes of Budget Controls

Budget controls let you know if you are on target and how well you are progressing as well as alert you to problems such as errors made, overexpenditures, items considered as emergencies, and exceptions or omissions.

For example, suppose that in checking your budget figures for the month of May, you discover that the total of your "Cash Out" column is equal to $876 and the total of all other expenditure columns is equal only to $832. The two figures should be equal if you have recorded all transactions and added all figures correctly. It is nearly futile to try to account for every single dollar because some cash is bound to "slip away" every month. However, a $44 difference ($876 − $832) indicates that something is wrong. More than likely you will have omitted some expenditure item. This is a valuable control check built into the recording process.

The controls used are not, of course, to be treated as absolute mandates with penalties should there be errors. They simply inform you that something needs to be remedied for the budgeting process to be properly completed.

Methods of Controlling the Budget

Eight means of controlling a budget are (1) using a checking account, (2) using a credit controlsheet, (3) checking accuracy, (4) monitoring unexpended balances, (5) justifying exceptions, (6) using the envelope system, (7) coding expenses, and (8) using subordinate budgets.

Using a Checking Account   If you use cash frequently instead of checks you have to keep track of the amount you spend, which can be difficult to control. You must hold onto many receipts and write the purpose of each expense on the back of its receipt as well as keep a daily log that includes expenditures for which you obtained no receipt. Using checks provides a record of to whom you wrote a check, and each check contains a space to record the purpose, as shown in Figure 3–6. It is also good control to deposit all checks received to your checking account; if you need money, write a check.

It is easy to write a check in haste without recording its purpose on the front of the check. The check stub or register (also shown in

FIGURE 3–6
Check with Explanation Space, Check Stub, and Register
Courtesy of Bank of Lexington & Trust Company.

Check

JAMES R. JONES
SSN 123-45-6789
1910 ROSE LANE   555-1289
LEXINGTON, KY   40509

104

_____ 19_____ $\frac{73-114}{421}$

PAY TO THE
ORDER OF_____ $ [   ]

_____ DOLLARS

Bank of Lexington
& Trust Company
LEXINGTON, KENTUCKY 40507

5-84

MEMO_____

⑆04210114 5⑆ 91160384⑈ 0104

Check Stub

IF TAX DEDUCTIBLE CHECK HERE ☐	BAL. FOR'D	380	71
	DEPOSIT		
	TOTAL	380	71
	THIS ITEM	11	40
	OTHER DED. (IF ANY)		
	BAL. FOR'D	369	31

Date *April 4* , 19*88* $ *11.40*   600
To *Pens and Pads*
For *school supplies*

Check Register

NUMBER	DATE	DESCRIPTION OF TRANSACTION	PAYMENT/DEBIT (−)	√ T	FEE (IF ANY) (−)	DEPOSIT/CREDIT (+)	BALANCE
		RECORD ALL CHARGES OR CREDITS THAT AFFECT YOUR ACCOUNT					$ 290 51
101	4-2	Angelo's Pizza supper	$ 9 80	$	$		9 80
							280 71
—	4-3	Deposit birthday from Aunt Lin				100 00	1 00 00
							380 71
102	4-4	Pens and Pads school supplies	11 40				11 40
							369 31

Figure 3–6) then becomes a handy place to record explanations of expenditures.

Using a Credit Controlsheet   Figure 3–7 shows a sample *credit controlsheet* that can monitor the use of credit, amounts owed, and to whom they are owed. This form can keep you abreast of outstanding credit obligations. A crosscheck can easily be made between the credit flow checksheet and credit statements received in the mail.

People who keep budgets on a cash basis sometimes do not keep track of credit transactions until they receive a statement noting what amount is due. For some this system works well. But there are many people who continue to buy on credit and who seem to be completely unaware of the detail and amount of their indebtedness until they receive a statement. Those who make credit purchases need to keep the receipts for future reference. By using a credit controlsheet (see Figure 3–7), you can record each credit transaction when it occurs, and if you misplace the receipt, some record is available for verification.

Checking Accuracy   Another way to control a budget is to double-check the accuracy of financial records. Many people increase the accuracy of the records by using a computer, a word processor, or a calculator. Accuracy in recordkeeping builds confidence in handling financial affairs.

Monitoring Unexpended Balances   The best method to control overspending is to *monitor unexpended balances* in each budget classification. You can accomplish this by using a budget design that keeps a declining balance, as illustrated by parts a and b of Figure 3–5. Other budget designs, such as those shown in parts c and d of Figure 3–5, need to be monitored differently. As illustrated in parts c and d, simply run subtotals every week or so, or as needed, during a monthly budgeting period.

Justifying Exceptions   *Budget exceptions* are the difference between budget estimates in various classifications and the actual expenditures. These are usually in the form of overexpenditures. There may also be exceptions in the over- or under-receipt of earnings. Allowing for exceptions is a way of keeping your budget flexible, but you still need to monitor them. For good control, set a limit on exceptions by type, number allowed, or amount spent. For example, an exception of $200 for sudden medical services need not be questioned. But $200 used to take a spontaneous weekend trip may be subject to question. You should record a written justification for going over budget. You will probably find that the more justifications you have to come up with to cover overages, the more *unlikely* they are to occur, as your "justifications" may be proof enough that certain expenditures were unwarranted. Of course, to stay within your budget allocations you must balance, or offset, overexpenditures with extra earnings received or with a reduction of spending elsewhere.

CREDIT FLOW FOR Jan-Mar _____ 19—

Date 19—	Purpose for Credit	VISA Chg/(Pay)	Balance	MASTERCARD Chg/(Pay)	Balance	SEARS Chg/(Pay)	Balance	AMES Department Store Chg/(Pay)	Balance	Summary: All Creditors Chgs	Paid	Balance
1-2	Has for Car	14.95	14.95							14.95		14.95
1-2	Clothing							32.00	32.00	32.00		46.95
1-15	Paid Visa	(14.95)	-0-								14.95	32.00
1-27	New Desk			320.00	320.00					320.00		352.00
2-12	Has for car	20.00	20.00							20.00		372.00
2-15	Bought Tools					75.00	75.00			75.00		447.00
2-28	Paid Ames							(32.00)	-0-		32.00	415.00

FIGURE 3–7
Credit Flow Checksheet

Using the Envelope System   The *envelope system* of budgeting gets its name from the fact that exact amounts of money are placed into envelopes for purposes of strict budgetary control. If you wish to use the envelope system, at the start of a budgeting period place in an envelope money equal to the budget estimates for each expenditure classification. Write the classification name and the budget amount on the outside of the envelope. As expenditures are made, simply record them on the appropriate envelope and remove the proper amount of cash. When an envelope is empty, funds are exhausted. This technique works well in controlling expenditures for variable expenses, such as entertainment, personal allowances, and food. It may be a good way for younger children to learn to budget allowances.

Coding Expenses   For a sophisticated system of budget control you may want to consider coding all income and expense classifications. As you pay a bill, write a check, or make a bank deposit, you can record the appropriate code. This enables you to sum up all budget classifications quickly and accurately.

Using Subordinate Budgets   Another useful method of budget control is to use *subordinate budgets.* These require explicit details in particular expense categories within the budget. Such extensive planning should result in improved control over expenditures. For example, a monthly estimate of $70 for gas, oil, and automobile maintenance could be estimated in detail at the beginning: gasoline, $38; oil, $6; tune-up, $26. Similarly, an allocation of $700 for a week-long summer vacation might last only four or five days if you lack subordinate budget estimate details for the vacation.

The Evaluating Phase of Budgeting

Evaluation is of extreme importance to the budgeting process. Indeed, evaluation provides feedback for reexamining achievement of short-term goals and, if needed, for reclarifying long-term goals. Your basic financial-planning values are reaffirmed or reorganized to fit your or your family's needs. More specifically, the purpose of evaluation is to determine whether the earlier steps in the budgeting process have worked.

Although evaluation is a continuous process, an important evaluation phase occurs at the end of a budgeting time period. It includes comparing actual with budgeted amounts, deciding whether the budget objectives have been achieved, and judging whether the overall process of budgeting has worked.

Comparing Estimated and Actual Amounts

It is practical to compare actual expenditures with the budget estimates. This is sometimes called *variance analysis,* as illustrated in Figure 3–8. In some budget expenditure classifications the budget estimates rarely agree with the actual expenditures, particularly in the variable expenses. Making comparisons is important if you want to understand why expenditures were higher or lower than you estimated. The "remarks" column, as illustrated earlier by parts c and d of Figure 3–5, can be of help here.

Carrying Forward Balances   At the end of the budgeting time period, some budget classifications may still have a positive balance. For example, perhaps you estimated the electric bill at $50 and it was only $45. You may then ask, "What do I do with the balance?" You may also ask, "What happens to budget classifications that were overspent?" The budgeting form in part d of Figure 3–5 allows for *carrying forward balances* to the next period.

Some people take the *net surplus* (the amount remaining after all budget classification deficits are subtracted from those with surpluses) and then deposit it in a savings account, such as their revolving savings fund. Others spend it like "mad money." Many carry the surpluses forward, which provides larger budget estimates for the following month. Some people carry forward deficits, hoping that having less available in a budgeted classification the following month will motivate them to try harder to keep expenditures low.

Because variable expense estimates are usually averages it is best not to change the estimate on the basis of a variation up or down over just one or two months. If the estimate is too high or low for a longer period, however, you will want to make an adjustment.

Be aware of any over- or underestimates of the amounts actually recorded for earnings or expenditures. Overages on a few expenditures may be of little concern. Perhaps the estimates were too low, and perhaps the total overage was not very much. Or perhaps earnings were more than estimated. Such findings should not be alarming. Essentially, these observations will tell you how well you followed the budget. It may also mean that some minor changes need to be made in estimates during the next budgeting time period. If excessive variances have occurred, preventing you from achieving objectives or making the budget balance, do something about it. New controls might have to be instituted or present controls might have to be tightened. Reflective thinking in this type of evaluation will ensure an improved budgeting process in the future.

Staying Within the Budget   You may feel quite critical of yourself if you did not stay within the budget estimates. On the other hand, pat yourself on the back if you deserve it!

If your objective was to stay within both the overall budget and the specific estimates for each classification, and you did not, make adjustments. Your next budgeting time periods will be more workable, and

FIGURE 3–8
Quarterly Budget Variance Analysis for Harry and Belinda Johnson

	January				February				March			
	Budget	Actual	Variance	Cumulative Variance	Budget	Actual	Variance	Cumulative Variance	Budget	Actual	Variance	Cumulative Variance
Income												
Harry's salary	1,450	1,450	—	—	1,450	1,450	—	—	1,450	1,450	—	—
Belinda's salary	1,900	1,900	—	—	1,900	1,900	—	—	2,100	2,100	—	—
Interest	15	5	(10)	(10)	20	5	(15)	(25)	20	5	(15)	(40)
Trust	—	—	—	—	—	—	—	—	—	—	—	—
Total income												
Expenses												
Fixed:												
Rent	400	400	—	—	400	400	—	—	400	400	—	—
Health insurance	65	65	—	—	65	65	—	—	65	65	—	—
Variable												
Food	380	390	(10)	10	380	400	(20)	(30)	380	390	(10)	(40)
Utilities	100	110	(10)	(10)	100	120	(20)	(30)	100	95	5	(25)
Telephone	70	60	10	(10)	70	55	15	25	70	45	25	50
Auto gas/maint.	45	48	(3)	(3)	45	46	(1)	(4)	265	268	(3)	(7)

your objectives more attainable. Experience and practice in the budgeting process will bring about greater success.

Achieving Budget Objectives

Whatever your objectives and goals, it is exciting to know that some or all of them have been achieved or that progress has been made toward those ends. A successful budget reflects upon the person who developed it and made it work. Even though achieving such objectives as staying within the budget estimates, or paying off a small debt, or saving a few hundred dollars within the budget period may seem unimpressive, you can say, "I achieved my goals because I made the plan and worked the plan successfully."

If you did not achieve some of your objectives, you can use the evaluation process to determine why and to adjust your budget and/or objectives accordingly. Suppose your objective was to save enough money to make a down payment for a new car, but you could not achieve it during the budgeting time period planned. By evaluating your budget, you realize that due to some unexpected medical expenses and a cross-country trip to visit a sick relative, you had to dip into savings. Under these circumstances you can easily understand why the objective was not achieved. You can still set your sights on it during the next budgeting time period.

Making the Budget Work

A final aspect of the evaluation process involves asking yourself some questions: "Did the budget, as put into practice, work?" "Did the budget give me enough information to refer to?" "Was I able to accomplish my objectives?" "Was the back-up detailed enough to prove my deductible expenditures when I filed my income tax forms?" If your answers are a resounding "yes!," you can be confident that your budget did work. Keep up the good work!

Remember, though, that if all these questions cannot be answered with a "yes," the entire evaluation or budgeting process should not be considered negative. This would merely illustrate that some part of the budgeting process did not work as intended. If your evaluation is negative in some way, accept it, and find out why. Then correct the problem so you will have a positive evaluation the next time.

Summary

1. Life-cycle financial activities of singlehood and couplehood include a variety of financial tasks, problems, and challenges. Both earnings and consumption are sharply affected by an individual's changes in periods and stages in the life cycle.

2. Today's younger generation numbers about 29 million, of which 30 percent are in school and 75 percent are single. Seven out of ten say that eventually they will be better off financially than their parents.

3. A budget is used to record estimated and actual income and expenditures for a period of time. Budgeting is a process of financial planning and controlling that involves using the budget to set and achieve short-term goals that are in harmony with long-term goals.

4. Establishing financial goals and objectives in budgeting requires that both long- and short-term goals be expressed explicitly when possible.

5. In the planning phase of budgeting—which focuses on the mechanical aspects of budgeting—you choose a recording format, select either the cash or accrual basis, choose various budget classifications, and select the time period for the budget. Throughout, it is important to have a positive attitude toward budgeting and to maintain flexibility.

6. The decision-making phase of budgeting focuses on the financial decisions that need to be made when setting up a budget. It requires understanding factors that can affect budgeting, making realistic budget estimates for income and expenses, and resolving conflicting needs and wants.

7. The implementing phase of budgeting includes recording actual income and expenditures, creating a cash flow calendar, establishing a revolving savings fund, determining totals for the time period, and preparing financial statements.

8. The controlling phase of budgeting includes the potential use of eight different means of control. Using a checking account, checking accuracy, and monitoring unexpended balances are popular controls. Stricter budgeting controls include the credit controlsheet and the envelope system.

9. The evaluating phase of budgeting includes comparing actual with budgeted amounts, deciding whether the budget objectives have been met, and judging whether the overall process of budgeting has worked or needs modification during the next budget time period.

Modern Money Management

The Johnsons' Budget Problems

The Johnsons enjoy a high income because they both work. They cannot believe that less than a year ago they were both living the difficult financial lives of college students. Times have changed for the better.

After developing their balance sheet and income and expense statements (shown at the end of Chapter 2) they made a budget for the year (shown in Table 3–6). They then reconciled some conflicting needs and wants until they found that total annual expenses did not exceed income. However, when developing their cash flow calendar for the year (Table 3–7) they noticed a problem: a series of substantial cash deficits over the first several months of the year. In fact, despite their high income they are broke!

The Johnsons have very little money in savings to cover planned deficits. Make specific recommendations to the Johnsons on how they could make reductions in their budget estimates. Do not offer suggestions that would alter their new lifestyle drastically; they would reject these. Make realistic suggestions to resolve their cash flow difficulties by modifying their needs and wants and reducing their budget estimates.

Key Words and Concepts

accrual basis budgeting, 66
budget, 53
budget estimates, 73
budget exceptions, 85
budgeting, 53
carrying forward balances, 88
cash basis budgeting, 66
cash flow calendar, 80
compound interest, 73
credit controlsheet, 85
envelope system, 87
expenditure, 77
future value, 72
impulsive buying, 71
life cycle, 53
long-term goals or objectives, 60

marginal cost, 72
monitoring unexpended balances, 85
net surplus, 88
opportunity cost, 71
personal spending style, 70
present value, 72
reconciling budget estimates, 77
recordkeeping, 65
revolving savings fund, 81
short-term goals or objectives, 61
simple interest, 73
subordinate budget, 87
time value of money, 72
variance analysis, 88

Review Questions

1. Provide a summary of the three life-cycle periods.
2. Give some examples of financial tasks, problems, and challenges for one period of the life cycle.
3. List some numerical characteristics of today's generation of youth.
4. What can budgeting do for you?
5. List and describe briefly the six phases of budgeting.

6. Why are a positive attitude and flexibility important in budgeting?

7. Why do people often prefer to design their own budgeting record formats rather than purchase them commercially?

8. Differentiate between cash and accrual basis budgeting.

9. Describe two ways that savings can be categorized in a budget.

10. Choose two spending styles and explain how they can conflict with each other.

11. What are opportunity costs?

12. Give an example of marginal costs.

13. Illustrate a financial situation for which you would need to consider the time value of money.

14. Cite some examples of where to obtain information to make realistic budget estimates.

15. How can you go about resolving conflicting needs and wants in budgeting?

16. What is the purpose of a cash flow calendar?

17. How can you use a revolving savings fund?

18. What are the purposes of budget controls?

19. How can you use a checking account as a budget control?

20. Explain how the envelope system of budget control works.

21. What is a subordinate budget?

22. What is the purpose of the evaluating phase of budgeting?

23. Explain variance analysis.

Case Problems

1. Bernard Gitman of Dayton, Ohio, thinks his two sons, who live at home, need budgeting advice. Ralph is 19, works as a sales representative for an electronics manufacturer, and regularly spends his entire $1,400 monthly income. Wilfred, 24, is a mid-level manager in a psychological testing company. He has completed three evening classes toward a master's degree and usually saves about 10 percent of his monthly salary of $2,400. Wilfred is contemplating marriage. Bernard is looking to you to offer suggestions to his sons in financial management.

   a. What advice would you offer Ralph regarding life's financial tasks, challenges, and opportunities?

   b. Realizing that Wilfred is contemplating marriage, what advice would you offer him regarding life's financial tasks, challenges, and opportunities?

2. Penny and Dick Stratton of Boston, Massachusetts, have just about decided to start a family next year, so they are looking over their budget (illustrated in Table 3–5 as the "married couple"). Penny figures that she can go on half salary ($800 instead of $1,600 per month) for about eighteen months, then return to full-time work.

   a. Looking at the Strattons' current monthly budget, identify categories and amounts in their $3,015 budget where they realistically might cut back $800. (Tip: Federal/state taxes should drop about $250 as their income drops.)

   b. Assume that Penny and Dick could be persuaded not to begin a family for another two to three years. What specific budgeting recommendations would you give them for handling (i) their fixed expenses, and (ii) their variable expenses, to help prepare them financially for an anticipated $800 loss of income for eighteen months.

3. Claude and Anne Marcus of Santa Ana, California, have two young children and have been living on a tight budget. Their monthly budget is illustrated in Table 3–5, "Married Couple with Two Young Children." Claude and Anne have been nervous about not having started an educational savings plan for their children. Therefore, Anne just started to work part time at a local accounting firm, earning about $160 a month, and this amount is reflected in their budget. They have decided that they need to save $200 a month for the children's education, but Anne does not want to work any more hours away from home.

   Review their budget and make suggestions to modify various budget estimates to point out how they could save $200 a month for the education fund. Also, describe the impact of your recommended changes on their lifestyle.

4. Ron Fernandes of Dover, Delaware, graduated from college eight months ago and is having a terrible time with his budget. Ron has a regular monthly income from his job and no really big bills, but he likes to spend. He goes over his budget every month, and his credit card balances are increasing. Choose three budget-control methods that you could recommend to Ron, and explain why each one will probably help him gain control of his finances.

Suggested Readings

"Financial Planners: What Are They Really Selling?" *Consumer Reports,* January 1986, pp. 37–44. Critical review of financial plans offered by nationwide financial service companies.

"Living Well on Less." *Changing Times,* March 1987, pp. 26–32. With planning, you can handle a cut in income.

"Ten Painless Ways to Get More out of Your Paycheck." *Working Woman,* July 1, 1987, pp. 72–73. Offers suggestions on spending, banking, controlling, and investing money.

PART TWO

Money Management

CHAPTER 4

Financial Services and Cash Management

OBJECTIVES

After reading this chapter, the student should be able to

1. contrast today's complex financial services industry with the heavily regulated industry of years ago.

2. describe the providers of today's financial services, including banks and banklike institutions, financial supermarkets, financial planners, brokerage firms, and insurance companies.

3. explain the fundamental value of effective cash management and summarize the four tools of cash management.

4. understand criteria for choosing a checking institution as well as how to use a checking account and how electronic funds transfer works.

5. recognize the benefits of opening a savings account at a nearby financial institution as well as what factors to consider in comparing savings accounts.

6. realize the value of placing excess funds in one of five types of money market accounts.

7. describe two low-risk savings opportunities.

U ntil just a few years ago, people practiced financial management primarily by using the banking industry. They maintained a checking account at a local bank because it was free and they deposited their savings money in a nearby savings and loan association because it paid a higher rate of interest. Not so now. Wider use of computers, improved communications technology, continued government deregulation of the traditional banking industry, and greater competition have brought about revolutionary changes in banking. In fact, the entire *financial services industry* (institutions offering checking, banking, and/or savings services) has been transformed in the past decade. Effective cash management now requires more careful management of money.

This chapter begins with an overview of today's financial services industry so you can better understand where to do your checking, savings, borrowing, insuring, investing, and other financial activities. We discuss the providers of such financial services, and then focus on the four tools of cash management: checking accounts, savings accounts, money market accounts, and other low-risk savings instruments.

The Changing Financial Services Industry

The effective financial manager endeavors to (1) protect against risks, and (2) provide for capital accumulation. To accomplish these ends financial managers must make numerous decisions and take appropriate actions, and must do so in a complex and changing financial services industry.

Yesterday's Financial Services Industry

Yesterday's financial services industry, comprised of banking, brokerage, and insurance services, was heavily regulated through the 1960s and 1970s by both the federal and state governments. The stock market crash of 1929 and subsequent decade of economic depression also brought an end to the carefree, competitive, laissez-faire era of the 1920s. More than 9,000 banks closed during the depression years. Elected officials then decided that if competition could not prevent a depression then government regulation would be the new order of the times.

The 1930s and 1940s saw the creation of the Federal Reserve System, including the Federal Reserve Board and the Comptroller of the Currency to oversee approximately 25,000 federally chartered banks. Banking commissions were established in all states to monitor the nearly 5,000 banks chartered at the state level. Congress also established the Securities and Exchange Commission, which was to regulate stock and bond transactions. Banks were prohibited from engaging in stock or insurance transactions. States then established insurance commissions to regulate that industry. In short, government regulators heavily influenced which financial services could be sold, how, by whom, and at what prices.

Today's Financial Services Industry

Today's financial services industry includes a host of intermediary institutions at which you can save or borrow money (such as banks, savings and loan associations, and credit unions) and numerous providers of financial transactions (such as insurance companies and stock brokerage firms). During the 1970s and 1980s elected officials have changed their long-standing approach to the businesses in the financial services industry. The key concepts of pre-1929 have returned through deregulation and competition because many Americans want less government regulation of the financial services industry.

The traditions are fading as banks are no longer required by law to pay a lower interest rate on savings deposits than savings and loan associations. They can pay whatever rates they please. Also, interest can now be paid on checking accounts. And, credit unions can offer their version of checking accounts too. Still greater changes are expected in the near future as Congress and various state legislatures rewrite the laws governing financial transactions that maintain the integrity of the industry.

In today's increasingly competitive financial marketplace, many firms not traditionally thought of as banks offer a variety of financial services to consumers. The automobile manufacturer General Motors now offers home mortgage loans. Sears Roebuck and Company sells insurance and stock brokerage services. American Express offers financial planning, brokerage services, insurance, and two credit cards. It is expected that soon you will be able to make a deposit at your local bank (or perhaps more appropriately your financial service institution), go on vacation several states away and make deposits and withdrawals at banks, supermarkets, and department stores while you are on vacation.

The result of all these changes has been an increasingly complex financial marketplace. You as a consumer must deal with these deregulated changes; you have no alternative. You must accept the responsibility to learn about the new financial marketplace and reap the benefits of higher interest rates on savings and new conveniences in the world of finance.

Providers of Financial Services

The providers of today's financial services include banks, financial supermarkets, financial planners, brokerage firms, and insurance companies. Table 4–1 lists these along with their financial products. We discuss these providers in detail in this and in following chapters. Also, at appropriate points, we offer suggestions about who might best use the various providers of financial services.

TABLE 4–1
Today's Financial Services Industry

Providers	Financial Products They Sell
1. Banks	
Banks Savings and loan associations Mutual savings banks Credit unions	Checking, savings, lending, credit cards, investments
2. Financial supermarkets	
Merrill Lynch Sears Roebuck American Express Company Prudential Bache	Checking, savings, lending, credit cards, real estate, investments, insurance, tax shelters, accounting and legal advice, financial planning
3. Financial planners	Various financial products and/or financial advice
4. Brokerage firms	
Stock brokerage firms Discount stock brokerage firms Real estate brokerage firms	Investments, tax shelters, real estate
5. Insurance companies	
Insurance companies	Protection against risks, tax shelters, retirement plans

Banks and Banklike Institutions

There are four types of financial institutions that offer various forms of both checking and savings accounts: commercial banks, mutual savings banks, savings and loan associations, and credit unions. Although each is a distinctive type of institution, and their characteristics will be detailed below, people often call them all *banks* or banking institutions.

Commercial Banks   Commercial banks are corporations chartered under federal or state regulations. Historically, they have offered the widest variety of financial services, and modern banks offer numerous consumer services, such as checking, savings, loans, safe-deposit boxes, investment services, financial counseling, and automatic payment of bills. There are approximately 14,000 commercial banks nationwide, with another 50,000 branch offices of banks in states that do not prohibit branch banking. Each account in a federally chartered bank is insured against loss up to $100,000 by an agency of the federal government, the *Federal Deposit Insurance Corporation (FDIC).* State-chartered banks are usually insured by the FDIC or sometimes through a state-approved insurance program.

Up until the 1970s, only commercial banks were permitted to offer *checking accounts.* These are technically known as *demand deposits;* a bank must withdraw funds and make payments whenever demanded by the depositor, which is typically done in the form of writing a check. Current law still permits only banks to offer demand deposits. However, both commercial banks and other types of checking institutions can now offer depositors a new kind of checking account, called a *negotiable order of withdrawal (NOW) account.* The money deposited in this account goes to a savings account, where it earns interest income. When the financial institution receives a negotiable order of withdrawal—which looks just like a check—the funds on deposit are used to make the payment. These NOW accounts are often called "NOW checking" or "interest checking," since users earn interest on their balances.

Mutual Savings Banks   A mutual savings bank (MSB) is quite similar to a savings and loan association. Historically, MSBs accepted deposits in order to make housing loans. They are called mutual because technically the depositors of savings are the owners of the institution. All MSBs are state-chartered and have either FDIC insurance or a state-approved insurance program amounting to $100,000 per account. MSBs are legally permitted in seventeen states, although most are located in the states of Connecticut, Maine, Massachusetts, New Hampshire, New Jersey, and New York. Like S & Ls, mutual savings banks compete for consumer loans and offer NOW accounts to checking customers.

Savings and Loan Associations   The original purpose of *savings and loan associations* (S & Ls) was to accept savings and to provide home loans. This remains a focus today, and S & Ls are still called "thrift" institutions. Many of the 3,200 associations, with 15,000 branches, also give loans for consumer products, such as autos and appliances. As mentioned, S & Ls are not permitted to provide demand deposits; however, they can offer NOW accounts to depositors, that are basically the same thing. The *Federal Savings and Loan Insurance Corporation (FSLIC),* a government agency, insures all federally chartered S & Ls ($100,000 per account) and some state-chartered institutions.

   The two kinds of savings and loan associations are mutual and corporate. In the more common *mutual savings and loan association,* depositors are the actual owners of the association, or share owners. A mutual savings and loan operation usually allows one vote per share owner (for example, for each $100 on deposit) when electing its board of directors. Alternatively, *corporate savings and loan associations,* located primarily in the Midwest and West, operate as corporations and issue stock to denote ownership.

   In recent years more than one hundred federally chartered savings and loan associations have changed their names to *bank* even though they are still S & Ls. Apparently they think there is a perception among the public that banks are better than S & Ls even though they each offer the same services. You can still recognize the renamed S & Ls because by law they must have the word *savings* in their title (for example, National Savings Bank of Missouri) or use the letters *FSB* for *federal savings bank* (such as Montgomery FSB Bank).

Credit Unions *Credit unions* were developed to serve members/ owners that have some common bond, such as the same employer, religion, union, or fraternal association. Of the 18,000 credit unions that exist, those with federal charters have their accounts insured to $100,000 cash through the National Credit Union Administration (NCUA). State-chartered credit unions are often insured by NCUA for $100,000 per account, and most of the others participate in state-approved insurance programs. Credit unions accept deposits and make loans for consumer products. They usually have payroll deductions, often offer free term life insurance up to $2,000, and sometimes offer free insurance to pay off a loan in the event of death or disability. Few have the financial resources to make home loans.

A *share draft* is the credit union version of a check; it looks just like a check from a NOW account or a demand deposit account. It is called a share draft because members of a credit union technically own the organization and their deposits are called shares. Thus, as with a NOW account, when a share draft arrives at the credit union, the money to pay for it is taken from an interest-bearing share account.

Financial Supermarkets

Continued government deregulation of the industry has not only eroded the traditional lines of business but also created opportunities for establishment of *financial supermarkets.* These are national or regional corporations that offer a great number of financial services to consumers, including the traditional checking, savings, lending, and credit cards, as well as advice on investments, insurance, real estate, and general financial planning. These financial service institutions are also referred to as *quasi-banks* or *nonbank banks,* as they provide limited traditional banking services in that they either accept deposits or make commercial loans, but not both. The firm Merrill Lynch became a pioneer in the nonbank area by offering its usual brokerage services in conjunction with other financial services that it either bought outright (real estate), established a corporate relationship with (banking), or developed expertise in (financial planning). Other large corporations in the business are Sears Roebuck, Prudential Bache, and Fidelity.

Financial Planners

Financial-planning advice is counseling you can receive about taxation, credit, money management, insurance, savings, housing economics, preservation of purchasing power, income from investments, growth in value of investments, and estate planning. This advice may come from financial publications, nonprofessional or quasi-professional advisers, and professional financial planners.

It is important to realize that most financial planners are biased because they sell something. The financial advice obtained from a

You may be able to get solid financial advice from friends, relatives, and coworkers. Quasi-professionals, such as the family lawyer, town banker, and local accountant, insurance agent, and stockbroker, can help you draw up a will, set up an individual retirement account, prepare taxes, buy life insurance, and purchase stock. But none of these people have high-level general expertise in financial planning.

If you have an annual income of $35,000 or more, you should consider relying on the expertise of a professional financial planner—a tax attorney, investment manager, or certified financial planner—but not until you have a thorough knowledge of personal finance.

Tax attorneys should be up to date on complex tax laws and regulations; a young tax attorney with access to older and more experienced legal partners might be especially helpful. Interview several prospects and choose someone with whom you feel comfortable. *Investment managers* take almost complete charge of your investment portfolio and give you periodic reports on the results of their efforts.

(Rock stars and movie personalities frequently use such services.) A *financial planner* is a person who calls himself or herself by that title. Many financial planners have undergone training and have met the qualifications for particular professional certifications. A *certified financial planner (CFP)* has been approved by the College for Financial Planning as having completed up to two years of a correspondence program in securities, insurance, taxes, and wills. CFPs must pass rigorous examinations and continuously update their financial-planning knowledge. A *Chartered Financial Consultant (ChFC)* takes courses in investments, real estate, and tax shelters given by American College in Bryn Mawr, Pennsylvania. CFPs and ChFCs may or may not sell services other than their own advice. They typically charge about $75 an hour and need three to four hours to analyze a client's financial situation thoroughly. You can locate a financial planner by using the Yellow Pages or by asking for a referral.

banker or broker is always slanted toward the transactions and/or products sold by the firm he or she represents. It is in the economic interest of the financial planner working for a brokerage firm to sell you stocks, bonds, or some other service from which a commission is earned. In a similar way, the insurance salesperson earns a commission and the banker gets a year-end bonus for successfully promoting their products.

In the face of this inherent bias you must be well armed with a knowledgeable background in personal finance. Then you can decide whether the economic interests of the financial planner coincide with your economic self-interest.

Brokerage Firms

Brokerage firms are licensed financial-service institutions that specialize in selling and/or buying securities or real estate. They usually receive a commission for the advice and assistance they provide and it is based on the buy/sell orders they execute. Chapter 17, "Buying and Selling Securities," examines stock brokerage services, and Chapter 9, "The Housing Expenditure," examines real estate brokerage services.

Insurance Companies

Insurance companies are state-licensed financial-service institutions that specialize in selling insurance policies. They must meet minimum standards of financial soundness and use approved policies and forms. Policies can be purchased directly from the insurance company or through insurance agents, and these are described in Chapter 10, "Insurance Fundamentals."

Tools of Cash Management

As your income increases you will have more and more cash to manage. *Cash management* is the task of earning maximum interest on all your funds, regardless of the type of account in which they are kept, while having sufficient funds available for living expenses, emergencies, and savings and investment opportunities.

The four tools of cash management are illustrated in Figure 4–1. First, you need to have a checking account from which to pay for monthly living expenses. Second, you might want to have a small savings account in a local financial institution that can assure you of a

FIGURE 4–1
Four Tools of Cash Management and the Options Available (with Illustrative Interest Rates Earned on Funds)

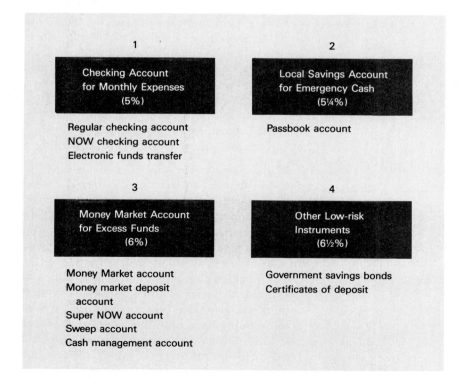

1
Checking Account
for Monthly Expenses
(5%)

Regular checking account
NOW checking account
Electronic funds transfer

2
Local Savings Account
for Emergency Cash
(5¼%)

Passbook account

3
Money Market Account
for Excess Funds
(6%)

Money Market account
Money market deposit
  account
Super NOW account
Sweep account
Cash management account

4
Other Low-risk
Instruments
(6½%)

Government savings bonds
Certificates of deposit

source of ready emergency cash. Third, when income begins to exceed expenses regularly you can consider opening a money market account so you can earn the highest interest rates on excess funds while considering other savings/investment options. Fourth, your cash management plan is complete after determining whether or not to use any other low-risk savings instruments.

Cash Management Tool 1: Checking Accounts

This section of the chapter focuses upon having a checking account from which to pay for monthly living expenses. First, we examine the criteria to use in choosing a checking account. Second, we discuss using a checking account. Third, we examine the electronic funds transfer.

Criteria for Choosing a Checking Institution

We will use the traditional term *checking* from this point on to include demand deposits, negotiable orders of withdrawal, and share drafts. The term *banking* will include commercial banks, mutual savings banks, savings and loan associations, and credit unions. In addition, you should know that the person who opens the checking account and writes the check is known as the **drawer** or **payer.** The name of the financial institution at which the account is held is the **drawee,** and the person or firm to whom the check is made out is the **payee.**

The Depository Institutions Deregulation Act of 1980 made it legal for each kind of depository institution to offer a variety of traditional banking services and compete for the business of the 88 percent of Americans who have checking accounts (averaging twenty-five checks per month) and write $40 billion worth of checks annually. With this blurring of differences, it is now more difficult for depositors to choose the best institution for their needs. For most people, five criteria can be applied: cost, safety, convenience, treatment of customers, and range of services.

Cost For many years, banks offered free checking, covering their expenses with other activities, such as lending. Very importantly, they also made money on their customers' checking account deposits, as by law interest was not paid on checking accounts. The trend in banking now is to assess charges for each service rendered. Thus, institutions usually charge customers from $5 to more than $15 a month to maintain a checking account. Some institutions offer free checking as a promotional device to bring in new customers, hoping that new customers will also want other, paid services. Some institutions that offer free accounts have only the name of the customer preprinted on the checks. Yet most merchants require that the full address appear on the check. This disadvantage of some free accounts encourages customers to open another account that has all the personal information preprinted on the checks.

Table 4–2 shows typical costs for different types of checking accounts. Few college students need the *package account,* which for a set fee per month permits unlimited free checking in addition to a few thousand dollars of accidental death insurance, limited use of a photocopying machine, free traveler's checks, a free safe-deposit box, and perhaps a few more services. With a *minimum balance account,* the customer must keep a certain amount in the account throughout the month (perhaps $300) to avoid a flat service charge or fee (usually $5 to $15). With the *average balance account,* a service fee is assessed only if the average daily balance of funds in the account drops below a certain amount (perhaps $300). Decision making gets difficult when the institution offers a NOW account in combination with either a minimum or average balance requirement. Check users have to consider the amount of interest the account will earn and how much of it will be offset by the occasional imposition of fees. A NOW account with no balance requirement is preferable, but rare. The effective cash manager should have a checking account that earns interest.

Safety Accounts with financial institutions that are chartered by the federal government are always insured for up to $100,000. Most of the

TABLE 4–2
Types and Costs of Checking Accounts

Type of Account	Balance Required to Avoid Fees	Monthly Fees	Who Should Use It
Free	$0	$0	People with a small amount of funds to leave on deposit
Transaction	$0	$.15–$.50 per check or deposit	Users of fewer than 10 checks a month
Average balance	$300–$1,500 daily average per month	None[a]	People who have some funds to leave on deposit and do not know about NOW accounts
Minimum balance	$300–$1,500 on every day of the month	None[a]	People who have some funds to leave on deposit and do not know about NOW accounts
NOW	$0–$1,500 average and/or minimum	None[a]	Anyone who wants to earn interest on checking funds
Package	$0	$5–$10	Those who want various free services

[a] Usually $5 to $15 if correct balance is not maintained.

remaining state-chartered institutions are either insured for a like amount through the same federal insurance programs or through a state-approved program. However, there are still some institutions that are uninsured and should be avoided. If an uninsured institution becomes insolvent, depositors will lose part or all of their money.

In recent years about one hundred insured financial institutions annually have been either forced out of business or permitted to merge with a financially stronger institution. Some have just gone bankrupt. Depositors with $100,000 or less per account in those failing institutions received all their money within forty-eight hours of closing. About one uninsured institution per year goes bankrupt. Note also that the state insurance programs in Ohio and Maryland had much difficulty in the mid-1980s repaying depositors when various state-insured financial institutions went bankrupt.

Convenience   Convenience is often the most important factor in deciding where to open a checking account. Find out if the main office, or at least a branch office, is located nearby. Does the bank have walk-up and drive-up services? Are the business hours set so that customers can make transactions before and after work and on Saturdays? Is there a nearby automated teller machine (ATM) available twenty-four hours a day?

Treatment of Customers   Frequent research studies by financial institutions show that lack of courtesy is a major reason why they lose customers to competitors. Most checking account customers expect courteous service both in person and over the telephone.

If a financial emergency arose and you needed a few thousand dollars, would you expect your financial institution to lend it to you? When you are comparing checking institutions, find out how loyal they are to preferred customers. When credit is hard to get, your institution may give you priority or even a lower rate of interest (by perhaps 1 percent) on a loan.

Range of Services   Financial institutions offer a variety of services, which you should consider in deciding where to open a checking account.

Waiting Periods for Check Writing   Many financial institutions require checking account customers to wait for the deposited check to clear before writing checks against those funds. A federal law effective September 1988 limits these waits to two days (one day by 1990) on checks drawn on local banks and six days (four days by 1990) on checks drawn on out-of-state banks. *Check clearing* is the process of transferring funds from the bank, savings and loan association, or credit union upon which the check was drawn to the financial institution that accepted the deposit. (The check-clearing process is discussed later in this chapter.) Some checking institutions may give preferred status to certain customers, permitting them to write checks immediately on a deposit under a set amount (perhaps $500).

Stop-Payment Order If you write a check in payment for a product you find is faulty, you may wish to issue a **stop-payment order** on the check. This assures that the check will not be honored when presented to your financial institution. Almost all stop-payment orders do in fact stop checks from being cashed if they are issued soon enough. However, realize also that most financial institutions probably have a contract clause relieving them of responsibility in case of an oversight. The cost for issuing a stop-payment order usually ranges from $5 to $15, and the order can last up to six months.

Overdrafts Some people have difficulty keeping track of how much money is in their checking account and occasionally write a *bad check*, that is, a check for which there are insufficient funds in the account. Less than 1 percent of all checks "bounce"; 60 percent of them are for amounts under $100. If you write a bad check, your financial institution can take one of four actions. First, your bank may stamp the check "insufficient funds" and return it to the payee. Your bank will charge you from $5 to $30 and the payee will probably also charge a fee. Second, if the check amount is not too large and/or if you are a good customer, your bank might honor the check by paying it and telephoning to remind you to put the funds in the account as soon as possible. Some smaller institutions still have this policy. Third, if you have arranged for **automatic funds transfer (AFT)** with your bank, the necessary amount to cover the check will be transferred from your savings to your checking account. Fourth, if you have an **automatic overdraft loan** agreement with your bank (often called "check plus" or "overdraft protection"), needed funds are automatically borrowed from your VISA or MasterCard account. Note that several states now allow merchants to sue bad-check writers for the amount of the original check plus a penalty of three times that sum, for a maximum of $500.

It does help your credit rating to avoid writing bad checks. But using an automatic overdraft loan can be expensive. Suppose, for example, that a $10 charge was assessed on a check that overdrew an account by $50. A $10 fee on a $50 check is 20 percent ($10 ÷ $50) for only a few *days* of credit. Practicing better cash management and using AFT will eliminate this problem completely.

Certified Check Occasionally a merchant will take your check only if there is a guarantee that the check is good. A **certified check** is a personal check on which your financial institution imprints the word *certified*, ensuring that the account has proper funds to cover the check. In practice, the financial institution freezes that amount in the account when the check is certified and then waits for the check itself to come back before subtracting the funds. This way the institution is absolutely sure that the payer will not draw the balance in the account down below the amount certified. Certified checks, which are initialed by an officer of the financial institution, have a service charge of $1 to $5.

Cashier's Check To be even more certain that a check is good, some merchants insist on receiving payment in the form of a **cashier's check.**

This is a check drawn on the financial institution itself and thus is backed by the drawee's finances. It is made out to a specific payee. To obtain a cashier's check, you would pay the financial institution the amount of the check and have an officer prepare and sign the check. Generally, a fee of $1 to $5 is charged.

Money Order Many financial institutions, and the U.S. Postal Service, sell money orders. A *money order* is a form of cash, bought for a particular amount and signed over by the purchaser to the payee. The drawee thus guarantees payment to the payee. Money orders are usually for amounts smaller than cashier's checks and the fee charged, usually from 35¢ to $3.50, is based on the amount.

Traveler's Checks Cashing a personal check in a distant city is usually most difficult. ***Traveler's checks*** are checks that are issued by large financial institutions (such as American Express, VISA, and Carte Blanche) and sold through smaller institutions such as a local bank or credit union. Traveler's checks are accepted almost everywhere. Purchasers pay a typical fee of 1 percent of the traveler's checks, or $1 per $100. Often this fee is waived by the seller if you are a regular customer. The checks come in selected denominations ($10, $20, $50, and $100) and should be immediately signed once by the purchaser. To cash a traveler's check, the purchaser need only fill in the name of the payee, date the check, and sign it for a second time. All traveler's check companies guarantee replacement if the serial numbers of lost checks are identified.

Automatic Payment of Bills You can direct your financial institution to pay certain recurring bills, such as mortgage payments, local taxes, and utilities, by telling your bank to write out actual checks or to transfer funds electronically. Some institutions permit customers to telephone directly into their own accounts to make payments by computer.

Safe-deposit Box Most banks have ***safe-deposit boxes,*** which are metal boxes that are locked inside a bank vault and can be rented for $10 to $150 annually. You can safely store jewelry, stocks, bonds, copies of wills, insurance policies, and other valuables in a safe-deposit box. It is extremely rare for burglars to get into a bank's safe-deposit boxes. In such instances, the bank is not liable unless there was gross negligence.

A married couple should put their safe-deposit box in both names, so that in case of the death of one person the other will have access to its contents. Otherwise, the box contents become part of the estate of the deceased, which sometimes cannot be touched for several days or even months.

Trust Services A trustee manages the financial assets of another. The will of a deceased person might establish a particular bank as a trustee to carefully distribute the estate to the heirs. Occasionally, trusts are established to oversee the finances of a minor. Fees for these services range widely, and the trust departments of large banks often manage many millions of dollars of other people's assets. Details on trusts are discussed in Chapter 22, "Estate Planning."

Using a Checking Account

There are numerous benefits to having a checking account. There is no need to carry much cash, and it is easier and less expensive to pay bills by mailing a check rather than traveling all over town to make payments. Some people prefer to use checks rather than credit, since the check represents an immediate cash payment. Having a checking account also helps in budgeting because a written record of each check is kept in an accompanying check register. Similarly, the canceled check provides proof of payment and a tax record.

Opening a Separate or Joint Checking Account

Your first step in opening a checking account is completing a *signature card,* which provides verification of the check writer's signature and which is compared against checks written in the future. Once you make an initial deposit, you will be assigned an account number. Then you must decide how much personal information to include on your checks, such as address and telephone number, and what your checks will look like. Checks of a solid color are usually less expensive than checks printed with halftones and exotic scenes.

To reduce checking account service charges, many couples decide to open a *joint account* in which case both must sign the signature card. The financial institution will honor a check written with either signature. An advantage of a joint account is that the couple can keep fairly good control of expenses, as both must keep track of checks written. Also, in case of death, the surviving account holder can have almost immediate access to the funds. It might take several months for a probate court to release the monies in a separate account to the deceased person's spouse.

A disadvantage of a joint account is that one person can withdraw all the money in the account without the other knowing. Also, some couples have trouble keeping an accurate record of the checks written or determining the current balance in the account. For these reasons, some couples decide to have separate accounts, each with his or her own money. For the tightest control, a couple can open an account where both signatures are required on each check; that way both parties always know the purpose and amount of every check.

Writing Checks

Checks are written in ink so as to avoid erasures and possible fraud. Figure 4–2 shows a properly written check. Record the date and the name of the payee, the person or firm to whom the check is written. Although some businesses offer to "stamp" this information for check writers, it is wise to either watch this process or personally record the information yourself. This eliminates the possibility of someone fraudulently putting another name in the space for the payee.

Write the amount of the check in numerals and also in words. Taking care not to leave blank spaces on either line will prevent some-

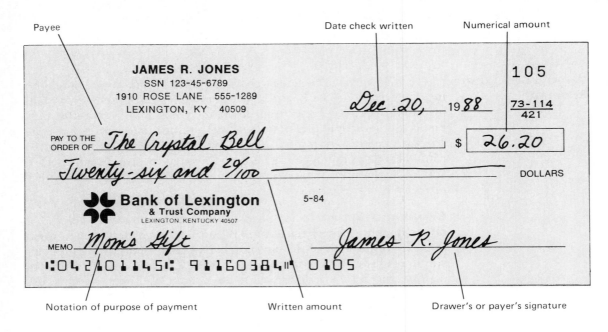

FIGURE 4–2
Properly Written Check and Stub
Courtesy of Bank of Lexington & Trust Company.

one from altering the amount of the check. If the amounts given in numerals and words differ, the financial institution will honor the words as legally correct. Sign your name on the signature line in the same manner as you signed the signature card. A checking institution can refuse payment if the signature appears to be a forgery. Finally, in the memo line along the lower left, write a brief notation that will help you identify the purpose of the check later.

Recording Checks and Deposits It is a good habit to record both checking and deposit information on your check register or check stub *before* actually writing out the check or making the deposit. Some sales clerks might become impatient while you take the time to record this information, but having accurate records justifies the wait. Return to Figure 3–6 for a sample check register and check stub or examine Figure 4–2.

Making Deposits and Endorsements Along with your checks, you will probably receive a supply of personalized *deposit slips,* such as the one illustrated in Figure 4–3. You need only record the date and the amount of cash and/or checks to be deposited.

Endorsement of checks is the process by which checks are transferred from one person to another. When you sign, or endorse, the back of a check written to you, it can then be either cashed or deposited. Figure 4–4 illustrates *blank, special,* and *restrictive* endorsements.

The Check-clearing Process *Check clearing* is the process in the banking system that transfers funds written on checks from the drawer's account to the payee's account. This is done by computer reading of the magnetic ink character recognition (MICR) numerals along the bottom edge of the check. Figure 4–5 identifies these MICR numerals. The first group is 042101145, which identifies the Bank of Lexington's complete transit symbol, including the Federal Reserve check-routing symbol for banks located in central Kentucky (0421) and the assigned number of the Bank of Lexington (01145; the last number, 5, is an internal check digit that verifies that the bank number is valid).

The second group of MICR numerals (91160384) identifies the specific account number of the check writer. The third group of MICR numerals (0103) represents the check number, which many banks also preprint in consecutive order in the upper right-hand corners of checks. On cashed checks returned to account holders, or canceled checks, a fourth group of MICR numerals appears at the extreme lower right (9826 in this example). To speed clearing in the system, the dollar amount of each check, $98.26 in this example, is entered on the check in the form of MICR numerals. These numerals are placed there by a

FIGURE 4–3
Sample Deposit Slip
Courtesy of Bank of Lexington & Trust Company.

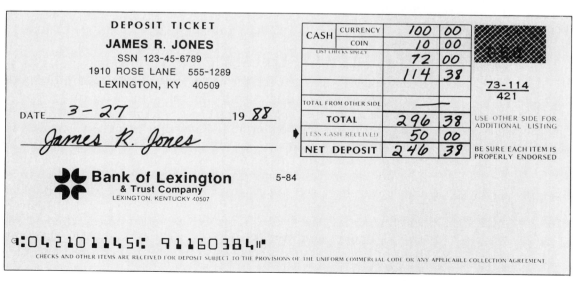

Checks made payable to you must be signed, or endorsed, on the back before they can be cashed or deposited. The endorsement should look exactly like the name on the front of the check.

> *E. Thomas Garman*

Blank endorsement: Once the check is endorsed this way it becomes a bearer instrument and anyone can cash it if it is lost or stolen. Be wise in not making a blank endorsement until just before making a deposit or cashing a check.

> *E. Thomas Garman*
> Pay to the order of
> Raymond E. Forgue

> *E. Thomas Garman*
> Pay to the order of
> Ideal Cabinets
> Ralph Chekani

Special endorsement: If you want to limit who can cash a check, sign it and then write "Pay to the order of X." The check is negotiable only by the person or firm to whom it is endorsed.

> *E. Thomas Garman*
> For Deposit Only

Restrictive endorsement: No one can cash a check with a restrictive endorsement, as the financial institution is thus authorized only to make a deposit. Checks mailed for deposit should be endorsed this way.

FIGURE 4–4
Endorsement of Checks

bank employee and should be exactly the same as the check amount. If a discrepancy exists between the check amount and this last group of MICR numerals, you should notify the bank of the error.

To visualize the check-clearing process, assume a check written on a Kentucky checking account to pay for some menswear is mailed to that company's headquarters in Boulder, Colorado. The menswear company receives the check a few days later and deposits it in the bank. The Boulder bank replicates the check amount by affixing the MICR numeral in the lower right-hand corner of the check. The Boulder bank then forwards the check to the Federal Reserve Bank in Denver, which sends it to the Federal Reserve Bank in Cincinnati, Ohio, which sends it to the check writer's bank in Lexington, Kentucky. Then, the Bank of Lexington subtracts the check amount from the check writer's account.

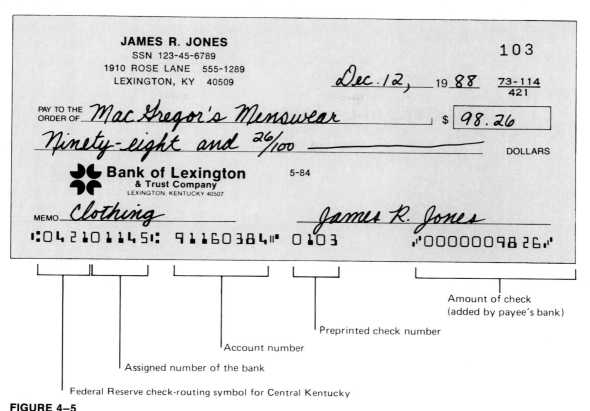

FIGURE 4–5
Check MICR Numerals
Courtesy of Bank of Lexington & Trust Company.

For such an out-of-state transaction, it could take from four to twelve days for the check to clear the original check writer's bank. The amount of time involved, called *float,* is the time the check writer actually has the funds in his or her local account until the check finally clears. Float is valuable, as it earns money in the form of interest for check writers who have their funds in an interest-bearing account. For a check written to a local business, the float is reduced to perhaps one or two days, since the check clearing is handled by a local check-clearing company or bank serving in that capacity.

Reconciling a Checking Account The task in account reconciliation is to compare the financial institution's records with the check writer's. Most checking account holders receive, as shown in Figure 4–6, monthly statements that itemize their checking transactions. Typically, the financial institution also returns checks and deposit slips. (To reduce costs, some institutions practice "check truncation," which means they do not return actual checks, or even deposit slips, unless they are specifically requested and a fee is paid by the check writer.) It is important to reconcile the accounts soon after you receive your monthly statement to avoid the extra mathematics of having numerous *outstanding checks* (checks written but presented for payment too late to

FIGURE 4–6
Sample Monthly Statement
Courtesy of Bank of Lexington & Trust Company.

STATEMENT OF ACCOUNT WITH

Bank of Lexington
& Trust Company
101 EAST VINE STREET • LEXINGTON, KENTUCKY 40507-1460
MEMBER FEDERAL DEPOSIT INSURANCE CORPORATION

James R. Jones
1910 Rose Lane
Lexington, Kentucky 40509

STATEMENT DATE/CREDIT LINE CLOSING DATE
11/30/88

91160384
ACCOUNT NUMBER

BALANCE LAST STATEMENT	DEPOSITS AND CREDITS		CHECKS AND DEBITS		SERVICE CHARGE	BALANCE THIS STATEMENT
	NO.	TOTAL AMOUNT	NO.	TOTAL AMOUNT		
65.10	4	1172.08	20	1146.13	2.88	91.05

#	Date	Amt		Bal
	11/03	715.33	CR	780.43
0280	11/03	3.50		776.93
0292	11/03	12.44		764.49
	11/04	200.00	CR	964.49
0310	11/04	65.17		899.32
0313	11/05	14.72		884.60
0312	11/06	15.50		869.10
0316	11/08	50.00		819.10
0315	11/09	10.00		809.10
0318	11/09	16.80		792.30
	11/10	6.75	CR	799.05
0317	11/11	21.37		777.68
0311	11/15	4.18		773.50
0314	11/16	8.00		765.50
0319	11/18	7.27		758.23
0322	11/18	30.00		728.23
0321	11/19	45.80		682.43
0326	11/20	24.83		657.60
0324	11/20	25.00		632.60
0328	11/21	132.00		500.60
0329	11/24	159.07		341.53
	11/29	250.00	CR	591.53
0331	11/30	497.60		93.93
	11/30	2.88	SC	91.05

DIRECT INQUIRIES ON ELECTRONIC DEBITS AND CREDITS
TO (606) 253-0511 OR WRITE TO ABOVE ADDRESS

NOTICE: SEE REVERSE SIDE FOR IMPORTANT INFORMATION.

appear on the statement). Most errors in account reconciliation come from two sources: (1) failure of the check writer to add and subtract correctly and (2) failure of the check writer to subtract from the check register certain charges of the financial institution (such as account activity fees, stop-payment charges, and costs for printing checks) or to add interest earned (on interest-bearing accounts).

Follow these steps in reconciling your checking account:

1. Place the checks in order by check number or issue date. Many financial institutions use the MICR number to arrange the checks on the monthly statement. See Figure 4–6 for an example of this.

2. Compare the canceled checks with the information in your check register to look for any recording errors. Place a check mark (√) by each correct amount in the check register.

3. In the check register, subtract any charges that appear on the monthly statement; also, add any interest earned.

4. List all outstanding checks, those which have been written but which were not presented for payment in time to appear on the statement. Total the amount.

5. Compare your deposit slips with the deposits listed on the statement and with deposit amounts noted in the check register. List *outstanding deposits* (amounts deposited too late to be included on the statement). Total the amount.

6. Finally, the moment of truth. Take the balance of the account as shown on the statement, add any outstanding deposits (from step 5), and subtract any outstanding checks (from step 4). The resulting amount should be the same as the amount in the check register. If not, first find out if you have committed the most common error of reconciliation—transposing digits, such as 786 for 876. This will show up if the difference between your balance and the bank's is divisible by 9. If so, seek and locate the transposition. If not, recheck the arithmetic and carefully follow these six steps again. As a last resort, an officer at the financial institution can, sometimes for a fee, assist you in balancing your account.

Electronic Funds Transfer

The most noteworthy feature of today's financial services industry is the advent of a wide variety of electronically assisted transactions. For example, you can go to an electronic terminal at a shopping mall, insert a plastic debit card, and withdraw cash from your own bank account. This differs from using a credit card, which provides a loan of money, although some credit cards can now also be used as debit cards. Credit cards are discussed in detail in Chapter 5.

You can use *electronic funds transfer (EFT)* to

1. authorize your financial institution to pay a monthly auto loan.
2. have your employer deposit paychecks directly into your account.

3. make a telephone call to your credit union to transfer funds from a share savings account to a share draft account.

4. allow a daily sweep transaction of funds out of a savings account into a NOW account (discussed further in this chapter).

5. obtain a $50 loan at midnight from a shopping mall terminal to pay for auto repairs in an unfamiliar city.

6. pay for groceries by punching a check-verification machine before giving the grocery clerk a personal check.

7. obtain a computer-chip card with "$100 of use on it" with which to make purchases, get cash, or play games at an arcade.

8. purchase items at a local store and have your funds instantly transferred from your account to that of the store.

9. make a deposit to your bank even when you are 1,500 miles away.

10. punch orders on a home computer, directing your bank to pay all the monthly bills as shown on the videoscreen.

11. purchase life insurance, stocks, or real estate through a financial institution offering a cash management account.

The most recognized forms of EFT are the use of debit cards, computer-chip cards, preauthorized payments and deposits, and computer money management through a home computer or telephone.

Debit Cards *Debit cards* permit holders to make immediate deductions from or additions to accounts through an automatic teller machine. In addition to the debit card, an EFT user will be issued a four- to seven-digit personal identification number (PIN), which is used to verify that the person using the debit card is authorized to do so. Some banks now issue "super smart" cards containing a computer chip or magnetic strip to confirm the user's identity. The PIN must be punched into the ATM whenever the card is used, which verifies that the account balance can cover the purchase. Personal identification numbers should not be written or stored near the debit card because if lost or stolen together they can "unlock" the account. Linkups with some retail stores (known as point-of-sale systems) permit the use of debit cards in making purchases; payment is electronically removed from the buyer's account and transferred to the store's account. Debit cards can be obtained from your local bank or companies such as VISA, MasterCard, and Shearson Lehman/American Express.

Computer-chip Cards A *computer-chip card* has a silicon memory chip embedded in a plastic card. It can keep track of how much money you have in your bank account and retain many details about you, such as your name, address, Social Security number, driver's license number, nearest relatives, and medical history. Such a card, with a certain amount of money "on" it, could be given to a child as a way of drawing a monthly allowance. It could also be used at stores or restaurants, for medical services, or for any item imaginable for which money is a medium of exchange. The use of a computer-chip card may also require submission of the personal identification number.

Preauthorized Deposits and Payments   You, or anyone else you so authorize, can make regular deposits, such as a paycheck, stock dividends, or Social Security benefits, to your account electronically. You can also authorize your financial institution to pay recurring bills in both regular amounts (such as a mortgage or auto loan) and irregular amounts (such as electric or telephone bills).

Computer Money Management   Many people do their banking by linking a home computer via telephone to their financial institution. This is called *computer money management.* Customers can summon an electronic checkbook to their television screen, double-check calculations and earlier payments, and push a few buttons to order payment of monthly bills. A printer attached to the computer can provide a hard-copy receipt for each transaction.

The monthly service charge for computer money management is around $25. Included in this service may be price quotations on stocks and bonds, current interest rates paid on government securities, comparative cost information on life insurance policies, investment advice from specialists, weather reports, access to white and yellow pages of telephone books, retail-store catalogs, and updated tax records. Such a service would allow you to apply for a loan, order traveler's checks, book airline reservations, reserve theater tickets, and purchase products and services. Probably a home computer isn't entirely necessary to computer money management; technology is yielding the "intelligent" telephone, which can function much like a home computer.

Regulation of Electronic Funds Transfers   Both state and federal regulations have been adopted to provide protection for EFT users. The 1978 Electronic Fund Transfer Act established guidelines on EFT-card liability. A valid EFT card can be sent only to a customer who has requested it. Unsolicited cards can be issued only if the card cannot be used until validated and the user is informed of liability for unauthorized use as well as of other terms and conditions.

Regarding lost cards, card holders are liable for only the first $50 of unauthorized use if they notify the issuing company within two business days after the loss or theft of their card or code. After two days, cardholder liability for unauthorized use rises to $500. You risk *unlimited* loss if, within sixty days after your bank statement is mailed to you, you do not report an unauthorized transfer or withdrawal. The logic is that if card holders examine their monthly statements, they will note unauthorized use of the account. These regulations are for specific EFT cards or for other cards (such as a VISA credit card) *used as* an EFT card to transfer funds. Note that it is difficult to dispute an item with a merchant (if the goods are faulty, for example) if the merchant has already been paid via EFT. Because the merchant already has the money, your only recourse is to ask for a refund.

In other EFT transactions, different state regulations apply. For preauthorized deposits, one such law requires that the customer receive written notification that the deposit has been made. Another requires that if financial institutions receive a request for payment in an amount different from that authorized, they cannot pay the bill unless the customer is notified or unless the customer has signed an agreement permitting payment of irregular amounts.

Stop-payment orders for EFT transactions may be difficult to manage because cash may have already been paid. For preauthorized payments, most state rules require that financial institutions set a maximum three-day notification period. Some states require that all EFT machines capable of providing cash also provide a written receipt.

General protection of customers' accounts exists in the form of periodic statements that financial institutions regularly send out. Some regulations also provide that when a customer suspects an EFT error and notifies the financial institution within ten days, the account holder must have use of the funds in question until the matter is examined and resolved. If the institution is correct in its analysis, the sum is later deducted from the account.

For all EFT transactions, your best protection is to carefully use and safeguard your PIN, which is the access number the financial institution issues to each user. Certainly, writing your number on a piece of paper you keep in your wallet along with your EFT card is not a good idea.

Cash Management Tool 2: Savings Accounts

After you have established a checking account to assist in payment of your monthly living expenses, the next phase of cash management is to consider opening a savings account. The major benefits of opening a savings account at a nearby financial institution are that it will provide you with a local source of emergency cash and it will serve as a personal financial reference if ever needed.

Savings are considered time deposits rather than demand deposits. *Time deposits* are savings that are expected to remain on deposit in a financial institution for an extended period and they are legal debts upon which the institution must pay interest as specified. (Technically, commercial banks pay interest while other financial institutions pay dividends on savings deposits.) Institutions usually have a rule requiring that savings account holders give thirty to sixty days' notice for withdrawals, although this is seldom enforced. Some time deposits, however, are *fixed-time deposits,* which specify a period that the savings must be left on deposit, such as six months or three years. In contrast, money in the form of demand deposits, such as checking accounts, must by law be paid immediately when demanded by the account holder.

The types of local financial institutions that generally handle time deposits are banks, savings and loan associations, and credit unions (these were described earlier in this chapter). Table 4–3 lists the agencies that insure checking and savings deposits in various financial institutions and summarizes the insurance coverage at those institutions.

How Much to Save

Personal savings in the United States averages about 6 percent of disposable personal income or take-home pay. Those with higher incomes generally save a greater proportion of income than those with lower incomes. Americans have a relatively low rate of savings because they find credit to be readily available; Europeans typically save more than 10 percent of their take-home pay.

Traditionally, many financial advisors have advocated that people should have two and one-half to three times their monthly take-home pay set aside as savings in readily accessible demand or time deposits. This is to serve as an emergency fund in case of job layoff, long illness, or other serious financial calamity. If your take-home pay is $1,700 a month and you follow this suggestion, you would need to have $4,250 to $5,100 in savings.

TABLE 4–3
Insuring Agencies for Savings Accounts

Agency	Insurance Coverage
Federal Deposit Insurance Corporation (FDIC)	Insures commercial banks and mutual savings banks up to $100,000 per account. Institutions are usually federally chartered for FDIC coverage; state-chartered institutions pay a higher fee.
Federal Savings and Loan Insurance Corporation (FSLIC)	Insures savings and loan associations up to $100,000 per account. Institutions are usually federally chartered for FSLIC coverage; state-chartered institutions pay a higher fee.
National Credit Union Administration (NCUA)	Insures federal and state-chartered credit unions up to $100,000 per account.
Private and state government insurance agencies	Insure accounts of various kinds that do not qualify for federal insurance coverage. Most coverage is for $100,000 per account.

Most people do not find it appropriate to keep such an amount in a local financial institution for four reasons. First, passbook accounts usually have such a low interest rate that they provide poor protection against inflation. Second, higher rates of interest generally can be obtained by placing such substantial savings amounts in long-term, fixed-time deposits or in nonlocal financial institutions. Third, people usually have ready access to credit when needed for emergencies. Fourth, people today typically feel that they have adequate job security as well as sufficient medical and disability insurance coverages to eliminate or greatly cushion the financial impact of such calamities.

Individual circumstances vary, of course, and some people definitely need to have a substantial local emergency fund. Most employed people with good job security and fringe benefits need to determine for themselves how much money they should set aside for emergencies in a local financial institution.

Types of Savings Accounts

Financial institutions offer various savings accounts to meet people's individual wants and needs. By examining the characteristics of passbook accounts as well as the values of separate and joint accounts, you can see how a certain type of account will meet specific needs.

Passbook Accounts

A typical passbook account costs nothing to open and is offered in two forms, the regular and club accounts. The term *passbook* refers to the bank book in which the customer records transactions. (Not all banks issue passbooks today even if they offer passbook accounts.)

Regular Account A *regular passbook savings account* permits frequent deposit or withdrawal of funds. It has the fewest restrictions and is the simplest for most savers to use. Generally, deposits and withdrawals are noted in the saver's record, or passbook. Today, however, many banks have replaced the passbook with printed receipts to indicate the account transactions. This is sometimes called a *statement account.*

About 12 percent of all bank and thrift deposits are in regular accounts. Figure 4–7 shows how a savings record is kept for regular accounts. The passbook withdrawals, deposits, interest, and balances recorded are illustrated at the top. At the bottom is a receipt of a deposit made.

Club Account The *club account,* a form of passbook savings account, is used to deposit money for a special purpose, such as saving for vacations, holidays, school, gift buying, or other reasons. For example, many people save in a Christmas club account. The amount deposited is generally quite small, ranging from $2 to $10 per week. The club account is offered in part to help discipline many heretofore nonsavers. It encourages saving on a regular basis because the amount to be saved is not large. Unfortunately, a club account does not generate much interest. It is usually not needed after a saver has launched a sound financial plan and budget.

FIGURE 4–7
Portion of Regular Passbook Account and Transaction Receipt
Courtesy of Bank of Lexington & Trust Company.

Bank of Lexington & Trust Company
Savings Department

101 East Vine Street
Lexington, Kentucky 40507-1460

Savings Account Number ___*8565 604 9*___

Name ___James R. Jones___

Address ___1910 Rose Lane___

City ___Lexington___ State ___KY___ Zip ___40509___

All accounts insured by the F.D.I.C.

This account is subject to rules and regulations governing savings deposits, and is not transferable, except on the books of this institution.

Date	Remarks	Interest		Withdrawal		Deposit		Balance	
1-28-87	New Acc't					432	88	432	88
2-12-87						50	00	482	88
3-14-87						50	00	532	88
4-1-87		4	13					537	01
4-12-87						50	00	587	01
4-26-87	Car Rep.			125	38			461	63
5-1-87	Tax Ref.					778	00	1239	63
5-12-87						50	00	1289	63

BANK OF LEXINGTON
& TRUST COMPANY
251 West Vine Street · Lexington, Kentucky 40507-1613

DEPOSIT RECEIPT

Items received for deposit are subject to the terms and conditions of this bank's rules & regulations governing accounts.

```
        MAIN OFFICE
    8565604920        $778.00      SAVD
0410      0014     5/01/87         0009
```

MEMBER FDIC—EACH DEPOSITOR INSURED TO $100,000

Separate and Joint Accounts   The several types of accounts that can be opened in a savings institution include the individual account, joint tenancy account, tenancy in common account, trustee account, and minor's account.

An *individual account* has one owner who is solely responsible for the account and its activity. A *joint tenancy account* lets each owner have access to the savings account, and both are responsible separately and collectively for deposits and withdrawals. This type of account is particularly attractive for married couples sharing a savings account. The *tenancy in common account* requires that both owners sign a withdrawal slip before it can be honored by the savings institution, thus preventing withdrawals by one owner without the knowledge of the other.

A *trustee account* may be set up by an adult for a child; the child is restricted from withdrawing money from the account without the adult's signature. Many parents set up trustee accounts for their children. The adult is responsible for the account's activity and any earnings generated from the account are income for the adult.

A *minor's account* can be opened with the permission of a parent or guardian when the child is not old enough to sign his or her name. In this type of account, the minor is the owner of the account and is ultimately responsible for the activity of the account. The minor is also the legal earner of the interest paid on the account.

Opening and Using a Savings Account

The basic procedures involved in the use of savings accounts are opening the account and making deposits and withdrawals.

Opening a Savings Account   The process of opening a savings account is similar to that of opening a checking account. You will need to supply personal information, fill out signature cards, and make a first deposit.

Making Deposits and Withdrawals   To make a deposit you would fill out a deposit slip indicating your name, account number, the date, the amount deposited, and a signature if cash is received as part of the deposit process. To withdraw money you would fill out a withdrawal slip with your name, account number, the date, the amount to be withdrawn in both figures and words, and your signature. Figure 4–8 shows examples of deposit and withdrawal slips (note that account numbers are preprinted). The completed forms will document the account's activity for the account holder and the bank.

Factors to Consider in Comparing Savings Accounts   You would think that if a savings institution advertises an interest rate of 6 percent you would earn more interest income there than at another financial institution advertising a rate of 5.75 percent. That may or may not be true.

The *nominal rate of interest* or *stated rate of interest* is the apparent interest rate that is applied to deposits before consideration of the time

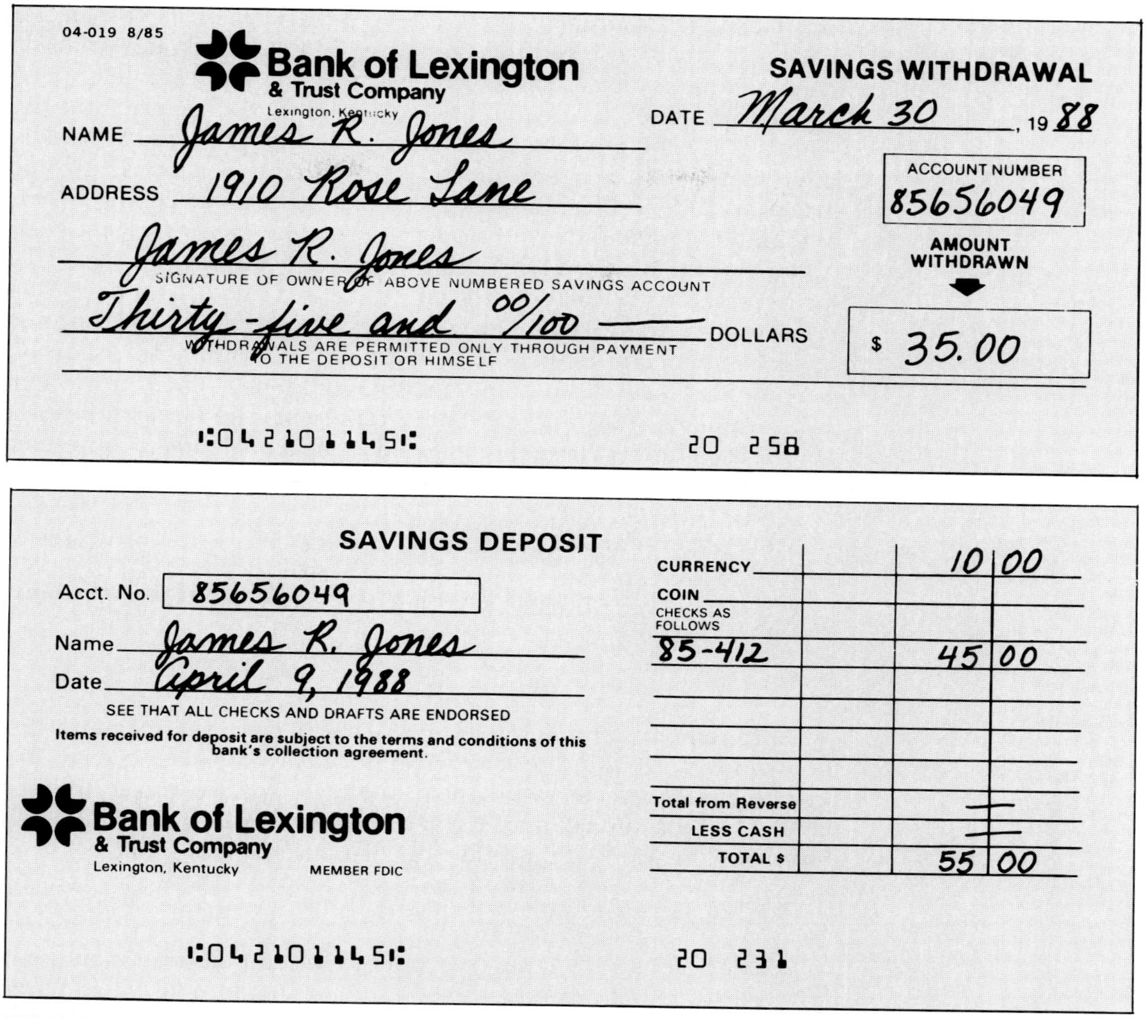
04-019 8/85

Bank of Lexington
& Trust Company
Lexington, Kentucky

SAVINGS WITHDRAWAL

NAME James R. Jones

DATE March 30, 1988

ADDRESS 1910 Rose Lane

ACCOUNT NUMBER 85656049

James R. Jones
SIGNATURE OF OWNER OF ABOVE NUMBERED SAVINGS ACCOUNT

AMOUNT WITHDRAWN

Thirty-five and 00/100 DOLLARS $ 35.00

WITHDRAWALS ARE PERMITTED ONLY THROUGH PAYMENT TO THE DEPOSIT OR HIMSELF

⑆04210114⑆ 20 258

SAVINGS DEPOSIT

Acct. No. 85656049

Name James R. Jones

Date April 9, 1988

SEE THAT ALL CHECKS AND DRAFTS ARE ENDORSED

Items received for deposit are subject to the terms and conditions of this bank's collection agreement.

CURRENCY	10	00
COIN		
CHECKS AS FOLLOWS		
85-412	45	00
Total from Reverse	—	
LESS CASH	—	
TOTAL $	55	00

Bank of Lexington
& Trust Company
Lexington, Kentucky
MEMBER FDIC

⑆04210114⑆ 20 231

FIGURE 4–8
Deposit and Withdrawal Slips
Courtesy of Bank of Lexington & Trust Company.

period, method of determining the savings balance, grace periods, and other costs and penalties. This is often the "high advertised interest rate." What you actually earn on your deposits is an ***effective rate of interest*** that is the actual rate at which deposits earn interest after consideration of all interest calculation variables, costs, and penalties. The business of calculating and comparing interest on deposits is potentially so detailed and confusing that Congress is considering passing a Truth in Savings Law in which the "cents per $100 per day" or other standardized periodic percentage rate is reported. Until such clarifications occur it will be necessary to examine the major factors affecting the return on savings deposits: how interest is calculated, method of determining the savings balance, grace periods, and costs and penalties.

How Interest Is Calculated The calculation of interest to be paid on deposits in financial institutions is primarily based on four variables: how much money is on deposit (the balance), the interest rate applied (the nominal rate), the method of determining the balance, and the frequency of compounding (annually, semiannually, quarterly, weekly, daily). With annual compounding, the amount of interest income earned on $1,000 left on deposit in a savings account paying 6 percent annual nominal interest is calculated as follows for the first year: $1,000 × 1.06 × 1 = $1,060. After two years the savings would be worth $1,123.60 ($1,000 × 1.06 first year = $1,060; $1,060 × 1.06 second year = $1,123.60). The compounding process would continue for each annual interest period. This example illustrates the discussion presented in Chapter 3 on the time value of money. The future value (*FV*) formula is shown here, where i represents the nominal interest rate for each interest period (expressed as a decimal) and n represents the number of compounding periods.

$$FV = \text{(sum of money)}(1.0 + i)^n \qquad (4\text{–}1)$$

Substituting the data in the illustration in formula 4–1 reveals the same answer:

$$\$1,123.60 = (\$1,000)(1.0 + .06)^2$$

If the amount were compounded *quarterly* (every three months) for the two years, the substitutions in the formula would be: (1) i is .015 because the 6 percent rate is paid quarterly and therefore must be divided by four annual quarters, and (2) n is 8 because over two years there are 8 quarters of time. The calculations are shown here.

$$\$1,126.49 = (\$1,000)(1.0 + .015)^8$$

Table 4–4 uses the same data and provides an illustration of quarterly versus annual compound interest. You should note four points: (1) you earn more interest on your deposited funds when compounding is used, (2) the effective rate is the same as the nominal rate when interest is compounded annually, (3) the more frequent the compounding the greater the effective return, and (4) the fullest value of compounding is realized over longer time periods as phenomenal differences occur. This is further depicted in Table 4–5.

Method of Determining Savings Account Balance Financial institutions calculate earnings on the balances in depositors' accounts in four different ways: FIFO (first in, first out), LIFO (last in, first out), low balance, and daily balance. Each method has advantages and disadvantages to a depositor.

Under the **FIFO (first-in, first-out) method,** withdrawals are first deducted from the balance at the start of the interest period and then, if the balance is not sufficient, from later deposits. This erodes the base

TABLE 4–4
Illustration of Quarterly Versus Annual Compound Interest ($1,000 Deposit at 6% Rate)

		Quarterly	Annually
First year	1st quarter	$1,000.00 earns $15.00, totaling $1,015.00	
	2nd quarter	1,015.00 earns 15.23, totaling 1,030.23	
	3rd quarter	1,030.23 earns 15.45, totaling 1,045.68	
	4th quarter	1,045.68 earns 15.69, totaling 1,061.37	
	End of first year	1,000.00 earns 61.37, totaling 1.061.37	$1,000.00 earns $60.00, totaling $1,060.00
Second year	5th quarter	1,061.37 earns 15.92, totaling 1,077.29	
	6th quarter	1,077.29 earns 16.16, totaling 1,093.45	
	7th quarter	1,093.45 earns 16.40, totaling 1,109.85	
	8th quarter	1,109.85 earns 16.64, totaling 1,126.49	
	End of second year	1,061.37 earns 65.12, totaling 1,126.49	$1,060.00 earns $63.60, totaling $1,123.60

on which the interest is figured. It means automatically losing interest on money on deposit early in the interest period if it is withdrawn.

Table 4–6 illustrates a hypothetical case of a savings account with various deposits and withdrawals over the quarter from July 1 to September 30. Below the example are shown the interest calculations for each of the four methods used. The FIFO method would earn only $39.29 for this saver.

Under the *LIFO (last-in, first-out) method*, withdrawals are first deducted from the most recent deposits and then from the less recent ones, and so on. The LIFO method does not penalize savers as much as the FIFO method does. In the case cited in Table 4–6, a total of $50.22 would be earned under the LIFO method.

TABLE 4–5
Effects of Compounding of Future Value of $1,000 at 6% Interest

Years	Compounding Period			
	Annually	*Quarterly*	*Weekly*	*Daily*
1	$1,060	$1,061.37	$1,061.80	$1,061.83
2	1,124	1,126.49	1,127.42	1,127.49
3	1,191	1,195.62	1,197.09	1,197.20
4	1,262	1,268.99	1,271.07	1,271.22
5	1,338	1,346.85	1,349.62	1,349.83
10	1,791	1,814.02	1,821.49	1,822.03
15	2,397	2,443.22	2,458.33	2,459.43
20	3,207	3,290.66	3,317.82	3,319.80
25	4,292	4,432.04	4,477.81	4,481.15

TABLE 4–6
Methods of Determining Savings Account Balances for
Interest Calculations

Savings Account Activity			
Date	Deposits	Withdrawals	Balance
July 1	$2,000		$2,000
12	2,500		4,500
Aug 8	1,000		5,500
15	500		6,000
Sept 5		$1,000	5,000
15		500	4,500
30		1,000	3,500

Methods of Determining Balance for Interest Calculation[a]

FIFO (first-in, first-out) method
$$\$2,000 \times .06 \times 81/365 = \$ \ 26.63$$
$$1,000 \times .06 \times 54/365 = \ \ \ \ 8.88$$
$$500 \times .06 \times 46/365 = \ \ \ \ 3.78$$
$$\text{Total interest, FIFO} = \$ \ 39.29$$

LIFO (last-in, first-out) method
$$\$2,000 \times .06 \times 92/365 = \$ \ 30.25$$
$$1,500 \times .06 \times 81/365 = \ \ \ 19.97$$
$$\text{Total interest, LIFO} = \$ \ 50.22$$

Low-balance method
$$\$2,000 \times .06 \times 92/365 = \$ \ 30.25$$
Total interest, low
 balance $\qquad \qquad \$ \ 30.25$

Day-of-deposit-to-day-of-withdrawal (DDDW) method
$$\$2,000 \times .06 \times 92/365 = \$ \ 30.25$$
$$2,500 \times .06 \times 81/365 = \ \ \ 33.29$$
$$1,000 \times .06 \times 54/365 = \ \ \ \ 8.88$$
$$500 \times .06 \times 46/365 = \ \ \ \ 3.78$$
$$-1,000 \times .06 \times 26/365 = \ - \ 4.27$$
$$-500 \times .06 \times 16/365 = \ - \ 1.32$$
$$-1,000 \times .06 \times \ \ 1/365 = \ - \ \ .16$$
$$\text{Total interest, DDDW} = \$ \ 70.45$$

[a] Using 6% and 365 days, with earnings including the day of deposit.

Under the *low-balance method,* interest is paid only on the least amount of money that was in the account during the interest period. This method, which discourages withdrawals, is the most unprofitable for the saver. It provides earnings of only $30.25 for the saver in our hypothetical case.

The *day-of-deposit-to-day-of-withdrawal (DDDW) method* is a way of determining and calculating account balances daily. The great majority of banks, savings and loan associations, and credit unions now use it. Each deposit earns interest for the total number of days it was actually in the institution. When withdrawals occur, interest is earned for the number of days the money remained before the day of withdrawal.

This method is costlier for the institutions, but it is the fairest for savers. In our hypothetical case, the saver would earn $70.45 under the DDDW method. With daily compounding, it provides the highest return of any of the methods used. Given the same nominal interest rates, savers should choose an institution using daily interest calculation methods.

Grace Periods A **grace period** is the time period in days in which deposits or withdrawals can be made and still earn interest on savings from a given day of the interest period. Generally, a ten-to-fifteen day grace period is allowed for deposits. This means, for example, that if deposits are made by the tenth day of the month, interest will be earned from the first.

For withdrawals, the grace period is more limited but generally ranges from three to five days. A saver might withdraw money from an account within three to five days from the end of the interest period and yet earn interest as if the money were in the account for the entire period. Wisely using a grace period increases a saver's real return. To illustrate, suppose you deposited $600 at 6 percent per year in a savings account on June 10. Normally, without a grace period, you would earn monthly interest of $2 ($600 × 0.06 × 20/360). With a grace period (deposits made by the tenth will earn from the first), you would earn $3 ($600 × 0.06 × 30/360). It is important to check with a savings institution to see if such a grace period is available. However, as more institutions adopt daily account balance and compounding procedures, the use of grace periods will diminish.

Costs and Penalties Costs and penalties frequently assessed on savings accounts are what savings institutions categorize as **account exceptions**. The wise money manager tries to be alert and avoid them. Table 4–7 lists these account exceptions along with the generally accepted criteria for assessing the costs or penalties. The costs and penalties noted here can be excessive. They are factors that you need to examine when you are choosing a place to save money. If you can find a savings institution that charges low costs and penalties, it may be a suitable place to have a savings account.

A significant penalty is usually assessed for early withdrawal of fixed-time deposits. This often occurs on certificates of deposit (CDs), which are examined later in this chapter. In this situation the penalty for early withdrawal from fixed-time deposits of short duration (usually forfeiture of interest for accounts of ninety days, six months, or a year) is less severe than for early withdrawal from those of longer duration (two years, four years, or longer). A one-year deposit may be assessed a penalty of ninety days' interest forfeiture, whereas a five-year deposit may be assessed a six-month interest forfeiture; also, the interest rate for the most recent period is usually lowered.

Some banks redeposit matured fixed-time deposits automatically into a lower-interest-bearing passbook account or another long-term deposit without consulting the original depositor of the money (for example, redeeming an 8 percent CD and redepositing the money in a passbook account paying only 5 percent). Be sure to check for these kinds of situations.

TABLE 4–7
Costs and Penalties on Savings Accounts

Account Exception	Criteria for Assessing Costs or Penalties
Early withdrawal	Amounts withdrawn before the end of a quarter earn no interest for that quarter.
Deposit penalty	Deposits made during the present quarter earn no interest until the beginning of the next quarter.
Delayed use of funds	Amounts deposited by check cannot be withdrawn until the check clears. More than half of all banks hold personal checks for 3 to 5 days.
Minimum account balance	A depositor's account balance falls below a set minimum balance. A set fee of $1 to $5 a month is often charged. An account could be reduced to zero.
Average account balance	A depositor's average account balance falls below a set amount. The cost varies but is usually based on a set fee, a scaled amount (the more the account falls below the average, the greater the cost), or a percentage of the amount the account falls below the average.
Variable balance	Passbook accounts earn varying interest rates depending on the amount on deposit, such as 4.5% on the first $500, 5% on amounts above $500 to $1,000, and 5.25% above $1,000. Some institutions charge a monthly maintenance fee if the balance drops below $500.
Telephone, computer, or teller information	Costs are assessed to those who request savings account information by telephone, by computer, or from the teller. Typically the assessment would come after a certain number of requests have been made. This is generally set at three per month, with a cost of $.50 per telephone or teller contact. The cost of computer information would be higher, often assessed at $1 or more per request.
Inactive accounts	A penalty may be assessed for inactive accounts. Usually there must be no activity for six months to a year before a penalty is assessed. The penalty varies, but typically it is $2 to $3 per set period. An account can be liquidated completely through these penalties.
Excessive withdrawals	To discourage too many withdrawals, some savings institutions assess a penalty (ranging from $1 to $3) on those accounts where withdrawals exceed a certain number in a quarterly period.
Early account closing	Charges are sometimes assessed if a depositor closes a savings account within a month or quarter of opening it. Charges range from $1 to $5.

Cash Management Tool 3:
Money Market Accounts

Most people establish their checking and savings accounts at local financial institutions as the cornerstones of their cash management efforts. They earn interest on both accounts.

When income begins to exceed expenses regularly, perhaps by $200 or $300 a month, a substantial amount of excess funds can quickly build up. This is a comfortable situation, to be sure; however, it is also wise from a cash management point of view to move excess funds to an account that pays the highest possible interest rate. Why earn only 5 percent on your money when 7 or 8 percent or more can be earned simply by opening a money market account?

A *money market account* is a generic term describing a variety of high-interest earning accounts (compared to passbook savings accounts) that have limited checkwriting privileges. Such accounts usually have daily compounding and are offered by banks, savings and loan associations, credit unions, stock brokerage firms, financial supermarkets, mutual funds, and other financial institutions. The types of money market accounts include money market funds, money market deposit accounts, super NOW accounts, sweep accounts, and cash management accounts.

Money Market Funds

A *money market fund (MMF)* is a mutual fund that pools the cash of thousands of investors and specializes in earning a relatively safe and high return by buying securities that have very short-term maturities, generally less than one year. The debt instruments include treasury bills and notes, certificates of deposit, commercial paper (IOUs of business), and other credit agreements. Because of the high quality of the securities, MMFs are considered extremely safe. Some money market funds buy only U.S. government securities and therefore are 100 percent safe and pay a return slightly lower than the other funds. Another group of funds invests only in tax-free securities, which earn lower yields but pay tax-free returns to depositors. The minimum deposit is from $500 to $1,000, and a service fee (usually .5 percent of the value of the fund per year) is charged. (Chapter 18 discusses mutual funds.)

Money market funds typically pay just about the highest interest rate of return that can be earned on a daily basis. An investor who keeps $4,000 in a local financial institution might earn $240 interest annually while the person with that amount in a money market fund could well earn $360, for a difference of $120 ($360 − $240). The rate fluctuates daily and in recent years has ranged from 5 to 17 percent. Money market funds are convenient to use for special financial needs because checks can be drawn on the account. The minimum check limit is often $200, which discourages use of a money market fund as a regular checking account.

Money Market Deposit Accounts

A *money market deposit account* is a government-insured money market account offered through a depository institution, such as a bank, credit union, or savings and loan association. Each account is insured by the appropriate federal agency (FDIC, FSLIC, or NCUA) for $100,000. Since there is no minimum maturity, depositors can withdraw their cash at any time. Five hundred dollars to $1,000 often must be deposited to open an account, with no minimums on additional deposits. Should the average monthly balance fall below a certain sum, such as $1,000, the entire account earns interest at the rate of the regular NOW account, which is likely to be about 5 percent. For this reason money market deposit accounts are sometimes called variable interest accounts. Financial institutions are allowed to guarantee a given rate for as long as thirty days but may change it daily. Account holders typically are limited to six transactions per month, three checks and three automatic transfers. Institutions are allowed to establish fees for transactions and maintenance.

Depositors consider placing cash reserves in this type of fund for the high rate of return and the convenience of local transactions. The interest rates paid may be .5 percent less than the best-managed money market funds, but many depositors like the extra margin of safety offered by these government-insured accounts.

Super NOW Accounts

A *super NOW account* is a government-insured high-interest NOW account offered through depository institutions. The initial minimum deposit ranges from $1,000 to $2,500, and yields are calculated weekly or monthly. If the average balance falls below a set amount, such as $1,000, the account will earn interest at the rate of the regular NOW account. Depositors can withdraw their funds at any time without penalty. Of great attraction to super NOW depositors are the account's unlimited checking privileges. Rates are almost as high as money market deposit accounts.

Sweep Accounts

A *sweep account* combines a regular NOW account with a money market fund. Banks, credit unions, savings and loan associations, credit card companies (such as American Express and MasterCard), and brokerage firms provide variations of sweep accounts. The essence of sweep accounts is that an investor's money flows between a regular NOW account and a money market fund, depending on the balance in the NOW account, and earns interest accordingly. For example, assume that the institution requires an initial deposit of $3,500. A target amount, perhaps $2,500, goes into the NOW account, where it earns perhaps 5 percent. The remaining portion, $1,000, goes into a money market fund, where it earns current market rates, which might be 8 percent.

Account rules vary among institutions, but a sweep occurs whenever the balance goes above or below specific minimum or maximum amounts. On an account with a $2,500 target, the minimum might be $2,400 and the maximum $2,600. A *sweep* is an automatic transfer of funds into or out of the sweep account's money market fund. This may occur daily or twice a week. If the investor above makes a deposit of $75, it will bring the NOW account balance to $2,575, which is not enough to trigger a sweep. With a subsequent deposit of $300, the balance rises to $2,875. Then the institution sweeps all the funds in excess of the $2,500 target ($375) into the money market fund.

Checks written are drawn from the NOW account. If the account is drawn down to less than the minimum, sufficient funds are taken from the money market fund to bring the balance back up to the target amount. For example, a sweep account with a balance of $4,000 would have $2,500 in the NOW account and $1,500 in the money market fund. A $500 check would draw the NOW account down to $2,000 ($2,500 target minus the $500 check), and the institution would "sweep" $500 from the money market fund into the NOW account to maintain the target balance. The result of the transaction would be $2,500 in the NOW account and $1,000 in the money market fund, for a sweep account balance of $3,500.

Charges vary on sweep accounts. Some have a monthly and/or annual fee, and others have a one-time initiation fee. Most institutions charge a transaction fee for each sweep.

Cash Management Accounts

A *cash management account (CMA)* is a multiple-purpose account that provides the same services as sweep accounts and more. It offers a checking account, money market fund, stock brokerage account, a credit card, and a debit card in one coordinated package. CMAs (often known as central assets accounts or by other names) are offered through brokerage firms, financial institutions, retailers, and mutual funds. A CMA offered through one of the financial supermarket institutions allows you to conduct all your financial business under one roof. The required minimum to open an account is $1,000 or more. One monthly statement conveniently serves as a written record of all transactions, as Figure 4–9 illustrates.

A computer program monitors and manages each account according to a predetermined set of rules. For example, say you open a CMA with $2,000 in cash and $8,000 in securities (stocks and bonds). The $8,000 amount goes to the securities account, and the cash is swept into a money market fund to earn current high market rates. Cash from stock dividends or from sales of stock go into the money market fund automatically. Large withdrawals of cash come first from any money in the money market fund, then from the securities account, and finally from the line of credit. Any deposit reduces a loan balance automatically even if the investor wanted to keep the loan balance outstanding while adding to the money market fund. Note that CMAs may be swept daily or weekly; in the latter case, recently deposited money may not

FIGURE 4-9
CMA Statement

```
                    CASH MANAGEMENT ACCOUNT


Franklin Marshall              Account Number  01234567891
123 Main Street                Date of Statement  March 1, 1988
Anytown, USA  01234
```

ACTIVITY IN ACCOUNT DURING MONTH OF FEBRUARY

Date	Activity	Description	Price	Amount	Cash Balance
1-31	opening balance	-	-	-	11,481.40
2-3	Bought	Cash Mgt Acct	1.00	1,000.00	12,481.40
2-6	VISA	Sheraton-Miami	-	310.00	12,171.40
2-9	Bought	ATT shares	77.50	7,750.00	4,421.40
2-13	Bought	Cash Mgt Acct	1.00	1,000.00	5,421.40
2-17	VISA	Gourmet Rest	-	90.00	5,331.40
2-22	Sold	ATT shares	84.50	8,450.00	13,781.40
2-22	Cash Div	Cash Mgt Acct	-	71.80	13,853.20
2-22	Check	Bandy Chevrolet	-	240.00	13,613.20
2-26	Cash div	Aetna shares	-	60.00	13,673.20
2-26	Bought	Kraft shares	48.50	4,850.00	8,823.20
2-27	Check	VISA	-	1,200.00	7,623.20
2-28	Cash div	Cash Mgt Acct	-	13.60	7,636.80
2-28	CLOSING BALANCE		-	-	7,636.80

SUMMARY OF PORTFOLIO

Quantity Long	Quantity Short	Description	Month End Price	Est Value	Est Ann Yield	Est Ann Income
200		IBM	46.00	9,200	2.10	193
100		Kraft	48.50	4,850	3.10	150
300		Aetna	33.00	9,900	2.40	238
CLOSING BALANCE FOR SECURITIES				23,950		481

SUMMARY OF SECURITY TRANSACTIONS IN FEBRUARY

Date	Activity	Description	Price	Amount	
2-9	Bought	ATT shares	77.50	7,750	
2-22	Sold	ATT shares	84.50	8,450	CR
2-26	Bought	Kraft shares	48.50	4,850	

earn interest for several days. Checks can be coded for budgeting purposes by some CMAs.

Initial fees range from $25 to $100, usually with a monthly charge of $2 to $12. Most CMA firms offer several free features to attract investors: a credit and/or debit card, a rebate of 1 percent on card purchases, traveler's checks, term life insurance, and various advisory newsletters.

Cash Management Tool 4: Low-Risk Savings Instruments

If you are a good manager of your personal finances, you have established a checking account, savings account, and money market account; you are earning interest on all monies until they are expended. You have maximized your economic self-interest. After all, *someone* is going to earn a return on deposited idle funds: it might as well be you.

At this point of financial security, you might consider making investments in the stock market or real estate or something else; these are covered in later chapters. Depending on your situation, these investments may be appropriate. However, you might decide instead to place additional money in various low-risk savings instruments. This is the fourth phase of cash management. These instruments include government savings bonds and certificates of deposit.

Government Savings Bonds

In 1980, the U.S. government began offering ten-year Series EE and Series HH savings bonds to replace the older Series E and Series H bonds. *Series EE savings bonds* are U.S. government bonds that are purchased for 50 percent of their face value. How long they have to be held to double in value depends on the interest rate set by the federal government. They pay no periodic interest, since the interest accumulates as the difference between the purchase price and the bond's value at maturity. For example, a Series EE bond can be purchased for $100 and redeemed at maturity for $200. Series EE bonds can be purchased in denominations from $25 to $5,000, with a maximum purchase limit of $15,000 annually. Series EE bonds cashed in early are penalized with a lower interest rate than stated on the bond. For example, a 6 percent Series EE bond would pay only 5.5 percent if *redeemed* (cashed in) after five years instead of at maturity. Series EE interest need not be reported to the IRS until it is received. If older savings bonds are held past November 1, 1987, they are eligible to pay a market rate if it is higher than the guaranteed minimum rate that the bond is already earning. The *market rate for savings bonds* is 85 percent of the latest six-month average rate on five-year treasury securities. For example, assume an EE bond paying 6.5 percent is held past November 1, 1987. If the market rate is 8.15 percent when the bond is redeemed, this higher rate will apply.

Series HH savings bonds are U.S. government bonds that are purchased at face value; they can be bought only by exchanging E and EE bonds. They pay interest semiannually until maturity five years later. For example, a $10,000 Series HH bond paying 7.5 percent interest annually will yield semiannual interest payments of $375 ($10,000 × 0.075 ÷ 2 = $375). Bonds redeemed early are cashed in at slightly less than face value, a penalty that in effect adjusts and reduces the interest rates paid earlier. For example, a $10,000 Series HH bond paying 7.5 percent at maturity will be redeemed at less than $10,000 if redeemed after four and one-half years to reflect an overall interest rate of perhaps only 6.8 percent.

Series EE and HH interest income is exempt from state and local income taxes. Federal income taxes can be deferred on Series EE bonds until they are redeemed.

Certificates of Deposit

Various fixed-time deposits available at savings institutions require savers to deposit money for a minimum amount of time, commonly ranging from thirty-two days to eight years (or even longer). Deposits can range from $1,000 to $100,000. These *certificates of deposit (CDs)* pay much greater interest rates than passbook accounts because financial institutions can count on having deposits for a specific time and can make investments accordingly. If money is withdrawn before the time limit is up, there are usually interest penalties. Interest rates, penalties, and maturities on CDs are no longer heavily regulated.

The savings investor with smaller sums would do well to consider *small certificates of deposit,* which are fixed-time deposits in minimum denominations of no less than $100. Interest is compounded daily, providing a yield higher than normal savings accounts but slightly less than the large certificates of deposit. CDs can be purchased through banks, savings and loan associations, and credit unions. With all CDs there are penalties for early withdrawal (on certificates held less than one year the depositor may lose a minimum of one month's interest; on certificates held more than one year the depositor may lose a minimum of three months' interest), so be certain that it is appropriate to tie up your funds. Note that if the penalty is greater than the interest, you will get back less than you deposited.

Summary

1. Today's somewhat deregulated financial services industry is competitive and increasingly complex. It is made up of banks, brokerage firms, insurance companies, financial supermarkets, and financial planners. Almost all financial planners are biased because they sell something.

2. Good cash management means that you try to earn interest on all your funds, often in different types of accounts, while also having sufficient amounts available for living expenses, emergen-

cies, and perhaps for various savings and investment opportunities. The first tool of cash management is a checking account from which to pay monthly expenses. In choosing a financial institution, one should consider such criteria as cost, safety, convenience, treatment of customers, and range of services.

3. The most recognized forms of electronic funds transfer (EFT) are debit cards, computer-chip cards, preauthorized payments and deposits, and computer money management.

4. The second tool of cash management is a local savings account. Most employed people with good job security and fringe benefits need to determine for themselves how much money they should set aside for emergencies in a local financial institution. A passbook account using the day-of-deposit-to-day-of-withdrawal method of determining the savings account balance will pay the highest effective interest rate.

5. The third tool of cash management is a money market account, which offers a higher interest rate than checking and savings accounts. Money market accounts include money market funds, money market deposit accounts, super NOW accounts, sweep accounts, and cash management accounts.

6. The fourth tool of cash management is other low-risk savings, such as government savings bonds and certificates of deposit. These types of fixed-time deposits pay higher interest rates than passbook savings accounts but also tie up your money for several months or longer.

Modern Money Management

How Should the Johnsons Manage Their Cash?

In January Harry and Belinda had $1,200 in monetary assets (see page 47): $570 in cash on hand, $190 in a passbook savings account at First Federal Bank earning 5 percent interest compounded daily, $70 in a passbook account at the Far West Savings and Loan earning 5.25 percent interest compounded semiannually, $60 in a share account at the Smith Brokerage Credit Union earning a dividend of 6 percent compounded quarterly, and $310 in their non-interest-bearing checking account at First Interstate.

1. What specific recommendations do you have for the Johnsons on using the first and second tools of cash management?

2. Their cash flow calendar (see Table 3–7) indicates that by September they will have an extra $1,854 available. They also expect continued surpluses of more than $200 a month from that point on because of anticipated salary raises. What specific recommendations do you have for the Johnsons on using the third and fourth tools of cash management?

Key Words and Concepts

Review Questions

1. Describe briefly the providers of financial services and the products they sell.
2. Explain why almost all financial planners are biased.

3. Explain what a professional financial planner does.
4. Summarize the four tools of cash management.
5. Differentiate among commercial banks, mutual savings banks, savings and loan associations, and credit unions.
6. Summarize the criteria used in choosing a checking account.
7. Explain the check-clearing process, including float.
8. Give five examples of electronic funds transfers.
9. What are the provisions for lost EFT cards?
10. Differentiate between time deposits and demand deposits.
11. Do most people need to keep a lot of money in a savings account at a local institution? Why or why not?
12. Explain the difference between the nominal and effective rates of interest.
13. Explain the effect of compounding.
14. Summarize three account exceptions.
15. Differentiate between a money market fund and a money market deposit account.
16. Summarize how a cash management account works.
17. Differentiate between the two types of government savings bonds.

Case Problems

1. Estelle Paradiso of Upper Montclair, New Jersey, has had a checking account at a commercial bank for three years. The bank has always required a minimum balance of $100 to avoid an account charge, and Estelle has always maintained this balance. Recently Estelle heard that a nearby savings and loan association is offering NOW accounts paying 5 percent interest on the average daily balance of the account. This institution requires a minimum balance of only $300 but a forfeiture of monthly interest is assessed when the account falls below this minimum. With her past habits at the commercial bank, Estelle feels the $300 minimum would not be too hard to maintain. She is seriously thinking about moving her money to the NOW account.
   a. Do you think it would be wise for Estelle to move to a NOW account? Why or why not?
   b. Explain why you think it is possible for a savings and loan association to offer NOW accounts paying 5 percent interest on a minimum balance of $300 and still operate profitably.
   c. Can you offer any suggestions to Estelle's commercial bank to keep her as a customer? Explain.

2. Celie Pollock of Portland, Oregon, pays a $25 fee every month for an electronic money management service. Her friend Valerie feels Celie is wasting her money. Celie has a net income of $3,000 a month, plus other earnings from some good investments. In addition, she is part owner of an apartment complex, which earns her approximately $1,000 a month. She always tries to put her reserve money into solid investments so that they might bring her future earnings and security.
   a. What specific services offered by electronic money management would help a person such as Celie?
   b. Justify Celie's paying the $25 monthly fee for computer money management.
   c. What are some alternative money management services Celie could use?

Suggested Readings

"A Dozen Painless Ways to Help a Nest Egg Grow." *U.S. News and World Report,* June 8, 1987, pp. 58–60. Useful suggestions on how to start saving.

"How Safe Is Your Money?" *Newsweek,* April 13, 1987, p. 55. How the FSLIC got into trouble and the likelihood of a congressional bailout.

"The Saving of America." *Forbes,* April 20, 1987, p. 71. Demographic shifts suggest that personal saving is becoming fashionable again.

"Troubled Temples of Thrift." *Time,* May 18, 1987, p. 56. Summary of the financial woes of the savings and loan industry.

CHAPTER 5

Credit Use and Credit Cards

OBJECTIVES

After reading this chapter, the student should be able to

1. discuss some considerations in the use of credit.
2. list and describe several different types of credit accounts.
3. describe the process of opening a credit account.
4. summarize the five criteria (five *C*'s) used to judge credit applications.
5. describe the features of credit statements and explain how finance charges are computed.
6. explain how the Equal Credit Opportunity Act prohibits discrimination in credit practices.
7. discuss the protection available to credit users under four major federal credit laws.
8. discuss the factors to consider when deciding how much open-ended credit to use.

M any people have strong feelings about the use of credit. On the one hand, you may be attracted to the ease of using a credit card to pay for gasoline on a cross-country trip or to finance the purchase of a stereo system with monthly payments. On the other hand, you may have vivid memories of a friend or relative who got too deeply into debt by overusing credit cards and ended up bankrupt. A recent survey revealed that one out of three households actually fears becoming overextended on credit. The purpose of this chapter is to show you how to use credit wisely.

The Use of Credit

Credit is a form of trust established between a lender and a borrower. If the lender believes that a prospective borrower has both the ability and the willingness to repay money, then credit will be granted. The borrower will, hopefully, live up to that trust and repay the lender.

Reasons for Using Credit

Credit is widely used in the United States by governments, businesses, and consumers. Many local governments finance the construction of high schools and community colleges by borrowing, and the federal government often borrows to meet its responsibilities, such as building highways and providing welfare benefits. Businesses that need to expand their production facilities to fulfill customer demand frequently borrow funds to build new plants.

Consumers borrow for a variety of reasons, as the following list shows:

1. Emergencies   Consumers use credit to pay for unexpected expenses, such as emergency medical services or auto repairs.
2. Early consumption   Buying a color television on credit allows the consumer immediate use of the product.
3. Convenience   Using credit, and credit cards in particular, simplifies making many purchases. It provides a record of purchases and it can be used as leverage in disputes over purchases.
4. The good life   An increasing number of younger persons (nearly two-thirds of the people under twenty-five) use credit as a tool for personal money management. Such credit users seem to want to have now what it took their parents perhaps twenty years to acquire.
5. Education   The growing costs of higher education forces many to borrow. The National Association of Student Financial Aid Administrators reports that for those who borrowed to attend school the average indebtedness was over $7,000. Those borrowers are devoting more than 4 percent of their current income to repay the debts.

6. Offsetting inflation   Many people borrow money to buy a product before inflation causes the price of the product to rise. These consumers assume that an inflated future income will enable them to repay the money in future years.

7. Debt consolidation   Many consumers who have difficulty making credit repayments turn to a **debt-consolidation loan.** Here the borrower exchanges several smaller debts with varying due dates and interest rates for one payment, which is usually lower in amount than the payments on the other debts combined. For the privilege of consolidating all debts into one, the consumer is charged a substantial interest rate (perhaps 28 percent) and the term of the loan is lengthened—which, in spite of higher interest charges, allows for lower monthly payments.

8. Free credit   Credit card users may be provided free credit for short periods of time, up to 50 to 55 days, depending on the timing of a purchase.

9. Identification   For many activities, such as renting an automobile or cashing a check, consumers often need to show one or two credit cards for identification.

Growth of Consumer Credit

Consumer credit is nonbusiness debt used by consumers for purposes other than home mortgages. (Borrowing for housing is considered an investment rather than an expenditure.) Attitudes toward the use of consumer credit have changed dramatically in the United States over the past forty years. Historically, people who needed funds borrowed only from members of their own family. As the extended family began to be replaced by the nuclear family after World War II, those in need of money had to look to banks and other financial institutions for loans.

The economic expansion following World War II provided greater income for many Americans and a growing number of dual-earner households. The typical family has had increasing amounts of money income to spend on items beyond necessities. Table 5–1 shows how outstanding consumer credit has risen tremendously in recent years. Much of this debt is for the purchase of automobiles and household goods.

Types of Consumer Credit

There are two types of consumer credit: installment credit and noninstallment credit. With **installment credit,** the consumer must, according to contract, repay the amount owed in a specific number of equal payments, usually monthly. Making monthly auto loan payments is an example. **Noninstallment credit** includes single-payment loans (such as paying the electric bill after using services for one month) and open-ended credit. With **open-ended credit,** also called *revolving credit,* the consumer may choose to repay the debt in a single payment or to make a series of equal or unequal payments. Most credit cards operate in this manner. Table 5–1 shows consumer credit outstanding in the United States since World War II. Although the definitions of installment,

TABLE 5-1
Consumer Credit Outstanding (Billions of Dollars)

| Year | Noninstallment Credit[b] | Installment Credit[a] | | | | | Total Consumer Credit |
		Total	Automobile	Revolving[c]	Mobile Home	Other	
1950	$ 10	$ 15	$ 6	$—	$—	$ 9	$ 25
1955	14	30	13	—	—	15	44
1960	19	44	18	—	—	26	64
1965	28	73	29	—	—	42	101
1970	35	104	36	5	2	59	139
1975	50	169	57	15	14	83	220
1980	74	308	116	55	17	118	382
1985	132	536	208	115	26	185	668
1990[d]	260	843	349	193	44	257	1,103

Source: Economic Report of the President, 1987 (Washington, D.C., 1987), p. 338.

[a] Installment credit covers most short- and intermediate-term credit extended to individuals to be repaid in two or more installments. Credit secured by real estate is generally excluded.

[b] Noninstallment credit is credit scheduled to be repaid in a lump sum, including single-payment loans, charge accounts, and service credit. Because of inconsistencies in the data and infrequent benchmarking, the series is no longer published by the Federal Reserve Board on a regular basis. Data are shown here as a general indication of trends.

[c] Revolving installment credit consists of credit cards at retailers, gasoline companies, and commercial banks, and check credit at commercial banks. Prior to 1968, it was included in "other," except for gasoline companies, which were included in noninstallment credit before 1971. From 1977, it has included open-ended credit at retailers, previously included in "other."

[d] Authors' estimates.

open-ended, and noninstallment credit are not the same as used in this book, the table gives a clear indication of the growth of the various types of credit. This chapter is concerned mainly with open-ended credit; installment credit will be discussed in Chapter 6.

Families headed by younger persons use consumer credit more than families headed by older persons. Similarly, higher-income groups use more credit than do lower-income groups. This may result partially from the unwillingness of lenders to make loans to lower-income families. Not surprisingly, young families with children have the greatest credit use. The per capita level of outstanding consumer credit has risen from about $680 in 1970 to over $2,500 today.

Problems of Credit Use

Perhaps the greatest disadvantage of credit use is the loss of financial flexibility in personal money management. For example, if you have installment debts taking 10 percent of your after-tax income, you have lost the opportunity to spend those dollars for something else. Credit use also reduces your future buying power, since the money you pay out in a three-year installment loan includes a *finance charge,* or what the lender charges you to borrow the money.

Credit use often leads to overspending. Buying clothes on a charge account for $25 a month for twenty months seem a lot easier than paying a full purchase price of $425. It is easier still to buy more clothes on credit the next month, especially if you have six credit cards; the average family does.

Overextension of credit can also be a real problem for credit users. By the time a consumer has installment debts amounting to 20 percent of take-home pay, he or she is seriously in debt. Instead of working at a job and spending the income, the consumer slaves at a job to pay the bills.

Misusing credit and not paying bills on time can give consumers a poor credit reputation or even result in the loss of items purchased. Suppose you buy an auto for $280 per month for forty-eight months. You make your payments for fourteen months, but then are unable to continue paying. You will have lost fourteen months of payments and will probably have to pay repossession costs, such as attorney and court fees, when the lender takes back the auto. Then you will have to arrange for new transportation. Clearly, it is wise to plan credit use carefully.

The Cost of Credit

For virtually all types of consumer credit, the federal Consumer Credit Protection Act (also known as the Truth in Lending Law) requires standardization of credit figures. Lenders must report both the total finance charge in dollars and the annual percentage rate of interest. The *annual percentage rate (APR)* is a measure of the cost of credit at a yearly rate expressed as a percentage. For example, a $1,000 single-payment one-year loan at 14 percent APR carries a finance charge of $140. Another lending source offering the same loan at 16 percent APR would require a $160 finance charge. Interest and all other loan charges required by the lender (such as those for a credit investigation or credit life insurance) must be included in both the calculation of the APR and the total finance charge in dollars. The annual percentage rate is a close approximation of the true cost of credit and can be used to compare credit contracts with different time periods, finance charges, and amounts borrowed. The lower the APR, the lower the true cost of credit.

Types of Charge Accounts

A *credit card* is a plastic card identifying the holder as a participant in the credit plan of a lender, such as a department store, oil company, or bank. Card holders can make merchandise purchases or, in some cases, obtain cash advances (loans). Most credit cards are used as open-ended credit accounts, or charge accounts, originally designed for the short-run money needs of consumers. Most of these accounts have a *credit limit*—the maximum outstanding debt on a credit account—and a flexible repayment schedule. The card holder can usually pay the entire balance due within the *grace period* (a period of twenty to twenty-five days after receipt of a bill, during which no finance charges are assessed) or repay according to a minimum-payment schedule. More than two-thirds of all cardholders maintain balances, and the average customer takes more than fifteen months to pay for the charges.

There are several types of charge accounts available to consumers. Some of these involve the use of credit cards, and some do not. Each is described in the following sections.

Thirty-day Account

Creditors expect debts incurred on a *thirty-day account* to be paid in full within thirty days. Consumers have such accounts with neighborhood businesses and local utility companies. Credit costs are not assessed because the companies expect full payment soon after mailing customers their bills. People with little or no credit experience can usually open thirty-day charge accounts.

Budget Account

A *budget account* is a somewhat limited charge account, typically offered by local department stores and specialty shops. Users must repay a specific portion of the charged amount (usually one-fourth to one-third) within 30 days, then pay the remainder over a period of a few months. An interest rate of 1.5 percent per month (18 percent APR) on the unpaid balance is usually charged. Of course, early repayment of all charges will reduce the finance costs.

Option Account

An *option account* permits either payment in full when the bill arrives (with no credit costs) or partial payment spread over several months (at a typical interest rate of 1.5 percent per month, or at 18 percent APR). A fixed dollar minimum or percentage of the bill outstanding each month must be repaid.

These accounts include most credit cards issued by local retail businesses, local shopping malls, national retail stores, and other major companies. Credit cards issued by a local retail business generally can be used only at that store, whereas cards from national retail chains (such as Sears Roebuck, Montgomery Ward, and J. C. Penney) and major companies (such as American Express Optima, Exxon, and Chevron) can be used almost everywhere. More than 60 percent of families use this type of credit card. The importance of option accounts to retailers can be seen in the fact that more than 50 percent of J. C. Penney Company sales are on credit.

Bank Credit Card Account

Bank credit card accounts, such as VISA, MasterCard, and Discover, are a form of option account and are used by more than 60 percent of all families. They can be used nationally (some internationally) in hundreds of thousands of retail outlets and thus offer the widest selection of goods and services of any credit card account. The user again has the option of paying the bill in full when it arrives or repaying over several months. At any time during the repayment schedule the card holder can pay the total balance due. More than 60 million MasterCards and 77 million VISA cards are in effect worldwide.

The cards are offered through a system of affiliated banks across the country, and the consumer applies to a local bank for service. An upper credit limit is established upon application, commonly $500 to $10,000. When a card holder requests a reasonable increase in the limit, it is usually given. In most states, banks are permitted to charge a card membership fee of $15 to $35 annually in addition to the finance charges. For $50 or more, users can have a "gold" or premium card, which has a higher spending ceiling and some added frills (travel insurance, for example). "Affinity" cards are sometimes available, too. Issued only to members of certain groups, such as the Sierra Club or a university, affinity cards are standard bank cards with the addition of the organization's logo; the bank pays a small fee to the organization based on members' usage, perhaps ½ of 1 percent of the charges. Revenues for bank credit cards are generated from membership fees, finance charges paid by those who do not pay their accounts in full, and by assessment on merchants of from 2 to 8 percent on the purchases billed through them.

Revolving Account

A *revolving account* is any charge account for which the user has the option to either pay the bill in full or spread repayment over several months. Thus, revolving accounts include budget accounts, option accounts, and bank credit card accounts.

Travel and Entertainment Account

The major *travel and entertainment account* (T & E) credit cards are American Express, Diners Club, and Carte Blanche. Generally the entire balance charged must be repaid within thirty days. T & E cards are used primarily by business people for food and lodging expenses while traveling. The cards are somewhat difficult to obtain (less than 15 percent of families have one) as applicants must have higher than average incomes to qualify and must pay an annual membership fee of $35 or more. However, the cards are not accepted at nearly as many outlets as are bank credit cards. T & E accounts are considered by some to be prestige cards; American Express has 15 million cards outstanding.

Opening a Charge Account

Obtaining credit is a three-step process. You must first fill out a credit application and then have your credit history investigated. The final step is credit scoring of your application.

Credit Application

Figure 5–1 shows a sample *credit application,* which requests information about your (1) ability to repay and (2) willingness to repay. Lenders must make educated decisions about whether they will be repaid.

FIGURE 5–1
Sample Credit Application
Courtesy of Bank of Lexington & Trust Company.

THIS CREDIT APPLICATION IS FOR:
☐ INDIVIDUAL ACCOUNT ☐ JOINT ACCOUNT ☐ VISA ACCOUNT and/or ☐ MASTERCARD ACCOUNT

Please complete the following about: YOURSELF

| FIRST NAME | INITIAL | LAST NAME | SOCIAL SECURITY NO | BIRTHDATE MO / DAY / YR | NO. OF DEPENDENTS * |

HOME ADDRESS | TELEPHONE NO | ZIP CODE | PREVIOUS ADDRESS

CITY | STATE | ZIP CODE | YRS. THERE | CITY | STATE | ZIP CODE | YRS. THERE

NAME OF NEAREST RELATIVE NOT LIVING WITH YOU | (RELATIONSHIP) | TELEPHONE NO | NAME & ADDRESS OF LANDLORD or MORTGAGE COMPANY

☐ OWN ☐ RENT ☐ LIVE WITH PARENTS | MONTHLY PAYMENTS | MORTGAGE BALANCE | ADDRESS | CITY | STATE | ZIP CODE

CHECKING ACCOUNT NUMBER | NAME OF FINANCIAL INSTITUTION | SAVINGS ACCOUNT NUMBER | NAME OF FINANCIAL INSTITUTION

YOUR JOB
PRESENT EMPLOYER | OCCUPATION | YRS. THERE | BUSINESS PHONE NUMBER | NET MONTHLY INCOME

STREET ADDRESS | CITY | STATE | ZIP CODE | LAST EMPLOYER | YRS. THERE

OTHER INCOME
Income from alimony, child support, or separate maintenance payments need not be revealed if you do not choose to have it considered as a basis for repaying this obligation.

SOURCE OF OTHER INCOME
ALIMONY, CHILD SUPPORT, SEPARATE MAINTENANCE RECEIVED UNDER ☐ COURT ORDER ☐ WRITTEN AGREEMENT ☐ VERBAL UNDERSTANDING

OTHER INCOME $ _____ PER _____

YOUR CREDIT REFERENCES CREDIT REFERENCES (CREDIT CARD, DEP'T STORES, BANKS, FINANCE CO, ETC.) & COMPLETE LIST OF ALL DEBTS NOW OWING OR PAID. ATTACH ADDITIONAL SHEETS IF NECESSARY.

NAME OF COMPANY & ADDRESS	ACCOUNT NO	MO. PAYMENT	BAL. DUE	NAME OF COMPANY & ADDRESS	ACCOUNT NO	MO. PAYMENT	BAL. DUE
NAME OF COMPANY & ADDRESS	ACCOUNT NO	MO. PAYMENT	BAL. DUE	NAME OF COMPANY & ADDRESS	ACCOUNT NO	MO. PAYMENT	BAL. DUE
NAME OF COMPANY & ADDRESS	ACCOUNT NO	MO. PAYMENT	BAL. DUE	AUTOMOBILE (MAKE & YEAR)	FINANCED BY & ADDRESS		BAL. DUE

CREDIT STATEMENT:
This statement is submitted to obtain credit and I(We) certify that all information herein is true and complete. I(We) also authorize the bank to verify or obtain further information the bank may deem necessary concerning My(Our) credit standing. I(We) authorize the bank to retain this application as its property and agree to the terms and conditions accompanying the bankcard for which I(We) hereby apply. Also accompanying the terms and conditions will be a copy of the Right to Dispute Billing Errors.

SIGNATURE OF APPLICANT | DATE | DRIVER'S LICENSE NO
SIGNATURE OF CO APPLICANT (if applicable) | DATE | DRIVER'S LICENSE NO
SIGNATURE OF AUTHORIZED USER OF THIS ACCOUNT

BANK USE ONLY

| VISA ACCOUNT NO. | CREDIT LINE | NO. CARDS | MASTERCARD ACCOUNT NO. | CREDIT LINE | NO. CARDS |

APP'D BY | DATE

CO-APPLICANT SECTION (Complete ONLY if joint account desired)

| FIRST NAME | INITIAL | LAST NAME |
SOCIAL SECURITY NO. | BIRTHDATE MO / DAY / YR | TELEPHONE NO
HOME ADDRESS | ZIP CODE | YRS THERE
CITY | STATE
PREVIOUS ADDRESS
CITY | STATE | ZIP CODE | YRS THERE
PRESENT EMPLOYER | OCCUPATION | YRS THERE
STREET ADDRESS | CITY | STATE | ZIP CODE
BUSINESS PHONE NO. | NET MONTHLY INCOME
LAST EMPLOYER | YRS. THERE
CHECKING ACCOUNT NO | NAME OF FINANCIAL INSTITUTION
SAVINGS ACCOUNT NO | NAME OF FINANCIAL INSTITUTION

REDDI RESERV SERVICE ____ CHECK BLOCK IF THIS SERVICE IS ALSO DESIRED

(1) I request and agree that, in the event my Bank of Lexington checking account(s) described below has insufficient funds to cover any checks or charges, presented against it for payment, the Bank shall deposit in my said checking account such funds in fifty dollar ($50.00) increments, as are required to pay the aforesaid obligation. (2) Each deposit shall constitute as a Cash Advance under my Bank Card and shall be governed by the Terms of Agreement thereof. Cash Advances may not be made if the Bank Card account is past due, over-limit, or the advance would cause the account to be over-limit. (3) This agreement shall be terminated automatically when the below designated demand account has been closed or when my credit source account is cancelled or otherwise terminated by the bank for any cause deemed sufficient by it. The Bank of Lexington may cancel this Reddi Reserv Service by a written notice mailed to me at the address shown on the bank's records and such cancellation shall be effective five (5) days after such notice has been placed in the United States mail. I may cancel this agreement by written notice to Bank of Lexington, Post Office Box 2010, Lexington, Kentucky 40594, and such cancellation shall be effective five (5) days after such notice has been mailed to the bank. (4) This agreement shall not be effective until I have received written notification of approval from Bank of Lexington.

CHECKING ACCT NO. _____ CHECKING ACCT NO. _____

AUTHORIZED SIGNATURE _____
AUTHORIZED SIGNATURE _____
AUTHORIZED SIGNATURE _____

**ALL AUTHORIZED SIGNATURES ON A JOINT ACCOUNT MUST SIGN THIS APPLICATION.

Department stores, for example, desire to keep their losses below 1 percent of all credit sales. Even though a major purpose of extending credit is to build sales through loyal customers, it is important for lenders to keep bad debts to a minimum.

The credit application process may include a brief interview with the lender, to review or clarify the information you provided on the form or to obtain additional information. Answering questions completely and honestly both on the application form and during the interview is important. If there are inconsistencies, the lender could refuse you credit.

Credit Investigation

Upon receiving your completed credit application, the lender generally conducts a *credit investigation* of your financial history and compares that information with your application. Lenders generally obtain information about you from a credit bureau. *Credit bureaus* provide lenders with financial information on millions of Americans, compiling information primarily from court records, various merchants, and creditors. More than two thousand local credit bureaus belong to national groups, such as TRW Information Services and Credit Bureau Inc. Members pay an annual charge and a fee for each credit report requested. The cost can vary from $1.50 for a telephone inquiry to $10.00 for a copy of the file on hand to $25 or more for an updated comprehensive report.

Credit Scoring

The lender, not the credit bureau, decides on your *credit rating,* which determines whether credit is granted to you. Scoring systems developed by most lenders help reduce subjectivity in decision making, avoid discrimination, and improve the likelihood of making correct decisions. Some risk is involved, of course, as at any time about 3 percent of consumer loans are past due. If lenders approved applications of only those who would repay with 100 percent certainty, few people would

---

How Would You Score on a Credit Application?

In the table below are twelve questions typical of those often asked of credit applicants. Each response carries, in parentheses, a hypothetical point score that may or may not illustrate the relative weight given to that characteristic in a particular credit-scoring scheme. Circle your response to each question and insert the point value in the blank at the right. Total the number of points you scored.

While we can't establish a real "approve/reject" cutoff score in this example, people with higher scores are likely to be better credit risks than those with lower ones. Note that you may gain or lose points because a creditor takes into account your credit-bureau report: Several accounts paid on time would increase your point total while overdue accounts, a tax lien, or a bankruptcy would decrease it. The scores needed for approval vary from lender to lender and depend on economic conditions, a lender's profit target, and its tolerance of risk. One lender, for example, might accept a 5.1 percent bad-debt ratio on our hypothetical Scorecard, below, and approve everyone who scored more than 75 points; another might be more conservative and approve only those who were able to score more than 125.

(cont. on next page)

A Hypothetical Credit-scoring Scheme

1. *What is your age?*
   Under 25 **(8)**   25–29 **(12)**   30–34 **(10)**   35–39 **(6)**   40–44 **(14)**
   45–49 **(18)**   50 or more **(25)**   _____

2. *How many years have you lived at your current address?*
   Less than 1 **(−10)**   1–2 **(−3)**   2–3 **(0)**   3-5 **(4)**   5–9 **(14)**
   10 or more **(26)**   _____

3. *Do you own your home or do you rent?*
   Own **(30)**   Rent **(−32)**   Other **(0)**   _____

4. *How many years have you held your current job?*
   Less than 1½ **(−14)**   1½–3 **(0)**   3–6 **(5)**   6–8 **(9)**   9 or more **(16)**   _____

5. *What bank accounts do you have?*
   Checking and savings **(24)**   Savings only **(11)**   Checking only **(6)**
   Neither **(0)**   _____

6. *Do you have a current bank loan?*
   Yes **(3)**   No **(0)**   _____

7. *Do you have a phone?*
   Yes **(9)**   No **(0)**   _____

8. *How many bank and travel-entertainment cards do you have?*
   0 **(0)**   1 **(12)**   2 or more **(21)**   _____

9. *How many major department-store credit cards do you have?*
   0 **(0)**   1–2 **(5)**   3 or more **(8)**   _____

10. *How many loans from a small-loan company do you have?*[a]
    0 **(0)**   1 **(−4)**   2 or more **(−12)**   _____

11. *How many marginal credit references would you have to use?*[b]
    0 **(0)**   1 or more **(−6)**   _____

12. *What is your annual family income?*
    0–$10,000 **(−7)** $10,000–15,000 **(0)** $15,000–19,000 **(5)**
    $19,000–25,000 **(8)** $25,000 or more **(13)**   _____

[a] Do not include loans from automobile-finance companies such as GMAC.
[b] In filling out an application form, a certain number of credit references are required. If you have to use small stores without an organized credit-reporting system, you'll lose points.

Total _____

	Scorecard				
If you scored	You would be in the top	Your group would have a bad-debt ratio of	If you scored	You would be in the top	Your group would have a bad-debt ratio of
151 to 175	3%	0.4%	26 to 50	67%	11.0%
126 to 150	8	1.0	1 to 25	84	14.7
101 to 125	16	2.5	−24 to 0	93	19.2
76 to 100	28	5.1	−49 to −25	98	22.7
51 to 75	46	8.0	−75 to −50	100	29.1

Source: Consumer Reports, May 1983, p. 257. Copyright 1983 by Consumers Union of United States, Inc., Mount Vernon, N.Y. 10553. Reprinted by permission from *Consumer Reports,* May 1983.

The Five C's of Credit

In evaluating a credit application, lenders consider the five C's of credit.

1. *Character* involves your honesty and reliability in meeting financial responsibilities. Your previous credit history indicates how highly you value paying bills on time.

2. *Capital* is a measure of your financial net worth. Questions about assets (home ownership, stocks, savings accounts) and liabilities (balance due on present credit accounts) reveal whether net worth is positive or negative (owing more than is owned).

3. *Capacity* is the income available to make repayment. Having a substantial income, having the same job for a number of years, and not having a lot of other debts suggests a strong financial capacity to repay.

4. *Collateral* generally includes all the assets you possess that could be available to meet liabilities. Specific collateral would be a named asset pledged to guarantee the loan repayment should you default. It makes good sense for a lender to rely more on an auto put up as collateral than on the smiling face of a credit applicant. Should the debtor later default, the auto would be sold and the proceeds applied against the loan.

5. *Conditions* are the general credit economy. When government and/or market conditions result in a restriction in the supply of money, less money is available for lending. In such cases, many applicants would be rejected who would normally have been approved for credit. Conversely, when large quantities of money are available, especially at low interest rates, it is much easier to obtain credit.

Establishing Credit

After examining a credit-scoring chart, most college-age people wonder if they will ever get credit when they need it. There are five ways to prove, to a limited extent, that you have the ability to manage credit.

1. *Act on some factors you can control.* Establish both a checking and a savings account. Avoiding overdrafts on a checking account and making regular deposits to a savings account may be good financial management, but the lender wants only to know that you *have* a checking and a savings account.

2. *Visit a local retail establishment.* Tell them that your intention is to establish a credit rating, and request an account. A local retailer is more likely to open a limited account if you visit the store in person and dress neatly. Once the account is open, use it to make a few purchases for which you typically use cash. When the bill arrives, pay it promptly and in full. Presto, a credit history is established.

3. *Request and acquire an oil company credit card.* Although more difficult to obtain than a local retail credit account, these are not impossible to get. Should one company refuse, apply at another, as scoring systems differ. Again, use the credit sparingly once obtained and repay promptly.

4. *Apply for a bank credit card.* Most bank card companies have a program of test credit for people without an extensive credit history. The limit on credit purchases may be $50 or $300, but once again the opportunity then exists to establish a credit rating. Later you can request an increase in the credit limit.

5. *Ask a bank for a small short-term cash loan.* Putting these funds into a savings account at the bank will almost guarantee that you will make the required three or four monthly payments. Also, the interest charges on the loan would be partially offset by the interest earned on the savings.

receive credit. Since types of credit and credit applicants vary, each lender uses different scoring techniques. Lenders typically use computers to analyze credit files and determine credit scores. A recent study revealed that about 12 percent of those applying for credit are denied. About half of the turndowns had no established credit history or their credit report contained adverse information. The box on page 150 shows a hypothetical credit-scoring chart combined with estimates of the probability of repayment.

Using a Charge Account

To use your charge account properly, you must become familiar with the details of credit statements and with how finance charges are computed.

Credit Statements

The significant features of most credit statements (also called a *periodic statement*) are the billing date, due date, grace period, payment schedule, and merchandise credit given. Figure 5–2 shows a monthly statement for a credit card.

Billing Date The *billing date* (sometimes called "statement date" or "closing date") is the last day of the month on which any transactions are reported; here it is 5/22/88. Any purchases or credits after this date will be recorded on the following month's bill. The statement is mailed to the card holder a few days after the billing date. The date of the billing period is generally the same each month.

Due Date The *due date* is the time by which the credit card company should receive payment from you. In Figure 5–2, this is 6/17/88. Most credit card companies permit payment to be made a few days past the due date, since mail is sometimes slow. However, if payment is received later than the due date the customer is legally obligated to pay finance charges. If no payment is received by the due date, the card holder is in *default* (has failed to meet legal financial obligations). The company will then begin collection efforts, usually by first mailing a notice that a payment is overdue.

Grace Period The days between the billing date and the due date, usually twenty in number, represent the grace period. During this time finance charges are usually not assessed on *current* credit card purchases, especially if there is no unpaid balance from the previous billing period. In Figure 5–2, the card holder has a previous unpaid balance, $228.39, and will be charged interest on the unpaid balance as well as on the charges made within the billing period. Only about one-third of all card holders pay their bills in full by the due date and thus may never have to pay finance charges. In effect, they get an interest-free

FIGURE 5–2

Sample Statement for a Revolving Charge Account

Courtesy of Bank of Lexington & Trust Company.

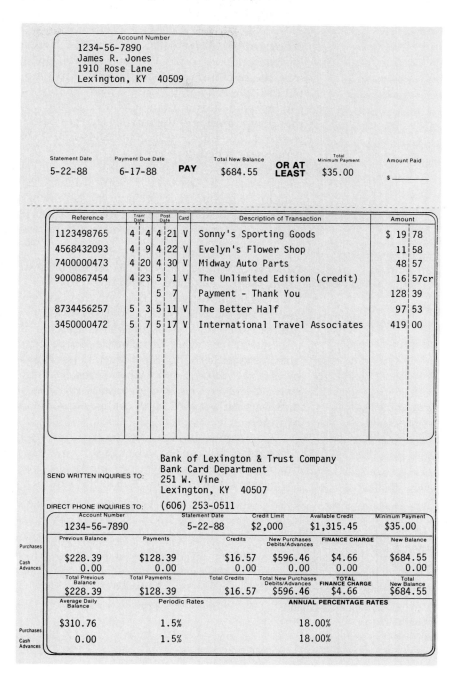

loan on their purchases for one month. One tactic is to make credit card purchases a day or two after the usual billing date and enjoy fifty to fifty-five days before having to make a payment (twenty days grace period, plus about thirty days until the next billing date).

Repayment Schedule As shown in Figure 5–2, the card holder has two options: to pay the total amount due ($684.55) or to make at least the minimum payment of $35. (Any amount above $35 could be paid.) If the full amount due is paid, finance charges in future months can be avoided. If a partial payment is made, such as $35, the amount due next month and the finance charges based on that amount will be reduced ($684.55 − $35.00 = $649.55). Table 5–2 shows a sample repayment schedule.

Merchandise Credit If you want to return merchandise you bought on credit, the merchant will issue you a *credit receipt,* written evidence of the item(s) returned and the sales price. This will be shown on your next monthly statement as a reduction of the amount owed.

Computing Finance Charges

Lenders generally charge whatever interest rates they need to assure a profit from credit card operations. However, many states have *usury laws* (legal interest-rate maximums that can be charged by lenders) that govern the charges assessed. In states with usury laws, people pay lower interest rates than in other states. Merchandise purchases are often assessed at one rate (for example, 15 percent) and cash advances at another rate (perhaps 18 percent). Lenders issue credit cards with *fixed* or *variable interest rates.* Most cards have fixed (constant) rates; for some, however, the interest rate is variable—that is, it moves up or down monthly according to changes in some index of the lender's cost of funds.

Companies that issue credit cards must tell consumers the annual percentage rate applied as well as what method they use to compute the finance charges. Typically the interest is calculated by first computing the *average daily balance.* This is the sum of the outstanding balances

TABLE 5–2
Sample Repayment Schedule

If new balance is:	less than $25	$25–100	$101–200	$201–300	$301–500	over $500
Your minimum monthly payment is:	balance amount	$10	$20	$30	$50	1/10 balance amount rounded to next highest $5 increment

June		July		August	
CHARGES, PAYMENTS, AND CREDITS		**CHARGES, PAYMENTS, AND CREDITS**		**CHARGES, PAYMENTS, AND CREDITS**	
6/09 Olsen's Shoes	$143.52	7/10 Taylor's Bookstore	$55.26	8/12 Big Canyon Souvenirs	$36.72
6/17 Children's Mart	95.46	7/15 Payment	−321.66	8/12 Notel Motel	276.57
6/22 Red Flame Cafe	82.68	7/25 Central Appliances	473.00	8/14 E-Z Car Rental	179.46
				8/17 Payment	−450.00

1. Free ride

Let's say your credit-card bill shows the purchases above over three months. A card that charges you nothing for any month in which you pay the full balance will have wording like this on each bill:

"If your previous balance is paid in full on or before the payment due date shown on the preceding billing statement, then the new purchases are added to the average daily balance on the first day of the billing period following the new purchases."

TOTAL FINANCE CHARGES FOR THREE MONTHS

$9.28

2. Retroactive interest

If the disclosure resembles this, you lose the previous month's free ride by not paying the next bill in full:

"If you paid the previous balance shown on the front of this statement in full by the due date, your average daily balance of credit purchases is zero. Otherwise get your last statement and go through that billing cycle one day at a time. For each day, start with a zero balance and add any credit purchases that were posted since the beginning of that cycle."

TOTAL FINANCE CHARGES FOR THREE MONTHS

$13.53

3. No free ride

You will pay a finance charge on every purchase if you use a card with language like this:

"The finance charge balance is the average daily balance owing on your account during the billing period ending on the date of this billing statement. Purchases are included in the balance owing on your account from the date the bank posts each purchase to your account up to the date payment is posted by the bank."

TOTAL FINANCE CHARGES FOR THREE MONTHS

$16.15

FIGURE 5–3
Computing Finance Charges (18 Percent) Three Ways
Source: Money, August 1986, p. 26. Used with permission.

owed each day during the billing period, divided by the number of days in the period. Next the interest rate is applied against that balance. But it can be confusing, as Figure 5–3 illustrates. Typical phraseology used in the three methods of computing finance charges (*free ride, retroactive interest,* and *no free ride*) are shown. Look for an interest-free grace period. Only about one-half the bank card companies utilize the free ride calculation. Perhaps it is no wonder that a recent survey revealed that 60 percent of the public is not aware of the wide variations in interest costs on credit cards.

Credit and Discrimination

Discrimination in lending against women, the elderly, and religious and racial minorities resulted in the passage of the Equal Credit Opportunity Act of 1975, which prohibits discrimination in granting credit. Rejecting a credit application due to poor credit history is legal, but rejecting a person on the basis of sex, race, age, or religion is not. By law, credit applications cannot probe for information that could be used in a biased manner. The Equal Credit Opportunity Act requires creditors to provide to the applicant a written statement, if requested, of the reasons for refusing credit. Should discrimination be proven in court, the lender may be liable for up to $10,000 in fines.

Lenders must use the same criteria to judge applications from single and married persons. A married man or woman applying for credit need not disclose marital status or a spouse's income unless he or she is dependent upon that income, in which case it is used as the basis for granting credit. Some states take exception to this, considering any property acquired by either the husband or wife, or *community property,* as jointly owned and equally shared.

Protection for Credit Users

The original Truth in Lending Law of 1968 required lenders to disclose the annual percentage rate and the finance charge as a dollar amount, to advertise credit information truthfully, to refrain from issuing unrequested credit cards, and to protect credit users who use their homes as security. Amendments in 1971 also provide for protection of lost or stolen credit cards.

Credit Card Liability

Unauthorized use of your credit card (including telephone credit cards) results in a maximum legal liability of $50 per card. This *credit card liability* occurs only if you receive notification of your potential liability, you accepted the card when it was first mailed to you, the company provided you with a self-addressed form with which to notify them if the card was lost, and the card was used illegally before you notified them of the loss. Although your financial liability is low, some companies specialize in selling lost credit card insurance; it is profitable for them and an unnecessary expense for you. As a gesture of good will, most companies waive the $50 fee for unauthorized use of credit cards.

Fair Credit Reporting Act

Most credit reporting is done by credit bureaus, which compile information about credit applications and forward it to the creditor. A creditor comes under the Fair Credit Reporting Act only when credit information from one firm is forwarded to another and a credit decision is based on the information. The objective of the act is to place certain restrictions on credit-reporting agencies to reduce errors.

If you are denied credit because of a poor credit report, the law requires disclosure to you of the name and address of any credit-reporting agency that supplied information about you. You can then request a summary of the contents of your file (except for medical information) at the credit-reporting agency without a fee. If you dispute an item, it must be reinvestigated. If the information was in error it must be corrected. You may also wish to tell your side of the story on a disputed item (in one hundred words or less). All such information (corrections or your side of the story) must be sent to anyone who received a credit report on you in the previous six months.

Even if you have not been denied credit, for a small fee (usually about $5 to $15) you can be told the contents of your file at a credit bureau. Negative information in your file must be removed after a period of seven years (except for data on bankruptcy, for which the time limit is ten years). If you have applied for life insurance or certain employment, your file may include comments from neighbors and friends about your morals, living habits, and the like. For these kinds of investigations, you must be informed when a report is being compiled.

Fair Credit Billing Act

This act went into effect in 1975 to help people who dispute their credit card bills. In the past, complaining about a bill often resulted in delays and in harmful information going into a consumer's credit file. Now, when a credit card company receives a billing error complaint within sixty days of when you were mailed your first bill, they have thirty days to acknowledge it and ninety days more to resolve the problem. Failure of the company to follow this schedule allows the card holder to keep any disputed amount up to $50 or to sue for a maximum of $100 in damages, plus attorney fees.

Consumers can legally withhold payment for a disputed item in certain circumstances. If you made a credit card purchase of a defective product or service for over $50 within your home state or within one hundred miles of your home (whichever is farther), you can withhold payment until the problem has been remedied. (If you used a bank card, provide the bank with a chronology and as much documentation as possible, so that the bank can contact the merchant to try to thrash things out.) During that time creditors cannot send *dunning letters* (notices that make insistent demands for repayment) to you or send negative information about your account to a credit bureau without stating additionally that "some items are in dispute."

This law states that bills must be mailed to card holders at least fourteen days before payments are due. Companies must also send a reminder of consumer credit rights to all customers twice a year. Another provision requires that retailers who voluntarily give price discounts of up to 5 percent to cash customers must publicly state that information. In this way, card holders might elect to pay cash and thus avoid the extra costs the merchant imposes on credit accounts.

Holder-in-Due-Course Doctrine

The *holder-in-due-course doctrine* held that if a merchant sold a product on credit to a consumer and then sold the credit contract to a sales finance company (the holder), a legally binding contract existed between the consumer and the finance company. Should the merchant go out of business or simply refuse to repair a defective product, the consumer still had to pay off fully the amount owed to the holder. The only other recourse was to find the merchant and sue, but payments to the finance company had to continue.

The Federal Trade Commission, in a 1976 ruling with the force and effect of law, has almost eliminated this practice. Now regulations permit withholding of payments to such third parties for defective products or services. This is true for credit card and noncredit card purchases. Both the seller and the holder are legally responsible should the consumer sue for replacement of the product or for payments already made. For a defective product, however, it may well be the manufacturer that is finally legally liable.

This protection does not apply when the borrower independently makes the lending arrangements directly with a creditor. In the great majority of cases, the ruling does not apply, as only the seller and the lender cooperate in arranging the financing.

Fair Debt Collection Practices Act

This 1977 legislation was aimed at improving the ethical practices of third-party collection agencies. Banks, dentists, lawyers, and others who do their own dunning are exempt. Collection agencies attempt to make collections that could not be obtained through the usual procedures. By law, collection agencies cannot telephone at unusual hours, make numerous repeated telephone calls during the day, use deceptive practices (such as claiming they are attorneys, unless they are), make threats, or use abusive language. They also cannot spread rumors that you are a "deadbeat." Even with these limitations, realize that collection agencies can be irritatingly persistent in collecting past-due accounts. If they are not successful they take the consumer to court as the last resort.

Deciding How Much Open-ended Credit to Use

We cannot really tell you how much open-ended credit you should or even could use. It partially depends on whether you use other types of credit, such as cash or installment loans. It also depends on how you view the purposes of open-ended credit. From a personal finance perspective, the purposes of open-ended credit seem to be twofold: (1) for convenience and (2) for emergencies. Keeping these two purposes in mind can help you avoid both overspending and the habit of saying "charge it." Then you can pay the open-end credit bills in full when they arrive.

It is often safer and easier to use credit to pay for items traditionally purchased with cash. But if you do not record the amount charged in your budget, your credit records can quickly become unmanageable. Similarly, carrying a pocketful of credit cards encourages you to use them.

The purchases made most frequently with credit cards, according to a study by General Mills, are clothing for adults, gasoline, major appliances, children's clothing, Christmas presents, and other gifts.

With the exception of major appliances, these items could probably be purchased with cash; hence such use of open-ended credit is not warranted. One rule can help govern your use of open-ended credit; if you need more than eighteen months to repay, get an installment loan because you will generally pay a lower interest rate. Installment loans are the subject of the next chapter.

Summary

1. People borrow for financial emergencies, to have things immediately, and to try to offset inflation.

2. Perhaps the greatest disadvantage of credit use is the loss of financial flexibility in personal money management.

3. Much of the growth in consumer credit over the years has been for luxury items, such as automobiles, installment loans for household goods, and credit card purchases.

4. Families headed by younger persons use more consumer credit than those headed by older persons.

5. The annual percentage rate (APR) is a close approximation of the true cost of credit.

6. Open-ended credit, such as that allowed by credit cards, permits the consumer to choose to repay the debt in a single payment or to make a series of payments of varying amounts.

7. The fairest method of calculating interest for both consumers and credit card companies is the average daily balance method.

8. There are several types of charge accounts, including thirty-day, budget, option or revolving, bank credit cards, and the national travel and entertainment cards.

9. Capital is one of the five C's of credit and is a measure of your financial net worth; this is one factor used in evaluating a credit application.

10. In the process of opening a credit account, the lender generally conducts an investigation into your credit history and assigns a credit rating accordingly.

11. Factors useful in establishing credit include opening checking and savings accounts as well as requesting a limited credit account from a local retailer.

12. The federal Equal Credit Opportunity Act requires creditors to provide a written statement of the reasons for any denial of credit or a statement that you have the right to request the reasons.

13. Major federal credit protection laws require that finance charges be disclosed, limit liability on lost credit cards, force credit reporting agencies to correct errors, and provide guidelines on

billing disputes for regular credit transactions as well as sales through third party lenders.

14. How much open-ended credit you should use depends on how you view the purposes of that type of credit.

Modern Money Management

The Johnsons' Credit and Cash Flow

Harry and Belinda have a substantial annual joint income, over $46,000. Yet they also have some cash flow deficits planned for the first some months of the year (see Tables 3–6 and 3–7).

To resolve that difficulty, they opened two VISA accounts and one MasterCard account and then obtained cash advances at interest rates above 19 percent. When they are supposed to pay on one account they just get the needed money from another bank credit card. They now owe over $1,200 and it will be some months until Harry's trust income arrives in September.

1. What do you think of the Johnsons opening more than one bank credit card account?

2. Comment on the costs involved in continually getting cash advances from one bank card to pay amounts due on the others.

3. Describe briefly two alternatives for the Johnsons to resolve their cash flow problem.

Key Words and Concepts

Review Questions

1. Describe the relationship between a lender and borrower that is vital for successful credit use.
2. Give several reasons to justify using consumer credit.
3. Identify the greatest disadvantage of using consumer credit and explain how it is a disadvantage.
4. What two items of credit-cost information must lenders report according to the Consumer Credit Protection Act (Truth in Lending Law)?
5. Distinguish between installment credit and open-ended credit.
6. Give one advantage of using a credit card account as compared to other types of credit accounts.
7. Distinguish among the following types of credit accounts: thirty-day account, budget account, option account, bank credit card account, revolving account, and travel and entertainment account.
8. Explain why travel and entertainment credit cards are sometimes called "prestige cards."
9. What types of information are requested on a credit application?
10. Explain what is involved in a credit investigation.
11. Of what value is a person's credit rating? Describe briefly how it is established.
12. Describe a type of credit-rating system that creditors use to reduce subjectivity in credit decisions.
13. Identify the five C's of credit and give an example of each.
14. Name and describe briefly five courses of action you can take to prove you can manage credit effectively.
15. What advantages accrue to the credit user from the grace period?
16. Explain how usury laws are associated with the use of credit.
17. Describe the differences among free-ride, retroactive interest, and no-free-ride methods of assessing credit charges.
18. Describe the purpose of the Equal Credit Opportunity Act of 1975.
19. Identify the conditions that must exist before a credit card holder can be liable for $50 for charges on a lost credit card.
20. Describe the purpose of the Fair Credit Reporting Act and its value to a credit user.
21. What disputes are typically covered through the Fair Credit Billing Act?
22. Describe the holder-in-due-course doctrine.

23. Describe some of the unethical practices of debt collectors that initiated the passage of the Fair Debt Collection Practices Act.

24. How much open-end credit should people use?

Case Problems

1. The use of credit has expanded greatly over the last several decades. This has been particularly true for consumer debt. Some people still advocate the old Ben Franklin adage, "Neither a lender nor borrower be." Examine this saying for a moment. Taken literally, and in view of the use and growth of credit, this adage seems somewhat outmoded today.
   a. What impact would the above adage have on our modern economy?
   b. If you were unable to use credit of any kind, what sorts of changes would you have to make in your money management goals? Explain.
   c. Justify the use of credit as a positive financial tool for consumers and for businesses.

2. Getting credit approval and using credit are goals of most people at some point. Unfortunately, credit approval (especially for large installment loans) may be difficult for young people in college or just out of college.

   Lenders have used many factors to judge credit potential, ranging from "how he or she looks" to credit scoring with a point system (see the box on page 150). Regardless of the method used, the five *C*'s of credit will continue to be factors considered carefully in any credit approval. Interpretation of these factors is still the issue.
   a. Assuming you are applying for credit, what would be a good way of assessing your application? Explain.
   b. What improvement, if any, is found in the point system of credit rating? Explain.
   c. Do you think lenders should hesitate to grant credit to college-age people? Explain.

3. Soon after his graduation, Geoff Dalrymple of Thibodaux, Louisiana, began work in the credit office of a regional chain of department stores. One of his assignments was to write a position paper for management to read, giving reasons why the company should change from computing finance charges using the free-ride method currently used to either the retroactive interest or the no-free-ride approach.
   a. Make a list of arguments Geoff can use in his position paper.
   b. Also make a list of arguments, which will not be used in the paper, *against* changing the methods of computing interest.

Suggested Readings

"Borrowing: Credit Card Junkies Overdose as Rates Stay High." *Money,* January 1987, p. 40. Monthly chart and comments on costs of credit cards.

"Credit Cards: Getting the Best Deal." *Better Homes and Gardens,* April 1987, pp. 24–28. Cost-cutting tips and how to shop for the best deal.

"Fixing Your Credit File." *U.S. News and World Report,* June 27, 1987, p. 49. Details on correcting errors in your credit file.

"It's Time to Rethink Debt." *Money,* April 1987, pp. 90–91. The mathematical wisdom of paying down credit card balances.

"Take a Card—But Not Just Any Card." *U.S. News and World Report,* March 23, 1987, pp. 64–65. Choosing among the premium credit cards.

"Up with Credit Cards: Despite the Critics, They've Never Been More Useful." *Barrons,* January 19, 1987, p. 9. Editorial on the benefits of credit cards.

CHAPTER 6

Borrowing

OBJECTIVES

After reading this chapter, the student should be able to

1. explain the roles of inflation and taxes in the decision to borrow or wait and pay cash.
2. discuss the planned use of credit, such as deciding when to borrow and establishing debt limits.
3. distinguish among the different types of consumer loans.
4. describe several sources of consumer loans.
5. calculate APR financing costs on both single-payment and installment loans.
6. describe the necessary components of a credit agreement.
7. identify seven signals of overextension of credit.
8. list places to obtain credit counseling and distinguish between the two types of bankruptcy.

A s mentioned in the last chapter, more people use installment debt than open-ended credit. This chapter examines the hows and whys of installment debt, more commonly called consumer loans. First we discuss the issue of saving versus borrowing. Next we discuss planning credit usage, then we examine consumer loans and where to get them. Then we explain how finance charges on consumer loans are computed and describe the features of a credit agreement. The chapter ends with the topics of credit overextension and bankruptcy.

To Borrow or to Wait and Pay Cash?

You may like the warm feeling of walking into a store and paying saved cash for a large purchase. Your conscience may tell you never to use consumer credit since you want to avoid getting into debt. There are times, however, when it may be wiser to use credit. Let's calculate the comparative costs of buying on credit versus saving the money to later pay cash.

Suppose a loan of $2,000 must be repaid in twelve monthly installments of $182 each, including interest. The dollar cost of credit would be $184 (12 months × $182 = $2,184; $2,184 − $2,000 = $184). Your alternative is to save $162 for twelve months at 6 percent interest. At the end of the year, you would withdraw the $1,944 deposited, plus $56 in interest, a total of $2,000, to make a purchase. At first glance it seems that the better course of action is to save. But is it? Only if you ignore two important factors—inflation and taxes—in your decision. It is fair to say that buying on credit may be wise when inflation is high or when the interest charged on loans is not much higher than the interest paid on savings.

In the example above, let's assume inflation is at 10 percent. The product will then cost $200 more at the end of the year, or $2,200, than it did at the beginning. This means that instead of saving $162 each month at 6 percent interest, you must save $178. After twelve months, $2,136 (12 months × $178) saved, plus $64 in interest, will total $2,200.

You must also consider taxes. Interest income earned on savings deposits is taxable on your federal tax return. Assuming that most people pay a marginal tax rate of 28 percent on income (discussed further in Chapter 7), the tax on the $64 interest income will be $18. That is $18 you no longer have available to spend on the product. Part A of Table 6–1 shows that the final dollar cost for the product, at inflation of 10 percent and taxes of 28 percent, is $2,218.

Part B of Table 6–1 reveals that the dollar cost of credit for a 15.5 percent loan is $184. Therefore, the cost to make a $2,000 purchase immediately on credit is $2,184. Thus, it is $34 less ($2,218 − 2,184) to buy on credit now than it would be if you waited and bought later, after

TABLE 6–1
Prices Rising Quickly or Slowly: Save or Borrow to Buy?
(assuming 6 percent interest on savings)

Prices rising quickly

A. Cost to save cash and purchase product next year (10% inflation):
   $2,200   purchase price assuming 10% inflation
   +   18   plus tax on interest earned (28% of $64 earned on savings of $178 per month)
   $2,218   final dollar cost

B. Cost to buy on credit now (15.5% loan):
   $2,000   amount borrowed to make purchase (monthly payment of $182)
   + 184   plus dollar cost of credit at 15.5%
   $2,184   final dollar cost

Prices rising slowly

C. Cost to save cash and purchase product next year (2% inflation):
   $2,040   purchase price assuming 2% inflation
   +   18   plus tax on interest earned (28% of $64 earned on savings of $178 per month)
   $2,058   final dollar cost

D. Cost to buy on credit now (12% loan):
   $2,000   amount borrowed to make purchase (monthly payment of $178)
   + 136   plus dollar cost of credit at 12%
   $2,136   final dollar cost

prices rose. Does this mean you should seriously consider buying most items on credit? No, but it should certainly demonstrate that buying on credit may be wise when inflation is high, the cost of credit is not prohibitive, and interest rates on savings are low.

What happens when inflation is low and the price of the product does not rise much? Part C of Table 6–1 shows the result of saving to make a purchase, assuming the price of the product rises only 2 percent. The final dollar cost of $2,058 is due to a $40 increase in the product price and $18 in taxes owed on the $64 interest earned. Part D shows that the cost of using credit is $2,136. That is $78 less for saving to make the purchase instead of using credit. Thus, when the price of the product does not rise much, the final dollar cost is lower if you pay cash rather than buy on credit (even at the lower interest rate of 12 percent).

Planning Credit Use

Using credit requires deliberate action and thinking. After you leave school, you may find that due to your new full-time employment and increased income some credit card companies will actually seek you out. To use credit intelligently, you should learn when it is best to borrow and how to establish your own debt limits. Setting debt limits for dual-earner households is a special problem.

Deciding When to Borrow

People use credit for four primary reasons: convenience, emergencies, planned expenditures for major purchases, and investments. It is convenient to use credit cards to purchase gasoline, to take advantage of a sales price on clothing, or to enjoy an expensive meal. It is important to pay these credit bills in full when they are due, since the proper uses of debt are (1) to finance a tangible asset (automobile, home, or education) and (2) to finance an investment (stock or real estate, such as an apartment building). Further, making payments on credit purchases of consumable items, such as food, entertainment, clothing, and gasoline, takes money in the form of cash flow and money for interest payments away from savings and investment purposes. It will be difficult to get ahead financially and achieve your goals if you commit dollars to monthly payments for convenience items.

Borrowing for an emergency is warranted, as it cannot be planned for in the budgeting process. If you have only $500 in savings and emergency auto repairs cost $1,600, your choice is twofold: either don't drive the vehicle or borrow funds to pay for the repairs. The money may be hard to find if your VISA card credit limit is $1,200 and you still owe them $950 for convenience purchases. Again, your financial management objective should be to pay off such debts as quickly and conveniently as possible. This will free funds for savings and investments.

Planned borrowing most typically includes purchases such as homes, automobiles, computers, electric typewriters, furniture, televisions, and other major appliances. For many people these items are too expensive to purchase without using credit. The financial management task is to determine when and how often to use credit for these purchases and how much credit to use. Your decisions will be based on your needs and wants as well as how effectively you can handle debt.

How to Set Debt Limits

A debt limit may be set for you if you go to a bank and try to borrow $35,000 to purchase a fancy sports car. The lender might be willing to loan you only $12,000 after carefully examining your assets, liabilities, level of income, job stability, and other factors. Those who succeed financially establish their own debt limits. There are three ways to establish debt limits: the disposable income, ratio of debts to equity and continuous debt methods.

Disposable Income Method   If you wish to use credit on a recurring basis, you will make monthly debt payments. When estimating a realistic debt level, do not include convenience debts that you will pay in full when the bill arrives. Also do not include first mortgage loans on homes; this becomes a factor when making an estimate of the mortgage you would qualify for (see Chapter 9, "The Housing Expenditure"). You must decide how much of your disposable personal income can be spent for regular debt payments. Your *disposable personal income* is the amount of your take-home pay left after all deductions are withheld for taxes, insurance, union dues, and the like.

Table 6–2 shows some monthly debt payment limits expressed as a percentage of disposable personal income. As illustrated, having a current debt of 16 to 20 percent of disposable personal income means that a borrower is fully extended and that taking on additional debt probably would not be wise. (As mentioned, current debt excludes the first mortgage loan on a home.)

Table 6–3 demonstrates the impact of increasing debts on a budget. After deductions, disposable monthly personal income is $1,800. Current budgeted expenses (totaling the full $1,800) are allocated in a sample distribution throughout the various categories.

You can see how assuming debt payments of $180 or $270 per month (to buy on credit a new automobile, television set, or stereo system, for example) affects this budget. The financial manager must make decisions about where to make cutbacks so that monthly credit payments can be met. Notice as the debt increases by each 5 percent how much more difficult it is to "find the money" and make the cutbacks. This person reduced expenditures on savings and investments immediately, then finally eliminated all allocations in the category. Food was cut back, but only so much. Utilities, auto insurance, and rent are fixed; it is hard to reduce these amounts without moving or getting a cheaper car. Entertainment was steadily reduced and charitable contributions were eliminated. Further reductions in other areas would seriously affect the person's quality of life.

Are you curious as to where you would have made the reductions? Perhaps spending a few minutes right now changing the figures in Table 6–3 will give you a feel both for your priorities and for how large a debt limit you might establish.

TABLE 6–2
Debt Limits as a Percentage of Disposable Personal Income

Percent	For Current Debt[a]	Take on Additional Debt?
10 or less	Safe limit; borrower feels little debt pressure.	Could be undertaken cautiously.
11 to 15	Possibly safe limit; borrower feels some pressure.	Should not be undertaken.
16 to 20	Fully extended; borrower hopes that no emergency arises.	Only the fearless and/or foolhardy ask for more.
21 to 25	Overextended; borrower worries about debts.	No, borrower should see a credit counselor.
26 or more	Disastrous; borrower may feel desperate.	Impossible; borrower will probably declare bankruptcy.

[a] Excluding home mortgage loans.

TABLE 6–3
Impact of Increasing Debts on the Budget[a]
(One person's decisions on where to cut back expenses to make
increasing monthly debt payments)

Gross income $26,000
Deductions for taxes,
  retirement, insurance 4,400
Disposable personal income $21,600
Monthly $ 1,800

	No Debt	10% Debt	15% Debt	20% Debt	25% Debt
Rent	$ 400	$ 400	$ 400	$ 400	$ 400
Savings and investments	200	100	100	60	–0–
Food	180	160	160	150	150
Utilities (telephone, electricity, heat)	150	150	150	150	150
Insurance (auto and life)	90	90	90	90	90
Transportation expenses	210	210	180	180	180
Charitable contributions	50	30	20	–0–	–0–
Entertainment	200	180	160	150	150
Clothing	50	40	30	30	–0–
Vacations and long weekends	25	25	20	15	15
Medical and dental expenses	20	20	20	20	20
Newspapers and magazines	10	10	10	10	10
Vices	40	40	35	35	35
Cable TV	15	15	15	15	15
Personal care	25	25	25	25	25
Gifts and holidays	25	25	25	20	20
Health club	40	40	40	40	40
Miscellaneous	70	60	50	50	50
Debt repayments	–0–	180	270	360	450
Total	$1,800	$1,800	$1,800	$1,800	$1,800

[a] Amounts in color are the changes—cutbacks—made in order to make the increasingly larger debt payments.

Ratio of Debts to Equity Method A second method of determining whether you have too much debt is to calculate the ratio of your debts (not including a first mortgage) to your equity, or net worth (excluding the value of a first home). Most people have more in assets than in liabilities, resulting in a positive net worth. For example, a person with $42,000 in assets who owes $14,000 has a debt-to-equity ratio of $1:2$ ($42,000 − $14,000 = $28,000 ÷ $14,000). This method gives a quick idea of your financial solvency. If debts equal or exceed equity ($1:1$ or $1.1:1$), you are probably at your maximum debt limit. Exceptions would be recent graduates, who often accumulate large educational loans. They would have a poor ratio of debt to equity, but their substantial earning power offsets the ratio. However, if five years later the situation has not changed, then a problem likely exists.

Continuous Debt Method A third method to use in determining when debts are too large is the continuous debt method. If you are unable to get completely out of debt every three years (except for mortgage and education loans) you probably lean too heavily on debt. You could be developing a credit lifestyle, in which you are never out of debt and continuously pay out income for finance charges.

Debt Limits for Dual-earner Households

It can be wonderful to double your income by joining incomes with another. Two people earning $26,000 a year each will gross $52,000! The net disposable personal income from this total may be around $39,000, or $3,250 monthly. Such an amount means a couple can afford a much higher level of living than before combining incomes.

After joining incomes, a couple must decide how much debt to establish, remembering to include any unpaid student loans in their calculations. The guidelines given in Table 6–3 are realistic, but this is a crucial decision for a dual-earner household. It is likely that never again will a couple have the opportunity to seriously expand an investment program than shortly after beginning couplehood. Taking on many new debt payments will surely constrain investment opportunities. Although some new debts are probably desirable and unavoidable, couples would be wise to pay early attention to making investments that will assure future income and financial security.

Types of Consumer Loans

Consumer loans are usually classified as installment or noninstallment credit. As discussed in the previous chapter, with installment credit the amount owed is repaid in equal payments, usually monthly. Examples include an automobile loan that is to be repaid in forty-eight equal monthly payments, and installment credit for home appliances, furniture, mobile homes, home improvements, travel, education, and medical expenses. Table 6–4 illustrates various monthly installment payments to repay loans at different interest rates. Most installment loans involve a *loan book*. This is a coupon booklet with perforated, tear-out pages that are to be remitted to the lender along with each payment. Each coupon gives details of each payment, such as the date and amount due. The loan book often has a stub, much like a checkbook stub, for the borrower to record details of payment.

Noninstallment credit is debt that is repaid in a single payment or repaid as open-ended credit. Examples of single-payment loans include those made to individuals (perhaps in anticipation of a federal income tax refund), charge accounts that require payment within thirty days of billing, and *service credit* extended by professionals (doctors, lawyers, and dentists) and service providers (utilities, hospitals, and laundries), who expect full payment soon after providing the service. Examples of open-ended credit include credit through a charge account or credit card in which the purchaser has the option to pay the bill in full or make a partial payment.

TABLE 6-4
Monthly Installment Payment (Principal and Interest) Required to Repay $1,000[a]

Terms of Installments	Annual Percentage Rate								
	4%	6%	8%	10%	12%	14%	16%	18%	20%
1 year (12 months)	85.14	86.04	86.94	87.85	88.75	89.65	90.56	91.46	92.36
2 years (24 months)	43.40	44.27	45.14	46.01	46.88	47.74	48.61	49.48	50.35
3 years (36 months)	29.49	30.35	31.20	32.06	32.92	33.77	34.63	35.49	36.34
4 years (48 months)	22.53	23.39	24.24	25.09	25.94	26.79	27.64	28.49	29.34
5 years (60 months)	18.36	19.21	20.06	20.90	21.75	22.60	23.44	24.29	25.14

[a] To illustrate, assume you want to know how much the monthly payments would be to finance an automobile loan of $9,000 at 10% for three years. To repay $1,000 the figure is $32.06; therefore multiply by 9 (for $9,000) to determine that $288.54 is required for 36 months of payments.

Loans are made on the assumption that they will be repaid. To help assure repayment, *creditors* (persons or institutions to whom money is due) frequently prefer to offer secured loans. A *secured loan* requires *collateral,* which is a certain asset that the borrower pledges to back up the debt, or a *cosigner,* another person who will agree to pay the loan should the borrower fail to do so. Cosigners have the same legal obligations for repayment as the original borrower. Hence, being a cosigner is a major responsibility. A loan secured with collateral means that the lender has a *security interest* in that collateral. Thus, the creditor can go to court to obtain possession of the property in the event the borrower defaults. Generally, the asset is sold by the lender and the proceeds received (minus expenses) are applied to the debt owed. Then the borrower is sued for any remaining balance due. By having a secure interest in the property, the lender can be fairly confident that most, if not all, of the loan eventually will be repaid. Lenders who make installment loans prefer to offer credit to those who have collateral; a new automobile, for example, could be the collateral for a three-year auto loan. Those who are late in making their loan repayment are often assessed a late payment charge, usually 5 percent of the amount due.

An *unsecured loan* has neither the assurance of collateral nor a cosigner. It is a loan given on the good character of the borrower, who is sometimes well known by the lender. Since there is a slightly greater risk with unsecured loans compared to secured debts, the interest rate charged is usually higher. Most single-payment loans are unsecured debts.

Besides credit card debts, consumers typically obtain credit in the form of cash loans and purchase loans. A *cash loan* means that a person borrows cash and then uses it to make purchases or to pay off other debts. For example, during the Christmas season some people borrow cash to buy gifts. A *purchase loan* (sometimes called *sales credit*) means that a consumer makes a purchase on credit with no cash transferring from the lender to the borrower. Cash flows from the lender to the seller (or the seller may be the lender). For example, buyers may obtain purchase loans from General Motors Acceptance Corporation (GMAC) to buy a new Chevrolet or from Sears Credit to purchase a new Sears television set.

A *second mortgage* is another loan on a residence in addition to the original mortgage, and in case of default what is owed on the original mortgage is paid first. With that additional risk, the interest rate on a second mortgage is often 2 to 5 percent higher than an original mortgage rate. Second mortgages are used primarily to help consumers purchase homes. Suppose Robert and Louise Bond of Van Nuys, California, wish to sell their $150,000 home to the Roget family. The Rogets want to assume the Bonds' remaining mortgage of $70,000, but they have only $50,000 available, which they obtained by selling their old home. A lender that thinks the Rogets can afford to make two mortgage payments will give them a second mortgage loan of $30,000 to make up the difference. Second mortgages often run from three to ten years in length, so the new homeowner can look forward eventually to having only one mortgage payment.

Sources of Consumer Loans

Table 6–5 summarizes the features of the four major sources of typical consumer loans: banks/S & Ls, credit unions, consumer finance companies, and sales finance companies. These are also discussed below, along with several other sources of consumer loans, including friends and relatives, life insurance companies, industrial banks, loans by mail, home-equity credit line loans, education loans, and pawnbrokers.

Banks/S & Ls

The term *bank* technically refers to commercial banks and mutual savings banks (described in Chapter 4) as they accept demand deposits *and* make commercial loans. However, from the consumer-borrower perspective deregulation has made savings and loan associations (S & Ls) very similar to commercial banks and mutual savings banks. Thus, all will be described as one source of consumer loans.

Banks are full-service institutions offering a variety of loans—secured, unsecured, installment, and noninstallment—to consumers and businesses. Many banks allow customers to use their passbook savings accounts for collateral and charge a lower interest rate, since this almost guarantees repayment.

TABLE 6–5
Major Sources of Consumer Loans

	Credit Source			
	Banks/S & Ls	Credit Unions	Consumer Finance Companies	Sales Finance Companies
Types of loans	Single-payment loans Installment loans Passbook loans Credit card loans Second mortgages Home-equity credit line loans Automatic overdrafts	Installment loans Credit card loans Automatic overdrafts	Installment loans Second mortgages	Installment loans
Lending policies	Loans to average and better credit risk people Often requires collateral Makes unsecured loans Rates vary according to type of loan and security Lower rates to their own customers	Lend to members only Average credit risk people approved Requires repayment by payroll deductions Makes secured and unsecured loans Provide free credit life and disability insurance for the amount of the loan Often have lowest interest rates available	Most credit risks acceptable Collateral often required Rates are high and vary according to risk, type of loan and security	Loans to average and better credit risk people Loans for collateral purchases only Loans tied in to seller (Sears, GMAC, etc.) who approves application Rates are usually competitive with banks/ S & Ls; special promotion rates are lower

Banks associated with a bank card company (such as VISA or MasterCard) can offer very small loans ($100 to $300) on the credit card, whereas most banks lose money on recordkeeping for loans of less than $500. Debit card loans are similarly available in small amounts from banks participating in a debit system. Both credit card and debit card loans are considered *cash advances*. Borrowers can obtain cash advances in small amounts ($10 to $200) simply by inserting a credit or debit card into an automated teller machine (ATM). These loans are based on the borrower's *line of credit*, which is the maximum approved amount that a person can borrow without completing a new credit application.

Many banks offer a similar line of credit along with an automatic overdraft loan (also discussed in Chapter 4). This system permits customers to write checks in amounts larger than the funds in their accounts. Instead of marking the check "insufficient funds" and returning it, the bank automatically makes a loan to the customer's account to cover the overdraft. Such loans are made either in the exact amount of the overdraft or in increments of perhaps $100. Thus, if you write a check for $75 when you have only $65 in your account, you may be charged interest on a loan of $100 when you really needed only $10. This particular form of loan may have a substantially higher annual percentage rate than other bank loans.

Banks tend to make loans to their own customers and to others who are good financial risks. However, research indicates that many people who go elsewhere for loans actually do meet the qualifications for bank lending. For most loans, banks are quite competitive in their rates; this is partially because funds loaned are obtained primarily from depositors. Commonly, the APR is 10 to 18 percent, which is quite competitive.

Credit Unions

Credit unions are cooperative thrift and loan associations that serve members only. People who wish to borrow or save at a credit union, and who qualify for membership, can easily join by purchasing a *credit union share,* making an investment of as little as $5 or $10, which earns interest like any other savings account. More than 50 million Americans are members of credit unions.

All loans are scheduled to be repaid in installments, and payments are typically withheld from the borrower's paycheck through an arrangement with the employer. This convenience for employees also lowers collection costs for credit unions. They prefer to make loans to good risks and will require collateral or a cosigner for large or higher-risk loans. Since some members of credit unions donate their time to the organization (the elected officers) and office space is inexpensive (sometimes subsidized by a company), costs are kept down. Also, because the funds lent almost always come from deposits made by members, credit unions do not have to borrow money at high rates to then lend to applicants.

Commonly, the APR is 9 to 18 percent, which is quite competitive. Credit unions usually offer free *credit life insurance* (where the loan is paid in full should the borrower die) on all loans. You can obtain information on credit unions in your community by writing the Credit Union National Association, P.O. Box 431, Madison, Wisconsin 53701.

Consumer Finance Companies

These lending institutions specialize in small loans and are therefore also known as small-loan companies. They range from the well-recognized Household Finance Corporation and Beneficial Finance Corporation to a local neighborhood lender. They make secured and unsecured loans on an installment basis. Each state has small-loan laws that regulate consumer finance companies. There are limits on the maximum amount that can be lent (commonly $2,000 to $5,000) and on the maximum interest rate that can be charged (perhaps 48 percent on loans of less than $500, 36 percent on amounts from $500 to $2,000, and 24 percent on amounts above $2,000).

Rates are higher because consumer finance companies make higher-risk loans, which require considerably more expense to collect. Higher rates also result because these companies accept no deposits; they borrow from commercial banks to obtain funds to lend to customers. Also, small loans are generally more expensive in terms of recordkeeping. Approximately one-fifth of the loans granted by consumer finance companies are for the purpose of debt consolidation. Other common purposes of such loans are for travel, vacation, education, automobiles, and home furnishings.

Sales Finance Companies

Sales finance companies are business-related lenders (such as General Motors Acceptance Corporation, Ford Motor Credit, and J. C. Penney Credit Corporation) who are primarily engaged in financing the sales of their parent companies. They specialize in making purchase loans, with the item being purchased as collateral. The seller of the item has the customer fill out a credit application. Then, because the seller often works in association with the sales finance company, credit can be approved almost immediately.

Since sales finance companies always require collateral and deal only with customers that are medium-to-good risks, their interest rates are competitive. Sales finance companies' rates are usually 1 or 2 percentage points higher than a bank's or credit union's. However, they may be a few percentage points lower if the seller subsidizes the rate to encourage sales (this occurs most often with car manufacturers).

Friends and Relatives

Friends and relatives were a more common source of loans in the past than they are today. Usually, people borrow from friends and relatives after traditional sources have refused them credit, perhaps because the borrower's investment scheme is too risky for conventional lenders or because the borrower has a poor credit history.

Two things are important when borrowing from friends and relatives. First, make out a promissory note, as it is more businesslike. In case of default, the lender will need such a document to take a tax loss. Second, establish a specific repayment schedule. Failure to follow these suggestions typifies situations in which the borrower decides that the loan was actually a gift and ill feelings develop in the lender. One special advantage of these loans is the generally low or nonexistent interest rate.

Life Insurance Companies

Policyholders can obtain loans from their life insurance companies if their policies have an accumulated cash value. *Term* policies have no cash value, and the policies that do have cash value take many years to build up to an amount sufficient to borrow. (This is discussed in detail in Chapter 13.) A significant advantage to borrowing on a life insurance policy is that the interest rate ranges from 5 to 8 percent, which is extremely low. The difficulty comes in paying back the loan, as there is no fixed schedule of repayment and no dunning letters reminding the borrower to pay off the debt. Of course, there is no risk for the lender because the policy is 100 percent security. If the insured dies before repaying the loan, the insurance company pays the beneficiaries the value of the policy minus the debt and any outstanding interest.

Industrial Banks

The term *industrial* comes from the early twentieth-century emphasis of these banks on making small loans to industrial workers. Although they have been largely replaced today by consumer finance companies, these usually small thrift and loan institutions are legally authorized in twenty-three states. They make small installment loans, and the interest rates charged are governed by state small-loan laws and are similar to rates charged by consumer finance companies. Industrial banks make loans to higher-risk customers and frequently require a cosigner.

Loans by Mail

Small-loan companies, such as industrial banks and consumer finance companies, sometimes specialize in making loans by mail. They advertise in magazines to attract borrowers, who complete a credit application and receive an approval by mail.

Higher-risk people are more apt to want to borrow by mail, especially those who have been turned down by other sources. Accordingly, the interest rate charged is higher than for a typical consumer finance company (perhaps 6 to 10 percent more). The rates charged are based on the usury or small loan laws of the state in which the lender is incorporated. Collateral and cosigners are often required to help ensure repayment, as there is the added expense and risk of having to collect a debt from out of state.

Home-equity Credit Line Loans

Banks, savings and loan associations, credit unions, bank credit card companies, financial supermarkets, and other lenders now make *home-equity credit line loans* to home owners. These are a form of second mortgage whereby the lender offers a line of credit up to a maximum loan value of perhaps 75 percent of the home's appraised value minus what might be owed on the first mortgage. Once such a line of credit has been established, for a fee of $50 to $1,500 or more, it can be tapped for years, perhaps by check, debit, or credit card. Interest rates are variable but tend to be lower than for other types of consumer credit. Failure to repay a home-equity loan may result in the forced sale of the home. Second mortgage loans are discussed in Chapter 9, "The Housing Expenditure."

Education Loans

Education loans are available directly from the federal government and from private sources, such as banks, savings and loan associations, and credit unions. Before applying for such loans, a student should check into obtaining an educational grant which does not have to be repaid. There are two main grant programs. Pell Grants, also known as Basic Educational Opportunity Grants (BEOG), are the largest government educational grant program. Pell Grant money is granted on the basis of financial need with maximum amounts varying from college to college but often up to $3,000 per year. Supplemental Educational Opportunity Grants (SEOG) are available to students attending higher-cost schools. Again the amounts vary but can be as high as $2,000 to $3,000 per year.

There are three federal loan programs for students. Both the National Direct Student Loan (now called Perkins loan) and the Guaranteed Student Loan (GSL) programs are for needy students while the Parent Loan for Undergraduate Students (PLUS) has no restrictions. These loans have relatively low interest rates and repayment usually begins after graduation. Education loans are also available from almost all state governments and these are often not based on need. Loan limits are usually $10,000 or more a year rather than the more restrictive federal loans. Many colleges also have special loan programs and a limited number of financial institutions offer reduced-interest education loans. You can get more information about these loan programs from college financial aid officers and state officers of higher education. Those who fail to repay their federal loans face the likelihood that the government will keep their income tax refunds.

Pawnbrokers

States regulate the lending policies of *pawnbrokers*—specialized businesses offering single-payment loans (typically for six months or less) to individuals based on the personal property of the borrower. Should the borrower fail to redeem the property by turning in the pawn ticket (no promissory notes are used) along with the amount due, plus interest, the pawnbroker can legally sell the item.

The interest rate charged can go as high as 120 percent, depending on state laws and the item being pawned. Clearly, a pawnbroker is a lender of last resort for borrowers. On the plus side, loans are made as soon as personal property is turned over to the pawnbroker.

As you have seen, the costs of credit vary among the different credit sources, and lenders offer credit for different purposes. Table 6–6 illustrates how much a two-year $2,000 unsecured loan would cost from various lenders.

Computation of Finance Charges

The federal Truth in Lending Law (Consumer Credit Protection Act of 1968) requires lenders to disclose to credit applicants the effective annual percentage rate (APR) as well as the finance charge in dollars. Borrowers can then compare rates for the best deal. When a borrower inquires about the interest rate that will be charged, the lender may respond verbally with the *stated rate* of interest which is simply the rate quoted by the lender. By law this stated rate must be the same as the

TABLE 6-6
Relative Costs to Borrow $2,000 as an Unsecured Loan for Two Years and Repay in Monthly Installments

Lender	Annual Percentage Rate	Monthly Payment	Total Finance Charge
Life insurance company	8%	$ 90.28	$166.72
Credit union	12	93.76	250.24
Commercial bank	16	97.22	333.28
Mutual savings bank	16	97.22	333.28
Savings and loan association	16	97.22	333.28
Bank credit card	20	100.70	416.80
Consumer finance company	24	105.74	537.81
Industrial bank	24	105.74	537.81
Loan by mail	36	118.09	834.28

effective APR. However, in practice this may not be the case. Some lenders are ignorant of the law, and others may attempt to hide the effective interest rate. In some cases, the effective APR will not be known until all the specifics of the transaction have been decided. Borrowers must be sure that they are being quoted the effective annual percentage rate and that the APR is the rate written into the credit contract. What follows is a discussion of the way the effective annual percentage rate is calculated for various types of loans.

Single-payment Loans

There are two methods of calculating interest on single-payment loans: the simple interest method and the discount method. The APR reveals the difference in the effective cost of credit.

Simple Interest Method With the simple interest method, interest is calculated only on the outstanding loan balance. The formula for the simple interest method is

$$I = PRT \tag{6-1}$$

where
I = *interest* or finance charges
P = *principal* amount borrowed
R = *rate* of interest
T = *time* of loan in years

Suppose you took out a single-payment loan of $500 for two years at a simple interest rate of 12 percent. Your interest charges would be $120 ($500 × 12 percent × 2 years). To calculate the effective APR, divide the average outstanding loan balance ($500 as the full amount was owed the entire time) into the average *annual* finance charge ($60, since $120 is the total for two years).

$$\text{APR} = \frac{\text{average annual finance charge}}{\text{average outstanding loan balance}} \qquad (6\text{--}2)$$

$$= \frac{\$60}{\$500} = 12 \text{ percent}$$

As you can see, the APR is 12 percent. When the simple interest method is used, the simple rate of interest and the APR are always equivalent for single-payment loans.

Discount Method Banks and consumer finance companies often use the discount method. With this method, interest is determined and then *subtracted* from the amount of the loan. The difference is the actual amount lent to the borrower. Essentially, the finance charges are pre-paid by the borrower.

If we use the same figures as in the last example to illustrate, only the denominator changes in formula 6–2. The average outstanding loan balance, or principal, is $380 [$500 − ($500 × .12 × 2)], because that is all the money the borrower got from the lending institution two years ago. Thus, $380 divided into the average annual finance charge of $60 gives an APR of 15.8 percent. It should be clear that if a borrower does not have full use of the money borrowed, the effective annual interest rate must be higher. The discount method always gives a higher APR than the simple interest method for single-payment loans at the same interest rates.

Installment Loans

The simple interest method and the add-on method are used to determine the APR of installment loans. The simple interest method is widely used to calculate interest on revolving charge accounts and by credit unions. The add-on method predominates at banks and finance companies in installment loans for automobiles, furniture, and other credit requiring collateral.

Simple Interest Method Again, with the simple interest method, interest is assessed only on the outstanding balance. Sometimes the lender designs a schedule to have the balance repaid in full after a certain number of months, such as in Table 6–7. Quite frequently, however, the borrower pays more than the schedule requires or even pays the bill in full. Thus it is impossible to know the credit charges in advance unless borrowers make no variations in repayment.

It is easy to apply the simple interest method to a credit account. As shown in Table 6–7, at the end of the first month an interest rate of 1.5 percent (18 percent annually) is applied to the beginning balance of $1,000 for an interest charge of $15. The required monthly installment of $91.67 goes toward payment of the principal and the simple interest. Since the simple interest method of calculating interest on installment

TABLE 6–7
Repayment Schedule for $1,000 Principal, Plus Simple Interest (1.5% per Month)

Month	Outstanding Balance	Payment	Interest	Principal	Ending Balance
1	$1,000.00	$91.67	$15.00	$76.67	$923.33
2	923.33	91.67	13.85	77.82	845.51
3	845.51	91.67	12.68	78.99	766.52
4	766.52	91.67	11.50	80.17	686.35
5	686.35	91.67	10.30	81.37	604.98
6	604.98	91.67	9.07	82.60	522.38
7	522.38	91.67	7.84	83.83	438.55
8	438.55	91.67	6.58	85.09	353.46
9	353.46	91.67	5.30	86.37	267.09
10	267.09	91.67	4.01	87.66	179.43
11	179.43	91.67	2.69	88.98	90.45
12	90.45	90.45	1.36	90.31	–0–

loans applies the rate to the outstanding loan balance, the effective APR and the simple interest rate are the same. (This method of paying off a loan, called *amortization*, is discussed further in Chapter 10.)

Add-on Method The add-on method is a traditional and widely used technique for computing finance charges on installment loans. Once again, formula 6–1 is used to calculate the finance charge or dollar cost of credit. (The interest rate used in formula 6–1 for the add-on method is an add-on rate and, as discussed below, is not to be confused with the APR.)

For example, assume that Laurie Mohr of Tallahassee, Florida, obtained a $2,000 loan for one year at 14 percent add-on interest. Using formula 6–1, the finance charge is $280 ($2,000 × 0.14 × 1). The finance charge ($280) is *added* to the principal ($2,000) for a total of $2,280, which is divided by the number of payments (12) for a monthly payment of $190. But we know that the effective APR must be higher than the add-on rate of 14 percent because Laurie does not have full use of the principal for the twelve months. The APR can be *approximated* by assuming that the borrower has use of only one-half of the funds ($1,000 instead of $2,000 in the example above). Then the calculation results in an approximate APR of 28 percent ($280 ÷ $1,000).

Calculating the Effective Annual Percentage Rate (APR)
Lenders use computer-generated tables or complicated formulas to calculate the precise *annual percentage rate*. Two rather basic formulas for computing annual percentage rates are illustrated in Table 6–8 using the data from the example above. Note that the *N*-ratio formula is more precise than the constant-ratio formula, as the latter generally overstates the correct rate. These formulas can be used to determine the effective APR for all add-on loans that require regular payments of

TABLE 6–8
Calculating the Annual Percentage Rate (APR)[a]

Constant-Ratio Formula (Formula 6–3)	N-Ratio Formula (Formula 6–4)

$$\text{APR} = \frac{2YF}{D(P+1)}$$

$$= \frac{2(12 \times \$280)}{\$2,000(12+1)}$$

$$= \frac{\$6,720}{\$26,000}$$

$$= 25.8\%$$

$$\text{APR} = \frac{Y(95P+9)F}{12P(P+1)(4D+F)}$$

$$= \frac{12[(95 \times 12) + 9]\$280}{12(12)(12+1)[(4 \times \$2,000) + \$280]}$$

$$= \frac{3,860,640}{15,500,160}$$

$$= 24.9\%$$

$\text{APR} = $ *annual percentage rate*
$Y = $ number of payment periods in one *year*
$F = $ *finance* charges in dollars (dollar cost of credit)
$D = $ *debt* (amount borrowed or proceeds)
$P = $ total number of scheduled *payments*

[a] For a $2,000 loan for one year at 14 percent add-on interest with equal monthly payments of $190.

equal amounts. For repayments of unequal amounts, ask a lender for the effective annual percentage rate.

The effective APR is considerably higher than the add-on rate because the add-on rate is applied to the initial principal even though the payments keep reducing the outstanding balance. Because the borrower does not have full use of the initial loan, the APR is much higher.

We have generally assumed that interest is the only finance charge on a loan. Although interest costs do make up the greatest portion of finance charges, some lenders charge fees for a credit investigation, a loan application, or for credit or disability life insurance (to pay the lender in case the borrower dies or becomes seriously disabled before completing repayment). When these fees are *required,* the lender must include them in addition to the finance charge in dollars as part of the APR calculations.

The Credit Agreement

When you finance an automobile or a color television set, for example, through the seller or a sales finance company, you must sign a credit agreement. This is known as a *retail installment contract.* The agreement has all the components necessary to effect the contract. It includes a sales contract, a security agreement, a note, an insurance agreement, and some credit clauses to safeguard the lender in case of default. Figure 6–1 shows a retail installment contract form which complies with the Truth in Lending Act.

RETAIL INSTALLMENT CONTRACT AND SECURITY AGREEMENT

© BANKERS SYSTEMS, INC. 1982. ST. CLOUD, MN 56301. FORM RS-PI-KY 1/23/84

Date _____
Number _____

Buyer(s) Name and Address _____ (A)

Seller(s) Name and Address _____

SALE: In this contract the words I, me, and my refer to the Buyer(s) listed above, jointly and severally. The words you and your refer to the Seller(s) identified above, and anyone to whom this contract is assigned. I have been given an opportunity to purchase the property described below for the cash price or the total sale price, which is the total price of the property if I buy it over time. I agree to buy this property from you at the total sale price stated below.

I agree to pay you the total of payments of _____

Dollars ($ _____) as specified below:

Payment Schedule

☐ a. in _____ installments of _____ each, beginning _____, 19 ____ and on the same day of each ☐ month
☐ _____ thereafter until paid in full. (D)
☐ b. _____

PAYMENTS: This is a precomputed contract, which means the sum I have agreed to pay already includes the finance charges payable hereafter to the maturity date.

PREPAYMENT: I may prepay this contract in full or in part at any time. Any partial prepayment will not excuse any later scheduled payments until this contract is paid in full.
Upon prepayment in full, or acceleration of the balance upon my default, I will receive a refund credit of the finance charge based on the rule of 78's. No refund less than $1.00 will be made.

☐ If checked, an acquisition fee of $ _____ will be deducted from the finance charge before application of the rebate formula. No part of this fee will be refunded.

DELINQUENCY: I agree to pay a late charge of 5% of the amount of a payment which is late by more than 10 days after it is due, but not less than $1.00 or more than $5.00.
I agree to pay the court costs you incur to collect this contract, if I default, and attorney's fees not exceeding 15% of the amount due and payable under the contract, if referred to an attorney, not a salaried employee of yours.

SECURITY: I give you a security interest in the property described below, including all accessions, attachments, accessories, equipment and all proceeds from the property.

DESCRIPTION	NEW OR USED	UNIT NO. OR SERIAL NO.	CABINET OR MOTOR NO.	SALE PRICE OF EACH
(C)				

If Motor vehicle, including: ☐ radio ☐ power seats ☐ automatic transmission ☐ power brakes ☐ power windows
☐ no. of cylinders ☐ air conditioning ☐ power steering

WARRANTIES: ANY WARRANTIES FOR THE PROPERTY DESCRIBED IN THE SECURITY SECTION ARE ATTACHED TO THIS CONTRACT, AND MADE A PART OF THIS CONTRACT BY REFERENCE. ALL IMPLIED WARRANTIES OF MERCHANTABILITY AND FITNESS FOR A PARTICULAR PURPOSE ARE DISCLAIMED BY THE SELLER AND EXCLUDED FROM THIS AGREEMENT. SELLER SHALL NOT BE LIABLE FOR CONSEQUENTIAL DAMAGES.

USE: This property will be used for ☐ personal, family or household ☐ farming ☐ business purposes.

LOCATION: The property will be located at my address stated above, or _____
If this property is to be attached to real estate, the legal description of the real estate is: _____
and the record owner (if not me) is: _____
I will furnish to you, at your request, a disclaimer signed by all persons having an interest in the above described real estate of any right, title or interest in or lien upon this property prior to the security interest created by this contract.

ANNUAL PERCENTAGE RATE The cost of my credit as a yearly rate.	FINANCE CHARGE The dollar amount the credit will cost me.	AMOUNT FINANCED The amount of credit provided to me or on my behalf.	TOTAL OF PAYMENTS The amount I will have paid when I have made all scheduled payments.	TOTAL SALE PRICE The total cost of my purchase on credit, including my down payment of $ _____
____% $	$	$	$	$

My Payment Schedule will be:	Number of Payments	Amount of Payments	When Payments Are Due
		$	(B)
		$	
		$	

Security: I am giving a security interest in: ☐ (brief description of other property) _____
☐ the goods or property being purchased.
Late Charge: I will be charged 5% of the amount of a payment that is late by more than 10 days after it is due, but not less than $1.00 or more than $5.00.
Prepayment: If I pay off this contract early, I ☐ may ☐ will not be entitled to a refund of part of the Finance Charge.
Filing fees $ _____ Non-filing Insurance $ _____ If the letter "e" is used, it means an estimate. I can see my contract
documents for any additional information about nonpayment, default, any required repayment before the scheduled date, and prepayment refunds and penalties.

FIGURE 6–1
Retail Installment Contract
Source: Banker's Systems, Inc., Box 1457, St. Cloud, Minn. 56301. Used with permission.

Two kinds of retail installment contracts are used. With an *installment purchase agreement* (also known as a collateral installment loan or chattel mortgage), the title of the property passes to the buyer as the document is signed. With a *conditional sales contract* (also known as a financing lease), the title does not pass to the buyer until the last installment payment has been paid. The installment purchase agreement provides full protection for the buyer, as the seller must follow all state-prescribed legal procedures when repossessing the property and suing for any balance of money due on the credit contract. With a conditional

ITEMIZED FINANCE CHARGE OF $ _____

1. Time price differential $ _____

2. _____ $ _____

Credit Insurance: Credit life insurance and credit disability insurance are not required to obtain credit, and will not be provided unless I sign and agree to pay the additional costs.

Type	Premium	Term
Credit Life		
Credit Disability	(E)	
Joint Credit Life		

I ☐ do ☐ do not want credit life insurance.
X _____

I ☐ do ☐ do not want credit disability insurance.
X _____

I ☐ do ☐ do not want joint credit life insurance.
X _____ XX

Property Insurance: I may obtain property insurance from anyone that is acceptable to you. If I get the insurance from or through you, I will pay $ _____ for _____ of coverage.
The property insurance premium is calculated as follows:

☐ Fire-Theft and Comb. Add'l. Cov. $ _____
☐ $ _____ Deductible Com. Cov. $ _____
☐ $ _____ Deductible Col. Cov. $ _____
☐ _____ $ _____
☐ _____ $ _____

Single Interest Insurance: I may obtain single interest insurance from anyone I want that is acceptable to you. If I get the insurance from or through you I will pay $ _____ for _____ of coverage.

The above insurance does not include liability insurance coverage for bodily injury and property damage unless such insurance is specifically described above.

SALES TAX

1. Sale Price .... $ _____
2. Less: Gross Trade-In Allowance .... − $ _____
3. Taxable Amount ....

Sales Tax Percent X _____ %

4. Sales Tax .... $ _____

ITEMIZATION OF AMOUNT FINANCED

1. Cash Price (excluding Sales Tax) $ _____
2. Down Payment Computation
   Description of Trade-In _____
   a) Gross Trade-In Allowance $ _____
   b) Pay-Off (if any) $ _____
   c) Net Trade-In (a - b) $ _____
   d) Cash Down Payment $ _____
   e) Total Down Payment (c + d) $ _____
3. Unpaid Balance of Cash Price (1 - 2) $ _____
4. Other Charges

	Paid in Cash	Being Financed
a) To Property Insurance Company	$ _____	$ _____
b) To Credit Life Insurance Company	$ _____	$ _____
c) To Disability Insurance Company	$ _____	$ _____
d) To Public Officials	$ _____	$ _____
e) _____	$ _____	$ _____
f) _____	$ _____	$ _____
g) _____	$ _____	$ _____
h) _____	$ _____	$ _____
i) _____	$ _____	$ _____
j) _____	$ _____	$ _____
k) _____	$ _____	$ _____

5. Principal Balance (3 + 4(a) through 4(k) if financed) $ _____
6. Prepaid Finance Charges $ _____
7. Amount Financed (5 - 6) $ _____

NOTICE TO THE BUYER: (1) Do not sign this contract before you read it or if it contains blank spaces. (2) You are entitled to a copy of the contract you sign. (3) Under the law you have the right, among others, to pay in advance the full amount due, and to obtain under certain conditions a partial refund of the finance charge. (4) This contract shall become effective only when signed and executed by the buyer and seller, and shall apply to and inure to the benefit of and bind the heirs, executors, administrators, successors and assigns of both parties to this contract.

Signed _____ Title _____
For Seller

Assignment

Seller assigns this contract on _____ , 19 _____
to _____
_____ in accordance with the
Seller's Assignment appearing on the reverse side. The assignment is 1. ☐ Without Recourse 2. ☐ With Recourse 3. ☐ Subject to a Separate Agreement.
(Seller)
By _____ Title _____

I AGREE TO THE TERMS SET OUT ON THE FRONT AND BACK OF THIS CONTRACT. I have received a copy of this document on today's date.

1. Signed _____ Buyer
2. Signed _____ Buyer
3. Signed _____ Buyer

Any person who signs within this enclosure does so to give you a security interest in the collateral described above, but assumes no personal obligation to pay this contract.
Name
X _____ Date _____

White First Copy - Original   Canary Second Copy - Seller/Assignee's Copy   Pink Third Copy - Buyer's Copy   Goldenrod Fourth Copy - Seller's Copy

FIGURE 6–1
(continued)

sales contract, the lender can repossess the property much more easily; in fact, in some states the lender can take the property back as soon as the buyer falls behind in payments.

Sales Contract

The *sales contract* discloses pertinent information about the borrower or lender, the merchandise being purchased, and the mathematical details of the contract. In Figure 6–1 the sales contract is the section marked "A" and the section marked "B." The Truth in Lending Act requires that items in the section marked "B" be written in a consistent manner, including in bold print the terms *finance charge* (in dollars) and the *annual percentage rate* in numbers.

Security Agreement

The security agreement is the portion of the contract that indicates whether the sales contract is an installment purchase agreement or a conditional sales contract. It is marked "C" in Figure 6–1. (This is an installment purchase agreement.) The *security agreement* gives the lender a legally secure interest in the item being financed. The lender files a *lien* (legal right to hold property or to sell it for payment of a claim) in court in order to make the security interest public. When the contract is paid, the lien is removed.

Note

The *note* is the formal promise of the borrower to repay the lender as detailed in the contract. It specifies what happens if the borrower defaults, who pays attorney's fees in that event, and what credit clauses are considered part of the terms of the note. The note is in the section marked "D" in Figure 6–1.

Insurance Agreement

The *insurance agreement* is the section marked "E" in Figure 6–1. It is a legal agreement by the borrower to purchase credit and/or disability insurance that would pay the lender the balance of the loan in full should the borrower die or become seriously disabled. Most states have laws prohibiting the sale of credit and disability insurance for exorbitantly high prices, and some states restrict a lender from forcing borrowers to purchase insurance as a condition of the lending agreement. The monthly premium for such insurance coverage might seem nominal, but similar coverage can be purchased through a traditional insurance agency for perhaps one-sixth the cost. A full discussion of disability and life insurance appears in Chapters 12 and 13.

Credit Clauses

A variety of credit clauses are included in contracts. Some of these you should avoid, if possible. Most clauses necessarily protect the lender from credit users who would try to skip town with the collateral property.

1. **Acceleration clause** The *acceleration clause* requires that after one payment is late (and therefore defaulted) all remaining installments are due and payable at once or on the demand of the lender.

2. **Repossession** After the borrower has defaulted, the act of physically seizing the secured property as described in the contract is known as *repossession.* In some states repossession can occur quite easily under a conditional sales contract. In most states where an installment purchase agreement is the contract, the lender must first get a court judgment of default and then follow legally prescribed procedures to regain possession of the

goods. The latter method provides more protection for the borrower.

3. **Balloon clause**   The *balloon clause* permits the last payment to be abnormally large in comparison to the other installment payments. Truth in Lending laws require any payment more than twice the size of others to be identified as a balloon payment.

4. **Prepayment penalty**   The *rule of 78s,* sometimes called the "sum of the digits method," is a commonly used method of calculating rebates of finance charges and the prepayment penalty charged the borrower who pays off an installment loan early. It takes into consideration that you pay more in interest in the beginning of a loan when you have the use of more money, and that you pay less and less interest as the debt is reduced. To illustrate, suppose on a $500 loan for twelve months, $80 in finance charges were scheduled to be paid. If the loan is paid off after only six months, the borrower will not have the interest reduced $40. To calculate the reduction, first add together all the numbers between 1 and 12 $(1 + 2 + 3 + 4 + 5 + 6 + 7 + 8 + 9 + 10 + 11 + 12 = 78)$. If the loan is paid off after one month, the amount of interest paid is assumed to be 12/78 of the total, with a reduction of 66/78 due the borrower. For a loan paid in full after two months, the amount of interest paid is assumed to be 23/78 of the total (12/78 for month one and 11/78 for month two). In this example, after six months the lender assumes that $58.46 (57/78) has been paid in interest, and the interest is reduced $21.54 (21/78). Thus, the borrower does not get 50 percent of the interest as a reduction for paying the loan off in half the time, but only 27 percent ($21.54 ÷ $80).

Signals of Credit Overextension

Many people in today's credit-oriented economy find themselves using more credit than they would like to. This uncomfortable feeling propels credit users to re-examine their own debt limits, as discussed earlier in this chapter. *Credit overextension* in which excessive personal debts make repayment difficult, is a more serious matter. Perhaps not surprisingly, numerous research studies have found that a primary reason for divorce is money problems. Seven signals of credit overextension are discussed below.

1. **Exceeding debt limits**   The debt limits established in Table 6–2 are only guidelines. Generally, however, spending more than 20 percent of disposable personal income on debt repayments (excluding mortgage loans) is a clear sign of difficulty ahead.

2. **Out of money** We all have emergencies and sometimes simply run out of money. But if you are running out of money on a month-to-month basis because a good portion of earnings goes to debt repayments, you may be overextended. Are you using credit cards where you previously used cash? Or using credit card cash advances and checking account credit lines to pay bills?

3. **Paying only the minimum amount due** When the revolving credit card bills come in, are you paying the minimum payment—or less—instead of the full balance owed?

4. **Requesting increases in credit limits** Department stores and bank credit card companies are usually quite pleased when customers request increases in their approved credit limits because it usually means more income for them. Raising your limit from $500 to $1,000 may make sense if you just graduated from school. However, if you request a raise of another $1,000 because you *need* the higher limit, it is time to think. On the one hand, some people have credit limits that are simply too low to permit much flexibility. On the other hand, you may get deeper into debt after obtaining an increase in your credit limit. Similarly, have you added new credit card accounts to increase your borrowing power?

5. **Missing credit payments** By the time you have missed a credit payment, you may have noticed some of the danger signals noted above. Of course, you can simply forget to mail a check. But when money is not available to pay your bills, trouble has arrived. Have you lost track of how much you owe and are avoiding adding up the total?

6. **Add-on loans** *Flipping,* or taking **add-on loans,** occurs when you take out a second loan for a larger amount before you repay your first loan. Say your original loan of $1,000 has been repaid down to $400. You decide to refinance the debt balance of $400 and borrow an additional $300 from the same lending source. It may be a wise course of action to increase an existing note, perhaps even at a lower interest rate. But it may also be a sign of both increasing debt and an inability to handle the repayments.

7. **Debt-consolidation loans** Many people who are in debt owe several creditors different amounts at varying interest rates. People in such situations often obtain a debt-consolidation loan to pay off all the bills and to make one payment that is less in dollars than all the others combined. It is less because the time period for prepayment is lengthened. Such action reduces pressure on the budget. It is also a sign that the credit user was simply using too much credit.

8. **Garnishment** *Garnishment* is a legal attachment to your wages directed by a court. Fortunately, the Truth in Lending Law offers some protections for credit users. Your wages cannot have more than two garnishments attached. Also, the total amount

garnished cannot be more than 25 percent of your disposable income for the pay period *or* more than the amount by which your weekly disposable income exceeds thirty times the federal minimum wage (whichever is less). Furthermore, the law states that having your wages garnished cannot be used by your employer as grounds for discharging you.

Credit Counseling and Bankruptcy

Whether you have serious financial difficulties or feel you are just getting in over your head, you should consider getting credit counseling. Many large employers offer credit counseling through their personnel offices. Most are willing to give many hours of advice and to work carefully through your bills and budget because they have an investment in you and want to help you remain effective in your job. You may also be able to find a credit-counseling program at your credit union or labor union. Another place to turn is to your creditor. Many creditors, such as banks and consumer finance companies, have programs that help debtors get out of financial trouble. Finally, excellent assistance is offered through the Consumer Credit Counseling Service, a nonprofit organization. You can locate a local office by writing the National Foundation for Consumer Credit, 8701 Georgia Avenue, Silver Spring, MD 20910. All the above services are provided at virtually no cost.

Some profit-making counseling services advertise that they will negotiate with your creditors to get repayment schedules changed so you can make smaller payments. Be aware that nonprofit counseling groups can also do this, and they won't charge you $250 to $1,000 to get you back on your feet.

When things are really bleak, you might seek the advice of an attorney and consider bankruptcy. Bankruptcy is a constitutionally guaranteed right of Americans and is available in two forms. Chapter 13 of the Bankruptcy Act (also known as the *wage-earner plan*) is designed for persons with regular income who might be able to pay off their debts given certain protections of the court. Under this plan, the court notifies all creditors of the petition for bankruptcy. At a scheduled hearing and with the help of a bankruptcy trustee, a repayment plan is designed to repay as much of the debts as possible, typically in thirty-six months. Interest charges and collection efforts by creditors generally stop at this point. Should the person make all the scheduled payments, he or she is judged free and clear of any remaining amounts due that could not be repaid within the period. Many responsible people choose this option to repay a portion, if not all, of what they owe.

Straight bankruptcy is available through Chapter 7 of the Bankruptcy Act. Many consumers choose this option because once the bankruptcy trustee has listed the debts and determined that it would be highly unlikely that substantial repayment could be made, all those debts are wiped out. The bankrupt person is then judged free and clear. Once a person has declared bankruptcy, he or she cannot be discharged from debts again for six years. Realize also that most of the bankrupt person's assets are given to the trustee and sold. Legally, bankrupt people are allowed to keep a small equity in their homes, an inexpensive automobile, and limited personal property. State or federal laws govern what can be kept, and some debts can never be excused, including education loans, fines, alimony, child support, and income taxes. Bankruptcy is the court of last resort for those overextended in debt and should be avoided if at all possible.

Summary

1. Important financial decisions, such as borrowing, often require considering the impact of both inflation and taxes.

2. People usually plan to use credit for three primary reasons: convenience, emergencies, and planned expenditures for major purchases.

3. Debt limits for personal use of credit can be established using three techniques: the disposable income method, the ratio of debts to equity method, and the continuous debt method.

4. Consumer loans are classified as either installment or noninstallment credit.

5. Both the simple interest and add-on methods are used with installment loans, but the annual percentage rate formula gives the correct rate in all cases.

6. Four major sources of consumer loans are banks, credit unions, consumer finance companies, and sales finance companies, with the latter specializing in collateral loans, often at competitive interest rates, for automobile or appliance purchases.

7. A credit agreement (also known as a retail installment contract) has all the components necessary to effect a contract: a sales contract, a security agreement, a note, an insurance agreement, and some credit clauses to safeguard the lender in case of default.

8. A contract may include a variety of credit clauses, some of which need to be avoided, if possible, as they could be detrimental to a borrower.

9. There are several signals of credit overextension, and some of the early ones are exceeding credit limit guidelines, running out of money too often, and requesting increases in credit limits.

10. People with serious financial difficulties can obtain professional assistance through credit counseling and/or by using Chapters 7 or 13 of the Bankruptcy Act.

Modern Money Management

The Johnsons' Credit Questions

Harry and Belinda need some questions resolved regarding credit.

1. They have a cash flow deficit projected for several months this year (see Table 3–7). Suggest how, when, and where they can finance the shortages by borrowing.

2. Also, their three-year-old car has been having mechanical problems lately. So instead of buying a new set of tires, as planned for in March (see Table 3–6), they are considering trading it in for a new vehicle so Harry can have a dependable car for commuting to work. They still owe $3,600 to the bank for their present car, or $200 a month for the remaining eighteen months of the forty-eight month loan. They want to buy a vehicle that lists for $14,800.

   Assume that the Johnsons want to buy the new car. Make recommendations to them regarding where to finance, how much to finance, what APR to expect, and what the monthly payments will be.

Key Words and Concepts

acceleration clause, 184
add-on loan, 186
annual percentage rate (APR), 180
balloon clause, 185
cash advance, 173
cash loan, 172
collateral, 171
conditional sales contract, 182
cosigner, 171
credit life insurance, 174
creditor, 171
credit overextension, 185
credit union share, 174
disposable personal income, 167

flipping, 186
garnishment, 186
home-equity credit line loan, 176
insurance agreement, 184
installment purchase agreement, 182
lien, 184
line of credit, 173
note, 184
pawnbroker, 177
purchase (or sales credit) loan, 172
repossession, 184
retail installment contract, 181

Review Questions

1. Explain how taxes and inflation can affect your decision to borrow rather than pay cash for products.
2. List the three primary reasons why people borrow.
3. How does setting a debt limit help the borrower?
4. Describe three methods for establishing debt limits.
5. Distinguish between noninstallment credit and installment credit.
6. Distinguish between a secured loan and an unsecured loan.
7. Describe how automatic overdraft loans work.
8. Describe how a credit union differs from a bank in terms of lending.
9. Explain what is meant by credit life insurance and of what value it is to the credit user.
10. Distinguish between a consumer finance company and a sales finance company.
11. Since life insurance companies are not noted for lending money to consumers, explain why they can be identified as a source for borrowing money.
12. What is the process followed by pawnbrokers in lending money to consumers?
13. Explain why the discount method of interest calculation raises the annual percentage rate.
14. Explain why the effective APR is always larger than the add-on rate of interest when installment payments are made.
15. What other costs besides typical interest charges could be included as part of finance charges?
16. According to the Truth in Lending Law, what two items must be shown in bold print on the disclosure section of an installment contract?
17. Why is the rule of 78s clause considered a prepayment penalty?
18. Describe the financial circumstances that would make debt consolidation necessary.
19. Name three of the seven signals of credit overextension and briefly describe each.

20. Distinguish between the wage-earner plan and straight bankruptcy.

Case Problems

1. Ricardo Millender of Santa Barbara, California, needs money to furnish his apartment. One store will finance his purchase of $1,800 at a 10.0 percent add-on rate, and he would be required to make monthly payments. This, of course, would mean paying an effective APR considerably greater than 10.0 percent. However, Ricardo desperately needs the new furnishings.
   a. Can Ricardo justify borrowing $1,800 at this rate? Why or why not?
   b. What other alternatives are available to Ricardo that may not be as costly?

2. Peter Nishi of Carson City, Nevada, had an old car that was operating fairly well but needed repairs to the extent of $800 per year. He recently saw new cars advertised at several hundred dollars less than those advertised previously. A particular model was priced at $1,700 below the regular selling price of $13,200. Peter gathered all the information and realized that to buy this car he would have to borrow $2,000 from his bank at an APR of 11.5 percent. Peter would also have to withdraw $2,000 from a savings account paying 7.5 percent interest annually. He is in the 28 percent tax bracket (meaning that 28 cents of each additional dollar earned goes to taxes), and inflation for the economy is projected to be 5 percent each year for the next two years. Peter is still undecided about what to do.
   a. What are some of the questions and concerns Peter must consider before making a decision?
   b. How does inflation enter into a decision of this type?
   c. What action would you recommend for Peter? Justify.

3. Nola Okimoto of Pearl City, Hawaii, recently entered into a sales contract to buy a new automobile. After signing the contract, she hurriedly left the office of the sales finance company with her copy of the contract. Later that evening Nola reread the contract and noticed several clauses—an acceleration clause, a repossession clause, a balloon clause for $900, and a rule of 78s clause. She was in a hurry when she signed the contract and was told these were standard clauses that should not concern her.
   a. Should Nola be concerned about these clauses? Why or why not?
   b. What are some fair warnings for Nola regarding the balloon clause?
   c. Considering the rule of 78s clause, what should Nola realize if she pays off the loan before the regular due date?

4. Keith Shildt of Indiana, Pennsylvania, had an unusual amount of debt. He owed $1,800 to one bank, $600 to a clothing store, $900 to his credit union, and several hundred dollars to other stores and persons. Keith was paying over $450 a month on the three major obligations and $425 a month for an apartment. He realized that with take-home pay of just over $1,200 a month he didn't have much excess cash. He discussed an alternative way of handling his major payments with his credit union officer. The officer suggested he pool all his debts and take out a consolidation loan. As a result he would pay only $230 a month for all his debts. Keith seemed ecstatic over the idea.

  a. Is Keith's enthusiasm over the idea of a debt consolidation loan justified? Why or why not?

  b. How is it possible for the credit union to offer such a "good deal" to Keith?

  c. To make payments of only $230 as compared to $450, what compromise would Keith make?

  d. If you assume that the consolidation loan will cost more in interest, what would be a justification for this added cost?

Suggested Readings

"Getting on Top of Your Debt." *Money,* April 1987, pp. 95–108. Helps you determine if you are too much in debt and what can be done to get out of debt.

"Home Equity Gold Rush." *Business Week,* February 9, 1987, pp. 64–70. The good news and bad news—and some horror stories—about home equity loans.

"How to Find the Best Loans Now." *Changing Times,* February 1987, pp. 22–29. Compare all places to borrow, showing advantages and disadvantages of each.

"How Lenders Size You Up." *Money,* April 1987, pp. 145–154. In-depth discussion of factors lenders use to accept or reject credit applications.

"A Savvy Borrower's Shopping Guide." *Money,* April 1987, pp. 161–170. Getting the best credit deals, from plastic to home equity.

"Sizing up Home Equity Deals." *Changing Times,* February 1987, pp. 31–35. Some home equity credit lines deserve a careful look.

CHAPTER 7

Managing Taxes

OBJECTIVES

After reading this chapter, the student should be able to

1. explain the principles of taxation.
2. describe the effects of tax rates on income.
3. determine whether to file an income tax return and define the three classes of filing status.
4. describe the two ways of paying taxes: payroll withholding and estimated taxes.
5. identify the nine steps of calculating income taxes.
6. calculate the tax liability for different types of tax payers.
7. discuss the philosophy of avoiding income taxes.
8. list the different methods of preparing tax returns and determine which method is best and why.
9. state some things to keep in mind to go successfully through the process of an IRS audit.
10. list numerous types of federal, state, and local taxes and explain their total effect on income available to spend, save, and invest.

B esides banking, credit use and credit cards, and borrowing, money management includes the crucial area of taxation. Taxation is of utmost importance in the study of personal finance for two reasons. First, taxes often take up 15 to 30 percent of your income—a considerable amount of money. Second, if through poor management you send more money in taxes to the government than is necessary, you will have less money available to spend, save, or invest.

This chapter examines the principles of taxation and the relationship among taxes, inflation, and your income. It then discusses who must pay taxes and ways of paying them, including both payroll withholding and estimated tax payments. Next, nine steps detail the entire process of paying taxes, from the determination of gross income through the final computation of taxes due. We provide examples of calculating tax liability. We also consider tax avoidance, tax-return preparation, and tax audits.

Principles of Taxation

Taxes are compulsory charges imposed by a government on citizens and property. To learn how to manage taxes effectively, you should know the origins and characteristics of taxes and how taxes are administered and classified.

Origins of Taxes

Governments must use a great deal of money to carry out the desires of people in our complex industrial societies. In the early history of this country, revenue was raised through the sale of lands in the West, import taxes on some products, and occasional use of a small (and constitutionally questionable) income tax. Over time, the growing financial need to pay for wars and social programs resulted in the Sixteenth Amendment to the Constitution in 1913. This amendment permitted the federal government to pass laws to tax income. In addition to federal income taxes on both individuals and corporations, governments use a wide variety of other taxes to raise revenue. Many of these other taxes will be discussed in the last section of this chapter.

Characteristics of Taxes

Most people agree that an ideal tax should have four basic characteristics.

1. **Fairness, or equity** Taxes should be free from bias or injustice and have some degree of impartiality. The preferred kind of tax is based on a citizen's ability to pay as indicated by income and assets.
2. **Ease of calculation and enforcement** A government and its tax-

payers should have some certainty that taxes will be computed accurately and will be paid.

3. **Ease of administration** A government should not have to go to great efforts to collect the taxes due. Further, the administrative program should be economical to operate. Currently, it takes less than $1 to collect $100 in federal income taxes.

4. **Positive economic benefits** Taxes should neither impair economic vitality nor negate the efforts of government to provide stable economic growth.

These ideas are certainly subject to interpretation and debate. Fairness, for example, is at the heart of arguments advocating elimination of state sales taxes on food and drug items. Critics maintain that because elderly and poor Americans spend proportionately more of their income on these items, they pay more than their fair share of sales taxes. A similar argument can be made on behalf of cigarette smokers, who pay a special user's tax on tobacco products.

Tax Administration

Taxes are administered at all levels of government. Because the largest amount of tax you pay is on your income, this chapter focuses on the personal income tax and on the Internal Revenue Service (IRS). The IRS is the agency charged with the responsibility of collecting federal income taxes based on the legal provisions in the Internal Revenue Service Code of 1986. The code represents the major tax laws written by Congress.

The IRS issues various *IRS regulations,* which are its interpretations of the laws passed by Congress. These have the force and effect of law and are contained in numerous thick volumes in large libraries. Dozens of *IRS rulings* are also annually issued; these are IRS decisions based on its interpretations of both tax laws and regulations. Tax rulings provide guidance to how the IRS will act in certain general situations. *IRS private letter rulings* are annually issued to several hundred individuals and corporations, giving the IRS advisory opinions on individual tax-management proposals. When these opinions are made public, all taxpayers gain some insight into IRS concepts; rulings often eventually follow issuance of several private letters on similar topics. In addition to the above, the tax courts issue many decisions each year giving the judicial interpretation of tax laws that Congress passes.

Ways of Classifying Taxes

Taxes can be classified according to a taxpayer's ability to pay as progressive or regressive. A *progressive tax* demands a higher percentage of a person's income as income increases. In this country, the federal personal income tax is a progressive tax because the tax rate increases as a taxpayer's income (or implied ability to pay) increases. Table 7–1 shows that under the federal income tax upper segments of a taxpayer's income are taxed at increasingly higher rates.

TABLE 7-1
The Progressive Nature of the Federal Income Tax[a]

This Segment of Taxable Income	Is Taxed at a Rate of
First $17,850	15%
$17,851 to $43,150	28
$43,151 to $89,560	33

[a] Rates quoted are for a single taxpayer.

A *regressive tax* operates in the opposite way. As income rises the tax rate remains the same or decreases, and so the tax demands a decreasing proportion of a person's income as income increases. Such taxes are not based on ability to pay. State sales tax is an example of a regressive tax. Assume that a stereo system costs $500, plus a 5 percent sales tax. Taxpayer *A,* with a monthly income of $1,000, and taxpayer *B,* with a monthly income of $5,000, each buy one. The sales tax would be $25 for both, yet it would represent 2.5 percent of *A*'s monthly income and only .5 percent of *B*'s income. Since the sales tax rate remains the same, 5 percent, it might appear that the tax is proportional, or fair to all. But as shown above, one person may pay proportionately fives times as much as another. Thus, the tax is regressive.

An often-proposed substitute for our progressive income tax system is the flat rate income tax. Billed as a proportional tax, the *flat rate income tax* would require all taxpayers' income to be taxed at the same flat rate, say 20 percent, with no exceptions. As soon as a single exception is permitted, such as certain kinds of income being nontaxable (such as retirement benefits) or deductions for certain expenses (such as for medical care), the flat tax would lose its proportionality and could become either progressive or regressive depending on the nature of the exception. As an example, consider the Social Security tax paid by wage earners. It is applied at a flat rate of 7.51 percent, but it is actually regressive because it is not applied to incomes above $46,800 (both figures based on projected 1988 data). Both the percent and the maximum income against which it is applied are scheduled to increase in future years.

Tax Rates and Your Income

Taxes have a major effect on your income. This section provides an understanding of marginal, true marginal, and actual tax rates.

Marginal Tax Rate

Later in this chapter and in subsequent chapters, you will see how the wise financial planner *carefully* considers the tax effects of financial decisions. Perhaps the single most important concept in personal finance is the *marginal tax rate.* This is the tax rate at which your last dollar earned is taxed. A *marginal tax bracket (MTB)* is each income range couplet shown in the tax rate schedules. To illustrate, in Table 7–2, Jean Van Name of Newark, Delaware, is a single person with a taxable income of $18,000. Table 7–2 indicates that she is in the 28 percent marginal tax bracket, as are all single taxpayers with incomes between $17,850 and $43,150. They will pay taxes at the 28 percent marginal tax rate. (In fact, most taxpayers are in the 28 percent MTB, so if they earn another $100, $28 of it goes to federal income taxes.) Taxpayers have three federal income marginal tax rates: 15 percent, 28 percent, and 33 percent.

For an example of how changes in income can affect taxes paid, assume Jane Hernandez, a single person from San Jose, California, has a total income of $48,000, and after subtractions a taxable income of $41,500. Her employer gives her a $1,000 year-end bonus to recognize the quality of her work. Table 7–3 shows that Jane pays an extra $280 in taxes on the fully taxable $1,000 bonus income; thus she pays a marginal tax rate of 28 percent on the last income earned.

For another example, assume that Jane receives a bonus of $4,000 instead of $1,000, which pushes up her taxable income from $41,500 to $45,500. Table 7–2 shows that the marginal tax rate for a taxable income of $45,500 is 33 percent. Thus, a small portion of the $4,000

TABLE 7–2
Tax Rate Schedules (for 1988 Tax Year)

	If taxable income is over	but not over	Tax is	plus following percent	of amount over
Joint return	$ 0	$ 29,750	$ 0	15%	$ 0
	29,750	71,900	4,462.50	28	29,750
	71,900	149,250	16,264.50	33[a]	71,900
	149,250			28[b]	0
Single	0	17,850	0	15	0
	17,850	43,150	2,677.50	28	17,850
	43,150	89,560	9,761.50	33[a]	43,150
	89,560			28[b]	0
Head of household	0	23,900	0	15	0
	23,900	61,650	3,585	28	23,900
	61,650	123,790	14,155	33[a]	61,650
	123,790			28[b]	0

Source: Internal Revenue Service.

[a] The value of paying only a 15 percent rate on the first part of taxable income is phased out for higher-income taxpayers with this 5 percent surtax on a portion of income.

[b] The value of personal exemptions is phased out for higher-income taxpayers by imposing a 5 percent surcharge. It is the lower of (1) $546 times the number of exemptions or (2) 5 percent of taxable income minus $149,250 on a joint return, 5 percent of taxable income minus $89,560 on a single return, or 5 percent of taxable income minus $123,790 on a head of household return.

TABLE 7–3
Marginal Tax Rate Illustrated (for Jane Hernandez)

Taxable Income	Tax[a]
$41,500	$2,677.50 + $6,622 ($41,500 − $17,850 = $23,650 × .28) = $9,299.50
$42,500	$2,677.50 + $6,902 ($42,500 − $17,850 = $24,605 × .28) = $9,579.50

Marginal Tax Rate with Bonus

$$
\begin{array}{rr}
\$42,500 & \$9,579.50 \\
-\ 41,500 & -\ 9,299.50 \\
\hline
\$\ 1,000 \text{ additional income} & \$\ 280 \text{ additional tax}
\end{array}
$$

$$\frac{280}{\$1,000} = 28\% \text{ marginal tax rate}$$

[a] From Table 7–2.

bonus is taxed at a rate of 28 percent, and the last dollars are taxed at a marginal rate of 33 percent.

Our discussion so far has focused on the tax rate schedules (Table 7–2), but most people use the tax table instead (such as Table 7–4) because they are convenient and do not require math calculations. Table 7–4 shows a portion of the tax table. You can calculate anyone's marginal tax rate from this table in the following way:

1. Assuming someone is single and has a taxable income of $42,500, find in the table the amount of tax on that income ($9,586).
2. Add $100 to that income for a total of $42,600, and find the tax on that amount ($9,614).
3. Calculate the difference between the two tax amounts ($9,586 − $9,614 = $28) and divide by 100 (28 ÷ 100 = 28 percent). Thus, the $28 higher tax resulting from an increase in taxable

TABLE 7–4
Illustration of a Portion of Tax Table[a]

If taxable income is		And you are filing		
		Single	Joint Return	Head of Household
At least	But less than		Your tax is	
$42,450	$42,500	$9,572	$8,025	$8,786
42,500	42,550	9,586	8,039	8,800
42,550	42,600	9,600	8,053	8,814
42,600	42,650	9,614	8,067	8,828

[a] Not the official IRS tax table, but derived from the tax schedules.

income of $100 reflects a marginal tax rate of 28 percent. (Note that the tax of $9,586 is slightly higher than the calculated amount using the tax rate schedules for Jane Hernandez in Table 7–3 because the IRS figures are rounded to account for the $50 income intervals in the tax tables.)

The marginal tax rate can have a great effect on tax deductions as well as savings and investment decisions. Consider someone with a 33 percent marginal tax rate who wants to make a $100 tax-deductible contribution to a charity. The charity receives the $100 and the taxpayer may deduct $100 from taxable income. This results in a $33 reduction in income tax ($100 × 33 percent), and the taxpayer is out only $67 ($100 − $33 = $67) for tax purposes. In effect, the taxpayer gives $67 and the government "gives" $33 to the charity.

True Marginal Tax Rate

For the majority of people who earn a gross income of $46,800 or less, the *true* marginal tax rate on income is even *higher* than that given in the discussion above. This is because there are two other taxes that must be subtracted from increases in income. Most workers pay about 7 percent of income in Social Security taxes and 6 percent or more in state income taxes. (Some cities have an additional income tax of perhaps 1 to 5 percent.)

To determine the true marginal tax rate on increases in income add these other taxes to the marginal tax rate. A single person with a taxable income of $18,000 (as discussed in the first example above) would have a marginal tax rate of 28 percent. A state income tax of perhaps 6 percent and a Social Security tax of 7 percent on an increase in income of $100 results in a "true" marginal tax rate of 41 percent (28 percent + 6 percent + 7 percent = 41 percent). People with incomes above the maximum income that can be assessed the Social Security tax would not have additional Social Security tax but would have applicable state and local income taxes to consider in determining their true marginal tax rate.

Average Tax Rate

The **average tax rate** is a calculated figure showing your tax liability as a percentage of total, gross, adjusted gross, or taxable income. People often confuse their marginal tax bracket with such a percentage. Realize that your total income is not fully taxed by the federal government. It can be reduced by exclusions, adjustments, exemptions, deductions, and credits; this all will be explained later in the chapter.

For example, Casey Lee of Summit, Mississippi, has a taxable income of $16,000 and a total income of $21,000. She can calculate her tax liability by using the official tax rate schedules shown in Table 7–2. Casey is single, so her tax liability is $2,400 ($16,000 × .15). A look at Table 7–2 reveals a marginal tax bracket of 15 percent. The average tax rate based on a total income of $21,000 is only 11.4 percent ($2,400 ÷ $21,000).

Therefore, Casey pays an average tax rate of 11.4 percent on her total income even though she is in the 15.0 percent marginal tax bracket. If she were to earn an additional $1,000, it would be taxed at the 15 percent marginal tax rate and the federal government would get another $150 from her. Meanwhile, her average tax rate would rise slightly to 11.6 percent [$2,400 + $150 = $2,550 ÷ ($21,000 + $1,000) = 11.6].

Filing a Tax Return

Most people who earn an income should file a tax return. It is fairly easy to determine whether you should file and what your filing status is.

Should You File?

U.S. citizens and residents of the United States or of Puerto Rico must file a federal income tax return if they have earned sufficient income ($4,950 in 1988). This includes U.S. citizens living abroad. Table 7–5 shows who is required to file.

There are three other cases where it is wise to file a tax return.

1. People who have had federal income taxes withheld but did not have enough income to be required to file a return should file to obtain a refund of those monies. (If you have neglected to file for refunds in the past, complete Form 1040-X, "Amended U.S. Individual Tax Return," to obtain deserved refunds for the previous three years.)

2. Dependent children with a gross income of up to $1,000 of unearned income, as opposed to earned income. *Earned income* includes salaries, wages, fringe benefits, and income from sole proprietorships. *Unearned income* includes rents, dividends, capital gains, interest, royalties, and *transfer payments* (payments by governments and individuals for which no goods or services are expected in return, such as welfare payments). Up to $1,000 of a dependent child's unearned income is exempt from taxes. If you

TABLE 7–5
Persons Required to File an Income Tax Return (1988 Tax Year)

Taxpayer	Must File if Total Income Exceeds
Single, no dependents	$4,950
Single, age 65 or older or blind	5,700
Head of household, 1 dependent	8,300
Married couple	8,900
Married couple, one age 65 or older or blind	9,500

have a child who owns Series E and EE savings bonds, reporting the income yearly on a separate return for the child (the taxes for this income will be nonexistent or quite low) will avoid the need to report the income when the bonds are redeemed and when the tax liability is likely to be higher.

3. If your adjusted gross income is less than $17,000 and a child lives with you for a whole year, filing an income tax return might qualify you for a refund of up to $800. (This is known as the earned income credit, which is discussed later in the chapter.)

Filing Status

The amount of tax people pay on their taxable income is determined partially by their tax status. Your tax status will be single, married, or head of household.

Single   Taxpayers who are not married on December 31 are considered single for the entire year and must file a separate return if their income exceeds the minimum income threshold. Partially as a result of IRS efforts to construct a truly fair tax system, single taxpayers pay at rates higher than most others because it is felt that single taxpayers have a higher ability to pay than a married couple or head of household with the same taxable income.

Married   For given levels of income, the lowest tax liabilities are paid by married taxpayers who file a joint return. In this case, one income or two combined incomes represent the income of the married couple. Married couples can file either separately or jointly. For most couples, filing jointly results in paying a lower tax. A couple need only be married on December 31 to qualify for this tax status. Filing jointly also means that the IRS can pursue either spouse for payments and can even attach assets held separately.

Head of Household   This special category is used most commonly by taxpayers with low to moderate incomes who are single and who pay the majority of expenses for a tax-qualifying relative, such as a child, parent, or sibling, who lives with them. The tax rate for heads of households is higher than for married persons filing jointly but less than that for singles.

Ways of Paying

When taxpayers complete their tax returns for mailing to the Internal Revenue Service by the April 15 deadline, they determine their exact *tax liability,* the actual tax owed on income earned during the previous year. However, the federal income tax is a pay-as-you-go tax, and taxpayers are required to use one of two methods to gradually discharge their tax liability during the year: payroll withholding or estimating taxes.

Payroll Withholding

Payroll withholding is a method of prepaying taxes in which your employer withholds a portion of each of your paychecks as an estimate of the tax you owe and forwards those funds to the government. The amount withheld is based on income earned, the number of exemptions reported by the employee on the W-4 form, called the "Employee's Withholding Allowance Certificate," and other factors. An *exemption* is the legally permitted reduction in the taxpayer's taxable income based on the number of persons supported by that income. Taxpayers can count as *personal* exemptions themselves and their spouses (if filing jointly) and receive extra partial exemptions if they are blind or over age 65. *Dependent* exemptions may be claimed for any qualifying dependents (for instance, children or parents).

If you had no income tax liability in the previous year and expect to have none in the current year (perhaps you are a student who works only summers), you can be exempt from withholding. Request a W-4 form from your employer and write in the word *exempt* in the appropriate place. This is not allowed if you are a student claimed as a dependent on your parents' tax return. Withholding for Social Security taxes occurs regardless of whether you are exempt from income taxes.

If your tax liability is anticipated to be lower than the federal government's withholding schedule, you are allowed to refigure your withholding allowances to lower the amount withheld. Those who deliberately have their taxes substantially underwithheld will be assessed a penalty.

Overwithholding occurs when employees have employers withhold more in estimated federal withholding taxes than the tax liability due the government. Approximately two-thirds of all taxpayers practice overwithholding, actually a form of forced savings. This way they get a refund approximately six weeks after filing their income tax return. However, the IRS does not pay interest on such refunded monies. The wise financial planner takes the necessary time to calculate estimated income tax liability and attempts to have the proper amount withheld. This way the refund money can be spent, saved, or invested as it is earned.

Estimated Taxes

Many people are self-employed or have substantial income from an employer who does not practice payroll withholding. Lawyers, accountants, consultants, movie stars, and owners of apartment buildings are examples. According to the pay-as-you-go requirements, the IRS directs such taxpayers to estimate their tax liability and pay it in quarterly installments during the year on the 15th of April, June, September, and the following January. Form 1040-ES, "Declaration of Estimated Tax for Individuals," must be filed if the estimated tax is $500 or more. No penalties are assessed for failure to file the form and pay the taxes unless the estimated tax paid in was underpaid by more than 10 percent.

Taxpayers who earn income in addition to income from an employer can avoid having to estimate taxes by completing another W-4 form to increase the payroll withholding to cover the anticipated extra liability. This directs the employer to overwithhold taxes so the taxpayer then has sufficiently prepaid the taxes on the other income.

Nine Steps in Calculating Income Taxes

There are nine basic steps in calculating federal income taxes.

1. Determine the gross income.
2. Determine adjustments to the income.
3. Claim exemptions.
4. Identify the standard deduction amount.
5. List itemized deductions.
6. Determine whether to use the tax tables or the tax rate schedules.
7. Determine tax liability.
8. Subtract tax credits to find the final tax liability.
9. Calculate the balance due or refund.

Our discussion of the nine steps in calculating income taxes will be general. Although we mention some limitations and qualifications, we do not examine them in depth. The wise financial manager will write the IRS to obtain Publication 17, *Your Federal Income Tax: For Individuals.* This booklet is less than two hundred pages and is revised annually. Since it represents IRS interpretation of tax policies, it is a most important publication to have when preparing your income taxes. It also includes a listing of the nearly one hundred other detailed IRS publications on specific tax topics.

1. Determine the Gross Income

In essence, all income is subject to the federal income tax. However, on the tax form *gross income* is all income received in the form of money, property, and services that is not legally exempt from tax. For married persons in community property states (such as Arizona, California, Idaho, Louisiana, New Mexico, Nevada, Texas, Washington and Wisconsin), half of any income described by state law as community income (such as stock dividends) is considered as having been earned by each spouse. To determine the gross income, we need to examine which kinds of income are excluded from the gross income and which kinds of income are included. It is also important to understand the concept and tax consequences of capital gains and losses.

Income Included as Gross Income Most people have their income reported to them annually on a W-2 form, "Wage and Tax Statement," sent by their employer by January 31. Types of taxable income include the following:

Wages and salaries

State and local income tax refunds (if the taxpayer itemized the previous year)

Barter (the fair market value of property or services received)

Interest income (and capital gains distributions from mutual funds)

Dividends

Annuities and pensions (portions excluded)

Alimony received

Scholarship and fellowship income spent on room, board and other living expenses

Awards for artistic, scientific, and charitable achievements unless assigned to a charity

Employee productivity awards

Value of personal use of employer-provided car

Grants and tuition reductions that pay for teaching or other services

Disability payments

Prizes and contest winnings

Gambling and lottery winnings

Net rents and royalties

Commissions and tips

Bonuses

Business and farm profits and losses

Capital gains or losses on sales or exchanges of property

Income Excluded from Gross Income *Exclusions* are sources of income that are not considered legally as income for federal tax purposes, thus such income is tax-exempt. Some of the more common exclusions are:

Interest received on municipal bonds

Federal income tax refunds

Proceeds from health and accident insurance policies

Portion of annuities and pensions

Life insurance death benefits

Gifts and inheritances

Veterans benefits

Welfare, black lung, and worker's compensation benefits

Damage payments from law suits for personal injuries or illnesses

Portion of strike benefits (food and rent)

First $125,000 of the capital gain on the sale of one residence (only for persons who are fifty-five years of age or older)

Income from a car pool

Child-support payments received

Amounts paid by employers for education expenses

Cash rebates on purchases of new cars and other products

Social Security benefits (subject to limits)

Scholarship and fellowship income spent on course-required tuition, fees, books, supplies and equipment (degree candidates only)

Rental income from vacation home (subject to limits)

Employer-provided dependent care assistance as well as amounts paid by employers for medical insurance premiums and group legal services

Capital Gains and Losses   A *capital gain* is income received from the sale of a capital asset above the costs incurred to purchase and sell the asset. It is generally taxed at the same rate as other income. A *capital loss* results when the sale of a capital asset brings less income than the costs of purchasing the asset. A *capital asset* is property owned by a taxpayer for pleasure or as an investment. Examples of capital assets are stocks, bonds, real estate, household furnishings, jewelry, automobiles, and coin collections. Gains and losses on investment properties must be reported. Gains from the sale or exchange of property held for *personal use* must be reported as income, but losses are *not* deductible.

The federal government requires that gains and losses be identified as short- or long-term. A *long-term capital gain (or loss)* occurs when the asset was held for more than six months. A *short-term capital gain (or loss)* occurs when the asset was held for six months or less. In the future, Congress may reestablish a preferential lower tax rate for long-term gains in an effort to encourage investments to help the economy grow.

It is important for taxpayers to realize that not all investments are profitable, so capital losses are deductible first against capital gains (a tax break that encourages venturesome investments) and then against up to $3,000 of other income. Any remaining loss is carried forward to successive years, each with a $3,000 maximum.

Selling your home results in a capital gain that receives special tax consideration. The cost of your home includes its price, broker's commissions, and any money spent to improve the value of the property. If you bought an $80,000 home five years ago and sold it for $120,000 today, less $10,000 in selling costs, you would have a capital gain of $30,000 ($120,000 − $80,000 − $10,000). That much additional income could push you into a higher tax bracket.

The capital gain on a home can be completely avoided if another, more expensive home is purchased within twenty-four months. Also, for persons age fifty-five or over, a once-in-a-lifetime capital-gains exclusion of $125,000 is permitted, providing they have lived in the home as their principal residence for three out of the previous five years. The tax aspects of housing are examined in more detail in Chapter 9, "The Housing Expenditure," and in Chapter 19, "Investing in Real Estate."

2. Determine Adjustments to Income

It is important to reduce total income as much as possible to bring your final tax liability to its minimum legal amount. *Adjustments to income* are a selected group of legal reductions to gross income generally related to employment. These reductions are permitted whether or not you itemize deductions or take the standard deduction amount (procedures explained next in this section). Adjustments are subtracted from gross income to give *adjusted gross income (AGI)*.

Adjustments to income include business expenses for self-employed persons (such as a portion of health insurance premiums), reductions attributable to rents and royalties, interest penalties for early withdrawal of savings certificates of deposit, alimony payments, and contributions to a qualified retirement program, such as Keogh plans for the self-employed and Individual Retirement Accounts for others. For example, a person with a gross income of $24,000 contributes $1,500 to an IRA. That contribution becomes an adjustment that reduces gross income to a $22,500 adjusted gross income. Contributions to retirement plans will be covered in Chapter 21, "Social Security and Other Retirement Plans."

3. Claim Exemptions

As noted earlier, an exemption is a legally permitted deduction of the taxpayer's taxable income based on the number of persons supported by that income. Each exemption you may claim reduces taxable income by $1,950 ($2,000 in 1989 with annual adjustments for inflation beginning in 1990). You may claim an exemption for yourself, a spouse, and for other dependents. The personal exemption is phased out for higher income taxpayers. (This is explained in the footnote to Table 7–2.)

The number of exemptions you claim on your tax return may be different from what you claimed on your W-4 form filed with your employer. For example, you may have chosen to claim fewer exemptions on your W-4 form so your employer would withhold more in taxes and you would get a refund.

To claim someone else as a dependent for tax purposes and claim their exemption value, the dependent must meet six criteria:

1. More than one-half of the dependent's total support must have been provided by you. (Exceptions include children of divorced parents, who can be claimed only by the custodial parent).

2. The dependent must have received less than $3,000 in income for the year (excluding tax-exempt income such as Social Security and welfare) or, if the person is a child under the age of nineteen or a full-time student, he or she can be a dependent regardless of income earned.

3. The dependent must be a relative or, if unrelated, must have resided in your home as a member of your household.

4. The dependent must not have claimed himself or herself as an exemption on his or her own income tax return. (However, regulations permit a person claimed as an exemption by a parent to file, not claiming himself or herself as an exemption, and still take up to $500 of the standard deduction to offset unearned income, such as interest or dividends.)

5. If married, the dependent must not have filed a joint return with his or her spouse.

6. The dependent must be a U.S. citizen or a legal resident of the United States, Canada, or Mexico.

4. Identify the Standard Deduction Amount

The *standard deduction* is the amount all taxpayers (except some dependents) may deduct whenever they file an income tax return, as it is the government's legally permissible estimate of any likely tax-deductible expenses that they might have. The amount of the standard deduction is the dollar threshold, or floor, for determining whether or not the taxpayer may itemize deductions. For example, for the 1988 tax year the standard deduction amounts are $3,000 for single people, $5,000 for married couples filing jointly, $4,400 for heads of households, and $2,500 for married couples filing separate returns. For those age 65 or over or blind, an extra standard deduction of $600 is allowed each qualifying married individual, or $750 if single. (Starting in 1989 the standard deduction will be adjusted upward for inflation.) Since a great number of people do not have itemized deductions in excess of the standard deduction, they use the standard deduction amount when calculating their income tax liability.

5. List Itemized Deductions

Taxpayers who have tax-deductible expenses in *excess* of the standard deduction amount may forgo the standard deduction and list itemized deductions. *Itemized deductions* are specific expenses that can be subtracted from adjusted gross income. The following classifications of itemized deductions are listed on the tax form: (1) medical, dental, and hospital expenses; (2) taxes; (3) interest expenses; (4) charitable contributions; (5) casualty or theft losses; and (6) miscellaneous expenses. Examples of deductions in each of these categories follow.

Medical, Dental, and Hospital Expenses in Excess of 7.5 Percent of Adjusted Gross Income (not paid by insurance)

Medicine and drugs

Medical insurance premiums (including contact lens insurance)

Medical portion of auto insurance policy

Medical services (doctors, dentists, nurses, hospitals) and medical equipment (hearing aids, eyeglasses, etc.)

Home improvements made for the physically handicapped

Transportation costs to and from obtaining medical services

Taxes

Real property taxes (such as on a home or land)

Personal property taxes (such as on an automobile)

State, local, and foreign income taxes

Interest Expenses

Interest on first and second home mortgage loans

Interest on "points" paid to purchase a home or secure a home mortgage loan for improvements of a principal residence

Portion of interest and finance charges on credit card accounts and other loans (limited to 40 percent of all interest in 1988, 20 percent in 1989, 10 percent in 1990, none after 1990)

Interest on home equity loans for loan amounts up to the cost of the home plus improvements or its fair market value, whichever is the lesser (if the loan is used for education or medical purposes, the interest up to the fair market value is deductible)

Interest on loans used for investments (up to the amount of investment income)

Charitable Contributions

Cash contributions to qualified organizations (churches, schools, and other nonprofit groups)

Noncash contributions (such as personal property) at fair market value

Travel expenses incurred while performing personal services for a charitable organization

Casualty or Theft Losses in Excess of 10 Percent of Adjusted Gross Income

Casualty losses (such as from storms, vandalism, and fires) in excess of $100 not reimbursed by insurance

Theft of money or property in excess of $100 not reimbursed by insurance (a copy of the police report provides good substantiation)

Mislaid or lost property if loss results from an identifiable event that is sudden, unexpected, or unusual (such as catching a diamond ring in a car door and losing the stone)

Miscellaneous Expenses in Excess of 2 Percent of Adjusted Gross Income (partial listing only)

Union or professional association dues and membership fees

Safe-deposit box used to store papers related to income-producing stocks, bonds, or other investments

Purchase and maintenance of specialized clothing that is not suitable for off-the-job use

Unreimbursed employee business expenses (but only 80 percent of the cost of meals and entertainment)

Tax counsel and tax preparation fees

Investment advisory or management fees

Tools used in profession

Books and periodicals used in profession

Expenses for investment publications

Business use of a personal residence

Fees paid to obtain employment through an agency

Travel cost between two jobs

Medical exams required by an employer to get or keep a job

Appraisal fees on taxable types of items

Education expenses for employees required by their employer to maintain and improve skills

Travel and living expenses for job hunting in your present career field

Expenses for typing, printing, and mailing resumes for jobs in your present career field

Miscellaneous Expenses Allowed as 100 Percent Deductions

Moving expenses to a new job location, including house hunting costs (must be at least thirty-five miles from old home and you must work thirty-nine of next fifty-two weeks)

Gambling losses (but only to offset reported gambling income)

Business expenses for handicapped workers and performing artists

Given the considerable list of deductions noted here, and numerous others for which you might qualify, it makes sense to make an estimate of your possible deductions. If the total estimates exceed the standard deduction amount or are even close, go back and itemize deductions more carefully. You get no tax benefit from the expenses you pile up if you take the standard deduction instead of writing off actual costs.

At this point you are ready to calculate your *taxable income.* Taxable income is the taxpayer's gross income, minus adjustments to income, minus either the standard deduction or total itemized deductions, minus the amount to be subtracted based on the number of exemptions allowed. It is the figure used to determine the taxpayer's tax liability. You can calculate taxable income by following the step-by-step, line-by-line instructions on the tax return. The process is similar whether you itemize deductions or not.

6. Determine Whether to Use Tax Tables or Tax Rate Schedules

You will use *either* the tax table or one of the tax rate schedules to find your tax liability. For taxable incomes up to $50,000, the IRS provides a tax table that you must use to determine your tax liability. Tables 7–4 and 7–6 are segments from the tax table.

If your taxable income exceeds $50,000, you must use the tax rate schedules (shown in Table 7–2). Although the IRS rules do not allow you to choose whether you use the tax table or tax rate schedule, in fact they are equivalent and will yield nearly equal tax liabilities (within $5 to $10) if used by the same taxpayer. The tax tables and schedules are adjusted each year for inflation. Taxpayers with extremely high income and/or substantial income from tax-exempt sources may also have to use a special formula in addition to the tax rate schedules to inevitably pay an *alternative minimum tax,* or AMT.

7. Determine Tax Liability

To minimize math errors on tax returns (one out of ten returns has an error), the IRS created the tax table for use by taxpayers with taxable incomes up to $50,000. These taxpayers need only find their taxable income in the table to find their correct tax liability. For example, according to the segment of the tax table found in Table 7–4, a married couple filing jointly with a taxable income of $42,620 would have a tax liability of $8,067. A single taxpayer with the same taxable income would have a tax liability of $9,614.

Taxpayers who must use the tax rate schedules are required to do some basic calculations once their taxable income has been determined. To prove the equivalence of the tax table and the tax rate schedules, we will again consider the examples of the married couple filing jointly and the single taxpayer, both with taxable incomes of $42,620. For the married couple, refer to the tax schedules in Table 7–2. Their tax liability would be calculated as follows. Find the income bracket in the first two columns that contains their taxable income. A taxable income of $42,620 for those filing a joint return falls between the limits of

TABLE 7-6
Illustration of Portions of the Tax Table[a]

| If taxable income is | | And you are filing | | |
At least	But less than	Single	Joint Return	Head of Household
			Your tax is	
5,000	5,050	754	754	754
5,050	5,100	761	761	761
5,100	5,150	769	769	769
5,150	5,200	776	776	776
20,300	20,350	3,371	3,049	3,049
20,350	20,400	3,385	3,056	3,056
20,400	20,450	3,399	3,064	3,064
20,450	20,500	3,413	3,071	3,071
22,400	22,450	3,959	3,364	3,364
22,450	22,500	3,973	3,371	3,371
22,500	22,550	3,987	3,379	3,379
22,550	22,600	4,001	3,386	3,386
24,000	24,050	4,407	3,604	3,620
24,050	24,100	4,421	3,611	3,634
24,100	24,150	4,435	3,619	3,648
24,150	24,200	4,449	3,626	3,662
24,500	24,550	4,547	3,679	3,760
24,550	24,600	4,561	3,686	3,774
24,600	24,650	4,575	3,694	3,788
24,650	24,700	4,589	3,701	3,802
30,950	31,000	6,352	4,805	5,566
31,000	31,050	6,366	4,819	5,580
31,050	31,100	6,380	4,833	5,594
31,100	31,150	6,394	4,847	5,608
31,150	31,200	6,408	4,861	5,622
31,200	31,250	6,422	4,875	5,636
31,250	31,300	6,436	4,889	5,650
31,300	31,350	6,450	4,903	5,664

[a] Not the official IRS tax table, but derived from 1988 tax schedules.

$29,750 and $71,900, as shown in the table. The tax liability is $4,462.50 plus 28 percent of the taxable income that exceeds $29,750, or $12,870 ($42,620 − $29,750). Since 28 percent of $12,870 is $3,603.60, the tax liability would be $8,066.10 ($4,462.50 + $3,603.60), or almost exactly the tax liability drawn from the tax table ($8,067). For practice, use the tax rate schedules to calculate the tax liability of the single taxpayer and check your answer against the one obtained from the tax table. They should be very close.

More than three-quarters of all taxpayers have itemized deductions that total less than the standard deduction amount for their filing status. For example, a single person might list all possible tax deductions and find that they total only $2,700, which is $300 less than the standard deduction amount permitted for single taxpayers. In such instances, calculating the tax liability is a straightforward process: determine gross income; subtract adjustments to income, which leaves adjusted gross income; subtract the $3,000 value of the standard deduction for singles; subtract $1,950 for each exemption claimed, which results in taxable income; and find the liability by using the tax table based on the taxable income and filing status.

The following examples show how to determine tax liability.

1. A married couple filing jointly has a gross income of $45,000, $5,150 in adjustments, $3,200 in itemized deductions, and two exemptions. They take the standard deductions of $5,000 since their itemized deductions do not exceed that amount.

Gross income	$45,000
Less adjustments to income	− 5,150
Adjusted gross income	39,850
Less value of two exemptions	− 3,900
Subtotal	35,950
Less standard deduction for married couple	− 5,000
Taxable income	30,950
Tax liability (from Table 7–6)	$ 4,805

2. A single person has a gross income of $37,000, $800 in adjustments, $2,600 in itemized deductions, and one exemption. The standard deduction of $3,000 is taken as itemized deductions do not exceed that amount.

Gross income	$37,000
Less adjustments to income	− 800
Adjusted gross income	36,200
Less value of one exemption	− 1,950
Subtotal	34,250
Less standard deduction for single person	− 3,000
Taxable income	31,250
Tax liability (from Table 7–6)	$ 6,436

3. A married couple filing jointly has a gross income of $48,000, $4,400 in adjustments, two exemptions, and $8,600 in itemized deductions. They deduct their total itemized deductions as the amount is in excess of the $5,000 permitted standard deduction value.

Gross income	$48,000
Less adjustments to income	− 4,400
Adjusted gross income	43,600

Less value of two exemptions	− 3,900
Subtotal	39,700
Less total itemized deductions	− 8,600
Taxable income	31,100
Tax liability (from Table 7–6)	$ 4,847

4. A single person with a gross income of $75,000 has $400 in adjustments, one exemption, and $3,150 in itemized deductions. The itemized deductions are taken because they exceed the standard deduction value of $3,000 for singles.

Gross income	$75,000
Less adjustments to income	− 400
Adjusted gross income	74,600
Less value of one exemption	− 1,950
Subtotal	72,650
Less total itemized deductions	− 3,150
Taxable income	69,500
Tax liability, calculated from the tax rate schedules in Table 7–2 because the taxable income is above $50,000, which is as high as the tax tables go. The tax liability is computed as follows: $9,761.50 + [.33 × ($69,500 − $43,150)] = $18,457).	$18,457

8. Subtract Tax Credits to Find the Final Tax Liability

After all your diligent efforts to itemize and to reduce your tax liability, you may lower it even more through *tax credits*. These are a group of items that you can subtract dollar for dollar from your tax liability, and you can do so whether or not you itemize deductions. Subtracting tax credits directly reduces tax liability to *final tax liability*, which is the amount you actually owe the government. It will be helpful to look now at Figure 7–1 which diagrams the entire process of income taxation.

There are many special tax credits. Tax credits are available to businesspersons for payment of foreign taxes and employment of special targeted groups. The elderly are allowed a credit while receiving public disability benefits. Tax credits are also available to taxpayers for making payments to care for a child or a disabled dependent, and there is also a credit for some people with a low earned income.

Child and Dependent Care Credit A credit of up to 30 percent of the cost for caring for a child or disabled dependent is available. The child or dependent care expenses must have been necessary because the taxpayer(s) was working, seeking work, or attending school full-time. A maximum of $720 can be claimed as a credit on expenses totaling a maximum of $2,400 ($2,400 × .30 = $720). For taxpayers with two or more qualifying dependents, the credit is permitted on a maximum of $4,800 in costs, resulting in a maximum $1,440 credit ($4,800 × .30 = $1,440). The credit is 30 percent of child or dependent care expenses if adjusted gross income is $10,000 or less. The 30 per-

FIGURE 7–1
The Process of Income Taxation

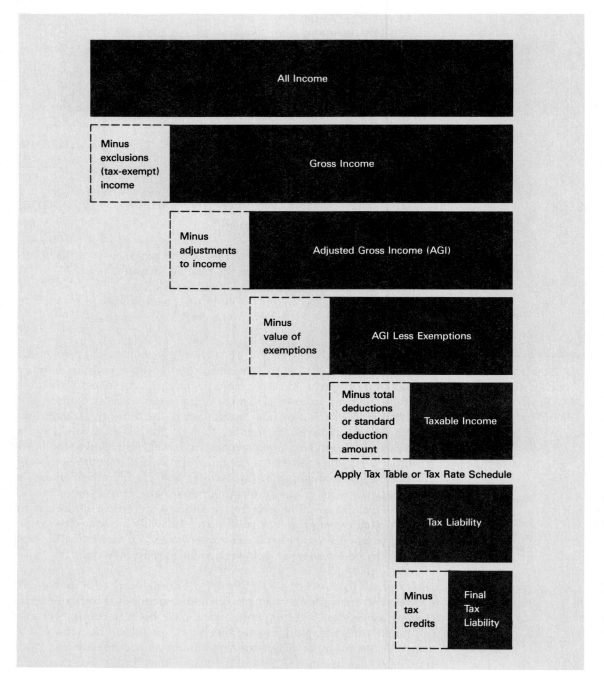

cent is reduced by one percent for each $2,000 of adjusted gross income, or part of $2,000, above $10,000 until the percentage is reduced to 20 percent for income above $28,000.

Such expenses could include home upkeep, cooking, and general care, such as a nursery. The taxpayer must have earned some income during the year; income from part-time employment qualifies. To get the credit, married taxpayers must file a joint return (unless they are living apart) and must have worked during the year. A spouse is also classified as working if he or she was a full-time student or incapacitated during five months of the tax year.

Earned Income Credit   The earned income credit is available for those whose earned income (wages, salaries, and so forth) and adjusted gross income are each less than $17,000 (even $0) and who have a child living with them for the whole year. The $17,000 of earned income does not include pensions or annuities (other than disability pensions), Social Security payments, worker's compensation, or unemployment compensation. A taxpayer filing as married or a qualifying widow or widower who seeks the credit must have a child who is a dependent (whether married or not); a taxpayer filing as head of household qualifies if there is a married child in the home even though the child is not a dependent. A person who might not otherwise have to file an income tax return could, if qualified, file for the earned income credit and obtain a refund (a form of negative income tax) of up to $800.

9. Calculate the Balance Due or Refund

After subtracting your tax credits, you have your final tax liability. Now look at your W-2 form, "Wage and Tax Statement," which summarizes your income and withholding for the year. The key figure is the federal income tax withheld. If the amount withheld is larger than your final tax liability, then you should receive a tax refund. If the amount withheld is less than your final tax liability, then you have a tax balance due. Before mailing your return, attach to it a check or money order made out to the IRS in the amount owed.

Taxpayers generally hear from the IRS within three weeks if they have failed to sign the tax return, neglected to attach a copy of the W-2 form, made an error in arithmetic, or used the wrong tax table or tax rate schedules. Refunds are usually received within six weeks.

Calculating Tax Liability: Some Examples

Below are examples of calculating tax liability for different types of taxpayers: college students, a single working person, and a married couple with two children and a dependent adult.

College Students

Joe Thales, who attends Michigan State University, plays football and receives a partial grant-in-aid of $4,800 ($2,000 was for room and board). In a part-time job last summer, he earned $1,600 ($290 was withheld for federal income taxes), and his savings account earned interest of $62. Joe owes no federal income taxes, as his total income totals $3,662 ($2,000 + $1,600 + $62), which is less than the value of his exemption ($1,950) and standard deduction ($3,000) combined. He should file Form 1040-EZ, which the IRS calls the "very short form," to obtain a refund of the income tax withheld by his summer employer.

Susan Blackstone graduated last year from California State University at Fresno, where she enjoyed a swimming scholarship in the amount of $1,600. She has worked since graduation and earned $9,100 last year ($944 was withheld for federal income taxes). She also earned $300 in interest on her savings account. Her tax-deductible expenses amounted to $390. Susan should file Form 1040A since she earned more than $4,950, but her itemized deductions are not enough to list. Her adjusted gross income of $10,000 includes $9,100 in salary, $300 in interest, and $600 in scholarship money (the portion allocated for housing; the remaining $1,000 was for fees and books and thus not considered taxable income). Susan subtracts the value of a personal exemption, $1,950, and another $3,000 for the standard deduction to determine her taxable income of $5,050. Using the tax table in Table 7–6, she determines her tax liability to be $761. Subtracting the $761 from the $944 withheld yields a refund due her of $183.

Single Working Person

Hanna Heine of Baton Rouge, Louisiana, took a position at a small engineering company two years ago. Last year she earned $28,400 and her employer withheld $3,850 in income taxes. Her gross income was reduced by a $1,000 contribution to an individual retirement account (IRA) as an adjustment to income. Her itemized expenses came to only $2,250, so she took the standard deduction of $3,000. Her taxable income, after subtracting $1,950 for herself as an exemption, was $22,450 ($28,400 − $1,000 − $3,000 − $1,950). Her tax as shown in Table 7–6 was $3,973. She was very upset at both the magnitude of her tax liability and the fact that she owed the government an additional $123 ($3,973 − $3,850).

This year, Hanna got a $1,600 raise to $30,000, and her employer withheld $4,100. She was determined to reduce her federal income taxes by becoming a home owner. She made a $500 contribution to an IRA, which reduced her adjusted gross income. She bought a condominium in January, and during the year she paid out $4,800 in interest expenses and $320 in real estate taxes. Hanna had $2,050 in other itemized deductions as well. Her total itemizations amounted to $7,170 ($4,800 + $320 + $2,050). Combining the $500 adjustment, the $7,170 in deductions, and $1,950 for the value of an exemption reduced her gross income to a $20,380 taxable income ($30,000 − $500 − $7,170 −

$1,950). The resulting tax liability was $3,385, and she received an income tax refund of $715 ($4,100 − $3,385).

Hanna was pleased that her tax bill had gone down, and as she was curious, she recalculated it assuming that she had not purchased a home. With a gross income of $30,000 less a $500 adjustment, a $1,950 exemption, and a $3,000 standard deduction (since she could not itemize without the housing deductions), she would have had a taxable income of $24,550 and her final tax liability would have been $4,561. Hanna's actual tax bill of $3,385 was $1,176 less than what it would have been had she not bought the condominium. She correctly concluded that the IRS actually "paid" $1,176 toward the purchase of her condominium and her living costs there, since she did not pay those dollars to the government.

Married Couple

Heinz and Rosetta Klingstead of Carbondale, Illinois, have a complex income tax return because they have both made it a habit to learn about possible tax deductions and to take advantage of them whenever possible. Table 7–7 shows the Klingsteads' income and various reductions.

The Klingsteads have two small children as well as Heinz's mother living at their home. By "thinking taxes," they have taken advantage of all applicable adjustments, deductions, and credits. Part of their income also comes from tax-exempt sources. Their deductions and tax credits, typical for a couple with two children, result in a final tax liability of $3,011.

The marginal tax rate for the Klingsteads is 15 percent. Their average tax rate compared to all income is 6.1 percent ($3,011 ÷ $49,550); compared to gross income, it is 6.7 percent ($3,011 ÷ $44,800); and compared to taxable income, it is 13.4 percent ($3,011 ÷ $22,450). For a family with such a substantial income, they have been quite successful in lowering their final tax liability.

Avoiding Taxes

At the beginning of this chapter, we defined taxes as compulsory charges imposed by a government on citizens and property. Although you must pay taxes, you do not have to pay more than is required. If you are knowledgeable about tax laws and regulations and assertive in your financial planning, you can avoid overpayment of taxes.

This section discusses ways to avoid overpaying taxes by (1) understanding the difference between tax avoidance and tax evasion, (2) recognizing the opportunity cost of a dollar paid in taxes, (3) avoiding the inherent bias in taxation against some married couples, (4) developing an attitude of "thinking taxes," (5) examining methods of reducing taxable income, and (6) increasing deductions.

TABLE 7–7
Income Tax Calculations for a Married Couple
(Heinz and Rosetta Klingstead)

All income
Heinz's salary	$27,700	
Rosetta's salary	15,000	
Capital gains (sales of stock)	450	
Rosetta's year-end bonus	1,000	
State income tax refund (itemized last year)	180	
Interest on savings account	350	
Dividends on stocks	120	
Interest on tax-exempt state bonds	2,000	
Gift from Rosetta's mother	2,500	
Car-pool income (Heinz's van pool)	250	
Total all income		$49,550

Minus tax-exempt income   − 4,750
    ($2,000 + $2,500 + $250)
Gross income $44,800

Adjustments to income
Payment to Heinz's retirement account	$ 1,000	
Payment to Rosetta's retirement account	1,000	

Minus adjustments to income   − 2,000
Adjusted gross income (AGI) $42,800

Deductions
Medical expenses	$3,500	
Exclusion (7.5% of AGI)	3,210	
Total		$ 290

Taxes
Real property	$1,800	
Personal property	210	
Total		$2,010

Interest expense
Home mortgage	$6,190	
Home equity loan	160	
Total		$6,350

Contributions
Church	$1,200	
Other charities	240	
Goodwill	300	
Charitable travel	90	
Total		$1,830

Casualty or theft
Loss—diamond ring	$4,500	
Insurance reimbursement	− 0	
Reduction	− 100	
Exclusion (10% of AGI)	−4,280	
Total		$ 120

Miscellaneous
Union dues (Heinz)	$ 280	
Safe-deposit box	30	
Investment publications	60	
Tax publications	20	
Subtotal	390	

TABLE 7–7
(continued)

Less 2% of AGI	− 856	
Total		0
Minus total itemized deductions		−10,600
Minus exemptions (5 @ $1,950)		− 9,750
Taxable income		$22,450
Tax liability (from Table 7–6)		3,371
Tax credits		
Child care	$1,800	
80% exclusion	−1,440	
Minus tax credits		360
Final tax liability		$ 3,011

Avoidance, Not Evasion

Tax evasion is illegal. It involves deliberately hiding income, falsely claiming deductions, or otherwise cheating the government out of taxes owed. A waiter who does not report tips received as income is guilty of tax evasion, as is a person who deducts $150 in church contributions but who has not contributed to a church in years. *Tax avoidance* is different. It is avoiding taxes by reducing tax liability through legal techniques. This involves applying knowledge of the tax code and regulations to personal income tax.

The U.S. Supreme Court in 1945 upheld the "legal right of a taxpayer to decrease the amount of what otherwise would be his taxes, or to avoid them altogether, by means which the law permits." Judge Learned Hand wrote further that "nobody owes any public duty to pay more than the law demands; taxes are enforced extractions, not voluntary contributions. To demand more in the name of morals is mere cant."

Tax evasion results in penalties, fines, excess interest charges, and an occasional jail sentence. Tax avoidance, on the other hand, results in paying less in taxes and having more money to spend, save or invest.

A Dollar Saved Is Really Two Dollars

Sufficient reason to avoid taxes can be illustrated in two ways. First, there is the concept of *opportunity cost*. This is the cost of a decision measured in terms of the value of forgone opportunities. By deciding to watch television at home for three hours on a warm summer day, for example, you give up enjoying those same hours on a nearby beach, or playing a neighborhood game of volleyball, or sleeping. Similarly, giving up an extra dollar in taxes also has a cost. By paying a dollar in taxes, you lose not only the dollar paid but also the alternative use for another dollar that must take the place of the dollar paid. Thus, a dollar saved in taxes is two dollars saved.

Second, a dollar also becomes two dollars (or more) when the concept of true marginal tax rate is considered. A single person earning a taxable income of $46,000 has a marginal tax rate of 33 percent. Adding 7 percent in Social Security taxes and a 6 percent state income tax results in a "true" marginal tax rate of 46 percent. Consequently, for every $2 earned, this person pays nearly $1 ($2 × .46 = $.92) in taxes. Conversely, for every $1 saved in taxes this person would have $2 available to spend, save, or invest. Taxpayers in the higher tax brackets realize the largest proportional benefit by saving a dollar in taxes.

The Marriage Tax Penalty

We are not advocating divorce, but it could actually save money for some people. One of the inequities in our current progressive income tax system is that it contains a *marriage tax penalty*. This is due to the fact that many two-earner married couples pay more in income taxes than they would if they were single because the pooled incomes boost them into a higher tax bracket than they faced as singles.

Here's how the system works. (These calculations are derived from Table 7–2.) A single person earning a taxable income of $25,000 pays income taxes in the amount of $4,679.50. Should that person get married to a person who has no income and they file a joint return, the tax is reduced to $3,157.60. The tax liability drops because by filing together they receive an extra exemption of $1,950 and a standard deduction amount of $5,000, instead of $3,000 for a single. The impression given is that marriage reduces tax liabilities. It does for a few, but for many the marriage tax penalty subjects millions of married persons to higher tax bills than singles. The inequity is serious. The marriage penalty exists when the spouse who earns less contributes approximately 25 percent or more toward total income.

To illustrate, Table 7–8 shows the final tax liabilities of married and unmarried couples earning a total taxable income of $50,000. Unmarried couples where one partner's taxable income is $37,500 and the other's is $12,500 have a $78 lower tax liability. As the income split nears $25,000 for each partner, the married couple must pay up to an additional $773.50 in taxes! Thus, a married couple would pay 8.3 percent ($773.50 ÷ $9,359) more taxes on precisely the same taxable income merely because they are married.

For $773.50, a married couple may not be willing to get a divorce. But for married couples with extremely high incomes there may be enough difference in tax liability to finance a divorce in late December

TABLE 7–8
Marriage Penalty Tax Illustration (Total Couple Taxable Income, $50,000)

Income Split		Income		Unmarried Tax Liability	Married Tax Liability	Extra Tax Liability
Spouse 1	Spouse 2	Spouse 1	Spouse 2			
75%	25%	$37,500	$12,500	$10,054.50	$10,132.50	$ 78.00
60	40	30,000	20,000	9,359.00	10,132.50	773.50
50	50	25,000	25,000	9,359.00	10,132.50	773.50

and a one-week vacation at a resort. Then upon their return in January, they could remarry, only to repeat the process the next year, in effect letting Uncle Sam pay for all their expenses. The IRS has ruled that quickie "tax divorces" are a form of tax evasion. Meanwhile, the marriage tax penalty remains, and an increasing number of married couples divorce but still live together, to save tax dollars.

"Thinking Taxes"

You have seen that considering the financial impact of taxation is important. The timing of decisions is crucial.

One problem confronting many young people is not having enough itemized deductions to exceed the standard deduction amount. By shifting the payment dates of some deductible items, you can increase your deductions. For example, if you have $2,700 of deductible expenses this year, you could prepay some items in December to push the total over the $3,000 threshold and receive the tax advantage of having excess deductions. The next year you can simply take the standard deduction amount. This process is known as *bunching deductions*. Some items that can be prepaid are medical expenses, dental bills, real estate taxes, personal property taxes, dues in professional associations, and church donations.

By *postponing income* you can have the same result. Say you expect a year-end commission check of $3,000; the extra income might be enough to push you into paying a higher marginal tax rate. If your employer is willing to date the commission check in January, the income need not be reported until the next year, when tax rates might not be as high. Or your tax bracket may be lower because you anticipate lower sales commissions or know that you will not work full time (if you return to school, have a child, decide to travel, and so forth).

It would be tax-wise for people earning similar incomes to wait until January to get married. The marriage tax penalty they save could help pay for the honeymoon! In the cases of divorce, if one spouse earns most of the income, a couple could save taxes by having the judge sign the divorce decree in January instead of December. Also in divorce situations, the former spouse with the higher income can claim the children as exemptions, and thus save a substantial amount of money, if the custodial parent signs a waiver for the exemption. (A $1,950 exemption is worth only $292.50 to someone in the 15 percent bracket but $643.50 to someone in the 33 percent bracket.)

Reducing Taxable Income

It may sound obvious that to lower tax liability you should reduce taxable income. This advice is often ignored, however. The wise financial planner will reduce taxable income through tax-exempt income, income splitting (or shifting), and tax shelters. Also, because the personal income taxes collected by states and municipalities are usually based on federal taxable income, reducing federal taxable income through adjustments to income will reduce other tax liabilities.

Tax-exempt Income   Taxpayers in higher income brackets (28 percent or higher) often can gain by purchasing tax-exempt bonds issued by various agencies of states and municipalities. For example, assume Joyce Bundy of Johnson City, Texas, currently has $5,000 in savings earning 9 percent, or $450 annually. She pays $126 in tax on that income at her 28 percent marginal tax rate. A tax-exempt $5,000 state bond paying 7 percent will provide her with a better after-tax return. She would receive $350 tax free from the state bond compared to $324 ($450 − $126) after taxes on the income from savings. The increase in after-tax income is $26 ($350 − $324). Finding tax-exempt income is a strategy to reduce your tax liability, sometimes considerably. This topic is discussed in detail in Chapter 16, "Investing in Bonds."

Income Splitting (or Shifting)   *Income splitting* takes place when one person with a high marginal tax rate shifts income to another person who is in a lower tax bracket (or who pays no taxes at all). Suppose a parent wants to create a college fund for a child and presently has $5,000 in a savings account earning 7 percent interest income ($350 annually). If the parent gives the child the $5,000, the parent will not have any interest income on which to pay taxes, perhaps at the 33 percent rate. To the parent, shifting income represents an immediate gain of $116 ($350 × .33), as that amount will not go to the government. Assuming that the child has no other source of taxable income, no taxes will have to be paid. After ten years with compound interest at 7 percent, the child's college fund will have grown to $9,835, although the child would have owed some small tax liabilities through some of the years.

Tax Shelters   Have you ever wished you could have a tax shelter like wealthy people do? People paying high tax rates can be easily enticed into investing in some rather risky ventures that most of us would never consider. This is because losses are partially "paid for" by the government since the high-income taxpayer reports the loss as a tax loss. If an investor in the 33 percent bracket puts $1,000 into an investment that fails, it could be a $1,000 tax loss used to offset $1,000 in other income. That means the investor does not have to pay $333 in taxes since the money was already lost in the investment, and in reality the investor is out only $667. Examples of such tax-shelter investments not covered in this text are cattle-feeding operations, leasing of business assets, production of films, and oil- and gas-drilling programs. Sophisticated investment "opportunities" become available, in part, because of our high marginal tax rates.

    Tax losses are paper losses, in the sense that they do not represent out-of-pocket losses, created when deductions generated from an investment (such as depreciation) exceed the income from the investment. By 1990, most investors will no longer be able to use passive activity tax losses to offset ordinary taxable income, such as wages, interest, dividends, and stock market profits. *Passive activity* means that you do not "materially participate" in the management of a trade or business. Passive tax losses can be used only to offset income from other passive sources.

An exception is allowed for real estate investors who (1) have an adjusted gross income of $150,000 or less and (2) actively participate in the management of the property, as they may deduct up to $25,000 of net losses from passive investments against regular income. For example, a residential real estate investment property could be generating an annual cash income $1,000 greater than the out-of-pocket operating costs. With depreciation expenses on the building taken as a tax deduction, however, the result could be a $1,500 tax loss, and this amount can be used to offset other income. Thus, useful tax shelters remain for most taxpayers, because tax losses may be taken for investments in real estate and limited partnerships, both discussed in Chapter 19, "Investing in Real Estate."

With few exceptions, a tax shelter does not permit an investor to avoid taxes. Rather, *tax shelters* are methods of deferring taxes until a later date when the tax rate might be lower. During the interim period the taxpayer gains an alternative use of the money not yet given the government as well as the time value of such funds.

The tax shelters emphasized in this text are individual retirement accounts (IRAs), salary reduction plans, and Keogh accounts. They are aimed at putting money that would be taxed at high rates into qualified retirement programs that will provide income during later years, presumably at much lower tax rates. It is sufficient to point out at this time that putting $2,000 into a qualified account permits the taxpayer to use that amount immediately as an adjustment to income, thus lowering the tax liability for the current year. These tax-sheltered programs are detailed in Chapter 21, "Social Security and Other Retirement Plans."

Increasing Tax Deductions

If, in an effort to reduce taxable income, you increase expenses, won't you have less money? Not necessarily. IRS Publication 17 and other tax-information publications describe what tax deductions you can take. An almost sure way to increase itemized deductions, for example, is to purchase a home with a mortgage loan. The large amounts of money home owners pay out for interest and real property taxes are deductible. (The pros and cons of obtaining a mortgage are examined in detail in Chapter 9, "The Housing Expenditure.") Remember that when you itemize, every dollar counts. If you are in the 28-percent bracket, an extra dollar in a found deduction puts twenty-eight cents back in your pocket.

Here are just a few ways to increase your taxable deductions and put more tax dollars back into your pockets. Assume you are in the 28 percent marginal tax bracket. Cash contributions made to people collecting door to door or at the shopping center during holidays are deductible, even though receipts are not given. (The IRS reasonably expects people to make such contributions). Fifty dollars in contributions deducted can save you $14 in taxes. Instead of throwing out an old television set, donate it. An $80 charitable contribution (get a receipt) will save you $22. Expenses for business-related trips can be a most fruitful area for tax deductions. If you take one business trip a year for $400 in deductible expenses, you will save another $112 in taxes assuming your miscellaneous deductions already exceed 2 percent of your AGI. In other words, Uncle Sam foots the bill for 28 percent of the cost of the trip.

Preparation of Tax Returns

It has been said that taxes are the price we pay for our free society. In reality we pay even a little more, by spending the time, and sometimes money, to prepare and send in income tax returns.

Superficially, the task seems easy enough. If you earn a moderate income and have no itemized deductions, you complete tax form 1040A or 1040EZ. All others send in tax form 1040 with extra supporting forms. Often, however, it is not so easy. Each year the directions for filling out tax forms are "simplified" but can still be confusing. And the tax code is frequently changed by Congress. Tax regulations and court rulings are published almost weekly. Completing your income tax return correctly *and* paying the lowest tax possible requires considerable effort. You have three options at tax preparation time. You can let the IRS do it, use a tax preparation service, lawyer, or CPA, or fill out the return yourself.

Aid from the Internal Revenue Service

The IRS makes tax publications available, handles questions from taxpayers on a toll-free hotline (mostly a busy signal around tax time), and will complete a taxpayer's form to determine final tax liability. To have the IRS compute your tax liability you must (1) have an adjusted gross income of $20,000 or less ($40,000 or less if filing jointly), (2) have income entirely from salaries, wages, tips, interest, dividends, pensions, or annuities, (3) have no itemized deductions, (4) complete the entire first page of the return, (5) complete all supporting schedules, and (6) mail the return by April 15. The IRS will look up your tax liability on the appropriate tax table and, if you qualify, calculate your earned-income credit.

Using Tax Preparation Services, Lawyers, and CPAs

If you can read and follow directions, you can fill out Form 1040A or Form 1040EZ, which do not permit itemized deductions and which are the tax forms filled out by most people. Taxpayers who have adjustments to income or who itemize deductions may want to turn to either a national or local tax preparation service.

National *tax preparation services* specialize in completing individual taxpayer's income tax returns and are affiliated with a nationally advertised tax service (such as H & R Block). Local tax preparation services do not have such an affiliation but typically offer tax advice year round to business customers as well as individuals. Both can help you list appropriate deductions, compute accurately, and determine proper tax liability. National services are not necessarily better than local ones. Choose a tax preparation service with a staff that asks lots of questions about possible deductions and searches for ways to legally reduce your liability.

Most taxpayers will not need the special services of a lawyer or a certified public accountant (CPA) to complete their tax forms. One reason to see a lawyer would be for a recommendation on alternative investments from a tax perspective. Help from a CPA, preferably one who is certified to represent clients before the IRS, should again be reserved for complicated tax matters. Lawyers and CPAs will complete your return just as accurately as a tax preparation service but will charge more.

Preparing Your Own Tax Return

When someone other than the taxpayer prepares a return, including friends and relatives, the law requires the preparer to put his or her name and address at the bottom of the form. You may be surprised to hear that getting help from others does not substantially reduce math errors, nor does it always result in obtaining advice on deductions with which the IRS will agree.

IRS Advice May Not Be Valid

IRS advice received over the telephone, in person, or even from IRS publications is not final. In audits, which are discussed below, the IRS frequently overrules tax advice given out by its representatives. Not all IRS personnel are well versed in all IRS policies. Various studies have shown that about one-half of returns prepared by all types of tax specialists have an error, such as inaccurate math or an incorrect deduction.

Taxes Can Be Fun

If income taxes are something you definitely do not want to get involved with, then by all means find someone to complete your tax returns. If, on the other hand, the prospect challenges you, you can have fun at it. You yourself can be the one best prepared to reduce your tax liability. Study Publication 17, *Your Federal Income Tax,* to learn what is deductible and what is not. Only you know the personal quirks in your expenditures that could qualify for tax deductions. Only you can review other commercially available tax preparation booklets (which are themselves tax deductible) to find overlooked areas for possible deductions. (Such publications do not give the narrow IRS perspective on deductions; they offer suggestions on what is probably deductible given certain circumstances.) Finally, only you have the assertiveness to take a deduction because you believe it is deductible. A tax adviser can give you guidance, but only you can make the decision.

We believe that taxpayers need to learn about taxes and complete the forms themselves. It is wise to seek professional assistance to see if there is some area of taxation you might have overlooked or if dramatic changes have occurred in your life (such as marriage or divorce, or a business opening or failure). In no time at all, you can become the expert on your own taxes.

What If You Are Audited?

With nearly one hundred million tax returns coming in annually, it is no wonder that the IRS can audit only a very small percentage. A *tax audit* is a formal examination of a taxpayer's tax forms for accuracy and completeness. This is done to motivate others to complete their tax returns properly (if you are audited, you usually tell friends about it) and to collect the proper amounts due.

With computer assistance, the IRS subjects *each* return to a series of reasonableness tests. These tests, revised each year, are numbers based on average deductions. For example, for a married couple with two exemptions, medical deductions usually amount to X and contributions amount to Y. Returns that exceed these averages are sorted for examination by a person who decides whether they will be audited. A police report attached to a return to document a large casualty loss (even though not required by the IRS) might convince the IRS person not to conduct an audit. Other returns are audited on a random basis. Chances of an audit are about one out of every one hundred earning an AGI of $10,000 to $25,000, two out of every one hundred earning $25,000 to $50,000, and four out of every one hundred earning over $50,000. For those deducting losses from an unusual tax shelter, the chances rise to two out of every three.

Types of Audits

Audits can be *complete, item,* or *section.* In most cases, subjects for the rarely conducted complete audit are selected randomly. In this audit, each deduction must be proven to the satisfaction of the auditor. (Complete audits help the IRS establish the numbers for their reasonableness tests.) Note, though, that the taxpayer needn't have a receipt for every deduction; the IRS takes estimates for many items.

Much more likely is an item audit, in which the IRS questions a particular deduction and wants documentation. It could be home mortgage loan interest of $6,800; it could be a contribution of $2,600. Most of these audits are conducted entirely by mail. A section audit requires the taxpayer to visit the nearest IRS office to document all items in a particular section of the form (such as "miscellaneous").

Advice If You Are Audited

If you are audited, consider it a challenge. Get prepared and enjoy the opportunity to see how the system works. Most auditors are well trained and courteous. They realize that you may be nervous and will attempt to put you at ease. But do not forget the purpose of the meeting: the IRS wants to get more dollars out of your pocket if possible. Therefore, do not (1) be overly chatty with the auditor, (2) offer a bribe (a federal marshal will arrest you even if you are kidding), (3) talk about other deductions that you took elsewhere on the form or took in an earlier year (the auditor can broaden the investigation if other problem areas are suspected), (4) bring any records not asked for in the letter explaining the purpose of the audit, (5) volunteer any extra information. However, *do* realize that if your judgment on the correctness of a deduction seems right you do not have to accept the auditor's judgment. Request an appeal on the item(s) about which you believe you are right, read more on the topic, and return in a few weeks to see the regional appeals officer, who will give you an opportunity to present your arguments. For a nominal fee you can further appeal an issue to the U.S. Tax Court (just like a small claims court). The court's decision on your case is legally binding for you but does not set a precedent for all other taxpayers as does the expensive process of proving a case in the federal courts.

Only about two hundred people a year go to jail for tax evasion. The IRS wants money, not jail sentences. If the IRS disagrees with your deductions and disallows something, you will owe them two or possibly three payments. First, you must pay the increased tax liability. For example, assume the IRS disallowed a $400 deduction and you are in the 28 percent bracket; your additional tax is $112 ($400 multiplied by .28). Second, interest on the additional tax liability is assessed from the date the tax "should have" been paid. If the audit takes place in April of the following year, the interest charge might be $12. (The IRS interest rate has varied from 9 to 14 percent in recent years.) Third, you may owe a penalty on the tax if the IRS concludes that you avoided the additional tax liability because of serious negligence on your part (a 5 percent penalty) or willful deception (a 50 percent penalty), which is also known as tax evasion. Having a deduction disallowed usually does not result in a penalty.

Other Types of Federal, State, and Local Taxes

There are other types of taxes besides the federal income tax. The most important is the Social Security tax, which is discussed in detail in Chapter 21. This tax results from the Federal Insurance Contribution Act (FICA), which is a combination of eleven different programs designed to prevent people from becoming destitute. Two of the larger programs are old-age benefits and Medicare.

The Social Security tax is a tax on earnings, and equal amounts are paid by employers and employees. To increase revenues, Congress regularly raises both the tax rate and the base upon which the rate is applied. For example, in a recent year the Social Security tax was 7.51 percent applied on earned income up to a maximum of $46,800 (maximum tax $3,514.68). Reducing your Social Security tax is extremely difficult to do, as the tax rate is applied to earned income.

Taxpayers also pay a considerable amount in personal income taxes to states and municipalities. Reduction of this tax liability generally can be accomplished by reducing your federal adjusted gross income as much as possible (using adjustments to income) and by studying the state and local tax guidelines, as they often permit other special deductions not allowed on the federal form. Most other federal, state, and local taxes are difficult to avoid.

Table 7–9 shows amounts of various taxes to be paid by Robert Chong of Brooklyn, New York, who earns $39,000 annually. More than 31 percent ($12,395 ÷ $39,000) of his income goes to pay various taxes—and this is the average for all Americans. Robert can probably reduce his federal income tax liability by finding more tax deductions. For instance, if he bought a home both real property taxes and mortgage loan interest expenses would be deductions. With careful analysis of income taxes, all taxpayers can increase monies available to spend, save, and invest—activities which are the focus of the rest of this textbook.

TABLE 7–9
Federal, State, and Local Taxes (for Robert Chong)

Gross income		$39,000
Taxes		
Federal income tax ($30,000 taxable income)	$6,080	
Social Security tax (assumed at 7.5%)	2,925	
State income tax (assumed at 6%)	1,800	
City or county income tax (assumed at 2%)	600	
Sales taxes (state/county/city assumed at 5% on $15,000 consumption)	750	
Use taxes (gasoline, cigarettes, liquor, assumed at various rates)	80	
Personal property taxes (assessed on three-year-old automobile)	160	
Estate taxes (assumes taxpayer lived)	–	
Inheritance taxes (assumes taxpayer did not inherit)	–	
Gift taxes (assumes taxpayer did not give large sums away)	–	
Total annual taxes		12,395
Money available to spend, save, and invest		$26,605

Summary

1. An important principle of taxation is fairness, or equity, but the most important is the concept of the true marginal tax rate.

2. United States citizens and residents of the United States or of Puerto Rico must file a federal income tax return if they have earned sufficient income.

3. The lowest marginal tax rates are paid by taxpayers who are married and filing a joint return.

4. To help ensure getting the tax liability due it, the government requires payroll withholding for most of us and estimated taxes for others.

5. Nine steps are involved in reducing gross income down to final tax liability using a variety of legal techniques, such as exclusions from total income, adjustments to income, deductions, exemptions, and credits.

6. A philosophy of legally avoiding taxes requires the development of the attitude to "think taxes" to reduce taxable income in achievable ways and to increase tax deductions.

7. Four choices are available in preparing a tax return: let the IRS do it, use a tax preparation service, have it done by a lawyer and/or CPA, and fill out the return yourself; the last technique allows the taxpayer to become the expert.

8. Besides the federal income tax, there exists a variety of other taxes, with Social Security being the largest for most people.

Modern Money Management

The Johnsons Calculate Their Income Taxes

Harry and Belinda are both working hard and earning good salaries. However, they feel that they are paying too much in federal income taxes. Calculate their income taxes this year and then give them some tax-planning advice.

The Johnsons' total income included Harry's salary of $17,850, Belinda's salary of $24,800, $355 interest on savings, $80 interest on checking, $3,000 from the trust, $90 refund from Belinda's health insurance claim, $210 state income tax refund (they did not itemize last year), $390 federal income tax refund, and a $400 cash gift from Harry's aunt.

1. What is the Johnsons' reportable gross income?
2. Harry put $500 into an individual retirement account last year, so what is their adjusted gross income?

3. Assuming that they file a joint federal income tax return, what is the total value of their exemptions?

4. How much is the allowable standard deduction permissible for the Johnsons?

5. They have $3,600 in itemized deductions; should they itemize or take the standard deduction?

6. What is the Johnsons' taxable income?

7. As the Johnsons have no tax credits, what is their final tax liability?

8. Since they had $8,160 in federal income taxes withheld, what will be their refund?

9. What is their marginal tax rate?

10. Based on gross income, what is their actual tax rate?

11. List four or five things the Johnsons can do to reduce their tax liability for next year. Even though they are renters, assume the Johnsons had a home with monthly payments of nearly $800, or $9,600 for the year. The sum of $8,400 might go for interest and real estate property taxes, both of which are tax deductible. That would give them $12,000 ($8,400 + $3,600) in itemized deductions. Calculate their taxable income and final tax liability, assuming the $12,000 instead of taking the standard deduction.

12. What is your advice to the Johnsons about the tax wisdom of purchasing a home instead of renting?

Key Words and Concepts

Review Questions

1. Describe the four characteristics of an ideal tax.

2. Which federal agency is charged with the responsibility of collecting federal income taxes? From what basis does this agency get its direction? What body is primarily responsible for writing the federal income tax laws?

3. Distinguish between a progressive and a regressive tax.

4. Explain and illustrate how your marginal tax rate from a tax table or schedule (see Table 7–2) will differ when you compare it with an average tax rate as a percentage of gross income.

5. When would a taxpayer need to use a tax table? A tax rate schedule?

6. Identify the factors used to determine the true marginal tax rate. Give an example of how a true marginal tax rate will differ from a marginal tax rate when these factors are applied.

7. Name two special instances in which it would be wise to file a tax return if not required by law.

8. Explain how your lifestyle determines your filing status.

9. Describe how an employer can be identified as a collector of taxes for the federal government. What is this way of paying taxes called?

10. Name one disadvantage that accrues to an employee if an employer overwithholds taxes from a regular paycheck. Identify both the short- and long-term effects of this practice.

11. List the nine steps used in calculating income tax and describe the important features of each step.

12. List five examples of exclusions to income.

13. List five examples of taxable income that must be reported to the IRS.

14. Identify two adjustments to income.

15. List five examples of tax-deductible items.

16. Describe what must be true for a parent to claim a child as an exemption.

17. What is the advantage of being able to qualify for and use tax credits?

18. Outline the general step-by-step process to follow to determine final tax liability.

19. Assume you go from being a college student to a successful employee with a substantial income. How will this affect your tax liability?

20. Name the five types of minuses or reductions that are subtracted from all income in the process of calculating final tax liability.

21. Give several examples of tax-related earnings or expenditures that might appear on a complex tax return.

22. State one reason why a taxpayer would want to be considered guilty of tax avoidance rather than tax evasion.

23. Illustrate the concept of opportunity cost with income taxes.

24. Explain why a married couple might consider divorce as a way of saving taxes.

25. Name four legal ways in which a person can reduce taxable income.

26. Give some reasons why taxpayers may want to have someone else prepare their tax returns.

27. List the guidelines to consider if the IRS cites you for a tax audit.

28. Name other types of taxes that are typically paid by taxpayers.

Case Problems

1. James Burton of Sacramento, California, is interested in the relationship between marginal tax rates and average tax rates.
   a. Given the information below, use Table 7–2 to calculate the tax liabilities and marginal tax rates based on the taxable incomes and appropriate filing status. Put the information in columns G and H of the table.
   b. Calculate the average tax rates based on gross income, adjusted gross income, and taxable income. Put the information in columns B, D, and F of the table.
   c. Briefly describe the relationships between marginal tax rates and average tax rates.

	Gross Income A	Average Rate B	Adjusted Gross Income C	Average Rate D	Taxable Income E	Average Rate F	Tax Liability G	Marginal Tax Rate H
James—single	$23,000		$22,000		$16,000			
Maria—single	29.000		28,000		22,000			
Phil—married	71,000		69,000		57,000			
Jane—married	46,000		41,000		30,000			

2. Juanita Linzey lives with her daughter in Portland, Oregon, and she needs your advice about her income taxes.
    a. Which of the following types of income of Juanita's must be included as total income for the IRS: $17,000 in salary, $10,000 life insurance proceeds of deceased aunt, $140 interest on savings, $4,000 alimony from ex-husband, $1,200 in child support, $500 cash Christmas gift from parents, $90 from a friend who rides to work in Juanita's vehicle, $60 lottery winnings, $420 state income tax refund as she itemized last year, $570 federal income tax refund, $170 worth of dental services traded for a quilt she gave the dentist, and $1,600 tuition scholarship she received to go to college part-time last year?
    b. What is the total of Juanita's reportable gross income?
    c. Juanita put $800 into an individual retirement account last year, so what is her adjusted gross income for tax purposes?
    d. How many exemptions can Juanita claim and how much is the total value allowed the Linzey household?
    e. How much is the allowable standard deduction for the Linzey household?
    f. Juanita has listed her itemized deductions, which total $4,000. Explain why she should itemize or take the standard deduction.
    g. What is Juanita's taxable income?
    h. What is her tax liability?
    i. Assuming she gets a credit of $140 for child care, what is Juanita's final tax liability?
    j. If Juanita's employer withheld $2,000 for income taxes, does she owe money to the government or does she get a refund? How much?

Suggested Readings

"The Executive Who Tried All the (Tax) Angles." *Working Woman*, March 1987, pp. 116–117+. Suggestions for executives on reducing income taxes.

"How to Survive a Tax Audit." *Consumers' Research*, March 1987, pp. 21–23. Techniques for defending your deductions.

"Is Your Return Audit Bait?" *Money*, February 1987, pp. 119–126. Techniques to avoid income tax audits; includes informative table of average tax deductions taken by others.

"A New Era for Tax Planning." *Consumers Digest*, January/February 1987, pp. 17–22. Guide to reaping the benefits of tax reform and avoiding the problems.

"The Smart Taxpayer's Guide." *U.S. News and World Report*, March 2, 1987, pp. 50–64. Annual article on money-saving tax strategies.

"Taxes: Play It Again Sam." *Changing Times*, January 1987, pp. 107–111. Suggestions on how to save on taxes as tax reform goes into effect.

PART THREE

Managing Expenditures

CHAPTER 8

Some Major Expenditures

OBJECTIVES

After reading this chapter, the student should be able to

1. list ways in which people waste money when purchasing goods and services.
2. explain the concept of life-cycle planning for making major expenditures.
3. discuss the seven steps of the buying process.
4. cite several major pieces of consumer legislation enacted in recent years.
5. identify the major consumer rights and responsibilities.

The last seven chapters examined the topics of financial planning and money management. Now that you understand the elements of budgeting, cash management, credit card use, borrowing, and taxes, we can get down to the enjoyable process of spending. Now the fun begins!

This chapter focuses first on ways that people waste money, habits important to study so that you can avoid them. We realize that many young people would like to start off with all the possessions it took their parents a lifetime to acquire—such as a three-bedroom home full of furniture, appliances, clothing, food, and recreational equipment. The section here on life-cycle planning will give you perspective on when to make major expenditures. The steps in the buying process are then examined and illustrated using a sample automobile purchase: determining needs and wants, fitting the budget, preshopping research, comparison shopping, negotiating, making the decision, and complimenting or complaining.

Ways That People Waste Money

Examples of ways that people waste money could fill the pages of dozens of books. The six most prevalent ways people waste money are (1) buying too much, (2) buying on credit, (3) not buying at the right time, (4) buying the wrong things, (5) going convenience, and (6) always going first class.

Buying Too Much

The small, inexpensive items placed near store check-out counters, such as diet booklets, pocket knives, magazines, fingernail clippers, and candy, are put there for people who practice impulse buying. Just $3 a week spent on impulse items can waste more than $150 a year.

Simple restraint will help you avoid impulse buying. Say, for example, you go to a discount store to pay $150 for a vacuum cleaner you've planned for a month to buy. While at the store, you also pick up a new lightweight fishing rod for $60. Of course, you have now spent $60 more than you intended to. Treat yourself now and then but don't get carried away.

Buying on Credit

Once you leave school, you may feel the need to go out and buy for yourself all those items owned by people who have been working for a while. Some people get around this problem by buying a lot of items on credit. As discussed in Chapters 5 and 6, overuse of credit can strangle you financially. By using credit, you may pay 15, 20, or even 30 percent more for products. For example, a $400 television might cost you $490 when financed at 15 percent for three years. Thus, using credit would cost 22.5 percent more ($90 ÷ $400) than paying cash. Overuse of credit wastes money that could be spent on other things, or saved or invested.

Not Buying at the Right Time

If you pay attention to sales and look for the right time to buy, you will waste less money. For example, you can save 30 to 60 percent on telephone charges just by making calls in the evenings and on weekends. Check the front of your telephone book for discount explanations. Even if you hate crowds, shop for groceries on weekends, because that is when the best sales occur. Many items, such as sporting goods and clothing, are marked down near certain holidays, and at the end of the season. Also, you can save $5 or $10 weekly on food simply by using coupons from newspapers and magazines and buying advertised specials.

Buying the Wrong Things

Some people have an "Excedrin headache" for thirty cents a dosage or an "Anacin headache" for twenty-five cents a dosage, and others have a plain headache for two cents a dosage. Scientific research (not the advertiser's research) consistently shows that the effectiveness of all aspirin is the same. Gasoline is a similar case. Most independent experts agree that there is not much difference between a national brand of gasoline and off-brand gasoline other than the extra you pay per gallon for the national brand. Plus, if you take advantage of self-service, you may pay up to thirty cents per gallon less. This could save you perhaps $225 annually (15,000 miles ÷ 20 miles per gallon × $.30).

Buying generic products is a good way to save money. Many physicians will write prescriptions for generic-equivalent drugs, which cost you 20 to 60 percent less than prescriptions for brand-name drugs. Also note that many less expensive, store-brand appliances (such as those sold at Sears and J. C. Penney) are actually made by the big manufacturers, such as RCA, Panasonic, Eureka, General Electric, and others.

In many cases, you must consider more than price when deciding what is the right item to buy. Should you purchase a new car for $470 monthly or pay cash for a used car that costs $50 to $75 in monthly maintenance? Should you buy new tires or recapped tires, which cost about one-third less than most other tires and pass the same safety standards? Should you use your savings of $3,000 to buy five pieces of quality furniture or to try to fill your entire home with used furniture?

Going Convenience

A six-pack of Pepsi or Coke bought at a supermarket probably costs fifty cents less than at a nearby convenience store, whereas bread and milk are priced about the same. Stopping once a week at a convenience store to buy a few items you forgot to get at the grocery store may cost you more than $100 a year extra. A well-planned trip to the grocery store will save you money. Also, although it may be convenient to shop for furniture and appliances in your local community, you may find better prices on the same items in larger, competitive shopping areas.

**Always Going
First Class**

Many people feel they should always go first class. When taking vacations they may stay at brand-name motels (Ramada, Holiday Inn, Hyatt, Sheraton) rather than save 40 to 50 percent at a high-quality budget inn, that has virtually the same accommodations and toll-free reservations. When going first class, people usually don't sample off-brand soft drinks or notice the savings they might get with a small, fuel-efficient automobile. It is important to make informed financial decisions consistent with your personal values. You can go first class if you truly want to, but you should realize how much money is involved.

Using Life-cycle Planning for Major Expenditures

"You can't have everything," as the old saying goes, but many Americans certainly try. Table 8–1 lists some of the items many people want to own during their adult years. These are relatively expensive items that usually require comparison shopping before purchasing.

**TABLE 8–1
Some Major-expenditure Items Desired by Adults**

Early years of singlehood

Bedroom furniture
Television
Living room furniture
Stereo system
Used automobile
Home computer

Middle years of singlehood or early years of couplehood

Microwave oven
New automobile
Better stereo system
Extra television set
Children's furniture
Video cassette recorder

Later years of singlehood or middle years of couplehood

Better living room furniture
Luxury automobile
Antiques
Piano
Second auto

What is important to realize is that although you cannot have everything *right now,* planning will help you achieve your financial goals. Intelligently setting goals and recognizing your budget limitations will enable you to reach goals for major expenditures as soon as possible.

As you can see, Table 8–1 categorizes purchases by life-cycle stage. This categorization has three major benefits. First, it helps plan expenditures by setting up an appropriate timetable. This makes it easier to delay some purchases knowing that the delay is not permanent. Second, it is a first step in setting up a budget category for saving in preparation for the purchase. Third, it makes clear that many major purchases are really replacements for obsolete items. The replacement process is a good opportunity to upgrade the quality of a basic model purchased when funds were more limited.

The Buying Process as Applied to Automobile Buying

There are seven steps in the buying process: (1) determining needs and wants, (2) fitting the budget, (3) preshopping research, (4) comparison shopping, (5) negotiating, (6) making the decision, and (7) complimenting or complaining appropriately.

Determining Needs and Wants

In Chapter 1 we distinguished between needs and wants. A need is something that is thought to be a necessity; a want is unnecessary but desired. For example, most people need transportation to and from work, but they do not need a *new* automobile for this purpose.

The task of separating needs from wants becomes harder when there are many ways of satisfying a need. For example, assume that Betti Sidwell of Tallahassee, Florida, finds that neither public transportation nor carpooling is available to get her to her new job; she needs an automobile. She likes Lincolns, Cadillacs, Nissans, Plymouths, and Fords. She may decide to fulfill her needs by purchasing an inexpensive Plymouth or Nissan. Or she may fulfill her needs *and* her wants by buying a Cadillac or a Lincoln. To make this decision, Betti used the worksheet in Figure 8–1. She found, to her surprise, that there were several features she did not want and that her wants were not as numerous as she had thought.

Fitting the Budget

The sticker price of the vehicle Betti has finally chosen is $10,600, including the four items she checked as needs because she would not consider buying a car without them. The other options she wants are priced as follows:

Tinted windows	$ 288
Automatic windows	250
Cassette player	338
Air conditioning	724
	$1,600

To buy a car that meets her needs and her four wants will cost Betti $12,700 ($10,600 + $1,600 + $500 for sales tax and title registration). She can use $1,700 in savings as a down payment and borrow the remaining $11,000. Assuming she could secure a 9 percent (APR) loan, the monthly payments would be $273 for 48 months. If she buys none of the options she wants, she would only need to borrow $9,350 ($11,000 − $1,600 − $50 in saved sales tax), for a monthly payment of $235. Or she could buy only one or two of the options.

The monthly payment that Betti must fit into her budget will depend on four factors: the price she actually pays for the car, the interest rate on the loan, the down payment she can make, and the time period for payback of the loan. We will choose the down payment of $1,700 and assume a forty-eight-month time period because that is currently typical. But what about the price and interest rate? Remember that the prices given above for the car and its options are sticker prices. The *sticker price* is the manufacturer's suggested price for a new car and its options as listed on the window sticker. It is usually possible to negotiate

FIGURE 8–1
Wants and Needs Worksheet (for Betti Sidwell)

Needs	Automobile Feature	Wants	Don't Care
✓	Power steering		
	Tinted windows	✓	
	Automatic windows	✓	
✓	Automatic transmission		
	Leather seats		✓
✓	AM-FM Radio		
	Cassette player	✓	
	Super sound system		✓
	Telescope and tilt steering wheel		✓
	Automatic light dimmer		✓
	Air conditioning	✓	
✓	Whitewall tires		
	Four-wheel drive		✓

a lower price because the dealer's cost of the car will average about 12 percent lower than the sticker price. By multiplying the sticker price by 12 percent you can get a rough estimate of the room you have for bargaining. For example, by driving a hard bargain, Betti could reduce the price of the car without the wanted options by $1,272 ($10,600 × 12 percent). This would reduce her monthly payment by about $32. Of course, the $1,272 represents the dealer's profit, so it might be too optimistic to assume that she could bargain the price all the way down to the dealer's cost: $9,328 ($10,600 − $1,272). You should always have a good idea of the dealer's cost for the car and its options when shopping for a new car. You could use the 12 percent figure; however, there are several sources of dealer cost information, such as the Nationwide Auto Brokers and Consumer's Union, publishers of *Consumer Reports* magazine. The $10 or so these services charge for a price report is a very wise investment.

The last important factor affecting Betti's monthly payment is the interest rate on her loan. She should shop around for the best rates. An important source of loans for new cars is sales financing, arranged through the car's manufacturer. In recent years, it has been possible to obtain such financing at interest rates of 2 or 3 percent APR on some makes and models (American Motors even offered interest-free loans for awhile). Often, such deals come with strings attached. You usually must buy a car already on the dealer's lot rather than order one from the factory. This reduces your ability to buy only the options you want. The time period of the loan is also usually limited to thirty-six months or less. The shorter time period will mean a higher monthly payment. For example, if Betti Sidwell pays the sticker price for the model without the options she wants, using a 2.4 percent loan for thirty-six months, her monthly payment would be about $270, as opposed to $235 at 9 percent for forty-eight months. But the finance charge for the shorter, less expensive loan is $1,560 less than for the longer, more expensive loan.

Table 8–2 shows Betti's monthly budget. Her monthly take-home pay of $1,130 is totally committed. Let's see what she has to do to be able to pay for an automobile. To buy the auto with no extra options, she will need $235 per month and will have to change her budget drastically. To get to her former job, she has used public transportation at a cost of $80 per month; those dollars can go toward a car payment. To get the rest of the money she could cut savings ($10 per month), cut entertainment and gifts in half ($50 and $25), cut back on food ($20), and cut back on clothing ($35). In all, these efforts would raise only $220 ($80 + $10 + $50 + $25 + $20 + $35), still $15 short of the amount she needs for the car. Note also that if Betti buys a car she will need additional funds for insurance, registration, license plates, gasoline, and maintenance; all of which could be avoided if she bought no car. Her alternatives are to make more cutbacks in her budget, to work overtime or get a part-time job, or to buy a cheaper or used car. We did not try to make the auto more affordable for her by lengthening the payments to sixty months because most people do not wish to have

TABLE 8–2
Fitting an Automobile Payment into a Monthly Budget

	Last Month	Possible Cutbacks	Budget with Auto
Food	$ 180	$ −20	$ 160
Clothing	100	−35	65
Transportation	80	−80	–0–
Housing	475		475
Entertainment	100	−50	50
Gifts	50	−25	25
Beautician	25		25
Savings	60	−10	50
Miscellaneous	60		60
Total	$1,130	$−220	$ 910
Car payment			235
Total with car payment			$1,145

monthly car payments on a five-year-old rusty vehicle with 60,000 to 75,000 miles on it.

Preshopping Research

Preshopping research is gathering information about products or services before you buy them. Manufacturers, sellers, and service providers are important sources of information on products and services during your preshopping research. Auto manufacturers publish many brochures on their products and sponsor auto shows that are used both to promote and to provide information on their cars. An auto dealer's sales staff can be helpful as well, but may be unwilling to spend time with you if they do not think you are seriously considering buying one of their automobiles. You will need to ask very specific questions and assure the salesperson that you are a serious customer. Two other sources of information are friends and consumer magazines. If someone you know drives an automobile you are thinking of buying, ask the person about his or her experience with the vehicle. You could also read about the car in a consumer magazine, such as *Consumer Reports,* which tests and reports on ten to twenty products monthly. In addition, *Consumer Reports Buying Guide Issue,* published in December of each year, lists facts and figures on numerous products. Monthly issues of *Consumer Reports* generally provide a two- to five-page narrative analyzing the products and summarizing the information in chart form. Figure 8–2 is an example of such a chart. The April issue of *Consumer Reports* each year is devoted entirely to the buying of new and used cars.

You can find *Consumer Reports* in your library. When you are shopping for any product, it may help to review publications on a more specific topic, such as *Photography, Car and Driver,* and *Stereo Review,* or of general consumer interest, such as *Changing Times.* Realize, however, that trade magazines that accept advertising for the products they report on are not likely to be as unbiased as *Consumer Reports,* which accepts no advertising.

Guide to the Ratings

Listed in order of estimated quality. Unless separated by bold rules, closely ranked models differed little in quality.

❶ Price. The *Panasonic* and the *Daikin* are not available nationwide; prices for those units are what we paid. Panasonic says that, as of June, its unit should be available in Atlanta, Baltimore, Chicago, Dallas, Los Angeles, and New York City. Daikin says its unit should be available this summer in all major cities.

❷ Cooling capacity. This is the key factor for matching an air-conditioner to the room. Use the worksheet on page 429 to determine the size you need.

❸ EER. This stands for energy-efficiency ratio. Other things being equal, a unit with a high EER will cost less to operate than one with a lower EER. Several states have minimum EERs for air-conditioners, with the strictest in California and New York. The *Amana* isn't efficient enough for either state's standards; the *White-Westinghouse* wouldn't pass muster in California.

❹ Dehumidification. The rates given here are from the manufacturers. A high rate will be more important to people in areas like Houston or St. Louis than in Phoenix or Denver.

❺ Thermostat performance. This test determined how well the units could maintain a specific temperature in a room. Each air-conditioner was mounted in a partition between two of CU's environmental chambers. We kept the "outdoor" side at 95°F, and set the air-conditioner to maintain the "indoor" side at 80°. The best maintained the set temperature within about three degrees.

Ratings

Air-conditioners

❶ Price

Brand and model	Average	Range	Cooling capacity (Btu/hr.) ❷	EER ❸	Dehumidification (pt./hr.) ❹	Thermostat performance ❺	Adverse conditions ❻	Temperature uniformity ❼	Directional control ❽	Ventilation ❾
Panasonic CW82JSX	$399	—	8000	9.0	1.5	⊙	⊙	⊙	◐	●
Friedrich SS08G10C	579	$446-$620	8000	10.0	1.4	◐	⊙	●	◐	○
General Electric AEX08FA	429	349-529	8000	9.3	1.5	⊙	◐	○	●	◐
Carrier 51DTA0081	504	398-592	8000	9.0	2.1	○	◐	⊙	○	◐
Sears 76088	442	360-500	8000	9.7	2.6	◐	⊙	●	◐	◐
Gibson AM08B6ESB	415	360-469	8000	9.6	2.0	◐	○	⊙	◐	◐
Kelvinator MH308C1Q	367	359-375	8000	9.6	2.0	◐	○	⊙	◔	◐
White-Westinghouse AC088K7B	376	280-520	7500	8.5	2.4	⊙	◐	◐	◐	◐
Emerson Quiet Kool 8AC73	405	349-490	8000	9.0	2.4	○	◐	◐	○	◐
Daikin W20MASAN	386	—	8300	9.0	2.7	◐	○	◐	◐	◐
Hunter 31075	305	296-320	7500	8.7	2.3	◐	⊙	◐	◐	◐
Whirlpool ACPS82XS	458	379-579	8000	9.5	1.9	○	◐	◐	◐	●
Airtemp L082WKRNDA	321	279-359	8000	8.7	⓵	○	⊙	◐	◐	◐
Fedders ASR08F2JA	417	349-500	8000	8.7	2.8	○	◐	◐	◐	◐
Amana ES8P2MR	383	330-450	7900	8.0	2.3	⊙	○	◐	●	○

⓵ Not supplied by mfr.

Specifications and Features

All: • Are designed for installation in double-hung window. • Can be run, local codes permitting, on single-outlet 15-amp circuit protected by circuit breaker or time-delay fuse. • Should be used only with grounded outlet. • Are rated at 7.5 to 8.5 amp but can draw more under adverse conditions. • Should be carried and installed by more than 1 person. *Except as noted, all have:* • Adjustable horizontal and vertical louvers. • 3 cooling-speed settings. • Convenient controls. • Windowsill support bracket. • Leveling provision. • Expandable side panels with plastic framing. • Protective guard on back. • 6- to 6½-ft. power cord. • 1-yr. parts-and-labor warranty on entire system, additional 4-yr. parts-and-labor warranty on compressor and some additional sealed-system components. (Diagnosis labor may not be covered during 2nd to 5th yr.)

Key to Advantages

A – On low setting, noise fluctuated much less than most when compressor cycled on and off.
B – On low setting, noise fluctuated less than most when compressor cycled on and off.
C – Has automatic Energy Saver setting, which turns fan off with compressor. Fan on *White-Westinghouse* continues to run for 3 min. after compressor shuts off. Energy Saver setting improved thermostat performance on the *Friedrich*, worsened performance on the *Sears*.
D – "Auto-saver" feature reduces cooling output when demand is low.
E – Can be set to dehumidify on days when minimal cooling is required.
F – Has indicator light for switch positions.
G – Has slide-out chassis to make installation and maintenance easier. *Daikin* chassis was somewhat difficult to slide.

H – Has at least 1 handle for carrying unit or steadying it during installation and removal.
I – Expandable side panels have metal framing; judged stronger than plastic.
J – Does not use fiberglass insulation in output duct (see story).
K – Filter can be removed without removing front panel. Wide windowsill may make that difficult on *Daikin* and *Hunter*. Filter slightly difficult to remove on *Friedrich*.
L – Indicator light reminds you to clean filter.
M – Some louvers can be closed to increase air thrust. Compressor on *Sears* cycled off while set in that position.
N – Louvers can be closed to increase exhaust air exchange through open vent.
O – Has On/Off timer; can start unit before you return home in the evening or shut it off automatically after you're asleep.

FIGURE 8-2
Consumer Reports Ratings on Air Conditioners

Source: *Consumer Reports*, July 1987. Copyright 1987 by Consumers Union of United States, Inc., Mount Vernon, N.Y. 10553. Reprinted by permission from *Consumer Reports*, July 1987.

The worst strayed as far as seven degrees from the setting—quite a noticeable fluctuation.

6 Adverse conditions. A worst-case test, designed to show how these units would perform during a power brownout in the middle of a heat wave. Many units operated normally through these severe tests; the rest had difficulty restarting after a three-minute rest or wouldn't restart at all.

7 Temperature uniformity. Nearly half the models delivered fairly even cooling throughout the room. Horizontal louvers tilted at a 35- to 45-degree angle produced the best distribution of air.

8 Directional control. These judgments reflect how well each air-conditioner directed cool air into the room. None of these units was particularly even-handed. Their louvers couldn't be set to balance left and right airflow, and none of them could send most of the cool air to their right.

9 Ventilation. These units, like virtually all air-conditioners, have an exhaust vent that can help remove stale room air. But even the best weren't as effective as a 20-inch window fan.

10 Noise. The noise from some models rose and fell as the compressor cycled on and off, a fluctuation that may bother some light sleepers. The ones with the steadiest drone are called out in the Advantages column.

11 Installation measurements. The **height, width,** and **depth** tell you the size of each unit. **Inside projection** tells how far the front of the air-conditioner projects past the window sash. **Window widths** tell you the range of window sizes each unit will fit. **Slide-out chassis** tells you which units should be easy to install.

◉ ◓ ○ ◒ ●
Better ⟵ ⟶ Worse

10 Noise: Indoors on high	Indoors on low	Outdoors on high	Outdoors on low	11 Installation measurements: Weight, lb.	Height, in. [2]	Width, in.	Depth, in.	Inside projection, in.	Window widths, in.	Slide-out chassis	Advantages	Disadvantages	Comments
○	◓	◒	○	85	14¾	22¼	23¾	4¾	26 to 38	✓	A,D,E,F,G,I,J,K,O	h,k	*A,B,C,D,G,L,P*
○	◓	◒	○	99	16	26	27½	4	28 to 41¾	✓	A,C,G,K	n	*E,H,N*
○	◉	○	○	96	16	26¼	22¾	4¼	29¾ to 41	✓	B,C,G,I,J,K,O	k	*C,D,G,J,L*
◓	◉	◒	○	104	16¾	24¾	24¾	5¼	30½ to 45½	✓	G	—	*E,F,I,L*
◒	◓	◒	○	84	15	22¾	23½	4½	26 to 38	—	C,I,M,N	l,m	*H*
◒	○	◒	○	87	16	23¼	20¾	5¼	27 to 40	—	A,C,J,K,N	c,e	*B,H*
◒	○	◒	○	85	15¾	23¼	18	2¾	27½ to 40	—	A,J,M,N	c,e,j	*H*
◒	○	●	○	66	13¼	19¼	17½	6¼	22¾ to 36	—	A,C,F,H,K,L,M,N	b,e,m	*C,O*
○	◓	◒	○	66	13¾	20¼	18¾	2	24¼ to 36	—	B,C,H,J,K	f	*K*
◓	◉	◒	○	88	15	22¼	21¾	4	27 to 41	✓	G,J,K	i,k	*D,G,L*
○	◓	◒	○	81	14¼	20¾	20¼	5¼	27 to 37½	—	A,H,J,K	—	*D,J,L,M,O*
◒	◒	●	◒	109	16¾	26¼	24½	4	26¼ to 40	✓	G,H	d,f,k,n,o	*D,H,O*
◒	◒	●	◒	78	12½	20¼	20½	3½	23½ to 39	—	—	f	*F,J,K*
◒	◒	●	◒	77	12½	20¼	20½	3½	23½ to 39	—	—	f	*J,K*
◒	○	●	◒	67	13¾	19½	20½	2	23 to 36	—	B,K	a,f,g,m	*H,K,O*

[2] *Minimum window-opening height required for installation.*

Key to Disadvantages

a – Cycled off during adverse-conditions test at 100 volts.
b – Compressor wouldn't restart during adverse-conditions test at 100 volts.
c – Compressor had difficulty restarting in thermostat-performance test.
d – In CU's tests at high humidity, unit dripped considerable amounts of condensate through drain fitting.
e – Dripped slightly during high-humidity test. Unit has no provision for drain fitting.
f – Fixed horizontal louvers.
g – Vertical louvers don't stay set.
h – Elaborate control panel; may force you to keep instruction book at hand.
i – Control markings can be hard to decipher.
j – Front panel must be removed with screwdriver in order to remove filter for cleaning.
k – Lacks leveling provision.
l – Has neither sill bracket nor leveling provision; judged least secure of all tested models during installation and removal.
m – Lacks guard on outside coils.
n – Side panels must be cut to fit.
o – Compressor made annoying buzzing sound.

Key to Comments

A – Sleep Setback mode raises room temperature by 1.8°F and by another 1.8° 1 hr. later.
B – Has motorized vertical louvers to alternate airflow from side to side; feature did not improve temperature distribution.
C – Has electronic controls.
D – Hose can be connected to drain fitting.
E – Vent control has provision for fresh-air intake as well as exhaust; judged relatively ineffective.
F – Has 5-ft. power cord.
G – Has 7½- to 8-ft. power cord.
H – Mfr. recommends periodic oiling of fan motor; difficult to do on models that lack slide-out chassis.
I – During 2nd to 5th yr., warranty covers entire unit with fixed labor allowances.
J – During 2nd to 5th yr., warranty covers compressor only.
K – During 2nd to 5th yr., warranty does not cover labor.
L – Assembly of side curtain panels required.
M – Shipping blocks around compressor must be removed before unit is turned on.
N – Has 5 cooling-speed settings.
O – Has 2 cooling-speed settings.
P – Unlike others, unit will not restart automatically after power interruption.

Comparison Shopping

Comparison shopping is the process of comparing products or services to find what you think is the best buy. A *best buy* is a product or service that, in your opinion, represents acceptable quality at a fair or low price for that level of quality. Note that buying the product with the lowest price does not necessarily assure you of a best buy. In comparison shopping, you should visit different stores to compare dealer service and reputation, warranty terms, and credit terms on various products.

Comparison shopping for cars does take time and effort, but when you are spending thousands of dollars the payoff can be worth the trouble. During the first three steps in the buying process you should narrow your choices to specific makes and models and the options that you feel you need and want. Then visit the various dealerships again. (You should have visited them during your preshopping research.) This time you will be much closer to the decision to buy and will be ready to discuss details. You tell the salesperson exactly what you are interested in and ask about price, availability, warranties, financing currently available, and any manufacturer's incentives, such as *rebates,* (refunds from the manufacturer) that apply. Your goal is to narrow the choice even further so that you can begin negotiating for the best deal, which is the next step in the buying process. To do so you first need to consider warranties, service contracts, and financing options.

Warranties Warranties are an important consideration in comparison shopping. Virtually all products have **warranties** (assurances by sellers that goods are as promised) because they have implied warranties. An **implied warranty** provides that products sold are warranted to be suitable for sale and will work effectively whether there is a written warranty or not. The first implied warranty in that definition is a "warranty of merchantability." The second is a "warranty of fitness for a particular purpose." Implied warranties are required by state law; the only time they are not in effect is if the seller states in writing that the product was sold "as is" or specifically states that there is no implied warranty. This is often the case with used cars.

Written warranties accompany many products and are offered by manufacturers on a voluntary basis to induce customers to buy. These are called *express warranties.* Companies that offer express warranties must do so under the provisions of the federal Magnuson-Moss Warranty Act if the product costs more than $15. This 1975 law provides that if a written warranty is offered it must be classified as either a full warranty or a limited warranty. A *full warranty* is a warranty that includes the stringent requirements that (1) a product will be fixed at no cost to the buyer within a reasonable time after the owner has complained, (2) the owner will not have to undertake an unreasonable task to return the product for repair (such as mail back a freezer), and (3) a defective product that cannot be fixed after a reasonable number of attempts will be replaced with a new one or the money will be returned. A *limited warranty* is a warranty that offers less than a full warranty. For example, a limited warranty may offer only free parts, not labor.

Note that one part of a product could be covered by a full warranty, perhaps the engine on a lawn mower, and the rest of the unit by a limited warranty. It pays to read warranties carefully. Note also that both full and limited warranties are valid only for a specified period.

New cars generally come with a warranty on most major components for 12,000 miles or one year, whichever passes first. This warranty often will also cover the drive train (engine, transmission, drive shaft, and so forth) for up to 60,000 miles.

Service Contract A *service contract* is an agreement between the contract seller (a dealer, manufacturer, or independent company) and the buyer of a product to provide free or nearly free repair services to covered components of the product for some specified time period. A service contract is generally purchased apart from the purchase of the product (which may be an automobile or appliance). The cost is either paid in a lump sum or may require small monthly payments by the purchaser. Service contracts are very similar to insurance. For example, a twenty-five-inch television selling for $600 could have a service contract that promises to fix anything free for the first two years of ownership after the full warranty expires. This contract could cost $60 or $5 per month for one year even if no servicing is done. You may want to buy a service contract for peace of mind in case an expensive product breaks down, but it is probably unwise economically. Find out if you can take the product back for repair without a service contract and simply pay for the servicing.

Service contracts have become increasingly prevalent in the new and used car market. All the major auto manufacturers and many dealers offer service contract plans. Ford offers more than twenty-five variations for its new cars. In addition, there are a number of independent companies not traditionally associated with the automobile market that offer service contracts for new cars. Names such as "extended warranty" or "buyer protection plan" are sometimes used rather than service contract. All these plans tend to extend the coverage provided under the new car's warranty, perhaps by extending the mileage and/or covering more components. The cost can be $400 or more and if the manufacturer or dealer offers the plan, it may be included in the purchase price and financed with the loan of the car. Often there is a deductible of about $100 that must be paid each time the car is repaired. Both preventive maintenance and repairs to covered components are included in some plans. Used car service contracts can cost $200 to $300 and usually provide protection for no more than two years.

Financing Options When comparison shopping for a car, you must consider financing options. It may be possible to take advantage of a special low interest rate when you use seller financing. However, you may have a higher monthly payment because of restrictions on the time period of the loan. Fortunately, most low-interest specials run concurrently with some type of rebate plan for people who pay cash or arrange their own financing. Thus, you might be able to get a higher-interest-rate loan for a longer period through your bank or credit union and use the rebate as compensation for the extra finance charges.

Leasing is another financing option that has become routinely available in recent years. With a lease you are, in effect, renting the car for three, four, or five years with the title remaining with the lease grantor. Usually the down payment is very small (less than $500). Your monthly payments are based on the price of the car minus its projected resale value at the end of the time period, divided by the number of months in the contract. Monthly lease payments are lower than monthly loan payments for equivalent time periods because with a lease you are only paying for the reduction in the car's value—not its entire cost. Sometimes auto insurance and a service contract are also included in the monthly payment.

You can obtain an open-end lease or a closed-end lease. An ***open-end lease*** is a leasing arrangement in which you must pay any difference between the projected resale value of the car and its true market value at the end of the lease period. If the car has had above normal wear or mileage it is likely that you will have to pay some difference. A ***closed-end lease*** is a leasing arrangement in which there is no charge if the true market value of the leased vehicle is lower than the projected resale value at the end of the lease period. The monthly payment for a closed-end lease is higher than that for an open-end lease. With either of these lease arrangements you may purchase the car for its resale value at the end of the lease period.

Many banking lenders have had their demand for auto loans slacken because of the popularity of auto leases. In response they have developed balloon auto loans. With a ***balloon auto loan*** the buyer takes title to the car, and the last monthly payment is equal to the projected resale value of the vehicle at the end of the loan period. This has the effect of lowering the other monthly payments to make them more competitive with lease payments. When the final balloon payment is due you have three options: (1) pay the balloon payment and keep the car, (2) return the car to the lender, or (3) sell the car and pay the balloon payment with the proceeds.

Negotiating

The next step in the buying process is ***negotiating,*** which is the process of discussing the actual terms of an agreement with a seller. We skip this step in most of the purchases we make because there is little room for individualizing the sale. But for many big-ticket items, especially appliances, furniture, automobiles, and real estate, it is expected that there will be offers and counteroffers to arrive at the exact price.

It is important to maintain a posture of being knowledgeable and in control. The salesperson will try to convince you to buy on his or her terms. You must be prepared to say no and buy elsewhere if the terms are not satisfactory; otherwise, the advantage will be the seller's.

How to Buy a Used Car

The average new car now sells for more than $14,000. For many people, these prices are simply more than they are able or willing to pay. For them a good, reliable, used car can do very nicely. However, you need to be careful when buying a used car. There are some basic steps you can follow to help ensure that you don't get a "lemon."

1. Decide on features and options. Your first step is to select the features you want, such as power steering, air conditioning, and stereo. In contrast with new cars, you do not need to be as careful about distinguishing between the options you need and want. If you want an option, you can usually obtain it without spending more simply by choosing an older model. Since there are many cars to choose from this is not a difficult task.

2. Decide how much you can afford to spend. You can purchase a used car for as little as $200 and as much as $20,000. Decide in advance how much you can afford and then search for cars in your price range.

3. Select several reliable makes and models in your price range. When you know what you can afford you can then select four or five makes and models that fit into your price range. The National Automobile Dealers Association publishes monthly reports on the average retail and wholesale prices of various makes and models of used cars. Your bank or credit union should have a copy of these "blue" and "red" books. The want ads in your local newspaper and used car advertising booklets distributed at supermarkets, convenience stores, and so forth also can be a source of price information. Or you can consult the most recent April issue of *Consumer Reports* for its list of recommended used cars in various price ranges. The same issue also lists the frequency-of-repair histories for most makes and models as reported by its readers. While these histories and price range recommendations only go back six years you can consult the April issues from past years to get information back ten to twelve years.

4. Start your search. Armed with your list of reliable makes and models in your price range, you can start looking for specific vehicles for sale. You may purchase a used car from a new car dealership, a used car dealership, a rental car company, a private individual, or even at a repossession auction. New car dealerships tend to offer the nicer, more expensive cars. Trade-ins are their major source of cars and they sell those that aren't in the best shape to wholesalers. Used car dealerships tend to have the widest range of choices. As a result your risk is greater. Some used car dealerships deserve the image that used car dealers sometimes have. Be careful. Private individuals deserve your attention because they own the car and know its history. Used cars sold by rental agencies such as Hertz and Avis can be a good choice because they have been regularly maintained. Regardless of the source, immediately rule out any car that seems to have a problem or raises a question in your mind. Do the same for sellers who do not seem cooperative. There are too many cars available to waste time with cars of poor quality or uncooperative sellers.

5. Check your selections carefully. By now you should have narrowed your choice to two or three specific cars. Inspect them inside and out. Take along a friend who is knowledgeable about cars if you are not. Test drive the car and check all its functions. Ask for maintenance records if the seller is an individual or a rental company. Ask dealers for the name and address of the previous consumer owner. Before you agree to buy any car have it examined by a mechanic. A $30 examination can save hundreds of dollars in repairs later.

6. Negotiate and decide. Never pay the asking price for a used car. Sellers expect to negotiate and set a higher than required initial price to give room for bargaining. Get *all* verbal promises and guarantees in writing. Verbal agreements are useless legally if problems come up later. If a seller will not put his or her words in writing, shop elsewhere. Go home to make your final decision.

Consider, for example, the case of Gary Joseph of Canyon Country, California. Gary had narrowed his choice of cars down to one model and two dealerships. To the first dealer, Gary presented his list of desired options and was shown a suitable car on the lot. He had arranged his own financing and was interested only in price and whether the dealer could offer cheaper financing than Gary had arranged at his credit union. When Gary asked about price, the salesperson asked him what monthly payment he could afford. Gary responded that what he could afford was unimportant and that he wanted to know the price, interest rate, and monthly payment, given his down payment. When the salesperson responded that it was policy to get the affordable payment before answering Gary's questions, Gary left the dealership with the salesperson in pursuit, seeking to continue the sale. The salesperson even called Gary later at home, but Gary had already bought his car at the other dealership. Had Gary responded to the salesperson's question, the salesperson could have tailored the price to Gary's figure; which would not necessarily have been the lowest price the dealership would have accepted.

Making the Decision

Most people make buying decisions inside a store or dealer's showroom. This may not be the best place because of pressures to buy that may be applied by the seller and/or by a customer's desire to get the process over with. This is especially true for big ticket items such as cars. It is better to wait until you get home to make the decision. There, you can retrace your steps rationally through the buying process, making sure that your decision is based on the proper facts. Then, you can return to the dealer's showroom and sign the necessary papers.

We should discuss one final problem: "lowballing." Lowballing, if used, occurs at the point of the close of the sale. The salesperson writes up the sale on the appropriate forms and, just before you sign, states that, as a formality, his or her superior's approval is necessary. While the salesperson is gone you are envisioning driving away in your new car, but then he or she returns and indicates that there is some problem and that the price will be higher. Perhaps the trade-in value is too high, or the sticker price can't be discounted by quite as much as planned, or the price of a certain option has gone up. In reality, of course, the dealer wants to get more money out of you. If this technique is used on you, quickly leave. Do not look back and do not apologize.

Complimenting or Complaining Appropriately

"A warm word goes a long way, but a nasty one will not, unless you know how to communicate it." This philosophy overviews the following material: complimenting, complaining, and seeking legal redress.

Complimenting In our increasingly complex society, which also seems a bit hurried at times, it is wonderful to find a competent salesperson who willingly gives the time necessary to inform consumers about many aspects of purchases. When a salesperson does this job effectively, it is clearly appropriate to give a word of thanks to both the salesperson and his or her boss. Give a sincere thank you to the salesperson and then to the manager on your way out of the store. Your comment is justified because it was deserved, because management likes very much to hear about employees, because business needs to hear some good news from customers now and then, and because it is your responsibility as a consumer to take special note of excellence in service. Some people offer compliments assuming that they will get even better service the next time. Whatever your motivation, try to provide a deserved compliment.

Complaining   Most Americans simply refuse to accept shoddy products or services. When you have a negative purchasing experience, make sure your complaint does the most good. Decide on the objective of your complaint. If your objective is to be treated a little better while in a store, just ask to see the person in charge. This may be the store manager or an assistant manager. Simply report the quality of service you received and request that someone more capable be provided so you can spend your money in the store. If your objective is *redress,* that is, to right a wrong, more work is necessary.

Table 8–3 shows the four channels of complaining: to business, to self-regulatory groups, to consumer-action personnel, and to the private-action legal arena. You can follow these channels individually or simultaneously, but it is important to begin with the merchant before moving to other levels or channels. For example, a complaint not resolved satisfactorily with a merchant could be brought to the attention of the manufacturer's consumer affairs department before communicating with the manufacturer's president or chief executive officer (CEO). Note that federal agencies, such as the Food and Drug Administration, the Consumer Product Safety Commission, and the Federal Trade Commission, are not included in this table. These federal agen-

TABLE 8–3
Complaint Procedure

Place to Bring Your Complaint	Channel for Complaint			
1. Particular business	Merchant	⟶ Manufacturer's consumer affairs department	⟶ Manufacturer's president or chief executive officer	
2. Self-regulatory groups	Chamber of commerce	⟶ Better Business Bureau	⟶ Trade association consumer panels	
3. Consumer-action personnel	Local consumer-action group	⟶ City or county consumer-protection office	⟶ State office of consumer affairs	⟶ State attorney general
4. Private-action legal arena	Small claims court	⟶ Regular civil court system		

cies can register consumer complaints but do not have the power to assist individual concerns. Seeking redress through the first three channels in the complaint procedure in Table 8–3 can rectify almost all consumer complaints.

Seeking Legal Redress Sometimes the first three forms of redress described above are not successful. As a result the wronged person can then consider legal action against the business. Most people think that the costs for this are too high, but costs depend on the case and the type of court chosen.

A *civil court* is a state court in which numerous civil matters are resolved and a written record is made of the happenings; the proceedings are completed with the assistance of attorneys, witnesses, a judge, and often a jury. The wronged person generally must hire an attorney

Consumer Protection Laws

There have been three notable eras of consumer activism at the federal level. The first spanned the twenty-five years preceding World War I, and the second took place during the 1930s. During these first two eras, the focus was primarily on the safety of foods and drugs and on antitrust laws. The third era began in the late 1950s and lasted until the late 1970s.

During this period, over forty major pieces of federal legislation focusing on consumer problems and concerns were passed. Today virtually every product and service offered in the marketplace is in some way covered by federal regulations. The table below describes the major laws enacted during the third era of consumer activism.

Law	Year	Synopsis
Food Additives Amendment	1958	Requires that all new food additives be proven safe.
Kefauver-Harris Drug Amendment	1962	Requires that all new drugs be proven safe and effective.
National Traffic and Motor Vehicle Safety Act	1966	Established programs for the setting of mandatory safety standards for new cars.
Truth-in-Lending Act	1968	Requires full disclosure of annual percentage rates and other information in credit contracts
Poison Prevention Packaging Act	1970	Authorized the establishment of standards for child-resistant packaging of hazardous substances.
Consumer Product Safety Act	1972	Created the Consumer Product Safety Commission with responsibility for the safety of virtually all products except foods, drugs, cosmetics, medical devices, and motor vehicles, which are regulated by other agencies
Fair Credit Billing Act	1974	Assists consumers in resolving disputes involving defective products purchased with a credit card.
Magnuson-Moss Warranty Act	1975	Authorizes the Federal Trade Commission to write rules governing warranties.
Fair Debt Collection Practices Act	1977	Restricts unfair techniques used by third-party debt collectors.

and pay additional fees. It is not unusual to spend $200 to $500 resolving an issue in this court.

A **small claims court** is a state court with no written record of testimony in which civil matters are often resolved without the assistance of attorneys (in some states attorneys are actually prohibited from representing clients in small claims courts). This court is also known as a **court not of record**. It is designed to litigate small civil claims with typical legal maximums of $500 to $2,500. Claims above the small claims court maximum must be filed in a regular civil court.

To file a small claims court action, you would go to the courthouse and inquire as to which court hears small claims. A small fee, often less than $10, is required, along with fees of normally $2.50 for each court summons (also called a subpoena) for each witness needed. When you complete the necessary forms, it is important to fill out the full legal name of the **defendant** (the person who allegedly committed the wrong deed and is the subject of the litigation) and to carefully describe the action with which the lawsuit is concerned. The court will subpoena all necessary witnesses and the defendant for the day of trial. The day the case is heard, you, the **plaintiff** (the person who has filed the small claims or civil court case and is suing the defendant), should be well prepared and have a clear understanding of the sequence of events that led up to the claim. Bring all relevant documentation. A written record of the court is not kept, and in most courts the decision of the judge can be appealed by the loser to a higher court (which, of course, results in considerable attorney fees and related costs). Most small claims court decisions are won by the plaintiff and are not appealed.

Consumer Rights and Responsibilities In 1962, President Kennedy proclaimed four basic rights of consumers: (1) the right to safety, (2) the right to be informed, (3) the right to choose, and (4) the right to be heard. Like all rights, these consumer rights carry with them corresponding responsibilities.

1. *Regarding the right to safety, consumers should*
   examine merchandise for safety features before buying.
   read and follow care and use instructions carefully.
   assume personal responsibility for normal precautions when using a product.
   inform retailers, manufacturers, trade organizations, and government agencies when a product does not perform safely.

2. *Regarding the right to be informed, consumers should*
   seek out accurate information about products and services.
   read advertisements and promotional materials carefully.
   ask questions of sellers about products and service when complete information is not available.
   become more knowledgeable about the American marketplace and the consumer's role in it.

3. *Regarding the right to choose, consumers should*

carefully select merchandise and services.

carefully choose from whom to buy.

compare products for both price and quality.

continue to buy when products and services are satisfactory.

refuse to buy when products and services are unsatisfactory.

4. *Regarding the right to be heard, consumers should*

seek redress when errors occur or when quality of products or service is inferior.

make suggestions for product and service improvements.

report favorable products and incidents to retailers and manufacturers.

become informed and speak up about issues that affect consumers in general.

Summary

1. The six main ways people waste money are buying too much, buying on credit, not buying at the right time, buying the wrong things, going convenience, and always going first class. Impulse buying is a good example of buying too much.

2. Although most people cannot have immediately all the expensive material possessions they may want, life-cycle planning for major purchases may help in achieving such goals.

3. The buying process generally includes determining needs and wants, determining if they will fit the budget, obtaining information during a preshopping search, comparison buying, negotiating, making the decision, and complimenting or complaining.

4. A best buy is a product or service that, in your opinion, represents acceptable quality at a fair or low price for that level of quality. Before you decide that something is a best buy, you need to do some comparison shopping.

5. Consumers have four basic rights (to safety, to be informed, to choose, and to be heard) and many related responsibilities.

6. Since the late 1950s, more than forty major pieces of federal legislation have been enacted to help protect consumers.

Modern Money Management

The Johnsons Decide to Buy a Car

It is now October and the Johnsons have decided that it is time to move out of their apartment and into some form of purchased housing. Though they have not decided on what type of housing they will buy, they do know that Belinda will no longer be able to ride the bus to work. Thus, they are in the market for another car. They have decided not to buy a new car and they think they have some room in their budget, given the raises each has received this year (see Table 3–6), for a car. They estimate that they could afford to spend about $3,000 on a used car by making a down payment of $600 and financing the remainder over twenty-four months at $120 per month.

1. Make suggestions about how the $120 might be integrated into their budget (Table 3–6) without changing the amount left over at the end of each month. Harry and Belinda want that extra money to help defray the added expenses of home ownership.

2. Which sources of used cars should they consider seriously? Why?

3. Assume that the Johnsons have narrowed their choices to two cars. Both have air conditioning, AM/FM radio, and automatic transmission. The first auto is a six-year-old Chevrolet Cavalier with 62,000 miles, being sold for $3,100 by a private individual. The car has a six-cylinder engine and is a hatch-back style. The seller has records of all repairs, tuneups and oil changes. The car will need new tires in about six months.

   The second car is a five-year-old Ford Escort two-door with 66,000 miles, being sold by a used car dealership. It has a four-cylinder engine. Harry contacted the previous consumer owner and found that the car was given in trade on a new car about six months ago. The previous owner cited no major mechanical problems but simply wanted a bigger car. There is a written thirty-day warranty on parts only. The asking price is $3,400. Which would you advise they buy? Why?

Key Words and Concepts

balloon auto loan, 248
best buy, 246
civil court, 252
closed-end lease, 248
comparison shopping, 246
court not of record, 253
defendant, 253
express warranties, 246
full warranty, 246
implied warranty, 246

limited warranty, 246
negotiating, 248
open-end lease, 248
plaintiff, 253
preshopping research, 243
redress, 251
service contract, 247
small claims court, 253
sticker price, 241
warranties, 246

Review Questions

1. Identify ways people waste money on major expenditures.
2. What is meant by impulse buying and how can you control it?
3. How can you waste money by buying groceries on weekdays?

4. Give an example of how you can waste money on food by going convenience.

5. Give an example of how you can waste money by going first class.

6. How does your life cycle affect your major expenditures? Give examples of changes in expenditures over the life cycle.

7. List the seven steps in the buying process.

8. Explain how preshopping research can help you save money.

9. Explain why magazines that accept advertising of products they rate for quality are not always reliable for product information.

10. Why doesn't getting the lowest price for several different products assure you of getting a best buy?

11. What is lowballing? What should you do if it is used on you when you are buying a new car?

12. What is the value of having a service contract? What is a disadvantage?

13. Explain the difference between an implied warranty and an express warranty.

14. Why does a kind word go a long way in buying merchandise?

15. How could you seek redress without going to court?

Case Problems

1. Martha Law of Plattsburgh, New York, is remodeling her kitchen. She has decided to replace her refrigerator with a newer model that has more conveniences. She has narrowed her decision down to a model that is 19.2 cubic feet in size and has a top freezer. Basic models in this size cost about $750. She has also drawn up a list of possible convenience options and their prices: automatic defrost—$125, ice maker—$50, textured enamel surface—$75, glass shelving—$30, and ice water port—$95. Martha's credit union will loan her the necessary funds for one year at 12 percent APR on the installment plan. Following is Martha's budget for her $1,115 monthly take-home pay. She lives alone.

Food	$150	Entertainment	$ 75
Clothing	50	Gifts	50
Car payment	232	Personal care	40
Auto expenses	75	Savings	75
Housing	325	Miscellaneous	43

a. What preshopping research should Martha do to select the best brand refrigerator?

b. Advise Martha on which convenience options you think she needs and which she should consider wants.

c. What would her monthly payment be for (1) the basic model, (2) the basic model with needed options, and (3) the basic model with needed and wanted options? (Use Table 6–4.)

d. Fit each of the three monthly payments into Martha's budget.

e. Advise Martha on her decision.

2. Ron McCord of Malibu, California, purchased a new automobile for $9,800. He used the car often and in less than nine months had put 14,000 miles on it. A 24,000-mile, two-year warranty was still in effect for most of the power-train equipment, and Ron did have to pay the first $100 on each repair.

   At 16,500 miles and the eleventh month of driving, Ron had some severe problems with the transmission. He took the car to the dealer for repairs. A week later he picked the car up, but some transmission problems still remained. When he took the car back to the dealer, the dealer said no more problems could be identified. However, Ron was sure the problem was still there and he was amazed that the dealer would not correct it. The dealer told him he would do nothing more.

   a. Was Ron within his rights to take the car back for repairs? Explain.

   b. What would be some logical steps to follow if Ron continues to be dissatisfied with the dealer's unwillingness or inability to repair the car?

   c. May Ron seek any help from the court system? If so, describe what he could do without spending money on attorney's fees.

Suggested Readings

"Great Bargains at Your Fingertips." *Consumers Digest,* May/June 1987, pp. 63–67. Quality merchandise is available from catalog outlets.

"Law: See You in Court." *Changing Times,* March 1987, pp. 65–70. How to go about suing someone.

"The 1987 Cars." *Consumer Reports,* April 1987, pp. 195–259. Entire annual issue focuses on choosing new and used automobiles; includes frequency-of-repair records.

"20 Top Used-Car Buys." *Consumers Digest,* March/April, 1987, pp. 14–18+. Detailed descriptions of which used cars are terrific.

"What's Best for Your Car." *Consumer Reports,* February 1987, pp. 88–109. Comprehensive care of oil, filters, batteries, and tire pressure gauges.

"When Leasing a Car Makes Sense." *Changing Times,* September 1987, pp. 39–47. An excellent overview of the lease-versus-buy decision for new cars in all price ranges.

CHAPTER 9

The Housing Expenditure

OBJECTIVES

After reading this chapter, the student should be able to

1. identify some housing values and goals.
2. discuss the question of whether renters or owners pay more for housing.
3. describe ways to determine how much buyers can afford for housing.
4. identify and describe the various types of rented and owned housing.
5. explain how taxes are assessed on real estate.
6. discuss the various aspects of financing a home, including how to obtain a mortgage loan and funds for a down payment.
7. identify the numerous costs of buying a home.
8. list and describe the steps in the home-buying process.
9. identify some concerns in the process of selling a home.

T he four major areas of expenditure are housing, food, transportation and clothing. Of these, the greatest expenditure is usually housing. People often spend up to 40 percent of their income on housing-related items. Consequently, it is extremely important for you to study the housing topic.

To begin, we will discuss some values and goals of housing seekers, particularly those involving housing space. This is followed by sections on the questions of renting versus buying and how much you can afford for housing. Since you will probably rent at some time in your life, we will discuss how to choose an apartment; and then we will describe owned housing and tax assessment on real estate. Next we will cover financing a home with a traditional or an alternative mortgage and explain how to estimate total home-buying costs. The chapter ends with a look at the processes of buying and selling a home. The important topic of real estate as an investment is covered later, in Chapter 19.

Housing Space and Your Values and Goals

The reasons people want more housing space are based on their values and goals. In housing, Americans generally value space, privacy, and an absence of noise. People tend to feel freer when they have extra room. Additional space permits more space compartments in the home, or opportunities for privacy, which are psychologically important. A practical value of additional space is for storage. Extra housing space can also help reduce noise, since family members can be engaged in different activities throughout the home without bothering others.

Most people have six housing goals that they pursue according to their values and personalities.

1. *Use and function* of housing space reflect the relationships among public, private, and work areas. Public space is normally for leisure activities. Private space is for sleeping, dressing, and bathing. Work space includes food preparation and storage areas, as well as a home office and workshop. Traffic patterns are important to use and function. For example, it is inconvenient to have the kitchen located too far from the dining area or to have to walk through a bedroom to get to the only bathroom.

2. *Ease of care* of the housing space partly reflects the dweller's lifestyle. A person who travels a great deal and spends little time at home might not need much total space, and small quarters should be easy to keep clean. The family that entertains often might prefer large, open spaces that can be easily kept up.

3. *Efficiency* of space is also important. A person who eats almost all meals out could easily live in a home with a small kitchen. A big

family might best enjoy a very large dining area adjacent to the kitchen. A family that buys a lot of groceries might prefer not to have to carry all those bags up to a fifth-floor apartment.

4. *Safety* is a goal many seek. Some people feel safe knowing there are sufficient fire-escape ladders, and some require an environment where a guard checks all who enter and a security force patrols the area day and night. Some people will not live in the country because it feels unsafe (even though the crime rate is one-tenth of what it is in some urban areas).

5. *Attractiveness* is another popular goal. Most people consider their homes a haven. Returning after work or a trip to an attractively decorated home can be a pleasure.

6. *Individuality* in housing reflects the dweller's personality. Outgoing, party-loving people should have large open spaces in which to entertain. More private people might want a floor plan with several smaller rooms and try to avoid singles apartment complexes.

Deciding Where to Live

One other group of concerns has to do with where your home is located. If an exciting job offer comes from a company six hundred miles away, some people would take it and others would not. Many people value greatly the local friends they have and simply refuse to move away. Others might insist on working in an area easily accessible to snow skiing or with year-round warm-weather boating. Your values will determine what decisions you make in the following five areas:

1. *Mobility* has to do with how easily you can change residences, for such reasons as obtaining a new job, getting married, or needing a change. Mobility is important to consider when making renting or buying decisions. Otherwise, you might be stuck in a depressed housing market trying to sublet an apartment with a two-year lease or trying to sell a condominium.

2. *Proximity* is also a key consideration. How close is your home to your job? How far is it to a shopping center, a laundromat, a church, mass-transit facilities, schools, parks, family, and friends?

3. *Neighborhood and location* of your home is important. Is your neighborhood made up of people who are all the same age? Do you like it that way? Is the neighborhood all high-rise buildings or a mix of buildings? Would you rather live in the middle of the block or on a corner? Is the neighborhood clean, attractive, and safe from crime? How far is the parking area, and is it well

lighted at night? Are there any environmental hazards nearby, such as a creek or busy highway. Realtors often say that there are three rules in choosing housing: location, location, and location.

4. *Pollution* of the air may not be avoidable if you live in an urban area. However, you can avoid noise and odor pollution, for example, by noticing a nearby industrial plant, airport, or pizza parlor (breathing pizza odors day and night can actually become very annoying). Many people would rather not have a children's playground, numerous humming air conditioners, or a noisy highway just outside their windows.

5. *Costs* for *total* housing are a vital concern. Your rent or mortgage loan payment does not reflect total housing costs. Also consider what type of energy is used to heat and cool the home, whether windows face the sun to reduce heating bills, if cable television is already hooked up, and if there are special charges for storage and recreational areas.

Who Pays More, Renters or Owners?

According to research studies, home owners have about a 1 or 2 percent advantage over renters. This is a generalization and involves total housing costs over the years. Renters generally pay out less money in terms of cash flow, but owners eventually see an increase in the value of their homes, which makes them financially better off.

Cash Flow: Renters Win

To compare renting and buying fairly, we must use comparable forms of housing. Comparing a house with an apartment is not a fair comparison, as differences are likely to exist in privacy, square footage, and neighborhood. Table 9–1 compares costs for an apartment renter with those for an apartment owner (examples of owned apartments, condominiums, and cooperatives, are discussed later in this chapter). As the table shows, the renter pays a yearly fixed amount of $6,600. The apartment owner has several expenses beyond the monthly mortgage payment, but both mortgage interest ($7,000 here) and real estate property taxes ($1,000 here) are tax-deductible. Assuming the owner is in the 28 percent tax bracket, this would mean that the $2,240 ($8,000 $\times$ .28) not going to the government in taxes would pay for housing costs. In this illustration, the net cost of buying is $7,760, or $1,160 more than renting.

Renting costs

Net renting cost ($550 monthly for 12 months) $ 6,600

Buying costs
Mortgage payment ($625 monthly for 12 months) $ 7,500
Plus real estate property taxes   1,100
Plus home owner's insurance   200
Plus home owner's association fee ($60 monthly for 12 months)   720
Plus maintenance (estimate of costs for year)   480

   Net outflow $10,000
Minus tax savings (on $7,000 interest and $1,000 in taxes as
   excess itemized deductions in 28% marginal tax bracket)   2,240

   Net buying cost $ 7,760

Advantages and Disadvantages of Renting Versus Buying Housing (Renting May Look Better)

ADVANTAGES

Renting	Buying
Easy mobility	Pride of ownership
Apartment amenities (pool, tennis courts, party rooms, laundry facilities)	Higher status for home owners
Lifestyle requires fewer responsibilities	Better credit rating
No maintenance or repairs	Monthly payment usually remains relatively constant for many years
No large down payment needed, only a security deposit	Income tax deduction for mortgage interest and real estate property taxes
Fixed housing expenditure (rent) makes it easier to budget	Potential for home to increase in value resulting in a significant gain
No chance for financial loss (beyond the amount of the lease)	Owner is forced to save by making payments on an asset that grows in value
Proximity of neighbors gives sense of security	Owner can borrow against owner's equity, as value of home increases against what is owed on it
Opportunity to look over the community and move again	More space available
Low moving-in costs	Freedom to make home improvements and alterations
Pride of occupancy	

Tax Advantage: Owners Sometimes Win Only with Ownership Value

To make the comparison fairer we should assume that both the renter and the owner have, say, $20,000 in down payment. The owner would have to put this money into the home, whereas the renter would have it available to save or invest. An after-tax interest rate of 6 percent would yield the renter $1,200. Subtract this amount from the $6,600 rent and the net cash outflow for the renter is reduced to $5,400.

Many buyers want to own because of the possibility of *appreciation,* or increase, in the home's value. Historically, in most areas of the country the value of housing has risen faster than the general inflation rate. Let's assume that over the next five years rents go up 4 percent a year while homes increase in value by 6 percent a year. A home valued at $80,000 would be worth $107,058 after appreciating at 6 percent a year for five years ($80,000 × 1.06 = $84,800; $84,800 × 1.06 = $89,888; $89,888 × 1.06 = $95,281; $95,281 × 1.06 = $100,998; $100,998 × 1.06 = $107,058). By then selling the home, the owner

---

DISADVANTAGES

Renting

No special tax deductions

No potential gain from the rising value of property

Usually less space for the money

Alterations cannot be made

Rent rises with inflation except where there are many rental units available

Many restrictions on noise level, pet ownership, or children

No pride of ownership

Buying

Substantial down payment needed

A big commitment in time, emotions, and money must be made to the home

Possibility that the home will decrease in value if the neighborhood deteriorates or changes quickly

Limited liquidity, as owner's money is tied up in the home

Possibility of limited marketability for resale

Cost of repairs and maintenance

Time and effort on repairs and maintenance

Difficulty in budgeting for repair, maintenance, and home improvements

Possibility that real property taxes could increase dramatically

Total housing costs might be more than the budget can handle

Higher moving-in costs, as new items may have to be purchased for a home

Possible feeling of less security if neighbors are not near

would have a gain of $27,058 ($107,058 − $80,000), minus selling costs of perhaps $7,000 and an income tax on the gain of about $5,000 for a net after-tax gain of approximately $15,000 ($27,058 − $7,000 − $5,000).

Meanwhile, the renter would continue to receive interest on the $20,000 never made as a down payment, perhaps in the cumulative after-tax amount of $6,765 ($20,000 × 1.06 = $21,200; $21,200 × 1.06 = $22,472; $22,472 × 1.06 = $23,820; $23,820 × 1.06 = $25,250; $25,250 × 1.06 = $26,765; $26,765 − $20,000 = $6,765). In this case the buyer is financially ahead of the renter by approximately $8,235 ($15,000 − $6,765).

However, note two immediate problem areas for buyers. First, the property might not appreciate in value very much, or it could possibly decrease. Second, the mortgage interest rates might be so high that instead of making a monthly payment of $625, the owner must pay $900, which cuts into assumed net gain.

So who pays more, renters or owners?

1. In terms of cash flow, most renters today pay out less than owners of similar types of homes.

2. Home owners today, even with the advantage of tax deductions, likely will not gain financially over renters until and unless their homes appreciate in value.

How Much Can You Afford for Housing?

Your decision to spend a certain amount of money on either renting or buying housing should be based on a careful analysis. Too often people take the first reasonably priced apartment they can find or quickly accept an offer to share expenses with a friend in a more expensive and larger home. Two important points to remember when deciding how much to spend on housing are (1) avoiding outdated rules of thumb and (2) figuring your housing budget.

Avoiding Outdated Rules of Thumb

"The purchase price of the home should not exceed two-and-one-half times gross income." "Monthly housing costs should not exceed 25 percent of gross income." "Housing expenses should not exceed 35 percent of take-home pay." These are outdated rules of thumb and only provide a ballpark figure for estimating borrowing capacity because housing costs have risen dramatically. Let's look at a couple of examples. Housing costs vary widely across the country.

The national median price of an existing home in 1987 was $86,000; the highest prices were in the Northeast, where the median

Qualifying to Buy a Home

This chart will give you a quick idea of how much income you need to have to buy a certain price home according to qualification rules followed by most lenders. For each price of home, the chart shows the monthly payment for principal, interest, taxes, and insurance (PITI) for various interest rates. It also shows the required gross annual income to qualify for the loan. The *top* figure in each row shows the monthly PITI payment; the *bottom* figure shows the required gross annual income. For example, an 11 percent loan on an $80,000 home requires a monthly PITI payment of $676, plus an income of $27,040 to qualify.

- Loans are 80 percent of purchase price; term is 30 years.

- Taxes and insurance (TI) are calculated at 1 percent of the purchase price (divided by 12 months).

- Most lenders require that annual PITI (monthly figure multiplied by 12 months) cannot exceed 30 percent of gross annual income.

Interest Rate	Price of Home				
	$60,000	$80,000	$100,000	$120,000	$140,000
8.0%	$402	$537	$687	$825	$962
	$16,080	$21,480	$27,480	$33,000	$38,480
9.0%	$436	$582	$744	$883	$1,041
	$17,440	$23,280	$29,760	$35,320	$41,640
10.0%	$471	$628	$785	$942	$1,100
	$18,840	$25,120	$31,400	$37,680	$44,000
11.0%	$507	$676	$845	$1,014	$1,183
	$20,280	$27,040	$33,800	$40,560	$47,320
12.0%	$544	$725	$906	$1,087	$1,268
	$21,760	$29,000	$36,240	$43,480	$50,720
13.0%	$581	$774	$968	$1,162	$1,355
	$23,240	$30,960	$38,720	$46,480	$54,200
14.0%	$619	$825	$1,031	$1,238	$1,444
	$24,760	$33,000	$41,240	$49,520	$57,760
15.0%	$657	$876	$1,095	$1,314	$1,533
	$26,280	$35,040	$43,800	$52,560	$61,320
16.0%	$696	$927	$1,159	$1,391	$1,623
	$27,840	$37,080	$46,360	$55,640	$64,920

Source: "So You're Looking for a Mortgage Loan?" Residential Tax Information, Inc., P.O. Box 27331, Denver, Colorado 80227. Used with permission. Figures for 8.0 and 9.0 percent calculated by the authors; other figures recalculated to correct rounding errors.

was $134,000. A three-bedroom condominium available in St. Louis for $90,000 might sell for $120,000 in Boston. To buy it, the "two-and-one-half times gross income" rule requires an income of $36,000 in St. Louis and $48,000 in Boston. Many people need to buy housing before making this much income. In addition, after you make a down payment of $10,000, the thirty-year monthly mortgage loan payment at 12 percent would be $823.20 in St. Louis or $1,131.90 in Boston. Perhaps another $200 per month must also be paid out for real estate property taxes and home owner's fire insurance. Thus, even if a buyer's income is $36,000 (approximately $2,250 take-home pay per month), the St. Louis condominium would have expenses of about $1,025, which is more than 50 percent of take-home pay.

Consider also the person earning $18,000 a year. If monthly housing costs should not exceed 25 percent of gross income, this person would theoretically have only $4,500, or $375 per month, available for housing. That sum would pay for a mortgage loan of only $31,000 and leave no money for insurance, taxes, maintenance, electricity, or heating and cooling. As you might guess, $375 does not go very far in the rental market either.

Figuring Your Housing Budget

You needn't become depressed about the high costs of housing, as this chapter will provide valuable suggestions to help you. Your alternative is to figure your housing budget using some of the budgeting tactics described in Chapter 3. Add up your living expenses *other than* for housing to determine how much income is left to spend on housing. Families buying housing today may well spend 35 to 45 percent of total income on the mortgage payment, taxes, insurance, and utilities. Table 9–2 shows a sample format to use.

Note that such calculations give you a figure for the *maximum* amount available for housing and assume that expenses other than housing costs will not go up, which they often do. It is good planning to pay less than the maximum available, if possible.

Finding a Home

A *realtor,* or *broker,* is a person licensed by a state to provide advice and assistance, usually for a fee, to both buyers and sellers of real estate. If you are unfamiliar with housing in an area or if you need special financing arrangements to pay for your housing, the services of a realtor could be invaluable. Realtors are also often a good source of information about rental housing.

Realtors earn a commission of 6 to 8 percent on the sales price of a home. Since the seller pays this commission, it is included in the sales price. A realtor can show you housing that is *listed* (under contract with

TABLE 9–2
Determining Monthly Amount Left to Spend on Housing

Annual family income

Salaries _____
Bonuses and commissions _____
Interest and dividends _____
Other income _____
   Total (divided by 12 months) _____

Annual expenses other than housing costs

Food _____
Automobile upkeep, insurance _____
Gasoline for auto _____
Other transportation costs _____
Commuting expenses _____
Medical and dental bills _____
Premiums for medical insurance _____
Entertainment and recreation _____
Vacations and long weekends _____
Education _____
Church and other contributions _____
Hobbies, books, magazines, tapes, vices _____
Personal gifts, holiday gifts _____
Luxuries and pleasures (sports, pets) _____
Cable television _____
Personal care (barber/beauty shop) _____
Life and/or disability insurance _____
Debt payments (auto, washer, television) _____
Savings and investments _____
Federal/state/local income taxes _____
Social Security payments _____
Pension contributions _____
Miscellaneous _____
Other expenses _____
   Total (divided by 12 months) _____

Amount available for housing

Monthly income _____
Less monthly expenses _____
   Maximum monthly amount available for housing _____

the seller and the realtor) by the realty firm. In addition, many communities have a *multiple listing service,* which is an information and referral network among real estate brokers allowing properties listed with a particular realtor to be shown by all other realtors as well. Although realtors primarily represent the seller in all transactions, by custom the realtor is supposed to be fair to both buyer and seller.

You can choose from a wide variety of rented and owned housing, depending on the amount available in your housing budget. Each type of housing has special features, which are discussed below.

Rented Housing

People who rent housing may not have the funds for a down payment or mortgage payments on a home, may prefer the easy mobility of renting, or may prefer to avoid many of the responsibilities of buying. Prospective renters need to consider the types of units available, the amount of rent and related expenses, the lease agreement and restrictions, and tenant rights.

Types of Rental Units Available After considering how close you want to live to work and the kind of neighborhood you like, you must choose from among various types of rental units. Recognize that amenities, such as a pool, tennis courts, party rooms, and laundry facilities, may or may not be available.

Checklist for Apartments

Building and grounds

Attractive, well-constructed building with professional landscaping

Good maintenance and upkeep

Locked, secure entrances

Clean, well-lighted and uncluttered lobby, halls and stairs

Reliable building management and supervision

Services and facilities

Laundry equipment

Adequate parking space (indoor or outdoor)

Locked mail boxes and receiving room for packages

Reliable and convenient trash collection and disposal

Accessible fire escapes

Storage lockers

Elevators

Engineer on call for emergency repairs

Extras—window washing, decorating, shops, doorman

Living areas

Adequate room sizes and storage space

Convenient floor plan with good traffic pattern

Suitable wall space for furniture

Soundproof (can you hear talking, footsteps, running water and the operation of equipment in the other apartments and in hallways?)

Attractive decorating and fixtures

Pleasant views, good natural light

Agreeable size, type and number of windows, affording good ventilation

Windows equipped with blinds or shades, screens, and storm windows

Easy upkeep, including attractive low-maintenance floors

Furnished appliances in good operating condition

Clean, effective heating, thermostatically controlled

Up-to-date and sufficient wiring

An adequate number of electrical outlets, conveniently placed

Well-fitted doors, casings, cabinets, and built-ins

Extras—air conditioning, carpeting, dishwasher, disposal, fireplace, patio

Source: This information comes from the Money Management Institute booklet *Your Housing Dollar*, published by the Money Management Institute of Household Financial Services, Prospect Heights, Illinois. Used by permission.

1. Multiunit structures   Buildings from three to more than thirty stories high vary sharply in the quality of lighting and ventilation. Apartment complexes usually have identical units, whereas some multiunit structures are mixed in with other types of housing. Multiunit structures have many types of floor plans.

2. Townhouses and row houses   The total number of attached units varies from perhaps four to twelve. Each apartment includes two or more stories and frequently contains ample storage space. Windows are limited to the front and back. Yard space is typically maintained by the landlord.

3. Duplexes   These are two-family dwellings broken up into two separate living spaces that look much like single-family homes and are commonly located in residential neighborhoods. A garage and basement may be available; yardwork is usually the tenant's responsibility.

4. Multiplex units   Often located in newer suburban areas, multiplex units are large houses with four, five, or six entrances. A variety of floor plans is available and common yard areas are often maintained by the landlord. Grouping several multiplex units together raises the noise level and decreases outside privacy.

5. Garages and basements of houses   These are often available in residential neighborhoods and afford privacy and less noise. Ventilation, heat, and amount of space vary.

6. Single-family dwellings   A number of home styles are available, with a wide variety of floor plans.

Rent, Deposit, and Related Expenses   *Rent* is the cost of using an apartment or other housing space and is usually due on a specific day each month. A late charge of perhaps an additional 5 percent of the rent payment may be assessed on tenants who are late in paying rent. A lost-key replacement fee of $10 is typically charged, as is a $15 fee to let in a tenant who has been locked out. Other fees could be for rental of a party room and the use of the pool, tennis courts, cable television, and storage and parking space.

The *security deposit* is the largest rent-related expense. This is an amount paid in advance to the landlord to pay for refurbishing the unit beyond what would be expected from normal wear and tear; it is sometimes charged in addition to prepayment of the last month's rent. Thus, to move into an apartment with a monthly rent of $500 might require prepayment of the first and last month's rent ($1,000 total), as well as a security deposit (of perhaps $300). If you leave the rental unit clean and undamaged, you should obtain a refund of your security deposit.

Lease Agreement and Restrictions   If you rent a unit on a month-to-month basis without signing any legal contract, you have few protections. A *lease* is a legal contract specifying the legal responsibilities of both the tenant and the landlord. It identifies the amount of rent and security deposit, the length of the lease (sometimes six months to two or three years, but typically one year), who pays for utilities and repairs, penalties for late payment of rent, eviction procedures and costs for continued nonpayment of rent, and what happens when the term of the lease is up. Leases often state whether interest is paid on the security deposit, how soon after the tenant vacates must the unit be inspected for cleanliness, and how soon the security deposit (or the balance) is to be forwarded to the tenant.

Lease agreements also contain restrictions. Pets may or may not be permitted; when permitted, a larger security deposit is often required. Excessive noise from musical instruments, stereos, televisions, or parties may also be limited. To protect all other renters from overcrowding, a clause often places some restrictions on the number of overnight guests. A most important restriction is on *subleasing* (leasing the property from the original tenant to another tenant). A tenant who moves before the lease is up may have to get permission from the landlord to permit someone else to take over the rental unit. The new tenant may even have to be approved, and the original tenant may have some financial liability until the term of the original lease expires.

Tenant Rights   Many legal rights are available to tenants under state and local laws. Some important ones are noted below.

1. Joining a tenant organization is not cause for eviction. These are groups whose aim is to improve the bargaining power of tenants.

2. Reporting building-code violations to a local government housing authority is not just cause for eviction or for harassment in the form of rent increases or utility shutoffs.

3. The habitability of the rental unit must meet some legally prescribed minimum standard (such as running water, heat, and a working stove), often in compliance with local housing codes. In most states an implied warranty covers the availability of heat and the safety of access areas, such as stairs.

4. In many states, tenants can legally make minor repairs themselves and deduct those costs from their next rent payment. This is subject to certain restrictions, such as giving sufficient notification to the landlord.

5. Security deposits must be returned, by law, in a timely manner in most states. Limits are placed on the kinds of deductions, and landlords must explain specific reasons for deductions. In some states interest must be paid on security deposits.

6. Filing a lawsuit against a landlord for nonperformance is permitted in all states. This is usually done in a small claims court, where for a nominal filing fee (perhaps $10) lawsuits in civil matters can be pursued without an attorney up to a certain dollar limit (perhaps $300 to $1,000 depending on state laws).

Owned Housing

Americans have historically favored single-family dwellings to satisfy their owned housing needs. However, because of rising construction and interest costs, other, less expensive, alternatives are increasing in popularity: condominiums and cooperatives, and manufactured housing and mobile homes.

Single-family Dwellings A housing unit detached from others is a *single-family dwelling*. It is traditionally located in residential neighborhoods. The four basic styles available are (1) the one-floor ranch, which requires more land for construction than do other styles; (2) the two-story, which offers a lower cost per square foot and the privacy of upstairs bedrooms; (3) the split-level, which requires more land than the two-story because each floor level is about a half-story above or below adjacent floors (this style fits well in rolling terrain); and (4) the Cape Cod (one-and-a-half story), which has second-floor windows protruding through the roof, can be built on a small lot, and has sloped ceilings upstairs. There are many variations on these basic styles.

In addition to choice of style, there is the choice between newer and older homes. Many people prefer the modern kitchens and other features found in new homes; others prefer the larger rooms, higher ceilings, bigger closets, and completed landscaping of older homes. Note, though, that some older homes have almost no closet space. Buyers considering an older residence should look for termite infestation and wood rot, as well as any sagging in the structure caused by a weak foundation. Additionally, check the wiring, heating and cooling system, insulation, plumbing, hot-water heater, roof and gutters, and the dryness of basements.

Condominiums and Cooperatives The terms *condominium* and *cooperative* describe a form of ownership rather than a type of building. These "owned apartments" are located in high-rise multiunit structures and multiplex units, as well as in townhouses and row houses. People often prefer these forms of ownership to single-family dwellings because of lower unit costs than for houses, the possibility of the value of the property increasing, availability of recreation facilities, reduced obligation for maintenance, and locations close to employment. More than 50 percent of all condominium purchasers are unmarried.

A *condominium* owner holds legal title to the specific housing unit within a building or project and a proportionate interest in the common grounds and facilities. The operation of the entire complex is run by the owners themselves through a home owners' association they elect. Operation must be in accordance with the association's bylaws, which detail what can and cannot be done. For example, the association could be in charge of swimming pool maintenance and of setting swimming hours. Also, improvements purchased by individual home owners may have to be approved by the association for consistency of design.

Besides making mortgage loan payments, the home owner must also pay a monthly *home owner's fee,* which is established by the home

Checklist for Houses

House exterior and yard

Attractive, well-designed house

In harmony with natural surroundings and neighboring houses

Lot of the right size and shape for house and garage

Desirable orientation on lot

Suitable use of building materials

Attractive landscaping and yard

Good drainage with dry, firm soil around the house

Mature, healthy trees, providing shade when needed

Well-kept driveway and walks

Patio, porch, deck, or yard

Convenient parking—garage, carport, or street

Enough distance between houses to afford privacy

Sheltered entry—well-lighted and large

Convenient service entrance with access to kitchen

Outside construction

Durable siding materials in good condition

Solid brick and masonry free of cracks

Solid foundation walls, six inches above ground level, eight inches thick

Caulked and weather-stripped windows and doors

Noncorrosive gutters and downspouts, connected to storm sewer or splash block to carry water away from house

Copper or aluminum flashing used over doors, windows, and joints on the roof

Inside construction

Sound, smooth walls with invisible nails and taping on dry walls; without hollows or large cracks in plaster walls

Well-done carpentry work with properly fitted joints and mouldings

Well-fitted, easy-to-operate windows

Level wood floors with smooth finish

Good possibilities for improvements, remodeling, expanding

Built-in cabinets with properly fitted and easy-to-work doors and drawers

Dry basement floor with hard smooth surface and adequate drain

Stairways with sturdy railings, adequate head room, not too steep

Leakproof roof, in good condition

Adequate insulation for soundproofing and year-round comfort

Living space

Satisfactory floor plan

Attractive entry with foyer and closet

Work areas (kitchen, laundry, workshop) with adequate storage and counter space, lighting and electrical power

Bedrooms and bathrooms located far enough from other parts of the house to afford privacy and quiet

Inviting social areas (living, dining and family rooms, play space, yard, porch, deck or patio) spacious enough for family and guests

Certain rooms conveniently located: the foyer and living room, dining room and kitchen, bedrooms and baths

Adequate storage—closets, cabinets, shelves, attic, basement, garage

Rooms of sufficient size to accommodate furnishings

Agreeable size and type of windows, placed to provide sufficient light and ventilation

Attractive decorating and fixtures

Usable attic and/or basement space

Extras—fireplace, air conditioning, porches, new kitchen and baths, built-ins, skylights, deck

Source: This information has been taken from the Money Management Institute booklet *Your Housing Dollar,* published by the Money Management Institute of Household Financial Services, Prospect Heights, Illinois. Used with permission.

owner's association. This amount pays for maintenance of common areas and facilities, repairs to the outside of any unit, real estate taxes on common areas, and fire insurance covering the exterior of the buildings. Some areas of concern for the potential buyer include rapidly increasing home owner's fees (developer-subsidized costs may be transferred to the home owners' association after all units are sold), limited marketability for resale (especially when new units in the development are still for sale), excessive rental of unsold units by the developer (which reduces the value of owner-occupied units), and the possibility that the developer might retain the right to charge increasingly higher fees for use of common areas instead of allowing the home owners' association to set fees.

A *cooperative* is actually a corporation that owns and manages groups of housing units. Buyers of cooperative housing purchase shares of ownership in the corporation equivalent to the value of their particular unit and also hold a proportional interest in all common areas. The cooperative holds legal title to the apartments and leases specific units to each buyer. The shareholders have some say in the rules and regulations and usually can change management firms if they desire. The monthly assessment covers the same types of items as does a condominium fee but also includes an amount for the professional management of the complex and payments on the cooperative's mortgage debt. (The pro rata share for interest and property taxes is deductible on an individual's tax return.)

A major concern for prospective buyers of cooperatives is the likelihood of rapidly increasing monthly fees due to numerous unexpected vacancies or nonpayment of fees by other owners. Typically, cooperatives have less marketability than single-family dwellings or condominiums. Also, shareholders in some cooperatives can legally prohibit the sale of shares to particular individuals they dislike. Purchasers of both cooperatives and condominiums should realize that operating costs might be much higher for older, converted apartment buildings than for newer complexes.

Manufactured Housing and Mobile Homes *Manufactured housing* is partially factory-assembled housing units designed to be transported (often in portions) to the home site, where finishing of the building requires another two to six weeks. The quality of such homes is generally good to excellent and many regional and national chains (for example, Jim Walter Homes, Inc.) are in this rapidly growing business. Square-footage costs drop dramatically, since much of the work is done inside a factory rather than on the building site. Further cost reductions are available to persons who purchase a partially completed home and finish it themselves. The manufacturer usually offers lower-than-market mortgage interest rates. Predesigned floor plans can be modified, and the wise buyer is encouraged to examine model homes to determine the quality of construction. More than one-fourth of all new single-family dwellings sold are manufactured units.

Mobile homes are fully factory-assembled housing units built to a certain size (for example, to a maximum of 14 feet by 70 feet) and designed to be towed on a frame with a trailer hitch. These homes are usually sold complete with appliances, furniture, carpeting, and curtains. Mobile home variations include a double-wide (two units connected side to side) and an expandable unit (an additional section perhaps attached to the living room area). Mobile homes are considered personal property, like automobiles, and are thus subject to lower taxes than those for real estate property. The building cost per square foot is about one-half that of a single-family dwelling. Although portable, today's mobile homes are generally sold rather than moved when the owners wish to move to a new location.

Of utmost importance is the quality of the mobile home park in which the home will be located and the protections offered to the person who leases the "pad" upon which the mobile home is placed. Mobile homes rarely appreciate in value like other forms of housing; in fact, they often depreciate. For this reason, purchasers are often limited to mortgage loans of no longer than fifteen years.

Tax Assessment on Real Estate

The major source of revenue for most communities, to provide for numerous community services and schools, is *real estate property taxes.* These are local (town, city, county, township, parish) taxes based on the determined value of buildings and land. Since a tax bill on a typical home could amount to $600 or even $3,000, prospective home owners need to learn something about the process of such taxation and how to legally avoid some of those taxes, if possible.

The process of determining real estate tax liability begins when local government officials establish a *fair market value* for the owner's home and land. This value should be what "a willing buyer would pay a willing seller." Next the *assessed* (or taxable) *value* of the property is calculated. This value is established arbitrarily by the local tax assessor, or by law is a fixed percentage of fair market value (perhaps 50 or 60 or 100 percent). A home with a fair market value of $100,000, for example, might have an assessed value of $60,000. The real estate tax rate is the percentage then levied on assessed valuations of property. Property with a taxable value of $60,000 at a tax rate of thirty mills (one-thousandth of a dollar) would have a tax liability of $1,800 ($60,000 × .030).

When you consider purchasing a home, find out how the property taxes are assessed, what the amount of the most recent tax liability was (by telephoning the tax assessor) and whether local officials expect the taxes to rise substantially in the next year or so. It is not enough to know that one community has a tax rate of twenty mills and a neighboring community has one of twenty-five mills. Table 9–3 shows how a change in the assessed value of a home affects the final tax bill. Although you can do little to affect the tax rate on real estate property, you can claim

TABLE 9-3
Calculating Real Estate Property Taxes

	Home in Community A	Home in Community B
Fair market value	$120,000	$120,000
Assessed (or taxable) value	$120,000	$80,000
Tax rate	20 mils	25 mils
Tax bill	$2,400	$2,000

that the assessed valuation on your home is too high. If your appeal is successful, your tax bill will be lowered accordingly.

Financing a Home

Buying a home probably represents the largest expenditure you will ever make. You should prepare for it thoroughly and become knowledgeable about traditional and alternative mortgage loans and how they work. It is also important to decide whether to buy now or to wait.

Preparing for Home Ownership

Your decision to become a home owner rather than a renter is based not only on your values and goals, but also on your finances. The financial aspect of buying includes money both for the down payment and monthly mortgage payments, plus all housing costs after moving.

You can use several strategies to get the needed finances. Establish a "home savings" fund while you are renting. Many young persons must rent for five years or more before they are able to purchase a home. Some couples decide to postpone beginning a family, and others cut back on entertainment and vacations and put off making major purchases.

Some home buyers obtain gifts or loans from relatives. A person may give up to $10,000 per year to another person without having to pay gift taxes, and the receiver does not have to pay income taxes on the amount. Thus, many younger persons ask affluent relatives for a cash gift to help buy a home now rather than wait a number of years for an inheritance. (This topic is further discussed in Chapter 22).

You can also prepare for home ownership by renting a home with an option to buy. Some landlords give renters the chance to buy the home they rent after one or two years. Obviously, if you live in a home for some time you are in a good position to judge its value.

In preparing for home ownership you should also plan to have funds for moving-in costs and home repairs. Additional costs might include furniture, lamps, draperies, carpeting, shrubbery, and lawn and power tools. You might want to establish a special cash reserve for repairing or replacing an item such as a water heater, furnace, or air conditioner.

Traditional Mortgage Loans and How They Work

A *mortgage loan* is an amount loaned to a borrower by a lender for the purchase of a home. In exchange for the loan the lender (*mortgagee*) has a *mortgage* on the real estate, which is the legal right (the security) to sell the property in the event the borrower (*mortgagor*) defaults on the loan. Mortgage loans are available from savings and loan associations, mutual savings banks, commercial banks, and credit unions. (These institutions were described in Chapter 4).

Traditionally, lenders have made loans to home buyers at a fixed rate and a fixed payment for a term of fifteen to thirty years. For example, a $70,000 loan could be granted at a 12 percent interest rate over a period of thirty years with a monthly payment of $720.03. The process of gradually paying off a mortgage loan through a series of periodic payments to a lender is *amortization.* Each payment goes toward repayment of both the *principal* (the original amount borrowed) and the interest. As the principal is paid off, this amount plus any appreciation in the value of the home become the home owner's *equity* (dollar value of the home in excess of that owed on it).

Most of the monthly payment during the early years of a mortgage loan goes for interest. Table 9–4 shows the interest and principal payment amounts for the first three months of a $70,000, thirty-year, 12 percent mortgage loan. For the first month, $700 goes for interest costs and only $20.03 goes toward retirement of the principal of the loan. The principal monthly payment increases very slowly over the life of the loan. The amortization schedule in Table 9–5 shows how this loan

---

TABLE 9–4
Amortization of Monthly Payment of $720.03 on a $70,000 Thirty-year Mortgage Loan at 12 Percent

First month

$70,000 × 12% × $\frac{1}{12}$	= $700.00	interest payment
$720.03 − $700.00	= $20.03	principal repayment
$70,000 − $20.03	= $69,979.97	balance due

Second month

$69,979.97 × 12% × $\frac{1}{12}$ =	$699.80	interest payment
$720.03 − $699.80	= $20.23	principal repayment
$69,979.97 − $20.23	= $69,959.74	balance due

Third month

$69,959.74 × 12% × $\frac{1}{12}$ =	$699.60	interest payment
$720.03 − $699.60	= $20.43	principal repayment
$69,959.74 − $20.43	= $69,939.31	balance due

TABLE 9–5
Amortization Schedule for a $70,000 Thirty-year (360-payment)
Mortgage Loan at 12 Percent

Month	Monthly Payment	Total Principal Payment	Total Interest Payment	Total Paid	Outstanding Balance
1	$720.03	$ 20.03	$700.00	$ 720.03	$69,979.97
2	720.03	20.23	699.80	1,440.06	69,959.74
3	720.03	20.43	699.60	2,160.09	69,939.31
4	720.03	20.64	699.39	2,880.12	69,918.67
5	720.03	20.84	699.19	3,600.15	69,897.83
6	720.03	21.05	698.98	4,320.18	69,876.78
7	720.03	21.26	698.77	5,040.21	69,855.52
8	720.03	21.47	698.56	5,760.24	69,834.05
9	720.03	21.69	698.34	6,480.27	69,812.36
10	720.03	21.91	698.12	7,200.30	69,790.45
11	720.03	22.13	697.90	7,920.33	69,768.32
12	720.03	22.35	697.68	8,640.36	69,745.97
24	720.03	25.18	694.85	17,280.72	69,459.73
36	720.03	28.37	691.66	25,921.08	69,137.18
48	720.03	31.97	688.06	34,561.44	68,773.73
60	720.03	36.03	684.00	43,201.80	68,364.18
120	720.03	65.45	654.58	86,403.60	65,392.34
180	720.03	118.91	601.12	129,605.40	59,993.42
240	720.03	216.02	504.01	172,807.20	50,185.23
300	720.03	392.44	327.59	216,009.00	32,366.69
360	715.89	708.80	7.09	259,210.80	–0–

will be eventually paid off. Many years pass before much of the monthly payment begins to reduce the outstanding balance of the loan.

The amortization table illustrated in Table 9–6 gives the amount of monthly payment required for each $1,000 of a mortgage loan at different interest rates. Using this table, we can calculate the monthly payment for mortgage loans of different sizes. For example, a $70,000 mortgage loan at 12 percent for thirty years costs $10.2861 per $1,000. Thus, 70 × $10.2861 equals $720.03.

There are four variations of the traditional mortgage loan: the conventional mortgage loan, a privately insured mortgage, an FHA-insured mortgage, and a VA-insured mortgage. Each is discussed below.

Conventional Mortgage Loan   The most traditional home loan is the conventional mortgage loan. This is the fixed rate, fixed-payment loan described above, which the home buyer obtains directly from a financial institution. Since a lender's only protection against possible loss is the home itself, most require a down payment of 20 to 30 percent of the loan amount. On a $100,000 home, for example, a savings and loan association would likely lend only $70,000 to $80,000. Then, should the borrower default, the lender probably could sell the home

TABLE 9–6
Monthly Payment on $1,000 Debt

Interest Rate	Payment Period (Years)			
	15	20	25	30
8	$ 9.5565	$ 8.3644	$ 7.7182	$ 7.3376
8.5	9.8474	8.6782	8.0528	7.6891
9	10.1427	8.9973	8.3920	8.0462
9.5	10.4422	9.3213	8.7370	8.4085
10	10.7461	9.6502	9.0870	8.7757
10.5	11.0539	9.9838	9.4418	9.1474
11	11.3660	10.3219	9.8011	9.5232
11.5	11.6819	10.6643	10.1647	9.9030
12	12.0017	11.0109	10.5322	10.2861
12.5	12.3252	11.3614	10.9035	10.6726
13	12.6524	11.7158	11.2784	11.0620
13.5	12.9832	12.0737	11.6564	11.4541
14	13.3174	12.4352	12.0376	11.8487
14.5	13.6550	12.8000	12.4216	12.2456
15	13.9959	13.1679	12.8083	12.6444
15.5	14.3399	13.5388	13.1975	13.0452
16	14.6870	13.9126	13.5889	13.4476

Note: Use this table to figure almost any monthly mortgage payment. For example, an $80,000, twenty-year loan at 11 percent will require a monthly payment of $825.75 ($10.3219 × 80); over thirty years it will require a monthly payment of $761.86 ($9.5232 × 80).

for at least the amount of the outstanding loan balance. Lenders feel more secure with larger down payments and often give a slight reduction in interest with them. Thus, with a down payment of $30,000, a lender might offer an interest rate one-quarter or one-half of 1 percent lower than with a $20,000 down payment.

Privately Insured Mortgage A conventional loan can be obtained by people with a good income and credit rating who are unable to make a substantial down payment. The lender simply requires the borrower to purchase *private mortgage insurance,* which insures the first 20 percent of a loan in case of default. For example, a lender could loan a home buyer $95,000 for a $100,000 home with only $5,000 down payment. The mortgage insurance company would insure 20 percent, or $19,000 ($95,000 × 20 percent), of the debt, which would assure the lender full payment of the loan even if the home is later repossessed for default and sold for perhaps only $85,000.

Private mortgage insurance for a borrower is typically arranged by the financial institution. The largest private mortgage insurer is the Mortgage Guaranty Insurance Corporation. On top of the mortgage payment for principal and interest, the cost is usually one-half of 1 percent of the mortgage loan for the first five years of the debt and one-quarter of 1 percent thereafter, or until the unpaid balance drops to 80 percent of the original loan. The waiting period for the credit investigation to obtain private mortgage insurance is usually less than two weeks.

FHA-insured Mortgage   To encourage lending, the *Federal Housing Administration (FHA)* of the federal government's Department of Housing and Urban Development (HUD) insures loans that meet its standards. The borrower must be creditworthy and the home must be approved. Most new homes meet the minimum-quality standards of the FHA and are approved.

The borrower goes to the usual lenders, and the FHA insures the mortgage so that the lender will not lose money if the borrower defaults. Like private mortgage insurers, the FHA charges borrowers a mortgage insurance premium. This premium is paid in total as an upfront, lump-sum payment, or may be financed.

Usually, only very small down payments are required, since this is a federally backed loan. Down payment minimums are calculated as follows: 3 percent on the first $25,000 of appraised value and 5 percent on amounts above $25,000. FHA-insured mortgage loans can be made on homes that do not exceed FHA lending limits, which change frequently but were recently $68,300 for single-family homes and $76,500 for two-family homes. Terms can be as long as thirty years and the waiting time to process an application is often sixty to ninety days.

VA-guaranteed Mortgage   The *Veterans Administration (VA)* promotes home ownership among veterans by providing the lender with a guarantee against buyer default. Mobile homes also qualify. In effect, the VA guarantee is much like that of the FHA or private insurers because the lender is protected for a portion of the value of the loan in the event the home must be repossessed and sold. Homes must meet VA standards of construction (most newer homes do), and only veterans qualify under this program. A low or no down payment is required on VA loans. Lending limits are set by the VA. Usually sixty to ninety days are needed to approve an application.

Alternative Mortgage Approaches

Mortgage loan rates in recent years have ranged from a low of 4.5 percent in 1972 to more than 20 percent in 1980. Such enormous swings created havoc in the lending industry, resulting in numerous bankruptcies and mergers as lenders found themselves with thousands of low-rate mortgage loans outstanding while having to offer high interest rates to savers. New borrowers also suffered, as monthly payments soared due to high interest rates: a $70,000 loan for thirty years at 9 percent has a monthly payment of $563.23; at 16 percent it is $941.33, or 67 percent more. Alternative mortgage approaches have come about in response to high interest rates. In general, most new alternative lending approaches eliminate the long-term, fixed-rate mortgage loan and include techniques to keep the monthly payment as low as possible. The lower rates also permit borrowers to purchase larger, more expensive homes than they could afford with a traditional fixed-rate loan.

Some of the newer mortgage loans allow smaller monthly payments than are actually necessary to pay the interest. This causes *negative amortization*, in which the principal loan balance actually rises. In later years the borrower repays the larger principal amount due. For example, Table 9–4 (page 276) illustrates that a payment of $700 is needed to repay the first month's interest on a thirty-year $70,000 mortgage at 12 percent. If the monthly payment in the early years was only $675, the principal balance owed would increase each month. Later higher payments, perhaps of $750, $800, or $900, would be required to amortize the larger total principal and interest amounts owed because of the earlier negative amortization.

The alternatives described below are the adjustable rate mortgage, graduated payment mortgage, renegotiable rate mortgage, shared appreciation mortgage, growing equity mortgage, seller financing, and assumable mortgage.[1]

Adjustable Rate Mortgage (ARM)   With the *adjustable rate mortgage*—sometimes called a variable rate mortgage—a borrower's interest rate can fluctuate up or down according to some index of interest rates. The monthly payment could increase or decrease, perhaps monthly or quarterly. Or the payment could remain fixed while the principal increased, causing negative amortization. Or both the payment and the principal could remain constant but the term of the loan might increase by several years. Lenders may offer rates at 1 percent to 3 percent or more below market rates to induce usage or guarantee that payments will not increase for perhaps a two- to five-year period; sometimes the rates are sharply discounted for the first year. Later increases in the rates make monthly payments greater and perhaps unaffordable, forcing some borrowers to sell. But, if rates drop, the costs would be lower than those of a conventional mortgage. *Interest-rate caps*, which place a limit on the amount an interest rate can increase (perhaps no more than 1 or 2 percent per year in one direction and no more than 5 percent in one direction over the life of the loan) are common. In recent years, this has been the most popular alternative mortgage.

Graduated Payment Mortgage (GPM)   Smaller-than-normal payments are required in the early years but gradually increase to larger-than-normal payments in later years, on the assumption that increased income will be available for the higher payments. Payments, for example, could increase 2.5 percent each year for five years and then level off. Or the payment could be level for five years and then rise 15 percent for the next five years, with another rise of 15 percent five

---

[1] A substantial portion of the following discussion on alternative mortgage approaches was adapted with permission from "So You're Looking for a Mortgage Loan?" Residential Tax Information, Inc., P.O. Box 27331, Denver, Colorado 80227.

years later, and so forth. Because payments in the beginning are less than the interest owed, the shortfall is added to the outstanding balance owed and results in negative amortization.

Renegotiable Rate, or "Roll-over," Mortgage (RRM) This mortgage is a series of short-term loans for two to five years, but with total amortization over the usual twenty-five to thirty years. It must be renewed each time period. If interest rates have increased, the borrower can increase the monthly payments, extend the term of the loan, or seek another mortgage loan from a different source. Rates usually cannot change more than one-half of 1 percent per year or more than a total of 5 percent.

Shared Appreciation Mortgage (SAM) The lender offers an interest rate about one-third less than the market rate for an agreement to receive perhaps one-third of any appreciation when the home is sold or after ten years. One question is, should the lender share in any increase as a result of home improvements made by the borrower? If so, how? Also, how does the borrower pay the lender's share of the appreciation after ten years if the home has not been sold?

Growing Equity Mortgage (GEM) The GEM is designed for people who want to pay off their mortgage loan early to reduce interest costs. The payments on the fixed-interest loan are scheduled to increase by a predetermined amount each year, perhaps 2 to 7 percent. The increase goes toward reducing the principal owed, so, for example, a thirty-year mortgage may be paid off in fifteen years.

One form of GEM requires biweekly payments (twenty-six per year), which results in an extra payment of one month per year. Of course, almost all types of mortgage loans will permit payment of additional amounts toward principal without penalty.

Seller Financing (SELF) Many variations exist, but many sellers are willing to make an installment sale with interest, with a balloon payment due after five or ten years. This requires that all principal and interest not paid at that point be paid. An extremely large sum thus would require refinancing, which would not be difficult to obtain if the home appreciates. However, interest rates could have risen dramatically, making it difficult to budget larger payments. In most installment sales, the buyer obtains the title to the property upon moving in. This is not the case with a contract sale, a land contract, and a contract for deed. These latter situations are more risky for the buyer because all terms in the contract must be satisfied before obtaining title, which could be thirty years.

Assumable Mortgage (ASM) More than one million mortgage loans a year are assumed by new purchasers through a written agreement made between the lender and the new owner. When an agreement is executed, the new buyer obtains the loan at either the original interest rate or a preferred rate (below market rate) offered by the lending institution. In order to pay off the seller's equity, the buyer must make a substantial down payment or must obtain a *second mortgage,* which is a secondary claim on the property after the claims of the first mortgage are met. A second mortgage often has a short term, such as three, five, or ten years. A new home owner paying off both first and second mortgages feels considerable budget stress.

Down Payment, Length of Maturity, and Points

Three factors that greatly affect mortgage loans are the amount of down payment, the length of maturity of the loan, and any "points" charged in making the loan.

Down Payment Perhaps you think of a down payment as the minimum amount you must pay to obtain a mortgage and move into a home. For those with limited cash, this may be true, but for those with an extra $5,000 or $10,000 available, the situation differs. Making a larger down payment than required lowers the amount of the total mortgage loan needed and the amount of the resulting monthly payments. A smaller loan also carries lower total interest costs.

Table 9–7 shows the progressively smaller monthly payments resulting from increasing the amount of the down payment. At 12 percent interest a thirty-year loan of $75,000 costs $771.46 per month. Making an extra $5,000 down payment reduces the monthly payment to $720.03, and an additional $5,000 reduces it further to $668.60.

People often prefer to make a smaller down payment so they can keep some funds to pay for moving-in expenses or to maintain a savings account. Others consider the after-tax return that might be earned on alternative investments if the extra down payment money was placed elsewhere. (Chapters 14 through 20 explore this topic in detail.) Also, it is sometimes easy to sell a home with a large mortgage loan by permitting a new buyer to assume the mortgage without having to make too large a down payment to buy the equity of the first owner (discussed as assumable mortgages earlier).

TABLE 9–7
Effect of Down Payment Size on Monthly Payment
(12 percent mortgage loan for thirty years)

Amount of Loan	Approximate Monthly Payment
$75,000	$771.46
70,000	720.03
65,000	668.60
60,000	617.17
55,000	565.74
50,000	514.31

TABLE 9–8
Monthly Payment and Total Interest to Repay a $70,000 Loan[a]

Length of Loan	Interest Rate					
	8%	10%	12%	14%	16%	18%
30 years	$514 $115,000	$614 $151,000	$720 $189,000	$829 $229,000	$941 $269,000	$1,056 $310,000
25 years	$540 $92,000	$636 $121,000	$737 $151,000	$843 $183,000	$951 $215,000	$1,063 $249,000
20 years	$586 $7?,000	$676 $92,000	$771 $115,000	$870 $139,000	$974 $164,000	$1,08? $189,00?

Note: Figures are rounded.
[a] The top in each pair is the monthly payment, and the bottom is total interest paid.

Length of Maturity   The total amount of interest on a loan is based on both the interest rate charged and the length of the repayment period. For loans with the same interest rate, the longer the term of repayment the smaller the payment size. For example, a loan of $120 could be repaid at $10 a month for twelve months or at $5 a month for twenty-four months.

However, the longer the term of repayment, the more interest charged. Table 9–8 illustrates the relationship among maturity length, monthly payment, and interest cost. The monthly payment goes up as the term of the loan becomes shorter. For example, the monthly payment on a 12 percent loan is $720 for thirty years and $771 for twenty years. Note also that when the loan is paid back sooner, perhaps in twenty instead of thirty years, the total interest costs are much lower ($115,000 rather than $189,000).

Buyers who can afford to make higher monthly payments than required on longer loans often choose a shorter-term mortgage loan. However, some buyers with that capability choose a longer-term loan anyway and place extra money in savings or make alternative investments.

Points   Lenders charge a special one-time fee to increase the yield on FHA and VA mortgage loans to what market conditions demand. The government-regulated loans have interest rates that are always set lower than conventional mortgage rates. For example, if mortgage loans average 12 percent, FHA and VA loans will probably be about 11 percent. Lenders must be encouraged to make such below-market-rate loans. Accordingly, the lender charges the seller or the buyer of a home one or more points. A *point* is a fee equal to 1 percent of the total loan amount, and it must be paid in full when the home is bought. For example, if a lender charges two points on a $60,000 loan, this amounts to a charge of $1,200. Note that by law these points do not have to be included in calculating the effective annual percentage rate. Each point charged increases the annual percentage rate approximately .125 percent.

Buyers of VA homes are prohibited by law from paying points. In reality, though, most sellers simply increase the sales price of the home by the amount of the points when quoting a price to a prospective purchaser who intends to use VA mortgage assistance. Home purchasers are protected to some extent from inflated prices, as the VA will not make loans for more than the appraised value of the home.

Additionally, points are often used in connection with a *loan origination fee.* This is what the lender charges the borrower for doing all the paperwork and setting up the mortgage loan. This fee usually ranges from 1 to 2 percent of the amount of the loan, or one or two points.

Deciding to Buy Now or to Wait

If you think you can predict the future and know when home prices and interest rates will drop, you should wait before buying. If not, you should buy as soon as you are able. Even during an economic recession, home prices generally rise every year.

Table 9–9 shows the financial consequences of waiting instead of buying now. Assume you are considering waiting to buy a $90,000 home with a thirty-year 12 percent mortgage loan, hoping that interest rates will drop next year. If the rate does drop to 11 percent and the price of the home rises only 6 percent, you may gain a little. Instead of a down payment of $9,000, you will pay $9,540. Furthermore, the monthly payment on the current 12 percent, $81,000 mortgage loan is $833.17, but next year on the 11 percent, $85,860 loan it will be $817.66, a savings of $15.51 per month. If you guess wrong about next year's interest rates and they remain at 12 percent, the monthly payment on $85,860 will be $883.16. This is an extra $49.99 per month and $17,996.40 over the life of the loan.

Estimating Home-buying Costs

Many prospective home buyers look at homes that are too expensive but end up buying them anyway. Such a buyer will have a nice home but will also have a budget that is "home poor." This home owner spends such a great proportion of income on housing costs that there is very little money left over for other items. To avoid becoming home poor, the wise financial planner estimates all costs of housing and thus makes more knowledgeable decisions.

In the discussion that follows, we assume that the prospective home owner has the funds necessary for the down payment to buy an $80,000 home. We use an alternative mortgage approach, so the down

TABLE 9–9
Buy a House Now or Wait? (Assumes a 6 percent increase in the price of a house in one year)

Cost to buy now

Price	$90,000
Down payment (10%)	9,000
Mortgage loan	81,000
30-year fixed mortgage monthly payment at	
8%	$ 594.35
9%	651.74
10%	710.83
11%	771.38
12%	833.17
13%	896.02
14%	959.74
15%	1,024.20
16%	1,089.26

Cost to wait a year and buy with 6% increase

Price	$95,400
Down payment (10%)	9,540
Mortgage loan	85,860
30-year fixed mortgage monthly payment at	
8%	$ 630.01
9%	690.85
10%	753.48
11%	817.66
12%	883.16
13%	949.78
14%	1,017.33
15%	1,086.56
16%	1,154.61

payment is only 5 percent ($4,000). All other costs are described below, and Table 9–10 shows a summary of estimated buying costs.

Principal and Interest

The mortgage loan requires repayment of both principal and interest (PI). The monthly payment schedule shown earlier in Table 9–6 (page 278) gives the amount needed per month to repay each $1,000 of mortgage loan at different interest rates. To estimate this amount, simply multiply the figures. For our thirty-year, 12 percent loan, the amount in the table is $10.2861. In our example, the loan amount is $76,000 ($80,000 − $4,000); multiplying 76 by $10.2861 equals a monthly payment of $781.74 to repay the principal and interest.

Taxes and Insurance

Taxes and insurance (TI) are the last part of the popular abbreviation *PITI,* which realtors and lenders often use to indicate a mortgage payment that includes principal, interest, taxes, and insurance. As dis-

TABLE 9-10
Estimated Buying Costs (Purchase price of home, $80,000; closing on July 1)

	At Closing	Monthly
Down payment	$4,000	—
Principal and interest (30 years, 12%, $76,000)	—	$781.74
Taxes (for first half-year)	450	75.00
Insurance (home owner's policy)	480	40.00
Private mortgage insurance	—	31.67
Loan origination fee	1,140	—
Title insurance (to protect lender)	190	—
Title insurance (to protect borrower)	190	—
Attorney's fee	200	—
Credit report	25	—
Recording fees	20	—
Appraisal fee	150	—
Termite inspection fee	50	—
Survey fee	100	—
Notary fee	25	—
	$7,020	$928.41
Less amount provided by seller	450[a]	
Subtotal	$6,570	
Warranty insurance (optional)	240	20.00
Mortgage life insurance (optional)	312	26.00
Totals	$7,122	$974.41

[a]Funds from seller to pay taxes for first six months of the year.

cussed earlier in this chapter, real estate property taxes must be paid to local governments. The total amount, $900 in our example, is due once a year when the government sends out its tax bill. This amount varies by community, usually ranging from 1 to 4 percent of the cost of the home. Most lenders require that the borrower prepay a pro rata share (one-twelfth) of the real estate taxes each month ($75 here) along with the monthly principal and interest. If a buyer takes possession at the midpoint of the tax year, the seller should make one-half ($450 here) of the taxes due available to the buyer on the day of *closing.* This is the day when the home is financially and legally transferred to the new buyer, which usually takes place in the office of the lender or an attorney.

Lenders always require home owners to insure the home itself in case of fire. Insurance on the contents of the home is up to the home owner. Both the home and its contents can be covered in a typical home owner's insurance policy. (Chapter 11 covers this information in detail.) The annual premium must be paid each year in advance. Most lenders require prepayment of a pro rata share (one-twelfth) each month ($40 here) of the next year's insurance premium. Additionally, on closing day the purchaser must be prepared to prepay one year's premium ($480 here).

Funds deposited with a lender for taxes and insurance go into an *escrow account,* which is a special reserve account used to pay third parties. Most lenders pay interest on funds deposited for taxes and insurance until the bills arrive at the financial institution; these are then paid out of the escrow account by the lender, who acts as the borrower's agent.

Private Mortgage Insurance

When a buyer makes a minimum down payment, a lender almost always requires the purchase of private mortgage insurance (described in the previous section). In this example, assume a premium charge totaling one-half of 1 percent of the mortgage loan (.005 × $76,000 = $380), which must be prepaid monthly ($31.67 here) to the lender, who forwards it to the mortgage insurance company.

Loan Origination Fee

The lender's charge for setting up the loan and completing necessary paperwork is the loan origination fee. In this example, assume a fee of 1.5 percent (1.5 points) of the mortgage loan, or $1,140 (.015 × $76,000). The buyer must pay this at the time of closing.

Title Insurance

The *title* to real property is the legal right of ownership interest. In real estate transactions, the title is transferred to a new owner through a *deed,* which is a written document used to convey real estate ownership. Usually with the assistance of an attorney at closing, the buyer reviews various documents to ensure having as clear a title as possible. Examples of claims against property include electrical work that a previous owner never paid for and the sale of mineral rights perhaps seventy-five years ago.

There are four types of deeds used: (1) a *warranty deed* is the safest, as it guarantees that the title is free of any previous mortgages; (2) a *special warranty deed* guarantees that only the current owner has not placed any mortgage encumbrances on the title; (3) a *quitclaim deed* transfers whatever title the current owner had in the property with no guarantee whatsoever; (4) a *deed of bargain and sale* conveys title with or without a guarantee with an assertion that the seller had an ownership interest.

If the quality of the deed is suspect, a title search and the purchase of title insurance can offer better protection. An attorney or title company can inspect court records and prepare a detailed written history of property ownership called an *abstract.* In a *title search,* an attorney examines the abstract and other documents and may issue a *certificate of title.* This is a legal opinion (not a guarantee) of the status of the title and is often provided when an abstract is unavailable or lost. The seller normally pays the fees for preparation of these documents.

A lender often requires a buyer to purchase *title insurance* because it protects the lender's interest if the title is later found faulty. A *separate* title insurance policy must be purchased by home owners if they wish to insure their own interest. Policies for home owners usually cover only the amount of the down payment, the beginning equity, rather than any appreciating equity occurring over the years. The premium for each title policy varies widely among title companies. The one-time charge at closing may amount to one-quarter of 1 percent of the amount of the loan for each policy ($190 here).

In areas where real estate transfers are frequent, the wise money manager might want to ask a title insurance company about a *reissue rate.* This is policy with lower-rate premiums because the property history has been checked in recent years. Some home owners do not purchase title insurance for themselves, assuming that the title insurance company will successfully fight any claims; this may not be true, however.

Attorney's Fee

About half of all home buyers hire an attorney to represent them during closing to review all documents and provide advice. Fees are commonly one-half of 1 percent of the purchase price of the home, although some attorneys do this work for as low as one-quarter of 1 percent. (The attorney's fee is $200 in our example.)

Miscellaneous Costs

A credit report normally must be compiled before a home buyer can obtain a loan. The borrower pays the fee for this report. Recording fees are charged to transfer ownership documents in the county courthouse. An *appraisal fee* may be required for a professionally prepared estimate of the value of the property by an objective party. A *survey* is sometimes required to certify the specific boundaries of the lot. Occasionally fees are charged for a termite inspection. Finally, separate *notary fees* may be charged for the services of those legally qualified to certify (or notarize) signatures.

The costs for most home-buying expenses are set by tradition and are subject to negotiation. The wise financial manager shops for better prices whenever possible. (Table 9–10 shows sample fee amounts.)

The federal Real Estate Settlement Procedures Act requires that on or before closing day a "good faith estimate" of all specific closing costs be given to the borrower. Each borrower must also receive a settlement information booklet that explains many details of the closing process. Depending on state laws, closing costs could vary from 1 percent of the mortgage loan up to 4 or 5 percent. Prospective home owners should visit a lender to get an idea of total closing costs in their community.

Warranty Insurance

All homes for sale carry some type of *implied warranty,* which is a legal doctrine in all states suggesting a promise of a certain level of quality that an ordinary buyer has a right to expect. Thus, the heating unit and air conditioner should work at the time the buyer purchases the home. This does not mean, however, that they must still be working two years from purchase of the home. Nor does an implied warranty mean that the roof will not have a small leak or that water will not slowly seep into the basement. A seller who knowingly hides such serious defects might be liable, but the buyer will have to hire an attorney and sue.

Warranty insurance provides another option for the home owner. Home protection warranty insurance is sold through real estate brokers for a one-time premium of perhaps $200 to $300. Buyers no longer need simply to trust the seller's assurances on the apparent good quality of the home. If the central air conditioning unit fails at a cost of $1,800, the home owner need pay only $250 and the insurance company will pay the rest. No inspection of the home is needed unless the policy also covers structural defects. The largest insurance company in the field is American Home Shield.

For new homes, the industry trade group, the National Association of Home Builders (NAHB), has established a Home Owners Warranty Corporation (HOW), made up of more than one hundred local councils of builders. Participating builders pay a beginning one-time insurance premium on all their homes, plus a service fee each of the years the warranty is in effect. These costs are built into the sales price of each home. The builder is responsible for repairs during the first two years and an insurance company for the remaining term, usually eight more years. About 40 percent of new houses being sold today are protected by the HOW program.

A little-known benefit of having a mortgage loan insured by the FHA or guaranteed by the VA is that newly built homes have a one-year warranty against the builder failing to meet specifications. Further, defects that seriously affect livability can be repaired at government expense during the first four years of ownership.

Mortgage Life Insurance

Home owners may consider the purchase of mortgage life insurance. This special type of term life insurance pays off the balance of the mortgage loan in the event the insured home owner dies. Thus, survivors inherit a home with no mortgage debt. The cost depends on the health and age of the insured and on the size of the mortgage. Of course, it may be in the beneficiary's best financial interest to keep the mortgage, particularly if it is at a low interest rate. (This topic is examined further in Chapter 13).

The Home-buying Process

After you find the home you really want, the buying process can move rapidly. Five steps are in order: (1) revise your budget, (2) make an offer to buy, (3) make a counteroffer to buy (if needed), (4) apply for a mortgage loan, and (5) sign your name on closing day.

Revising Your Budget

The wise financial manager adds a few more budget items when considering buying a home. Some estimate ought to be made for maintenance. It could range from $15 to $20 monthly for a small owned apartment up to $30 to $40 for a single-family dwelling. Other budget items could be for moving-in costs and new furniture and tools. These expenses are likely to be much higher during the first year of ownership than in later years. Research shows that people spend in excess of $2,000 on such items. It may be helpful to estimate the cost of utilities as well. The previous owner may agree to show you receipts of the past year with which to develop your estimates. Budgetary forms to help in estimating costs are shown in Chapter 3 and in Table 9–2.

Making an Offer to Buy

Sellers of homes generally put a sales price on the property 3 to 10 percent higher than what they expect to get for it. Housing is an area in which buyers are expected to dicker. Therefore, you probably should make an offer to buy for less than the asking price. The formal legal document that conveys your dollar offer and any list of conditions you might want is called a *purchase contract* or a *sales contract*. It is wise to use preprinted forms available from real estate professionals and attorneys, as they often include protective clauses.

Examples of conditions you might want to list are a seller-paid termite inspection; certification of the plumbing, heating, cooling, and electrical systems; and inclusion of the living room drapes and kitchen appliances in the purchase price. Make sure that your *earnest money* (a deposit in advance of the down payment) will be refunded by the seller if you cannot obtain satisfactory financing within a specified time period, usually thirty days. This protects you if lending conditions suddenly become unfavorable. Earnest money is usually kept in an escrow account. Of course, if you simply change your mind about buying, you may forfeit your earnest money.

Making a Counteroffer

Most people who sell their homes do not accept the first offer. They assume that if a buyer is willing to make a formal offer of X amount of dollars, that buyer may be willing to pay X plus a few thousand more dollars. The seller might make you an official *counteroffer*, which is a legal offer to sell (or buy) a home at a different price and perhaps with different conditions. Realize that if a seller is willing to make you a counteroffer, he or she may be willing to sell even at a slightly lower price. Thus, if you then make a counteroffer between the two prices, a sale will usually result. However, if you push the seller too far, you risk having the seller back out of the negotiations altogether. Remember that while all this dickering is going on, the seller could be receiving offers from other prospective buyers.

Applying for a Mortgage Loan

Assuming you have talked with lenders to get a good idea of the financial terms available in your community, you apply for a mortgage loan on the specific home you have selected. The financial institution usually approves or disapproves the loan within ten days. Your exact interest rate may be the current rate at the time of application or the rate at the time of closing.

Signing Your Name on Closing Day

The buyer and seller and their representatives generally meet in the lender's office on closing day and sign all required documents in less than one hour. If the buyer chooses a closing date just past the sixteenth of the month, the first payment on the new mortgage loan may not be due until the first of the month after next, six weeks hence.

Selling a Home

Although most of this chapter deals with buying a home, there are important considerations in selling a home. Generally, it helps to do some minor painting, cleaning, and repairing before listing your home for sale. Let's examine the pros and cons of listing your home with a realtor, note some of the costs of selling, become aware of the dangers of seller financing, and consider some aspects of income taxes.

Listing with a Realtor or Selling a Home Yourself

Knowing that the sales commission to a realtor on a $100,000 home could easily be $6,000 or $7,000 is usually enough motivation for home owners to consider selling the home themselves. About one-third of home sales each year do not involve realtors. The key is to know what price to ask for your home. Asking too little could cost you much more than the services of a realtor.

As a wise compromise, many home owners begin by contacting a few realtors to get their opinions on how much their home is worth. Realtors are often most willing to give their opinions, since the home owner might list the home with them if it does not sell quickly. A "For Sale" sign on your lawn and about $100 in advertising should keep your telephone ringing for a month or so with all types of inquiries. If your home does not sell by then, perhaps you should list with a realtor.

Realtors request that home owners sign a *listing agreement* permitting them to list the property exclusively and/or with a multiple listing service. When there may be only a few prospective buyers, a multiple listing service may work best, since every broker in the community can show and sell the home. Brokers are invaluable in qualifying prospective customers, distinguishing between serious buyers and people who are just looking or others who want to visit homes they simply cannot afford. If your broker cannot find a buyer within sixty days, you should consider signing an agreement with another broker who might be more aggressive in advertising and selling your property. Any sale that occurs (or begins) during the time period of the listing agreement will result in a commission paid to the realtor even if you find the buyer on your own.

Costs of Selling

A realtor's commission is the greatest selling cost, and most sellers are unaware that many brokers will negotiate the commission. Most sellers also pay for the cost of updating the title with a title search. Some sellers get a professional appraisal as well.

An often-overlooked selling cost is a *prepayment fee* charged by the mortgage lender. This fee is designed to discourage people from refinancing a mortgage every time interest rates drop. Most mortgage loans are paid off before maturity because people move and have to sell. Almost all mortgage loan contracts, therefore, include a clause that specifies the prepayment penalty, if any. This is often 1 to 3 percent of the original mortgage loan. On an $80,000 mortgage loan, for example, the charge would be from $800 to $2,400.

A *due-on-sale clause* requires that the mortgage be paid if the home is sold. It can impose a particularly heavy burden on the seller, as it generally prohibits a seller from letting a new buyer assume the mortgage loan. Home owners often have an existing loan with an interest rate well below market. If no due-on-sale clause is in the original mortgage loan agreement, it could be easier to sell the home through a loan assumption than if the buyer must obtain his or her own mortgage. The U.S. Supreme Court has upheld the constitutionality of such clauses whether expressly written in the loan agreement or implied by various state laws. Avoid this clause if possible when buying, as it eliminates one selling option. If you are unclear about your present mortgage loan clause, simply telephone your lender for clarification.

Dangers of Seller Financing

Sellers having trouble marketing their homes have successfully resorted to many variations of *seller financing,* although difficulties can become quite serious. Suppose you have a home worth $100,000 with a mortgage loan balance of $45,000. The buyer assumes the existing 10 percent mortgage loan, puts up $20,000 in cash, and takes out a second mortgage from you of $35,000 with a five-year term at 12.5 percent. At closing the broker gets $6,000 in commission and you come away with a net of $14,000 cash. This is a small sum for you to use to make a down payment on another home. Since you probably would be depending on the income you receive from the second mortgage payments to make mortgage payments on another home, think what could happen if the buyer cannot make the second mortgage payments to you.

Income Taxes

If you sell a home for more than you paid, you will have a taxable gain. Such gains are taxed at the same rates as income from ordinary sources. A home bought for $80,000 and sold for $100,000, for example, would yield proceeds of $20,000. If your marginal tax rate is 33 percent, the tax on the $20,000 would be $6,600.

IRS regulations permit deferring tax payment on capital gains from home sales if all the proceeds from one sale are invested in another home or in a newly constructed home within twenty-four months. You can defer taxable gains for years by buying another, higher priced home within the IRS time limits each time you sell. At age fifty-five a most generous tax break becomes available: home owners aged fifty-five and older who have lived in their last home for three of the past five years before selling it are allowed a once-in-a-lifetime capital gains exclusion amounting to the first $125,000 of accumulated gains. That might be a prize worth waiting for.

Remember that the IRS requires proof of tax-deductible expenses. Keep accurate records of any home improvements you make, such as constructing a new garage or adding shrubbery, that add to the value of your property. These can be subtracted from any taxable gains resulting from the sale of a home. (See Chapter 2 for an example of such a record.)

Summary

1. Most people have six goals in housing that reflect to some extent their values, financial goals and aspirations: use and function, ease of care, efficiency, safety, attractiveness, and individuality.

2. There are five areas of decision making about where to live: mobility, proximity, neighborhood and location, pollution, and costs.

3. When we compare the pros and cons of renting versus buying housing, renting looks pretty good.

4. Renters generally pay out less money in terms of cash flow while owners/buyers usually see an increase in the value of the home, permitting them to be financially better off.

5. The decision to spend a certain amount of money on housing should be based on careful financial analysis.

6. Among other factors you should compare when considering rental units are security deposit requirements, late charges, and restrictive subleasing clauses.

7. Tenants have several legal rights; in some states this includes withholding rent for landlord noncompliance with the lease, as

well as requiring that security deposits be returned in a timely manner.

8. Condominiums and cooperatives are increasing in popularity as apartment-style homes in part because they are less expensive than single-family dwellings.

9. The major source of revenue for local communities is often the real estate property tax, which is calculated on the basis of the assessed value of the property.

10. Successful strategies to get needed finances to purchase a home include gifts from relatives and renting a home with an option to buy.

11. Traditional mortgage loans for homes are amortized. Amortization is the process of gradually paying off a mortgage through a series of periodic payments to a lender.

12. Numerous alternative types of mortgages are available that have reduced the importance of the long-term, fixed-rate mortgage loan in addition to devising techniques to keep the monthly payment as low as possible.

13. Mathematics show that most people considering buying a home might be wise to buy it as soon as possible instead of waiting, even if interest rates are slowly declining.

14. The wise financial planner tries to avoid becoming "home poor" by carefully estimating all housing costs, such as principal and interest, taxes and insurance, title insurance, and attorney's fee.

15. Five steps that expedite the process of buying a home include revising your budget, making an offer to buy, making a counteroffer to buy (if needed), applying for a mortgage loan, and signing your name on closing day.

16. When selling a home, it is wise to consider the pros and cons of listing with a real estate broker or selling the home yourself; the extent of selling costs; the dangers of seller financing; and the impact of income taxes.

Modern Money Management

The Johnsons Decide to Buy a Condominium

Belinda's parents and maternal grandmother have combined their finances and presented Harry and Belinda with $15,000 for them to use to purchase a condominium. They have shopped and found two that they like very much. The financial alternatives are presented in the accompanying table.

1. Which of the five mortgage alternatives (developers A and B or lenders C, D, and E) has the lowest monthly payment? Why? (Create a table to present the information.)

2. Which plan has the lowest total closing costs? Highest?

3. If the Johnsons had enough spare cash to make the 20 percent down payment (which they do not), would you recommend lender C or D? Why?

4. Assuming that the Johnsons will need about $2,500 for moving-in costs (in addition to closing costs) and they have to choose between developer A and B, which would you recommend. Why?

5. Choose the best of the five options for the Johnsons and explain briefly why you recommend that developer or lender.

Financing Details on Two Condominiums Available to the Johnsons

Condo 1 Price, $85,000	Developer A will finance with a 10 percent down payment and a 9 percent ARM 30-year loan with 2 points as a loan origination fee. The initial monthly payment for principal and interest is $615.53 ($76,500 after the down payment results in 76.5 × $8.0462). After 1 year the rate goes to 10 percent. At that point, the rate can go up or down as much as 2 percent per year, depending on the cost of an index of mortgage funds. There is a cap of 5 percent over the life of the loan. Taxes are estimated to be about $600 and the home owner's insurance premium should be about $240 annually. A mortgage insurance premium of $48 a month must be paid for 5 years.
Condo 2 Price, $81,000	Developer B will finance with 5 percent down payment and an 11 percent GPM 30-year loan with 3 points as a loan origination fee. The initial monthly payment for principal and interest is $710. After five years the monthly payment increases to $740, after 10 years it goes to $768, after 15 years $784, after 20 years $806 and after 25 years $829. Taxes are estimated to be about $550 and the home owner's insurance premium should be about $240 annually. A mortgage insurance premium of $2,600 must be paid in full at the closing.
Other lenders	Lender C offers a conventional 30-year mortgage loan at 12 percent with a 20 percent down payment on either condo, a 1-point loan origination fee, and a mortgage insurance monthly premium of $40. On condo 1, the monthly payment for principal and interest will be $699.45. On condo 2, it amounts to $666.54. Lender D offers a 15-year mortgage loan at 11.5 percent with a 20 percent down payment in either condo, a 1 point loan origination fee, and a mortgage insurance monthly premium of $40. On condo 1, the monthly payment will be $794.37; on condo 2, it will be $756.99. Lender E offers a 20-year renegotiable (every 5 years) rate mortgage at 9.5 percent with a 10 percent down payment on either condo, a 3 point loan origination fee, and a mortgage insurance monthly premium of $44. Initial monthly payments would be $713.08 on condo 1 and $679.52 on condo 2.

Key Words and Concepts

Review Questions

1. List four major areas of expenditure and identify the largest one.
2. What three housing features do Americans value most?
3. Identify the six goals that most people pursue in acquiring housing.
4. What five factors influence where people decide to live?
5. List some arguments in favor of renting over buying.
6. List some arguments in favor of buying over renting.
7. Give support for the statement, "Renters do better financially on a cash-flow basis than home buyers."
8. Why are the several so-called rules of thumb for housing affordability outdated today?

9. Identify one procedure to use in determining whether you can afford the housing you want.

10. Distinguish among the several types of rented housing.

11. Explain the purpose and value of a lease.

12. List some tenant rights and explain how they work to the advantage of the tenant.

13. Distinguish among the several types of owned housing.

14. Distinguish between the fair market value of a house and its assessed value.

15. Explain the advantage of renting a home with an option to buy.

16. Define the term *amortization*.

17. Explain the reduction of the principal of a home loan as a result of monthly payments over several years. Include what happens to principal and interest amounts with each subsequent payment.

18. Give one reason for and one reason against using a longer maturity period for a loan payback.

19. Explain the purpose for using points in home loans. Who is responsible for paying points?

20. Explain why it may be advantageous to use a multiple listing service to locate and buy a home.

21. Describe what is meant by a *home poor* budget.

22. Why is it necessary for a mortgage lender to require a home owner to carry property insurance on the home?

23. Why would a new home owner want to have title insurance?

24. Why would a home owner consider buying warranty insurance or mortgage life insurance?

25. Name the five steps in the home-buying process.

26. What is the purpose of making a counteroffer when attempting to buy a home?

27. Give one reason for and one reason against a home owner selling a home personally rather than through a real estate broker.

28. What is the once-in-a-lifetime capital gains exclusion?

Case Problems

1. Grant Higginbott and Richard Van Ness of Binghamton, New York, are trying to decide whether each should rent or purchase housing. Grant is in favor of buying and Richard leans toward renting, and both seem able to justify their particular choice. Grant thinks that the tax advantage is a very good reason for

buying. Richard, however, believes that cash flow is so much better when renting. See if you can help these two single men decide by responding to the issues listed below.

   a. Is there a tax advantage for the home buyer? Explain.

   b. Discuss Richard's belief that cash flow is better with renting.

   c. Suggest some reasons why Grant should consider renting, rather than purchasing, housing.

   d. Suggest some reasons why Richard should consider buying, rather than renting, housing.

   e. Is there a clear-cut basis for deciding either to rent or to buy housing? Why or why not?

2. Sally Donelan of Boston, Massachusetts, has examined several options for new-home financing. She has been favoring alternative mortgage plans due to high current mortgage rates. She hopes that the market rate will drop in a couple of years.

   a. What broad concerns are there with alternative mortgages?

   b. What financing option could you suggest for Sally, assuming she is able to use any type available? Why?

3. Jeremy Jorgensen of Salt Lake City, Utah, is concerned about the costs involved in selling his home, so he has decided to sell his house himself rather than pay a broker to do it.

   a. What problems will Jeremy encounter, if any, when selling his own home?

   b. How would you advise Jeremy if he asked you whether he should sell the house himself or list with a broker? Explain your answer.

   c. Would Jeremy really save money by selling his home himself if he considers his time as a large part of his costs? Why or why not?

   d. Can you suggest any ways that Jeremy could use to reduce selling costs without doing the selling himself? Explain.

4. Walt and Mary Jensen of Atlanta, Georgia, a couple in their late twenties, currently are renting an unfurnished two-bedroom apartment for $550 per month, with an additional $62 for utilities and $10 for insurance. They have found a condominium they can buy for $80,000 with a 20 percent down payment and a thirty-year, 11 percent mortgage. Closing costs are estimated at $2,400 in addition to property taxes of $1,680 per year and a homeowner's insurance premium of $360 per year. The monthly home owner's association fee and utility costs are estimated at $175. The Jensens have a combined income of $33,000 per year, with take-home pay of $1,980 per month. They are in the 28 percent tax bracket, pay $225 per month on an installment contract (twelve payments left), and have $19,000 in savings and investments.

   a. Can the Jensens afford to buy the condo? Support your answer with data.

b. Walt and Mary think their monthly housing costs would be lower the first year if they buy the condo. Do you agree? Support your answer.

c. How much will they have left in savings to pay for moving expenses?

Suggested Readings

"Building the Assets You Live In." *Money*, June 1987, pp. 70–71. Graphic illustration of how to move up from one home to another, all the way to retirement.

"Housing Affordability Index." *Consumers' Research*, April 1987, p. 33. Discussion and table on how much easier it is now to own your own home.

"How to Sell Your Home Yourself." *Reader's Digest*, March 1987, pp. 89–93. Good suggestions to those who want to avoid paying the real estate agent's commission.

"Mortgages That Go Bump in the Night." *U.S. News and World Report*, July 13, 1987, p. 54. Overview of potential problems for home owners using adjustable rate mortgages.

"Signs of the Times—Sale by Owner." *U.S. News and World Report*, June 29, 1987, p. 43. Suggestions on how to sell your home without using a broker.

"Starter Home: Your First Step Is the Biggest." *Money*, June 1987, pp. 72–82. Detailed suggestions on every step of buying a first home.

PART FOUR

Income and Asset Protection

CHAPTER 10

Insurance Fundamentals

OBJECTIVES

After reading this chapter, the student should be able to

1. define *insurance*.
2. explain the relationship between risk and insurance.
3. apply the risk management process to personal financial affairs.
4. describe the various types of insurance and explain the contractual nature of an insurance policy.
5. discuss the origins, goals, and methods of government regulation of the insurance industry.
6. discuss the important points to consider when buying insurance.

So far, this book has focused on the planning and management of financial resources. You have learned ways to maximize those resources and to use them to achieve your personal financial goals. This knowledge will help you become a competent financial manager, but you must also know how to protect what you have attained or plan to attain from the possibility of financial loss. You can provide some of this protection for yourself by locking doors, being careful with fire, driving safely, and similar efforts. You need additional protection from the financial losses that can result from auto accidents, fires, illness, death, and many other events. Such protection can be provided by insurance.

This chapter begins by discussing the concept of insurance. The connection between risk and insurance is also explored. Insurance is then considered as a part of total risk management. Sections on insurance as a product and on insurance regulation follow. The chapter closes with a discussion of how to buy insurance.

What Is Insurance?

Insurance is a mechanism for reducing risk by having a large number of individuals share in the financial losses suffered by members of the group. Insurance protects each individual in the group by substituting a certain but relatively small fee for an uncertain and possibly large financial loss. This fee for insurance protection is called the *premium*. It includes the individual share of the group's losses, a proportional share of the expenses of administering the insurance plan, and an allowance for profit if the plan is administered by a profit-seeking company.

The history of insurance can be traced to ancient civilization. Babylonian merchants found it necessary to protect themselves from losses resulting from theft by the traveling sellers hired to trade their wares. Thus began the form of insurance called bonding. In more recent times, casualty insurance was designed to protect shippers from the possibility that their cargoes might be lost at sea. The famous Lloyd's of London began as providers of this marine insurance. In the United States, the first fire insurance plan was established in Philadelphia by Benjamin Franklin.

Today insurance is a major component of the American economy. The insurance industry controls assets of more than $1 trillion. More than $250 billion was spent on insurance in a recent year, and approximately two million people are employed by the nearly 5,600 companies in the industry. According to the National Insurance Consumer Organization, the average family spends about 11 percent of its disposable income on insurance each year. This exceeds the percentages spent on clothing, gasoline, or entertainment.

Modern insurance provides a vast and complicated assortment of products designed to help us protect our assets and our income. Yet insurance is one of the least understood purchases we make. Many people buy too little insurance. Others buy too much. Still others comprehend their insurance needs but do not understand insurance sufficiently to make the most of the protection it provides. This and the next three chapters will help you recognize the need for financial protection and act as a risk manager, planning and organizing the many mechanisms available for minimizing your financial losses.

The Risk and Insurance Relationship

A thorough understanding of insurance requires a knowledge of its basic terms and concepts. These meanings will bring insurance into a sharper focus and clarify its role as a protection from financial loss. This section examines such terms as *peril* and *hazard,* and the concepts of loss, indemnity, risk, and the law of large numbers. These terms take on special meanings and applications when used in the field of insurance.

Perils and Hazards

The protection that insurance provides is often associated with the occurrence of some event, such as a fire or auto accident. Any event that causes a financial loss is called a *peril.* Fire, theft, illness, and accidents are among the many perils that could occur to you or your property. Insurance does not provide protection from perils, but rather from the financial losses that result from their occurrence.

Protection from the actual occurrence of a peril requires an elimination or reduction of hazards. A *hazard* is any condition that increases the probability that a peril will occur. Driving under the influence of alcohol is an example of an especially deadly hazard.

Three types of hazards are important in insurance. A *physical hazard* is a particular characteristic of the insured person or property that increases the chance of loss. An example of a physical hazard is high blood pressure in a person covered by health insurance. A *morale hazard* exists when a person is indifferent or does not care if a peril occurs. A *moral hazard* exists when a person wants and causes a peril to occur. These latter two types of perils are of special concern to insurance companies. A morale hazard exists if the insured party, knowing that theft insurance will pay the loss, becomes careless about locking doors and windows. An example of a moral hazard would be the temptation to cause a loss intentionally in order to collect on an insurance policy. Insurance companies often limit or deny coverage if a loss occurs as a result of a morale or moral hazard.

The Concept of Loss

The major reason for buying insurance is to provide reimbursement for financial loss. A *financial loss* is any decline in value of income or assets in the present or future. Certain minimum requirements must be met for a loss to be insurable: the loss must be fortuitous, financial, and personal. *Fortuitous losses* are unexpected both in terms of their timing and their magnitude. A loss caused by lightning is fortuitous. A loss caused by the decline in the value of a corporate common stock is not fortuitous because it is reasonable to expect stock value to go up and down with the market. *Financial losses* can be measured in dollars and cents. When you are sick, you suffer due to discomfort, inconvenience, lost wages, and medical bills. But insurance will cover only the lost wages and medical bills because these are the only losses that can be objectively measured. Finally, *personal losses* can be directly attributable to specific individuals or organizations. This means that losses occurring to society as a whole cannot be insured against.

In order to buy insurance, an individual or organization must have an insurable interest in the property or person insured. An **insurable interest** exists when a person or organization stands to suffer a financial loss resulting directly from a peril. You can buy fire insurance on your own home, but you cannot buy it on a friend's home. Nor could you purchase insurance on the life of a total stranger. You would suffer no loss should these perils occur. However, because businesses might suffer a loss if one of their major executives were to die, they often buy life insurance on their top managers.

The requirement of insurable interest separates insurance from gambling. If you bought insurance on a friend's house, you would actually be gambling, since you would gain if your friend's house burned down. Insurance is not gambling because there is no potential for gain.

The Principle of Indemnity

The **principle of indemnity** states that insurance will pay no more than the actual financial loss suffered. For example, an automobile insurance policy will pay only the actual cash value of a stolen automobile. This principle, like the requirement of insurable interest, prevents a person from gaining financially from a loss. Thus, if a windstorm causes $500 worth of damage to a home, the amount paid to the home owner will not exceed $500.

A possible exception to the principle of indemnity occurs in the case of life insurance. The financial losses suffered from an untimely death are very difficult to measure because they involve lost future income. Life insurance policies are written for a specific *face amount,* which is the amount of money that will be paid upon the death of the insured party. The face amount allowed by an insurance company depends on the likely loss and the relationship between the person whose life is covered and the person who will receive the benefits.

Although the principle of indemnity states that insurance will pay no more than the loss suffered, it does not guarantee that insured losses will be totally reimbursed. Insurance policies are not open-ended agreements to pay. Every policy will have *policy limits,* which are the maximum dollar amounts that will be paid under a policy. Insurance purchasers must be careful that the policy limits are sufficient to cover losses they might suffer.

The Concept of Risk

Insurance was defined earlier as a mechanism for reducing risk. In insurance, *risk* is uncertainty about whether a financial loss will occur. There are two types of risk. *Speculative risk* exists whenever there is potential for gain as well as loss. Gambling is an example of speculative risk, as is buying corporate stock. *Pure risk* exists when there is no potential for gain but a possibility of loss. Fires, auto accidents, premature death, illness, and theft are examples of events involving pure risk. Insurance can be bought to reduce pure risk but not speculative risk.

The definition of risk as uncertainty differs somewhat from the usual definition of risk as "odds," "chance," or "probability." The difference is subtle but very important. A peril with a 95 percent chance of occurrence is highly certain to occur. Thus uncertainty and therefore risk are low. When the probability of financial loss is high, it is usually best to provide for loss in the household budget rather than pay the high insurance premiums that would be required. When a peril has a lower probability of occurrence, 10 percent for example, the uncertainty and risk are relatively high, because it is difficult to predict the one person in ten to whom the loss will occur. In such cases, insurance is often a wise choice for reducing uncertainty.

The Law of Large Numbers

The *law of large numbers* states that as the number of units in a group increases, predictions about the group become increasingly accurate. This increased accuracy decreases uncertainty and therefore risk. For example, consider a city of 100,000 households in which the probability of a fire striking a household is one in a thousand, or .1 percent. If we focus on groups of ten or even a hundred households at a time, we cannot predict very accurately whether a fire will strike a house in a given group. Some groups might have two or three fires and others might have none. However, if we combine all the households into one group, we can accurately predict that there will be a hundred fires (100,000 × .1 percent). Even if there are only 98 or 103 fires, our prediction would be in error only by a small percentage. Insurance companies, which often have millions of customers, can be even more accurate in their group predictions.

Insurance thus consists of just two basic elements: the reduction of risk and the sharing of losses. Risk is reduced by the application of the law of large numbers. Each insurance customer trades the uncertainty of a potentially large financial loss for the certainty of a fixed insurance premium. Loss sharing occurs as the insurance company pools all of the premiums into a fund for the payment of individual losses.

When viewed in this way, the benefits of insurance become clear. Individual insurance purchasers benefit whether or not they suffer a loss. If a loss is suffered, the obvious benefit is the reimbursement that will be made. But even if no loss is suffered, the reduction of risk is itself a benefit. Reduced risk provides the freedom to drive a car, own a home, and plan financially for the future, knowing that some unforeseen event will not result in financial disaster. Society also benefits from insurance. No major business activity, whether it be the construction of a house, the drilling of an oil well, or the establishment of a law firm, would be undertaken without insurance protection. Without insurance, the only sure way to handle risk is to avoid risky situations.

Risk Management

People usually have one of three personal reactions to risk. Some people are *risk takers* who are not upset by uncertainty and may even enjoy risky situations. Others are *risk neutral,* neither fearing nor enjoying risk. Still others are *risk averse.* These people are very uncomfortable with risk and will avoid it whenever they can. These chapters on insurance will start you on your way to becoming a successful risk manager with a knowledgeable eye to the risks you face now and in the future.

You may view insurance as the wisest way to handle risk. It is, however, only one of many ways and is not always the best choice. Each risky situation must be identified and analyzed to determine the best way to manage it. This analysis is called *risk management* and will enable you to choose among the many alternative ways of handling risk. The risk management process involves three basic steps: (1) analyzing risk, (2) deciding how to handle risk, and (3) implementing the risk management program. Table 10–1 details the steps in the risk management process.

TABLE 10–1
The Risk Management Process

Step 1: Risk analysis

A. Determine source of risk:

Possession	Activity	Accompanying peril
Car	Driving	Accident
House	Smoking	Fire
Jewelry	Traveling	Theft

B. Determine potential magnitude of loss
C. Determine level of risk

Step 2: Deciding how to handle risk

A. Avoid risk
B. Assume risk
C. Reduce risk
D. Transfer risk

Step 3: Implementing the risk management plan

A. Refrain from certain activities
B. Take extra precautions
C. Buy insurance

Risk Analysis

Sources of risk are the items you own and your activities that expose you to the risk of financial loss. These items and behaviors are called *exposures.* Consider, for example, the very common exposure of owning an automobile. One loss that could occur is the destruction of the auto by fire or an accident. There is additional exposure to loss when you drive the car, since you may cause an accident and be held liable for losses suffered by others. You should take an inventory of what you own and what you do to identify your exposures to loss.

Next you need to identify the perils that cause losses. Some very common perils are fire, theft, death, illness, and accidents. Some perils are associated more with some exposures than with others. For example, the theft peril does not apply to a dwelling, but does apply to the contents of a dwelling. Also, similar losses may result from an accident and an illness, but the way you handle the risks associated with these two perils may differ.

Risk management also requires you to determine how much you might lose if the peril occurs, or the magnitude of the loss. When you identify this amount, you can decide how best to handle the risk. If you decide to purchase insurance, you can use this figure to choose the policy limits.

Finally, the most difficult step is identifying the level of risk, that is, identifying whether there is high or low uncertainty. Level of risk cannot be easily quantified. Knowing the probabilities of a peril occurring and the variation in these probabilities over time and for different groups, you might be able to calculate the risk associated with a peril. However, this figure would still be an inadequate measure of risk; of utmost concern to the risk manager is the uncertainty regarding the loss, not the uncertainty of the peril. Nonetheless, if you estimate the level of risk as carefully as possible, you will be better able to manage risk effectively.

Deciding How to Handle Risk

Once you have identified the sources and levels of the risks you face, you can consider how to handle the risks. The four major ways to handle risk are to avoid it, to assume it, to reduce it, and to transfer it. Each of these methods is described below.

Avoiding Risk   The first and simplest way to handle risk is to avoid it. To do this, you must refrain from owning items or engaging in activities that provide exposure to risk of financial loss. For example, choosing not to own an airplane or not to sky dive limits your exposure. However, avoiding risk is not always practical. You can avoid some of the risks of home ownership by renting, for example, but then you will lose the benefits of owning a home.

Assuming Risk   A second way to handle risk is to assume it, or to recognize and accept risk as part of everyday life. The breakage of glassware in the home is usually an assumed risk, as is the risk that your shrubbery may die during a dry spell. Although this approach might seem somewhat fatalistic, risk assumption has a role to play in risk management. Some losses are so small that they can be borne without hardship. Also, insurance may be unavailable for a specific type of loss; an example is pet health insurance, unavailable in most states. Lastly, risk assumption seems practical when the probability of loss is very high. These losses are best provided for in the basic financial plan. For example, a person who races motorcycles will have a high probability of loss due to repair expenses and should consider repairs a cost of the hobby and provide for them accordingly.

There are two cases in which risk assumption is inappropriate. The first is risk assumption due to ignorance. If people do not understand the risks they face, they take no action and engage in risk assumption by default. The second is risk assumption due to inaction. Many people assume the risk of loss associated with premature death by putting off the purchase of life insurance because they feel it is a morbid, unpleasant task. Such uses of risk assumption are the opposite of effective risk management.

Reducing Risk A third way to handle risk is to reduce it to more acceptable levels, or to reduce the uncertainty of financial loss. Risk reduction invariably entails the use of the law of large numbers. The greater the number of exposures, the easier it is to predict collective losses accurately. For example, a chain of retail stores will have a reduced level of fire risk as the number of stores increases. Ultimately the stores' fire losses may become so predictable that they will be able to set aside funds to pay fire losses as they occur. This type of plan is called *self-insurance.* It is not risk assumption because it involves a formal setting aside of funds. Households cannot reduce risk through self-insurance because they cannot make use of the law of large numbers. However, they can buy insurance individually to reduce their risk.

People sometimes think that they can obtain insurance whenever they want to reduce risk. There are, however, certain situations and types of losses for which insurance may *not* be obtainable. The following rules describe such situations:

1. **Too few exposure units** When there are too few exposure units, the law of large numbers will not operate and uncertainty will not be reduced. Thus, the major rationale for insurance will be lost.

2. **Inability to determine the probability of loss** Without an accurate assessment of the probability of losses it is impossible to determine the premium (the share of the total losses) to be paid by each policyholder. There may be too few exposure units or insufficient time to establish a loss history for a type of exposure. For some time after condominiums became popular in this country, it was difficult to find insurance specifically for condominium owners. Such policies became available as more people bought condominiums and their losses became more predictable.

3. **Intentional losses**   Insurance covers only unexpected or accidental losses. If this rule were not followed, insurance could be used to achieve financial gain. The arson problem faced by many large cities occurs because property values fall below the level at which many buildings are insured. When these buildings burn, their owners can benefit financially. Unfortunately, this creates an incentive for owners to intentionally set fires. Since it is very difficult to prove that arson by the owner may have caused a loss, many of these losses are reimbursed.

4. **Small losses**   Insurance cannot be purchased for occurrences such as glassware breakage and other small losses. The reason is simply that the cost of providing the coverage would exceed the probable loss.

5. **Many losses occurring at the same time**   If the peril to be insured against is likely to occur to many policyholders at the same time, an insurance company may not be able to pay all the claims. To avoid such situations, property insurance companies will not write policies on all the homes in a neighborhood for fear that a common disaster such as a tornado or uncontrolled fire might generate unmanageable losses. It is very difficult to obtain flood or earthquake insurance for the same reason.

It should be stressed that these rules are not necessarily completely adhered to in practice. For example, you can buy flood insurance from the federal government. This form of protection is not technically insurance but is a way of handling risk called risk transfer.

Transferring Risk   The fourth major way of handling risk is to transfer it. This is an arrangement by which another party agrees to reimburse you for a financial loss. At first glance, insurance may appear to be an example of risk transfer. However, whereas insurance reduces risk via the law of large numbers, risk transfer does not use the law of large numbers. Instead, an insurance company simply assumes the risk the insured wishes to transfer. An example would be an insurance policy taken out on the legs of a football team's star running back. There is no combination of exposure units. In fact, there is only one exposure unit (or two, if you count each leg). The uncertainty is simply transferred (for a not-so-small fee) from the running back or his team to an insurance company or companies. We call such transfers insurance, but technically they are not.

In deciding how to handle risk, you must weigh each source of risk with each risk-handling method to select the proper method(s) for each source. Remember that you cannot rely on any one method in all cases. The mix of risk avoidance, assumption, reduction, and transfer that you choose will depend on the source of the risk, the size of the potential loss, your personal reactions to risk, and your financial resources available to pay for losses. These financial considerations are especially important when you choose insurance as a risk-handling method.

Implementing the Risk Management Program

Selecting a risk-handling method is not the final step in risk management. You must then implement the methods you have chosen. For risk avoidance, this might mean refraining from a certain type of activity, such as drinking and driving. For risk assumption, it might mean taking extra precautions to protect items that may not be insured, such as jewelry. For most households, the risk-handling method of most significance is risk reduction through insurance. The remainder of this chapter will address the general subject of insurance. The next three chapters will closely examine property and liability, health, and life insurance.

The Insurance Product

Insurance differs from most other products and services that consumers buy. Unlike an object, insurance cannot be physically measured or aesthetically evaluated. Unlike a service, insurance does not directly entail someone doing something for another. Nevertheless, insurance is certainly a product offered in the marketplace. It is designed, packaged, advertised, promoted, bought and sold, and consumed, and it becomes obsolete and often needs to be replaced.

Types of Insurance

Insurance can be classified according to the type of loss it covers. The five main types of insurance are property, liability, health, life, and income insurance.

Property insurance protects against financial losses resulting from damage to or destruction of property or possessions. Property insurance can pay for repair or replacement of property and cover other expenses that might result from the occurrence of a peril. If a fire damages your home, property insurance can pay for repair of the structure and replacement of your home's contents and cover your temporary living expenses. People most commonly purchase property insurance to protect homes and automobiles.

Liability insurance protects against financial losses suffered by others for which you are responsible. Such responsibilities can arise when you are negligent or when a contract, a law, or court judgment requires you to pay for the losses of another. Automobile owners typically carry liability insurance to cover damage to another's property in the case of a car accident. Doctors, dentists, and other professionals usually purchase professional liability insurance.

Health insurance protects against financial losses resulting from illness, injury, and disability. Health insurance benefits pay hospital and doctor bills and can offset the income lost as a result of an illness or accidental injury.

Income insurance protects against the loss of future income. Individuals can purchase *disability income insurance* to provide income if you cannot work due to an injury or prolonged illness. Two kinds of income insurance are purchased by employers: *unemployment insurance* provides income for employees who may be laid off when business is slow, and *workers' compensation insurance* provides medical care and replacement of lost income for employees who are injured on the job.

Life insurance protects against financial losses resulting from death. Such losses can include burial expenses, expenses for the settlement of the estate, and lost future income needed to provide for the dependents of the deceased. People who financially support families probably need life insurance.

The Insurance Policy

An *insurance policy* is a written agreement between a person *buying* insurance (the *insured*) and an insurance company (the *insurer*). Few people read an entire insurance policy before or even after they purchase one, relying instead on the salesperson to describe the coverage for them. This often leads to misunderstandings when a loss occurs and is a major reason why insurance consistently ranks among the top ten sources of consumer complaints.

Insurance policies historically have been written in complex legal language. However, in recent years a number of states have enacted legislation requiring that insurance policies be written in plain English. This trend has helped make policies more understandable but the responsibility still remains with the insured to read and understand their insurance policies.

You can best comprehend an insurance policy by separating it into its component parts and studying each part separately. Insurance policies have five basic components, each of which serves a specific purpose and provides specific information. These five, in order of their usual location in the policy, are as follows: declarations, insuring agreements, exclusions, conditions, and endorsements.

Declarations provide the basic descriptive information about the insured person and/or property, the premium to be paid, the time period of the coverage, and the policy limits. Also included may be promises by the insured to take steps to lessen the hazards associated with the peril insured against. For example, a home owner may promise to install a smoke alarm and maintain a fire extinguisher in exchange for paying a discounted premium. The information in the declarations is used to set the premium and for identification purposes.

The *insuring agreements* are the broadly defined coverages provided under the policy. These are promises that the insurer makes in return for the premium paid by the insured. For example, in an auto insurance policy, the insurer will promise to pay medical expenses to the driver and passengers in the event of an accident. The insuring agreements will often include definitions of *motor vehicle* or *insured premises* in order to specifically focus the promises made.

Exclusions narrow the focus and eliminate specific coverages broadly stated in the insuring agreements. These are exceptions and special circumstances for which the insurer will make no promise to pay. One exclusion might deny coverage under a family's automobile policy if the car is used primarily for business purposes. Another would deny coverage if the insured intentionally sets a fire. Exclusions eliminate unnecessary coverage, reduce moral hazards, lower the cost of the policy, and generally make the promises made by the insurer more specific. People who do not understand the exclusions in their policies often believe they are covered for a loss when in fact they are not.

Making Sense of an Insurance Policy

Insurance policies do not invite casual reading. As a result, many people fail to read their policies until a loss occurs, only to find that they had misunderstood the terms of the agreement. Avoid these problems by carefully and systematically reading a policy before you purchase it. Although the language of the policy may not be entirely familiar to you, your understanding of the policy provisions can be enhanced if you focus on eight key points.

1. *Perils covered* This information can be provided in two ways. Some policies will list only those perils that are covered. Other policies will cover all perils *except* those listed. This latter type of policy will provide more comprehensive coverage. Realize that the definition of *peril* may differ from that used in everyday language. Such definitions are often provided in the policy itself; if not, consult the insurance seller.

2. *Property covered* Like perils, the property covered under a policy may be listed individually, or only the excluded property may be listed. When the property is listed individually, any new acquisitions must be added to the policy.

3. *Types of losses covered* When a piece of property is damaged or destroyed by a peril, three types of losses can result: the loss of the property itself, extra expenses that may arise because the property is unusable for a time, and loss of income if the property was used in the insured's work. The extra expenses and the lost income may exceed the dollar loss of the property itself.

4. *People covered* Insurance policies will often cover only certain individuals. This is especially true of auto, life, and health insurance. This information is usually contained in the policy declarations but may be subsequently changed in the exclusions and endorsements.

5. *Locations covered* Where the loss occurs may have a bearing on whether or not it will be covered. It is especially important to know what locations are not covered.

6. *Time period of coverage* Policies are sometimes written to cover only specific time periods. These restrictions may exclude coverage during specific times of the day and/or during certain days of the week, month, or year.

7. *Hazards that nullify coverage* Hazards increase the chances of a peril occurring. Insurance policies often stipulate that if a certain hazard exists, coverage will be suspended. For example, coverage on a restaurant may be denied if the owner fails to maintain an adequate fire-extinguisher system.

8. *Amount of coverage* All insurance policies specify the maximum amount the insurer will pay for a loss. The amount specified will vary greatly from policy to policy and for the various types of losses covered under a policy.

Finally, note that the information on these eight points may be spread throughout a policy. In fact, coverage which appears to be provided in one location may be denied elsewhere. Study the entire policy to fully determine what protection it provides.

Conditions impose obligations on both the insured and the insurer by establishing the ground rules of the agreement. This section contains information on how claims are to be made in the event of a loss and what procedures the insurer will follow when settling the claim. Other items might be the time limits for making a claim after a loss, rules for cancellation of the policy by either party, rules for obtaining estimates of damages, and procedures for changing the terms of the policy. The insured who fails to adhere to procedures or obligations described in the conditions risks being denied coverage when a loss occurs.

Endorsements and *riders* are amendments and additions to the basic insurance policy. Insurance policies are almost always preprinted forms. The insured may wish to alter the form to suit specific needs, and endorsements and riders are the mechanisms for accomplishing the alterations. These can both expand and limit coverage provided in the body of the policy. Therefore, when the terms of an endorsement or rider differ from the terms of the basic policy, the endorsement will be considered valid. Endorsements may be added at any time during the life of the policy to expand coverage, raise the policy limits, and make many other changes.

Insurance as a Contract

Insurance policies are contracts. A *contract* is a legally binding agreement between two or more parties. *Legally binding* means the provisions of the agreement can be enforced in a court of law. *Agreement* means the two parties involved have had a meeting of the minds and promise to honor the provisions of the contract.

Contracts are formed when one party makes an offer that is accepted by another. In most selling situations, the seller offers and the buyer accepts. For example, the seller of a car would stipulate the price of the car, and a buyer would accept or reject the offer.

With insurance the process is reversed. The initial offer is made by the purchaser in the form of an application for coverage. The decision to accept or reject is then made by the insurance seller. Usually, the insurer gives temporary acceptance when an applicant submits full or partial payment of the initial premium. This temporary insurance contract, called a *binder,* is either replaced at a later date with a written contract (the policy) or allowed to expire.

The promissory nature of insurance contracts holds high potential for disputes over the agreement. Each party is vulnerable to dishonest acts on the part of the other. Legally, therefore, insurance is a contract of utmost good faith. This means that all parties to the contract are held to higher-than-usual standards of honesty and good faith. Insurers will be able to avoid their promises only with difficulty, and the insured will not be able to collect on a loss if they intentionally or unintentionally withhold information or make erroneous statements to the insurer.

Regulation of Insurance

Like many other businesses, the insurance industry is subject to government regulation. Insurance is regulated due to its status as a contract of utmost good faith. This section discusses the history of insurance regulation, what is regulated, rate regulation, and insurance redress.

History of Insurance Regulation

The regulation of insurance dates back to the 1830s, when several states began chartering insurance companies and overseeing the financial solvency of insurers. Historically, the regulation of insurance was a state, rather than a federal, responsibility. This pattern was affirmed in 1869, when the U.S. Supreme Court ruled that insurance was not commerce and was therefore exempt from the power of the federal government to regulate interstate commerce. For seventy-five years the regulation of insurance remained a function of the individual states.

Then in 1944 the U.S. Supreme Court reversed its earlier ruling and held that insurance was indeed commerce and that when such commerce was transacted interstate (across state lines) it was subject to federal control. This new ruling did not cancel the right of states to regulate insurance, and so the insurance industry was faced with the prospect of regulation on two levels. Of particular concern to some insurers was the prospect of being subject to federal antitrust laws. Insurance companies often share data on losses in an effort to jointly set rates based on large pools of insureds, and many feared that federal antitrust laws would forbid such sharing of information. To head off such an application of federal law, proposals were presented to Congress to establish the primacy of state regulation of insurance. In response, Congress passed the McCarran-Ferguson Act in 1945. This law exempted the insurance industry from federal regulation until July 1948, at which time the exemption would expire unless states had acted to regulate insurance. By July 1948 all states had moved to provide such regulation, and to this day the regulation of insurance remains a state function.

What Is Regulated?

State regulation of insurance focuses on four areas: (1) licensing of companies and agents, (2) financial solvency of insurance companies, (3) insurance policies and forms, and (4) insurance rates.

Licensing of Companies and Agents In order to sell insurance in a state, insurance companies must be licensed by the state insurance commissioner or other officials responsible for regulating insurance. Such licensure is granted only to those companies that exhibit minimum standards of financial soundness and use approved insurance policies and forms.

Insurance agents sell, modify, and terminate contracts of insurance between the insured and the insurers. Agents are legally permitted to act on behalf of an insurer and to establish contractual obligations that are binding on the insurance company. They must be licensed by each state in which they wish to operate. The license is granted only after the prospective agent passes a test covering knowledge of insurance products and procedures.

Insurance Company Solvency   The promissory nature of the insurance contract makes the regulation of insurance company solvency a primary responsibility for insurance regulators. Regulators monitor insurance companies' finances to ensure that the companies can pay the claims of the insured as losses occur. Insurance companies do not keep the premiums of their policyholders until loss payments must be made. Instead, they invest these funds in real estate, stocks and bonds, and other forms of investment; income from these investments is a primary source of revenue to insurance companies. Insurance regulators restrict the types of investments insurers can make and require that insurers keep some funds in reserve for the payment of losses. If an insurance company should fail, regulators in every state require that all other insurers provide funds to pay the claims of customers of the insolvent company.

Insurance Policies and Forms   Because insurance policies are very technical, the potential for misunderstanding or for the inclusion of policy provisions unfavorable to the insured is high. State regulators generally require approval of the policies and forms used by insurers in order to prevent the use of vague or deceptive policies. Some states require that standardized, identical policies be used by all companies selling certain types of coverage, such as basic fire insurance.

Insurance Rates   In most forms of business activity in the United States prices are set through the mechanism of the marketplace and the workings of supply and demand. Historically, though, this has not been the case for the insurance product, especially property and liability insurance. Each state has enacted some type of rating law that establishes procedures for the submission and approval of proposed insurance rates.

An *insurance rate* is the cost to the insured for each unit of insurance coverage. Units are usually stated in dollars of coverage but may also apply to individual pieces of property to be covered. The price of insurance, the premium, is determined by multiplying the rate by the number of units purchased.

Insurance Rate Regulation

The insurance rating laws of all fifty states have the same objectives, but the mechanisms and procedures by which these objectives are reached vary from state to state.

Goals of Rate Regulation The three goals of insurance rate regulation are (1) to ensure that rates are adequate, (2) to prevent excessive rates, and (3) to prevent unfair rate discrimination.

Adequate rates generate sufficient premium revenue to provide the funds necessary to pay losses that will occur. The goal of adequacy benefits both those insured and the insurers. Those insured benefit because they can be confident that funds will be available to pay for their losses. Insurers benefit because the requirement of adequacy prevents unfair competition from unscrupulous insurers who may attempt to cut the price of their coverage without concern for future loss payments. Such a company could steal customers from companies who take their promises to pay future losses more seriously.

Excessive rates generate premium revenue that exceeds the amount needed for the payment of future losses, the expenses of providing coverage, and a fair rate of profit for the company. Overpriced policies are, of course, harmful to those insured.

Unfair rate discrimination exists when insurers charge different insureds different rates without sufficient statistical justification for the differences. People who own brick houses pay lower fire insurance rates than do owners of frame homes. Poor drivers pay higher auto insurance rates than do careful drivers. Nonsmokers may pay lower life insurance premiums than do smokers. These types of discrimination are considered fair. Discrimination is considered unfair when it is not based on accurate and verifiable probabilities of loss or when it is based on unacceptable social criteria, such as race or religion.

Methods of Rate Regulation States use two basic methods to achieve the three objectives of rate regulation. The first method requires prior approval of insurance rates. In the prior-approval states, insurance companies must file their proposed rates with the insurance regulatory body and must receive approval before putting the new rates into effect. A second method of rate regulation, called competitive rating, is used by a growing number of states. Competitive rating laws allow companies to change their rates as needed without prior approval. The philosophy behind such laws is that the competitive marketplace will keep insurance rates under control. However, even when companies use competitive rating, they must have statistical evidence to support the rates they set. In competitive-rating states, monitoring of insurance company solvency is used to ensure that companies have the funds to pay future losses.

Insurance Redress

Insurance transactions sometimes result in disputes between the insured and the insurers. Disputes over policy language, premium levels, coverage, and the amount of the reimbursement are typical disagreements that may arise. If you have a complaint in any of these or other areas, you have three places to turn. First, contact the insurer itself. This will usually entail making the problem known to the agent who sold you the policy or the agent to whom the policy is currently assigned. Many insurance disputes are simply the result of a misunderstanding that can be most easily handled this way. If the agent cannot or will not handle the dispute satisfactorily, you should contact the appropriate representative of the insurance company. Most large insurers maintain a staff of consumer representatives whose job it is to resolve disputes.

If the first contact is unsuccessful, notify the state insurance regulatory office, which may be called the department of insurance or the office of the commissioner of insurance. One of the regulatory functions of these offices is to resolve disputes between the insured and the insurers. In some states these offices offer toll-free telephone services. However, it is best to put a complaint in writing with full documentation and to keep copies of all correspondence.

Finally, if necessary you can contact the state consumer protection office. Each state has consumer protection legislation that prohibits unfair and deceptive business practices and identifies a state agency for the resolution of consumer problems. In most states this function is the responsibility of the state attorney general. Most state consumer protection offices provide toll-free telephone services. If you do phone, remember also to put a complaint in writing.

Buying Insurance

Buying insurance requires a knowledge of the product and the means by which it is sold and distributed. You also need to understand the procedures for creating an insurance contract, the concept of group insurance, and how to minimize the cost of insurance.

Types of Insurers

An insurer is any individual or organization that provides insurance coverage. The major function of insurers is to combine the premiums paid by the insured into a fund for the payment of losses. Some insurers are in business to make a profit; others operate on a nonprofit basis. The major types of insurers are stock companies, mutual companies, reciprocal exchanges, and producer cooperatives.

Stock insurance companies are owned by stockholders and provide insurance coverage in return for the opportunity to earn a profit for their owners. Like any other business, they sell stock to raise capital, use the proceeds to sell a product or service, and distribute any profits to the owners. These distributed profits are called *dividends*.

Like all insurers, stock insurance companies derive their earnings from underwriting profits and investment profits. Figure 10–1 diagrams the sources of insurance company profits. Underwriting profits result when the premiums collected exceed the expenses of providing coverage and the losses paid by the company. Investment profits result

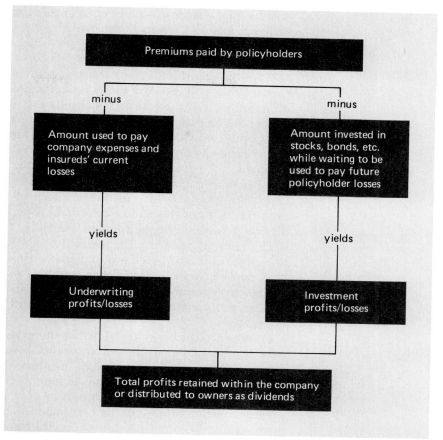

FIGURE 10–1
Sources of Insurance Company Profits

when there is return on the investments made with premiums collected from the insured. Insurers need not make an underwriting profit in order to be profitable. For example, auto insurers often have underwriting losses that are more than offset by their investment profits.

Some stock insurance companies may make *insurance dividends* payments to their policyholders. These dividends differ from those paid to the owners of the company in that they are not a distribution of the company's profits. Instead they are considered a partial refund of premiums paid by the policyholders. These refunds can result from a lower-than-anticipated level of losses for an entire group of policyholders or lower-than-expected losses for an individual policyholder, or are simply one of the benefits written into the contract. Insurance policies with such provision for dividend payments are called *participating policies.* The Internal Revenue Service and most students of insurance view these insurance dividends not as profits but as refunds for overpayment. *Nonparticipating policies* do not pay dividends to policyholders. Many stock insurance companies offer both participating and nonparticipating policies, and participating policies often require higher premiums.

Mutual insurance companies are owned by their policyholders and operate on a nonprofit basis. Mutual insurance companies sell only participating policies. Any funds remaining after expenses and losses are paid are returned to the policyholders. In addition to receiving dividends, the policyholders of a mutual company maintain voting control of the company. In practice, however, most policyholders in mutual companies do not take active roles in the management of the company.

Reciprocal exchanges are self-insurance mechanisms through which the insureds share in the provision of insurance. Assume, for example, that one thousand Fire Island property owners wish to obtain insurance coverage on their homes. Instead of buying insurance from a stock or mutual company, the members of the group agree to provide a proportional share of each group member's insurance needs. If a member's house is destroyed, all other members will contribute their share of the loss reimbursement. The automobile insurance provided by the American Automobile Association (AAA) is an example of a reciprocal exchange.

Producer cooperatives are owned by individuals or organizations that have come together to provide insurance coverage. One type of producer cooperative is formed when insurers provide each other with coverage for exposures too large to handle individually. In a second type of producer cooperative, businesses not primarily established to provide insurance do so for their customers. The best-known examples of this second type of producer cooperative are the Blue Cross and Blue Shield health insurance plans. Under Blue Cross, hospitals come together to provide insurance for their patients. Blue Shield is a producer cooperative of physicians that provides insurance to patients to help pay medical bills.

Types of Insurance Sellers

Sellers of insurance, called insurance agents, act as representatives of one or more insurance companies. They have the power to enter into, change, and cancel insurance policies on behalf of the companies they represent. There are two types of insurance agents, independent agents and exclusive agents.

Independent insurance agents represent two or more insurance companies. They are independent businesspersons who act as a third-party link between insurer and insured. Independent agents earn a commission from the companies they represent and will place each insurance customer with the company that best meets the customer's needs. Legally, the agent represents the insurance companies, not the customer, but an insurance agent who neglects customers will not be successful for very long. Insurance companies that rely on a sales force of independent insurance agents are called *agency companies*.

Exclusive insurance agents represent only one insurance company. They are employees of the insurance company they represent. Life insurance is often sold through exclusive insurance agents. Since World War II, the proportion of insurance sold through exclusive agents has grown steadily, mainly because commissions paid to exclusive agents tend to be lower than those paid to independent agents. Because insurers using exclusive agents save on commissions and may be more selective in whom they insure, they can sometimes offer protection for a lower premium.

Not all insurance is sold and serviced through agents. Many companies are *direct sellers,* selling their policies through salaried employees, mail-order marketing, newspapers, and even vending machines. Although any type of insurance can be sold directly, the most common are supplemental health insurance, life insurance, and airplane accident life insurance.

From Whom to Buy?

When you are ready to purchase insurance, you face two decisions regarding your source of insurance protection. You must decide which company will best provide the desired protection and whether to purchase it through an agent.

Selecting an Insurance Agent Choosing among independent agents, exclusive agents, and direct sellers is not an easy task. Each seller has advantages and disadvantages. Independent agents may be able to provide more personalized service and can select one company among many that best fits your needs. Because they are independent, they know that their success depends as much on their personal services as on the reputation of any one company they represent.

Exclusive agents can also provide personalized service. But they are limited in what they may offer by the one company they represent. They can advise you on your insurance needs and how their company fits those needs, but when your needs do not match the offerings of the company there is nowhere else for the exclusive agent to turn. Nonetheless, premiums may be lower through exclusive agents. If you know what you need and want, and understand insurance, you may do better with an exclusive agent.

Direct sellers represent a unique challenge for insurance customers. This is especially true when the solicitation is based on a mail-order or newspaper advertisement. You must be careful to understand the policy fully, particularly its exclusions and conditions. Many policies sold through direct sellers are virtually worthless.

Selecting an Insurance Company The selection of an insurance company is tied to the selection of an insurance agent. Independent agents initially make the company selection, and final approval is made by the customer. With exclusive agents, the customer first chooses the company and then chooses among the agents who represent the company. With direct sellers, of course, there is no agent.

Insurance companies spend millions of dollars a year on advertising, but these ads do not provide much useful information to insurance purchasers. There are three major sources of information on insurance companies. The first, *Best's Key Rating Guide*, is available in most public libraries. This book rates companies on the basis of financial strength. By consulting this guide, you can avoid the companies that have shaky finances. However, because most of the prominent insurance companies receive *Best's* top rating, the guide is not usually helpful in choosing among these companies. Further, *Best's* rates companies only for financial soundness and avoids other important attributes such as price, service, and speedy payment of claims.

A second source of information is the insurance regulatory agency in your state. Such agencies sometimes publish insurance buyer's guides that discuss how to buy specific types of insurance and rate the companies providing such insurance. Insurance regulatory agencies may also report on the reputation of a company for fairness and competent handling of complaints.

A third source of information is *Consumer Reports* magazine, published by Consumers Union. *Consumer Reports* regularly includes articles on insurance, especially life insurance. It periodically publishes feature articles that rate various types of insurance policies on the basis of price.

In general, selecting insurance companies and agents is much like making any other purchase. You must know your needs, the product, and the sellers, and you must shop around for the best buy. It is essential to obtain premium quotations from more than one insurer, since insurance premiums can vary 300 percent and more for essentially the same coverage. Many agents will provide quotes over the telephone, so don't hesitate to use the Yellow Pages when considering a new policy or renewal of an existing policy. Finally, do not ignore service and convenience. A good company and agent will be one that combines a low price with quick and efficient service when a loss occurs.

Creating an Insurance Contract

The procedure for the creation of an insurance contract involves four distinct, although sometimes nearly simultaneous, steps: the application, underwriting, premium determination, and issuance of the policy.

Application   The creation of the insurance contract begins with an offer by the purchaser in the form of a written or an oral application for coverage. Generally, an oral application is followed later by a written application. The application provides the insurer with information about the persons or property to be insured, the perils insured against, the policy limits, the existence of hazards that may affect the premium, and other relevant matters. Figure 10–2 shows an application form for life insurance.

When the application is accepted by the agent or seller, a legally binding insurance contract is formed. Even when the application is oral or not directly accompanied by payment, a contract may be formed if

application for insurance

This application is for your use

Please print
Be sure to answer every question;
go by question number

TIAA Teachers Insurance and
Annuity Association of America
730 Third Avenue, New York, New York 10017

1 first name | middle name/initial | last name | social security no | **2** ☐ male ☐ female

3 addresses: State both, mail will be sent to residence unless otherwise requested
number | street | city/town | state | zip code | telephone
residence:
business: ( ) ( )

4 nonprofit employer. Please state (a) name of college, university, private school or other educational or scientific institution by which you are currently employed and check boxes indicating (b) type of institution, and (c) your duties. **NOTE:** If you are eligible for TIAA because your spouse is employed by a qualifying institution, check here ☐ and indicate spouse's employer as well as your own (if any) in (a) _____

(b) ☐ 4 yr. college/univ. ☐ grad school ☐ library ☐ 2 yr college ☐ private school ☐ research institution ☐ other ____
(c) ☐ teaching ☐ research ☐ maintenance ☐ administration ☐ clerical ☐ other ____

5 date of birth | month | day | year

6 ☐ married ☐ single ☐ divorced ☐ widowed ☐ separated

7 State title of new policy(ies) you want
(e.g., 20-Yr. Decreasing Term, 5-Yr. Ren. Term etc.) | amount of insurance

10 List all insurance policies on your life
(if none, so state)

name of company	amount	plan	year issued

8 How are premiums to be paid?
☐ annually ☐ semiannually ☐ quarterly

9 To whom shall the insurance benefits be paid at your death? Indicate full name (e.g., Mary A. Smith, not Mrs. John Smith) A married person with children usually names his/her spouse as primary beneficiary and simply "my children" under contingent beneficiary. When the term "my children" is used, the date of birth and relationship columns are left blank. Unless you specify otherwise, this term provides equally for all your children present and future, born of any and all marriages or legally adopted at any time. If primary beneficiary is other than spouse, child or parent, please explain purpose of insurance in details below

primary beneficiary(ies) (class I) | date of birth | relationship to you

contingent beneficiary(ies) (class II) if any

The right to change beneficiaries is reserved to me
Note: If no primary beneficiary (class I) is living at time of insured's death, benefits are payable to the contingent beneficiary (class II). If a class includes more than one person, the benefits are divided equally among the living beneficiaries of the class

11 thru 16 For all "yes" answers, please explain in details below
yes no

11 Will this insurance replace any existing insurance or annuity?
(If yes, state which and give name of company.) ☐ ☐

12 Are other applications for insurance on your life now pending?
(If yes, state companies and amounts.) ☐ ☐

13 Have you changed employers within the past two years or do you plan to do so? ☐ ☐

14 Are you now a member of, or planning to join, any active or reserve military service? ☐ ☐

15 Do you plan foreign travel or residence within the next 12 months? (If yes, state dates, places & purpose.) ☐ ☐

16 Have you ever applied for life, health or disability insurance which was declined, postponed or rated substandard?
(If yes, state companies, dates and reasons.) ☐ ☐

details—Use reverse side if necessary

I understand that the policy will include the Disability Waiver of Premium benefit provision, if the issue age is below 56. I also understand that if this application is for other than Term insurance, the Automatic Premium Loan Option will be included, if I so elect. This option provides a loan to me from the cash value if it is sufficient, to pay a premium not paid by the end of the grace period. I may revoke this option at any time. I elect to include the option in my policy by checking this box: ☐

To the best of my knowledge and belief, each and all of the above answers are true and complete. These answers, together with those provided on the Statements to Examiner form, are my application

I hereby tender $_____ the amount of the first premium for the plan of insurance and the frequency of payment chosen above. This will be returned to me if TIAA does not grant the insurance

signed at _____
city and state

on _____
date

signature of proposed insured

The insurance herein applied for will become effective upon receipt by TIAA of this application and the report of your medical examination, both properly completed, and your first premium payment, provided that all are received, and you are then insurable according to TIAA's underwriting standards

18.28 (7/82)   **Please review your application to be sure that all questions have been answered.**   305E

FIGURE 10–2
Life Insurance Application

Source: Teachers Insurance and Annuity Association of America. Used with permission.

the offer is accepted. Often the contract is a conditional and temporary binder and becomes permanent only after the insurance company underwrites and issues the policy.

Underwriting   *Underwriting* is the insurer's process of deciding which insurance applicants to accept. Some underwriting is done by agents when they decide to accept or reject an applicant. In general, however, most underwriting is done by the insurance company when it receives the written application. To best describe the process of underwriting, we must first discuss how insurance rates are set.

Insurance rates were previously defined as the price per unit of coverage. Rates represent the average cost of providing coverage to various groups of insureds. These groups, called *classes*, are made up of the insureds who share characteristics that are associated with the potential for suffering losses. For example, auto insurance policyholders are classified by their age, sex, marital status, and driving record, as well as by the make and model of their car and several other characteristics. Insurance companies use statistical information about losses to establish rates for the various classes of insureds.

When underwriters receive an application for insurance, they assign the applicant to the appropriate class and then determine whether the rates established for that class are sufficient to provide coverage for that applicant. Remember that rates are averages for a class. Some applicants will generate higher-than-average loss expectancies, and others lower-than-average expectancies for their class. Underwriters divide insurance applicants into three groups. The first group consists of applicants with average loss expectancies for their class. These standard applicants are accepted for coverage. The second group has loss expectancies that are much too high. These applicants are deemed ineligible for coverage and are rejected. The third group has loss expectancies that deviate only somewhat from average. These applicants are accepted with some modifications to their premiums or changes in their coverage. Preferred applicants have lower-than-average loss expectancies and usually qualify for lower premiums. Substandard applicants have higher-than-average loss expectancies and may be charged higher premiums or have restrictions placed on the types or amount of coverage they may purchase.

Premium Determination   After underwriting, the premium determination is relatively easy. The premium is equal to the rate multiplied by the number of units of coverage. Rates are sometimes stated as per $1,000 of coverage. For example, the rate on a life insurance policy may be $3 per $1,000 of coverage per year. Thus a $50,000 policy would require payment of a $150 premium per year ($3 × 50 units of $1,000).

Issuance of the Policy   The final act in the formation of the insurance contract is the issuance of the policy. At least partial payment of the premium will be made at this point if this has not occurred previously. The policy then becomes a legally enforceable agreement between insured and insurer.

Group Insurance

The process described above for the creation of an insurance contract applies most directly when individuals seek insurance coverage on their own. Alternatively, *group insurance* is sold collectively to an entire group under one policy. The most common example of group insurance is the health insurance provided employees by their employers. Other types of insurance often available on a group basis are life and disability insurance.

Group insurance may be more desirable than individual insurance for two reasons. First, an insured may be able to obtain group insurance at lower rates. Second, employers often provide group insurance as a fringe benefit for employees. Underwriting is done on the basis of the group, and employees are not parties to the contract. They simply participate as recipients of the benefits of the policy.

The policy itself is not provided to the individual group members. Instead, members are given booklets or pamphlets describing the coverage. If you are covered under a group policy, you should know what coverage the policy provides so you can then purchase supplemental insurance, if necessary, without duplication.

Minimizing the Cost of Insurance

A discussion of the process of buying insurance would be incomplete without a description of how to minimize insurance costs. As we mentioned earlier, you can save a good deal of money by shopping around and comparing premiums among companies. There are also specific features of insurance policies that can lower premiums without significantly lowering protection. These features are deductibles, coinsurance, hazard reduction, and loss reduction.

Deductibles are requirements that you pay an initial portion of any loss. For example, automobile insurance is often written with a $100 deductible. The first $100 of loss to the car must be paid by you. The insurer then pays the remainder of the loss, up to the limits of the policy. Deductibles are most often included in health and property insurance policies. They are sometimes required and sometimes optional, and you usually have a choice of deductible amounts. The higher the deductible you choose, the lower your premiums will be.

Coinsurance is a method by which insured and insurer share proportionately in the payment for a loss. For example, it is common in health insurance for the insured to pay 20 percent of any loss and the insurer to pay the remaining 80 percent. Coinsurance is most common in health and home owners' insurance and will be discussed in more detail in later chapters. Substantial premium reductions can be realized through coinsurance, but you must be prepared to pay your share of losses.

The following formula can be used to determine the amount of a loss that will be reimbursed when there is a deductible and a coinsurance clause:

$$R = (1 - CP)(L - D) \tag{10-1}$$

where

R = reimbursement (i.e., the amount the insurance company will pay)
CP = coinsurance percentage required of the insured
L = loss
D = deductible

Assume a health insurance policy with a $100 deductible per hospital stay and a 20 percent coinsurance requirement. If the hospital bill is $1,350, the reimbursement will be $1,000, calculated as follows:

$$\begin{aligned} R &= (1.00 - .20)(\$1,350 - \$100) \\ &= .80 \ (\$1,250) \\ &= \$1,000 \end{aligned}$$

Hazard reduction is action by the insured to reduce the probability of a loss occurring. Insurance companies will sometimes offer reduced premiums to the insured who practices hazard reduction. For example, some life insurance companies offer lower premiums to nonsmokers.

Loss reduction is action by the insured to lessen the severity of loss should a peril occur. Many property insurers offer reduced premiums to the insured who practices loss reduction. For example, premium discounts are often offered to homeowners who install smoke alarms and fire extinguishers in their homes. These items will not prevent fires but may lessen the severity of the losses a fire would cause.

Summary

1. Insurance is a mechanism for reducing risk by having a large number of individuals share in the losses suffered by members of the group.

2. Insurance is designed to provide reimbursement for financial losses. It cannot be used in a risky situation in which there is a potential for gain as well as loss. Nor can insurance be used to provide payment in excess of the actual financial loss suffered. Insurance basically consists of two elements: the reduction of risk through the application of the law of large numbers and the sharing of losses.

3. Personal financial managers must practice risk management in order to protect their present and future assets and income. Risk management entails identifying the sources of risk, selecting the appropriate risk-handling method, and implementing the risk management plan.

4. The major types of insurance are property, liability, health, income, and life insurance. The purchase of insurance involves the establishment of a contract (the policy), and all the major components must be fully understood by the purchaser.

5. Because an insurance policy is a contract of utmost good faith, the insurance industry is carefully regulated by the states. The principal focus of this regulation are the rates charged for coverage. The goal is to ensure that the rates are adequate, not excessive, and not unfairly discriminatory.

6. There are four types of insurers: stock insurance companies, mutual insurance companies, reciprocal exchanges, and producer cooperatives. Most insurance is sold through either independent or exclusive agents. Extreme care must be taken when buying insurance through direct sellers. Two ways of reducing the cost of insurance are through the use of deductibles and coinsurance.

Modern Money Management

The Johnsons Decide How to Manage Their Risks

The financial affairs of the Johnsons have become much more complicated since we began following them in Chapter 2. Both Harry ($75 per month) and Belinda ($200 per month) have been given raises at work. They have purchased an $85,000 condominium that has added about $400 per month to their cost of housing. They have purchased a $3,000 used car, adding about $120 per month to their expenses. As a result of these changes, Harry and Belinda have begun to realize that they are facing more risks in their financial affairs. They have decided to step back and take a look at their situation with an eye toward managing their risks more effectively. Use Table 10–1, their net worth and income and expense statements at the end of Chapter 2, and other information in Chapter 10 to answer the following questions.

1. What are Harry and Belinda's major sources of risk from home and auto ownership and what is the potential magnitude of loss from each?

2. Given the choices listed in step 2 of Table 10–1, how would you advise they best handle the sources of risk listed in question 1?

Key Words and Concepts

binder, 314
coinsurance, 325
conditions, 314
contract, 314

declarations, 312
deductibles, 325
direct sellers, 321
endorsements, 314

Review Questions

1. What is insurance?

2. In what way does insurance affect your personal financial management?

3. How are insurance and risk related?

4. Define *hazards* and *perils*.

5. How does the requirement of insurable interest affect your ability to buy insurance?

6. Why is the principal of indemnity so important to insurance sellers?

7. State the relationship among insurance, risk, and the law of large numbers.

8. Distinguish among the four ways of handling risk.

9. What characteristic of the insurance product makes it unique among other products or services for sale in the marketplace?

10. List the five main types of insurance typically offered for sale to individuals.

11. Describe what an insurance policy is and name and distinguish among its components.

12. Why are insurance contracts considered to be legally binding?

13. What are the four aspects of insurance activity that are typically state-regulated?

14. Describe three goals of insurance rate regulation.

15. What three contacts can you use to get insurance redress? Describe each one.

16. Name and describe the three steps in the risk management process.

17. What is the difference between a stock insurance company and a mutual insurance company?

18. List and characterize the four steps in the procedure for creating an insurance contract.

19. What are two advantages of being covered by group insurance?

20. Specify four ways in which you can minimize the cost of insurance.

Case Problems

1. Carmen Telimen of Mishawaka, Indiana, recently moved out of her parents' home and into her own apartment. When she moved, she was no longer covered by her parents' family automobile insurance policy. Her parents' agent suggested that Carmen simply buy the same coverage under her own name. He quoted a premium of $380 every six months, which was a shock to Carmen. She wanted to take a hard look at her policy to see if she could cut back on some of the coverage to save some money, but she could not make sense of the policy.
   a. Advise Carmen on how an insurance policy is organized.
   b. What key points should she focus on to help her understand the policy.

2. Larry Larsen of Green Bay, Wisconsin, wanted to buy life insurance after he graduated from college. He knew something about auto insurance but most other types of insurance were really only names to him. He certainly didn't know how much insurance to buy or when to buy it. Nor did he know much about insurance agents, companies, or costs.
   a. Advise Larry about the basic purpose of insurance.
   b. What sources would you tell Larry to contact to learn more about insurance?
   c. What guidelines would you suggest to Larry concerning the selection of a company and agent?
   d. Assuming Larry decided to buy more types of insurance (for instance, auto insurance or renter's insurance), how could he keep his insurance costs low?

3. Assume that you have been talking to some friends about how much more you know about insurance. One young married couple in the group says that they believe insurance is really a waste of money in most cases. They argue that "the odds of most bad events occurring are so low that you needn't worry." Further, they say that "buying insurance is like pouring money down a hole; you rarely have anything to show for it in the end." Based on your reading in this chapter, how might you argue against this couple's point of view?

Suggested Readings

"AIDS Testing Insurance." *Newsweek,* June 8, 1987, p. 55. The dilemma of proving insurability before being insured.

"Car Insurance—Is It Ever Smart *Not* to File a Claim?" *Better Homes and Gardens,* September 1987, p. 91. Discusses situations in which an insured may benefit from not filing an insurance claim and the consequences of not doing so.

"The Damage Is Mounting in Property and Casualty." *Business Week,* August 10, 1987, p. 32. A discussion of problems with regulation focusing on insolvent insurers.

"Saving $500—The Easy Way." *Esquire,* September 1987, p. 90. Ways to decrease unnecessary costs while maintaining adequate homeowner's, auto, and disability insurance protection.

C H A P T E R 11

Property and Liability Insurance

OBJECTIVES

After reading this chapter, the student should be able to

1. identify the types of losses that give rise to the need for property and liability insurance.

2. design a homeowner's insurance program to meet his or her needs and keep the cost of the plan to a minimum.

3. design an automobile insurance program to meet his or her needs and keep the cost of the plan to a minimum.

4. describe property and liability insurance policies designed for special groups of insurance purchasers.

5. specify the steps to take when making a claim against a property or liability insurance policy.

On the average, an automobile accident occurs once every second in the United States. Every seven seconds someone is injured in an auto accident. Every forty-nine seconds a residence is damaged by fire. And every three seconds a crime against property is committed. Each of these events results in a financial loss. Who pays for these losses? As a society we all do, as these costs take away resources that could be put to more productive uses. On a more personal level, however, the victims of these events will pay the costs unless they have purchased property and liability insurance.

Property insurance protects you from losses resulting from the damage to or destruction of your property or possessions. *Liability insurance* protects you from losses suffered by others for which you are responsible. Individuals spend over $75 billion per year for property and liability protection, and businesses spend over $80 billion. Automobile insurance accounts for over 40 percent of these expenditures. The list of perils that could be covered by property and liability insurance is virtually endless. Fire, wind, flood, automobile accidents, falling objects, medical malpractice, and theft are covered perils that are familiar to most people.

This chapter will first discuss the need for property and liability insurance and then cover the two major types of property and liability insurance, homeowner's insurance and automobile insurance. The next section will describe several other types of property and liability insurance. The final section will discuss the process of collecting when a property or liability loss occurs.

Why Property and Liability Insurance?

When you own property, you may suffer three kinds of losses. First, the property itself can be damaged or destroyed. When the value of the property is low or the chance of loss is low, this risk can be assumed. However, the risk (uncertainty) associated with property losses caused by many perils is very high. People commonly purchase fire insurance to reduce such risks.

A second type of loss results from the loss of the use of property. The need to rent a car because yours has been damaged in an accident is an example of this second type of loss.

Third, a liability might arise from the use of the property. The best example is the liability that arises out of the ownership and operation of an automobile. The owner of a car may be held liable if the driver of the car causes damage to others by destroying property or injuring individuals. More than thirty states require automobile owners to purchase liability insurance in order to drive on public roads.

Liability can also arise out of the various activities that people engage in at work or for enjoyment. Many professionals, such as doctors, dentists, dental hygienists, and lawyers, can be held liable for damages their clients suffer as a result of their negligence, errors, and omissions. These people buy professional liability insurance to provide reimbursement for such losses.

Homeowner's Insurance

Whether you own a home or a condominium or rent an apartment, you face the possibility of suffering property and liability losses. *Homeowner's insurance* combines liability and property insurance coverage needed by home owners and renters into a single-package policy. Today there are five types of homeowner's insurance for those who own a house, one type for the owners of condominiums, and another type for those who rent. All will be referred to here as homeowner's insurance.

Coverages Provided by Homeowner's Insurance

The standard homeowner's insurance policy is divided into two sections. Section One provides protection from various types of property damage losses. Included are coverages for losses due to (1) damage to the dwelling, (2) damage to other structures on the property, (3) damage to personal property and dwelling contents, and (4) expenses arising out of the loss of the use of the dwelling (for example, food and lodging). Additional coverages are usually provided for such things as debris removal, trees and shrubs, and fire department service charges. An important variable related to Section One is the number of loss-causing perils that are covered. Some homeowner's insurance policies are *named-perils policies* and cover only those losses caused by perils specifically named in the policy. Others are *all-risk policies,* which cover losses caused by any peril other than those specifically listed as excluded. This type of policy provides broader coverage because there are hundreds of perils that could cause property losses but only a few would be excluded. Table 11–1 summarizes the prominent types of homeowner's policies and the coverages provided.

Section Two is the liability insurance section. *Homeowner's general liability protection* covers situations where you are legally liable for the losses of another. Such a loss might be a broken leg suffered by a visitor who trips on a broken sidewalk on your property. You will be liable because you have an obligation to keep sidewalks in good repair. Whenever you are negligent or otherwise do not exercise due caution in protecting visitors to your property, there is a potential for suffering a liability loss.

You may wish to take responsibility for the losses of another regardless of the legal liability. Say, for example, a guest of yours suffers burns from touching a hot barbecue grill even though you warn him that the grill is hot. *Homeowner's no-fault medical payments protection* will pay for injuries to visitors regardless of who was at fault for the loss.

TABLE 11-1
Summary of Homeowner's Insurance Policies

	HO-1 (Basic Form)	HO-2 (Broad Form)	HO-3 (Special Form)
Perils covered (descriptions are given below)	Perils 1–11	Perils 1–18	All perils except those specifically excluded for buildings; perils 1–18 on personal property except glass breakage
Property coverages/limits			
House and any other attached buildings	Amount based on replacement cost, minimum $15,000	Amount based on replacement cost, minimum $15,000	Amount based on replacement cost, minimum $20,000
Detached buildings	10% of insurance on the home	10% of insurance on the home	10% of insurance on the home
Trees, shrubs, plants, etc.	5% of insurance on the home, $500 maximum per item	5% of insurance on the home, $500 maximum per item	5% of insurance on the home, $500 maximum per item
Personal property	50% of insurance on the home	50% of insurance on the home	50% of insurance on the home
Loss of use and/or add'l living expense	10% of insurance on the home	20% of insurance on the home	20% of insurance on the home
Credit card, forgery, counterfeit money	$500	$500	$500
Liability coverages/limits[a]			
Comprehensive personal liability	$25,000–$100,000	$25,000–$100,000	$25,000–$100,000
Damage to property of others	$250–$500	$250–$500	$250–$500
Medical payments	$500–$1,000	$500–$1,000	$500–$1,000

Special limits of liability[a]

For the following classes of personal property, special limits apply on a per occurrence basis (e.g., per fire or theft): money, coins, bank notes, precious metals (gold, silver, etc.), $100 to $200; securities, deeds, stocks, bonds, tickets, stamps, $500–$1,000; watercraft and trailers, including furnishings, equipment, and outboard motors, $500–$1,000; trailers other than for watercraft, $500–$1,000; jewelry, watches, furs, $500–$1,000; silverware, goldware, etc., $1,000–$2,500; guns, $1,000–$2,000.

List of perils covered

1. Fire, lightning
2. Loss of property from premises that are endangered by fire or other perils (has been discontinued by many companies)
3. Windstorm, hail
4. Explosion
5. Riots
6. Damage by aircraft
7. Damage by vehicles owned or operated by people not covered by the homeowner's policy
8. Damage from smoke
9. Vandalism, malicious mischief
10. Theft
11. Glass breakage
12. Falling objects
13. Weight of ice, snow, sleet

Note: This table describes the standard policies. Specific items differ from company to company and state to state.
[a] Where two figures are given, they represent the range of possibilities; most companies using one or the other as their standard limit. When you want a limit that exceeds the standard limit for your company, you usually can increase the limit by paying an additional premium.

HO-5 (Comprehensive Form)	HO-8 (For Older Homes)	HO-4 (Renter's Contents Broad Form)	HO-6 (For Condominium Owners)
All perils except those specifically excluded	Perils 1–11	Perils 1–18	Perils 1–18
Amount based on replacement cost, minimum $30,000	Amount based on actual cash value of the home	10% of personal property insurance on additions and alterations to the apartment	$1,000 on owner's additions and alterations to the unit
10% of insurance on the home	10% of insurance on the home	Not covered	Not covered
5% of insurance on the home, $500 maximum per item	5% of insurance on the home, $500 maximum per item	10% of personal property insurance, $500 maximum per item	10% of personal property insurance, $500 maximum per item
50% of insurance on the home	50% of insurance on the home	Chosen by the tenant to reflect the value of the items, minimum $6,000	Chosen by the home owner to reflect the value of the items, minimum $6,000
20% of insurance on the home	20% of insurance on the home	20% of personal property insurance	40% of personal property insurance
$500	$500	$500	$500
$25,000–$100,000	$25,000–$100,000	$25,000–$100,000	$25,000–$100,000
$250–$500	$250–$500	$250–$500	$250–$500
$500–$1,000	$500–$1,000	$500–$1,000	$500–$1,000

14. Collapse of building or any part of building
15. Leakage or overflow of water or steam from a plumbing, heating, or air-conditioning system
16. Bursting, cracking, burning, or bulging of a steam or hot water heating system, or of appliances for heating water
17. Freezing of plumbing, heating, and air-conditioning systems and home appliances
18. Injury to electrical appliances and devices (excluding tubes, transistors, and similar electronic components) from short circuits or other accidentally generated currents

Such coverage would help pay for the medical treatment of your guest's burns. Members of your immediate family are not covered under no-fault medical payments and should be covered by health insurance.

Types of Homeowner's Insurance

There are seven distinct types of homeowner's insurance policies: HO-1 through HO-6 plus HO-8. They are described in detail in Table 11–1 and more generally in the following text. The terms and numbers used to identify each are generally recognized, as they are used by most companies.

Basic Form (HO-1)   The basic form homeowner's policy is a named-perils policy that covers eleven of the eighteen major property-damage-causing perils and provides protection from the three liability exposures. Fire and lightning, explosion, windstorm, and smoke are the most common perils that can cause property damage. Each is included in the basic homeowner's policy.

Broad Form (HO-2)   The broad form homeowner's policy is a named-perils policy that covers the eighteen major property-damage-causing perils and provides protection from the three liability exposures.

Special Form (HO-3)   The special form homeowner's policy provides protection from liability exposures, as well as all-risk protection for four property coverages: losses to the dwelling, losses to other structures, landscaping losses, and losses for additional living expenses. Contents and personal property are covered on a named-perils basis for seventeen of the eighteen major homeowner's perils. The exception is the peril of glass breakage. In all other respects, the coverage under HO-3 is the same as under HO-2.

Renter's Contents Broad Form (HO-4)   The renter's contents broad form homeowner's policy protects the contents of a dwelling rather than the dwelling itself. HO-4 is a named-perils policy; it covers all eighteen major perils and provides liability protection. It is ideal for renters in that it provides protection from losses to the contents and personal property, and assures additional living expenses if the dwelling is rendered uninhabitable by one of the covered perils.

Comprehensive Form (HO-5)   The comprehensive form homeowner's policy provides all-risk protection. Whereas the HO-3 affords "all-risk" coverage on the dwelling and other structures but named-peril coverage on personal property, the HO-5 affords all-risk coverage on the dwelling, other structures, and personal property. Many companies will not write the Comprehensive Form because they do not want to pick up the losses to personal property on an all-risk basis. Such things as breakage, ripping, tearing, and spilling may be covered under "all-risk," and companies do not want to obligate themselves for these types of losses.

Condominium Form (HO-6)

The condominium form homeowner's policy protects condominium owners from the three principal losses they face: losses to contents and personal property, losses due to the additional living expenses that may arise if one of the covered perils occurs, and liability losses. HO-6 is very similar to HO-4 in that it is a named-perils policy covering the eighteen major perils. There are two additional coverages, however, that meet the specific needs of condominium owners. The first is protection against losses to the alterations and additions that condominium owners sometimes make to their units. The second is coverage for the dwelling unit, which will pick up where the building owner's coverage leaves off. This coverage is needed to protect the condominium owner if the owner of the building (usually the condominium association) is not sufficiently insured.

Older Home Form (HO-8)

An older home may have a replacement value that is much higher than its market value. The HO-8 policy provides actual cash value protection and does not provide that the dwelling be rebuilt to the same standards of style and quality, which may be prohibitively expensive today. Instead, the dwelling will be rebuilt to make it serviceable.

Buying Homeowner's Insurance

As with all other forms of insurance, you can purchase homeowner's insurance with varying coverage amounts, exclusions, and limitations. You must tailor protection to your needs, considering how homeowner's insurance is priced and how you can save on premiums.

Determining Your Homeowner's Insurance Needs

Both property and liability losses can occur during the ownership or rental of a home. The easiest way to identify the property losses is to make an inventory of the property and its contents and then determine the dwelling's replacement value. To determine the value of the buildings, you could (1) use the services of a professional property appraiser, (2) use the value of the property used to figure property taxes, or (3) consult with your insurance agent to assist in determining replacement value.

Homeowner's insurance policies usually contain a replacement cost requirement that stipulates that a home must be insured for 80 percent of its replacement value for the policy to pay the full reimbursement for any losses to the dwelling. If you fail to meet the replacement cost requirement, the amount of reimbursement for any loss will be calculated using the formula

$$R = L \times [I \div (RV \times .80)] \qquad (11-1)$$

where

R = reimbursement payable
L = the amount of the loss less any deductible
I = amount of insurance actually carried
RV = replacement value of the dwelling

Consider the example of twin brothers, John and Jim Otto, of Independence, Missouri. Each owns a home with a replacement value of $100,000 and each home suffers a $40,000 fire loss. John, who took a personal finance class in college, has insured his home for $80,000. Jim, in an attempt to save some money, has insured his home for $72,000. Applying formula 11–1, each brother determines the amount he will be reimbursed for the loss to his dwelling. John's calculations are

$$R = \$40,000 \times [\$80,000 \div (\$100,000 \times .80)]$$
$$= \$40,000 \times [\$80,000 \div \$80,000]$$
$$= \$40,000$$

Thus, John will be fully covered for his losses. Jim's calculations are

$$R = \$40,000 \times [\$72,000 \div (\$100,000 \times .80)]$$
$$= \$40,000 \times [\$72,000 \div \$80,000]$$
$$= \$40,000 \times .90$$
$$= \$36,000$$

Thus, Jim will be reimbursed for only $36,000 of his loss. His failure to insure his house for the full amount of his policy's coinsurance requirement means he must pay 10 percent of any loss; in this case, $4,000.

Making an inventory of and placing a value on the contents of your home is a more time consuming task. Table 11–2 shows the inventory and valuation for the contents of and personal property in an average living room. Such an inventory should be conducted for each room, the basement, garage, shed, and yard possessions. The values are especially important, since when totaled they allow the selection of the proper policy limits. Most homeowner's policies will automatically cover contents and personal property for up to 50 percent of the coverage on the home. If your home is insured for $100,000 but contains $55,000 worth of personal property, you probably need to purchase an extra $5,000 worth of contents coverage. Furthermore, some items of personal property may have specific policy limits. For example, a homeowner's insurance policy might provide a maximum of $2,500 theft coverage for precious metals (gold, silver, etc.). If the inventory reveals a higher valuation on such items, extra coverage might be needed.

Notice that Table 11–2 lists three estimates for the value of the contents of a room: the purchase price, the actual cash value, and the replacement cost. Historically, property insurance policies paid only the *actual cash value* of an item, which represents the purchase price of the property less depreciation. The formula for determining the actual cash value (ACV) is

$$\text{ACV} = P - [CA \times (P \div LE)] \tag{11-2}$$

TABLE 11-2
Personal Property Checklist

Item	Date Purchased	Purchase Price	Actual Cash Value	Replacement Cost
		Valuation		
Living room				
Furniture				
Couch	8–83	$750	$375	$950
Chair	11–81	250	100	375
Lounger	12–84	575	300	695
Ottoman	12–84	100	50	120
Bookcase	4–86	275	225	300
End table (2)	7–87	300	250	300
Appliances				
TV	1–88	550	500	600
VCR	6–86	400	300	400
Wall Clock	7–80	60	10	100
Furnishings				
Carpet	6–80	375	50	600
Painting	12–84	125	225	225
Pole lamp	4–82	150	50	225
Table lamp	4–82	75	40	100
Table lamp	5–87	125	100	135
Throw pillows	7–83	45	20	60
Totals		$4,155	$2,595	$5,185

where

P = *purchase* price of the property
CA = *current age* of the property in years
LE = *life expectancy* of the property in years

As an example, consider the case of Ruby Jones, of Minneapolis, Minnesota, whose eight-year-old color television set was stolen. The TV cost $500 new and has a total life expectancy of ten years. Its actual cash value at the time it was stolen was

$$ACV = \$500 - [8 \times (\$500 \div 10)]$$
$$= \$500 - (8 \times \$50)$$
$$= \$100$$

Ruby would be hard pressed to replace the TV for $100. A more realistic replacement cost for the TV might be $600. **Contents replacement cost protection** is an option now available in many homeowner's insurance policies; it pays the replacement cost of any personal property. This option has become more common in recent years as inflation has pushed up the price of home furnishings. Note that the standard limitation that applies to contents (50 percent of insured value of the dwelling) is still in effect if contents replacement cost protection is purchased. This overall limit may need to be raised since it is easier to reach the 50 percent figure when replacement cost valuation is used.

Determining the need for liability loss coverage is not as complicated as that for property losses. For example, many standard homeowner's policies provide $100,000 of general liability coverage, $250 of no-fault property damage coverage, and $1,000 of no-fault medical expense coverage. It would be wise to increase the policy limits for all three liability coverages.

How Homeowner's Insurance Is Priced Many factors affect the pricing of homeowner's insurance. The first is the amount and type of coverage and the perils insured against. Other factors are less well understood by many policyholders. The loss experience of the company affects the premium paid because the company must collect sufficient premiums to pay the loss claims made by the insured. You can avoid this problem by comparing policy premiums among companies and choosing one with a lower premium cost. Insurance companies vary their premiums by the adequacy of the firefighting system in a town or city. Even the distance of a fire hydrant from the home can affect the premium. The type of construction used to build a house will also affect the homeowner's insurance premium. When all other factors are equal, it will cost more to insure a frame house than a brick house. Some neighborhoods generate higher and more frequent losses than others. Usually, inner-city neighborhoods and extremely rural areas have higher homeowner's insurance costs than do suburban neighborhoods.

Lowering the Cost of Homeowner's Insurance Earlier we focused on the need to buy the proper type and amounts of coverage to obtain sufficient protection from property and liability losses. Equally important is the need to purchase no more protection than required to keep the cost of homeowner's insurance low. You can lower the cost of protection by making use of four policy features: the policy limits, deductibles, exclusions, and discounts.

Each of the property and liability coverages provided under a homeowner's insurance policy is subject to specific policy limits. Most people focus on the policy limit for the coverage on the dwelling itself, but although this limit is important, you must also select the proper limit for the coverage on the contents, other structures, and general liability. Match each limit in your homeowner's insurance policy as closely as possible with the potential for loss.

Insurance experts frequently advise homeowner's insurance purchasers to select higher deductibles as a means of lowering the premium. Twenty years ago the $100 deductible was commonplace in homeowner's policies. Yet in the period since 1965, prices and income levels have more than tripled, and some companies have raised their standard deductible. You can reduce your premium if you choose an even higher deductible. If you wish to reduce the cost of your homeowner's insurance policy, you can select a lower face amount than that required under the replacement cost requirement. In effect, you will be agreeing to pay a percentage of any loss suffered. The percentage you will pay is the percentage by which the face amount fails to meet the coinsurance requirement (see formula 11–1). Select such a premium reduction technique cautiously. Lowering the face amount of the policy by as little as 10 percent can result in your paying thousands of dollars of unreimbursed losses if your home is damaged by an insured peril.

The final way to lower the cost of homeowner's insurance is to use any discounts offered by the insurance company. Most discounts are offered to the insured who reduce the probability or severity of a loss. For example, some companies offer a discount if you install dead-bolt door locks and a fire extinguisher in your home. The locks reduce the probability of a theft loss and the fire extinguisher can reduce the severity of small fire losses. Another discount is commonly offered for the installation of smoke alarms.

Automobile Insurance

By owning and driving an automobile, you risk the potential of devastating financial losses. One split-second error in driving judgment can result in a loss of thousands of dollars in property damage and personal injury. In a recent year, more than 33 million automobile accidents occurred in the United States. These accidents resulted in injury to more than 5 million people, more than 46,000 deaths, and economic losses of more than $80 billion. It is not surprising that more automobile insurance is in force than any other type of property and liability insurance. *Automobile insurance* combines liability and property insurance coverage needed by automobile owners and drivers into a single-package policy. More than thirty states require auto owners to purchase automobile insurance, and the remainder require auto owners to show financial responsibility for any accident that might occur. This requirement is most commonly fulfilled through the purchase of auto insurance.

Losses Covered by Automobile Insurance

Automobile insurance offers a package of protection from two types of losses. The first type of loss includes the property losses to the covered vehicle and its contents due to collision, fire, theft, and other perils. The second type of loss includes those losses suffered by others for which the insured is legally liable.

Property Losses   A number of perils can cause property losses to an insured automobile. The most common peril is, of course, collisions with other vehicles or objects. Table 11–3 gives the frequency and the average loss payment per collision claim and the average loss payments

TABLE 11–3
Collision Claims for Various Cars

Make and Series	Body Style	Relative Average Loss Payment per Insurance Vehicle Year[a]	Average Loss Payment per Insurance Vehicle Year
Models with the best collision coverage loss experience			
Mercury Grand Marquis	Station wagon	43	$ 72
Dodge Aries	Station wagon	47	79
Chevrolet Impala	4-door	49	82
Dodge Caravan	Pass. van	49	82
Plymouth Voyager	Pass. van	50	84
Plymouth Gran Fury	4-door	52	87
Mercury Grand Marquis	4-door	53	89
Pontiac Parisienne	Station wagon	55	92
Pontiac Parisienne	4-door	57	96
Ford Crown Victoria	4-door	58	97
Chevrolet Celebrity	Station wagon	58	97
Models with the worst collision coverage loss experience			
Volkswagen Scirocco	2-door	256	430
Nissan 300ZX	Sports	234	393
Nissan 300ZX 2 + 2	Sports	231	388
Pontiac Firebird	Sports	208	349
Toyota Celica Supra	Sports	197	331
Nissan 200SX	2-door	194	326
Chevrolet Corvette	Sports	194	326
BMW 318i	2-door sports	192	323
BMW 325i	2-door sports	188	316
Porsche 944 Coupe	Sports	186	312

Source: Highway Loss Data Institute. Used with permission.
[a] 100 represents $168, the average loss payment per insured vehicle year for all 1985 models in their first year.

for various car models. In general, the cars with the highest collision losses per vehicle tend to be the smaller, sportier models offered by foreign manufacturers.

Other perils can cause property losses to automobiles. The most common of them is theft. About 1 out of every 160 autos is stolen each year. Again, the sportier models have the highest frequencies of theft claims.

Liability Losses   Two types of liability can arise out of the owner-ship and operation of an automobile. *Automobile property damage liability* occurs when a driver or car owner is legally responsible for damages to the property of others, such as another vehicle, a building, or roadside signs and poles. *Automobile bodily injury liability* occurs when a driver or car owner is legally responsible for bodily injury losses suffered by others. Table 11–4 lists the average automobile property

TABLE 11–4
Average Auto Insurance Liability Claims[a]

Year	Bodily Injury	Property Damage	Year	Bodily Injury	Property Damage
1976	$2,583	$490	1981	$4,453	$ 889
1977	2,890	544	1982	5,041	958
1978	3,123	622	1983	5,699	1,020
1979	3,559	715	1984	6,163	1,125
1980	4,010	787	1985	6,815	1,217

Source: Insurance Information Institute. Used with permission.
[a] Dollar averages include all loss-adjustment expenses and exclude data from Massachusetts and most states with no-fault auto insurance laws.

damage and bodily injury claims in recent years. Note that the average bodily injury liability claim is more than five times greater than the average property damage liability claim. The cost of insurance claim settlements and court awards resulting from auto accidents has risen steadily in recent years.

Types of Automobile Insurance

There are many different variations of the standard automobile insurance policy. Each provides coverage for essentially the same types of losses and is organized in nearly the same way. The *family auto policy (FAP)* and the *personal automobile policy (PAP)* are the types of automobile insurance most commonly selected by individual consumers and households. As you might expect, the FAP is designed for autos owned by families in which there are several persons who might drive the car and the PAP is designed for autos owned by an individual who is likely to be its only driver. Since the basic components of the FAP and PAP will vary little from company to company, we will combine our discussion of the two. Two other types of auto insurance of interest to you are automobile insurance plans and no-fault automobile insurance. These also will be discussed below.

Family Automobile Policy   The family automobile policy is designed to meet the insurance needs of families. It provides coverage for you, relatives living in your household unless specifically excluded, and persons who have your permission to operate the insured vehicle. Your relatives living in your household and other persons acting on your permission will also be covered when driving a vehicle not owned by you provided you have the permission of the car owner. The FAP (and the PAP) is a package of four distinct types of coverage: (1) liability insurance, (2) medical payments insurance, (3) property damage insurance, and (4) protection against uninsured motorists. Each of the four will generally have its own policy limits, conditions, and exclusions. Table 11–5 summarizes the coverage provided by family and personal auto policies.

TABLE 11–5
Summary of Family and Personal Automobile Policies

Policy Part	Type of Coverage	Persons Covered	Property Covered	Recommended Limits
1	Bodily injury liability	Nonexcluded relatives living in insured's household driving an owned or nonowned auto	Not applicable	At least legally required minimums or $50,000/$100,000, whichever is greater
	Property damage liability	Nonexcluded relatives living in insured's household driving an owned or nonowned auto	Automobiles and other property damaged by insured driver while driving	At least legally required minimums or $25,000, whichever is greater
2	Medical payments	Passengers in insured auto or nonowned auto driven by insured family member	Not applicable	$30,000
3	Collision	Anyone driving insured car with permission	Insured automobile	Actual cash value
	Comprehensive	Not applicable	Insured automobile and its contents	Actual cash value
4	Uninsured motorists	Anyone driving insured car with permission and insured family members driving nonowned autos with permission	Not applicable	$10,000/$20,000

Liability Insurance Part 1 of the FAP provides protection from both property damage liability and bodily injury liability. The policy limits for Part 1 are quoted with three figures, such as $10,000/$50,000/$15,000. The first of the three figures is the maximum that will be paid for one person's bodily injury losses resulting from an auto accident. The middle figure represents the overall maximum that will be paid for bodily injury liability losses resulting from an auto accident. The third figure represents the maximum that will be paid for property damage liability losses resulting from an accident.

In a PAP, the Part 1 liability limits would be stated as a single figure, such as $100,000. Any property and bodily injury liability losses from an accident would be paid until the limit is reached. In both the FAP and PAP, Part 1 cannot be used to pay for bodily injuries suffered by the driver at fault or for property damage to that driver's car. Passengers of the at-fault driver may collect under Part 1 for their losses but usually only after exhausting the coverage provided under Part 2 (discussed below).

Consider the following example as an illustration. On September of last year, Donna Redman, of Monterey, California, caused a serious accident when she failed to yield to an approaching vehicle while attempting to make a left turn. Donna suffered a broken arm and facial cuts resulting in medical costs of $1,254. Her passenger, Phillip Windsor, was seriously injured with head and neck wounds requiring surgery, a two-week hospital stay, and rehabilitation. Phillip's injuries resulted in medical costs of $17,650. The driver of the other car, John Miner, suffered serious back and internal injuries and facial burns resulting in some disfigurement. His medical care costs were $22,948. His passenger, Annette Combs, suffered cuts and bruises requiring minor medical care at a cost of $423. Both cars were totally destroyed. Donna's ten-year-old Buick was valued at $2,150. John's two-year-old Ford Taurus was valued at $9,350. The force of the impact spun John's car around, causing it to destroy a traffic-signal control box (valued at $3,650) and catch fire. Fortunately, both Donna and John were covered by a family auto policy.

In our example, both Donna's and John's FAPs had liability limits of $20,000/$50,000/$15,000. Donna's policy paid $20,000 (the per-person policy limit) toward John's injuries and the $423 loss suffered by Annette Combs. Donna's policy also paid a total of $13,000 in property damage liability losses ($9,350 for John's car, plus $3,650 for the traffic-signal control box).

Two additional points need to be raised before ending our discussion of the liability portion of auto insurance. The first point concerns situations in which an accident victim suffers serious, permanent injuries that are not fully reimbursed by the insurance policy protecting the driver at fault. In our example, John Miner suffered very painful injuries resulting in permanent disfigurement. He may wish to sue Donna for his pain and suffering and his unpaid medical expenses. If he were to file such a suit, Donna would be provided legal assistance by her insurance company. However, any judgment that exceeds the policy limits (remember that Donna's per-person policy limit has already been reached) will be Donna's responsibility. The second point involves situations where a covered family member causes an accident while driving a borrowed car. In such a situation, the insurance on the car is considered to be the primary coverage. Only after such coverage is exhausted will the coverage under the driver's policy be applied to any losses.

Medical Payments Insurance   Part 2 of the FAP/PAP provides *automobile medical payments insurance,* which will pay for the personal injury losses suffered by the driver of the insured vehicle and any passengers regardless of who is at fault. Medical losses occurring within one year and as a direct result of an accident will be reimbursed up to the limits of the policy. Automobile medical payments insurance will also cover insured family members when injured as passengers in any car, as pedestrians, or while riding a bicycle. Medical payments coverage is subject to a single policy limit, usually $5,000 or $10,000, which is applied per person per accident.

Consider Donna Redman's accident again. The FAPs in our example each have medical payments policy limits of $5,000. Donna and

Phillip Windsor were reimbursed for their medical losses by Donna's FAP. Because Phillip's losses ($17,650) exceeded Donna's medical payments policy limits, he also made a liability claim against her policy. John Miner's FAP also comes into play. Remember that medical payments insurance will pay regardless of who is at fault for an accident. Therefore, John and Annette Combs were initially reimbursed by John's FAP for $5,000 (the policy limit) and $423, respectively. Then John made a claim against Donna's insurance company in order to be reimbursed for the remainder of his bodily injury losses. Also, John's insurer exercised its subrogation rights and made a claim against Donna's insurer in order to collect the $5,000 it had paid John and the $423 it had paid Annette. **Subrogation rights** allow an insurer to take action against a negligent third party (and that party's insurance company) to obtain reimbursement for payments made to an insured.

Property Damage Insurance   Part 3 of the FAP/PAP provides protection against property damage losses to the insured car through collision insurance and comprehensive automobile insurance. Two minor but sometimes important coverages are also available under Part 3. The first is towing coverage, which will pay the cost of having a disabled auto transported for repairs. Towing coverage usually has a limit of between $25 and $50 per occurrence. The second minor coverage will provide a rental car when the insured vehicle is being repaired or has been stolen. Such rental reimbursement often has a daily limit of $10 or $20 and, therefore, provides only part of the funds needed to obtain a replacement.

Collision insurance reimburses you for losses resulting from a collision with another car or object or from a rollover. Collision insurance applies when you are at fault for the accident or when fault cannot be determined. When the other driver is at fault, reimbursement is obtained through his or her property damage liability protection. Collision insurance is invariably written with a deductible, usually $100 or $200. Donna Redman collected $2,050 for her car, as her collision coverage included a $100 deductible.

When you make a claim for payment under collision insurance, you must get an estimate of the repair cost. If the estimate exceeds the book value of the car, the lower of the two figures is paid, less any deductible. The *book value* of a car is based on the average current selling price of cars of the same make, model, and age. In the case of vintage, restored, or specialty cars, the book value may be much less than the true value of the particular car being insured. The wise owner of such a car will obtain additional coverage. At the other extreme, many auto insurance purchasers forgo collision insurance on cars that have lost much of their resale value due to old age or high mileage.

Comprehensive automobile insurance provides payment for property damage losses caused by perils other than collision and rollover. Such perils include fire, theft, hail, and wind, among many others. Comprehensive insurance is written on an all-risk basis, and it may include coverage for personal property in the insured car. Comprehensive automobile insurance may or may not be written with a deductible.

Uninsured Motorist Insurance Part 4 of the FAP/PAP addresses the problems that can arise when the driver at fault for an automobile accident is uninsured. ***Uninsured motorist insurance*** protects the insured driver and passengers from bodily injury losses (and, in a few states, property damage losses) resulting from an auto accident caused by an uninsured motorist. Uninsured motorist insurance provides protection above that provided by the automobile medical payments insurance in Part 2. The limits for uninsured motorist insurance are quoted in a manner similar to that for automobile liability insurance. Where available, uninsured motorist insurance carries a very low premium (often under $10 per year) and should be included in an auto insurance policy.

Automobile Insurance Plans

In more than one-half of the states it is illegal to operate a motor vehicle without being covered by auto insurance. Even where insurance is optional, it is unwise to be uninsured because of the potentially devastating effects of automobile accidents. Insurance companies will not voluntarily accept every applicant for automobile insurance. Drivers with very poor driving records may find it difficult, if not impossible, to obtain coverage at any price. Because auto insurance is so vital, most states have established a mechanism to provide coverage for drivers who are otherwise uninsurable. These ***automobile insurance plans (AIPs)*** assign a proportional share of the uninsurable drivers to each company writing auto insurance coverage in a state, according to each company's share of the total auto insurance premiums written in that state. As you might assume, the premiums for such coverage are extremely high. In addition, coverage is usually limited to liability insurance for the minimum legal policy limits. Drivers assigned to one of these plans by an insurance company should check with various insurers for more affordable prices.

No-fault Auto Insurance

During the late 1960s several problems in the auto insurance market provoked calls for reform. One problem was the long delay between an accident and the receipt of payment by the person who suffered the loss. A second problem was that a high proportion of the auto insurance premium was allocated to the determination of who was at fault for accidents. A third problem was the rapidly increasing cost of auto insurance. The most prominent reform was based on the concept of no-fault auto insurance. ***No-fault auto insurance*** allows you to collect directly from your insurance company for losses resulting from an auto accident without regard to who was at fault. Proponents of no-fault insurance argued that delays in the payment of claims and claims-handling expenses would be greatly reduced, thereby lessening the pressure to increase premiums.

Over the past 20 years, approximately one-half of the states have enacted some variation of the no-fault concept. The results have been mixed. Studies have shown that in states with strong no-fault auto insurance laws, payment delays have been reduced, claims-handling expenses have come down as a proportion to the premiums collected, and premiums, although continuing to rise, have done so at a lower rate than in states without a no-fault system. In general, however, the benefits envisioned after the enactment of no-fault plans have not been fully realized because only two states (Mich. and Mass.) have fully implemented the no-fault concept by severely restricting lawsuits.

Buying Automobile Insurance

The personal risk manager must shop very carefully for auto insurance because its cost can be as high as $1,000 or more per year. The proper auto insurance program must be selected while keeping the premiums as low as possible. Several methods of reducing premiums are available and need to be considered.

Determining Your Automobile Insurance Needs The first step toward designing an adequate auto insurance program involves identifying the losses that might occur. This is not a difficult task because the personal and family auto policies cover most of the losses that you can reasonably expect to face as a result of owning and driving a car. It is sometimes possible to eliminate some of the coverages provided in a policy to reduce the overall premium. The only way to obtain a significant reduction, however, is to eliminate collision insurance. The collision premium represents from 30 to 40 percent of the total insurance bill. Cars with a book value under $1,000 are candidates for collision insurance elimination. Other nonessential coverages, such as comprehensive, towing, or uninsured motorist insurance, would not yield significant savings if eliminated.

The more difficult step is determining the amount of coverage you need. At a minimum, you must conform to the financial responsibility requirements in your state (see Table 11–6). Most auto owners, even in states that do not require auto insurance, will choose auto insurance as the means to show the required financial responsibility. Yet the policy limits needed to conform to the financial responsibility laws are truly only minimums. In the light of current health-care and auto repair costs, it is wise to buy as much coverage as possible. A recommended program would provide liability protection with limits of $100,000/$300,000/$25,000, and you can obtain even higher limits for a small increase in premium. Similar limits for uninsured motorist insurance are advisable unless lower maximums are legally mandated. The recommended limits for automobile medical expense coverage are at least $30,000 per person.

How Auto Insurance Is Priced The premium charged for an auto insurance policy is based on fifty-two different characteristics that describe the driver, the car itself, and the usage of the car. These characteristics are used to place the insured in one of 260 classes. Members of each class have a similar probability of loss. The same price per unit of insurance is assigned to each member of the class and is then adjusted for the individual driver's accident and traffic violation experience, as well as any discounts for which the driver qualifies. The resulting price per unit is then multiplied by the number of units to obtain the premium charged.

TABLE 11–6
Automobile Financial Responsibility Limits

State	Liability Limits[a]	State	Liability Limits[a]
Alabama	20/40/10	Nebraska	25/50/25
Alaska	50/100/25	Nevada	15/30/10
Arizona	15/30/10	New Hampshire	25/50/25
Arkansas	25/50/15	New Jersey	15/30/5
California	15/30/5	New Mexico	25/50/10
Colorado	25/50/15	New York	10/20/5[b]
Connecticut	20/40/10	North Carolina	25/50/10
Delaware	15/30/10	North Dakota	25/50/25
Florida	10/20/5	Ohio	12.5/25/7.5
Georgia	15/30/10	Oklahoma	10/20/10
Hawaii	25/unlimited/10	Oregon	25/50/10
Idaho	25/50/15	Pennsylvania	15/30/5
Illinois	15/30/10	Rhode Island	25/50/10
Indiana	25/50/10	South Carolina	15/30/5
Iowa	20/40/15	South Dakota	25/50/25
Kansas	25/50/10	Tennessee	20/40/10[b]
Kentucky	25/50/10	Texas	20/40/15
Louisiana	10/20/10	Utah	20/40/15
Maine	20/40/10	Vermont	20/40/10
Maryland	20/40/10	Virginia	25/50/10
Massachusetts	10/20/5	Washington	25/50/10
Michigan	20/40/10	Washington, D.C.	25/50/10
Minnesota	30/60/10	West Virginia	20/40/10
Mississippi	10/20/5	Wisconsin	25/50/10
Missouri	25/50/10	Wyoming	25/50/20
Montana	25/50/5		

Source: Insurance Information Institute. Used with permission.
[a] The first two figures refer to bodily injury liability limits and the third figure to property damage liability. For example, 10/20/5 means coverage up to $20,000 for all persons injured in an accident, subject to a limit of $10,000 for one individual; and $5,000 coverage for property damage.
[b] 50/100 in cases of wrongful death.

Most of the characteristics used to classify the insured generate little controversy. Some of these characteristics are the miles driven to work or per year, the make and model of car insured, whether the car is used for business or pleasure, and where the car is garaged (more congested city traffic generates more frequent accidents). Several of the characteristics have generated considerable controversy in recent years, however. These are the age, sex, and marital status of the driver. Unmarried males under the age of twenty-five pay higher premiums than any other group. Insurance industry representatives argue the validity of the classifications being used. For instance, young drivers are involved in a disproportionate share of the auto accidents in the United States (see Table 11–7), as are unmarried drivers and males. Opponents of these classifications point out that although the statistics used by the industry may be actuarily valid, the result is still discrimination

TABLE 11–7
Accidents by Age of Driver

Age Group	Accident Involvement Rate	
	All Accidents[a]	Fatal Accidents[b]
14–19	34	53
20–24	36	65
25–34	23	42
35–44	17	30
45–54	14	25
55–64	13	24
65–74	11	25
75+	26	59
All drivers	21	38

Source: National Safety Council, 1986. Used with permission.
[a] Drivers in all accidents per 100 drivers in each age group.
[b] Drivers in fatal accidents per 100,000 drivers in each age group.

based on age, sex, and marital status, which is prohibited in other commercial activity. They question why a young, male driver who operates a car safely should pay a higher premium solely because of his age and gender. Legislators and insurance regulators in many states have proposed abolishing the use of age, sex, and marital status as determinants of auto insurance premiums, although less than ten states have enacted such laws. It is difficult to predict what actions will be taken in the future.

Lowering the Cost of Auto Insurance   There is no point in paying more for auto insurance than is absolutely necessary. The best way to save on premiums is to shop around for the lowest cost coverage. Auto insurance is one purchase where shopping around can pay off handsomely. The range of premiums is truly astounding. You may obtain quotes that differ by as much as $500 per year for essentially the same protection. To obtain a quote, call an agent and provide some basic descriptive information. Most agents are happy to call back later with a quotation in the hope of obtaining a new customer.

You can also reduce premiums by carefully selecting policy limits, deductibles, and exclusions. Policy limits can be reduced to lower the premium, but take care that you don't lose needed coverage. The savings achieved by a 50 percent reduction in policy limits for liability coverage will reduce the liability premium only by 10 to 15 percent. Raising the deductible can be an effective way of lowering the premium, especially for collision insurance. Doubling the collision deductible from $100 to $200 can lower the collision premium by 25 percent.

Certain exclusions can also be beneficial. If the car is never driven for business or to work, make sure that is reflected in the policy. Or if certain drivers in the family are the source of high premiums, it might be wise to exclude them from coverage and use of the car.

You can also save on premiums by taking advantage of the discounts offered by insurers. If your family owns more than one car, all should be insured with the same company if possible. Most companies will insure two cars without doubling the premiums. The rationale behind such discounts is that two cars will not be driven twice as much as one. Most auto insurers provide discounts when a driver has attained a certain number of accident-free years. This provides an added incentive to keep losses to a minimum. Auto insurance agents are the best source of information concerning the discounts available.

The final way of lowering the cost of auto insurance is to make certain that you have been placed in the proper class for premium determination purposes. Insurers will classify a car driven just a few miles to work each day differently than one driven a greater distance. If a job change results in a shorter drive to work, you should notify your auto insurance agent. Verifying that you are in the proper class is also important for obtaining the protection desired. If you use your car regularly in a manner not anticipated when the premium was determined, a claim may be denied when a loss occurs.

Other Property and Liability Insurance

Homeowner's and automobile insurance are the types of property and liability insurance most commonly purchased by individual risk managers. However, many individuals need other types of protection. This section will discuss some of the less well known but equally important property and liability policies.

Other Property Insurance

In addition to the property protection provided under homeowner's and auto insurance, there are three other types of property insurance commonly purchased by individuals.

Floater Policies *Floater policies* provide all-risk protection for accident and theft losses to movable personal property regardless of where in the world the loss occurs. Floater policies can be purchased as an addition to a homeowner's policy or as a separate policy. Some of the personal property items commonly protected under a floater policy are stereo equipment, sporting goods, cameras, and gifts. *Scheduled floater policies* provide insurance protection for specifically identified items of personal property. *Unscheduled floater policies* provide insurance protection for certain classes of property or all movable property owned by the insured.

Antique and Specialty Cars As mentioned earlier, the collision and comprehensive coverage under an auto insurance policy will pay only the book value when an automobile is destroyed. Antique and specialty cars are often worth more than their book value. In order to avoid receiving inadequate payment after a loss to such a vehicle, you can purchase special coverage from an auto insurance company. The amount of coverage should be based on a professional appraisal of the worth of the vehicle.

Government-provided Property Insurance Crop insurance and flood insurance are two types of property insurance provided through the federal government. *Crop insurance* provides all-risk protection from losses to crops between planting and harvest. The Federal Crop Insurance Corporation is the major source of such insurance. The policy limits for crop insurance are stated as a certain dollar amount per acre. *Flood insurance* protects property from losses caused by floods and mud slides provided that the property is located in areas eligible under the National Flood Insurance Act of 1968. The U.S. Department of Housing and Urban Development and the National Flood Insurers Association jointly administer the program. Eligibility is based on the existence of flood control measures in the community and the proximity of the property to the flooding source.

Other Liability Insurance

In addition to the liability insurance provided by homeowner's and automobile insurance, there are three other types of liability insurance commonly purchased by individuals.

Comprehensive Personal Liability Insurance Owning a home and driving a car are not the only sources of potential liability you face. Consider, for example, the case of Michael Hunt, of Golden, Colorado. While climbing in a restricted area, Michael accidentally loosened some rocks, which fell down the slope and seriously injured hikers below. Because Michael had failed to warn the hikers that he was above them, he was held liable for their injuries and was ordered to pay a court judgment of $78,458. Fortunately for Michael and the injured hikers, he was protected by a *comprehensive personal liability insurance* policy, which provides protection from liability losses that might arise out of any activity.

Remember that the standard homeowners' insurance policy includes a specified limit of personal liability coverage. For those without such coverage or who wish higher limits, a separate "umbrella" liability policy is advisable. When such coverage is designed to pay for only the excess of that provided in an auto or homeowners' policy the premiums are generally affordable.

Group Legal Insurance   Personal liability insurance policies will provide reimbursement for legal expenses if you are sued or held liable for the losses of others. However, legal services are often needed in situations not involving a question of liability. In response to such needs, a **group legal insurance plan** provides reimbursement for legal expenses to eligible members of a group. Most group legal insurance plans currently in effect have been provided as an employment benefit.

Professional Liability Insurance   Professionals, such as doctors, lawyers, dental hygienists, and accountants, can be held legally liable for losses suffered by their clients or patients. Such losses can arise out of a breach-of-contract dispute or as a result of negligence on the part of the service provider. **Professional liability insurance** protects individuals and organizations that provide professional services when they are held liable for the losses of their clients. Policy limits, deductibles, and other characteristics of such policies vary considerably depending on the profession involved. Generally, professional liability policies are written with policy limits of $1,000,000 and more. The premiums for such policies can also vary considerably. A $1,000,000 professional liability policy written for a dental hygienist may cost as low as $120 per year. Yet some surgeons pay in excess of $50,000 per year for professional liability insurance.

Collecting on Your Property and Liability Losses

For most people, the peace of mind and reduction of risk that insurance can provide is worth its cost. But the real value of owning insurance becomes evident when a loss occurs and reimbursement is obtained. Collecting this reimbursement can be very frustrating, however, if you do not understand the processes involved and are not prepared to present timely and accurate evidence of loss.

The first step in making an insurance claim is to contact as soon as possible the insurance agent or other company representative designated to handle claims. Keep the agent informed of everything relevant to the loss. This may mean almost daily contact until the claim is settled. The tenacious claimant is most likely to collect fully on a loss.

Documenting Your Loss

The burden of proof is on you whenever a property or liability loss occurs. Adequate documentation of the circumstances and the amount of the loss is essential. In the absence of such documentation, the agent and the company will interpret the situation in the manner most favorable to their interests. While essentially the same in principle, the documentation needed for homeowner's and automobile insurance differs in detail.

Documenting Claims for Homeowner's Insurance The best way to document a theft, fire, or other personal property loss is with pictures. Photograph or videotape all valuable property in your home when you purchase it or when you obtain insurance coverage. Write the date of purchase, price paid, description, model name and number, and serial number (if any) of the property on the back of the photograph or verbally record it on the videotape. Keep the documentation and a list of any unphotographed property (with a complete description) separate from the property itself. Ideally, these items should be kept in a safe-deposit box. A trusted friend or relative could also keep the photos and list.

When a loss occurs, file a report with the police or fire department, and present a copy of this report and copies of the photos and list to the agent or company when you file your claim for reimbursement. If your home has been damaged in a way that might allow for subsequent damage from rain or wind, the opening should be boarded up or otherwise secured. Often the insurance agent will arrange for these temporary repairs. No permanent repairs should be attempted until the insurance company has been notified and inspected the premises.

Documenting Claims for Automobile Insurance Contact the police and file a report whenever an auto accident occurs. The potential for misunderstanding or intentional deception between the drivers of the cars involved and their respective insurance companies is too great to rely solely on any verbal statements made by the drivers at the time of the mishap. Consider the case of Lisa Chen, of Santa Fe, New Mexico, who was involved in an accident with a driver who had struck her car after attempting to pass on the right shoulder. Such a maneuver is illegal and the other driver was clearly at fault and admitted as much. Because the accident caused no bodily injury and both cars could be driven afterward, Lisa agreed to the other driver's request that the police not be contacted. Instead, Lisa and the other driver exchanged information. Later, Lisa found out that the other driver's insurance had been canceled and that he had given her a false address and telephone number. Because she had no collision or uninsured motorist insurance on her car, Lisa paid the $638 repair bill herself. Had she filed a police report, her chances of collecting from the other driver would have been greatly increased, as she would have had evidence of his liability.

If you are involved in an accident, prepare a written report for your own records. This report should include a diagram of the accident scene showing the location of the vehicles before, at, and after the time of impact, plus the location of traffic lights and signs and any landmarks (for example, road construction or repairs). Also include a written description of the accident giving the time and place, the direction of travel and speed of the cars involved, road and weather conditions, and behavior of the parties involved. Obtain the names and addresses of at least two witnesses if possible.

Filing the Claim

An *insurance claim* is a formal request to the insurance company for reimbursement for a covered loss. All the information described in the section above will be requested by the insurance agent or *claims adjuster,* who is a person designated by the insurance company to assess whether the loss is covered and the dollar amount the company will pay. A claims adjuster can be an employee of the insurance company or an individual who provides these services for a fee. Generally, the insurance agent oversees the settlement process and should be the principal contact for the insured.

Insurance companies require that requests for payment be made in writing. Figure 11–1 shows the form used by many insurance companies for an auto insurance claim. Some companies will require you to fill out the forms, and others will complete the forms for you.

The most common problem occurring in the claims process is disagreement over the dollar amount of the loss. When property is damaged rather than destroyed or stolen, most companies request that you obtain repair estimates. Some companies, to speed up the settlement of claims, allow the claims adjuster to estimate the repair costs and issue a check to you to use for repairs. Although this process is faster, it is not always easy to find a source willing to make the repairs for the amount paid. Disputes over the dollar amount of a loss are most common when property is totally destroyed or stolen, especially when policies cover only the depreciated value of the property rather than its replacement cost. People invariably feel that their property had a greater value than that established by the insurance company. The best solution to this dilemma is to purchase replacement cost insurance, but this lesson is often learned too late.

Signing the Release

The final step in the claims settlement process is the signing of the *release,* which is an insurance document affirming that you accept the dollar amount of the loss settlement as full and complete reimbursement and that you will make no further claims for the loss against the insurance company. The legal effect of signing the release is to absolve the insurance company of any further responsibility for the loss. Never sign a release prematurely since the full extent of the loss often does not manifest itself until some time after the loss occurs. This is especially true for bodily injury losses. Sometimes the insured is pressured into signing the release quickly in order to receive payment as soon as possible, but you should resist the temptation to acquiesce to such pressure. When dealing with your insurance company, gently but firmly insist that adequate time elapse so that the full magnitude of the loss has a chance to become evident. You may face significant problems when dealing with the insurance company of the party at fault for the losses, but you can avoid most of them by insisting that the other insurance company negotiate through your agent. A qualified agent has the experience and expertise to resist undue pressure and insist on full payment of your losses.

FIGURE 11–1
Automobile Insurance Claim Form
Source: Acord Corporation. Used with permission.

SET TAB STOPS AT ARROWS

acord® AUTOMOBILE LOSS NOTICE

DATE (MM/DD/YY)

PRODUCER | PRODUCER PHONE (A/C, NO., EXT.) | FOR COMPANY USE ONLY

COMPANY | POLICY NUMBER | CAT. #

CODE | SUB CODE | POLICY EFF. DATE (MM/DD/YY) | POLICY EXP. DATE (MM/DD/YY) | DATE (MM/DD/YY) & TIME OF LOSS | A.M. | P.M. | PREVIOUSLY REPORTED | YES | NO

INSURED

NAME AND ADDRESS | INSURED'S RESIDENCE PHONE (A/C, NO.) | INSURED'S BUSINESS PHONE (A/C, NO., EXT.)

PERSON TO CONTACT | WHERE TO CONTACT | WHEN

CONTACT'S RESIDENCE PHONE (A/C, NO.) | CONTACT'S BUSINESS PHONE (A/C, NO., EXT.)

LOSS

LOCATION OF ACCIDENT (INCLUDING CITY & STATE) | AUTHORITY CONTACTED & REPORT NO. | VIOLATIONS/CITATIONS

DESCRIPTION OF ACCIDENT (USE REVERSE SIDE, IF NECESSARY)

POLICY INFORMATION

BODILY INJURY | PROPERTY DAMAGE | SINGLE LIMIT | MED. PAY. | OTHER THAN COLL. DED. | OTHER COVERAGES & DEDUCTIBLES (UM, NO-FAULT, TOWING, ETC.)

LOSS PAYEE | COLLISION DED.

INSURED VEHICLE

VEH. NO. | YEAR, MAKE, MODEL | V.I.N. (VEHICLE IDENTIFICATION) | PLATE NO.

OWNER'S NAME & ADDRESS | PHONE (A/C, NO., EXT.)

DRIVER'S NAME & ADDRESS (CHECK IF SAME AS OWNER) ☐ | RESIDENCE PHONE (A/C, NO.) | BUSINESS PHONE (A/C, NO., EXT.)

RELATION TO INSURED (EMPLOYEE, FAMILY, ETC.) | DATE OF BIRTH | DRIVER'S LICENSE NUMBER | PURPOSE OF USE | USED WITH PERMISSION ☐ YES ☐ NO

DESCRIBE DAMAGE | ESTIMATE AMOUNT $ | WHERE CAN VEHICLE BE SEEN | WHEN | OTHER INSURANCE ON VEHICLE

PROPERTY DAMAGED

DESCRIBE PROPERTY (IF AUTO, YEAR, MAKE, MODEL, PLATE NO.) | OTHER VEH. OR PROPERTY INSURED ☐ YES ☐ NO | COMPANY OR AGENCY NAME & POLICY NO.

OWNER'S NAME & ADDRESS | BUSINESS PHONE (A/C, NO., EXT.) | RESIDENCE PHONE (A/C, NO.)

OTHER DRIVER'S NAME & ADDRESS (CHECK IF SAME AS OWNER) ☐ | BUSINESS PHONE (A/C, NO., EXT.) | RESIDENCE PHONE (A/C, NO.)

DESCRIBE DAMAGE | ESTIMATE AMOUNT $ | WHERE CAN DAMAGE BE SEEN

INJURED

NAME & ADDRESS	PHONE (A/C, NO.)	PED.	INS VEH	OTHER VEH	AGE	EXTENT OF INJURY

WITNESSES OR PASSENGERS

NAME & ADDRESS	PHONE (A/C, NO.)	INS VEH	OTHER VEH	OTHER (SPECIFY)

REMARKS (INCLUDE ADJUSTER ASSIGNED)

REPORTED BY | REPORTED TO | SIGNATURE OF PRODUCER OR INSURED

ACORD 2 (6/84) NOTE: IMPORTANT STATE INFORMATION ON REVERSE SIDE ACORD CORPORATION 1984

Summary

1. The ownership of property exposes an individual to two types of losses. First, the property itself can be damaged or destroyed. Second, the use of the property can result in losses to another person for which the owner is legally liable.

2. Homeowner's insurance is designed to protect home owners and renters from property and liability losses. There are seven different types of homeowner's insurance. Homeowner's policies can be purchased on a named-peril or all-risk basis. In order to be fully reimbursed for a loss, the insured must fulfill the policy's coinsurance requirement.

3. Automobile insurance is designed to protect the insured from property and liability losses arising out of the use of a motor vehicle. The most commonly purchased type of automobile insurance is the family automobile policy. The premium for automobile insurance is based on the characteristics of the insured driver, including age, sex, marital status, and driving record.

4. Other important types of property and liability insurance include floater policies to protect personal property regardless of its location, flood insurance provided by the federal government, and professional liability insurance.

5. Responsibility for documenting and verifying a loss lies with the insured. Photographs or a videotape of the insured property are ideal for documenting losses under a homeowner's insurance policy. A police report provides the best documentation for losses under an automobile insurance policy.

Modern Money Management

The Johnsons Change Their Insurance Policies

The recent purchase of a condominium and a used car have forced the Johnson's to change their homeowner's and auto insurance policies. Their personal property and furniture are now valued at about $12,000. Their used car is a seven-year-old Chevrolet Citation with 87,000 miles on the odometer. They currently carry a 30/60/20 family auto policy with $200 deductible collision, $100 deductible comprehensive, and a $10,000 medical expense protection on their Toyota.

1. What type of homeowner's insurance policy will they need to buy?

2. What should be the face amount of the policy and what major property and liability coverage will it provide?

3. In addition to adding their new car to their existing auto insurance policy how might the Johnsons change Parts 1, 2, 3, and 4 of their policy?

4. Should the Johnsons buy collision insurance on the used car? Why or why not?

Key Words and Concepts

actual cash value, 338
all-risk policies, 333
automobile bodily injury
    liability, 342
automobile insurance, 341
automobile insurance plans
    (AIPs), 347
automobile medical payments
    insurance, 345
automobile property damage
    liability, 342
book value, 346
claims adjuster, 355
collision insurance, 346
comprehensive automobile
    insurance, 346
comprehensive personal liability
    insurance, 352
contents replacement cost
    protection, 339
crop insurance, 352
family automobile policy
    (FAP), 343

floater policies, 351
flood insurance, 352
group legal insurance plan,
    353
homeowner's general liability
    protection, 333
homeowner's insurance, 333
homeowner's no-fault medical
    payments protection, 333
insurance claim, 355
liability insurance, 332
named-perils policies, 333
no-fault auto insurance, 347
personal automobile policy
    (PAP), 343
professional liability
    insurance, 353
property insurance, 332
release, 355
subrogation rights, 346
uninsured motorist
    insurance, 347

Review Questions

1. Who pays for financial losses suffered from various kinds of accidents, such as automobile accidents and fire, and from crimes against property?

2. Of the amounts spent for property and liability protection from losses, what proportion is allocated to automobile-related losses?

3. Why would you purchase property and liability insurance?

4. Name the five types of losses covered under the property insurance portion of a homeowner's policy.

5. Identify two perils that are commonly excluded from homeowner's policies.

6. Give an example of a homeowner's liability loss that could be covered under general liability insurance.

7. Briefly distinguish among the seven types of homeowner's insurance polices identified as HO-1 through HO-6 and HO-8.

8. If you do not insure your home for the full amount of the coinsurance requirement, what would be the result in case of a loss?

9. In most homeowner's insurance policies contents and personal property are covered up to what percentage of the coverage on the dwelling itself?

10. Name the five principal factors that will affect the price of most homeowner's policies.

11. Why might it be wise to purchase contents replacement cost protection?

12. What five policy features can a home owner use to lower the cost of insurance coverage?

13. Name and distinguish between the two types of losses covered by automobile insurance.

14. Identify the two automobile insurance policies most often purchased by individuals or families and name their four parts.

15. Many auto insurance policies may identify dollar coverage for the insured as $20,000/$50,000/$15,000. Explain what each amount means.

16. Explain the type of coverage provided under automobile medical payments insurance.

17. What are subrogation rights?

18. Distinguish between collision and comprehensive automobile insurance coverage.

19. What is the benefit to the insured of no-fault automobile insurance? What is the benefit to the insurer?

20. How many different characteristics do insurers use to classify the insured when determining the premium for an automobile insurance policy?

21. What are the three most controversial characteristics insurers use to assess an automobile insurance premium?

22. What type of property loss would be covered under a floater policy?

23. Briefly distinguish among the following liability coverages: comprehensive personal liability insurance, group legal insurance, and professional liability insurance.

24. What is the best way to document a theft, fire, or other loss to personal property in the home? Also, identify the documentation process.

25. Describe what you should do to file a claim most effectively when involved in an auto accident.

Case Problems

1. Joe and Pam Cleve of Buffalo, New York, recently suffered a fire in their home. The fire began in a crawl space at the back of the house, causing $24,000 of damage to the dwelling. The garage, valued at $8,400, was totally destroyed but did not contain a car at the time. The damage to their personal property in the home and garage came to $18,500. Also, $350 in cash and a stamp collection valued at $3,215 were destroyed. While the damage was being repaired the Cleves spent three weeks in a motel and spent $1,350 on food and lodging. The house had a value of $95,000 and was insured for $68,400 under an HO-5 comprehensive form homeowner's policy with a $250 deductible. (Use Table 11–2 to answer this problem. Use the higher figure where two are given for the limits of coverage.)
   a. Assuming that the deductible was applied to the damage to the dwelling, calculate the amount covered by insurance and the amount paid by the Cleves for each loss listed: the dwelling itself, the garage, the personal property, the cash and stamp collection, and the extra living expenses.
   b. What amount and percentage of the total loss was paid by the Cleves?
   c. What two things could the Cleves have done to prevent their having to pay anything more than the deductible?

2. Louise Miller of Denver, Colorado, drives a three-year-old Plymouth Horizon valued at $5,600. She has a $75,000 personal auto policy with $10,000 in medical payments coverage and both collision ($200 deductible) and comprehensive. David Smith of Fort Collins, Colorado, drives a two-year-old Chevrolet Celebrity valued at $8,500. He has a 25/50/15 family auto policy with $20,000 in medical payments coverage and both collision ($100 deductible) and comprehensive. Late one evening, while he was driving back from Rocky Mountain National Park, David's car crossed the center line, striking Louise's car and forcing it into the ditch. David's car also left the road and did extensive damage to the front of a roadside store. The following table outlines the damages and the dollar amounts of each.

Item	Dollar Amount
Bodily injuries suffered by Louise	$ 6,800
Bodily injuries suffered by Fran, a passenger in Louise's car	28,634
Louise's car	5,600
Bodily injuries suffered by David	2,700
Bodily injuries suffered by Cecilia, a passenger in David's car	12,485
David's car	8,500
Damage to the roadside store	14,123

a. How much will Louise's policy pay Louise and Fran?

b. Will subrogation rights come into play? How?

c. To whom and how much will David's bodily injury liability protection pay?

d. How much will David's property damage liability protection pay?

e. To whom and how much will David's medical protection pay?

f. How much reimbursement will David receive for his car?

g. How much will David be required to pay out of his own pocket?

3. Donald Kriminshaw, of Burlington, Vermont, has frequently questioned the basis for setting the premium he pays for automobile insurance. He takes issue with three factors: his age (he is twenty), his sex, and his marital status (he is single). He feels that being judged a greater financial risk on the basis of these factors is discriminatory and thinks many other factors should be given overriding consideration.

a. Is Donald correct in his assessment of the use of age, sex, and marital status being discriminatory? Explain.

b. Why do you think insurance companies consider these factors when determining premium rate for automobile insurance?

c. Describe other factors that could be used in addition to or instead of these three that would result in a more equitable premium charge.

d. Will Donald ever be able to overcome these three negative factors and pay lower insurance premiums? How?

Suggested Readings

"Car Insurance: Picking the Policy." *Changing Times*, February 1987, p. 62. Tips on choosing a policy.

"Home: After the Smoke Clears," *Changing Times*, February 1987, pp. 65–70. What to do before and after a fire.

"Insurance in the Fast Lane." *Forbes*, January 12, 1987, pp. 276–278. The high cost of insuring a luxury or high-performance auto.

"Rental-Car Insurance: Don't Get Taken for a Ride." *Business Week*, January 19, 1987, p. 106. What coverages your regular insurance policy covers when you rent a vehicle.

CHAPTER 12

Health Insurance

OBJECTIVES

After reading this chapter, the student should be able to

1. identify the major reasons for buying health insurance.
2. describe the process used to determine health insurance needs.
3. identify and describe the major types of health insurance available and list the health-care expenses covered by each.
4. describe the purpose and major features of disability income insurance.
5. explain the major provisions and exclusions contained in health insurance policies and identify the benefits and negative aspects of each.
6. identify the major sources of health insurance, including health maintenance organizations and preferred provider organizations.
7. design a health insurance program to meet his or her health insurance needs and select the most appropriate sources for the policies included in this program.

Although the American population is healthier now than at any time in our history, illness and injury still strike frequently. By 1991 the total expenditure for health care in the United States will exceed $750 billion per year. This will represent more than 11 percent of the gross national product and amount to more than $3,000 each for every man, woman, and child in the country.

Fortunately, about 85 percent of Americans are covered to some extent by some form of health insurance. *Health insurance* provides protection against financial losses resulting from illness, injury, and disability. The development of health insurance is a relatively recent event. The first insurer that offered sickness insurance was organized in 1847, but not until 1930 or so did health insurance begin to be widely established. In 1929 the first health maintenance organization (HMO) was established, as was the first Blue Cross plan. In 1935 the passage of the Social Security Act brought the federal government onto the health insurance stage.

Private health insurance and government programs now account for about two-thirds of the annual health-care expenditures in this country. The remaining one-third represents out-of-pocket expenditures by individuals. In truth, however, the entire health-care bill comes out of the pockets of individuals since government expenditures are supported by taxes and insurer expenditures are supported by premium payments.

The decisions you make regarding health insurance can be the most complicated of any decisions about insurance. This chapter is designed to remove some of the mystery surrounding the subject. The first section addresses the question of why you need health insurance. Then we discuss how to determine your health insurance needs. A thorough discussion of the types of health insurance follows. The next section covers the important topic of disability income insurance. The final two sections of the chapter address important provisions in health insurance policies and guidelines for buying health insurance.

Why Health Insurance?

The reason for buying any type of insurance is to reduce the risk of loss that might result from the occurrence of a peril. In health insurance the major perils are illness and injury.

It is the almost infinite variety of illnesses and injuries that can beset us that makes health insurance so complicated. There are varying degrees of illness and injury, and the type of illness or injury has everything to do with the magnitude of the resulting loss. This makes it very difficult to decide whether you need more health insurance, how much you need, and what perils you need to cover.

Health insurance reduces the risk of financial loss due to illness or injury. But risk reduction is only one of many ways of handling health-related risks. Risks can also be assumed. Most people assume the risk of small health-related losses when they buy health insurance policies that call for the payment of a deductible. Likewise, they assume the risk of a very large health-related loss when they buy health insurance with policy limits.

A quick look at health-care expenditures shows why you need health insurance. The bill for a one-day hospital stay can exceed $275, excluding physicians' charges, drugs, or the cost of any medical procedures performed. The bill for a one-day stay in an intensive-care unit can easily exceed $1,000. The birth of a baby can cost $2,500 even if there are no complications. The average American spends more than $350 on doctors' services per year. None of these figures represents extraordinary medical treatment. On the other hand, an illness or injury that requires advanced medical science (such as CAT scans, nuclear medicine, or microsurgery) can quickly wipe out family savings or, worse, go untreated due to lack of funds.

If you are among the 85 percent of Americans covered by some form of private or government health insurance, you can receive financial assistance when injury or illness strikes. But will the assistance be sufficient to meet your needs? Do you have the correct type of coverage? Do you understand your policy? Have you gotten the most from your premium dollar and obtained coverage from the best source? This chapter will help you answer these questions.

Determining Health Insurance Needs

You must match your health insurance coverage to your needs. It is just as possible to be overinsured as it is to be underinsured. Your first step is to assess the types and magnitude of losses that can occur. You can then match these against the resources available to cover the losses. The difference between the potential losses and the resources available can be taken care of through the purchase of insurance.

Health-related Losses

There are four categories of losses that can result from an injury or illness. The most obvious is the expense for direct medical care. The other three are often overlooked, although they may result in larger dollar losses than medical care. They are losses resulting from the need for recuperative care, for rehabilitation, and for replacement of income lost while you are unable to work.

Direct Medical Care Expenses When illness or injury strikes, little attention usually is paid to the cost of medical care. It is much more important to treat the problem and restore the health of the patient. But eventually the bills come rolling in and are often met with disbelief. Not only are the amounts a shock, but there are usually many more people requesting payment than the patient had anticipated.

Consider the case of Irma Hayenga of Minneapolis, Minnesota, who fell while ice skating and suffered a compound fracture of her right arm. An ambulance transported her to the hospital and she was admitted through the emergency room and seen by a physician. There will be separate charges for the ambulance and emergency room, and the admitting physician may send a separate bill. Irma's first stop was the x-ray department. There will be a charge for each x-ray, and any technologists or physicians needed to read the x-rays will also charge for their services. Irma then underwent a series of blood tests and other lab work, which will each carry a separate charge. For surgery and postoperative recovery, Irma will be charged for a variety of items: professional services of an anesthesiologist, a surgeon, and an assisting surgeon; intravenous fluid and drugs; two days' stay in a hospital room (with extra charged for a telephone and television); personal items, such as tissues and water jug; and possible follow-up complications.

As you can see from this example, the variety of direct medical expenses can seem endless. Irma would probably pay a total of around $4,200. These costs increase dramatically with more complicated medical treatments.

Recuperative Care Expenses The need for health care may not end when a patient is discharged from the hospital. Sometimes there is a need for a period of confinement in a convalescent center or nursing home. Even after the patient returns home, there may be a need for home nursing care, possibly twenty-four hours per day. These expenses can exceed the cost of hospitalization. Unfortunately, many people fail to anticipate the possibility of such expenses when they purchase health insurance.

Rehabilitation Expenses Some illnesses or injuries are so severe that they result in a partial disability. A *partial disability* is an injury or illness that prevents you from performing one or more functions of your regular occupation. Examples of partial disabilities might be the loss of full use of a limb or the loss of sight in one eye. *Rehabilitation* is the retraining of disabled persons for their previous, or a new, occupation. The cost of this rehabilitation can represent an enormous sum of money.

Lost Income The average worker in the United States misses five work days per year due to illness or injury. An occasional work day lost will not put much of a strain on the family budget. But when an illness is severe or becomes chronic, serious budget disruptions can result. When a partial disability strikes, income may be lost because the victim may not be up to full-time work or may be forced to take a lower-paying, less-demanding position. A more extreme situation occurs when a total disability strikes. A *total disability* is an injury or illness that prevents you from performing any of the tasks of your previous occupation or of any other occupation. The result may be a period of no income lasting weeks, months, or even years. It takes little imagination to visualize the hardships if such a disability is permanent. Although three-fourths of all Americans are covered by life insurance, about one out of five American workers is covered by insurance to replace income lost from a long-term disability. Yet for young workers the probability of a long-term disability, though small, is greater than that of death.

Resources Available to Cover Losses

You need not purchase health insurance if you have sufficient resources available to cover health-related losses. Three types of resources need to be considered: (1) monetary and other assets, (2) other insurance, and (3) skills and education.

Monetary and Other Assets Assets such as savings and investments can lessen the need for health insurance. However, the assets that most families accumulate during a lifetime are often specifically intended to cover retirement expenses, not health-related losses. Further, retirement needs can be predicted with some degree of accuracy. Not so with health-related losses. Therefore, there can be little certainty that the assets accumulated will be sufficient to cover losses that might occur.

Other Insurance Health-related losses may be reimbursed through types of insurance other than health insurance. Auto insurance policies often contain medical payments coverage that will meet the medical bills of family members injured in auto accidents. Most workers are covered by workers' compensation insurance, which will pay for health care needed when injured on the job. Both of these types of insurance are helpful, but they provide only limited coverage. They can only supplement, not replace, health insurance.

Skills and Education A disabled person's skills and education will have a bearing on the amount of rehabilitation needed following a partial or total disability. The amount of education is not as important as the types of skills the disabled person possesses. For example, a physical disability such as paralysis might not prevent an accountant from doing his or her job, but blindness might require a change of careers.

Amount of Health Insurance Needed

To determine the amount of health insurance you need, you must subtract the losses that can result from an injury or accident from the resources available to pay for such losses. The differences will be in terms of both the dollar amount and the type of coverage you need. The next section will cover types of health insurance available, and a later section will discuss the dollar amounts of coverage.

Types of Health Insurance

The term *health insurance* is a general name for a wide variety of insurance policies and plans that cover financial losses resulting from illness, injury, or disability. No one policy or plan provides coverage for all types of losses that can occur. The health insurance purchaser faces a situation not unlike that of a diner who must choose from an á la carte menu. You must select coverages for medical expenses, recuperative care, rehabilitative care, and lost income. Note that insurance companies pay for losses in one of two ways; by paying the health care provider directly, or by reimbursing the insured for expenses paid. The sections below discuss the health insurance "menu."

Hospital Insurance

Hospital insurance (also called hospitalization insurance) protects you from the costs arising out of a period of hospitalization. The expenses usually addressed under such a plan include the room and board charges, routine laboratory expenses, operating-room charges, general nursing services, basic supplies, and drugs. Approximately 80 percent of all Americans are covered by hospital insurance. Many, however, are not adequately protected.

There are three types of hospital insurance: hospital expense insurance, hospital indemnity insurance, and hospital-service-incurred plans. *Hospital expense insurance* provides cash reimbursement for specific hospital expense items incurred during a hospital stay. These expenses include the per-day hospital room charges and miscellaneous hospital expenses (operating room, drugs, supplies, etc.). If the charges for covered items during the first day of hospitalization are $350, and the second day $200, the reimbursement will be $500 (subject to deductible and coinsurance requirements). Such insurance may have a daily maximum reimbursement, an overall per-stay maximum, and a maximum number of days for which reimbursement will be provided.

Hospital indemnity insurance provides a cash payment of a specific amount per day of hospitalization. No attempt is made to match the payment to a specific item of expense. Such a plan might pay $75 per day of hospitalization up to a maximum number of days. Even if the charges for the first day are $350, and the second $200, the reimbursement will be $75 per day.

A *hospital-service-incurred plan* pays the hospital directly for the covered services provided to the insured. Such plans do not provide cash reimbursement to the insured for hospitalization expenses. In all other respects they are much like hospital expense insurance plans.

Surgical Insurance

Surgical insurance protects you from the expenses of surgical procedures. *Surgical expense insurance* reimburses you directly for up to fifty (sometimes more) listed surgical procedures. Dollar maximums will be established for each procedure listed, and provision will be made for determining the reimbursement to be made for unlisted procedures. A *surgical-service-incurred plan* pays the surgical service providers (surgeon, anesthesiologist, hospital, and others) directly for their services. Surgical-service-incurred plans usually do not have dollar maximums per procedure. Instead they pay the usual, customary, and reasonable charge, based on what most service providers are charging for like services in a specific geographic area.

Medical Expense Insurance

Medical expense insurance provides reimbursement for physicians' services other than those connected with surgery. Medical expense insurance may pay for doctors' visits, drugs, nonsurgical outpatient procedures, drugs, x-rays, and other bills. Such plans usually include a dollar maximum per year, as well as a coinsurance clause and a deductible clause. The deductible clause is often written on an item basis rather than in terms of a dollar amount. This means, for example, that the policy will not cover the first few doctor's visits or x-rays. Like hospital and surgical insurance, medical expense insurance may be written on a service-incurred basis.

Major Medical Expense Insurance

The three types of health insurance discussed thus far are sometimes referred to as providing "first dollar" protection. They will pay the first dollar, or nearly so, of a covered health-care expense. As discussed, however, these plans do place limits on the amount to be reimbursed. Expenses beyond these limits are your responsibility. In a sense, this violates one of the principles of buying insurance: assume the risks that you can afford; insure the risks you cannot. If you rely solely on hospital, surgical, and medical expense insurance, you may be reimbursed for small losses but could be wiped out by a serious illness with costs beyond the limits of your protection.

Major medical expense insurance provides reimbursement for a broad range of medical expenses (including hospital, surgical, and medical expenses) and has policy limits as high as $1 million and deductibles as high as $1,000. Major medical insurance is usually a supplement to your hospital, surgical, and medical expense insurance. This means that the major medical insurance will pay only expenses not covered by the more basic plans and only after the deductible has been met.

Most major medical plans include a coinsurance requirement that you pay a proportion of any loss suffered (for example, 20 percent). Thus, you will pay a portion of losses above the deductible. Sometimes, there is a cap on the coinsurance requirement. A *coinsurance cap* is a stipulation in a health insurance plan that establishes a maximum loss beyond which a coinsurance requirement is not applied. Table 12–1 shows how a supplemental major medical plan might apply to the $200,000 health-care emergency incurred by Joe Peters, of Bloomington, Indiana. Note that with even a $150,000 limit on the major medical policy and reimbursement from hospital, surgical, and medical expense insurance, Joe will still have out-of-pocket expenses of

TABLE 12-1
Supplemental Major Medical Plan[a] Applied to Joe Peters's
Open-heart Surgery

	Total Expenses $200,000	
	Paid by Joe	Paid by Insurer
Items covered by "first-dollar" protection (hospital, surgical, and medical expense insurance)		$ 23,400
Major medical deductible	$ 500	
First $10,000 subject to major medical coinsurance clause	2,000	8,000
Remainder covered by major medical insurance		142,000
Expenses beyond major medical policy limit	24,100	
Totals	$26,600	$173,400

[a] $150,000 aggregate policy limits, $500 deductible, 20%/80% coinsurance requirement, $10,000 coinsurance cap.

$26,600. With health-care costs as high as they are today, a major medical policy with an overall limit of $500,000 may not be sufficient.

Comprehensive Health Insurance Plans

A *comprehensive health insurance* plan combines the protection provided by hospital insurance, surgical insurance, medical expense insurance, and major medical expense insurance into one policy. It is simply a package of protection that provides the coverage of the basic plans and the broad, high-limit coverage of major medical. Comprehensive health insurance plans usually have a $100 or $200 deductible and a 20 percent coinsurance requirement for all expenses up to the coinsurance cap. A benefit of comprehensive policies is that there is no need to determine which policy applies to a given expense. Comprehensive health insurance plans are primarily available on a group basis, and many employers who wish to provide a full line of health insurance coverage to workers do so under one comprehensive policy.

Dental Expense Insurance

Dental expense insurance provides reimbursement for dental-care expenses. Dental expense insurance is similar to other forms of health insurance in that there are deductibles, coinsurance requirements, maximum payments for specific procedures, and overall policy limits. Most dental expense insurance is written on a group basis as an employment benefit.

Eye Care Insurance

Eye care insurance provides reimbursement for the expenses related to the purchase of glasses and contact lenses. Such a policy would cover eye examinations, refraction tests, fitting of the lenses and the cost of the lenses and frames. Most eye care insurance is written on a group basis as an employment benefit. For an individual, eye care insurance is probably not a good buy. The cost of glasses is not high enough nor is the risk great enough to prevent such expenses from being paid out of the regular budget. Further, the greatest expense for eye care arises out of diseases and injuries to the eyes. These expenses would be covered under general health insurance plans.

Supplemental Health Insurance Plans

Taken together, the health insurance plans discussed thus far would cover virtually all the health-care expenses you might have. Each plan does, however, have limitations in terms of dollar amounts and procedures covered. *Supplemental health insurance* plans fill the gaps in coverage of the standard health insurance plans or provide reimbursement in addition to that provided by the standard plans. Often supplemental health insurance is advertised directly through the mail or on television. Many of these plans are not all they claim to be and/or their prices are too high. Often these policies contain severe limitations on the coverage provided or the amount to be paid under the policy. Purchasers are sometimes unaware of these limitations until they request reimbursement.

Accident Insurance   *Accident insurance* pays a specific amount per day (for example, $100) for a hospital stay arising out of an accident and/or a specific amount for the loss of certain limbs or body parts (for example, $2,000 for the loss of an arm). Often the premium for such a policy is very low and the benefits are not that generous, perhaps $50 per day. Such per-day hospitalization benefits are too low to be helpful, and often the benefits begin only after the hospitalization exceeds seven, ten, or fourteen days. The average cost of a semiprivate hospital room in the United States is more than $200 per day (room charges only) and the average hospital stay is seven days.

Dread Disease Insurance   *Dread disease insurance* provides reimbursement for medical expenses arising out of the occurrence of a specific disease. Cancer is the disease most commonly addressed by this type of policy. The fear of cancer and the staggering costs of its treatment lead many people to consider buying cancer insurance. Yet this purchase, as of all dread disease insurance, is not a wise use of scarce funds. It would be better to buy a major medical or comprehensive policy with high limits or to increase the limits of an existing policy that covers more than one type of illness.

Medigap Insurance   Closely associated with dread disease insurance, *medigap insurance* supplements the protection provided by Medicare. Medicare is a federal government health insurance plan for the elderly and others that includes coverage for hospital, surgical, and medical expenses. Medicare does have certain limitations that make the purchase of a supplemental policy seem desirable. As reductions in Medicare coverage have occurred or been predicted, the volume of television and print ads for medigap insurance has increased dramatically. Unfortunately, many medigap policies fall far short of the benefits provided by major medical insurance, and the endorsement of a celebrity is no guarantee of quality. The best supplement to Medicare would be very similar to a standard major medical policy.

Disability Income Insurance

None of the types of health insurance discussed thus far is designed to provide reimbursement for the income loss resulting from an illness or accident. *Disability income insurance* replaces a portion of the income lost when you cannot work due to illness or injury. It is probably the most overlooked type of insurance yet is vitally important for all workers. For example, a twenty-two-year-old man without dependents would probably need no life insurance. Yet he would need disability insurance to support himself during a period of disability. Further, at age twenty-two the chances of becoming disabled for at least three months are seven and one-half times greater than the chances of death (the probability of death at age 22 is 18.9 per 10,000; the likelihood of disability is 142.8).

There are a number of sources of income protection during a period of disability. Many workers have sick pay benefits. These can help ease the burden of a short period of disability. Social Security disability benefits are available to many disabled workers and their families. (See Appendix B for an illustration of how to calculate these benefits.) Other government programs provide disability protection for veterans, railroad workers, and civil servants. Some employers provide or make available group disability income insurance, although typically only for a short term (less than two years). In addition, pension plans may provide benefits to workers who become disabled. In many cases these plans fall short of a worker's needs and he or she will have to seek more protection by buying more through the group plan provided by his or her employer or buy a policy individually from an insurance company that provides disability income insurance.

Determining the Level of Need

The first question to ask is, "How much disability income insurance do I need?" One way to find out is to determine your current monthly after-tax wages. From that figure, subtract the amounts you would receive from insurance currently in force, Social Security disability benefits, and other sources of disability income. The resulting figure would be the amount of extra coverage you would need to obtain.

There are several problems with this method. First, some of the benefits listed above may not be available for all disabilities. For example, Social Security disability benefits begin only five months after the

TABLE 12–2
Determining Disability Income Insurance Needs

Current monthly after-tax income	_____
Minus	
Estimated monthly Social Security disability benefits	_____
Monthly benefit from employer-provided disabililty insurance	_____
Monthly benefit from private disability insurance	_____
Monthly benefit from other government disability insurance	_____
Reduction of monthly life insurance premiums due to waiver of premium options	_____
Total subtractions	_____
Estimated monthly disability income needs	_____

disability occurs and are only payable if you are unable to perform any gainful employment. Fully 70 percent of all applicants are rejected. It is possible that a less severe disability that does not qualify for Social Security may result in the need for a larger income replacement than a more severe disability that does qualify for Social Security. A second problem is that some disability benefits may cover short-term but not long-term disability. In spite of these reservations, it would be wise to complete the calculations (see Table 12–2) using the figure obtained as a starting point in your shopping for disability income insurance protection. The dollar limits on disability income policies are either written in increments of $100 per month or as a percentage of monthly income. Most companies will not write policies for more than 60 to 80 percent of after-tax earnings. The major factors affecting premiums are the amount of coverage desired and your age, health status, occupation, and gender.

Important Policy Provisions

Once you have estimated your level of need, you can begin the search for a disability income insurance policy. The key is to look among the major policy provisions for those that meet your needs in terms of short-term and long-term protection and in terms of full versus partial disability. This section includes a discussion of these important policy provisions.

Elimination Period The *elimination period (waiting period)* in a disability income policy is the time period between the onset of the disability and the date the disability benefits begin. The longer the elimination period is, the lower the premium will be. Increasing the disability period from thirty to ninety days can reduce the premium by one-third. If you have sick pay benefits from your employer, you can coordinate the elimination period in a policy with the number of sick days you have accrued. Or if you have some savings set aside as an emergency fund to carry you through several months without income, your elimination period can be lengthened. Because disability income benefits are paid monthly, the first check will not arrive until thirty days after the elimination period ends.

Benefit Period The *benefit period* in a disability income policy is the maximum period of time for which benefits will be paid. It begins when the elimination period ends. The benefit period is usually stated in years and can be from one year to "to age sixty-five." Most disability income policies will not pay past age sixty-five. It is to your advantage to select a long benefit period. The extra premium required can be offset by a longer elimination period.

Residual Clause Recall that Social Security disability protection covers only total disabilities. The same is true for some disability income policies. Yet many injuries or illnesses result in partial disabilities whereby the victim may be able to work part-time at his or her old job or work at a less demanding, lower paying position. In such cases some, but not all, income is lost. A *residual clause* allows for some reduced level of benefits when income is reduced but not eliminated. Consider the case of Shirley Whitaker, a criminal lawyer in Kansas City, Missouri, who had purchased a $3,000-per-month disability policy. Shirley suffered from high blood pressure and was forced to cut back her work load by 50 percent, thereby taking a 50 percent pay cut. Her disability policy had a residual clause so she received $1,500 (50 percent × $3,000) per month during her disability.

Social Security Rider If you have figured your disability income insurance needs assuming that you would receive Social Security benefits, you may find yourself with inadequate protection if your application is denied. A *Social Security rider* may be added to your policy, providing an extra dollar amount of protection should you not qualify for Social Security disability benefits. Consider the dilemma faced by Sharon Senn of New Orleans, Louisiana. Sharon determined her disability insurance needs to be $1,400 after assuming that she would receive $1,000 from Social Security if she were to become disabled. She could have purchased a $2,400-per-month policy and remove all uncertainty, but the premium would be more than she could afford. Instead she bought a $1,400 policy with a $1,000 Social Security rider for a premium savings of 30 percent.

Continuation Provisions Like other forms of health insurance, disability income insurance policies will contain clauses that dictate how or whether the policy may be discontinued at the discretion of the company. It is advisable to buy at least guaranteed renewable disability insurance so that you can always maintain the coverage even though the premium may increase at renewals. (See page 379 for a more complete discussion of these concepts.)

Cost-of-living Adjustments   Your need for disability income insurance will increase over your lifetime because of inflation and increases in your earnings. You should include a cost-of-living clause in your policy, which will increase your benefit amount with inflation. You might also consider buying a policy that uses a percentage of income as a limit on benefits rather than a specific dollar amount per month. That way, your potential monthly benefit would increase automatically with increases in your salary.

The Health Insurance Policy

The most important source of information about health insurance benefits is the health insurance policy itself. The policy outlines the general benefits and, most importantly, includes the limitations and conditions that affect the amount reimbursed. When your health insurance is provided by a group policy, you will not receive a copy of the policy but a *certificate of insurance,* which is a document that outlines the benefits and policy provisions for individuals covered by group insurance. The group policy will remain on file with your organization, and you should be allowed to consult it if you choose.

You will find important information throughout a health insurance policy. This section describes important provisions, especially those that limit payment and coverage provided. Make a note of which provisions to include in your health insurance policies and which to avoid. Remember that the inclusion of restrictive provisions usually lowers the cost of health insurance. Similarly, the inclusion of liberal provisions increases premiums.

General Terms and Provisions

The first section of a health insurance policy contains general terms and provisions that define the terminology used in the policy and outline its basic provisions. Important parts of this section are (1) the application, (2) the insuring agreements, (3) the definitions, (4) who is covered, and (5) the time period of the protection.

The Application   Your application for health insurance becomes part of your policy. The application contains specific information about you that is used to establish the premium to be charged, such as your health status and possibly the results of a medical exam. Also important are your age and occupation. You must not falsify an application or even unintentionally include erroneous information. Errors in an application can result in a denial of payment.

Insuring Agreements   As defined in Chapter 10, insuring agreements describe in general language the type of coverage being provided. This information is the first indication of whether the policy will meet your needs, but it is unwise to rely solely on the insuring agreements as a sign of appropriate coverage. Other policy information can greatly modify the terms of the agreement. Probably the only benefit of the insuring agreements is that they can be used to eliminate a policy from consideration. Benefits not outlined in the insuring agreements will not be available under the policy.

Definitions   Of vital importance are the definitions of the terms used in the policy. For example, a policy may promise to pay $100 for each day of a hospital stay. But what is a hospital? Would such a policy cover nursing-home care? Probably not. Would it cover a stay in an osteopathic hospital? Maybe. A veterans hospital? Probably not. Definitions of *hospital* in many policies include the stipulation that the hospital must be nongovernmental. Two of the more critical definitions in health insurance policies are those for *injury* and *sickness*. Expenses resulting from an injury may be covered to a greater or lesser degree than those for a sickness. Consider the case of a person who suffers a hernia. Is a hernia an injury or is it a sickness? It depends on the policy. Read the definitions very carefully.

Who Is Covered   Health insurance policies can be written to cover an individual, a family, or a group. When an individual is the focus of the coverage, there is little chance of a misunderstanding, but family policies can be more complex. Generally, a family is a husband, wife, and dependent children. But at what age are children no longer covered? Are children who are born while the policy is in effect automatically covered from the moment of birth? Each policy may answer these questions differently.

The question of who is covered under a group policy is also very important. All group members are usually covered, but there may be a waiting period for newer members. If the group consists of the employees of a business, there may be different protection for full-time and part-time employees. The family of the group member may also be covered, but again the definition of *family* needs to be considered.

The Time Period   Individual and group health insurance policies are usually written on an annual basis. An annual policy beginning on January 1 will start at 12:01 A.M. that day and end at 12:01 A.M. on January 1 the following year. Any illness that begins during the year will be covered. But will coverage end if the policy expires while you are still in the hospital? The answer is usually no. Similarly, a surgical procedure performed after a policy expires but for an illness or injury for which treatment was sought during the policy period will be covered.

A time period concern may arise with accident insurance policies. Many of these policies are in effect only during specific hours of the day and in specific locations. For example, an accident policy may cover a child only while he or she is at school or traveling to and from school.

Payment Limitations

A health insurance policy will contain a number of provisions that limit the level of payments to reimburse covered expenses. These provisions include (1) policy limits, (2) deductibles, (3) coinsurance requirements, and (4) coordination of benefits requirements.

Policy Limits *Policy limits* are the maximum amounts an insurance policy will pay to reimburse a covered loss. Health insurance policies may employ up to four types of policy limits. To illustrate these, we will consider the case of Jim Foulks, of Marquette, Michigan, who owns a five-year hospitalization policy. *Item limits* specify the maximum reimbursement for a particular health-care expense. Foulks's policy contains a $200 maximum for x-rays. Jim suffered a stroke, and had x-ray expenses of $317. The policy will pay $200 of this expense and Jim will pay the remainder. *Episode limits* specify the maximum payment for health-care expenses arising from a single episode of illness or injury. Each episode is considered separately. Foulks's policy contains an episode limit of $10,000 for hospitalization expenses. Jim was hospitalized for two weeks after his stroke and incurred $11,223 in hospital charges. His policy will pay $10,000 of these charges. One month later, Jim suffered burns from a cooking accident at home and was hospitalized for five days, incurring hospital-care costs of $1,310. His policy will pay these expenses in full because the second hospitalization is considered a separate episode.

Time period limits specify the maximum payment to be made for covered expenses occurring within a specified time period, usually one year. Consider again Foulks's stroke and burn hospitalizations. If his policy contained a $10,000 annual time period limit rather than an episode limit, the hospital expenses from Jim's second hospitalization would not have been covered. *Aggregate limits* place an overall maximum on the total amount of reimbursement that can be made under a policy. Foulks's policy might have an aggregate limit of $25,000. This means that during the five-year period of the policy, no more than $25,000 will be reimbursed for hospitalization expenses he incurs.

The dollar amounts of these policy limits increase in the order in which they were discussed. Aggregate limits are always higher than time period limits, which are higher than episode limits. A policy with high aggregate limits may seem attractive, but if the episode limits are too low the policy may not be a good buy. Analyze each limit separately to determine if it allows for sufficient protection.

Deductibles Deductibles are clauses in insurance policies that require you to pay an initial portion of any loss before receiving insurance benefits. Deductibles may apply to specific types of expense items. For example, a medical expense plan may require you to pay the first $50 of any x-ray expense during a year. Deductibles may also apply to each episode of illness or injury. A hospitalization policy might require you to pay the first $200 of expenses from a hospital stay. If you are hospitalized five times during a year, you would have to pay the deductible each time, for a total of $1,000. Deductibles can also apply per time period. Major medical policies often have annual deductibles requiring you to pay the first portion of expenses each year before collecting under the policy.

Generally speaking, annual deductibles are best. Family policies warrant special attention. Sometimes the deductible applies to each family member. A policy with the same deductible applied to the family as a whole is better.

Coinsurance   As you recall, a coinsurance clause requires you to pay a proportion of any loss suffered. In health insurance, this share is usually 20 or 25 percent. A variation of coinsurance, a *copayment clause,* requires you to pay a specific dollar portion of specific covered expense items. Copayment is often required for prescription drug coverage. You would pay a specific amount (for example, $1) for each prescription and the insurer would pay the remainder. A copayment differs from a deductible in that a deductible might require that you pay the first $100 of x-ray expenses during a year but a copayment clause might require that you pay the first $10 of each x-ray.

Coordination of Benefits   Recall from Chapter 10 that the principle of indemnity prevents you from collecting insurance benefits that exceed the loss suffered. This principle is maintained in health insurance through the inclusion of coordination-of-benefits clauses. A *coordination-of-benefits clause* prevents you from collecting more than 100 percent of a loss and designates the order in which policies will pay benefits if multiple policies are applicable to a loss. The primary policy is the insurance policy which will be first applied to any loss when more than one policy provides coverage for the loss. If the primary policy fails to reimburse 100 percent of the loss, secondary (or excess) policies, if any, will be applied in order until the loss is fully paid or benefits are exhausted, whichever occurs first.

Coverage Limitations

In addition to limits on the dollar amounts reimbursed, health insurance policies may contain a number of provisions that limit the types of expenses covered by the policy. For purposes of discussion, these coverage limitations will be grouped in three categories: (1) limitations based on the timing of the loss, (2) general exclusions, and (3) maternity benefits.

Limitations Based on the Timing of the Loss   For losses to be insurable, they must be unexpected. Say, for example, you develop an ulcer and are told by your doctor that surgery will be needed. If you are not covered by surgical expense insurance, you might be tempted to buy such a policy before having the surgery. However, because the surgery is expected, it would not be covered under the new policy. Health insurance policies contain provisions that prohibit coverage for a *pre-existing condition,* which is a medical condition that becomes evident and for which treatment is received before the issuance of the policy. Group policies exclude fewer pre-existing conditions.

Disputes often arise as to whether or not a medical loss is the result of a pre-existing condition. In order to clarify matters and prevent such disputes, insurance policies may contain specific waiting periods before coverage will be provided for specific losses. The most common example is the one-year wait that is generally required for maternity benefits to be payable under a new health insurance policy.

Disputes also arise when episode deductibles and limits are applicable under a policy. The dispute may center on whether a recurrence of an illness is or is not a separate episode. If the recurrence is considered a separate episode, the deductible will need to be paid but reimbursement will be available up to the full episode limits. If the recurrence is considered a continuation of the original episode, the deductible will not apply but the loss may exceed the episode limit. A *recurring clause* clarifies whether a recurrence of an illness is considered a continuation of the first episode or a separate episode. Recurring clauses will often stipulate a minimum number of days between hospital stays for a recurrence to be considered a separate episode. Usually, the best recurring clause is one that has a short waiting period before a recurrence is considered a separate episode. This is because it is usually less expensive to pay a deductible than to pay expenses exceeding the episode limit. Nonetheless, you should judge each policy individually in terms of the recurring clause, the amount of the deductible, and the amount of the episode limit.

General Exclusions   Exclusions narrow the focus of and eliminate specific coverages provided in the policy. Reimbursement for injuries resulting from war, riot, and civil disturbance are generally excluded from health insurance policies, as are the expenses for voluntary cosmetic surgery. Many policies will deny coverage if the illness or injury occurs outside the United States. Expenses resulting from self-inflicted wounds are commonly nonreimbursable, especially in the first two years of the policy.

Maternity Benefits   Maternity benefits are often considered separately from other benefits in a health insurance policy, and specific limits and exclusions may apply. The best policies consider maternity care similarly to any other health-care requirement. A common limitation on maternity benefits restricts payment for the hospitalization of the newborn once the mother is discharged from the hospital.

Nonmedical Provisions

In addition to the medical expense payment provisions, each health insurance policy contains important provisions that regulate the payment of premiums and the terms under which the policy may be renewed and canceled. These nonmedical provisions are (1) continuation provisions, (2) waiver-of-premium benefits, (3) grace period, and (4) convertibility.

Continuation Provisions   Health insurance policies are not written for life. They will expire and need to be renewed or changed. Even during the policy period they may be canceled. The following terms apply to the continuation of health insurance policies:

1. *Cancelable policies* may be canceled or changed at any time at the option of the insurer. Such policies are not as common now as they were in the past and should be avoided.
2. *Optionally renewable policies* may be canceled or changed by the insurer only at the time of expiration.
3. *Guaranteed renewable policies* must be continued in force as long as the insured pays the required premium. Premiums may change but only if the change applies to an entire class of the insured rather than to an individual insured. This prevents the company from raising the premium to force the insured individual to cancel. This is the most common and desirable policy.
4. *Noncancelable policies* must be continued in force without premium changes (up to the age of sixty-five) as long as the insured pays the required premium. Noncancelable policies may be prohibitively expensive.

Waiver of Premium   Health insurance policies can include a waiver-of-premium option. This allows the insured to stop making premium payments during a period of disability and have the policy remain in force.

Grace Period   Health insurance policies may contain provisions for a grace period, commonly thirty-one days. This prevents the lapse of a policy if a payment is late. The policy remains fully in force during the grace period only if the premium is paid before the end of the grace period.

Convertibility   Many people are covered by group health insurance through their employer. Federal law requires that employers with more than twenty employees who offer group health insurance continue to offer coverage for eighteen months after an employee has quit or been laid off. However, the employee generally must pay both the employee and employer premiums plus a 2 percent fee. (Widows, widowers, divorced spouses, and their dependents must be provided this option for thirty-six months.) Eventually, however, eligibility to remain a member of the group will expire. Convertibility allows you to convert the group coverage to an individual basis without proving insurability. You will usually have to pay a higher premium, but waiting periods and pre-existing condition provisions will not apply.

Buying Health Insurance

As a purchaser of health insurance, you should ask yourself a number of questions. Is group insurance best? Where can I obtain health insurance? How are the premiums determined? How can I make comparisons? What type of coverage should I buy and how much protection do I need? The following section will help you answer these and other questions.

Group Versus Individual Health Insurance

Health insurance is most commonly sold on a group basis. More than one-half of all Americans are covered by a group health insurance policy, mainly because group health insurance is so often one of the fringe benefits provided by employers. Employers benefit from offering group policies because the premiums are a tax-deductible business expense. Employees benefit because such fringe benefits are not subject to the federal income tax. Even if employers did not provide group coverage, it would still be popular because premiums are lower and underwriting criteria are less restrictive for group insurance than for individually purchased policies. This latter feature is especially attractive to anyone who has a negative medical history.

The only major problem with group insurance is that it cannot be tailored to the needs of an individual or family. However, in today's health insurance market there are numerous supplemental and major medical plans that can be purchased to fill gaps in group policies. If you are eligible for group health coverage, do not overlook it.

Sources of Health Insurance

Health insurance protection is available from several different sources. You can choose from among Blue Cross/Blue Shield plans, private insurance companies, and health maintenance organizations. Even if you are fully covered by group insurance through your employer, you will usually have options to choose from there. The federal government is also a source of health insurance protection, and this may lessen the need to obtain coverage elsewhere. Table 12–3 summarizes the sources of health-care protection.

Blue Cross/Blue Shield   Blue Cross/Blue Shield plans are probably the best-known sources of health insurance protection. Technically, these plans are not insurance but are producer cooperatives that provide health-care protection on a service-incurred basis. Originally, Blue Cross provided hospital insurance and Blue Shield provided surgical insurance. However, major medical and comprehensive insurance are now available through Blue Cross/Blue Shield. The "Blues," as they are sometimes called, also provide dental insurance through their Delta Dental Plan subsidiary.

TABLE 12–3
Summary of Health Insurance Plans

Type of Plan	Sources			Basis		
	Private Insurers	Service-incurred	Government	HMOs	Group	Individual
Basic plans						
Hospital	X	X	X[a]	X[b]	X	X
Surgical	X	X	X[a]	X[b]	X	X
Medical expense	X	X	X[a]	X[b]	X	X
Major medical	X	X		X[b]	X	X
Comprehensive	X	X		X[b]	X	X
Dental care	X	X	X[c]		X	X
Eye care	X			X[b]	X	X
Supplemental plans						
Dread disease	X					X
Accident	X				X	X
Medigap	X					X
Disability income insurance	X		X		X	X

[a] Medicare and Medicaid
[b] Prepaid health care
[c] Medicaid

The Blues provide group or individual health-care protection. There are more than eighty individual Blue Cross and/or Blue Shield plans operating in the United States. Each is a separate organization of doctors and hospitals in a geographic area that provides health-care protection on a nonprofit basis. Participating doctors and hospitals accept Blue Cross or Blue Shield reimbursement as payment in full. Nonparticipating doctors and hospitals do not accept Blue Cross or Blue Shield reimbursement as payment in full and may require patients to pay the difference between the reimbursement and their higher fees for services.

The Blues have come under criticism in recent years because they are managed by the very doctors and hospitals that depend on these plans for payment. The Blues have historically reimbursed hospitals and doctors for whatever they charge for a service, as long as the charge is usual, customary, and reasonable. Many critics argue that this system provides no incentive for service providers to hold down costs. The insureds do not object to high health-care costs because the insurer pays their bills. Although these increased costs are reflected in rapidly rising premiums, the premiums are most likely paid by employers providing group benefits. In response, many employers have begun to require workers to pay a larger portion of premiums. An individual insured might therefore have an incentive to exert pressure on service providers to hold down costs. Another solution to this problem has been the institution of Fair Allowance Reimbursement Effort (FARE) plans by some Blue Cross/Blue Shield companies. Under a FARE plan, a health-care provider (hospital, clinic, doctor, etc.) is paid a specific, preestablished amount for the service provided rather than an amount that the provider feels is reasonable.

Private Insurance Companies   The hundreds of individual private health insurance companies operating in the United States (Aetna and Travelers are but two examples.) provide protection for over one-half of the people in this country. Because there are so many different companies, you may know little about the ability and willingness of a company to live up to its promises. Do not trust advertising to provide the necessary information. Ads will describe the coverage in the broadest terms and use ideal situations when discussing the benefits that could be paid. Ads never mention the serious exclusions that can reduce benefits.

Health Maintenance Organizations   *Health maintenance organizations (HMOs)* are health-care providers who operate on a prepaid basis. Health maintenance organizations do not provide health insurance. They provide health care. HMOs provide their services to groups as well as individuals. For a specific monthly fee, HMO members will receive a wide range of health-care services, including hospital, surgical, and preventive medical care. Some HMOs also provide eye examinations, psychiatric care, and ambulance service. If an HMO is not set up to provide certain types of care, it will contract with a local hospital or clinic that does.

HMOs have grown to be a major force in the American health-care system. There are more than four hundred HMOs providing services to more than 20 million Americans. The reason for this popularity may lie in the HMOs' emphasis on preventive care and efficiency. Because HMOs do not charge for services over and above the monthly fee, patients are motivated to seek care whenever symptoms appear, or even before. (Some plans have a small, $1 to $5 copayment per office visit for those wishing to pay a lower monthly fee.) This means that problems tend to be caught early or are prevented, thereby reducing the probability of a high-cost medical emergency. Also, because HMOs collect only the monthly fee, there is an incentive to keep costs and unnecessary procedures to a minimum. Some critics of HMOs argue that cost-cutting measures lead to a reduction in the quality of services provided. Another common criticism is the reduced freedom of choice among doctors. Members are assigned a primary-care physician but members are seen by another physician if their primary-care physician is not on duty when they are seeking treatment.

Federal law requires that employers of more than twenty-five workers who provide group health insurance benefits to their employees to offer HMO membership as an alternative but only if an HMO in the area has solicited their business. It would certainly pay to investigate the HMO alternative if it is available to you either through a group or as an individual. Often the HMO fee is higher than the group or individual health insurance premium but the avoidance of deductibles and coinsurance costs can more than offset the extra monthly cost. When considering an HMO, ask questions about turnover rates among the physicians (high is bad, low is good), the level of satisfaction among current members, whether you will be reimbursed for all or just emergency medical expenses required when you are out of town, and the waiting time for a nonemergency appointment (ten to fourteen days should be the maximum).

Preferred Provider Organizations   A *preferred provider organization (PPO)* is a group of medical care providers (doctors, hospitals, and so forth) who contract with a health insurance company to provide services at a discount to policyholders. The discount is then passed along to the policyholders in the form of reductions or elimination of deductibles and/or coinsurance requirements when they choose the PPO providers for their medical care. The discounts do not apply if the policyholders choose to be served by non-PPO members. In addition, if the nonmembers charge more than what the insurer feels is reasonable, you will pay the excess as well as the deductible and coinsurance. Employers who provide group health insurance to their employees as a fringe benefit of employment have become increasingly interested in PPOs in recent years. This is because they usually pay reduced premiums for PPO-associated health plans. Consider the case of Professor Ralph Brite, who teaches at a large southern university. His health insurance plan has contracted with a PPO representing the university's teaching hospital and its affiliated physicians. Because he chose the university hospital for treatment of a broken ankle he saved $150 on the $250 deductible and did not have to pay his 20 percent coinsurance share of the bill. Of course, he gave up the right to go to his family doctor who is not a PPO member, but he could use that doctor for any further health-care needs.

Government Health-care Insurance   Since the establishment of the Social Security program in 1935, the federal government has steadily expanded its role as a provider of health insurance protection. Federal, state, and local programs account for about 40 percent of health-care expenditures each year. There are four major federal programs. *Social Security disability income insurance* provides benefits that will help replace the lost income of eligible disabled workers. *Medicare* is a program administered by the Social Security Administration that provides payment for hospital and medical expenses of persons aged sixty-five and over and some others. *Medicaid* is a jointly financed program of the federal government and the states that pays some medical expenses of the poor. These programs will be discussed below. Finally, many military veterans are eligible for free or low-cost health care provided at Veterans Administration hospitals around the country. *Veterans Administration hospitals* are medical care facilities designed exclusively to provide care to veterans.

Employee Fringe Benefits (Choices of Harry and Belinda Johnson)

You may be understating your true income by thousands of dollars if you think only of your gross salary as your payment for employment. A *fringe benefit* is any payment for employment that is not provided in the form of wages or commissions. Many employees receive 40 to 50 percent over and above their salary in the form of fringe benefits. Some of the most common benefits are paid or subsidized group health insurance (about 75 percent of companies providing health insurance benefits require that employees pay some share of the cost of a family plan), group life insurance, retirement programs, savings programs, tuition subsidies, unemployment insurance, child care, clothing allowances, and employee discounts. The value of these benefits is even greater since the income they represent is often nontaxable or tax deferred.

About 95 percent of the employees of medium-sized and large U.S. firms are covered by health insurance, according to a 1987 Labor Department survey. Ninety-six percent have life insurance, 89 percent have a retirement plan, 80 percent have protection against catastrophic

medical expenses, 74 percent have dental benefits, and 49 percent also have some protection against long-term disability.

Traditionally, employees had little choice as to what fringe benefits they would receive. For dual income households this often resulted in duplication of some benefits. For example, both Harry and Belinda's employers provide partially subsidized family health insurance plans as fringe benefits. They chose to be covered under Belinda's policy because it provides more protection and is less expensive. The net effect of this choice is that Harry does not benefit as much from his fringe benefits as his coworkers.

Harry's employer, like many others in recent years, has decided to use a more flexible approach toward providing fringe benefits. Employees are provided with a maximum dollar amount that can be used for benefits. They then choose from a menu of fringe benefits those that they desire the most. Harry has decided to continue to forgo his health insurance in order to receive master's degree tuition support and some additional life insurance protection.

Social Security disability income insurance provides eligible workers and their dependents with income during a period of disability expected to last twelve full months or until death. There is a five-month waiting period for benefits to begin, and the disability must be total. This means that recipients must not be able to engage in any substantial, gainful activity. If they can do any work for pay, they will be ineligible for benefits. Social Security disability income protection may provide upwards of $15,000 in tax-free income to the family of a fully insured disabled worker.

Medicare is a hospital and medical expense insurance program for the elderly and other eligible persons. It is funded via the Social Security payroll tax. Those eligible for Medicare include persons aged sixty-five and over who are eligible for Social Security retirement benefits, federal civilian employees aged sixty-five and over who retired after 1982, persons who are disabled and eligible for Social Security disability benefits, and individuals with kidney disorders that require kidney dialysis treatments.

Medicare is divided into two parts. Part A is the hospitalization portion of the program and requires no premium. Part B is the medical expense insurance portion of the program. It is optional and is open to all Part A recipients and anyone else aged sixty-five or over upon payment of a monthly premium ($17.90 in 1987).

Medicare Part A will pay benefits for up to ninety days of hospitalization per benefit period. A benefit period begins on the first day of any hospitalization and lasts until the patient goes sixty consecutive days without hospitalization. There are no limits on the number of benefit periods that a person may use.

For a longer hospital stay a patient may draw on a lifetime maximum of sixty reserve days of benefits. Part A will also pay benefits for up to one hundred days of care in a nursing facility following a three-day or longer episode of hospitalization. Additionally, it will provide benefits for home health-care visits after a three-day or longer period of hospitalization. As with other hospital insurance plans, Medicare Part A requires the payment of deductibles, which can result in substantial out-of-pocket expenses for the insured. In 1987 the hospitalization deductible was $520 for the first sixty days of a benefit period, $130 per day for each of days sixty-one through ninety, and $260 per day for any reserve days used. Deductibles also apply to nursing facilities and home health-care visit benefits.

Medicare Part B will pay benefits for surgical procedures and medical expenses for surgery, outpatient care, hospitalization, or certain other services. Part B requires the payment of a $75 (in 1987) annual deductible and has a 20 percent/80 percent coinsurance requirement. Part B will reimburse 80 percent of the reasonable approved charge for covered expenses. If the service provider will not accept the approved charge designated by the Social Security Administration, the insured must pay the difference. Part B will also pay a portion of the expenses for treatment of mental illness, chiropractic services, dental care, and physical therapy.

Medicaid is a program of health care for the poor that is jointly administered and funded by the federal and state governments. Eligibility for Medicaid is based on household income, and the program is generally available to those households receiving Aid to Families with Dependent Children (AFDC) benefits. Health services provided through medicaid vary from state to state. Benefits generally include hospital, surgical, and some medical care and in some states may cover dental care for children.

Workers' Compensation   If you are injured on the job or become ill as a direct result of employment, state law requires your employer to pay the medical costs that result. *Workers' compensation insurance* protects employers from liability for injury or disease suffered by employees which result from employment related causes. The benefits to the employee include health care, recuperative care, replacement of lost income, and, if necessary, rehabilitation. Thus, the full range of health-related losses is covered by workers' compensation insurance. However, because only those losses resulting from work-related accidents or injuries are covered, workers' compensation can only supplement your total health insurance plan.

How Health Insurance Is Priced

When you apply for health insurance, the decision of whether to accept you is based on a number of underwriting factors, including your age, sex, occupation, family and personal health history, and physical condition. Each of these factors has a bearing on the likelihood of health-related losses. If you have a hazardous occupation or a history of heart disease, you may be required to pay higher-than-standard rates for any policy you select. Applicants who exhibit severe health problems may be denied coverage.

If you are accepted for coverage at the standard rates, the price you will pay for health insurance will be based on three factors: age, occupation, and sex. Age will not affect the premium unless the applicant is a child or is over forty years old. Occupation will be more of a factor for accident insurance coverage than for sickness coverage. If your occupation is extremely hazardous, this will be factored in during the underwriting process. Women pay higher health insurance premiums than men because they generally suffer somewhat more frequent and more severe health losses.

It is very difficult to provide estimates of the cost of health insurance. There is such a wide variety of plans, limits, deductibles, and exclusions that there is no standardized pricing mechanism as there is for life insurance. Without doubt, however, health insurance is expensive and becoming increasingly so. The rapid price increases in the health-care industry and the general aging of the population indicate that there is little prospect of substantial relief in the near future. A sound health insurance program for the typical family of four can easily cost more than $250 per month. There is little mystery as to why employer-paid group health-care programs are so popular. For the individual purchaser of health insurance, careful comparisons of plans and policies are absolutely necessary in order to stretch the health-care dollar.

Shopping for Health Insurance

Shopping for health insurance requires careful comparison of the many options available. In addition to the premium to be charged, you should focus your attention on three areas: (1) the company, (2) the policy, and (3) claims procedures.

The Company Although Blue Cross/Blue Shield is the most widely known provider of health insurance protection, many other companies offer health insurance. Many are more familiar as marketers of life insurance. As in the selection of a life insurance company (see Chapter

13), health insurers should be rated A+ or A by *Best's*. It is also a good idea to consult the insurance regulatory agency in your state to determine if there have been any problems with a company. Such agencies will not be able to recommend a company but may be helpful in eliminating those that engage in questionable practices. The company itself can be a source of information. Wise financial planners always ask about the company's *claims ratio,* which represents the percentage of premiums collected by an insurance company that are subsequently paid out to reimburse the losses of the insured. The formula for the claims ratio is

$$\text{Claims ratio} = \text{losses paid} \div \text{premiums collected} \qquad (12\text{--}1)$$

Blue Cross/Blue Shield companies typically have claims ratios that exceed 90 percent. At the other extreme, there are many companies that have claims ratios of less than 25 percent. The lower the claims ratio, the lower the return on the premium dollar paid.

Pay special attention to the purchase of any health insurance policy through the mail. The advertising for such policies cannot possibly detail what is covered and what is not. Unfortunately, many of these ads intentionally leave out important restrictions and exclusions. No insurance policy should be purchased sight unseen. If an agent or company will not allow you to study a policy for a few days, buy elsewhere.

The Policy   The variety of health insurance policies seem to render futile any attempt at making comparisons. The most effective way to compare health insurance policies is to set some criteria for judging whether a policy provides the needed coverage. Those policies that do provide the needed coverage can then be compared for price. Table 12–4 outlines a set of criteria to use in judging the merits of various types of policies. These criteria reflect the need to obtain adequate coverage and to keep premiums affordable. Many policies will greatly exceed the criteria in this table, but they will do so for a price you may not be willing to pay. Similarly, you may find lower-priced policies, but the lower price may be at the expense of adequate coverage.

Claims Procedures   An often-overlooked aspect when comparing health insurance policies is the procedure used to make a claim when a loss occurs. Service-incurred plans and HMOs have the advantage in that they require little or no paperwork on your part. Some other plans require you to submit the appropriate forms yourself. Figure 12–1 shows a typical health insurance claim form that requires both the insured and the health-care provider to complete certain segments.

Another important aspect of the claims procedure is the method of payment. Service-incurred plans, HMOs, and some other insurers do not require you to pay for your health care and then wait for reimbursement. Insurers who will reimburse only may cause you some hardship, especially if the health-care provider wants payment in full soon after or even before services are rendered.

TABLE 12–4
Recommended Health Insurance Criteria

Plan[a]	Policy Limits	Deductible	Coinsurance/ Copayment	Coordination of Benefits	Exclusions
Hospital insurance	Should pay usual, reasonable, and customary charges for a period of 180 days per episode; semiprivate room recommended.	Small deductible ($100) can be used to lower premium; deductible should apply on an annual basis	None	Primary	Exclusions should be kept to a minimum; maternity benefits can be excluded, as can mental illness benefits and hospitalization for elective cosmetic surgery
Surgical insurance	Should pay usual, reasonable, and customary charges with no limit	None	None	Primary	Should be few exclusions; elective cosmetic surgery can be excluded; outpatient and doctor's office surgical procedures should not be excluded
Medical expense insurance					
Drugs	$500 annually	$100 annually	$1 or $2 copayment recommended	Primary	Drugs provided during hospitalization should be covered under hospital insurance; will not cover nonprescription drugs and medicines
Home nursing care	Full payment for 30 days per episode	None	None	Supplement to hospital insurance	None
X-rays	$500 annually	$50 annually	$5 copayment per x-ray may help lower premium	Supplement to hospital insurance	None

Maternity	Maternity protection should treat a maternity event like any other hospitalization episode and surgical procedure				
Major medical	$500,000 per episode	$500 annually	20%/80% with $5,000 cap	Supplemental to basic plans	Very few exclusions recommended, such as cosmetic surgery
Comprehensive	Any comprehensive plan chosen should have at least the same features as the basic and major medical plans outlined above.				
Dental	$3,000 annually	$100 annually	10% or 20% coinsurance would help lower premium	Primary	Exclusion of orthodontic procedures may help reduce premiums; cleaning and other preventive care should not be excluded
Eye care	Not recommended				
Supplemental					
Dread disease	Not recommended				
Accident	Not recommended				
Medigap	See major medical recommendations				

[a] All policies should be written on a guaranteed renewable basis.

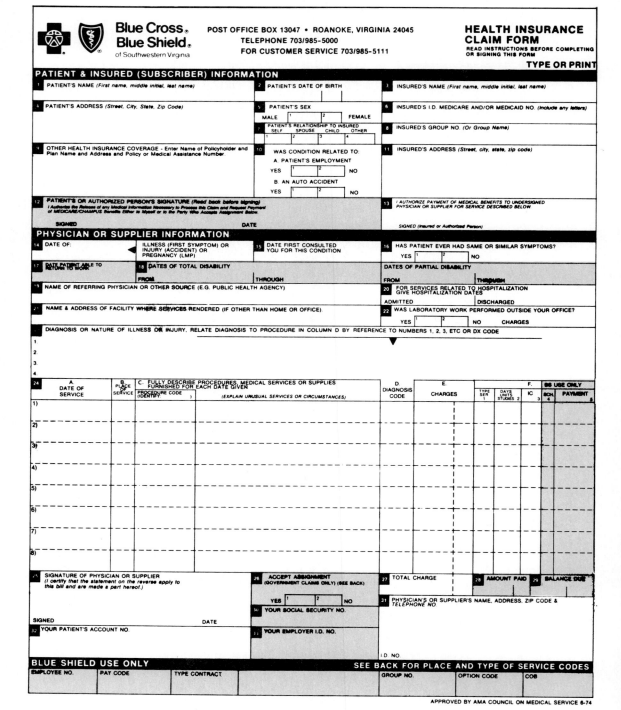

FIGURE 12–1
Health Insurance Claim Form

Source: Blue Cross & Blue Shield of Southwestern Virginia. Used with permission.

NATIONAL AND LOCAL
PLACE OF SERVICE CODES

1 - Inpatient Hospital
2 - Outpatient Hospital
3 - Practitioner's Office
4 - Patient's Home
5 - Daycare Facility-Psychiatric
6 - Nightcare Facility-Psychiatric
7 - Domiciliary Facility-Nursing Home
8 - Extended Care Facility
    (Convalescent, Rehabilitation)
9 - Ambulance Service (Licensed Only)
0 - Other Not Classified

RECIPROCITY ⟨◁══⟩

Place in Block 6 in front of the subscriber's contract number, the three digit code indicating "Reciprocity." This code is located in the "red" arrow on the subscriber's identification card.

SIGNATURE OF PHYSICIAN (OR SUPPLIER):

I certify that the services listed above were medically indicated and necessary to the health of this patient and were personally rendered by me or under my personal direction.
NOTICE: This is to certify that the foregoing information is true, accurate and complete.

NATIONAL BLUE SHIELD
TYPE OF SERVICE CODES

0 - Surgical Assistance
1 -
2 - Surgery
3 - Maternity-Termination of Pregnancy
4 - Anesthesia
5 - Outpatient Diagnostic X-Ray
6 - Medical Care - Inpatient
7 - Dental - Free Standing
8 - Outpatient Diagnostic Laboratory and Pathology
9 - Consultation - Requested by Attending Physician
A - Medical Care - Emergency Care Including X-Ray and Laboratory (Physician's Office and Outpatient Hospital)
B - Concurrent Care - Medical Care by Other Than Attending Physician
C - Psychiatric Care - Mental, Nervous, Alcoholism, Drug Addiction
D - Physical Therapy/Medical
E - Therapeutic X-Ray - X-Ray Radium, Radioactive Isotopes
F - Ambulance
G - Durable Medical Equipment, Supplies, Optical, Othopedic, Prosthetic (Purchase Only)
H - Durable Medical Equipment - (Rental Only)
J - Home Care Service
K - Drugs
L - Visiting Nurses Services
M - Vision Care
N - Pulmonary TB
P - Professional Component When PC Separate from TC (Inpatient X-Ray or Laboratory)
R - Donor Surgery and Related
T - Radioimmunoassay (RIA) or Competitive Protein Binding Analysis
U - Supplemental Accident - Service Not Covered by or Exceeding Basic
V - Hearing Care
W - Second Opinion Consultation/Surgery
Z - Medicare Plus

FOR INSTRUCTIONS ON COMPLETION OF THIS FORM, REFER TO BLUE SHIELD OF SOUTHWESTERN VIRGINIA'S <u>PHYSICIAN'S MANUAL</u>

Summary

1. Health insurance is purchased to provide reimbursement for expenses arising out of injury, illness, and disability.

2. Health insurance needs are determined by balancing the medical losses likely to occur against the resources available to cover those losses. The medical losses most likely to occur include direct medical care expenses, recuperation expenses, rehabilitation expenses, and lost income. Resources that might be available to cover these losses include savings, other insurance, and education.

3. The major types of health insurance are hospital insurance, surgical insurance, medical expense insurance, major medical expense insurance, comprehensive health insurance plans, dental expense insurance, eye care insurance, and supplemental health insurance plans.

4. Disability income insurance replaces a portion of the income lost when you cannot work due to illness or injury. The amount you need is equal to your monthly after-tax income less any benefits such as Social Security to which you are entitled. By selecting among various policy provisions you can tailor a policy to fill the gaps in your existing disability protection.

5. The health insurance policy outlines the general provisions of the coverage and most importantly includes the limitations and conditions that affect the amount reimbursed under the policy. Some of the more important policy provisions include who is covered under the policy and the time period for the coverage. Important limitations include the deductible, the coinsurance requirement, and limitations on the types of losses covered.

6. The decision to buy health insurance must be based on the consideration of the sources of coverage, the premium to be paid, and the company, the policy, and the claims procedures. The ideal health insurance program provides protection from catastrophic losses and smaller losses that the insured may find unaffordable.

Modern Money Management

The Johnsons Consider Buying Disability Insurance

Although the employee benefit program Belinda receives is generous, it does not provide disability income protection other than eight sick days per year that may accumulate to thirty days if she does not use them. Harry also has no disability income insurance. Although both have worked long enough under Social Security to qualify for disability benefits, Belinda has estimated that they would only receive about $200 per month each. Harry and Belinda have come to realize that they could not live up to their current standards on one salary alone. Thus, the need for some disability income insurance has become evident even though they probably cannot afford such protection at this time. Advise them on the following points.

1. Use Table 12–2 to determine how much disability insurance each needs. Use the December salary figures from Table 3–6.
2. Use the information on pages 372, 373, and 379 to advise them as to their selections related to the following major policy provisions: elimination period, benefit period, residual clause, continuation provisions, and cost of living adjustments.

Key Words and Concepts

accident insurance, 370
aggregate limits, 376
benefit period, 373
certificate of insurance, 374
claims ratio, 387
coinsurance cap, 368
comprehensive health insurance, 369
coordination-of-benefits clause, 377
copayment clause, 377
dental expense insurance, 369
disability income insurance, 371
dread disease insurance, 370
episode limits, 376
eye care insurance, 369
elimination period (waiting period), 372
fringe benefit, 384
health insurance, 363
health maintenance organization (HMO), 382
hospital insurance, 367
item limits, 376

major medical expense insurance, 368
Medicaid, 383
medical expense insurance, 368
Medicare, 383
medigap insurance, 370
partial disability, 365
pre-existing condition, 378
preferred provider organization (PPO), 383
recurring clause, 378
rehabilitation, 365
Social Security disability income insurance, 383
supplemental health insurance, 370
surgical insurance, 367
time period limits, 376
total disability, 365
Veterans Administration hospitals, 383
workers' compensation insurance, 385

Review Questions

1. What major perils are covered by health insurance?
2. What are the four categories of losses that can result from an injury or illness?

3. What resources might be available to cover losses due to injury or accident?

4. What are the three types of first-dollar health insurance?

5. Explain the differences among the three types of hospital insurance.

6. How does major medical insurance differ from the three types of first-dollar health insurance?

7. What is comprehensive health insurance?

8. What is the greatest expense in eye care?

9. Explain supplemental health insurance plans.

10. Define disability income insurance.

11. Identify the major policy provisions to consider when purchasing disability income insurance.

12. Distinguish among item limits, episode limits, time period limits, and aggregate limits as used in health insurance policies.

13. What are the usual coinsurance percentages used in health insurance policies and how does a coinsurance cap apply to these percentages?

14. What is a pre-existing condition?

15. Explain the various nonmedical provisions typically included in a health insurance policy.

16. What are HMOs and PPOs?

17. Name the four major federal health-care programs.

18. Distinguish between Medicare and Medicaid.

19. What variables are used to determine health insurance premiums?

20. What three areas should you focus on when shopping for health insurance coverage?

Case Problems

1. Bernard Goldhart of East Lansing, Michigan, aged sixty-one, recently suffered a severe stroke. He was in intensive care for twelve days and hospitalized for eighteen more days. Then he was in a nursing home forty-five days for medically necessary nursing and rehabilitative care. Bernard had hospital, surgical, and medical expense insurance through his employer. He had also purchased major medical insurance through a group with a $1,000 deductible and $50,000 episode and $250,000 aggregate limits. The major medical policy had a 20 percent/80 percent coinsurance clause with a $20,000 coinsurance cap. All of his policies covered medically necessary services performed in a

nursing home setting. Bernard's total medical bill was $125,765. His insurance from his employer covered $42,814 of these charges.

   a. Of the remainder, how much did the major medical policy pay?

   b. How much did Bernard pay?

2. Jim Alford of Richmond, Kentucky, recently took a new job as a manufacturer's representative for an aluminum castings company. While looking over his employee benefits materials he discovered that his employer would provide ten sick days per year that he could accumulate to a maximum of sixty days if any went unused in a given year. In addition, his employer provided a $1,000 per month short-term (one year) total disability policy. After calling the employee benefits office where he worked, Jim found that he probably would qualify for $400 per month in Social Security disability benefits. Jim also knew that he could cease paying $50 per month in life insurance premiums if he became disabled under a waiver of premium option in his life insurance policy. Jim earns a base salary of $1,500 per month and expects to average about that same amount per month in commissions. After considering this information, Jim became understandably concerned that a disability might destroy his financial future.

   a. What is the level of Jim's short-term (one year) disability insurance needs?

   b. What is the level of Jim's long-term disability insurance needs?

   c. Help Jim select from among the important disability insurance policy provisions to design a disability insurance program tailored to his needs.

3. Your good friend, Amy Short of Tulsa, Oklahoma, recently started a new job in a moderately sized CPA firm. Knowing that you were taking a personal finance course she asked your advice about the selection of her health insurance plan. Her employer offered four options.

   Option A: A package of hospital, surgical, and medical expense insurance plus a major medical policy. The first-dollar coverages provide for forty-five days per year of hospitalization and otherwise would pay the usual, customary and reasonable charges for most any event including maternity. The major medical policy has a $500 annual deductible and a 20 percent/80 percent coinsurance clause with a $20,000 coinsurance cap. The major medical policy has a $100,000 aggregate limit.

   Option B: A comprehensive health insurance policy with a $250 per year annual deductible, a 20 percent/80 percent coinsurance clause with a $10,000 coinsurance cap, and a $250,000 aggregate limit.

Option C: Same as option B except that there is a PPO associated with the plan. If Amy agrees to have services provided by the PPO, her annual deductible drops to $100 and the coinsurance clause is waived. As an incentive to get employees to select Option C, Amy's employer will also provide dental expense insurance worth about $20 per month.

Option D: Membership in an HMO. Amy would have to contribute $25 per month extra if she chose this option.

a. Explain to Amy why her employer requests her to pay extra if she joins the HMO.

b. Why might Amy's employer provide an incentive of dental insurance if she chooses option C?

c. To help her make a decision, Amy has asked you to make a list of three positive and three negative points about each plan. Prepare such a list.

Suggested Readings

"Are The Elderly Overinsured?" *Consumers' Research,* March 1987, pp. 16–19. An examination of policies suggests that the best insurance is a savings account.

"Catastrophic-Illness Insurance: Not If, but When." *Business Week,* January 12, 1987, pp. 46–47. Whether government-provided catastrophic-illness insurance is likely, and what form it might take.

"Health Insurance: Covering the Bills." *Changing Times,* February 1987, p. 160. How to be sure that you are not caught between your parent's coverage and your employer's.

"The Real Health Care Catastrophe: More than 30 Million Uninsured." *Business Week,* February 9, 1987, p. 29. Details on who is not covered by health insurance and why.

C H A P T E R 13

Life Insurance

OBJECTIVES

After reading this chapter, the student should be able to

1. state the purpose of life insurance and identify the reasons for buying it.

2. discuss the procedures used to determine life insurance needs.

3. define and distinguish among the various types of term and cash value life insurance policies.

4. describe the major provisions of life insurance policies and explain the value of each.

5. discuss the important points to consider when choosing and buying life insurance.

T

he average life expectancy for people born between 1988 and 1991 will exceed seventy-seven years for women and seventy-two years for men. Although no one knows how long he or she will live, people tend to think of every death as a premature death, as an unwanted interruption of life. With the uncertainty of when death will occur comes the uncertainty of the financial losses that will result from it. As discussed earlier, one way to reduce uncertainty or risk is to purchase insurance. *Life insurance* reduces the risk of financial loss resulting from death.

The first life insurance company in the United States, the Corporation for Relief of Poor and Distressed Widows and Children of Presbyterian Ministers, was established in 1759. Since then life insurance has grown to be an immense industry, with today more than $6.5 trillion worth of life insurance in force in this country. Life insurance companies control assets of more than $850 billion. Seven out of eight U.S. families own some life insurance, and their coverage averages more than $75,000 per family. The importance of life insurance for the individual, the family, and the entire economy should not be underestimated.

This chapter will focus on the role of life insurance in your overall personal financial management plan. Topics to be covered include why you need life insurance, how to determine your life insurance needs, the many types of life insurance, the life insurance policy and its major provisions, and how to buy life insurance.

Why Life Insurance?

The term *life insurance* is in a sense a misnomer. Obviously, the person whose life is insured will not be protected from death, nor will he or she benefit financially from the proceeds of the policy paid after death. The primary reason for buying life insurance is to obtain financial protection from losses suffered by others when the insured party dies. (Perhaps it should be called death insurance.)

In another sense, however, life insurance is appropriately named. Life insurance can allow the survivors and heirs of the deceased to continue the financial aspects of their lives free from the financial burdens that death can cause. The death of a breadwinner is particularly devastating when there are young children in the home; life insurance can at least allow the family's financial needs to be satisfied. Home ownership can be safeguarded, and the remaining parent may be able to stay at home for a time rather than have to take a job immediately. College or other educational plans can remain intact. Benefits such as these are some of the whys of life insurance.

Some statistics are useful to consider. Insurance companies employ *actuaries,* who calculate the probabilities of death for individuals based on such characteristics as age, health, and lifestyle and then use these probabilities to establish the rates an individual must pay for life insurance. The *death rate* represents the probability that an individual will die at a given age. A *mortality table* is a compilation of death rates for each year of life. Table 13–1 shows a mortality table for persons covered by life insurance. As you would expect, the death rate increases as a person grows older. In recent years, death rates for all age groups except one have declined due to medical advances in the treatment of heart disease, stroke, and cancer. The exception is the fifteen- to twenty-four-year-old age group. Death rates for this group have increased recently due to increased numbers of auto accidents, suicides, and homicides.

The death rate for the population as a whole is expected to continue to decline. Table 13–2 ranks the top ten causes of death and contains a clue to why the death rate should continue to decline. Note that the top three causes of death are those for which medical advances are taking place. As people survive these diseases, their prospects for longevity increase. Some actuaries believe that life expectancies of ninety to one hundred years are not too far in the future.

Though most people live to retirement age, approximately 25 percent of today's adults will die during their working years. Life insurance purchased as part of an overall financial management plan will enable you to deal financially with this potential loss.

Life Insurance over the Life Cycle

The whys behind life insurance vary over the life cycle. During childhood and singlehood the need for life insurance is nonexistent or very small. This is because few, if any, other people are relying on the income of the person under consideration. With marriage comes the increased responsibility for another, although life insurance needs will probably remain low: each spouse usually has the potential of self-support if the other were to die. The arrival of children, though, triggers a sharp increase in life insurance needs unless other financial resources are available in sufficient amounts. Children often require up to twenty-five years of financial support with little ability to provide for themselves. As they grow older, the number of years of dependency declines. This may seem to indicate declining insurance needs, but the impact of inflation and higher income levels may keep insurance needs high. A married couple will see a much reduced need for life insurance once their children become independent. This is partly because their responsibility for others is reduced and partly because their investments will have matured to be used for income. Retirement and the likelihood of another period of singlehood reduce the need for life insurance even further—if not eliminating it altogether.

TABLE 13–1
Commissioner's Standard Ordinary Mortality Table

Age	Male Mortality Rate per 1,000	Male Expectancy, Years	Female Mortality Rate per 1,000	Female Expectancy, Years
0	4.18	70.83	2.89	75.83
1	1.07	70.13	0.87	75.04
2	0.99	69.20	0.81	74.11
3	0.98	68.27	0.79	73.17
4	0.95	67.34	0.77	72.23
5	0.90	66.40	0.76	71.28
6	0.85	65.46	0.73	70.34
7	0.80	64.52	0.72	69.39
8	0.76	63.57	0.70	68.44
9	0.74	62.62	0.69	67.48
10	0.73	61.66	0.68	66.53
11	0.77	60.71	0.69	65.58
12	0.85	59.75	0.72	64.62
13	0.99	58.80	0.75	63.67
14	1.15	57.86	0.80	62.71
15	1.33	56.93	0.85	61.76
16	1.51	56.00	0.90	60.82
17	1.67	55.09	0.95	59.87
18	1.78	54.18	0.98	58.93
19	1.86	53.27	1.02	57.98
20	1.90	52.37	1.05	57.04
21	1.91	51.47	1.07	56.10
22	1.89	50.57	1.09	55.16

Age	Male Mortality Rate per 1,000	Male Expectancy, Years	Female Mortality Rate per 1,000	Female Expectancy, Years
50	6.71	25.36	4.96	29.53
51	7.30	24.52	5.31	28.67
52	7.96	23.70	5.70	27.82
53	8.71	22.89	6.15	26.98
54	9.56	22.08	6.61	26.14
55	10.47	21.29	7.09	25.31
56	11.46	20.51	7.57	24.49
57	12.49	19.74	8.03	23.67
58	13.59	18.99	8.47	22.86
59	14.77	18.24	8.94	22.05
60	16.08	17.51	9.47	21.25
61	17.54	16.79	10.13	20.44
62	19.19	16.08	10.96	19.65
63	21.06	15.38	12.02	18.86
64	23.14	14.70	13.25	18.08
65	25.42	14.04	14.59	17.32
66	27.85	13.39	16.00	16.57
67	30.44	12.76	17.43	15.83
68	33.19	12.14	18.84	15.10
69	36.17	11.54	20.36	14.38
70	39.51	10.96	22.11	13.67
71	43.30	10.39	24.23	12.97
72	47.65	9.84	26.87	12.28

23	1.86	49.66	1.11	54.22	73	52.64	9.30	30.11	11.60
24	1.82	48.75	1.14	53.28	74	58.19	8.79	33.93	10.95
25	1.77	47.84	1.16	52.34	75	64.19	8.31	38.24	10.32
26	1.73	46.93	1.19	51.40	76	70.53	7.84	42.96	9.71
27	1.71	46.01	1.22	50.46	77	77.12	7.40	48.04	9.12
28	1.70	45.09	1.26	49.52	78	83.90	6.97	53.45	8.55
29	1.71	44.16	1.30	48.59	79	91.05	6.57	59.35	8.01
30	1.73	43.24	1.35	47.65	80	98.84	6.18	65.99	7.48
31	1.78	42.31	1.40	46.71	81	107.48	5.80	73.60	6.98
32	1.83	41.38	1.45	45.78	82	117.25	5.44	82.40	6.49
33	1.91	40.46	1.50	44.84	83	128.26	5.09	92.53	6.03
34	2.00	39.54	1.58	43.91	84	140.25	4.77	103.81	5.59
35	2.11	38.61	1.65	42.98	85	152.95	4.46	116.10	5.18
36	2.24	37.69	1.76	42.05	86	166.09	4.18	129.29	4.80
37	2.40	36.78	1.89	41.12	87	179.55	3.91	143.32	4.43
38	2.58	35.87	2.04	40.20	88	193.27	3.66	158.18	4.09
39	2.79	34.96	2.22	39.28	89	207.29	3.41	173.94	3.77
40	3.02	34.05	2.42	38.36	90	221.77	3.18	190.75	3.45
41	3.29	33.16	2.64	37.46	91	236.98	2.94	208.87	3.15
42	3.56	32.26	2.87	36.55	92	253.45	2.70	228.81	2.85
43	3.87	31.38	3.09	35.66	93	272.11	2.44	251.51	2.55
44	4.19	30.50	3.32	34.77	94	295.90	2.17	279.31	2.24
45	4.55	29.62	3.56	33.88	95	329.96	1.87	317.32	1.91
46	4.92	28.76	3.80	33.00	96	384.55	1.54	375.74	1.56
47	5.32	27.90	4.05	32.12	97	480.20	1.20	474.97	1.21
48	5.74	27.04	4.33	31.25	98	657.98	.84	655.85	.84
49	6.21	26.20	4.63	30.39	99	1,000.00	.50	1,000.00	.50

Source: National Association of Insurance Commissioners. Used with permission.

TABLE 13–2
Leading Causes of Death in the United States

Cause of Death[a]	Death Rate[b]	Number of Deaths
Diseases of the heart	296.7	765,622
Cancer	192.5	453,648
Stroke	58.7	151,113
Accidents and their effects	38.2	94,723
Motor vehicle accidents	20.1	47,380
All other	18.1	49,343
Major lung diseases	27.0	69,511
Pneumonia and influenza	25.0	59,474
Diabetes	15.4	36,292
Suicide	10.7	28,203
Chronic liver disease	11.0	26,208
Hardening of the arteries	9.2	24,175

Source: U.S. Department of Health and Human Services, *Monthly Vital Statistics Report,* September 26, 1985.
[a] As of 1987, AIDS was not one of the top ten causes of death.
[b] Per 100,000 people

Determining Your Life Insurance Needs

Life insurance needs are highly individualized and can vary from zero to more than $1 million. This section will cover the four areas to consider when determining your life insurance needs: (1) the types of losses that will occur, (2) the projected dollar amount of losses, (3) resources that may be available to cover losses, and (4) the amount of life insurance needed.

Losses Resulting from Premature Death

In addition to substantial personal loss, survivors may experience severe financial losses when a loved one dies. These include lost income and costs such as final expenses, readjustment period expenses, and debt repayment expenses.

Lost Income The major financial loss resulting from premature death is the lost income of the deceased. This is especially true for the death of family breadwinners. Included in this lost income should be the value of any essential employment fringe benefits, such as health insurance. However, often overlooked are the contributions of a full- or part-time homemaker. The dollar income of homemakers is not indicative of the financial contributions they make to family life. The best way to allow for funds needed after the death of a family's homemaker is to estimate the annual cost of hiring the lost services. The amount would be an estimate of lost income. Since the majority of married-person households have two earners, there is a temptation to think that the income of the surviving spouse would support the family. In most cases, however, both incomes are needed to maintain the desired level of living and will need to be replaced.

Final Expenses *Final expenses* are those outlays occurring just prior to or after a death. Probably the greatest of these expenses is the cost of the funeral. It is not unusual for a modest funeral to cost more than $3,000. Emergency travel expenses for family members during terminal illness and to attend a funeral can also be quite high. Food and lodging expenses for mourners are often overlooked. The severe and costly disruptions of family life can often last up to a month. Unless otherwise provided for in some type of emergency fund, final expenses should be covered by life insurance.

Another type of final expense includes the final health-care expenses of the deceased. Although life insurance can provide funds for the payment of these charges, it is best to provide for them through health insurance. (Health insurance is covered in Chapter 12.)

Readjustment Period Expenses A period of readjustment is often necessary after the death of a loved one. This period may last for several years, and the readjustment will have financial aspects that may require life insurance proceeds. For example, the death of a sole breadwinner with infant children may be such a shock that the spouse must forgo seeking employment for a while. Similarly, a working spouse may need to take time off from a job, or a nonworking spouse may wish to obtain further education. Parents mourning the death of a child may need special counseling or travel to let the wounds heal.

Debt Repayment Expenses Many people feel that life insurance should cover family debts should a breadwinner die. No doubt there will be a need to pay debts, and difficulties may arise, but a family that has provided adequately for the replacement of lost income will probably not need to make specific insurance provisions for the payment of debts. Lenders will sometimes require borrowers to purchase life insurance as a condition for granting a loan; such insurance will help lessen the need for insuring for debt repayment.

Dollar Amount of Losses

Determining the magnitude of the possible losses resulting from a premature death can be difficult since the amounts of final expenses and lost income are relatively unknown. Several approaches can be used. A relatively unsophisticated and imprecise approach is trying to put a dollar value on the life to be insured based on some notion of the psychological loss that would be felt by survivors. This *value-of-life* approach is particularly hazardous because it carries so much potential for error. It should not be used.

Multiple-Earnings Approach A great improvement over the value-of-life approach, the *multiple-earnings approach* involves estimating the funds needed to replace the lost income by multiplying the annual take-home pay of the person involved by the number of years the income will be needed. However, this will overestimate the needed funds for two reasons. First, approximately 25 percent of an individual's take-home pay is spent on his or her own personal expenditures. Thus, only about 75 percent of the take-home pay of the deceased will need to be replaced. Second, if the funds needed to replace lost income are received shortly after death (as life insurance benefits are), they can be invested and earn interest. This interest can also be used to help replace lost income.

Needs Approach The *needs approach* involves estimating the total dollar loss due to a premature death. It builds on the calculations of the multiple-earnings approach by including an accurate assessment of lost income, and the dollar losses likely to result from final, readjustment period, and debt repayment expenses. It also takes into account government benefits that lessen the need to replace lost income.

Most families—widows, widowers, or surviving children—may collect *Social Security survivors' benefits* if a breadwinner dies, with the level of benefits depending on the amount of Social Security taxes paid by the deceased. If eligible, a family can receive from $8,000 to $19,000 per year, but these benefits will generally cease when the children reach the age of nineteen. This period of ineligibility for Social Security benefits is called the Social Security blackout period. It ends when the surviving spouse reaches the age of sixty and may then begin collecting Social Security benefits based on his or her own contributions or on the contributions of the deceased, whichever results in the higher payment.

The formula for the needs approach is

$$DL = (.75AI - AGB)PVIFA + FE + RE + DR \qquad (13-1)$$

where

DL = *dollar loss* from premature death

AI = *annual income* of person insured including fringe benefits that survivors depend on and/or the cost of replacing their household services

AGB = *annual government benefits* available if insured dies

$PVIFA$ = the *present-value interest factor of an annuity* from Appendix A4, which incorporates the number of years the income will be needed and the interest rate (*after* taxes *and* inflation) earned by invested life insurance proceeds

FE = *final expenses*

RE = *readjustment expenses*

DR = *debt repayment* expenses

To illustrate the application of the needs approach, consider the Martin family of Grand Rapids, Michigan. John Martin is thirty-three years old and his wife, Joan, is twenty-eight. They have two children, aged seven and four. John is a landscape architect. His annual salary is $52,000 before taxes and $40,000 after taxes, including fringe benefits. John applies formula 13–1 to find the dollar loss from his premature death as follows:

AI = $40,000 (take-home pay)

AGB = $17,000 rounded (Social Security survivors' benefits while children are under the age of nineteen; see calculations in Appendix B)

$PVIFA$ = 11.118 (income needed for fifteen years; 4 percent return, after taxes and inflation, on invested life insurance proceeds; see Appendix A4)

FE = $10,000 (assumed)

RE = $40,000 (to replace lost income in the first year after death)

DR = $2,000 (assumed)

DL = [(.75 × $40,000) − $17,000]11.118 + $10,000 + $40,000 + $2,000

= ($30,000 − $17,000)11.118 + $52,000

= $196,534

Thus, John estimates that his death would result in financial losses of $196,534. The level of potential losses will not, however, dictate the amount of life insurance needed. First, John must determine whether existing resources can meet the financial losses.

Resources Available to Cover Losses

There is no need to purchase life insurance if resources will be available to cover the losses resulting from a premature death. Savings accounts and investments are the most obvious resources, and others are existing insurance, education, and asset equity.

Savings and Investments   As time passes, individuals and families usually develop at least a minimal nest egg of savings and investments. Usually, these are specifically intended to meet some special purpose, such as retirement, travel, or college for children. If necessary in the event of a premature death, these funds can be used to meet final and readjustment expenses and to replace lost income. As children grow older and leave the nest, the potential losses that would result from the death of a parent will lessen. At some point savings and investments may exceed potential losses and eliminate the need for life insurance.

Existing Insurance   Life insurance is often a fringe benefit paid for employees by their employers. In addition, automobile insurance will often pay a specific sum when death results from a traffic accident. This is an important consideration for young people, since auto accidents are the leading cause of death for persons aged twenty-four and under.

Skills and Education The level of skills and education attained by a surviving spouse will affect whether he or she can earn enough to replace the lost income of the deceased. A spouse who had been working part-time outside the home could take a full-time position. A spouse who had not been working outside the home could begin or renew a career. In either case, the potential for extra income can reduce the loss and thereby reduce the need for life insurance. Spouses returning to work should increase their own life insurance coverage to reflect the income that would be lost if they were to die.

Asset Equity As time passes, individuals and families acquire physical assets that can provide services or funds after the death of a family member. *Equity* is that portion of the dollar value of an asset that is owned by an individual. For example, if you drive a car with a market value of $10,000 on which you still owe $4,400, your equity is $5,600. You can build up equity by paying for an asset, by paying off a loan used to purchase an asset, or through appreciation of an asset. For most families, the equity built up in the home represents their largest asset. When one spouse dies, the other may decide to sell the home and use part of the income to buy or rent a less-expensive house or apartment. The remainder of the equity could then be used for living expenses or other needs.

Amount of Life Insurance Needed

The death of any individual may result in some financial losses for family, friends, business associates, and others. This does not mean that every individual should have life insurance coverage, however. Figure 13–1 shows the calculation for determining the amount of life insurance needed. The resources available are subtracted from the losses resulting from premature death. If the result is a negative number, life insurance is probably not needed because assets can cover the losses. However, some people in this situation may wish to buy life insurance anyway, so that they can pass resources on to heirs.

FIGURE 13–1
Determining Life Insurance Needed

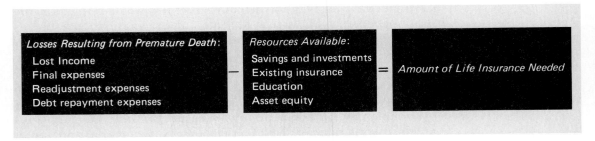

Losses Resulting from Premature Death:
Lost Income
Final expenses
Readjustment expenses
Debt repayment expenses

— Resources Available:
Savings and investments
Existing insurance
Education
Asset equity

= Amount of Life Insurance Needed

Life Insurance for Young Professionals

When you graduate from college, your name and accomplishments may become known to many people through listings in your hometown newspaper and other sources. Life insurance agents use such lists to obtain prospects for their sales efforts. Don't be surprised if you are solicited by mail or by phone for a life insurance "consultation." The key question is, "Do you really need life insurance?" Let's look at a typical example of a recent college grad.

Amy Dee of Lexington, Kentucky, recently graduated with a degree in hotel management and has a position as night desk manager at a major resort hotel. She earns $24,000 per year in gross salary. Amy is single and owes $7,500 on a car loan as well as $11,800 in education loans. Among her fringe benefits are an employer-paid term insurance policy equal to her annual salary and an option to buy an additional $24,000 for $1.25 per year per thousand. Thus, for an additional $30 per year (24 × $1.25), Amy can increase her employer-related life insurance coverage to $48,000.

Amy has been approached by a life insurance agent whose calculations suggest that she needs a $120,000 policy. Does she? If we apply the needs approach formula to Amy's situation, we see the following:

$$DL = (0.75AI - AGB)PVIFA + FE + RE + DR$$

where

DL = *dollar loss* from premature death

AI = *annual income* required to support survivors dependent on that income. In Amy's case, this would be $0.

AGB = *annual government benefits* to survivors. In Amy's case, this would be $0, as she has not qualified for Social Security benefits as yet and she has no qualifying survivors.

$PVIFA$ = *present value interest factor*, which Amy estimates at 4 percent, but which is irrelevant for her as there is no need to replace lost income.

FE = *final expenses*. Amy figures that her burial would cost about $8,000.

RE = *readjustment expenses*, which Amy has determined would be $0.

DR = *debt repayment*. Amy would like to see her $19,300 in auto and education loans repaid in the event of her death. She feels better knowing that her college loans would be repaid and that her younger brother could inherit her car free and clear.

The resulting calculations show that Amy has a likely dollar loss of $27,300 ($8,000 + $11,800 + $7,500), which can easily be met by the $48,000 in insurance available through her employer. Clearly, she does not need further insurance at this time. When her circumstances change, Amy should reappraise her needs.

If losses exceed resources available, life insurance is probably needed. The amount needed will depend on the magnitude of the losses, the resources available, and the individual's willingness to assume the risk of premature death. The amount of life insurance purchased will depend on all three of these factors, plus the funds available to buy life insurance. Once you determine how much life insurance you need, you must decide what type of life insurance is best and from whom to buy your policy. The remainder of this chapter covers these topics.

Types of Life Insurance

Most people seem confused by the variety of life insurance policies. However, there are really just two types of life insurance: term life insurance and cash value life insurance. Term life insurance is often called pure protection because it will pay benefits only if the insured person dies. Cash value life insurance also pays benefits at death but includes a savings element that allows for payment of benefits to the insured prior to death. Included under the cash value type of life insurance is interest-sensitive cash value insurance. This savings element adds to the cost of cash value life insurance and should be evaluated separately from the death benefits provided under the policy.

A life insurance policy is more than just a contract between the purchaser and the company. Several other parties might be named in the policy. The **policyholder** (also called the *owner*) is the person who pays for the policy and retains all rights and privileges granted by the policy, including the right to amend the policy and the right to designate who shall receive the proceeds. The insured is the person whose life is insured. The **beneficiary** is the person or organization that will receive the life insurance or other benefit payment upon the death of the insured. The **contingent beneficiary** is the person or organization that will become the beneficiary if the original beneficiary dies before the insured does. The owner and the insured are often the same person, but it is possible for four different people to be named in a policy. For example, a father (the owner) might insure the life of his son (the insured) and name the boy's mother as beneficiary and sister as contingent beneficiary. This section will cover term and cash value life insurance and their variations, and briefly examine annuities.

Term Life Insurance

Term life insurance pays benefits only if the insured party dies within the time period of the contract. If the insured survives the specified time period, the beneficiary receives no monetary benefits. You can purchase term insurance contracts in face amounts in multiples of $1,000, usually with a minimum face amount of $25,000.

Term life insurance contracts are most often written for one, five, ten, or twenty years. A new contract is required to continue coverage past the end of the contract period. Unless otherwise stipulated in the original contract, this means that you must apply for a new contract and may be required to submit the results of a medical examination. If you have a health hazard, you may be denied a new policy or have to pay higher premiums. (You can avoid this medical requirement if you include a "guaranteed renewability" option in the term policy.) Even if your health status remains the same the premium will increase, because you will be older and thus more likely to die while the new policy is in force. Thus, term insurance premiums rise with each renewal, and a change in health status may disqualify an applicant for coverage. For example, a $50,000, five-year term policy for a man aged twenty-five might have an annual premium of $90; at age thirty-five the policy will cost him $105, and at age forty-five it will cost $200. Nonetheless, term policies are *less* expensive than cash value policies, since there is no savings element in term insurance.

You can avoid premium increases as you grow older by purchasing a term policy with a long time period, say twenty or thirty years. Under such a policy the premiums remain constant throughout the period, increasing only for a renewal after the policy expires. Such policies initially cost more than policies written for shorter time periods, but they cost less toward the end of the policy period. This is because premiums are higher than necessary in early years to balance out the higher premiums that would have been necessary in later years. To illustrate, consider two $100,000 term policies for a man aged twenty-five, one on a twenty-year basis and one on a five-year basis. A typical annual premium for the twenty-year policy would be $225 for each of the twenty years. The annual premium for the five-year policy might be $150 for each of the first five years. After renewal, the premiums would increase to $200 for each of the second five years. Annual premiums for the third five years might be $250, and for the fourth five years $325. Thus the annual premiums for the twenty-year policy remain constant and are higher in the early years and lower in the later years than those of four five-year policies.

The premiums paid for the twenty-year policy would total $4,500, and premiums for the four five-year policies would total $4,625. There is a difference in total premiums because the insurance company (1) will save expenses by writing one policy rather than four and (2) will invest the excess premiums paid in the early years of the twenty-year policy and use the income on these investments to reduce later premiums paid by the insured. Given the figures cited in this example, it appears that the twenty-year policy is less expensive than four five-year policies. However, a policyholder could buy the five-year policies, invest the premium differences from the early years, and earn enough interest on the investments to more than offset higher premiums in later years. A method of comparing the price of insurance policies that takes into account the potential investment effects of policy price differences is discussed later in this chapter.

All term life insurance has a face amount that is payable if the insured dies during the contract period, but there are several variations that add to the flexibility of term life insurance: decreasing term insurance, a guaranteed renewability option, a convertibility option, credit life insurance, and group life insurance.

Decreasing Term Insurance   With *decreasing term insurance,* the face amount declines annually and the premiums remain constant. You can choose a face amount and a contract period; the face amount of the policy gradually declines to some minimum, such as $5,000, in the last year of the contract. As expected, the premiums for a decreasing term policy are lower than those for a comparable term policy with a fixed face amount. For example, a woman aged twenty-five could buy a thirty-year, $50,000 decreasing term policy for about $110 per year. A thirty-year, $50,000 term policy that does not decline would cost about $150 per year.

Typically, around the age of forty-five, people's insurance needs decrease. The major benefit of decreasing term policies is that they can more closely fit your changing insurance needs. It is important to realize, however, that decreasing term policies vary in the rate at which the face amount declines. Some decline at a constant rate, such as 5 percent per year for twenty years, and some have accelerating rates of reduction. The rate of reduction in the face amount must closely fit the rate at which your insurance needs decrease. A second caution concerning decreasing term insurance: inflation may cause life insurance needs to *increase* even when your financial obligations appear to decline as you age.

Guaranteed Renewability Option   Term life insurance policies may be written with a *guaranteed renewability option,* which eliminates the need to prove insurability when you want to renew a policy. Proving insurability may be difficult if you developed any health problem during the period of the original policy. In a sense, the renewability option insures against the possibility of becoming uninsurable. The renewability option is usually not available for one-year term policies. There may also be a limit to how many renewals you can make without proving insurability, and a maximum age for these renewals. Unless you are positive you will not need a renewal, it is always best to buy term life insurance with a guaranteed renewability option.

Convertible Term Insurance   *Convertible term insurance* allows you to convert a term policy to a cash value policy. Usually, this conversion is available only in the early years of the term policy. Some life insurance policies provide for an automatic conversion from term insurance to cash value insurance after a specific number of years.

There are two ways to convert a term policy to a cash value policy. One is to simply request the conversion and begin paying the higher premiums required for the cash value policy. The savings element of the cash value policy will begin accumulating as of the date of the conversion. A second conversion method entails paying the savings that would have built up had the policy originally been written on a cash value basis. Although this lump sum may be a considerable amount, it does represent an asset to the policyholder. Furthermore, with this method the new premiums are based on your age at the time you bought the original term policy, which can result in substantially lower premiums. No proof of insurability is required to convert the policy.

Credit Life Insurance   *Credit life insurance* will pay the remaining balance of a loan if the insured dies before repaying the debt. Basically, credit life insurance is a decreasing term insurance policy with the creditor named as beneficiary. Some lenders will require credit life insurance as a condition of granting you a loan. If so, you may buy the insurance through the lender or obtain coverage elsewhere, often for lower premiums.

If the lender merely offers credit life insurance, you must decide whether insurance is really needed and if the premiums offered by the lender are competitive. Such coverage is not needed if you are otherwise adequately insured. Credit life insurance requires no proof of insurability. Individuals who have health problems that make life insurance expensive or difficult to obtain might use credit life insurance to help meet their overall life insurance needs.

Group Life Insurance   Group life insurance is issued to people as a group rather than individually. The typical policy is written for a group of employees, with premiums paid in full or in part by their employer. Group life insurance premiums are generally lower for individuals than are premiums for individual policies. If you are insured under a group plan, you need not prove your insurability, and if you leave the group, you may be able to convert the policy to an individual basis without proof of insurability. Most group life insurance is term insurance and has no savings element.

Cash Value Life Insurance

Cash value life insurance pays benefits upon the death of the insured and has a savings element that allows the payment of benefits prior to death. Cash value life insurance is sometimes called whole life insurance or permanent life insurance because the time period of coverage under the policy is the entire life of the insured. You need never renew the policy nor prove your insurability again, and the annual premiums for cash value policies usually remain constant.

The premiums for cash value policies are always higher than those for term policies providing the same amount of coverage. This is because only a portion of the cash value life insurance premium is for payment of a death benefit. The remainder is used to build cash value, the savings element. Figure 13–2 illustrates the premium differences between cash value and term life insurance policies.

One way of thinking of cash value insurance is that it is nothing more than a combination of decreasing term insurance and an investment/savings account. Initially, you might have $100,000 of insurance and no savings. Several years later you might have built up $5,000 in savings within the policy. If you were to die, your beneficiary would collect $100,000 and $5,000 of the payment would be your own money. Thus the actual insurance amount paid would be only $95,000, hence the decreasing term insurance analogy. If you lived long enough, the cash value would equal—and might surpass—the $100,000 figure, and your beneficiary would collect your savings account rather than an insurance payment.

The rate at which the cash value accumulates in a policy will depend on the size of the premiums and the rate of return paid. Most cash

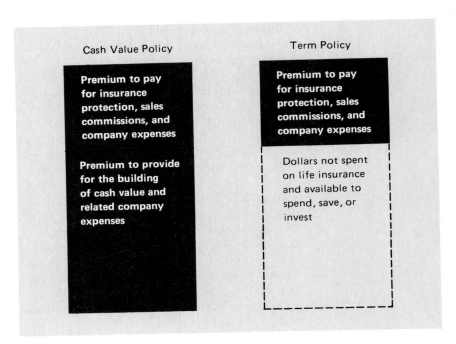

FIGURE 13–2
Comparison of Premium Dollars for Life Insurance*

*For example, the annual premium for a $100,000 cash value policy might be $1,200 for a twenty-five-year-old female but only $300 for a $100,000 term policy.

value policies have a guaranteed minimum interest rate. Policies written before 1978 may have guaranteed rates as low as 2 or 3 percent, but more recently issued policies have guaranteed rates of up to 6 percent. Some newer varieties of cash value policies will pay even higher rates depending on prevailing interest rates in the economy. Table 13–3 shows the cash value accumulations for a typical cash value policy with a guaranteed rate of return of 4 percent.

The cash value of a life insurance policy accumulates throughout your life, and upon your death the face amount of the policy will be paid. Prior to death you have the option of cashing in the policy for the accumulated cash value, or you may borrow all or part of the cash value. What you borrow you must repay with interest, and the amount owed will be subtracted from the face amount of the policy if you die while the debt is outstanding. The specifics of cashing in a policy and borrowing cash values will be discussed in more detail later. For now, remember that cash values represent a kind of forced savings that allow the build-up funds while you buy life insurance.

There are several different types of cash value life insurance. Each of the major types will be discussed.

Whole Life Insurance   *Whole life insurance* is a form of cash value life insurance that provides life insurance protection for your lifetime and requires you to pay premiums for life. In developing insurance

TABLE 13–3
Illustrative Cash Value
Accumulations[a]
(4 Percent Guaranteed Rate)

Policy Year	Cash Value
1	$ 0
2	0
3	585
4	1,280
5	1,993
10	5,816
15	10,089
20	14,738
25	17,492
30	22,197

[a] For a $50,000, whole life insurance policy for a male aged thirty-five with an annual premium of $658.

rates, insurers assume that all insureds die at the age of one hundred. Therefore, premium payments cease when the insured turns one hundred and the face amount of the policy is paid. *Straight life* and *ordinary life* are sometimes used interchangeably with *whole life.*

Modified Life Insurance   *Modified life insurance* is whole life insurance with reduced premiums in the early years and higher premiums thereafter. The period of reduced premiums can vary from one to five years. Modified life insurance is primarily designed for those whose life insurance needs are high but who cannot immediately afford the premiums required, such as a young family. The reduced premiums in the early years are attained by relying on term insurance protection during that time period and on cash value insurance in later years. Because of the lower premiums in early years, modified life insurance accumulates cash value more slowly.

Limited Pay Life Insurance   *Limited pay life insurance* is whole life insurance that allows premium payments to cease before you reach the age of one hundred. Two common examples are *twenty pay life* policies, which allow premium payments to cease after twenty years, and *paid at sixty-five* policies, which require payment of premiums only until the insured turns sixty-five. An extreme version of limited pay life insurance is the *single-premium* life insurance policy, which is fully paid for in a lump sum. As you might expect, the annual premiums for limited pay policies are higher than for ordinary policies because the insurance company has fewer years to collect premiums. Although premiums need be paid only for the time period specified, death benefits last your lifetime. Limited pay policies are said to be *paid up* when the time period for the payment of premiums ends. Paid-up policies will continue to accumulate cash values because the insurer continues to pay a return on the funds. Many young adults have small paid-up life insurance policies that were purchased by their parents and paid in full when they turned eighteen or twenty-one years old.

Endowment Life Insurance   *Endowment life insurance* provides for payment of the face amount either at your death *or* at some previously agreed-upon date, whichever occurs first. The date of payment, called the endowment date, is most commonly some specified number of years after issuance of the policy (say, twenty or thirty years) or some specified age (such as sixty-five). Many such policies name a child as beneficiary and endow when the child turns eighteen. Sometimes the beneficiary of the policy is a different person from the one who is to receive the endowment. For example, one spouse may name the other as beneficiary but designate the children as recipients of the endowment.

Endowment policies are the most expensive form of life insurance per dollar of coverage. Insurers have a limited time to collect premiums and must also pay the face amount by the endowment date. Furthermore, premiums must be large enough to provide the funds needed for a rapid accumulation of cash value.

Adjustable Life Insurance   The three cornerstones of cash value life insurance are the premium, the face amount, and the rate of cash value accumulation. *Adjustable life insurance* allows you to change any of the three with corresponding changes in the other two. Adjustable life insurance was developed recently in response to policyholder demands for more flexibility in policies. Say, for example, you feel that inflation has increased your need for life insurance. Adjustable life insurance would allow you to increase the face amount. In response, your premiums could go up or the cash value accumulation could slow, or both. With more traditional life insurance policies, these changes can be made only if you purchase a new policy or cash in an existing one. Adjustable life insurance allows changes under the existing policy with no added proof of insurability.

Interest-sensitive Cash Value Life Insurance   Traditionally, the cash value life insurance policies discussed thus far have paid a fixed, guaranteed rate of return on the accumulated cash value. You will recall from earlier chapters that fixed interest rate arrangements in credit and savings often have been replaced by more flexible interest rate arrangements in response to variable inflation and interest rates in the economy. Life insurance has not been immune to these pressures and several new forms of cash value life insurance that employ variable rates of return that are sensitive to changing conditions in the economy have come on the market. A further pressure for such a change in life insurance has come from those who have criticized the low rates paid on cash value life insurance and advised buyers to "buy term and invest the rest" in ways that pay a better rate of return. The more prominent among these new products are variable life insurance, universal life insurance, and a hybrid of the two called variable-universal life.

Universal Life Insurance *Universal life insurance* provides both the pure protection and cash value build-up of whole life insurance but with variability in the face amount, rate of cash value accumulation, premiums, and rate of return. Essentially, the purchase of universal life insurance represents combining the purchase of annual term insurance (allowing for variations in face amounts and premiums) with an investment program (allowing for variations in premiums, cash value, and other characteristics of the policy). Universal life policies are usually available only in initial face amounts of $100,000 or more. The rate of return is tied to some interest rate prevailing in the financial markets or is more commonly dictated by the company. In either case, the rates of return are higher than commonly available under other types of cash value policies. With some universal life policies, the payment of a higher premium allows payment of both the face amount and the accumulated cash at the death of the insured party.

An examination of a universal life policy requires an understanding of four elements: the premium, the cost of the death benefit, the interest rate, and the company expense charges. Table 13–4 includes these four elements in a summary comparison of term, whole life, and universal life policies. There are literally thousands of variations among

TABLE 13–4
Comparisons of Three Popular Life Insurance Policies

Feature	Term Insurance	Whole Life Insurance	Universal Life Insurance
Face amount	Fixed or declining during term of the policy; changeable at renewal	Fixed	Variable
Premiums	Low with increases at renewal	High and fixed	High but variable within limits
Cash value accumulation	None	Fixed rate of accumulation	Variable accumulation as premium and interest rate vary
Rate of return paid on cash accumulations	Not applicable	Fixed	Variable with interest rates in economy or as specified by company
Cost of the death benefit portion	Low and fixed	Unknown	Known but can vary and may hide some expense charges
Expense charge	Low but unknown; hidden in premium	Unknown; hidden in premium	Known; may be high

universal life policies, so comparisons are extremely difficult. Even brand names vary with names such as "Target Life II," "Designer III," and "Exceptional Life" all coming under the generic heading of universal life.

Initially the purchaser selects a face amount and an annual premium is quoted. The annual premium goes into the cash value fund. From this fund the cost of providing the death benefit and charges for company expenses are deducted. As time goes by the insured may reduce or increase the premium with corresponding changes in the death benefit or amount added to cash value. If premiums drop below that necessary to cover the death benefit and expenses, funds are removed from the cash value account to cover the shortfall. Sometimes universal life policies are promoted as allowing the cessation of payment of the premiums after five, seven, or ten years. While this may be possible, it should be clear that the funds to support these unpaid premiums come at the expense of cash value accumulation.

The portion of the premium that is required to provide the death benefit is clearly disclosed in universal life insurance policies. This is not the case with whole life and other traditional cash value policies. This disclosure is of great benefit because it allows the insured to compare the cost of protection with other universal life policies and, more importantly, a similar amount of term insurance. Most policies have two tables of charges for various death benefit amounts. One table lists the charges that are currently being assessed to purchasers. The second table lists the maximum that can be charged for various death benefit levels. Most companies charge less than the maximum and the lower charge is the one emphasized by the agent. But the company is within its rights to raise the charges for death benefits up to the maximum in the contract.

The rate of return applied to the cash value balance and the amount of the premium paid are the two determinants of the rate of cash value accumulation under a universal life policy. This rate is clearly disclosed but usually two rates are quoted. One is the guaranteed minimum rate and the other is the current rate. It is the current rate that is emphasized by the agent, who will often present a table illustrating the rate of cash value accumulation resulting from the two rates. Table 13–5 is an example of such a table. Note the differences in the two cash value columns. It is easy to understand why the agent would emphasize the current rate. Note also that initial cash value accumulations ($500 to $5,000) under some policies will earn only the guaranteed rate. A high current rate of return that is not applied to the entire cash value is a misleading indicator of the true annual rate of return.

The company expense charges are the last of the four elements necessary for an understanding of universal life insurance. Like the rate of return and the death benefit charges, the company expense charges are disclosed clearly in a universal life policy. The most typical of these involves a deduction of from 5 to 10 percent from each annual premium. Such charges are referred to as a front-end load. Some com-

TABLE 13–5
Cash Value Build-up: Guaranteed Versus
Current Rates

Policy Year	Guaranteed Cash Value (4% Rate)	Cash Value at Current Rates (11.2% Rate)
1	$ 0	$ 0
2	0	472
3	585	1,187
4	1,280	1,977
5	1,993	2,852
6	2,723	3,851
7	3,470	4,955
8	4,234	6,177
9	5,016	7,528
10	5,816	9,022
15	10,089	19,408
20	14,738	36,886

panies will charge a back-end load, which is a charge assessed if you wish to withdraw some or all of the cash value accumulated. This type of charge is often highest in the early years of the policy and is eliminated in later years. The policy illustrated in Table 13–5 has a back-end load in the first few years that accounts for the initially low cash values. Be very wary of policies that have both front- and back-end loads.

Variable Life Insurance *Variable life insurance* allows you to choose the investments made with your cash value accumulations and to share in the gains and losses. The face amount of your policy and the policy's cash value will rise and possibly fall as the rates of return on the investments vary. The face amount of the policy usually will not drop below the originally agreed-upon amount. What will fluctuate is the cash value. Because you are continually paying premiums, the cash value will increase, but it may increase slowly if poor investments are made.

To complicate matters further, holders of variable life insurance policies have control over the types of investments made with their premiums. If you are unfamiliar with markets for corporate stocks and bonds and money market securities, you should probably avoid variable life insurance. Another negative aspect of variable life insurance is that many policies contain provisions calling for the payment of fees and sales charges before the policyholders can share in investment returns. Variable life insurance policies require very careful reading and analysis before purchase.

Variable-universal Life Insurance *Variable-universal life insurance* is a form of universal life insurance that allows the policyholder to choose the investments made with the cash value accumulated by the policy. It is sometimes called flexible-premium variable life insurance or universal life II. It is probably the life insurance product that most closely embodies the philosophy of "buy term and invest the rest." Because you choose the investment vehicles (a combination of stocks, bonds, or money market mutual funds), there is the potential for a higher rate of return than under a universal life policy. With this potential for a higher rate of return comes the risk of a lower rate of return. In fact, variable-universal life policies have no minimum guaranteed rate of return. It is possible that you might lose cash value and even be required to come up with a higher premium payment to keep the policy in effect. Prospective purchasers of variable-universal life insurance need to consider carefully how much risk they are willing to accept in their life insurance program.

Annuities

An *annuity* is a contract (generally with a life insurance company) that provides income for a set period of time or for life in return for the payment of a premium (or premiums). In a sense, an annuity is the opposite of a life insurance contract. Life insurance reduces the financial risk of the insured dying prematurely; whereas annuities reduce the financial risk that the insured will live too long, that is, longer than income will be available for support.

Annuities are not life insurance. But they are often sold by life insurance agents and companies as a way of investing life insurance or

---

Single-Premium Life Insurance

Historically, the cash value that builds up in a life insurance policy is not subject to income taxes while it grows. When withdrawn, only the portion that exceeds the total premiums paid will be taxable. This makes cash value life insurance a tax shelter of sorts. The 1986 tax law left this tax advantage intact while eliminating many other types of tax shelters. In response to this competitive advantage, many life insurance companies began vigorously promoting something called single-premium life insurance. With such a policy you pay only one initial premium, which provides an immediate insurance amount and immediate cash value, which will grow tax-sheltered as the years pass. For example, a person aged thirty-five might pay a single $35,000 premium for a $100,000 policy, which would have about $34,000 in cash value at the end of the first year and, say, $60,000 by the end of year ten.

Are such policies a good idea? Maybe, but probably not. First of all, if you do not need more life insurance, why should you buy another policy? The insurance is not free; you pay for it through the premium (note the difference between the premium and the cash value for the first year in the preceding example) and through reduced cash value build-ups in subsequent years. Second, some policies require a lower rate of return or a surrender charge during the first few years to discourage people from cashing in their policies too early. Third and probably most important, the rate of return on the cash value build-up must be competitive with the after-tax rate of return for other investment options if single-premium life insurance is to be an intelligent choice. In many instances this is simply not the case.

---

endowment proceeds. Because annuities provide income, they are investments and should be compared with the many investment options available in today's financial marketplace. Annuities will be covered more fully in Chapter 21, "Social Security and Other Retirement Plans."

The Life Insurance Policy

A life insurance policy is the written contract between the insurer and the policyholder. The policy contains all of the information relative to the agreement. Even though individual policies vary somewhat, most of them contain the following common provisions: (1) general terms and provisions, (2) living benefits, (3) optional living benefits, and (4) settlement options.

General Terms and Provisions

Life insurance policies define the terminology used in the policy and outline the basic provisions. The purpose of such information is to clarify the meaning of the policy and the protections afforded the insurer and the policyholder.

Death Benefit   The *death benefit* of a life insurance policy is the amount that will be paid upon the death of the insured person. The amount of the death benefit will differ somewhat from the face amount. The face amount will be slightly adjusted up or down to allow for such items as any dividends accumulated but not yet paid, outstanding cash value loans, premiums paid in advance, or unpaid premiums. For example, consider a $100,000 participating whole life policy with annual premiums of $1,380. If the insured were to die halfway through the policy year, with an outstanding cash value loan of $5,000 and earned but unpaid dividends of $11,000, the death benefit would be $106,690 calculated as follows:

$100,000	Face amount
11,000	Unpaid dividends
+ 690	Premiums paid in advance (one-half year)
$111,690	Subtotal
− 5,000	Outstanding cash value loan
$106,690	Death benefit

Beneficiary   In addition to the naming of the beneficiary and contingent beneficiary, the policy will give the procedure for payment of the death benefit if both of these people die before the insured does and the policyholder has not named a new beneficiary. Occasionally, there may be a dispute as to who died first, the beneficiary or the insured. Procedures for settling this type of problem and for changing beneficiaries will be included in the policy.

Insurable Interest   As we discussed in Chapter 10, you have insurable interest if you stand to suffer a financial loss when a peril occurs. It is sometimes difficult to determine exactly who has an insurable interest in the life of an insured and what the dollar value of that interest is. Life insurance companies will question an application for life insurance that seems to request more coverage than warranted by the nature of the relationship among the policyholder, the beneficiary, and the insured. Sometimes policies will be issued and appear suspect only after a loss occurs. In such a case the company may challenge a loss claim and may refuse to pay the death benefit. Policies contain general language giving the company the right to make such challenges.

The Application   The life insurance application is the policyholder's offer to purchase a policy. The application requests specific information and becomes part of the life insurance policy. Any errors or omissions in the application may allow the insurance company to deny a request for the payment of the death benefit.

Incontestability   Life insurance policies generally have an *incontestability clause,* which places a time limit—usually two years—on the right of the insurance company to deny a claim after the death of the insured. This clause applies to the problems arising out of questionable insurable interest and false statements in the application. The only exception to this limit is a denial based on the failure to pay the premium.

Suicide   Life insurance policies will generally have a *suicide clause,* allowing the life insurance company to deny coverage if the insured commits suicide within the first few years after issuance of the policy. If the specified number of years has elapsed (usually two), the full death benefit will be paid. If not, only the premiums that had been paid will be payable to the beneficiary.

Living Benefits

Life insurance policies often include provisions for benefits to an insured prior to death. Such benefits are most likely to be included in cash value policies. Least likely to include living benefits are one-year term insurance policies.

Dividends   Life insurance dividends are the return of a portion of the premium paid for a life insurance policy. Policies that pay dividends are called *participating policies,* and policies that do not pay dividends are called *nonparticipating policies.* Both term and cash value policies may pay dividends. Dividends are paid when losses and/or company expenses are below those anticipated. Dividends can also be the result of a higher-than-anticipated return on the insurer's investments. It is not unusual for an insurance company to charge higher-than-necessary premiums in order to pay high dividends. Carefully evaluate the premiums charged and the dividend likely to be paid when you compare participating and nonparticipating policies.

Owners of participating policies may receive dividends in one of several ways. One option is to receive the dividends as a cash payment at the end of the policy year. A second option is to have the dividends remain with the insurance company to accumulate and earn interest. A third option is to use the dividends for the purchase of small amounts of paid-up life insurance. With some policies this paid-up insurance, plus accumulated cash values, grows to a sufficient level over the years to allow the insured to discontinue paying premiums and still maintain the same amount of coverage. A fourth option is to allow the dividends plus interest to accumulate until retirement, when the funds are used to purchase an annuity. Until the dividends are actually withdrawn from the policy, the policyholder is free to change the option chosen.

Grace Period The prompt payment of the premium is crucial to the continuation of coverage provided by any insurance policy. A *lapsed policy* is an insurance policy that has been terminated due to the policyholder's failure to pay the required premium. Approximately 12 percent of all life insurance policies written will lapse each year.

If your life insurance policy lapses, you must prove insurability and pay any missed premiums plus interest in order to be reinstated. You will pay a higher premium for a new policy, reflecting your current age. In order to help prevent a lapse, most cash value and multiyear term policies include a *grace period*, which is a period of time, usually thirty-one days after the premium due date, during which late payment may be made without a lapse of the policy. During the grace period all provisions of the policy remain intact, but only if payment is made before the grace period ends. For example, assume that payment was due but not paid on January 1. If the insured were to die on January 15, the policy could be reinstated as long as payment is made by January 31, given a 31-day grace period.

Nonforfeiture Options *Nonforfeiture options* prevent you from losing the accumulated cash value if your policy lapses or is cashed in. You can receive these accumulated funds in one of three ways. The first option is simply to receive the funds as a cash payment. A second option is to continue the policy on a paid-up basis. A new and lower face amount for the policy will be established based on the amount that can be purchased with the accumulated funds. The new face amount will generally be lower than the policy's original face amount. The third option is to continue the policy with the original face amount but for a time period shorter than the original policy. Effectively, this means that the accumulated funds will be used to purchase an equal amount of term insurance for as long a time period as the funds will allow. Table 13–6 illustrates the year-to-year changes in the value of the nonforfeiture options for a paid at sixty-five cash value policy. Note that when the

TABLE 13–6
Table of Nonforfeiture Values[a] (3.5 Percent
Guaranteed Rate)

Policy Year	Cash or Loan Value	Face Value of Paid-Up Insurance	Period of $10,000 Term Insurance	
			Years	Days
1	$ 0	$ 0	0	0
2	0	0	0	0
3	60	240	2	81
4	190	720	7	35
5	310	1,140	10	282
10	1,000	3,160	19	351
15	1,790	4,900	22	346
20	2,690	6,410	23	122
30	4,350	8,260	21	228
35	5,390	9,140	20	286
40	6,520	10,000	For life	
45	7,110	10,000		

[a] For a $10,000, "paid at 65" limited payment cash value life insurance policy for a male aged 25. The annual premium is $180.

insured reaches the age of sixty-five (policy year forty) the policy will continue on a paid-up basis without further premium payments.

Policy Loans   You may borrow against the accumulated cash value of your policy. The maximum amount you may borrow is the total cash value accumulated. Interest rates charged for the loan will range from 2 to 8 percent depending on the terms of the policy. Because interest rates in general have been high in recent years, policies issued since about 1980 have higher policy loan interest rates. In addition to paying interest on borrowed funds, you will lose the return that would have been earned had the funds remained in the policy.

The charging of interest on cash value policy loans is controversial. Many people argue that the cash value in a policy really belongs to policyholders, who have merely deposited the funds with the insurance company, and that policyholders should not be required to pay interest on their own money. Insurers, unlike most lenders, do not require proof of creditworthiness prior to granting a policy loan and will not require any repayment schedule other than annual payment of the interest charges. The principal may remain outstanding indefinitely. However, any policy loan outstanding when the insured dies will be deducted from the death benefit.

Optional Living Benefits

The living benefits discussed thus far are generally available on most policies. They are automatically included in the agreement and require no increased premiums. However, there are several other living benefits that you can obtain for slightly higher premiums. These optional benefits are guaranteed insurability, waiver of premium, automatic premium loan, and multiple indemnity.

Guaranteed Insurability The *guaranteed insurability option* allows you to buy additional cash value life insurance without proving insurability. This option differs from the guaranteed renewability option for term insurance in that guaranteed insurability enables you to increase the face amount of the policy or to buy an additional policy.

There are usually limits to the number of times you may exercise this option and the additional face amount that you may purchase. For example, consider the purchase of a $20,000 cash value policy by a twenty-two-year old woman. The policy could include a guaranteed insurability option at an extra cost of $30 per year. The option would allow the purchase of an extra $20,000 in coverage on a maximum of five different occasions. The policy might allow the exercise of these options when the insured turns twenty-five, thirty, thirty-five, or forty, or when she gets married or has children.

Waiver of Premium A *waiver-of-premium option* allows you to keep a life insurance policy in force without having to pay premiums. It usually will apply when a policyholder is totally and permanently disabled but may apply under other conditions depending on the policy provisions. In effect, the waiver-of-premium option is insurance against the risk of becoming disabled and unable to pay premiums.

Automatic Premium Loan An *automatic premium loan* provision allows any premium not paid by the end of the grace period to be paid automatically with a policy loan if sufficient cash value or dividends have accumulated. In the first few years of a policy, this provision may not be of much benefit because cash value and dividends accumulate slowly. Eventually these funds may become sufficient to pay premiums for a considerable length of time and may effectively prevent the lapse of the policy.

Multiple Indemnity A *multiple indemnity clause* provides for a doubling or tripling of the face amount if death results from certain specified causes. This type of clause is most often used to double the face amount if death is the result of an accident. A multiple indemnity clause is often included automatically as part of the policy at no extra cost; sometimes there is a charge for it. If you are adequately insured, a multiple indemnity clause will add little to your insurance protection and is probably not worth any extra premium. If you are not adequately insured, the money used to obtain a multiple indemnity clause would best be spent on raising the face amount of the policy.

Settlement Options

Settlement options are the choices the life insurance beneficiary and/or the insured have concerning the form of payment of the death benefit of a life insurance policy. The option may be chosen by the insured before death or by the beneficiary after the insured's death. One option is simply to receive the death benefit in a lump sum immediately after death. Upon receipt of the death certificate, the insurance company will pay the funds, usually within two weeks. The other settlement options are to receive *interest income, income for a specific period, income for life,* and *income of a specific amount.* Under each of these four settlement options, the death benefit is left on deposit with the company to earn interest. The funds (death benefit and/or interest) are then paid to the beneficiary over time according to the settlement option chosen. If the beneficiary dies before the proceeds are fully exhausted, the remaining funds will be paid in a lump sum to the estate of the beneficiary. The rate of return is determined by the company at the time of death of the insured, although the policy will stipulate some minimum rate (for example, 4 percent).

Interest Income   Under this settlement option, the beneficiary will receive the annual interest earned from the death benefit. For example, the beneficiary would receive $7,000 each year from a $100,000 death benefit earning 7 percent interest. Payments may be made monthly, quarterly, semiannually, or annually at the beneficiary's option. The $100,000 principal would remain intact to earn interest until the death of the beneficiary and then become part of his or her estate.

Income for a Specific Period   Under this option, the beneficiary will receive an income from the death benefit for a specific number of years. For example, a widow with small children may choose to receive an income for eighteen years. The insurance company would calculate a level of income that would allow for equal proceeds each year, with all funds being exhausted at the end of the eighteenth year.

Income for Life   Under this option, the beneficiary will receive an income for life. The insurance company would use the life expectancy of the beneficiary to calculate the level of income that would allow for equal annual payments so that funds would be exhausted by the expected date of the beneficiary's death. If the beneficiary lives longer than expected, the income payments will continue. This option is similar to the purchase of an annuity.

Income of a Specific Amount   Under this option, the beneficiary will receive a specific amount of income per year from the death benefit. Payments will cease when the death benefit and interest are exhausted. For example, a $100,000 death benefit earning 5 percent interest would provide a $15,000 annual income for approximately eight years. (To find this, divide the death benefit by the desired annual income. Then find the factor in the 5 percent interest rate column in Appendix A4 that comes closest to the figure obtained. The year corresponding to that factor is the approximate number of years the death benefits will last.)

Buying Life Insurance

In a recent year, more than eighteen million new individual life insurance policies were purchased. Did each individual really need to be covered by life insurance? Was the price paid too high? Was the policy purchased the right one, and was it purchased from a reputable company and agent? This section will help you, as an insurance purchaser, answer these questions.

Should You Be Insured?

Anyone whose death will result in financial losses to others should be covered by life insurance unless there are sufficient assets to cover the losses. As a practical matter, obtaining insurance also depends on the financial resources available to pay the insurance premiums. Most American families do not own enough life insurance. On a more positive note, more than 90 percent of the male heads of households with children are covered by at least some life insurance. However, almost one-third of all female heads of households are not insured at all.

The bulk of any family's life insurance expenditures and protection should be concentrated on the principal breadwinner. If other breadwinners are currently providing income for the family, they should be covered in order to protect that income. The remainder should be concentrated on persons who would become breadwinners should the other breadwinners die. Life insurance coverage should have a renewability or guaranteed insurability option.

Many families purchase life insurance for members who are not breadwinners. Most often these individuals are children. If breadwinners are sufficiently protected, buying a small amount of life insurance for the children is perhaps understandable. But when the breadwinners are not sufficiently insured the family would be much better off buying more term insurance for the breadwinner. Others who are sometimes unnecessarily insured are the elderly. Since life insurance premiums for those over the age of sixty are extremely high, such people would be better off by saving or by keeping only a small policy for funeral expenses.

College students nearing graduation and young, single, working persons are often approached by life insurance agents. The sales pitch is that it is best to buy life insurance while you are young and healthy and while premiums are still low. The fact that life insurance needs are low or nonexistent at this time is not mentioned by many agents. Furthermore, young adults have more chance of becoming disabled than of dying. If they buy insurance to protect their income, it should be disability income protection.

Young people without dependents sometimes purchase a small life insurance policy sufficient for their burial and final expenses. While it can be argued that it would be better to set aside funds for this purpose, such a life insurance purchase is of course an individual decision. It

Tips on Life Insurance for Students

Students are often approached by life insurance agents. Here are some tips from consumer-minded insurance experts:

1. If you have no dependents, you probably don't need life insurance. Life insurance is essentially protection against loss of income for dependents.

2. There is no mathematical advantage to buying life insurance at an early age. Premiums increase at the same rate for everybody regardless of the age at which you start the policy.

3. If you need protection for your dependents, term insurance can do the job at the lowest cost.

4. Be wary of offers of "free" insurance or cash value policies for only a few dollars the first year. Agents who make such claims are probably hiding vital details. A small initial premium may be only a down payment on a sizable loan for the rest of the first year's cost.

5. There are disadvantages to financing the first year's premium. Signing a promissory note binds you to a long-term debt and substantially raises the price of insurance. If you cannot afford to pay the full first year's premium, you probably should not sign up.

6. If you fail to pay *any* premium on time during the years when a promissory note is in force, the entire note becomes due immediately.

7. Before you buy life insurance, get the advice and approval of people you trust—such as your parents—and at least one insurance expert other than the agent selling the policy.

8. Read everything carefully. If an agent does not allow you time to read, don't sign anything. Don't be afraid to ask questions or take a few days to think it over.

9. Bring a friend with you when you meet with an agent. Take notes on the sales presentation. An agent will be less likely to misrepresent the policy if he or she realizes you are paying close attention.

10. Don't be pressured into buying anything you do not want. If you think an agent is misleading or dishonest, report him or her to state insurance officials and to officials at your school.

11. If you buy a policy and then run into a problem that cannot be solved by the insurance company, call your state insurance department. Many companies will make adjustments in hardship cases referred to them by state insurance officials.

would be best for such a small policy to contain a renewability or guaranteed insurability option that would later allow a continuance or increase in protection.

Cost Comparisons in Life Insurance

The price people pay for life insurance depends on their age, their health, and to a lesser degree their lifestyle. Age is important, of course, because the probability of dying increases with age. Health also affects mortality, and a person who has a health problem such as heart disease or diabetes may pay considerably higher life insurance rates or may not be able to obtain coverage at any price. People with extremely hazardous lifestyles or occupations (stunt pilot, grand prix racer) or who engage in hazardous hobbies (sky diving, hang gliding) historically have been required to pay higher life insurance premiums. Recently, life insurance companies have begun offering lower prices to applicants whose lifestyles suggest longevity, such as nonsmokers and joggers.

Premium per $1,000 of Coverage Comparing life insurance prices is a difficult task because policies and plans vary from company to company. Life insurance premiums are usually quoted in dollars per $1,000 of coverage. Generally, the higher the face amount of the policy, the lower the rate per $1,000. For example, a company might sell term life insurance for $1 per $1,000 per year when purchased in face amounts of $100,000 or more. You can see the problems involved in comparing this policy with, say, a cash value policy with a different face value. Simply comparing the premium per $1,000 of coverage will not tell you which policy is the better bargain. Table 13–7 lists annual premiums that are typically required for various types of insurance policies.

There are several sources of information about the prices for life insurance policies. Popular magazines such as *Changing Times* and *Money* regularly feature articles that give average or typical premiums for different types of policies. In 1986, *Consumer Reports* magazine (June, July, and August issues) published a comprehensive report on life insurance. In addition to providing excellent explanations of life insurance, the report compared the premiums for typical policies offered by more than a hundred insurance companies. Another source of information is your state department of insurance. Many such departments publish life insurance buyers' guides that provide price guidelines useful for evaluating quotes from agents.

The Net Cost Method The most obvious source of information about the cost of life insurance is the agent selling the policy. Agents will discuss the price of a life insurance policy in terms of the premium

TABLE 13–7
Typical Premiums for Various Types of Life Insurance (Face Amount $100,000)

Policy Type	Premium[a]							Age 65
	Policy Year							
	1	2	3	5	10	11	20	
5-year renewable term (guaranteed insurability to age 70)	$ 100	$ 100	$ 100	$ 100	$ 140	$ 140	$ 190	$2,700
5-year convertible term	185	185	185	185	940	940	940	940
Whole life	870	870	870	870	870	870	870	870
Limited pay life (paid at age 65)	920	920	920	920	920	920	920	0
Endowment (at age 65)	1,070	1,070	1,070	1,070	1,070	1,070	1,070	0

[a] Premiums quoted are for a twenty-one-year-old male nonsmoker.

per $1,000 of coverage and the annual premium. Regarding cash value life insurance, many agents will also mention the net cost of the policy under consideration. The *net cost* of a life insurance policy is the total of all premiums to be paid minus any accumulated cash value and accrued dividends. The net cost is calculated for a specific point in time during the life of the policy, say, at the end of the tenth or twentieth year. The formula for calculating the net cost is

$$\text{Net cost} = \text{premiums paid} - \text{dividends accrued} - \text{cash value}$$
(13–2)

Consider the following example of determining the net cost of a cash value life insurance policy. Sarah Nelson of Dubuque, Iowa, is considering the purchase of a $100,000 participating cash value life insurance policy. Her annual premium will be $1,444. Total dividends accumulated for the first twenty years will be $10,500. The policy will also have a cash value of $26,348 at the end of twenty years. The net cost of the policy after twenty years will be

$$\begin{aligned} \text{Net cost} &= (\$1,444 \times 20) - \$10,500 - \$26,348 \\ &= -\$7,968 \end{aligned}$$

Because this net cost is a negative figure, it appears that the policy will pay for itself within twenty years. Many life insurance agents have been known to make this claim for cash value policies by using the net cost method.

Of course, Sarah's policy will not really pay for itself. The net cost method fails to consider the opportunity cost of the forgone interest she could earn by investing the premiums rather than buying life insurance. This failure to consider the opportunity cost of the forgone interest is the basic flaw of the net cost method. You should ignore net cost calculations provided by a life insurance agent.

Interest-adjusted Cost Index   Ask an agent to provide the interest-adjusted cost index for the policy you are considering. Reputable agents should have this information at hand and are required in thirty-eight states to disclose it if asked. However, in most of these states the disclosure need only be made after the sale is closed and then the buyer has ten days to cancel if he or she feels that the index is too high. You should insist on being told the index before you agree to buy a policy and shop elsewhere if the agent refuses, resists, or tries to imply that the index will be of no help.

The *interest-adjusted cost index (IACI)* is a measure of the cost of life insurance that takes into account the interest that would have been earned had the premiums been invested rather than used to buy insurance. The lower the IACI, the lower the cost of the policy. The interest rate usually used to calculate the IACI is 5 percent. This figure was chosen because a reasonably sophisticated investor would generally be able to invest funds to earn 5 percent after taxes. Like net cost, the IACI is calculated for a specific point in time, usually the twentieth year, during the life of the policy.

To illustrate the IACI, consider again Sarah's purchase of a $100,000 cash value policy for $1,444 per year. At 5 percent interest, she could invest $1,444 per year for twenty years and accumulate $47,747. Total dividends of $10,500 would also be adjusted for 5 percent interest, to $14,719. Subtracting the interest-adjusted dividends of $14,719 and the cash value of $26,348 from $47,747 yields $6,680. This figure represents the interest-adjusted cost of buying the policy. Because this cost is spread over twenty years, it must be divided by a constant, 34.719, to obtain the interest-adjusted cost index. The same constant would be used whenever calculating a twenty-year IACI. The IACI is $192.40, or $1.92 per $1,000 of coverage.

Sarah may use this figure to compare similar policies from other agents and companies. Interest-adjusted cost indexes vary considerably among policies and companies. IACIs as low as -3.00 are available. Yet some high-cost policies will have an IACI as high as $+5.00$. Certainly policies with a positive IACI should be avoided. Sarah need not make the IACI calculations herself. She needs only to ask the agent to provide the twenty-year interest-adjusted cost index. She should receive a quick, accurate response.

Interest-adjusted Net Payment Index   The IACI assumes that the policy will be cashed in at the end of a certain period rather than remain in force until the death of the insured. If, however, the policy is to remain in force until death, the twenty-year IACI will not be an accurate measure of the cost of the policy. To overcome this deficiency, you can use the *interest-adjusted net payment index (IANPI)* to measure the cost of cash value insurance held until death. This method does not subtract the accumulated cash value, as the IACI does, because policies held for life do not pay cash value. Instead, the face amount is paid at death. Using the previous example as an illustration, the IANPI after twenty years for Sarah's $100,000 policy would be $9.51 per $1,000 of coverage. This is obtained by subtracting the interest-adjusted dividends ($14,719) from the interest-adjusted premiums paid ($47,747) and dividing by the same constant (34.719) and then 100 (to obtain the IANPI per $1,000 of coverage). Notice that the IANPI is about five times greater than the IACI. This higher figure reflects the fact that no cash value is paid if the policy is held until death.

Preferred Method of Cost Comparison   We have examined four measures of the cost of life insurance policies: (1) premium per $1,000 of coverage, (2) net cost, (3) interest-adjusted cost index, and (4) interest-adjusted net payment index. Although none of these measures provides a means for comparing among all the different types of policies, the interest-adjusted cost index has been adopted by the National Association of Insurance Commissioners as the recommended measure to be used in the industry. However, some insurance companies have been accused of manipulating the timing of dividend payments and cash value accumulation in order to make their policies appear less expensive at the twenty-year point than they really are. Further, the

IACI does not provide an accurate means of comparing among greatly different types of policies. It is totally inappropriate, for example, when comparing term insurance and cash value insurance. It is best to decide beforehand which type of policy you need and then to use the IACI to compare policies of that type.

Linton Yields   Many people who buy cash value life insurance want to know the rate of return they will earn on the cash value accumulated under the policy. With such knowledge they can compare different policies and compare buying cash value insurance to buying a term policy and investing the difference in premiums in some other investment vehicle. The most frequently used measure of the true rate of return on cash value insurance is the *Linton yield*. The mathematical formula for calculating Linton yields is complicated. The annual premium for an equivalent amount of low-priced term insurance is subtracted from the cash value policy annual premium. The result is the "extra" premium that goes into the building of cash values. This figure is then compared to the cash value (plus dividends for participating policies) that would be accumulated after a given number of years (five, ten, twenty, and so forth) to determine an annual rate of interest at the end of the given time period.

Agents are often unprepared to answer questions about rates of return and Linton yields but it would not hurt to ask, being aware that the response may not be accurate. An even better idea would be to consult *Consumer Reports'* 1986 life insurance report. The Linton yields after five, ten, and twenty years are given for the policies the magazine staff examined. Five year Linton yields ranged from −100.0 percent to more than 7 percent with most being negative. The reason for such low rates of return is the slow or nonexistent cash value accumulation in the early years of most policies. Twenty-year Linton yields ranged from less than 5 percent to more than 12 percent. It should be obvious that when rates of return vary so widely it pays to shop for policies that pay the better rates of return.

Choosing the Type of Life Insurance Policy

A fundamental decision to make when buying life insurance is whether to buy term insurance or cash value (including universal life) insurance. Cash value policies are often recommended because the premiums stay the same and because they provide protection for life and have a savings element. They can also be a method of forced savings for people who lack the discipline to save for retirement. Life insurance companies and agents generally recommend cash value life insurance. This is not too surprising, since cash value policies are more profitable for them than are term policies.

Historically, more people bought cash value insurance than term insurance. Since the mid-1970s, however, term insurance has become more popular. Now the volume of term insurance sold each year is greater than that of cash value insurance. This trend toward the purchase of term insurance seems to be reversing somewhat with the growth of universal life insurance. These changes have resulted from several factors, two of which are the inflation and interest rates. When inflation rates are high, life insurance needs increase rapidly, and buying term insurance is the least expensive way to increase life insurance protection. When interest rates are high, cash value policies lose their attractiveness because many pay relatively low interest rates on their cash values. When inflation and interest rates moderate as they did in the mid-1980s, cash value insurance becomes more competitive.

Another factor is an increasing sophistication among life insurance purchasers. Many people have come to agree with the adage "Buy term and invest the rest." This means that you are better off buying term insurance to meet your life insurance needs and investing the extra funds you would have spent on cash value insurance. Most cash value policies pay guaranteed interest rates below 6 percent. Careful investors can earn after-tax rates of return that exceed this percentage (see Chapters 7 and 16). Of course, the decision to buy term and invest the rest requires some planning on your part. If you do not invest the funds systematically, you will lose the benefits of a higher rate of return and compounding. Some investment plans will automatically deduct funds from your paycheck or checking account, and others will bill you monthly or annually (see Chapter 18).

Although term insurance provides more coverage for the same premium than does cash value insurance, term policies do have some negative features. You can avoid these by purchasing renewable and convertible term insurance. The convertibility option allows you to convert to cash value insurance if you wish. Make sure that convertibility is an option and not required at some future date. The renewability option allows continuation of the same amount of term insurance without requiring you to prove insurability. Neither of these options will prevent the cost of term insurance from increasing at renewal, however. You can avoid a cost increase by purchasing decreasing term insurance or a twenty- or thirty-year term policy, or by decreasing the face amount of the policy at renewal.

Most independent insurance advisers do not recommend the purchase of large amounts of cash value insurance. However, a small cash value policy may prove advantageous, even for the young. Regardless of age or financial responsibility, most people face a potential loss of up to $10,000 from a premature death. This basic minimum could be provided on a permanent basis through the purchase of a $10,000 whole life policy. This small policy should include a guaranteed insurability option, which would allow you to purchase more coverage if a change in your health prevents you from buying term insurance.

Figure 13–3 diagrams a recommended life insurance and investment plan for the income-producing years in an individual's life cycle. The plan is built on two cornerstones. The first is the purchase of term insurance for the bulk of life insurance needs, since term insurance is more flexible than cash value insurance and provides more protection for each premium dollar. The second is a systematic, regular investment program. Because the rates of return on cash value policies are often low, it is wise to make other investments.

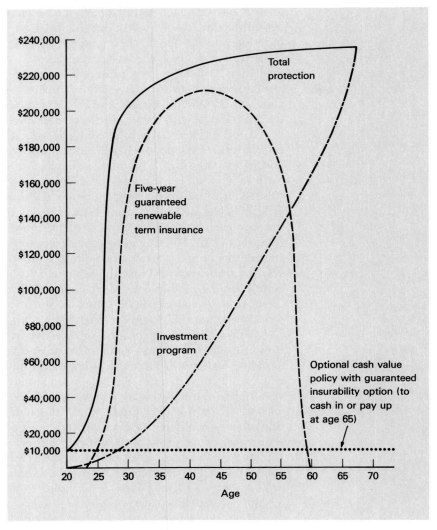

FIGURE 13–3
Life Insurance and Investment Plan over the Life Cycle

At the age of twenty, as diagrammed, the average person needs little or no life insurance. If desired, a small cash value policy with guaranteed insurability is sufficient. Over time, however, an individual's responsibilities for the financial well-being of others may increase. These responsibilities will in turn increase the need for protection from the risk of premature death. Since the early years of an investment program will not yield enough protection, life insurance must be purchased. The amount purchased will depend on the individual's needs, and the amounts in Figure 13–3 are only examples. At about the age of forty-five, the probable losses from a premature death will begin to diminish because the investment program started at the age of twenty will have grown sufficiently to provide some of the protection from a premature death. Thus there will be a leveling off or decrease in the need for life insurance around the same time that term insurance premiums become prohibitively expensive. By the age of sixty-five, life insurance needs will be greatly reduced or eliminated and the investment program will have grown sufficiently to provide retirement income. (Investments are examined in detail in Chapters 14–20.)

Life insurance companies have begun to realize that a program such as the one described above is in the best interest of policyholders. In response, many companies now offer interest-sensitive life insurance (discussed earlier), which gives the flexibility of term insurance, the permanence of cash value insurance, and the high rates of return available in the financial markets. Universal and variable life insurance are no panacea, however. You should still compare the term insurance component with policies that can be purchased separately, and evaluate the investment component against other available investments. Investments are covered in the next section of the book.

Choosing a Company and Agent

Life insurance in the United States is commonly sold through agents who represent one company exclusively. It is also sometimes sold directly through the mail. It is critical to your financial security to select a financially sound company and a qualified, reputable agent.

The most important feature of a life insurance company is its ability to pay its obligations. The company must have the stability and financial strength to survive for the many years your policy will be in force. A. M. Best Company publishes *Best's Key Rating Guide,* which rates the financial strength of life insurance companies on a scale from A+ to C. A rating of A+ or A indicates that the financial strength of the company has been judged excellent. There is really no need to consider any company with less than an A+ rating, as this rating has been given to over two-hundred companies. More than two-hundred other companies have received an A rating.

Choosing an agent is somewhat more difficult than evaluating individual insurance companies. Your relationship with your life insurance agent is both professional and personal. The agent must be qualified to design a program tailored to your specific needs and must understand the dynamics of family relationships, which are the source of life insurance needs. The agent should have earned a professional designation, such as *chartered life underwriter* (CLU). To earn the CLU, an agent must have three years of experience and pass a rigorous ten-course program in life insurance counseling. Some agents may also have earned the *certified financial planner* (CFP) or *chartered financial consultant* (ChFC) designation. If possible, choose an agent with these qualifications. Also be sure the agent is willing to take the time to provide personal service and answer all questions about the policy both before and after you purchase it. An agent who is a friend or relative is not necessarily the best choice.

Summary

1. Life insurance is designed to provide protection from the financial losses that result from a premature death.

2. Life insurance needs are determined by subtracting the financial resources that will be available at death from the financial losses likely to result from the death. The losses likely to occur include lost income, final expenses, readjustment period expenses, and debt-repayment needs. The resources available to cover these losses include savings, other insurance, skills and education, and asset equity.

3. There are basically only two types of life insurance, term life insurance and cash value life insurance. Variations of term life insurance include decreasing term insurance, convertible term insurance, and credit life insurance. Variations of cash value insurance include whole life insurance, limited pay life insurance, endowment life insurance, and interest-sensitive life insurance.

4. An examination of four elements is necessary for an understanding of universal life insurance: the premium, the cost of the death benefit, the interest rate, and the company expense charges.

5. A life insurance policy is a written contract between the insurance purchaser and the insurance company, spelling out in detail the terms of the agreement. When buying life insurance, it is important to pay attention to the policy's general terms and conditions, living benefits, optional living benefits, and settlement options.

6. You should purchase life insurance only after you determine the actual dollar amount and type of policy you need and analyze comparative premiums. Term life insurance provides the most insurance protection for each premium dollar. The interest adjusted cost index can provide a means of comparing similar policies, but its use is limited when comparing dissimilar policies.

Modern Money Management

The Johnsons Change Their Life Insurance Coverage

Harry and Belinda spend $9 per month on life insurance. This represents the premium on a $10,000 paid-at-sixty-five cash value policy on Harry. Belinda receives a group term insurance policy from her employer with a face amount of $37,800 (1.5 × her annual salary). By choosing a group life insurance plan from his menu of fringe benefits, Harry now has $18,300 (his annual salary) worth of group term life insurance. Harry and Belinda have decided that since they have no children, they could reduce their life insurance needs by protecting each other's income for only four years, assuming the survivor would be able to fend for himself or herself after that time. They also realize that their savings fund is so low that it would have no bearing on their life insurance needs.

1. Should the $3,000 in Harry's trust fund be included in his annual income for the purposes of calculating the likely dollar loss if he were to die? (See the discussions about the Johnsons at the end of Chapter 2.) Explain your response.

2. Based on your response to question 1, how much more life insurance does Harry need? Use formula 13–1 and the information in Figure 13–1 to arrive at your answer. Justify any assumptions you make about the final expenses, readjustment expenses, and debt repayment figures used in formula 13–1.

3. Make the same calculations to arrive at the additional life insurance needed on Belinda's life. Again, justify your assumptions.

4. How might the Johnsons most economically meet any additional life insurance needs you have determined they may have?

5. In addition to their life insurance planning, what might the Johnsons begin to do now to prepare for their retirement years? See Figure 13–3.

Key Words and Concepts

Review Questions

1. Briefly explain why the term *life insurance* may be considered a misnomer.
2. Identify the role actuaries play in the life insurance business.
3. What purpose does a mortality table serve in the life insurance industry?
4. What is considered to be the major financial loss suffered upon the death of a family's breadwinner?
5. Name three other types of losses resulting from a premature death of a family's primary wage earner.
6. What is the multiple-earnings approach toward estimating lost income for a family or individual?
7. What is the basic difference between the multiple-earnings approach and the needs approach in estimating income losses?
8. Identify four resources that may be available to cover the losses resulting from a premature death.
9. What is the calculation used to determine the amount of life insurance needed?
10. What is the basic difference between term life insurance and cash value life insurance?
11. Why might you want to buy a decreasing term policy?
12. Why might you want to have a convertibility option on a term life policy?
13. What is the major reason for not buying credit life insurance?
14. Give two reasons why you might want to buy group life insurance.
15. Explain why endowment policies are the most expensive form of life insurance to buy.
16. What three things do universal life insurance purchasers know about their policies that purchasers of more traditional cash value policies do not know?
17. How does variable-universal life insurance differ from variable life insurance?
18. Why is an annuity considered the opposite of a life insurance contract?
19. What are the general terms and provisions contained in a life insurance policy?
20. What benefit can you gain through a life insurance policy prior to your death?
21. What benefit does a grace period offer to life insurance policyholders?

22. Of what value is a guaranteed insurability option to life insurance policyholders?

23. What is meant by the term *settlement options*, and what options are available to life insurance beneficiaries?

24. Name several factors that influence the cost of life insurance.

25. Give the names of three publications that can provide information on the cost of life insurance.

26. What is the interest-adjusted cost index?

27. What is a Linton yield as it relates to cash value life insurance?

28. What might you gain by "buying term and investing the rest"?

29. What is the most important factor to consider when choosing a life insurance company?

Case Problems

1. Tracy and Clark Cristner of Savannah, Georgia, are a young married couple in their late twenties. They have two children, aged five and three, and Tracy is pregnant with their third child. Tracy is an interior design consultant for medical and dental offices and last year earned $15,000. Because she does much of her work at home it is unlikely she will need to curtail her work after the baby is born. Clark is a family therapist with a thriving practice; he earned $42,000 last year.

    Because both are self-employed, Tracy and Clark do not have access to group life insurance. They are covered by a $50,000 universal life policy they purchased three years ago. Clark is also covered by a $50,000 five-year renewable term policy, which will expire next year. They feel that now is a good time to reassess their life insurance program. As a preliminary step in this reassessment they have determined that Tracy's account with Social Security would yield the family an $8,000 annual benefit if she were to die. For Clark the figure would be about $10,000. Both agree that they would like to support each of their children to age twenty-two, hoping that the children would be able to obtain the necessary extra college expense funds. They expect it would take about $6,000 each for burial, and they would like to have a lump sum of life insurance clearly marked for paying off their $70,000 home mortgage. They also feel that each would want to take a six-month leave from work if the other were to die.

    a. Calculate the amount of life insurance that Tracy needs.
    b. Calculate the amount of life insurance that Clark needs.
    c. If Tracy and Clark purchased term insurance to cover their additional needs, how much more would they each need to spend?

    d. How might the Cristners lower their need for more life insurance without greatly affecting their financial protection?

2. Just-married couples sometimes overindulge in the type and amount of life insurance they buy. Arnold and Jayne Tucker of Barberville, Kentucky, however, took a different approach. Both were working and had a small amount of life insurance provided through their respective employers—Arnold, $35,000, and Jayne, $15,000. During their discussion of life insurance needs and related costs, they decided that if Jayne completed her master's degree in industrial psychology she would have better employment opportunities. Consequently, they decided to take money they had available for more life insurance to help pay the costs for Jayne's education. They both feel, however, that they do not want to become "life insurance poor."

    a. In what way does Jayne's returning to school alter the Tuckers' life insurance concerns?

    b. Would you agree that the amount of life insurance provided by the Tuckers' respective employers is adequate while Jayne is in school? Explain your response.

3. Jim Howe is a college friend of yours from Santa Ana, California. Jim is about to graduate from college and was approached recently by a life insurance agent who set up a group meeting for about a dozen members of Jim's fraternity. During the meeting, the agent presented about six life insurance plans and was very persuasive about the benefits of a plan his company calls Affordable Life II. It allows the students to buy $100,000 of permanent life insurance for a very low premium during the first five years and then a higher premium later when their income presumably will be higher. Jim felt pretty confused after the meeting, as did his friends. Knowing that you were taking a personal finance course, they asked you to meet with them and answer some of their questions.

    a. Do you think this Affordable Life II is a good deal for these young men? Why or why not?

    b. How can they decide how much life insurance they need?

    c. Is life insurance really as confusing as the agent made it seem? If not, what more simple explanation would you give?

    d. What type of life insurance program would you advise for the fraternity brothers?

    e. How do you know if a life insurance policy is offered at a fair price?

Suggested Readings

"The Hot Air in 'No-Load' Insurance." *Changing Times*, April 1987, pp. 89–92. Details how growing number of cash-value policies that do not have a sales charge still get their commission costs.

"Insurance: A New Policy on Life." *Esquire,* March 1987, p. 65. Description of flexible-premium variable life policies, also known as Universal II.

"Insure the Parent Not the Child, Even When the Policy Is a College Fund." *Money,* January 1987, p. 51. Why it is financially smarter to insure the parents.

"Life Insurance: How to Protect Your Family." Three-part series in *Consumer Reports* ("Term Insurance," June 1986, pp. 371–402; "Universal Life Insurance," July 1986, pp. 515–530; "Whole Life Insurance," August 1986, pp. 447–470). Comprehensive analysis and ratings of companies.

"Life Insurance: Should Your Protection Double as an Investment?" *Money,* March 1987, pp. 140–148. Newer life insurance policies combine various types of investment opportunities that are tempting to consider.

"Universal Pain." *Fortune,* February 16, 1987, pp. 8–9. The unprofitability of universal life insurance policies.

"Your Life as a Tax Shelter." *Money,* March 1987, pp. 153–167. The high costs and definite income tax benefits of cash-value life insurance.

THE WALL STR

WEDNESDAY

NASDAQ NATIONAL MARKET ISSUES

PART FIVE

Investment Planning

C H A P T E R 14

Investment Fundamentals

OBJECTIVES

After reading this chapter, the student should be able to

1. list some motivations for starting an investment program and some ways to obtain funds to invest.

2. describe important elements of investment goals.

3. determine his or her own investment philosophy.

4. recognize the variety of choices among the alternative investments available.

5. identify several major factors that affect the return on investments.

6. describe some pitfalls to avoid in order to achieve investment goals, as well as three steps to help him or her invest successfully.

7. summarize descriptive characteristics of numerous alternative investments.

aking investments might seem to be an activity that is too far in the future for you to consider now. However, if you see the importance of practicing good financial management and protection of income and assets, you will recognize the related benefits of investment planning. Investments can increase your income and help maximize your enjoyment of life, whether you most enjoy reading a good book and taking long walks or dining in fine restaurants, taking exotic vacations, and driving expensive automobiles.

To begin the general study of investments, you must understand the investment fundamentals. This chapter first examines why and how people start to invest and then discusses how to set *your* investment goals. Next is a section to help you identify *your* investment philosophy. Alternative investments are then introduced. The following section describes factors that affect return on investment, especially such factors as risk and yield, diversification, leverage, taxes, and inflation. The next section offers reasons why people fail to succeed financially as well as ideas on how to succeed. The chapter concludes with a detailed summary of characteristics of many of the investment alternatives examined in later chapters.

Starting to Invest

Before starting your investment plan, you need to know why people invest, some prerequisites for investing, how various types of investments earn returns, and how to go about getting money to invest in the first place.

Why Invest?

People invest for one or more of four general reasons: (1) to achieve specific financial goals (new car, down payment on home, child's education, and so forth), (2) to increase income, (3) to gain wealth and a feeling of financial security, and (4) to have funds available during retirement years. People report these kinds of specific motivations for investing:

"I like the feeling of 'money in the bank.'"

"I have too much money just 'sitting' in the bank."

"I want to get rich quickly."

"I want to get rich slowly."

"I want to buy a Mercedes-Benz automobile."

"I hate paying money to the Internal Revenue Service."

"I want to retire with a secure income."

"My parents might have to depend on me financially after their retirement."

"I want to protect my spouse's finances in case I die first."

"My children should not have to support me in my old age."

"My children should not have to suffer financially when I die."

"The return on my current investments is not beating the rate of inflation."

"My investments should provide an income equal to one-quarter of my salary income by age fifty."

Prerequisites to Investing

Before you embark on an investment program, make sure you

1. **Live within your means** If you can live within your financial means, you will have financial control over your life. If you find yourself constantly running short of cash toward the end of the month, you may need better budget controls and probably won't have any money available for investments. On the other hand, if you are not overly indebted and generally have money available for unexpected automobile repairs, small gifts, and occasional self-indulgences, you can begin thinking about an investment program.

2. **Continue a savings program** Good financial managers save regularly, to acquire goods and services and/or to build an emergency fund. Investors save so they can make periodic investments with accrued savings or so they will have cash reserves if they need additional investment funds in a hurry.

3. **Establish a line of credit** Having a line of credit will help you meet personal financial emergencies and reduce the need to have large amounts of readily available savings. For example, you might have a line of credit of $3,000 at a local bank, $5,000 at a brokerage firm, and $4,000 on a bank credit card.

4. **Carry adequate insurance protection** Liability insurance will protect your assets and lifestyle in the event you are sued and health insurance will help defray costs if you or a member of your family falls ill. Life insurance is frequently purchased in conjunction with investments to protect the lifestyle of dependents in the event of an investor's death.

Returns on Investments

Two broad types of investment are available. With *savings investments,* you would expect virtually no risk for either the *principal* (amount placed in the investment) or the *interest* (amount earned on the principal). Various types of savings investments were discussed in Chapter 4. *Alternative investments* are riskier, since monies are placed in assets that guarantee neither return of the principal nor earnings, but they have the possibility of a greater return than savings investments.

The return on investment may come from two sources: current income and capital gains. In the field of investments, *current income* is money received from an investment, usually on a regular basis, in the form of interest, dividends, rent or other such payment. Interest is the payment you receive for allowing a financial institution (or an individual) to use and invest your money. Banks, credit unions, and savings and loan associations typically take funds on deposit, invest them profitably, and pay interest to depositors. *Dividends* are distributions of profits you receive for holding stock in a corporation. Generally, corporations retain some profits to use for continued growth of the company and distribute the remainder as dividends. *Rent* is the payment received in return for the use of property, such as land or a building.

A *capital gain* is income resulting from an increase in the value of an investment and it is calculated by subtracting the total amount paid for the investment (including commission costs) from the higher price at which it is sold, less any sales commissions and costs. Of course, a *capital loss* results if the selling price (plus expenses) is less than the original amount invested (plus commissions). The value of a small apartment building you own could increase over a few years from $200,000 to $275,000. The value of a common stock you own could increase from $80 to $100 a share in six months. You could realize a capital gain on each of these investments by selling the assets.

Yield is the *rate of return* on an investment; it is reported as a percentage and it is usually stated on an annualized basis. Say, for example, that Geoffrey Heagney purchases $1,000 of H & M stock, including broker's commissions, and receives $50 in cash dividends during the year. If he then sells the stock of $1,100, minus $60 in broker's commissions, he will have a capital gain of $40 ($1,100 − $1,000 − $60). Adding this $40 to the $50 in cash dividends provides a total return of $90, or a 9 percent annual yield on the investment ($90 ÷ $1,000).

Getting Money to Invest

Obtaining a return on an investment means earning money above and beyond your salary income. This is an attractive idea, of course, but you must first have the funds to invest. Unless you inherit money, you must save to build up some principal. Some suggestions follow.

1. **Pay yourself first** We recommend two ways to save in your budgeting (see Chapter 3). First, you should treat savings as a fixed expense and pay it regularly along with other dollar commitments. Second, when budgeted costs do not exceed income for a given time period, you should place the surplus (or part of it) in savings.

2. **Use forced savings plans** When asked, most employers will direct a portion of your salary to a savings account at a bank, credit union, savings and loan association, or even a special company savings plan. This way you never "see" the money, since it is deposited automatically. Another form of forced savings is to have the IRS overwithhold money from your paycheck and to receive a larger tax refund (a disadvantage of this method is that the IRS does not pay interest on withheld funds). An advantage of forced savings plans is that you have to take forceful action

not to save, thus making it easier to continue saving. Forced saving often works best when you save for a goal.

3. **Save—don't spend—windfalls** When unexpected money arrives, you may have the impulse to spend it quickly. However, if you save such windfalls rather than spend them, you will be able to add substantially to your savings account. Examples of extra money are a year-end bonus from an employer, the amount of a raise above your previous salary, money gifts, and an income tax refund.

4. **Keep making installment payments** If you make installment re-payments on a consumer debt, you have an unusual opportunity to save. After making the last payment on the debt, simply con-tinue to make payments—to your savings account. You will build up funds quickly over a few months.

5. **Scrimp one month per year** If one month a year you make a concerted effort to scrimp on all expenses, you can accumulate a sizable amount of money for savings and investment. To do this, cut back on some planned expenditures and question every pos-sible variable expense. Knowing that this level of frugality will end after thirty days will help motivate you toward success.

Setting Investment Goals

Investment goals are partially based on motivations, which are some-times hard to pinpoint. For example, what exactly is a "feeling of secu-rity"? The goal of "being financially successful over a lifetime" is a laudable objective, but it is not specific enough. Investment goals need to be specific so you can (1) prioritize them and (2) know when you have achieved them. Having a single purpose for each goal gives clarity to your investment efforts. For example, Randall Allman of Bakersfield, California, wants retirement income of $6,000 from his investments, a clear, single-purpose goal. Randall's second goal of trading in his sail-boat for a larger boat within three years is also clear, but because it might conflict with his investing for retirement, Randall needs to prioritize the two goals.

To clarify and achieve your investment goals, you need to consider the dollar amount of the goal, the maturity date for the goal, invest-ment income versus growth, investment liquidity and safety, invest-ment risk versus return, and your risk disposition.

Dollar Amount of Goal

It is not too difficult to place a dollar value on a current goal of buying an automobile, a sailboat, or a home, but it can be a problem to estimate the dollar value of a future goal.

Assume that Elaine Arno of Columbus, Georgia, finds that the home she wants to buy currently costs $100,000 and decides to make a

20 percent down payment. If she buys it today she will need to put $20,000 down. What if she waits a year or more? If prices on homes rise five percent per year, she will need a larger amount for a down payment. In one year the price would rise to $105,000 ($100,000 × 1.05), requiring a 20 percent down payment of $21,000 ($105,000 × .20). In two years the price would be $110,250 ($105,000 × 1.05) and the down payment $22,050; in three years the price would be $115,763 ($110,250 × 1.05), and the down payment $23,153. In order to have the proper amount of funds available to reach her goal when she decides to buy, Elaine must try to estimate the dollar amount she needs.

Maturity Date for Goal

The preceding example shows that as prices rise the longer the time period for goal achievement, the more money will be required. Thus, if you set too long a maturity date for your goal, it could become too difficult to reach. Set maturity dates that are not too unreasonably far in the future. Three years is probably enough time to save for an expensive automobile, and five years is enough time to set up a sizable fund to make a down payment on a home. (See Appendix A1 for illustrations of calculations for lump sum investments and Appendix A3 for calculations for annual investments.)

Investment Income Versus Growth

As we discussed, returns on investments take the form of current income from dividends, interest, rent, and/or capital gains realized through growth in the value of the asset. The likely investment goal of retired persons would be income rather than growth, since they probably need additional money for living expenses. Younger persons might choose growth as an investment goal. Earning extra income is always nice, but the possibility of long-term growth in the value of an investment could be more appealing. Investing in a small company in the high-technology field, for example, could be an alternative that pays little or no dividends but has promising potential for growth. For most investments, there is a tradeoff between growth and income. Investments with high growth potential often pay little income; investments that pay substantial income generally have little or no growth potential.

Investment Liquidity

Occasionally you might urgently need cash, and at that moment liquidity is very important. *Liquidity* is the speed and ease with which an asset can be converted to cash. Cash is 100 percent liquid, a check slightly less. It usually takes a considerable amount of time to sell real estate holdings. If you are forced to quickly convert an asset to cash, you may have to accept a selling price lower than you expected.

Investment Risk Versus Return

Risk is the uncertainty that the yield on an investment will deviate from what is expected. Placing money in a federally insured savings account is virtually a no-risk situation, as the government guarantees both the principal and the yield. Buying stock in a corporation is riskier since no one guarantees the future success of a company. For most investments, the greater the risk, the greater the possible yield.

<table>
<tr><td>

Your Risk Disposition

</td><td>

Have you ever known someone who received a substantial inheritance and quickly lost it on poor investments? This happens when people forget to match their financial decisions with their usual manner of thinking, feeling, and acting. For example, many people are simply unwilling to take much risk and probably would lose sleep at night worrying about investments made in the risky commodities market (see Chapter 20).

As an investor, you need to determine your SSQ—"stomach and sleep quotient." What is your basic temperament or natural disposition? How strong is your stomach? How well do you sleep at night? Will your financial decisions cause loved ones to worry? Answering these questions honestly will help you match investments to your temperament.

</td></tr>
</table>

Your Investment Philosophy

If you decide to invest in any type of alternative investment, such as stocks, bonds or real estate, you need to develop an ***investment philosophy***—a personal investment strategy that anticipates specific returns and risks and contains tactics for accomplishing your investment goals. If you record your strategy and tactics in writing, you can avoid inconsistent investment decisions.

The financial goal of having a certain rate of return is accompanied by varied degrees of risk. If your goal is to obtain a very high return, and thus to accept a high degree of risk, your investment philosophy is *speculative.* You could be characterized as a "risk seeker." Your tactics might be to place most of your investment funds in a single stock in the hope that it will rise sharply and then to sell those shares in ninety days to have money to invest elsewhere unless the price has risen 10 percent (which would be an annual rate of more than 40 percent). You must be willing to suffer substantial temporary losses, perhaps a downward swing in price of 30 percent, with the expectation that an even stronger upswing in price might occur in the near future.

If your investment philosophy is *moderate,* you invite only a fair amount of risk. Your tactics might include selling stocks when the price has risen 20 percent, selling if value drops by 20 percent, and spreading your investment funds among three or four stocks.

If you have a *conservative* investment philosophy, you accept less risk and are generally rewarded with low rates of return. You could be characterized as a "risk averter." Your tactics could include selling stocks when the price has risen 15 percent, selling if value drops by 15 percent, holding bonds until maturity or a 15 percent rise is realized, and spreading your investment funds among several alternatives in different industries.

Choosing Alternative Investments

Two of the most important decisions you must consider when choosing alternative investments are making lending versus owning investments and making short-term versus long-term investments.

Lending Versus Owning

You can invest money in two ways, by lending and by owning. You can earn interest income by lending money to banks, credit unions, savings and loan associations, governments (treasury bonds), businesses (corporate bonds), mortgage-backed securities, and life insurance companies (cash value policies). Lending investments generally have both a fixed maturity and a fixed income. With a *fixed maturity*, the borrower agrees to repay the principal to you on a specific date. With a *fixed income*, the borrower agrees to pay you a specific rate of return for use of the principal. What people like most about lending investments is being confident that they will receive a certain amount of interest income for a specific period and that all the loaned funds will be returned to them.

The other way to invest money is through ownership. You can buy common or preferred corporate stock (for part ownership in a corporation), purchase shares in a mutual fund company (which then invests in corporate stock), put money into your own business, buy investment property (usually through a syndicate), purchase real estate, or buy investment collectibles (such as gold, rare antiques, fine art, or stamps). Many people enjoy ownership investments, especially when the value of ownership increases.

For a lender, the return is somewhat assured. But no matter how much profit the borrower makes with your funds, you get only the fixed rate. As an investment owner, on the other hand, you face a greater possible return but also a greater risk. If your ownership is unsuccessful, you could lose your entire investment. Some forms of ownership (sole proprietorships and unlimited partnerships, for example) might even render you personally liable for ownership losses. During times of inflation, lenders often lose because the fixed maturity and fixed rate result in a fixed value of the investment. Ownership investments, however, may be a hedge against inflation as the value of most assets increases somewhat during inflationary periods.

Making Short-term Versus Long-term Investments

Most individual investors lack the expertise, time, and money to reap substantial short-term financial gains from investments (*short-term* meaning less than one year). You may find it difficult to monitor an investment carefully and too expensive to get professional advice. Or, any short-term gains may be offset by payments of sales commissions.

For these kinds of reasons, most individual investors make long-term investments, keeping funds working in the investment for two, five, or even ten years. Regardless of the length of the investment period, you should periodically re-examine your investments with an eye toward maximizing return.

Choosing from among Alternative Investments

This chapter on investment fundamentals provides the tools of analysis to permit you to decide which types of alternatives probably suit your needs. Should you lend or own? Do you prefer short-term or long-term investments? The following six chapters examine the details of alternative investments to enable you to make wise financial decisions.

You will observe that stocks and bonds are the most popular of all alternative investments and each is examined separately in the next two chapters. Chapter 17 delves into the complexities of buying and selling securities and outlines many successful tactics of profitable investing. Chapter 18 covers the important subject of mutual funds as an investment. Millions of Americans have been turning to this alternative in recent years. No textbook on personal finance would be complete without an examination of real estate. The upcoming chapter on this alternative (Chapter 19) does not take the point of view of real estate for personal use (see Chapter 9) but covers real estate as an investment. Finally, the subject of high risk investments (such as gold, diamonds, and options) is examined in Chapter 20.

Two important points should be noted. First, in *all* investment chapters, we will provide you with enough details to help decide which alternatives are suitable for you. Second, we also provide specific guidelines on when each investment should be sold. In sum, your goal in these chapters should be actually to learn enough about alternative investments to make your own wise investment decisions.

Factors Affecting the Rate of Return

Several factors affect the rate of return on an investment: the risk and yield relationship, various types of risks, diversification, leverage, taxes, and inflation. Each of these is discussed below.

Risk and Yield Relationship

On the average, the greater the potential risk of an investment, the greater the potential yield. Pure risk, concerning the uncertainty of events occurring with no potential for gain was discussed in Chapter 10. The risk referred to here, however, is *speculative risk,* which involves potential for gain as well as loss. Common stock, for example, may rise or fall in value; whether it will rise or fall is an unknown. Since this feeling of speculation surrounds many alternative investments, many people choose conservatively to keep their risks small; others who want higher yields accept greater unknowns and higher risks.

Figure 14–1 diagrams the relationship between risk and knowledge of the future. Where the curve intersects the vertical axis, there is total knowledge of the future and thus virtually no risk. An investment in U.S. Treasury bonds could be placed near this point as they are loans from the people to the government and are guaranteed with the full

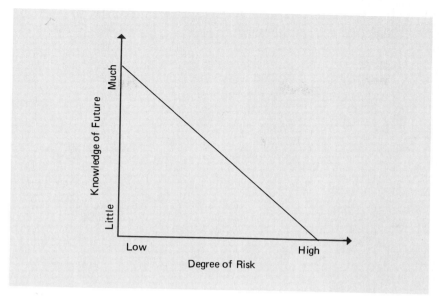

FIGURE 14–1
Risk and Knowledge Relationship

faith and credit of the United States government. A bond issued by a large corporation with a long history of financial stability would be slightly riskier because it carries no government guarantee. To make up for increased risk, the yield on the corporate bond must be higher. Figure 14–2 gives sample investments with increasing degrees of risk relative to yield. The government bond has virtually no risk and the corporate bond has a slight risk. Most corporate common stock would be placed further along the risk curve, and ownership in a new business to convert coal to a liquid-burning state, a highly speculative investment, even further.

Types of Investment Risks

There are eight major types of risks in investments.

1. **Inflation risk**   During inflationary times, there is a risk that the general price level will rise faster than the value of an investment. Cash held in a savings account will lose purchasing power unless the interest rate earned is significantly higher than the inflation rate; this is because you *also* pay taxes on income earned. Investments in bonds suffer similarly; if the interest received is less than inflation, the principal itself declines in purchasing power.

2. **Deflation risk**   Should prices decline, as has happened a few times in U.S. history, the value of the dollar actually increases. Houses and other real estate investments are subject to deflation, as their values might decline.

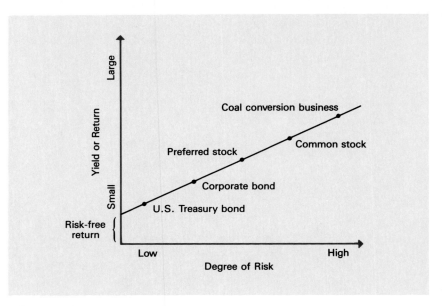

FIGURE 14–2
Investment Risk and Yield Relationship

3. **Interest rate risk** Because of fluctuations in the level of interest rates in the economy as a whole, there is some risk that an investment will lose part of the value of the principal if the investment has to be sold. This can occur with fixed interest rate obligations such as bonds and preferred stocks, investments that have an almost guaranteed dollar income. For example, suppose that a corporation sells you a twenty-year, $1,000 bond at 6 percent. This obligates the corporation to pay you $60 a year ($1,000 × .06) and to repay the $1,000 principal in twenty years. Should bond interest rates rise substantially, perhaps to 8 percent, the market value of the 6-percent bond will decline. Other investors could buy a new bond for $1,000 that pays 8 percent or offer to buy your old bond for $750, which would raise the effective yield of 6 percent to 8 percent ($60 ÷ $750).

4. **Financial risk** You might expect that most investments are profitable, but this is not the case. There is some financial risk that the investment will be unable to pay a return to the investor. A corporation could experience difficult financial times and not be able to pay interest on corporate bonds or dividends on shares of stock. And there is always the financial risk that the company could go bankrupt. An insured savings account carries minimal financial risk.

5. **Market volatility risk** Even in times of economic prosperity, the value of individual investments can change dramatically. Gener-

ally, prices on real estate do not fluctuate nearly as much as prices on corporate stocks do. Residential real estate in a suburban area is likely to increase steadily, whereas the value of stock in a food company could change sharply when a new product is successfully introduced to the public.

6. **Liquidity risk** The ease with which an investment can be sold or bought also presents a risk. In times of economic recession, it is usually quite difficult to sell real estate since so few buyers can afford to make such a purchase. Coin and stamp collections also might be difficult to sell. Common stocks, on the other hand, usually have good liquidity.

7. **Marketability risk** This risk has to do with regaining the amount of principal or expected value in an investment. If you have to sell an asset quickly, you may not be able to regain the amount of money you originally invested. Selling real estate swiftly often requires the seller to make price concessions.

8. **Political risk** The political environment can often sharply affect the value of investments. Imposition of wage and price controls, government efforts to settle labor strikes, and election of officials who change defense-spending and tariff policies can all affect investments negatively or positively.

Table 14–1 summarizes the degrees of each type of risk for each type of investment. You may want to refer back to this table as you read in more detail about these types of investments in the following chapters.

TABLE 14–1
Types of Investments and Degrees of Risk

Type of Investment	Type of Risk							
	Inflation	Deflation	Interest Rate	Financial	Market Volatility	Market-ability	Liquidity	Political
Savings account	Medium	Low	Medium	Low	Low	Low	Low	Low
Money market funds	Medium	Low	Low	Low	Low	Low	Low	Low
Insurance (cash value)	Medium	Low	Low	Low	Low	Low	Low	Low
Insurance annuities	High	Low	Low	Low	Low	Low	Low	Low
Bonds (best quality)	High	Low	High	Low	Medium	Low	Medium	Low
Bonds (high quality)	High	Low	High	Medium	Medium	Low	Medium	Low
Common stocks	Medium	Medium	Medium	Medium	High	Low	High	High
Mutual funds	Medium	Medium	Medium	Medium	High	Low	High	High
Real estate	Low	Low	Low	Low	Low	Medium	Medium	Low
Precious metals, options, and commodities	Low	Low	Low	High	High	Low	High	High

Diversification

Diversification is the process of reducing risk by spreading investment monies among several alternative investments. It also results in a potential rate of return on all the investments that is generally lower than the return on a particular investment alternative. If you were absolutely sure that the rate of inflation would decline in future years, you might be wise to put $10,000 into high-yielding corporate bonds (perhaps paying 10 percent) before the rate of return slipped lower. If you were wrong and inflation went up, pulling bond rates upward too, the value of your bonds would decline sharply. (If the rate of return on new bonds rose to 12 percent, the market value of a $10,000, 10-percent bond might drop to $8,333). The first column in Table 14–1 shows that bonds have a high risk to inflation and that real estate has a low risk to inflation (real estate prices generally rise during inflationary times). By making investments in several areas, say, in both bonds and real estate, you can reduce your risk.

Other types of diversification will be discussed as appropriate in the following chapters. For example, in buying common stocks, you might want to purchase a speculative stock along with an income stock to reduce the possibility of losing everything with the speculative stock (see Chapter 15, "Investing in Stocks"). The potential return is reduced somewhat by diversification, since in this example some funds are invested in the income stock rather than all monies put in the speculative stock. The lower return on investment is the opportunity cost of reducing the risk of loss.

Leverage

Another factor that can affect return on investment is *leverage*. This is using borrowed funds to make an investment in which the goal is to earn a rate of return in excess of the after-tax costs of borrowing. Investing in real estate to rent out provides an illustration of leverage. Assume you can buy a small office building either by making a $10,000 down payment and financing the $90,000 remainder or by paying $100,000 cash. Assuming that rental income is $13,200 annually ($1,100 per month) and your income tax bracket is 28 percent, it would be better to use credit to buy the building, as Table 14–2 shows.

There is a potentially negative side to using leverage. In the example above, if you used credit, you would need a rental income of more than $11,000 to be able to pay the mortgage loan payments. A couple of vacant months and/or expensive repairs to the building could result in a losing situation. Even though some cash losses are tolerable for tax purposes (as shown in later chapters), you can become financially overextended by using leverage for investments, a risk that you should consider.

A plus for using leverage is that capital gains can occur, sharply boosting the return on the investment. Assume that at the end of one year the building has appreciated 10 percent and you could sell it for $110,000 (excluding commission costs). If you had bought it for $100,000 cash and then sold it for $110,000, the capital gain on the sale would be 10 percent ($10,000 return ÷ $100,000 originally invested).

TABLE 14-2
Illustration of Leverage (Buying Real Estate as an Investment)

	Pay Cash	Use Credit
Purchase price of office building	$100,000	$100,000
Amount borrowed	0	90,000
Amount invested	$100,000	$ 10,000
Rental income	$ 13,200	$ 13,200
Minus tax-deductible interest (12.5%, 30-year loan on $90,000)	0	11,113
Net earnings before taxes	$ 13,200	$ 2,087
Minus income tax liability (28% bracket)	3,696	584
Rental earnings after taxes	$ 9,504	$ 1,503
	$ 9,504	$ 1,503
	÷ 100,000	÷ 10,000
Percentage return on amount invested	9.5%	15.0%

However, if you had bought it using credit, the capital gain would be 100 percent ($10,000 return ÷ $10,000 originally invested). Other examples of leveraged investments appear in Chapter 17.

Taxes

You should analyze investments carefully in terms of (1) annual income, (2) possible capital gains, and (3) the after-tax effects of total investment income. Sending your investment income on a one-way trip to Washington guarantees a lower rate of return on investments than if you could keep some tax-free dollars. Increasing the after-tax return on your investments requires an understanding of the marginal tax rate and taxable versus tax-free income.

Marginal Tax Rate   This concept was first discussed in Chapter 7, but a reminder from the perspective of after-tax return is appropriate. In the example illustrated in Table 14–2, whether you pay $100,000 cash or make a down payment of $10,000 for the building, you will receive $13,200 in before-tax rental income. If you pay cash, you earn a before-tax rate of return of 13.2 percent ($13,200 ÷ $100,000). If you use credit, you have expenses of $11,113, which reduce before-tax income to $2,087. On an investment of $10,000, this provides a before-tax rate of return of 20.9 percent ($2,087 ÷ $10,000). In this example, the rental income received is subject to a 28 percent marginal tax rate, which reduces the respective yields to 9.5 percent and 15.0 percent.

Taxable Versus Tax-free Income   Chapter 7 covered various techniques of legal tax avoidance, including tax-free investment. Many states and municipalities issue bonds that are exempt from federal and state income taxes. (See Chapter 16, "Investing in Bonds," for more details.)

Investors should consider the after-tax return of comparable taxable and tax-free alternatives. For example, Nancy Jeries of Ames, Iowa, is comparing a $1,000 corporate bond paying a 7.6 percent return with a municipal bond paying 5.9 percent. Since she is in the 28 percent marginal tax bracket, $21 of the $76 interest earned annually on the corporate bond would go to income taxes ($76 × .28). This provides Nancy with an after-tax return of 5.5 percent ($76 − $21 = $55 ÷ $1,000). The municipal bond annual interest of $59 is exempt from federal income taxes. Nancy should choose the municipal bond because the after-tax return is 5.9 percent ($59 ÷ $1,000), which is .4 percent higher than the corporate bond (5.9 percent − 5.5 percent). Whether you should invest in tax-free opportunities depends upon the yields available and your marginal tax rate.

Inflation

You should recognize by now that inflation reduces the purchasing power of the dollar. Inflation is an extremely important factor for investors to consider because it consistently takes from the unwise and gives to the wise. Consider Richard Belisle of Shepherdstown, West Virginia, who thought he had a hedge against inflation by depositing $10,000 in a bank account paying 5 percent interest. His account earned $500 interest during the year, but unfortunately the inflation rate was 6 percent. Richard's bank won, since it wisely invested his deposit at rates somewhat above 6 percent.

Many investors expect inflation to continue, and the only question is how quickly prices will rise. During periods of high inflation, the value of many assets declines and the value of others rises. Historically, common stocks and real estate rise with inflation over several years. However, during the double-digit inflation of the late 1970s and early 1980s, stocks did poorly while real estate values increased sharply.

Calculating the Real Return (after Taxes and Inflation) on Investments

Step 1—Identify anticipated total return.
Perhaps you think that a stock is expected to pay a total return of 11% in one year, including current income and capital gain.

Step 2—Subtract the impact of your marginal tax rate on anticipated total return to get net return after taxes.
You are in the 28 percent federal income tax bracket, so .28 × .11 = .0308, which when subtracted from 11 percent total return leaves a net return after taxes of 7.9 percent (.11 − .0308 = 7.92, or 7.9 percent).

Step 3—Subtract estimate of anticipated inflation from net return after taxes to get real return (after taxes and inflation).
You estimate annual inflation of 5 percent for the coming year; therefore 7.9 percent − 5 percent = 2.9 percent. Moreover, your anticipated total return provides a real return of but 2.9 percent after taxes and inflation.

TABLE 14-3

Common Investment Choices and Real Returns (after Taxes and Inflation) for People with Different Investment Philosophies*

Conservative (2–3%)	Moderate (4–5%)	Speculative (6%+)
Fixed-dollar investments (Chapter 4)	Growth stocks (Chapter 15)	Speculative stocks (Chapter 15)
Blue-chip income stocks (Chapter 15)	Mutual funds (Chapter 18)	Options, rights, warrants and futures (Chapter 20)
Preferred stocks (Chapter 15)	Real estate (Chapter 19)	Raw land real estate (Chapter 19)
Treasury bonds (Chapter 16)	Corporate and municipal bonds (Chapter 16)	Junk bonds (Chapter 16)
Municipal bonds (Chapter 16)	Unit investment trusts (Chapter 18)	Precious metals (Chapter 20)
	Real estate investment trusts (Chapter 18)	
	Collectibles (Chapter 20)	

* For example, a moderate investor may invest in a well-known growth common stock, hoping to receive an annual total return of 11% (perhaps 2% from cash dividends and 9% in price appreciation), which might provide a real return of 2.9% after subtracting 3.1% for income taxes (11.0% × expected marginal tax bracket of .28%) and 5% for the effects of inflation.

Bonds lose value during inflationary times because they are fixed-dollar investments that offer the return of a certain number of dollars rather than dollars with their original purchasing power.

The challenge to you is to analyze carefully the risks of making alternative investments to earn the highest possible *real return on investment* (the yield after subtracting the effects of taxes and inflation). This is difficult to accomplish during periods of high inflation, but it is important if you expect to stay ahead of inflation. Table 14–3 shows common investment choices and real returns for people with different investment philosophies.

Achieving Investment Goals

Whether you achieve your investment goals helps determine how financially successful you will be. Below are some pitfalls to avoid in your financial behavior and some guidelines to follow toward successful investing.

How Not to Succeed Financially

There are ten major reasons why people fail financially.

1. Procrastination You will have a difficult time attaining financial success if you keep spending your income and continually postpone planning and implementing savings and investments programs.

2. **Lack of specific goals** Although saving may give you feelings of security and success, to provide yourself with a true incentive to save and invest you must make specific short- and long-term financial goals and prioritize them.

3. **Lack of commitment to pursue goals** You may be able to list your financial goals but lack the commitment or determination to reach them. For example, if you need to save $150 a month for a year to make a substantial down payment on an automobile, then twelve months of saving are necessary, not eleven or ten or nine. Although a financial emergency might prevent you from saving during a particular month, your commitment to your goal will enable you to make up the difference over the following months.

4. **Ignorance about investments** With all the information available on different types of investments there is no excuse for not learning as much as you can.

5. **Ignoring investments** Many people simply make an investment and look back a few years later to see if it has gained value. Such optimism is foolhardy. You need to keep track of the annual rate of return of each of your investments.

6. **Following ill-advised tips** Every year there is a new investment fad. Following ill-advised tips, whims, and hunches can quickly deplete your investment funds. So, investigate before you invest.

7. **Ignorance about taxes** Understanding how your marginal tax bracket works and the impact of tax-free investments can help you make wise investment decisions.

8. **Payment of high insurance premiums** An overly insured person may not be able to afford to invest. You may determine that some insurance protection is a necessity, but make sure that you do not purchase too much insurance or pay exorbitant premiums for it.

9. **Lack of diversification** People who put all or most of their funds into just one kind of investment hope for a world that does not change. Some kinds of investments are better than others depending on the climate of the economy. Economic change is absolutely certain, and you must establish strategies and tactics to diversify investments to control risks.

10. **Lack of discipline in following investment tactics** You should set your own tactical guidelines for taking profits or cutting losses and for moving into and out of particular investments, and you should follow them. Say you decide to sell an investment when its value rises by 25 percent, sell if its value slides 20 percent, and sell regardless of value during the late stages of a sharply rising market. If you fail to follow your guidelines, you invite considerably more risk and an increased likelihood of losses or smaller gains. For example, assume that your investment increased 30 percent in value and you didn't sell, hoping instead

to see the value increase by 40 or even 50 percent. In reality, your gain could drop swiftly to perhaps 5 percent as the market declines after peaking.

How to Succeed in Investments

Getting ahead financially through investments requires willingness, ability, and discipline. Willingness involves understanding your own motivations. Ability has to do with knowing alternative investments, finding investment funds, and making intelligent investment decisions. And discipline describes the courage to act responsibly in financial matters. You will not accumulate savings very quickly without the discipline to budget expenses carefully; success in investments requires disciplined effort, too. To achieve your investment goals, follow the three steps described below.

1. **Prioritize investment goals** Your first task is to prioritize your goals. This requires making decisions on what is important and what is not. Figure 14–3 illustrates a list of goals for Ellen Campbell of Palos Verdes, California, who decided to stop her habit of "spend, spend, spend" because it was beginning to hurt her financially. Ellen has only $1,000 in a money market fund and no real investments. As shown in Figure 14–3, she recorded her three most important goals—savings or investment of $1,200 per year, a new automobile, and a European vacation—and excluded others that were less important.

2. **Calculate the amount of investment needed annually** Ellen's next task is to calculate how much she will need to invest annually to achieve her goals. For her first goal, she simply records $1,200 in the last column. For her second goal, she estimates that with a trade-in a new car will cost $10,000. Using Appendix A1 and assuming that inflation is 6 percent, Ellen finds the inflation factor 1.124 (at the intersection of 6 percent and two years) and multiplies it by the current amount needed ($10,000) to determine the inflated amount needed ($11,240) in two years. Ellen thinks that her money market fund will continue to pay an estimated return of 8 percent. Using Appendix A3, she finds the factor 2.080 for two years; this factor divided into the inflated amount needed ($11,240) gives an annual investment amount of $5,404. Ellen calculates her third goal in a similar manner. Assuming that vacation costs will rise 8 percent (faster than 6-percent inflation), Ellen figures, using Appendix A1, that a $4,000 trip will cost $5,876 in five years. Using Appendix A3, she finds the factor 5.867 (at 8 percent and five years), this factor divided into the inflated amount needed ($5,876) gives an annual investment amount of $1,002. Adding together the three annual amounts ($1,200 + $5,404 + $1,002) gives a total of $7,606. This will require Ellen to put $634 a month ($7,606 ÷ 12) into her money market fund.

Goals	(1) Current Amount Needed	(2) Years Before Funds Are Needed	(3) Assumed Rate of Inflation	(4) Inflation Factor [a]	(5) Inflated Amount Needed (1 × 4)	(6) Estimated Return on Investment	(7) Return Factor [b]	(8) Annual Investment Amount Needed (5 ÷ 7)
Save/Invest $1,200 a year	—	—	—	—	—	—	—	$1,200
New automobile $10,000, plus trade-in	$10,000	2	6%	1.124	$11,240	8%	2.080	$5,404
European vacation (two weeks)	$4,000	5	8%	1.469	$5,876	8%	5.867	$1,002

FIGURE 14–3
Goals Worksheet for Ellen Campbell

3. **Re-evaluate investment goals**   Because of her habit of spending virtually all her income each month, it may be difficult for Ellen to save $634 a month. She may have to cut back on entertainment, food, clothing, even vacations. She may have to find another source of funds, perhaps a part-time job.

Ellen might also want to change her investment goals. For example, if she drops the idea of a vacation, she would need $1,002 less annually, or about $84 less a month. Or if she drops the goal of an automobile and continues to plan for a vacation, she would need only $184 a month ($1,200 + $1,002 = $2,202 ÷ 12 months).

Summary of Investment Characteristics

The next six chapters will examine alternative investments available to most investors. Table 14–4 summarizes the characteristics of each investment. As you read later chapters you may want to look back at this table for perspective on the alternatives.

Summary

1. Investing requires an understanding of the motives for investing as well as the types of investments.
2. Some suggestions for getting money to invest include paying yourself first, using forced savings plans, and saving windfalls.
3. Having specific goals that can be prioritized, placing accurate estimates of the dollar amounts needed on the goals, and matching one's disposition toward risk to compatible types of investments will help in the achievement of investment goals.
4. Investors with different investment philosophies must choose between lending or owning their investments as well as between short-term and long-term investments.
5. The factors affecting the rate of return on investments include risk/yield relationship, types of risk, diversification, leverage, taxes, and inflation.
6. Steps necessary to achieve investment goals include listing investment goals in priority order, calculating the annual investment amounts needed, and doing some re-evaluation to find appropriate amounts needed.

TABLE 14–4
Characteristics of Common Investments

	Financial Risk	Protection Against Inflation	Yield Range in Recent Years	Yield Relative to Alternative Investments	Relative Yields During Economic Prosperity	Relative Yields During Economic Decline
Savings accounts	Low	None	4½–6%	5½%	5½%	4½%
Savings bonds	Low	None	5–7%	6½%	6½%	5%
Certificates of deposit	Low	None	6–16%	7½%	10%	5%
Money market funds	Low	Some	6–18%	8%	12%	5½%
Insurance (cash value	Low	None	4–8%	6%	6%	4%
Insurance annuities	Low	None	4½–8%	6%	6%	4½%
Treasury bills and notes	Low	None	5–16%	8%	13%	6%
Treasury bonds	Low	None	5–15%	7½%	11½%	5½%
Municipal bonds (best quality)	Low	None	3½–13%	5%	9%	5½%
Corporate bonds (best quality	Low	None	5½–14½%	7%	11%	5½%
Corporate bonds (high quality)	Medium	None	6–15%	7½%	12%	5¾%
Common stocks	Medium to high	Good	0–20%	5%	6%	4%
Preferred stocks	Low to medium	Good	0–12%	6%	6%	2%
Mutual funds	Medium	Good	0–16%	5%	6%	2%
Real estate	Medium to high	Good	4–20%	9%	10%	4%
Real estate investment trust	High	Good	0–20%	9%	12%	5%
Precious metals, options and commodities	High	Good	0–30%	11%	18%	16%

Minimum Initial Investment Required	Associated Costs and Commissions to Start	Personal Management Time Required	Liquidity/ Maturity	Tax Aspect
$1	—	None	Immediate to 90 days	—
$25	—	Some	Varies with interest rates	On some bonds taxes are deferred until maturity
$200–$500	—	Some	30 days to 8 years	—
$500	—	None	Immediate	—
$200–$400	30–55% of 1st premium is commission	None	14 days	Refunded cash value has already had taxes paid on it by the investor
$10,000	—	None	1 month to 10 years	Income taxes deferred until payments are received
$10,000	$20+	Some	Immediate to 1 year	—
$1,000	$20+	Some	Immediate to 30 years	—
$1,000	½% or less	Some	Immediate to 30 years	Interest is tax-free; capital gains/ losses upon sale
$1,000	½% or less	Some	Immediate to 30 years	Income taxes on interest; capital gains/losses upon sale for bonds issued on or before 7/18/84; otherwise gains are fully taxable
$1,000	½% or less	Some	Immediate to 30 years	
$100 or less	2–18%	Some to much	1 to 2 weeks	Capital gains/losses upon sale
$100 or less	2–18%	Some	1 to 2 weeks	—
$100 or less	8–9%, but only on load funds	Some to much	1 to 2 weeks	—
$2,000–$10,000	—	Much	2 weeks to 2 years	Some income tax sheltered because of depreciation and other costs; capital gains/losses upon sale
$5,000	—	Some	1 month to 1 year	Same as for real estate
$500 or less	1–3%	Much	Intermediate	Capital gains/losses upon sale

7. Numerous investment alternatives are available to most investors that typically differ on such characteristics as financial risk, protection against inflation, yield, personal management time required, and liquidity/maturity.

Modern Money Management

The Johnsons Want to Start an Investment Program

Harry and Belinda's finances have improved in recent months, even though they have incurred new debts for an automobile loan and a condominium. This has come about because they cut back a little in their spending on discretionary items (clothing, food, and entertainment) and because Harry recently got a sizable raise after changing employers. The new job is assistant head designer at Medical Facilities Incorporated, which pays $6,000 more than his other job, and it is one mile closer to home, which reduces Harry's commuting time.

The Johnsons have decided to concentrate on getting a solid investment program underway while they have two incomes available. They are willing to accept a moderate amount of risk and expect to invest between $200 and $400 a month over the next five years. Assuming that they have an adequate savings program, respond to the questions below.

1. In what types of investments (choose only two) might they place the first $2,000 for that purpose? (Review Table 14–4 for available options and consider the types of investment risks apparent in the options.) Give reasons for your choices.

2. In what types of investments might they place the next $4,000 for that purpose? Why?

3. What types of investments should they choose for the next $10,000? Why?

Key Words and Concepts

Review Questions

1. Identify the four reasons why most people are motivated to invest.
2. What are the prerequisites to investing?
3. Distinguish between savings and alternative investments.
4. Distinguish between current income and capital gain.
5. Name five ways you can get money to invest.
6. Why do investment goals need to be specific?
7. Distinguish among the three types of investment philosophies.
8. Explain the importance of assigning a specific dollar amount to an investment goal.
9. Compare and contrast returns on investments from income with returns on growth.
10. Explain the difference between the risk of buying stock in a corporation and the risk of putting money in a bank savings account.
11. Explain the concepts of the liquidity and safety of investments.
12. Explain how your ability to handle risk relates to the investment process.
13. Describe the difference between lending investments and owning investments and give examples of each.
14. Why do more investors make long-term, rather than short-term, investments?
15. Describe the relationship between risk and knowledge of the future as it relates to investments.
16. Describe the relationship between risk and yield as it relates to investments.
17. List and briefly describe four types of investment risks.
18. Explain the importance of diversification.
19. Identify the advantage of using leverage in the investment process.
20. How can a knowledge of taxes influence investment decisions?
21. Describe the effect of inflation on investments and the bearing it has on investment decisions.
22. How is the real return on investment calculated, and why is it important to know?
23. Explain four reasons why people fail financially.
24. Summarize how to succeed in investments.

Case Problems

1. Gerald Beardsley of San Luis Obispo, California, has worked for four years for a large accounting firm. He has earned a fairly good income and has had bonuses of more than $1,000 every year. Gerald feels frustrated because he has not started to make any investments. He simply seems to spend too much every month and has less than $400 in savings. Often he has to get cash advances on his VISA card. Gerald owes the credit union at work more than $2,000, which he borrowed to pay off some bills last summer. Following the prerequisites for investing, how would you advise Gerald on these matters?
   a. Living within his means
   b. Having a savings program
   c. Having a line of credit
   d. Having insurance protection

2. Susan Hayenga of Galveston, Texas, is hoping to continue her savings and investment program for three more years before making a down payment on a condominium. The home that interests her is currently priced at $70,000.
   a. If inflation is 5 percent for each of the next three years, how much will the condominium probably cost? (See Appendix A1.)
   b. If she wants to make a 20 percent down payment now, how much money will she need at that time?
   c. Should Susan invest her money during the next three years by lending or owning? Why?

3. John Knox of Fennimore, Wisconsin, has a sister, Kate, who is dissatisfied with the low rate of return she is earning on the $4,000 in her savings account and she has asked John for advice. Kate says that she is a bit nervous about risky things and would not want to lose any of her money in some foolish venture. Further, she says she views the $4,000 as money for long-term investment, perhaps even to be used in her retirement years. She has been told by a friend at work to consider investing in bonds or common stocks. If you were John, explain how you would advise your sister about the following:
   a. The financial risk of bonds and common stocks
   b. Interest rate risk
   c. Liquidity risk

Suggested Readings

"Risk Takers." *U.S. News and World Report,* January 12, 1987, pp. 60–67. Includes self-test to measure financial risk-taking potential.

"A Rough Road Ahead." *Time,* May 25, 1987. Rising inflation threatens economic growth.

"The Sky Is Not Falling." *Gentlemen's Quarterly,* March 1987, pp. 183–186. Logical thinking shows the future to be kind to investors.

"Taking the Plunge: How to Start Investing." *Changing Times,* April 1987, pp. 22–28. Suggestions on how to begin investing, including how to chose a stockbroker.

"Where to Get Great Investment Advice for Free," *Money,* September 1987, p. 131. Information on how to lower the cost of getting investment advice by tapping sources that are free.

"Will the Real Yield Please Stand Up." *Changing Times,* January 1987, pp. 125–132. How to spot the correct yields among all the confusing advertisements: Some tricks of the trade.

CHAPTER 15

Investing in Stocks

OBJECTIVES

After reading this chapter, the student should be able to

1. explain what stocks are and how they are used by corporations and investors.
2. define twelve important stock investment terms.
3. classify stocks according to several descriptive categories.
4. discuss three theories about what affects the price of stocks.
5. describe advantages and disadvantages of owning common stock.
6. explain why preferred stock is probably not a good investment for the average investor.

A fter you have accumulated a certain amount of savings, your good feeling of financial security may be accompanied by a new sense of frustration. If inflation is higher than the after-tax rate of return on savings, you will realize that you are losing ground. Even if inflation is just less than the after-tax yield on savings, you will be gaining by only a very small amount. Consequently, you may begin to think about increasing risk so as to increase yield. This requires an alternative investment to savings.

The variety of investments available offers you numerous opportunities to gain substantial returns on your money. Of course, there is the possibility that you can lose money, too. This increased risk keeps many people from considering investments other than savings. However, if you increase your knowledge about investments and choose investment alternatives with common sense, you can increase returns significantly while increasing risks only slightly.

Common stocks are investments with opportunities for both conservative investors and speculators. In this chapter we begin by examining what stocks are and how they are used. A review of important investment terms follows. Next are discussed the several classifications of stocks (such as growth stocks) as well as some theories about what affects the price of stocks. Then a section on the advantages and disadvantages of common stocks will help you discover whether they are for you. Finally, the chapter examines preferred stocks and the individual investor.

What Stocks Are and How They Are Used

Stocks are shares of ownership in the assets, earnings, and future direction of a corporate form of business. Stocks finance corporate goals and represent potential income for investors.

Forms of Business Ownership

There are three forms of business ownership. The *sole proprietorship* is a business owned by one person who is responsible for and has control over all aspects of the operation. Net profits earned are taxed as ordinary income and the owner's liability for business losses is unlimited. Most small businesses are run as sole proprietorships. Since the business could fail upon the death of the proprietor, he or she should provide for future management of the firm in a legally executed will. This topic is examined in Chapter 22, "Estate Planning."

A *partnership* is a business owned by two or more persons and operated in the interests of all partners. Net profits earned are normally taxed as ordinary income and the owners' liability for business losses is usually unlimited. The benefits of having a partner include obtaining more capital to run the business, getting additional expertise, and sharing the risks. Articles of partnership define responsibilities and restrictions and how profits and losses are to be divided. A partnership is dissolved upon the request of a partner to withdraw, incapacitation, or death.

A *corporation* is a state-chartered legal entity that can conduct business operations in its own name and be totally responsible for its actions as well as its debts. Net profits earned are taxed at corporate rates. Corporations sell shares of ownership (stock) to investors and thus have the potential to raise large sums of money for expansion. An investor's liability is limited to the amount of stock purchased. Corporations continue to exist even as many shares of ownership change hands.

Types of Corporate Stock

Since a corporation may have a great number of investors, this form of business ownership offers a company the potential to develop into a firm of some size. A corporation's financial needs may differ from time to time. To begin, a new corporation will need money for start-up *capital* (funds invested in a business enterprise). During its life, a corporation may need additional monies to expand and grow. To raise capital and finance its goals, a corporation issues different *securities* (negotiable instruments of ownership or debt). Common stock and preferred stock are securities discussed in this chapter, while bonds are examined in the next chapter.

Common Stock *Common stock* is the most basic form of ownership of a corporation. The owner of common stock—called a *shareholder* or *stockholder*—has a residual claim on the assets of the firm after those made by bondholders and preferred stockholders (discussed later). Sale of common stock conveys legal ownership of such shares to the shareholder. A corporation may have one owner or sell millions of shares to numerous owners. Each shareholder has a proportionate interest in the ownership and therefore in the income of the corporation. For example, if you own two hundred shares of a company that declares a $5 million dividend to be paid on two million outstanding shares, you will receive $2.50 per share, or $500 [($5,000,000 ÷ 2,000,000) × 200].

Each shareholder may vote to elect a board of directors, which names the principal officers of the company to set policy and run the day-to-day business of the firm. The number of votes each shareholder has depends on the proportionate number of shares owned. A shareholder's liability for business losses is limited to the amount invested in the shares of stock owned. In the case of bankruptcy, the common stockholder's equity is what is left after the claims of all debtors are met. This risk of loss is met by the potential to share in substantial profits. The common stockholder expects that (1) the corporation will be profitable enough to pay *dividends* (a share of profits distributed in cash) and that (2) there will be an increase in the market value (or market price) of the stock held (the current price that a buyer is willing to pay a willing seller).

Preferred Stock   *Preferred stock* is a special type of fixed-income ownership security in a corporation. Preferred stockholders have the legal right to assets and earnings before the claims of common stockholders but after those of bondholders. Generally, preferred stock pays a fixed dividend per share that must be paid before any dividends are made to common stockholders. Usually, preferred stockholders have no voting privileges and do not share in any extraordinary profits made by a corporation.

Concerns of the Investor

Of particular concern to the stock investor are the factors of investment income, price appreciation, and total return. Those are discussed below and then illustrated in an example.

Investment Income   The revenues of a profitable corporation generally are used to pay expenses, interest to bondholders, taxes, cash dividends to preferred stockholders, and cash dividends to common stockholders, in that order. The average corporation pays out 40 to 60 percent of its after-tax earnings in cash dividends to stockholders; the remainder, called retained earnings, is used by the company most often to facilitate growth.

Cash dividends to preferred stockholders are a set amount per share and usually remain the same each year, despite good or bad economic conditions. The common stockholder has no guarantee of income. However, most profitable companies pay common stockholders a small regular dividend on a quarterly basis until increased earnings justify paying out a higher amount. On a $30 share of Greenfield Computer's common stock, for example, the dividend for several past years might have been 30 cents quarterly, or a total of $1.20 annually. If the company has higher profits this year, the dividend might be raised to $1.90 annually. It is this cash dividend, or more accurately the anticipation of it, that is of interest to the investor. Over the years, the rate of return from cash dividends on common stocks has been between 3.5 and 5.0 percent.

Characteristics of Stockholders

- Forty-seven million persons in the United States own stock; this means that shareholders make up 20 percent of the population.

- Twenty-two and one-half million stockholders are men, 22.5 million are women, and 2 million are children.

- The median age of stockholders is forty-four.

- The median income of stockholder households is $36,800—compared to $22,400 for the whole population.

Source: New York Stock Exchange 1986 Fact Book. Used with permission.

Price Appreciation Given the low rate of return in cash dividends relative to savings accounts, you may wonder why people invest in stock. There are two reasons. First, as a company becomes more efficient and profitable, the cash dividend to common stockholders can rise. Second, the market value of the stock can also go up as more investors become interested in the company.

Total Return Many common stockholders look only at the amount of cash dividend that a corporation has paid in recent years rather than also at the potential for capital gains upon sale of stock. (Preferred stockholders rarely share in capital appreciation since their stock pays a fixed dividend.) *Total return* is the combination of the dividend yield *and* the potential capital gains. The *dividend yield* is the relationship between the current cash dividend and the cash dividend return to an investor expressed as a percentage value of a security. It is determined by dividing the dollar amount of a recent annual dividend by the current market value of the stock or purchased price if the stock is already owned. Say that Greenfield Computer's preferred stock, currently selling at $104, has an annual dividend of $8 which is a preferred stock cash dividend yield of 7.69 percent ($8 ÷ $104). Greenfield's common stock is now selling for $30 and its recent quarterly cash dividend suggests an annual dividend of $1.90; this would provide a common stock cash dividend yield of 6.3 percent ($1.90 ÷ $30).

The capital gain or *price appreciation* (net income received from the sale of capital assets beyond the expenses incurred in the purchase and sale of those assets) is actually realized when the stock is sold. Until then such gains are known as *paper profits,* or unrealized gains. If you purchased Greenfield common stock at $30 a share and sold it at $35 a share, you realized a capital gain of $5 a share. Assuming that you bought two hundred shares for a commission of $60, your cost would have been $6,060 ($30 × 200 + $60). If you sold at $35 per share and paid $70 sales commission, the proceeds would be $6,930 ($35 × 200 − $70). Your capital gain is thus $870 ($6,930 − $6,060). Based on the invested amount of $6,060, the capital gain of $870 represents a 14.4 percent yield ($870 ÷ $6,060). Thus, if you sell your Greenfield common stock after one year, the return would include $870 in capital gains plus $380 in cash dividends (200 shares × $1.90) for a total return of $1,250 or a 20.4 percent yield on $6,130 invested ($6,000 + $60 + $70 in commissions).

An alternative would be to hold the shares in anticipation of a further increase in the market value of the stock. The price of Greenfield stock could rise to $38 in the next several months. Of course, the price could also drop to $31 and reduce your gain, or it could drop to $29 and result in a capital loss if you sold the stock.

Running Paws Catfood Company—An Example To visualize better how a corporation finances corporate goals with common and preferred stock while achieving returns for stockholders, consider the following illustration. Running Paws Catfood Company, a small family business, was started in New Jersey by Linda Webtek. She developed a wonderful recipe for catfood and sold it to the local grocery store. As sales increased, she decided to incorporate the business and to expand operations. Running Paws issued 10,000 shares of stock at $10 each. Three friends bought 2,500 shares each, and Linda signed over the catfood formula and equipment to the corporation in exchange for the remaining 2,500 shares. Running Paws then had a four-person board of directors.

Capacity quickly expanded and sales increased. Soon more orders were coming in from New York City than the firm could handle. After three years, the owners of Running Paws decided to expand again. They needed an additional $100,000. They wanted to borrow it, but their business was so new that lenders demanded an extremely high interest rate. They considered issuing bonds as debts of the corporation but again found that their new business was viewed as quite risky for investors to consider making a loan through the purchase of bonds. They then decided to issue 5,000 shares of preferred stock at $20 a share, paying $1.20 a share annually. When they found that no one wanted to buy preferred shares with that yield ($1.20 ÷ $20 = 6 percent), they voted to increase the dividend to $1.80 annually, providing 9 percent yield to investors. The preferred stock then sold and the original investors retained control of the company, since the preferred stockholders could not vote for the board of directors.

Following its consistent philosophy of expanding into new markets, Running Paws soon developed new lines of catfood, which sold well. After a new plant in Los Angeles opened, sales picked up so much that the income of the four-year-old business finally exceeded expenses. That year it earned $13,000. The board of directors declared a dividend payment of $9,000 to the preferred stockholders but none for the common stockholders. The following year, net profits after taxes amounted to $28,000. Again the board paid the preferred stockholders but retained the remainder to be reinvested in the firm for continued expansion and efficiency of operations.

One of the original partners wanted out of the business and needed to sell her 2,500 shares of stock, for which she had paid $25,000 five years earlier. Fortunately, because Running Paws was beginning to show a profit as a corporation, other private investors recommended by a local stockbroker made offers to purchase her shares. The shares were sold at $16 a share: 1,500 to one investor and 1,000 to another. Now there were five owners of the common stock who voted for the board of directors.

During the following year sales were good and earnings amounted to $39,000. This time the board voted $9,000 for the preferred stockholders and $5,000 ($.50 a share) for the common stockholders and retained the remaining $25,000. After all these years, the common stockholders finally began to receive some cash dividends.

With all its success, Running Paws faced another difficult decision. To distribute its products nationally would mean another $200,000 to $250,000 in expansion costs. After much discussion, the board voted to sell an additional 10,000 shares of common stock at $25 a share. This action diluted the original owners' proportion of ownership by half, but the potential for profit was assumed to be much higher with such an increased production capacity.

It was somewhat difficult to sell all the new common stock at $25 a share since so few people knew the company had stock available for sale. Various stockbrokers took selling commissions totaling $16,000, leaving $234,000 available to use for expansion. If things continue well for Running Paws, the board might work toward having its stock listed on a regional or national stock exchange to facilitate trading of shares and enhance the image of the company.

The Language of Stock Investing

Before you study stocks as an investment, you need to understand the everyday terms in the language of stock investing. Some of these terms describe ways of measuring investments, and others describe important concepts.

Earnings per Share (EPS)

Earnings per share (EPS) is a measure of the profitability of a firm on a common stock per-share basis; it is a dollar figure determined by dividing the corporation's total after-tax annual earnings (before common stock cash dividends but after payment of dividends to preferred stockholders) by the total number of shares of common stock held by investors. Usually, companies calculate this figure and report it in the business section of many newspapers. For example, assume that Running Paws Catfood Company has a net profit of $34,000 after payment of dividends to preferred stockholders. With 20,000 shares of company stock the EPS would be $1.70 ($34,000 ÷ 20,000). Thus the company has that amount available for common stockholders, although a portion is typically retained to finance growth of the business.

Price/Earnings Ratio (P/E Ratio)

The *price/earnings ratio (P/E ratio* or *P/E multiple)* is simply a ratio of the current market value (price) of a common stock to its earnings per share (EPS), which shows in ratio form how the market is valuing the stock. For example, if the market price of a share of Running Paws stock is currently $25 and its EPS is $1.70, the P/E ratio will be 15 ($25 ÷ $1.70 = 14.7, which is rounded up to 15). This could also be called a "15-to-1 ratio," or a "P/E multiple of 15." The price/earnings ratio or multiple for many corporations is also widely reported as financial news. In general, the lower the P/E ratio, the better the value of the stock.

The only valid reason for buying stock in a company is to realize income from dividends or capital gains. The company must have substantial earnings out of which to pay cash dividends or the market value of the stock needs to rise over time. The P/E ratios for most corporations have ranged between 5 and 25. Financially successful companies that have been paying good dividends through the years might have a P/E ratio of 7 or 8. Companies that are growing, such as Running Paws, would most likely have a higher P/E ratio. High-growth and speculative companies might have P/E ratios of 40 or 50, since they are primarily interested in growth for future earnings.

Cash Dividends per Share

As mentioned, *cash dividends* are distributions in cash by a corporation usually paid out of earnings to holders of common stock. The board of directors of a firm usually declares a dividend on a quarterly basis according to the fiscal year, typically at the end of March, June, September, and December. Dividends are ordinarily paid out of current earnings. In the event of unprofitable times, the money could come from previous earnings. Occasionally, a company will borrow to pay the dividend in order to maintain a reputation of consistently paying dividends to its stockholders. Of course, later profits will be needed to repay any funds borrowed.

Dividends per share translate total cash dividends paid out by a company to common stockholders into a per-share figure. For example, Running Paws Catfood Company could declare a total cash dividend of $11,000 for the year. Thus, cash dividends per share amount to $.55 ($11,000 ÷ 20,000 shares). The *dividend yield* can also be determined. For example, the $.55 cash dividend of Running Paws Catfood Company divided by the current $25 market price reveals a dividend yield of 2.2 percent ($.55 ÷ $25). Growth and speculative companies typically pay little or no cash dividends.

Dividend Payout Ratio

The *dividend payout ratio* is a measure of the percent of total earnings paid out to the stockholders as cash dividends. For example, Running Paws Catfood Company earned $34,000, paid a cash dividend of $11,000, and retained the remaining $23,000 to facilitate growth of the company. This is a dividend payout ratio of .32 ($11,000 ÷ $34,000). For that year Running Paws paid a dividend equal to 32 percent of earnings. The remaining $23,000 is called *retained earnings*. These are amounts of past and current earnings not paid to shareholders but instead are left to accumulate and finance the goals of the company. Newer companies usually retain most of their profits to facilitate growth. An investor interested in growth would want to invest in a company with a low payout ratio.

Price-sales Ratio

The *price-sales ratio (PSR)* is a ratio obtained by dividing the total current market value of a stock (current market price multiplied by the number of shares outstanding) by the total sales over the past year. It is a measure of how good a buy a particular stock is at its current market price. For example, if Running Paws Catfood Company common stock is selling for $25 per share and there are 20,000 shares outstanding, the total current market value is $500,000. If sales of the company were $750,000 over the past year, the stock's PSR is .67 ($500,000 ÷ $750,000). The lower the ratio, the better the marketability of the stock. Market analysts generally suggest that investors avoid companies with a ratio greater than 1.5 and stay with those that have PSRs of less than .75.

Book Value

Book value is the net worth of a company, determined by subtracting the total of a company's liabilities (including preferred stock) from its assets. *Book value per share* is the book value of the company divided by the number of shares of common stock outstanding. For Running Paws, the net worth is $230,000, which when divided by 20,000 shares gives a book value per share of $11.50. This figure is relevant only in the likelihood of bankruptcy, when the firm would be liquidated. There is little relationship between the book value of a company and its earnings or market price. Note, though, that the market price for a company's common stock is usually higher than its book value. Otherwise, something is wrong with the usefulness of the assets.

Par Value

Historically, *par value* meant the dollar amount assigned to a share of stock when it was issued by a corporation. Par value is sometimes printed on the front of a share of stock. In the past, many people assumed that this was a minimum price, but par value bears no relation to the current market value of common stock. Common stocks nowadays are issued at *no par* (zero par value) or at *low par* (usually $1 or $2). Dividends paid on preferred stocks are based on the par value. After issuance, the price of preferred stocks may rise or fall but dividends paid are calculated on the original par value.

Market Value or Market Price

The *market value* or *market price* of an investment is the current price that a willing buyer would pay a willing seller for the asset. Sales commissions are not included. In stock transactions, the market value is the current price of a single share of stock. This may be estimated by looking at prices quoted in financial newspapers. True market value is the price you actually receive in selling an investment. For example, if the price of Running Paws stock has recently been selling at $25 a share, that is the market value. The true market value at the exact time you sell your Running Paws stock might be $24 a share.

Beta

An important aspect of a common stock is its price stability or volatility, a characteristic called *beta*. This is a statistically determined measure of the relative risk of a common stock compared to the market for all stocks. The historical performance of each stock has been examined in relation to stock market averages. The average for all stocks in the market is +1.0. Betas can be positive or negative. Most are positive because most stocks move in the same direction as the general market.

Most individual stocks have betas of between +0.5 and +2.0. A beta of zero suggests that the price of the stock is independent of the market, similar to a risk-free U.S. Treasury security. A beta of zero to +0.9 means that the stock price moves in the same direction as the general market but not to the same degree. A beta of +1.1 to +2.0 (or higher) indicates that the price of the security moves in the same direction as the market but by a greater percentage.

For an example, assume that you are willing to accept more risk than the general investor and you buy a stock with a beta of 1.5. If the average price of all stocks rises over time by 20 percent, it is probable that the price of the stock you chose will rise by 30 percent, which is the beta of 1.5 multiplied by the increase in the market (1.5 × 20 percent = 30 percent). Should the average market drop in value by 10 percent, the price of the stock you chose might drop by 15 percent (1.5 × 10 percent = 15 percent).

Note that the statistical averages used by brokerage firms, advisory services, and other investment companies to determine the betas for individual stocks assume that each stock is owned along with a well diversified portfolio of other stocks. A *portfolio* is a collection of securities and other instruments. Note that the performance of just one particular stock with a certain beta may be in error compared to its historical activity. On the other hand, if you own several stocks, the betas as a group are more likely to be reliable estimates of price volatility. If you own 20 different stocks, for example, it is likely that the beta for the entire portfolio will be a good indicator of volatility. This would be even more likely for a large institutional investor than for an individual.

Stock Dividends

A *stock dividend* is issuance of additional new stock certificates to existing stockholders on the basis of current proportional ownership. For example, the board of directors of Running Paws could decide to declare a 10 percent stock dividend to stockholders who currently own the 20,000 shares outstanding. Thus, if you owned 2,000 shares, the company would mail you an additional 200 shares. If you owned 55 shares, the company would mail you 5 shares and ask how you would like to handle the value of the remaining half share. You might have the option of either receiving the cash equivalent of the half share or paying for an additional half share so you could receive 6 full shares.

Many people assume that when they receive a stock dividend the value of their holdings increases. Although the price of the stock might rise for a few days after a stock dividend is declared, it then corrects for the additional shares of stock now available and drops accordingly. Assume that the 20,000 shares of Running Paws stock were currently valued at $25 per share and last year paid a cash dividend of $.55. With a stock dividend of 10 percent, there are now 22,000 shares of ownership. If you had owned 2,000 shares of the 20,000 total you would have owned 10 percent of the company. After the stock dividend, you own 2,200 shares out of a total of 22,000. You still own exactly 10 percent.

The value of a company is not affected by a stock dividend, although the value of each share is. If after declaring a stock dividend the company continues to pay the same cash dividend per share, many people may think that the additional cash dividends are the result of the stock dividend. For example, suppose Running Paws continues to pay a $.55-per-share cash dividend the year following a 10 percent stock dividend. To do this will require greater earnings because the company will be paying out $12,100 rather than $11,000, a cash dividend 10 percent greater than the previous year. Alternatively, the company could have kept the number of shares at 20,000 and simply increased the cash dividend by 10 percent. Some companies offer stock dividends knowing that some stockholders will think they have gained something of value. The result of a stock dividend is to slightly dilute stock ownership and reduce the market price of the stock by a like percentage while not changing the actual value of each stockholder's holdings.

Stock Splits

A *stock split* is a trade of a given number of old shares of stock for a certain number of newly issued shares. A two-for-one stock split usually results in a 100 percent increase in the number of shares outstanding and a 50 percent reduction in cash dividends per share. For example, in a stock split at Running Paws, the owners of the 22,000 shares (remember the 10 percent stock dividend) would be issued 44,000 new shares. If the market price of the old stock was $22.50 per share, the new stock will be worth approximately $11.25, or 50 percent, since the number of shares was doubled. A three-for-one or a three-for-two stock split might also occur.

The net effect of a stock split is threefold: (1) no change in the proportion of ownership held by the original stockholders, (2) no change in the proportion of cash dividends per share, and (3) a sharp change in the market price of the stock. A company whose stock is selling at $90 per share might want to have a stock split to reduce the market price to $45 (two for one) or even $30 (three for one), to encourage more investors to buy and sell stock. Stock splits, therefore, can have the effect of opening up trading to a greater number of investors. For this reason stock splits sometimes require the consent of two-thirds of the current stockholders. A reverse stock split is opted for when a company wishes to increase the market price of its stock. For example, a company with stock selling at $10 per share could have a one-for-three or one-for-four reverse split to increase the price per share to $30 or $40.

Voting Rights

Owners of common stock normally have *voting rights*. This is the proportionate authority to express an opinion or choice in matters affecting the company. Each share of common stock gives the holder one vote. (Very rarely does a company issue nonvoting common stock.) At the annual meeting of the company, the board of directors is elected (or re-elected) and matters of special interest are voted on. Each stockholder gets an opportunity to take part in these activities by either attending the meeting or voting by *proxy.* This is a legal procedure of assigning one's voting rights to another. (It is often easier to vote by mail through a proxy than attend the meeting in person.) In reality, most issues facing a corporation are foreseen by the board of directors, which then obtains control via proxies of a large voting bloc to ensure that its desires are met. On rare occasion, a proxy battle occurs, as two competing forces (often the existing board of directors and an outsider group perhaps seeking a merger or buyout) actively bid for the individual voting rights (proxies) of each stockholder to gain control of the company. Most common stockholders also have a *pre-emptive right* to purchase additional shares in the company so they will maintain their proportionate ownership interest. Thus, new issues of common stock may have to be offered to the current stockholders before being sold to the public.

Classifications of Common Stock

Although the terminology is imprecise, many investment brokers, securities analysts, and individual investors find it helpful to group certain stocks according to specific characteristics. This is often an aid when matching an investor's preferences with stock investment options.

There are four basic classifications of stock: (1) income stocks, (2) growth stocks (well known), (3) growth stocks (lesser known), and (4) speculative stocks. In addition, other terms are used to characterize classifications.

Income Stocks

An *income stock* has a cash dividend that is higher than average year after year because the company has fairly high earnings and chooses to declare high cash dividends regularly and retain only a small portion of the earnings. This requires the company to have a steady stream of income, as, for instance, utility companies do. Stocks issued by telephone, electric, and gas companies are normally labeled income stocks. Investors in these companies usually are not too concerned with the P/E ratio or the growth potential of the value of the stock. Betas are often less than 1.0. Elderly or retired persons often are interested in income stocks.

Growth Stocks (Well Known)

Stocks of companies that are leaders in their fields and have several consecutive years of above-average earnings are considered *growth stocks (well known).* Such companies grow rapidly and retain most earnings (usually about 75 percent) to assist that growth. Investor awareness of such corporations remains high, and expectations of continued growth are also high. For this reason the P/E ratio is high, too. Many growth stocks have a glamorous reputation that improves or declines sharply with the market. Thus, they often have betas of 1.5 or more. Investors generally seem to prefer growth stocks of well-known companies, as they typically offer some dividends and a good opportunity for price appreciation. In the past, well-known growth stocks were offered by such companies as Abbott Laboratories, Apple Computer, and Xerox.

Growth Stocks (Lesser Known)

Some excellent companies that are not necessarily the industry giants have had higher-than-average earnings in recent years and have good prospects for the future. They are considered *growth stocks (lesser known).* Since they are not the most popular with investors, their P/E ratios are generally lower than those of the more glamorous, well-known growth stocks (although the P/E ratios are still high). Often such firms are regional businesses with strong earnings, for instance, Crazy Eddie Inc. (in the East) and Popeye's Chicken (in the South). Others may be the third- or fourth-leading firm in an industry or may have less name recognition, such as Wendy's, Cray Research, and The Limited, Inc. Their betas are usually 1.5 or more.

Speculative Stocks

A *speculative stock* may have a spotty earnings record but has an apparent potential for substantial earnings at some time in the future, even though such earnings may never be realized. Investors in these types of firms take a bit of a gamble, since the recent history of earnings and dividends is likely to be very inconsistent. With little or no dividends anticipated, the investor hopes that the company will make a new discovery or invent a new product or generate some type of valuable information that later may both push up the price of the stock and result in substantial dividends. Examples of speculative companies include small oil companies, genetic engineering firms, and some drug manufacturers. The P/E ratio fluctuates widely along with the fortunes of the company and a beta above 2.0 is common. For every speculative company that succeeds there are many others that do poorly or fail. The investor willing to accept a high risk of financial loss with little or no dividends might consider such an investment.

Other Characterizing Terms

A variety of other terms are used to better describe particular stocks within the four basic classifications. These include *blue-chip, cyclical,* and *countercyclical* or *defensive.* A *blue-chip stock* indicates a company with a well-regarded reputation and a long history both of good earnings and consistent cash dividends. The earnings of blue-chip companies (usually an income stock or well-known growth stock) are expected to grow at a consistent but unspectacular rate because these firms are the leaders in their industries and are usually the most stable of firms. Examples are Sears, Du Pont, and H. J. Heinz. Investing in such companies is considered much less risky than investing in other firms.

A *cyclical stock* has a price that typically follows the general state of the economy and the various phases of the business cycle. During times of prosperity and economic expansion, the company's earnings are high; during a recession, earnings decline sharply. Examples are stocks of firms in the basic industries: housing, automobiles, steel, and heavy machinery. Of course, some blue-chip, income, growth, and speculative stocks also can be classified as cyclical stocks. Most cyclical stocks have a beta of about 1.0. Investors buying cyclical stocks necessarily aim to buy at or near the bottom of a recession and sell at a high point during the expansionary days of prosperity before the price begins to slide downward again.

Despite a general decline in economic activity, some companies maintain substantial earnings because their products are needed. These are considered *countercyclical (defensive) stocks*. Most smokers, for example, do not quit during a recession, and people usually continue to go to movies, drink softdrinks, and buy groceries. Similarly, the earnings of utility companies generally hold up well during periods of economic decline. Countercyclical stocks, by definition, usually have a beta of less than 1 and are often negative. Investors interested in consistent cash dividends through the years sometimes choose these stocks.

What Affects Stock Prices: Some Theories

The prices of some stocks rise when others fall. The television news commentator tells us why the market acted the way it did or asks for the analytical commentary of a "Wall Street expert." Do these people know why stock prices rise or fall? Not really. They are simply offering their opinions or theories about what is occurring. If they actually knew what made stock prices rise or fall they would be billionaires. There are three general areas of stock theory: fundamental theory, technical theory, and efficient-market theory.

Fundamental Theory

The premise of fundamental theory is that a particular stock has an intrinsic, or true, value based on its expected future earnings. If the company expects to be extremely profitable in coming years, this should be reflected in a high P/E ratio. If prospects look dismal and earnings are expected to be quite low, the price of a stock and the P/E ratio should be low. Fundamental theory assumes that because knowledge about the futures of companies is not perfect, some stocks are underpriced and others are overpriced. The investor's task is to study certain fundamental factors that may enable them to select undervalued stocks for purchase and sell overvalued stocks. These fundamentals are the historical profitability of an industry, the leading companies in the industry, the economic outlook for the profitability of the industry as a whole, and the outlook for the general economy. The potential investor then estimates the value of one company by comparing the history and expected future profitability of this company with competing firms. Such comparisons are based on much subjective information.

The P/E ratio is one piece of objective data that can be used in fundamental analysis. However, it too is subjective when used to forecast the future. Investors often compare the expected P/E ratio of a firm with its competitors and the industry as a whole. In a growth industry, such as robotics, all such P/E ratios would be high. In a cyclical industry, such as automobiles, all such P/E ratios would be low. The task for the common-stock investor is to analyze the fundamental factors at work and choose the best company. Most investors believe in fundamental theory.

Technical Theory

Some people believe that stock prices are not affected by fundamental factors but instead vary due to technical factors in the stock market as a whole. Technical theory is not based on forecasted earnings, and consequently the intrinsic value of a stock is ignored. Technical analysts, or "chartists," carefully plot price movements in conjunction with various market indexes and other technical data that when combined into a theoretical model indicate when to buy or sell. Factors included in such a model could be the total volume of shares traded, the ratio of the number of stocks that rose compared with those that declined, published information on the amount of insider sales (to officers of companies), the ratio of short sales (sales of borrowed shares to be replaced later when the price may be lower) to other sales, high-low indexes, odd-lot trading, and moving average lines.

The individual investor can do some charting, but the more complex models are constructed by professionals. A number of investment advisory services sell subscriptions to technical theory indicators, such as the one shown in Figure 15–1. Different services weigh various factors differently, hoping to offer more reliable advice. Given the difficulty of trying to outguess the market, it is not surprising that many technical theorists have been unsuccessful over the years.

Efficient-market Theory

Many researchers have concluded that short-term stock price movements are purely random. This idea has been called the random walk hypothesis and has evolved into the efficient-market theory, which

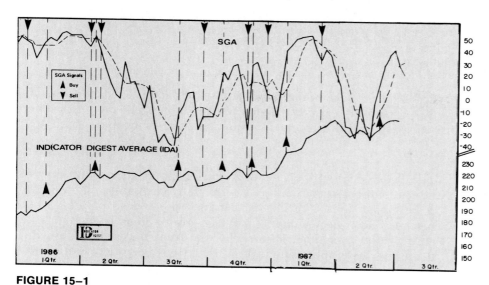

FIGURE 15-1
Technical Theory Indicator

Source: Indicator Digest, May 22, 1987, p. 5. Used by permission of Indicator Research
Group, Palisades Park, N.J.

holds that knowledge of stock market investors as a group is considered
to be perfect and the price of each stock accurately reflects all available
and anticipated information. Thus the market reacts swiftly to all unexpected information and properly prices each stock. The conclusion is
that no one can consistently do better than the average. Efficient-market theorists believe that some do better than average because of luck.
In fact, they suggest that the traders—those who buy and sell their
stocks frequently—do less well than the stock market averages by an
amount equal to the commissions they pay.

The data for this theory come from the large institutional investors, such as mutual funds, pension plans, and bank trusts, for which
information about investment activities is publicly available. Because of
their immense size, these institutions are restricted to investing in only
the largest several hundred companies. Otherwise, their individual
actions could affect the price of a stock. If, for example, an institutional
investor determined to sell off all holdings of a relatively small company, the sale of such a large block of stock would then further reduce
the price because quite likely there would not be enough buyers available. Conversely, if several investment companies all wanted to buy the
stock of the same corporation, the price would skyrocket as they bid
against each other.

Most investors reject the efficient-market theory. They believe in
using the fundamental and technical theories to improve the likelihood
of investment success and claim that such knowledge improves their
investment expertise.

Advantages and Disadvantages of Owning Common Stock

People invest in common stock because they want to make money. For the possibility of earning a higher return, they assume more risk. There are several advantages and disadvantages of investing in common stock.

Advantages

The likelihood of cash dividends and price appreciation motivates most investors to consider common stocks. Many companies might declare relatively small cash dividends, perhaps with a yield of only 2 or 3 percent. But these companies may also offer a good chance for price appreciation over time. Historically, the combined annual cash dividend and price appreciation of all stocks has been between 8 and 9 percent; this includes times when inflation was 10 percent and when it was 1 percent. Supposedly, common stocks offer a probable hedge against inflation, since the combined cash dividends and price appreciation has exceeded inflation over time, although certainly not in every year.

Common stocks also offer the potential of high returns. Greater-than-average returns are possible if you wisely buy and sell stocks. In fact, the potential for very large returns is there as well.

Another popular advantage of common stocks is the low minimum investment amount required. A share of stock could sell for as little as $5 or $10 (although it is rare to buy one share at a time). This encourages savers to consider investing. Two other advantages are limited liability (if the corporation goes bankrupt, all you lose is the price of the stock) and marketability (stocks can generally be sold with considerable ease).

Disadvantages

Risks of various types are present with common stock investments. There is the financial risk that the company will go bankrupt. There is the liquidity risk that the price of a stock might be quite low when you want to sell it. Inflation risk is also present. During times of extremely high inflation, many common stock prices are depressed. As inflation rises, interest rates rise, which increases the costs of doing business (thus lowering profits) and provides much higher rates of return to savers. When interest rates are high, common stockholders often sell their somewhat riskier stocks and put their money in safer forms of savings. This continues to depress stock prices. A market in which stock prices are generally declining is called a *bear market.* In a *bull market,* average stock prices are increasing. (Similarly, a "bull" in the market is an optimist who expects prices to go up; a "bear" is a pessimist who expects the general market to decline.)

A bear market of two or three years can play havoc with your investment timing. For example, assume that your child's college fund was made up of common stock investments, and a severe bear market existed when the child turned eighteen. At that point the value of the investments could be sharply depressed.

Uncertainty of yield is another disadvantage of common stocks. Even a company with an excellent record of paying cash dividends might have to skip one or two quarterly dividends during times of low profitability. Or the company might declare dividends of varied amount, say, quarterly dividends of $.40, $.45, $.30, and $.40 during a year. Investors who want to depend with high certainty on regular dividends as income should probably not own most common stocks.

Because many common stocks vary in price with certain news events, world happenings, and economic and political variables, they require a significant amount of personal management. Investors need to be alert to current happenings in order to know when to sell quickly in order to reap profits or reduce losses. Also, it is probably true that the riskier an investment, the more attention it requires.

A final disadvantage is your risk disposition. If you are averse to much risk taking, then most common stocks are not suitable investments for you. You will sleep better with less risky investments. Also, if you cannot take the pressure of knowing that the price of your common stock could vary weekly and monthly up or down by 10 or 20 percent or more, then your disposition may not be suited to common stocks.

Preferred Stock and the Individual Investor

Probably 90 percent of all stock outstanding today is common stock, since it has a broader appeal to investors than preferred stock. As we noted earlier in the chapter, a preferred stock is a fixed-income ownership security with the right to assets and earnings of a corporation before the claims of common stockholders but after those of bondholders. U.S. tax laws do not permit a corporation to deduct as an expense the dividends paid to common or preferred stockholders. Because interest paid to bondholders is tax deductible, most corporations today find it less expensive to sell bonds to raise money than to sell preferred stock. This section describes some characteristics of preferred stock.

Fixed Dividends

The dividends to preferred stockholders are usually fixed and represent a financial obligation of the firm. When a company profits, first in line are the preferred stockholders, and any remaining profits may then be distributed to common stockholders. Since preferred stockholders are offered only a strong assurance that a specific cash dividend will be made to them, there is still some risk involved.

Since the yield is fixed, the price of preferred stock generally will not increase as the company becomes more profitable and successful.

Thus, the typical preferred stockholder does not benefit from price appreciation as would a common stockholder. Instead, the price, or market value, of preferred stock is primarily based on prevailing interest rates. (Generally, the yields on preferred stocks will be slightly lower than investments with comparable risks—long-term certificates of deposits or corporate bonds—because other corporations bid up the prices of preferred stocks. Corporations are the main buyers of preferred stocks because tax laws allow them to avoid taxes on 85 percent of the dividends they receive.) In times of rising interest rates, the market value of a preferred stock will drop so that the real yield will remain competitive with similar risk investments. For example, a preferred stock that cost you $100 and paid an annual cash dividend of $7 would provide you with a 7 percent return. If returns on other investments of similar risk later climbed to around 9 percent, the market price of your preferred stock would have to drop to reflect the differences in return. After all, no investors would pay $100 for your preferred stock paying $7 when they could put their money into a similar investment and receive $9. With a cash dividend of $7, the market price of the preferred stock would have to drop to about $78 to increase the yield to approximately 9 percent ($7 ÷ $78 = .089).

Participating or Nonparticipating Stock

A few companies offer *participating preferred stock,* which allows the preferred stockholder to receive extra dividends above the stated amount after the common stockholders have received a certain amount. This is sometimes called a *bonus dividend.* Most preferred stock is nonparticipating and permits the owner to receive only the fixed amount per share. The enticement of participating preferred stock is sometimes offered by firms experiencing difficulty in raising money through more conventional sources.

Cumulative or Noncumulative Stock

Preferred stocks that are *cumulative* are desirable. This means that if the board of directors votes to skip (pass) making a cash dividend to preferred stockholders (if the firm was unprofitable at that time), the dividend must be paid before any future dividends are distributed to the common stockholders. For example, assume that a company passes on two quarterly dividends of $2.25 each to preferred stockholders, who are accustomed to receiving $9 a year. If in the third quarter the company profits and wants to give a cash dividend to its common stockholders, it must first pay the cumulative preferred stockholders their passed $4.50. Further, the usual cash dividend of $2.25 must be made to the preferred stockholders for the third quarter before any dividends can be paid to the common stockholders.

In the case of noncumulative stock, the preferred stockholder would have no claim to previously skipped dividends. However, during the third quarter preferred stockholders would still have preference over common stockholders. Thus, preferred stockholders would receive the $2.25 but not the skipped $4.50 ($2.25 + $2.25). Most preferred stock sold in the past thirty years is cumulative.

Callable Stock

Most preferred stock is *callable,* which means that the company can repurchase it by paying a slight premium (often 5 percent above par value) if the price reaches a certain level. The call price is stated in advance as either a specific amount or a proportion of the original par value. A company with preferred stock generally would like to call it in when interest rates have dropped substantially. For example, assume that the company issued preferred stock for $100 paying a $9 annual dividend. This presumably provides a good return to the investor. Should interest rates drop to about 7 percent, the price of the preferred stock would rise to reflect a yield comparable to investments of similar risk. A price increase to $128 would result in a yield of 7.03 percent ($9 ÷ $128 = 7.03 percent).

The issuing company is not trying to cheat the preferred stockholders out of a nice capital gain (from $100 to $128) but, rather, is looking to keep its operating costs down. If it is currently paying preferred stockholders $9 per share, it would be prudent to pay a 5 percent penalty to retire the stock. Then it can issue new preferred stock or sell bonds at around 7 percent to regain use of the capital at a substantial savings. (Would you choose to pay $900,000 in dividends to preferred stockholders or to pay them a 5 percent penalty and sell a new issue that costs the company only $700,000 in dividends?)

Convertible Stock

Preferred stocks that are *convertible* can be exchanged for a certain number of shares of common stock during a specified time period. A small but growing number of firms are offering convertible preferred stock. Because the conversion feature is attractive to some investors, this stock can be sold with a lower fixed dividend. For example, assume that one share of preferred convertible stock bought at $100 is convertible to two shares of common stock until October 1, 1994, and the current market price of the common stock is $30. Should the company prosper in coming years and the value of the common stock increase, it may be wise for preferred stockholders to convert. Thus, the convertible preferred stockholder does have a chance to share in a part of the price appreciation of common stock. Note, though, that the conversion ratio might be unrealistic. If only two years were left to convert the above stock, it might seem unlikely that a $30 common stock would rise to above $50 to make conversion profitable for the investor. In this instance, the conversion privilege is almost worthless.

It's Not for the Average Investor

Preferred stock with its fixed cash dividend seems to attract investors who are interested in reliable and relatively high dividends, not in price appreciation. Additionally, all convertible preferred stocks are also callable, thus limiting the potential for price appreciation. Preferred stocks are also susceptible to the risk of rising interest rates, as the price of preferred stocks drops under such conditions. Thus, for most individual investors, preferred stocks are not the best investment alternative. In sum, preferred stocks have many of the disadvantages of common stocks without the same advantages.

Summary

1. Stocks are important from the perspectives of both the corporation (to finance corporate goals) and the investor (in terms of income and price appreciation).

2. In the study of investments, several important terms need to be understood, such as earnings per share, price/earnings ratio, market value, beta, and stock splits.

3. Stocks can be classified according to their characteristics, such as speculative stock (with which earnings may have been spotty but a potential for substantial earnings is present) and cyclical stock (with which price movements typically reflect or follow the general trend of the economy).

4. There are three general theories about why stock prices rise or fall: fundamental theory, technical theory, and efficient-market theory. The last concludes that short-term stock price movements are purely random.

5. The likelihood of dividends and price appreciation is perceived as a major advantage of common stock while its disadvantages include financial risk, liquidity risk, and inflation risk.

6. Preferred stock with its fixed cash dividend seems to attract investors who are very interested in reliable and relatively high dividends, and not in price appreciation.

Modern Money Management

The Johnsons Want to Invest in Stock

After reviewing various types of investment alternatives, Harry and Belinda have decided to invest $1,200 now and then $200 to $400 a month in the stock market for the next two years. At that point they will decide whether to continue with their stock selection or invest in something else. They want a regular income in the form of cash dividends from the stock and expect some price appreciation as well.

1. The Johnsons were considering preferred stock but a friend of Belinda's advised against it. What is your advice to the Johnsons about buying preferred stock?

2. You need to give the Johnsons your views to help them decide between two stocks, each with a market price of $100, classified accordingly: (1) blue-chip income stock and (2) well-known growth stock. For a typical stock in each of those classifications, give the Johnsons your estimates *and* reasoning on the following: price/earnings ratio, dividend payout ratio, and beta.

3. If the Johnsons invested in a blue-chip income stock for the two years while the general market for stocks rose 30 percent what would the likely market price of the stock be at the end of the two years?

4. If the Johnsons invested in a well-known growth stock for the two years while the general market for stocks rose 30 percent what would the likely market price of the stock be at the end of the two years?

Key Words and Concepts

Review Questions

1. Distinguish among the three forms of business ownership: sole proprietorship, partnership, and corporation.
2. Explain how a corporation raises funds to meet its financial needs.
3. Describe the differences between common and preferred stock.
4. Explain why the revenues of a profitable corporation are not paid out totally to the stockholders.
5. Explain and illustrate the two components making up total return.
6. What does *price/earnings ratio* mean, and how would you interpret a P/E ratio of 8 to 1?
7. Explain why one company has a dividend payout ratio of .65 and another a ratio of .30.
8. Explain the likely relationship of the market price of a stock with its par value and its book value per share.
9. What does *beta* mean, and how can it be used by an investor who hopes to select stocks that will go up much more than average during a rise in the stock market?
10. What is the effect of stock dividends on the individual investor who already owns shares of stock in a company?
11. Identify some reasons why some companies have stock splits.
12. Discuss the value of voting rights for a stockholder.
13. Differentiate between blue-chip growth and speculative stocks.
14. Explain how a particular growth stock could also be called a cyclical stock.
15. Explain the basic differences between the fundamental and technical theories as to what affects stock prices.
16. What is the efficient-market theory, and why do most investors reject this approach?
17. List some advantages of buying common stock instead of keeping all of your investment money in a savings account.
18. Distinguish between a bull and a bear market, and explain why it is important to know the difference.
19. Give reasons why most investors do not buy preferred stocks.

Case Problems

1. Robert Chisholm of Memphis, Tennessee, opened his successful food-service business as a sole proprietorship three years ago. Phyllis Stevens and her partner, William Pyeatt, recently opened their second retail toy store in Memphis after becoming partners four years ago.
   a. Justify opening a business as a sole proprietor and as a partnership.
   b. What are some arguments for Chisholm as well as Stevens and Pyeatt to change to a corporate form of ownership?

2. Richard Ford of Riverside, California, has $5,000 that he wants to invest in the stock market. Richard is in college on a scholarship and does not plan on needing the $5,000 or any dividend income for another five years, when he plans to buy a new automobile.
   a. What classification of common stock would you recommend to Richard? Why?
   b. What would be a likely price/earnings ratio for this classification of stock?
   c. What would be a likely dividend payout ratio for this classification of stock? Why?
   d. Identify the components of the total return Richard might expect, and estimate how much he might expect annually from each component.

3. Jean Maynard of Evanston, Illinois, graduated from college three years ago and is now a successful salesperson for a real estate firm. She bought a condominium to live in last year (primarily for the tax advantages) and is now considering the stock market as an area for investments. Jean has $6,000 in cash to invest.
   a. Give Jean some reasons why she should consider buying common stock as an investment.
   b. Advise her also on major cautions she should recognize by investing in common stocks.
   c. If Jean bought a stock with a market price of $50 and a beta value of 1.8, what would be the likely value of her $6,000 investment after one year if the general market for stocks rose 20 percent?
   d. What would the investment be worth if the general market for stocks dropped 20 percent?

Suggested Readings

"The Biggest Bull Market." *Newsweek,* April 20, 1987, p. 57. Review of previous bull markets and what is expected next.

"The Forbes 500s on Wall Street." *Forbes,* April 27, 1987, pp. 232–275. Annual *Forbes* list of companies with vital facts, including earnings predictions.

"Hot Growth Companies." *Business Week,* May 25, 1987, pp. 82–97. One hundred top-growth companies and many reasons for their success.

"New Tools for the Armchair Investor." *Forbes,* March 23, 1987, p. 150. Telephone and personal computer programs to help monitor investments.

"Stocks That Reinvest Your Dividends." *Money,* September 1987 pp. 147–150. How to reinvest dividends in 150 companies offering discounted prices.

"Super Stocks for Tomorrow: Computers." *Changing Times,* September 1987, pp. 40–46. What you need to know to invest in the best computer hardware and software producers.

"Super Stocks for Tomorrow: Robotics." *Changing Times,* August 1987, pp. 60–64. How to choose a robotics company for an investment.

"Where Were the Cops?" *Forbes,* April 6, 1987, pp. 60–62. Identifying scams that hurt the small investor.

CHAPTER 16

Investing in Bonds

OBJECTIVES

After reading this chapter, the student should be able to

1. distinguish among three types of fixed asset investments.
2. describe the nine major characteristics of bonds.
3. differentiate among the three general types of bonds.
4. explain the effect of changing market interest rates on bond prices, current yield, and yield to maturity.
5. list the advantages and disadvantages of investing in bonds.
6. explain factors to consider when buying and selling bonds.

M any people who make investments in stock do not understand the important part bonds can play in their portfolios. Bonds are easier and less expensive to purchase now than they were some years ago, and often provide a much better total return than savings accounts, certificates of deposit, and many stocks.

This chapter first discusses fixed income investments and then details the characteristics of bonds. After describing the major types of bonds, we will cover the general advantages and disadvantages of owning bonds and how to determine yields on bonds. The chapter ends with sections on selecting and selling bonds.

Fixed-asset Investments

Fixed-asset investments require a specific amount of money to be invested for a certain amount of time. You can be reasonably certain of receiving periodic income (often interest received quarterly or semiannually) as well as getting back the amount you originally invested. For this small financial risk you usually earn a relatively low return. Examples of fixed-asset investments are savings accounts, certificates of deposit (both discussed in Chapter 4), government bonds, corporate bonds, and annuities. (Annuities are discussed in Chapter 21.) Fixed-asset investments can be classified according to whether the value and yield of the asset are variable or fixed.

Fixed Value and Fixed Return

An asset has a fixed value and a fixed return when its value (or price) and the rate of return do not change during the time period. For example, a thirty-six-month, $5,000 certificate of deposit paying 8 percent that is purchased through a savings institution has a fixed value and yield guaranteed by the government. At any time during the thirty-six months the asset is always worth $5,000, and no matter what happens to interest rates in the general economy, the rate of return is fixed at 8 percent, which provides an investor with a $400 annual return ($5,000 × .08) on the original amount invested.

Fixed Value and Variable Return

Government savings bonds (EE and HH) and funds deposited in savings accounts in banks, S & Ls, and credit unions are examples of fixed-asset investments with a fixed value but a variable return. (These were examined in Chapter 4.) With these investments, the government guarantees the value of the asset. Over time, however, the return can vary. For example, the interest rate on savings bonds was 6.5 percent in 1979, 8.5 percent in 1982, and 6 percent in 1987. When the rate on newly issued savings bonds is higher than that on old bonds, the rate on the older bonds is raised; otherwise, a guaranteed minimum rate is offered. The rate paid on savings accounts has fluctuated from 4 to 5.5 percent in recent years, too.

Variable Value and Fixed Return

Bonds are interest-bearing negotiable certificates of long-term debt issued by corporations and governments. The most common denomination for a bond is $1,000. Normally when bonds are first issued they have a *stated interest rate* (also called *coupon* or *nominal rate*), which remains fixed. This is the interest rate printed on the bond certificate. The value (or price) of bonds fluctuates with the interest rates in the general economy. This is known as *interest rate risk,* which is the uncertainty of the market value of an asset that results from possible interest rate changes. For example, assume that you bought a twenty-year, $1,000 bond with a stated annual interest rate of 8 percent, or for an annual return of $80 ($1,000 × .08). If after one year interest rates in the general economy jump to 12 percent, no one will want to buy your bond for $1,000 because it pays only $80 per year. Should you want to sell it at that time the price of the bond will have to be lowered, perhaps to $700. It is important to realize that if the bond is held to maturity (nineteen more years in this example), the issuer is obligated to repay the *face value* (the stated price or par value printed on the certificate) of $1,000. On the other hand, if after one year interest rates slip to 6 percent, the value of your bond will increase sharply (perhaps to $1,333) because people would like to own your bond paying 8 percent when other rates are 6 percent. Because of the possibility of capital gains, bonds offer a unique investment opportunity for the moderate and speculative investor as well as the conservative investor.

Characteristics of Bonds

Bonds have nine major characteristics: legal indenture, denomination of value, maturity time, sinking fund, being secured or unsecured, being senior or subordinated, being registered or bearer, callability and convertibility, and warrants. Each of these is discussed below.

Legal Indenture

An *indenture* is a legally written agreement between a group of bondholders and the debtor as to the terms of the debt. For corporate bonds, this lengthy document specifies many of the debtor's responsibilities regarding what the borrowed money will be used for, the date(s) the bond principal must be repaid (*maturity date*), and the dates interest payment must be made. A trustee, a bank or trust company, is normally appointed to represent the bondholders and ensure that the obligations of the indenture are completed. State laws require issuers of corporate bonds to pay interest due to bondholders even if a company is not profitable. Government bonds usually do not have indentures, as the authorizing statute typically details responsibilities of the public agency issuing the bond.

Denomination of Value

Bonds are usually issued in units of $1,000. This amount is a bond's *face value, stated value,* or *par value.*

Maturity Time

Bonds are paid off, or *retired,* at the maturity date specified in the indenture. When bonds mature, the issuing agency is obligated to pay the face value to the bondholder. Most corporate bonds mature in twenty to thirty years, government bonds usually in ten to twenty years. The maturity time could be as short as five years on some government issues or as long as forty years on a corporate bond.

Sinking Fund

Investors in bonds want to be as confident as possible that interest payments will be made on time *and* that the principal will be repaid as scheduled. For this reason, many bonds have a *sinking fund,* which is a requirement in the indenture that monies be set aside each year to repay the debt. The trustee receives the funds and oversees this responsibility. The added assurance of a sinking fund reduces risk and permits the agency to issue bonds at interest rates lower than rates on similar secured or unsecured bonds. Occasionally, bonds are retired *serially,* whereby each bond is numbered consecutively and matures according to a prenumbered schedule.

Secured or Unsecured Bonds

Bonds are issued on the financial reputation of the issuing agency as either secured or unsecured. A corporation issuing a *secured bond* would pledge specific assets as collateral in the indenture or have the principal and interest guaranteed by another corporation or government agency. In the event of default, the trustee could take legal action to seize and sell such assets. Three types of secured bonds are *mortgage bonds* (land and buildings as collateral), *collateral trust bonds* (stocks and perhaps other bonds as collateral), and *equipment bonds* (certain equipment, such as airplanes or railroad cars, as collateral). In the event of bankruptcy, the claims of secured creditors are paid first.

An *unsecured bond* has no collateral named as security for the debt and is backed only by the good faith and reputation of the issuing agency. All government bonds are unsecured. Any unsecured bond is called a *debenture.* You may think that secured bonds are safer than unsecured, but often this is not the case. U.S. government bonds are backed by the full faith, credit, and taxing power of the government. Also, the fine financial reputations of many large corporations enable them to offer unsecured bonds that are safer than the secured bonds of many other companies.

Senior or Subordinated Bonds

A corporation that issues bonds several times over the years must rank the bonds for repayment in the event of default. These details are spelled out in the indenture of each issuance of bonds. A *senior debenture* gives holders a right to all assets not pledged to secured bondholders. A *subordinated debenture* gives holders a lesser claim to assets perhaps similar to those of the stockholders. Of course, the riskier a bond is, the higher the interest rate should be.

Also, if husband and wife file separate returns, they cannot get a credit for child care expenses — a credit that may be important to remarried persons with children, said Blockman.

If one spouse filing separately itemizes deductions, the other must do so as well, even if it is not to the benefit of the second spouse to do so, Blockman said.

But separate returns may work out well for a couple in which one partner has relatively low income but relatively high medical expenses and miscellaneous deductions. That's because only medical expenses exceeding 7.5 percent of adjusted gross income and miscellaneous expenses such as union dues and uniform costs exceeding two percent of the adjusted gross may be deducted.

But joint returns mean joint liability: Each spouse is liable for the collective tax, penalties and interest of both partners, Blockman said.

Because of the changes in the tax situation and the filing options, newly married persons should take a new look at the W-4 forms they file with employers, said Ms. Dunn. The information on those forms is used to figure out how much federal tax is withheld from a worker's paycheck.

Ms. Dunn said a couple should estimate taxes they will owe once married, then check to see if current withholding will cover those taxes.

In many cases, people will find they are having too little withheld because of the generally higher tax burden imposed on married couples. If that's the case, they should have the amount withheld increased, she said.

Persons planning to get married who are more than 55 years old when both partners own a home have another piece of tax planning to do, said Blockman. If the husband- and wife-to-be decide to sell both homes, they should make the sales before they marry, Blockman said.

Federal tax laws allow a once-in-a-lifetime exclusion of up to $125,000 in capital gains on a home sale by persons 55 years old or older. If both homes are sold before the marriage, each partner gets to use that exclusion, said Blockman. If the couple waits until after the marriage, only one exclusion may be used.

Marriage also changes insurance and estate needs.

Most single persons think little about life or disability insurance, said Ms. Dunn. "They say, 'There's nothing to protect, so why spend that mony?'" she said. But after marriage there's the other spouse's lifestyle to think about.

For example, a husband and wife earning $20,000 each buy a house and take out a $50,000 mortgage. With two incomes, they meet the payments easily, but if one does or becomes disabled and loses his income, the couple, or survivor, may not be able to meet the payments and may have to sell the house, said Ms. Dunn. Life insurance ance and disability coverage can take care of that.

Also, persons who have or plan to have children should draw up wills, said Kelman.

Although state law covers what will happen to a person's estate if he or she has children and dies without a will, the process is faster and less expensive if the person has a will, Kelman said.

(David Flaum is a business writer for The Commercial Appeal in Memphis, Tenn.)

When couples get married — as so many do this time of year — they spend hours picking out wedding gowns, booking reception halls, addressing invitations and selecting flower arrangements.

But few take minutes to talk about finances or taxes.

"People are too busy planning the wedding to plan how the marriage is going to go (financially)," said Memphis accountant Vicki Dunn.

They shouldn't be, said Ms. Dunn and other financial advisers.

Especially when both newlyweds work, marriage may mean a major overhaul of personal finances.

The first step is for the man and woman to discuss their values and feelings about money and how it should be handled, said Cheryl Williams, financial planner with Kelman-Lazarov Inc. in Memphis, Tenn. .

"Finances play a large role in a relationship, so you want to make sure you understand each other's values before you start planning," she said.

For example, one partner may be conservative in spending habits, the other may be less careful. "You must come to a consensus," Ms. Williams said.

Also, the couple must decide which partner will take primary responsibility for handling the family finances. One may want to take charge, the other may not want the responsibility, she said.

Next, the newly marrieds must decide how to set up their accounts.

The easiest arrangement is often putting all the income in one pot — a joint account — and paying the bills out of that account, said Martin Kelman, certified financial planner in Kelman-Lazarov.

"A problem with a joint account is that sometimes one spouse forgets to make an entry and that could cause friction with the other spouse who likes to keep things in neat order," he said.

In some cases, it is important for the husband and wife to have individual accounts, Kelman said.

If the partner who earns the least has his own account — and his own credit card — that spouse can establish a credit history, he said.

If the couple gets a divorce or the higher-earnings spouse dies, the other partner will then find it easier to get credit in the future, Kelman said.

Another possibility is to set up several joint accounts, said Ms. Williams. One should be for fixed expenses — those that must be paid every month, like rent and utilities. A second account may be opened for flexible expenses — entertainment, clothes and travel — that can be cut or eliminated in tough times, she said. Still another account can be established for savings.

Once the mechanics of how the money will be handled are in place, financial planning should start.

Kelman believes newlyweds should wait for three or four months, "see how your life together is, your lifestyle," then analyze where the money is coming from and how it's being spent. After that, the couple can plan a budget, which should be flexible enough to handle possible changes in income and lifestyle, Kelman said.

Having a budget will eliminate problems before they crop up, said Ms. Williams.

"Most young newlyweds don't have the funds available just to go out and spend," she said. Making a budget is also a good way for newlyweds to communicate, work with each other and build their relationship, she said.

Part of the planning process should be setting financial goals — such as providing a cushion in case one partner loses a job, taking time off to have children or buying a house, even retirement, said Ms. Williams.

"Try to have answers to these questions before they occur so you won't make an emotional decision," she said.

Each partner may be earning $20,000 and while $40,000 per year "sounds like a lot of money," taxes will take a larger bite out of the combined incomes than out of the earnings of two single persons, said Ms. Dunn.

Tax rates are generally higher for married couples filing separate returns than if they file joint returns, said Sanford Blockman, tax partner with Uiberall & Co., a Memphis Certified Public Accounting firm. In the example, the couple would owe $4,868.50 by filing separately.

Registered or Bearer Bonds

Historically, all corporations issued *bearer bonds,* also called *coupon bonds.* The owners of such bonds were unknown to the corporation; a series of postdated coupons attached to the bond represented their ownership. When the interest payment was due, a bondholder detached the proper coupon and presented it to the corporation, a paying agent, or a bank for payment. The principal was received in the same manner. By law, all bonds now issued are *registered bonds,* which provide for the recording of the bondholder's name so that checks for interest and principal can be safely mailed when due. The Internal Revenue Service is therefore notified as well. Older issues of coupon bonds are still traded. The term *coupon* or *coupon yield* refers to the interest rate printed on the certificate when it is issued.

Callable Bonds

It would be nice if you could buy a $1,000 bond scheduled to pay 15 percent annually for a long time period, such as twenty years. During times of low interest rates, such a bond would be highly attractive. Often, however, bonds carry provisions requiring that they be sold back to the issuing agency if the agency so requests.

Probably 80 to 90 percent of long-term bonds are classified as *callable bonds,* which means that the issuing agency may retire the bond prematurely. If a bond is callable, the call date is specified on the certificate. It may even be in the issuer's interest to pay a premium of perhaps 5 or 10 percent (as specified in the indenture) to pay off, for example, bonds paying 11 percent if rates have dropped to 8 percent.

Bond investors consider the callable feature a negative one because they stand to lose their high interest rate if the bonds are called. As a result, callable bonds usually have a higher stated rate than similar bonds without such a feature. A good strategy is to purchase bonds that are not callable during the first five or ten years. Also, all other things being equal, it is wise to choose the bond with the higher call premium.

Convertibility and Warrants

Convertible bonds and bonds sold with warrants are attempts to attach some of the benefits of stock ownership to bondholders. A *convertible bond* may be exchanged during a specified time period before maturity for a predetermined number of shares of stock of the same corporation. Assume you have a $1,000 Running Paws Catfood Company bond that is issued at 9 percent, and it has a convertibility feature permitting conversion to thirty shares of Running Paws common stock at any time during the next twenty years. During this time, you will receive interest from the bond and hope that the stock price will rise. The conversion right starts to affect the value of the bond when Running Paws stock rises above $33.33 per share ($1,000 ÷ 30 shares). If the stock price rises to $36, for example, the bond value will rise to $1,080 (30 shares × $36), regardless of general interest rates, which normally affect the prices of bonds. As the common stock price continues to rise, so will the value of the bond. Of course, if the bond is also callable the issuer may force the bondholder to convert to common stock equal to the par value of the bond plus a small penalty. If the common stock price stays below $33.33 the conversion privilege makes no difference. Note, however, that since the possibility exists that the price will rise, the inclusion of a convertibility option has value, and this permits the original bond to be issued at a slightly lower interest rate than it could be otherwise.

A *warrant* is an option attached to a bond, a preferred stock, or some issues of common stock to purchase a specific number of shares of stock at a set price over a certain number of years. It is also called a **purchase warrant.** For example, assume that you have a Running Paws bond with a market value of $1,000 and an 8 percent interest rate. For the next five years the warrant gives you the privilege of buying ten shares of common stock for $30 per share. If the price of the common stock rises above $30, the warrant will have substantial value. If the price rises to $36, say, you can purchase ten shares at $30, for a total of $300 (saving $60 on the market price of $360). Thus, in this example, the warrant has a value of $60, and the value of the bond will rise by the same amount. If you do not want to use the warrant, you may sell it, assuming it is "detachable" from the bond. If the common stock price never rises above $30 per share, the warrant will be valueless. But because the price has the potential to rise, the interest rate on bonds with warrants is a little lower than it would be otherwise.

Types of Bonds

There are three general types of bonds: corporate bonds, U.S. government securities, and municipal bonds (also called state and local bonds). Some specialty bonds are also available.

Corporate Bonds

Bonds are an important source of funds for corporations. Corporations can obtain long-term financing of projects (typically, twenty to thirty years) through bonds at relatively lower cost because of tax regulations. In fact, for every dollar of newly issued common stock there are three dollars of newly issued corporate bonds. Payments of dividends to common and preferred stockholders are not tax deductible for corporations, but interest to bondholders is. Because a corporation must by law make interest payments on time (usually semiannually), companies in financial difficulty usually pay bondholders before paying short-term creditors. Corporations are sometimes profitable and sometimes not; during the early 1980s hundreds of corporations went bankrupt. It is important for investors to size up the financial quality of a company, considering both current profitability and the likelihood of long-term profits before buying its bonds.

Bonds are sold in organized securities markets where investors (lenders) compare the risks and potential rewards of investments. To help you in appraising such risks, two major advisory services give

TABLE 16-1
Summary of Municipal and Corporate Bond Ratings

Moody's Rating	Standard & Poor's Rating	Interpretation of Rating
Aaa Aa A	AAA AA A	High investment quality suggests ability to repay principal and interest on time
Baa	BBB BB	Medium-quality investments that also may have some speculative characteristics
B Caa Ca	CCC CC C	Lack characteristics of strong investments and have decreasing assurance of repayment as the rating declines
C	DDD DD D	In default with little prospect of retaining any investment standing

unbiased ratings of both corporate and municipal bonds: Moody's Investors Service, Inc., and Standard & Poor's Corporation (S & P). They examine each bond offering and assign it a quality rating according to the likelihood that the interest and principal will be repaid as detailed in the indenture. These are measures of the **default risk**, which is the likelihood of not receiving the promised interest and bond redemption when due. Moody's and S & P examine the financial strength of each bond issuer, the quality of its management, its prospects for the future, how strong it is compared to competitors or other municipalities, future directions of the industry or region, and a variety of other factors. Ratings for each bond issue are constantly re-evaluated. The higher the rating, the greater the probable safety of the bond. Table 16-1 shows the rating scales used by Moody's and S & P. The lower the rating value of the bond, the higher the stated interest rate, as more risk is involved. So-called **junk bonds** are often unsecured bonds of low quality rated below Baa or BB; they pay two to five more interest points than quality bonds. Higher ratings denote confidence that the issuer will not default and, if necessary, the bond can readily be sold before maturity. You can obtain the Moody's and S & P ratings for specific bond issues from libraries, banks, and brokerage firms.

U.S. Government Securities

There are several types of U.S. government securities: (1) Treasury bills, notes, and bonds, and (2) federal agency issue notes, bonds, and certificates. The interest rates on federal government securities are usually lower than on corporate bonds because they are almost risk-free: the possibility of default is near zero. Conservative investors like the certainty of U.S. government securities. Unlike U.S. savings bonds (discussed in Chapter 4), these government securities are transferable. This means that you may purchase a U.S. Treasury security directly from the government or in the securities markets. When buying U.S. government securities, you are required to provide the government with your Social Security number as well as the name of your financial institution so the latter can report correct tax information. You do not receive certificates; rather, purchases are recorded electronically, with all interest, principal, and other payments deposited with your local financial institution. One major advantage of government securities is that the interest income is exempt from state and local taxes.

Treasury Bills, Notes, and Bonds Treasury bills, notes, and bonds—collectively known as Treasury issues—are debt instruments used by the federal government to finance the *public debt,* or national debt.

Treasury bills, also called *T-bills,* are U.S. government securities that mature in ninety-one days, six months, nine months, or one year. New issues are generally sold only in $10,000 denominations. The ninety-one-day and six-month bills are sold every week, and the nine-month and one-year bills are sold every two weeks. No current interest income is paid on Treasury bills; they are sold on a "discount basis," with the gain on maturity representing the interest for federal income-tax purposes. The return on such investments is called a *discount yield.* For example, if you purchased a one-year $10,000 T-bill for $9,200, it would mature in twelve months and the U.S. Treasury Department would mail you a check for $10,000. The discount yield is 8.7 percent ($10,000 − $9,200 = $800 ÷ $9,200) because your investment was only $9,200.

You may purchase Treasury issues directly from any Federal Reserve Bank or branch office. You may buy T-bills on a noncompetitive bid basis. The price you pay for the bill will be the average of all the competitive offers made by large institutions that buy millions of dollars' worth of T-bills. Simply submit a certified or cashier's check for the face amount along with the proper form. A few days later you will receive the T-bill and a refund check in the amount of the difference between the face value of the bill and the purchase price. You can also make the purchase through a securities broker or a bank, but you must pay a $15 to $30 fee.

U.S. Treasury notes are U.S. government securities in $1,000 and $10,000 denominations that have a maturity of one to ten years and pay interest semiannually. These notes are registered and sold with a fixed interest rate, and the rates are slightly higher than those of Treasury bills. *Treasury bonds* are U.S. government securities that have a maturity time of more than ten years and are sold in $1,000 and $10,000 denominations. Interest is paid semiannually on these registered bonds. The fixed interest rates are higher than on notes because they are longer-term issues.

Federal Agency Bonds, Notes, and Certificates   More than a hundred different bonds, notes, and certificates are issued by various federal agencies, such as the Federal Home Loan banks, Government National Mortgage Association, Federal Intermediate Credit banks, Banks for Cooperatives, and Federal Land banks. They are often called *agency issues.* Since these certificates are not backed by the full faith and credit of the U.S. government and are not as popularly known as Treasury securities, they often pay a yield that is one-quarter of one percent or more higher.

The actual certificate of ownership of agency issues is held in trust in a bank. Interest is either mailed directly to you or credited to your account with a broker. Redemption of government securities is not automatic at maturity. You must submit evidence of ownership either to a financial institution or to a Federal Reserve Bank.

Municipal (State and Local) Bonds

Municipal bonds, also called *munies,* are long-term debts issued by local governments (cities, states, and various districts and political subdivisions) and their agencies. Moody's *Bond Record* lists some twenty thousand municipalities, and there are twice as many unrated issues. The range could be from a triple-A, $30-million state highway bond to an unrated $50,000 issue by a local parking authority.

Among the dozen or more types of specialized municipal bonds, two are frequently issued: general obligation and revenue bonds. *General obligation bonds,* the more common, are backed by the full taxing authority of the issuing agency. Since the local government has a primary responsibility to repay these debts, they usually have the highest safety rating and pay lower yields than other municipal bonds. Massachusetts and other states have recently offered *mini-bonds* issued directly to the public in denominations as small as $100 and $500. *Revenue bonds* are backed by the revenues from the projects built or maintained by the bond's proceeds, such as dormitories, sewers, waterworks, and toll roads. Revenue bonds typically have yields about 20 percent higher than general obligation bonds of the same quality, as they are less safe.

Municipal bonds almost always offer a lower return than other bonds because of tax regulations. Interest paid on almost all munies is exempt from federal income taxes and is normally exempt from state and local taxes if the investor lives in the state that issued the bond. A single taxpayer in the 28 percent bracket would have to earn more than 10 percent on a taxable investment to equal the yield on a tax-free muni earning 7.2 percent [7.2 percent = $.10 \times (1.00 - .28)$]. (Tax-equivalent yields are discussed in detail on page 505.)

Note that capital gains on the sale of munies are taxable. Gains are possible because bonds may be bought at a discount and then sold at a higher price or redeemed for full value at maturity.

During the Great Depression, hundreds of local governments failed to pay their bond obligations in a timely manner. In the 1970s and 1980s, numerous municipalities experienced difficulty in paying their debts on time. Examples include New York City, Cleveland, and the Washington Public Power Supply System (often known as "Whoops") utility. This is evidence that, although municipal bonds are generally safer than corporate bonds, they are not as safe as U.S. government securities. Both Moody's and S & P rate municipal bonds.

Specialty Issues

The types of bonds that interest most investors are those that simply pay interest semiannually and are redeemed at maturity. Two newer variations issued by some corporations and municipalities are floating-rate bonds and zero coupon bonds. *Floating-rate bonds* (or *variable-rate bonds*) are long-term corporate or municipal bond issues, usually redeemable at the option of the bondholder after two or three years, and with an interest rate fixed for only six to eighteen months, after which it varies according to an index or government interest rate. Since the investor shares in the risk when interest rates decline, such bonds are issued at higher rates than other corporate bonds. *Zero coupon bonds* (also called *zeros* or *deep discount bonds*) are municipal or corporate bonds, issued at prices far lower than their face value; they pay out no interest income to the investor (thus no coupons are cashed) and the return to the investor comes from redeeming them at their stated face value. The interest, usually compounded semiannually, accumulates within the bond itself. Thus, they are similar to EE savings bonds and U.S. Treasury bills. For example, an investor might purchase a ten-year, zero coupon corporate bond for $250. The Internal Revenue Service requires that the assumed interest of $75 ($1,000 − $250 = $750 ÷ 10) per year must be reported annually. Zero coupon bonds are usually advantageous only to investors utilizing tax-sheltered investments. (The uses of tax-sheltered investments for retirement planning are discussed in Chapter 21.)

Bond Prices and Yields

Both the price and yield of a bond are functions of current market interest rates, prices for similar bonds, the stated interest or coupon rate on the bond, and the number of years that must elapse before the bond matures. Transaction costs and taxes also affect yields significantly.

Market Interest Rates

The state of the economy as well as the supply and demand for credit affect *market interest rates.* These are the current interest rates charged on various types of corporate and government debts that have similar risks. When the economy slumps, the federal government often lowers the interest rates on Treasury issues in an attempt to stimulate economic activity. Market interest rates for various investments on a particular day might be: Treasury bills providing a return of 5.6 percent;

U.S. notes, 6.2 percent; U.S. bonds, 7.6 percent; high-quality corporate bonds, 9 percent; and high-quality municipal bonds, 6.4 percent. (Munis are lower because the income is tax-exempt.) These market interest rates would change frequently. In order for a bond to be attractive to investors, it must return the market interest rate or better for debts with similar risks.

When a bond is first issued it is sold at its *face value* (the value of the bond as stated on the certificate; it is also the amount the investor receives when the bond matures), at a *discount* below its face value, or at a *premium* above its face value. Since the stated interest rate on the bond is fixed, it is the price that changes to provide a competitive return. For example, assume that Running Paws Catfood Company decided to issue twenty-year bonds at 8.8 percent. In the time it took to print and prepare the bonds for sale the market interest rate on comparable bonds might have risen to 9 percent. In this instance, Running Paws bonds will sell at a slight discount in order to provide a competitive return. Discounts and premiums are factors of market interest rates and the number of years to maturity.

Current Yield

The *current yield* of a bond is a measure of the current annual income (the semiannual interest payments in dollars) expressed as a percentage when divided by its current market price. For example, if Glenda Champion of Williamston, North Carolina, owns a bond paying $70 a year and its current market price is $980, the bond's current yield is 7.1 percent, as shown below:

$$
\begin{aligned}
\text{Current yield} &= \frac{\text{current annual income}}{\text{current market value}} \\
&= \frac{\$70}{\$980} \\
&= 7.1\%
\end{aligned}
\tag{16--1}
$$

Financial sections of larger newspapers publish the current yields for a great number of bonds. Note, however, that the total return on a bond investment is made up of the same components as stock or any other investment: current income *and* capital gains.

Yield to Maturity

Yield to maturity (YTM) is the total annual rate of return earned by a bondholder on a bond when it is held to maturity; it reflects both the current income and any difference if the bond was purchased at a price other than face value. If a bond is purchased at face value, the yield to maturity is the same as the stated or coupon yield printed on the certificate.

For example, recall that Glenda Champion bought a Running Paws Catfood Company twenty-year bond with a stated interest rate of 7 percent. If Glenda bought it at a discount for $980, her yield to maturity is greater than the stated rate because she will receive $20 more than she paid for it when she receives the $1,000 at maturity.

Alternatively, if she bought it at a premium (because market rates were lower than the stated rate on Running Paws bonds), her yield to maturity is lower.

You can find exact YTMs in detailed bond tables available at large libraries or a broker's office. You can calculate the approximate yield to maturity when contemplating a bond purchase, as seemingly comparable bonds may have different YTMs. The YTM varies for each bond at various prices. The YTM formula shown below factors in the approximate appreciation when a bond is bought at a discount or at a premium.

$$YTM = \frac{I + \left(\dfrac{FV - CV}{N}\right)}{\left(\dfrac{FV + CV}{2}\right)} \qquad (16\text{--}2)$$

where

I = *interest* paid annually in dollars
FV = *face value*
CV = *current value*
N = *number* of years until maturity

For example, Glenda paid $980 for a twenty-year, 7 percent stated rate bond. The YTM of 7.17 percent is calculated as follows:

$$YTM = \frac{\$70 + \dfrac{(\$1{,}000 - \$980)}{20}}{\dfrac{(\$1{,}000 + \$980)}{2}}$$

$$= \frac{\$71}{990}$$

$$= 7.17\%$$

If you plan to buy and hold a bond until maturity, you should compare YTMs instead of current yields, because YTMs fairly represent all factors. The current yield on a bond is not an effective measure of the total annual return to the investor, and the fewer years until maturity the worse an indicator it becomes. Using the data above, if Glenda's bond with a current yield of 7.1 percent matured in ten years, the YTM becomes 7.27 percent; in five years the YTM becomes 7.47 percent; and in two years the YTM is 8.1 percent. Large-circulation newspapers publish yields to maturity, but only for Treasury issues.

| Effect of Transaction Costs on Bond Yields | The purchase and the sale of bonds often involves *transaction costs*, which include fees charged by the broker and the seller to pay for the expenses of transferring ownership of the certificate(s). You can avoid fees for U.S. securities only if you purchase the bonds directly from a government agency and later redeem them. Other bonds almost always have transaction costs. |

Payment of transaction costs, of course, reduces the yield. Since such expenses are usually incurred at both the purchase and sale of bonds (but not at retirement), they can cause sharp reductions in yield on a bond with a short maturity or in a small denomination. For example, the 10 percent coupon rate on a $1,000 corporate bond would be quickly reduced to about 4 percent if the bondholder had to pay a $30 fee to purchase the bond and another $30 to sell it a year later. The wise investor will (1) avoid transaction costs when possible (by buying T-bills or buying directly from the issuer if possible), (2) place a large amount of funds in bonds to reduce the effect of transaction costs (on a $10,000 bond the above $60 in fees would amount to only six-tenths of 1 percent), and (3) purchase bonds with a longer maturity to reduce the effect of the transaction costs ($60 in fees on a $1,000 bond would be a reduction in yield of about 6 percent over one year, 3 percent over two years, and 2 percent over three years). Some banks charge maintenance fees of up to $5 a month to serve as custodian of bonds; you can avoid this fee by locating a bank that does not charge it.

Tax-equivalent Yields

In Chapter 7 we illustrated the effect of the marginal tax rate on your income. The less you pay in taxes, the more you have available for spending, saving, and investing. Because municipal bonds receive special tax treatment, many investors consider buying them.

In general, the higher your federal tax bracket, the more favorable municipal bonds are as an investment compared to taxable bonds. The following formula calculates the federal *taxable yield* (TY):

$$TY = \frac{\text{tax-exempt yield}}{1.00 - \text{federal marginal tax rate}} \qquad (16-3)$$

For example, assume that you are a taxpayer paying at the 28 percent federal marginal tax rate. This means that any extra income earned over a certain amount will be taxed at that rate. You are considering buying a tax-exempt bond yielding 7 percent. Substituting in formula 16-3 gives

$$TY = \frac{.07}{1.00 - .28}$$
$$= \frac{.07}{.72}$$
$$= 9.7\%$$

Therefore, a 9.7 percent taxable yield is equivalent to a tax-exempt 7 percent yield. Thus, you would have to earn a yield greater than 9.7 percent on a taxable bond (or any other taxable investment) in order to earn more than the tax-exempt yield of 7 percent. Restated in the opposite way, you would have to get a tax-exempt yield greater than 7 percent to do better than a taxable yield of 9.7 percent.

When you know the taxable yield, you can reverse the problem. For example, assume that you are a taxpayer paying at the 33 percent federal marginal tax rate and you are considering investing in a taxable corporate bond yielding 10.6 percent. How much of a *tax-exempt yield* (*TEY*) would you need to do better than you would with the taxable bond? Simply reverse formula 16–3:

$$TEY = TY \times (1.00 - \text{federal marginal tax rate}) \qquad (16-4)$$

Substituting figures, we have

$$
\begin{aligned}
TEY &= 10.6 \times (1.00 - .33) \\
&= 10.6 \times .67 \\
&= 7.1\%
\end{aligned}
$$

Therefore, you would have to earn a tax-exempt yield above 7.1 percent to earn more after taxes than on a 10.6 percent taxable investment.

The *real* marginal tax rate also includes the effect on an investment of both state and local taxes. Residents of New York State and New York City who buy *local* municipal bonds, for example, enjoy exemption from state and local income taxes on the earnings from these bonds, and the equivalent yields on their bonds rise accordingly.

Advantages and Disadvantages of Bond Investments

The advantages and disadvantages of investing in bonds are explained below.

Advantages

1. **Higher interest rates than savings accounts** You receive a higher current income yield than you do on savings accounts. When market interest rates are declining many conservative investors purchase bonds with a three- to four-year remaining maturity to "lock in" the higher rates.

2. **Safe return of principal** Choosing a highly rated bond provides excellent assurance that the principal will be returned when the maturity date arrives. There is less financial risk with bonds than with common stocks. A bond issued from a highly regarded company provides security to an investor who has almost a guarantee of return of principal.

3. **Regular income** The fixed interest payments of bonds represent a known amount of money that almost assuredly will come in on a regular basis.

4. **Diversification of investment portfolio** The investor who wishes to spread out the risk of losing capital can choose among several different types of investments. Placing funds in common stocks, in real estate as well as in some bonds provides diversification.

5. **Low purchase cost** You may purchase most bonds in denominations of $1,000, and some municipals are available for as little as $100.

6. **Ease of management** Although you should never ignore your investments, bonds need less careful attention than most alternatives. If you choose government or other top-rated bonds and hold them to maturity, they will need minimal management.

7. **No taxes on municipal bonds** Interest earned on municipal bonds is exempt from federal, and sometimes state and local, taxes. Thus persons in higher marginal tax brackets might find them attractive.

Disadvantages

1. **Interest rate movements affect bond prices** Bond prices are influenced partially by supply and demand and mostly by the cost of money. If you paid $1,000 for a twenty-year, 7 percent bond and needed to sell it when current interest rates were at 9 percent, you might lose more than $200. You can estimate the selling price of an old bond (assuming it is not just a couple of years from maturity) with the following formula:

$$\text{Selling price} = \frac{\text{annual interest income in dollars}}{\text{current interest rate}} \qquad (16\text{--}5)$$

Substituting figures, the selling price equals $70 ÷ .09, or $777.78. If you bought the bond for $1,000, you will lose $222.22 if you sell it for $777.78. (Keep it until maturity and the issuer will retire it for $1,000.)

2. **Volatile bond prices** Since interest rates vary after a bond has been issued, bond prices can change rapidly on occasion. They are most volatile when (a) bonds are sold at less than face value when first issued, (b) the stated rate is low, and (c) the bond maturity time is long. The investor who holds a bond to maturity might ignore such information, but the person considering selling before maturity might be shocked to see price swings of 20 percent or more. The speculator might see such rapid price changes as opportunities.

3. **No hedge against inflation** During inflationary times, market interest rates rise, which pushes bond interest rates up as well. Thus, the bond investor earns a current return that may or may not stay even with the inflation rate.

4. **Principal does not appreciate** Unlike common stocks, bonds do not increase in value with increased profitability of the firm or good expectations for the future. Bond prices are instead tied to general interest rates. Except for convertible bonds, price appreciation is unlikely to occur unless the financial rating rises or interest rates decline.

5. **Difficulty of compounding** Unlike many stockholders, bondholders cannot reinvest dividends to receive the benefits of compounding (earning interest on principal and interest). They must instead hold interest payments in lower-yielding savings accounts or money market accounts until they accumulate enough to purchase another bond.

6. **High taxes** Except for tax-exempt bonds, the interest and capital gains on bonds are subject to an investor's marginal tax rate.

7. **Possible poor marketability** Although all bonds are marketable, holding lots of five or fewer makes selling a bit more difficult. A premium commission of as much as $50 might be charged for odd-lot sales. Further, prices of tax-exempt bonds are not published daily except for the larger issues.

8. **Poor diversification** Because most bond issues sell at $1,000 each, it may be difficult for some small investors to diversify if all their investments are in bonds.

Buying and Selling

If you want to make money on bonds, the timing of their purchase and sale can be crucial. This section discusses the selection of bonds and when it is best to sell a bond.

Selecting Bonds

Deciding whether to buy bonds as an investment depends on your investment needs, the current yields of investment alternatives, and your estimate about the future of interest rates. Conservative and moderate bondholders generally desire income rather than the opportunity for appreciation. Also, most bonds held to maturity carry little financial risk as compared to common stocks and real estate.

The total annual after-tax return on bonds is normally about one-half that of stocks. This is not true, however, during economic downturns. During an economic recession, declining profits reduce dividends, and the prices of common stocks, while current yields on bonds tend to increase and may equal or even exceed those on stocks.

Advice for the Conservative Bond Investor*

- If interest rates are volatile or show little movement, put money in a money market fund, short-term CDs, or Treasuries.

- When interest rates are low, take profits on bonds and keep money in a money market fund, short-term CDs, or Treasuries.

- When interest rates are rising, stay liquid; be alert for bargains, as eventual falling prices and rising yields will create opportunities.

- If interest rates are falling, move your money out of money market funds and into short-term CDs and Treasuries.

- If interest rates are falling, lock in yields among intermediate and long-term securities.

* Especially if you have some well-reasoned opinions on the direction of interest rates, inflation, and the economy for the next year or more.

How to Select a Bond

The process of selecting a bond involves the following four decisions:

1. **Decide on risk level** The level of financial risk is related to the likely rate of return; the safest bonds offer the lowest yields. U.S. government securities offer virtually no risk. For slightly more risk, consider the highest-rated corporate and municipal bonds. Note that most commercial banks do not invest in a bond with a rating lower than Baa or B. Lower-rated bonds offer substantial risk as well as higher yields.

2. **Decide on maturity** Consider the time schedule of your financial needs. Bonds with a short maturity generally have a lower current yield but greater price stability. For people who desire a maturity time of a year or less, a Treasury bill rather than a savings certificate of deposit is often a better investment. Remember that you buy T-bills at a discount, so you need less cash. Also, T-bills calculate interest based on a 360-day year but actually earn interest for 365 days, which increases the yield.

3. **Decide on tax equivalents** Carefully consider the impact of the return from bonds on the total income taxes to be paid. As shown in formulas 16–3 and 16–4, tax-exempt securities may be a better investment than taxable alternatives.

4. **Decide on highest yield to maturity (YTM)** Given similar bond issues with comparable risks, maturity, and tax equivalency, investors should choose the one that offers the highest yield to maturity (YTM), which was illustrated in formula 16–2.

Knowing When to Sell a Bond

In a few distinct instances, a bondholder should consider selling before a bond matures.

1. **When interest rates have dropped** When interest rates drop, the price of a bond necessarily increases. If, for example, you have an 8 percent bond and interest rates decline to 6 percent, the price of your bond could rise to over $1,333 (as determined by formula 16–5).

2. **When the bond rating has slipped** In spite of your efforts to choose a quality bond, unexpected events can cause a bond's rating to change. Perhaps the corporation suffered some economic setbacks; perhaps the municipality had a loss in taxing authority. Be alert to any changes in bond ratings. A decreased bond rating can mean greater financial risk and a lower market price.

3. **When shifts in interest rates are definitely expected** Interest rates are constantly changing. But some events clearly suggest that substantial changes in interest rates are ahead. Perhaps a conservative (or liberal) government is elected; perhaps federal budget deficits are growing larger (or smaller) with confident

forecasts of greater deficits (or surpluses) in the future. How you might react to a likely interest rate shift depends on what bonds you own and the direction of the shift. You could sell short-term bonds and reinvest the proceeds should interest rates be expected to rise. In a market of falling interest rates, you can realize capital gains by selling bonds with higher coupon rates.

Summary

1. Fixed-asset investments are classified according to variability of value and yield, such as fixed value and fixed yield, fixed value and variable yield, and variable value and fixed yield. Bonds are in the last category.

2. As evidences of debt, bonds have several characteristics: legal indenture, denominations of value, maturity time, being secured or unsecured, senior or subordinated, and registered or bearer, sinking fund, callability and convertibility, and warrants.

3. The three general types of bonds are corporate bonds, U.S. government securities, and municipal bonds, and the last one is exempt from federal income taxes.

4. Both the price and yield of a bond are functions of current market interest rates, prices for similar bonds, the stated interest or coupon rate, and the number of years until the bond matures.

5. The advantages of investing in bonds include higher interest rates than on savings accounts, safe return of principal, regular income, and ease of management. Some of the disadvantages are that interest rate movements affect market value of a bond before it reaches maturity, the principal does not appreciate, and interest is not compounded.

6. The yield on bonds is described by various terms, such as *current yield* and *yield to maturity*.

7. Four steps are involved in selecting a bond for investment: deciding on risk level, maturity, tax equivalents, and highest yield to maturity.

8. A bondholder should consider selling when interest rates have dropped, when the bond rating has slipped, and when interest rate shifts are definitely expected.

Modern Money Management

The Johnsons Compare Some Investments

Harry and Belinda have saved $6,000 toward a down payment on a very expensive luxury automobile they hope to purchase in the next three to five years. Because they are not getting too high a return on their money market account, they seek the greater yields of bond investments. Examine the table here, which identifies eight investment alternatives; respond to the questions that follow.

Name of Issue	Bond Denomination	Coupon Rate	Years until Maturity	Moody's Rating	Market Price	Current Yield	YTM
Corporate ABC	$1,000	9.0%	4	Aa	$ 980		
Corporate DEF	1,000	9.5	20	Aa	1,020		
Corporate GHI	1,000	8.4	12	Baa	735		
Corporate JKL	1,000	8.8	5	Aaa	990		
Corporate MNO	1,000	10.1	15	B	820		
Corporate PQR	1,000	6.0	11	B	450		
Treasury note	1,000	8.1	3	—	995		
Municipal bond	1,000	6.6	20	Aa	960		

1. What is the current yield of each investment alternative? (Put your responses in the proper column in the table.)

2. What is the yield to maturity for each? (Put your responses in the proper column in the table.)

3. Knowing that the Johnsons are moderate in investment philosophy, which one of the six corporate bonds would you recommend? Why?

4. As the Johnsons are in the 28 percent federal marginal tax bracket and given the one municipal bond choice, what is the tax-equivalent yield? Should they invest in your recommendation in questions 3 or in the municipal bond? Why?

5. What three of the eight alternatives would you recommend as a group so that the Johnsons would have some protection for their $6,000 because of diversification? Why do you suggest that combination?

6. Assume that the Johnsons bought all three of your recommendations in question 5. If market interest rates drop by 2 percent in two years (from 9.4 to 7.4 and 6.9 to 4.9), what are your recommendations for buying or selling each alternative? Why?

Key Words and Concepts

Review Questions

1. Explain the characteristics of a fixed-asset investment, and give an example of one.

2. Identify a type of fixed-asset investment that has a fixed value but a variable yield.

3. Explain how bonds have a variable value and a fixed yield.

4. List several characteristics of bonds.

5. Explain how an indenture works and why government bonds do not have indentures.

6. Distinguish between secured and unsecured bonds.

7. Explain the difference between a senior debenture and a subordinated debenture bond.

8. Identify the purpose of a bond sinking fund and explain its value to a bond investor.

9. What is the difference between coupon bonds and registered bonds?

10. Describe a situation in which a bond issuer would exercise a bond's callable feature.

11. What is the value of having a convertible bond?

12. Name the three general types of bonds and distinguish among them.

13. Describe the differences among Treasury bills, notes, and bonds.

14. Why are U.S. government bonds the safest bonds to buy?

15. Distinguish among the two most popular types of municipal bonds.

16. What tax characteristic is unique to municipal bonds?

17. Explain the difference between current yield and yield to maturity.

18. Explain how changes in market interest rates cause bonds to be sold at a premium or at a discount.

19. What are transaction costs and how can they be reduced or avoided?

20. Illustrate how your federal marginal tax rate can influence your decision to invest in different types of bonds.

21. Explain the four-step procedure of selecting bonds.

22. Describe three situations in which it may be wise to sell bonds.

Case Problems

1. Mary Ellen Boyer of Taos, New Mexico, has purchased several types of bonds over the years. Her total bond investment exceeds $40,000. She prefers a variable value and fixed yield investment. Her sister Margaret, on the other hand, has more than $50,000 invested in various blue-chip income common stocks in a variety of industries.
   a. Justify Mary Ellen's attitude toward bond investments.
   b. Justify Margaret's attitude toward stock investments.

2. Johnson Edwards of Henderson, Tennessee, is interested in investing $10,000 in bonds because he believes that market interest rates are going to decline during a business slowdown over the next eighteen months or so. Johnson is in the 28 percent marginal tax bracket and is a conservative investor. Assuming that his conclusion is correct, give him appropriate advice in response to the questions below.
   a. Should Johnson buy corporate or government bonds? Why?
   b. If Johnson is in the 33 percent federal marginal tax bracket and he has to choose between a corporate bond with a current yield of 11.1 percent and a municipal bond yielding 7.0 percent, which would you recommend? Why?
   c. If high-quality corporate bonds have a current yield of 11.2 percent, long-term government bonds have a current yield of 8.7 percent, and Treasury notes are yielding 8.4 percent, which type do you recommend to Johnson and why?
   d. If Johnson was to purchase municipal bonds, would you recommend general obligation or revenue bonds? Why?
   e. Assume that Johnson bought a twenty-year $1,000 corporate bond with a coupon rate of 9 percent for $950. Calculate his current yield and also tell him what the selling price of his

bond might be if interest rates drop 2 percent over the next year.

3. Charlotte Chang of Martin, Tennessee, is a speculative investor who believes that interest rates will drop over the next year or two because of an economic slowdown. Charlotte wants to profit in the bond market by buying and selling during the next several months. She seeks your advice on how to invest her $15,000.

   a. If Charlotte buys corporate or municipal bonds, what rating should her selections have? Why?

   b. Assume that Charlotte has a choice between two comparable $1,000 corporate bonds. One has a coupon rate of 7.4 percent. The other is a convertible bond with a coupon rate of 7 percent. The convertible right is for thirty shares of Running Paws common stock with a current market price of $30, over the next five years. Tell Charlotte which bond is the better choice and give your assumptions about the market value of the stock.

   c. If Charlotte buys fifteen $1,000 thirty-year corporate bonds with a 9.8 coupon rate for $960 each, what is her current yield?

   d. If market interest rates drop 2 percent over the next twelve months (from 10.2 to 8.2 percent), what will be the approximate market value of each of Charlotte's bonds in part c?

   e. Assuming rates do go down 2 percent in twelve months, how much is Charlotte's capital gain on the $14,400 investment? How much was her current return for the two semiannual interest payments? How much was her total return both in dollars and as an annual yield? (Ignore transaction costs.)

   f. If Charlotte is wrong about projecting the future and interest rates go up 1 percent over the year, what would be the probable market value of each of her bonds? Tell why you would advise her to sell or not to sell.

Suggested Readings

"*Fortune* Forecast: Equilibrium Ahead for Interest Rates." *Fortune*, March 20, 1987, pp. 63–64. *Fortune's* predictions for the future on the direction of interest rates.

"Municipal Garbage." *Forbes,* March 9, 1987, pp. 42–43. Not all municipal bond investments are safe.

"Seizing the Golden Moment in Tax-Free Bonds." *Money,* January 1987, pp. 106–110. How to shop smart in the municipal bond market.

"Where to Get up to 20% on Your Money." *Consumers Digest,* May/June 1987, pp. 21–25. A variety of fixed-income and other investments are available.

CHAPTER 17

Buying and Selling Securities

OBJECTIVES

After reading this chapter, the student should be able to

1. explain the operation of primary and secondary securities markets.
2. list the major sources of investment information.
3. calculate the potential total return of a stock.
4. discuss the factors to consider when selecting a broker.
5. describe the elements in the process of buying and selling securities.
6. explain the six-step investment process.
7. specify some investment approaches for long-term and short-term investors.
8. list three guidelines to use when deciding whether to sell securities.

T his chapter will give you more specific information about how to buy and sell securities. The sequence of topics follows the investment process. You must first understand how the securities markets operate. Then you can begin to explore information about general economic conditions, securities markets indexes, various industries, and specific companies. Next comes the important task of calculating a stock's potential total return as this tells you whether or not you want to invest in a particular company. Then you need to choose a securities broker to perform your buying and selling transactions. A six-step process on how to invest is then presented. Finally, you need to select the long- or short-term investment approach that is most acceptable to you and anticipate the best times to consider selling your securities.

Securities Markets

Securities are traded in primary and secondary markets. A *primary market* is where issuers and buyers of new offerings of stocks and bonds are brought together. For example, when Linda Webtek sold the original shares in Running Paws Catfood Company to her three friends, the primary market was her living room, where the transactions took place (see Chapter 15). More complex primary markets will be discussed below. A *secondary market* is where the trading of previously purchased securities occurs. Such markets include organized stock exchanges and over-the-counter markets. The activities of securities markets are regulated by the securities industry and by various government agencies.

Primary Markets

In the primary markets, companies that need capital to begin or expand their operations sell new issues of stocks or bonds or both to the investing public. However, later capital needs, perhaps for expansion, may also be financed by corporate profits. *Investment banking firms* are specialized sellers of new securities and serve as middlemen between the issuing company and the investing public in the primary markets. (This task of raising money for corporations is called *underwriting,* as distinguished from insurance underwriting.) Investment banking firms, either individually or acting as a syndicate, typically purchase the entire new stock or bond issue of a corporation and then resell it to the investing public.

For example, assume that Running Paws, now a successful small corporation, wants to expand and sell its products nationally. The owners have calculated that they will need about $5 million. After careful analysis, they estimate that the likely per-share market value of their new 100,000 shares of stock is probably $25. (The remainder of the needed funds will be raised by issuing long-term bonds and out of profits.) The underwriting firm negotiates a purchase price, perhaps $24, after assessing the likely marketability of the stock and the anticipated expenses in selling it. The $1 difference between the purchase

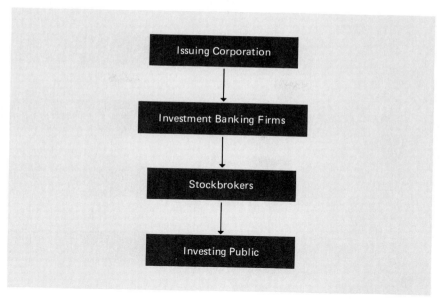

FIGURE 17-1
Flow of Stocks and Bonds in the Primary Markets

price and the expected resale price, or **spread,** is the potential profit for the investment banker. The underwriter then publicly announces the availability of the stock as of a certain date. The underwriter may sell blocks of shares to stockbrokers who in this case might pay $24.50 per share, with 50 cents representing the brokers' per-share profit when they sell shares to the investing public for $25. Normally, stockbrokers charge no sales commissions on the sale of new securities. Figure 17-1 illustrates this flow of stocks and bonds in the primary markets.

Secondary Markets

After securities have been sold in the primary markets, they are further sold and bought in the *secondary markets,* composed of organized stock exchanges and the over-the-counter market. These are commonly known as *securities markets* or *stock markets.*

You can buy or sell securities in the secondary markets through a **stockbroker,** who collects a commission on each purchase or sale of securities. A stockbroker may be called an account executive or a registered representative and work for a brokerage firm, broker dealer, or brokerage house. The stockbroker may either buy securities for the firm's own account to then sell to investors or arrange the transactions between buyers and sellers. Stockbrokers must disclose when they are selling securities owned by the firm. Figure 17-2 shows the flow of stocks, bonds, and other securities in the secondary markets. Note that the issuing corporations are no longer involved.

Organized Stock Exchanges   An *organized stock exchange* is a market where agents of buyers and sellers meet and trade a specified

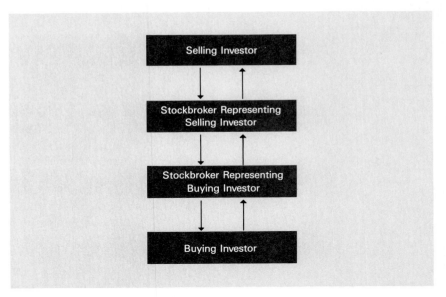

FIGURE 17–2
Flow of Securities in Secondary Markets

list of securities, which are usually those of the larger, well-known companies. More than three-fourths of all securities bought and sold are traded on one of the organized exchanges, such as the New York Stock Exchange, the American Stock Exchange, or a regional stock exchange (the Pacific Stock Exchange, for example). Each exchange trades only *listed securities*. This is a designation by a stock exchange meaning that the companies have met various criteria regarding number of stockholders, numbers of shares owned by the public (outstanding shares), market value of each share, and corporate earnings and assets. Such minimum requirements provide some assurance to investors that the stocks traded are issued by reputable companies.

Securities are traded on the floor of each exchange only by members of the stock exchange, whose number is generally fixed (there are 1,366 members of the New York Stock Exchange). A *member firm* is an organization that has purchased a *seat on the exchange* (the legal right to buy and sell securities on the exchange) with the approval of the board of directors of the exchange. In recent years, the price of a seat sold on the New York Stock Exchange has ranged from $425,000 to over $1 million. The largest brokerage firm (Merrill, Lynch, Pierce, Fenner & Smith) owns more than twenty seats on the New York exchange.

The *New York Stock Exchange* (NYSE), founded in 1792, is by far the largest exchange in the world and has the most stringent requirements for listing. It also is called the Big Board. Corporations must have minimum earnings of $2.5 million before taxes, net assets of at least $16 million, a minimum of 1.2 million shares publicly held, a market value of outstanding stocks of no less than $18 million (which varies according to market conditions), and a minimum number of two thousand shareholders owning at least one hundred shares each. In addition, the company must be of interest to investors nationally, have stability in its industry, and be able to improve its competitive position within that industry. As with all exchanges, companies may be delisted if they later fail to meet the minimum requirements. As Table 17–1 shows, over 2,400 common stock securities of the approximately 1,449 companies on the NYSE account for about 97 percent of the market value of *all* listed stocks on the various exchanges. The average per share price on the NYSE is $33.

The *American Stock Exchange* (ASE or AMEX), also located in New York City, represents the second largest exchange in the country. It is a distant second, with about 3 percent of the listed dollar volume traded. The AMEX was started in 1849 when people traded securities on a street corner on Wall Street, now the financial nerve center of the United States. Today the American Stock Exchange lists more than 940 stocks and 260 bonds. Since the AMEX lists smaller and younger companies than does the NYSE, its listing requirements are less stringent: $750,000 in earnings, $4 million in net assets, a minimum of 400,000 shares outstanding, $3 million in market value of outstanding shares, and a minimum of 800 shareholders owning a least 100 shares each. Note that these firms still have substantial investor interest.

Regional stock exchanges trade securities of interest primarily to investors living in certain areas of the country. Many stocks listed on the NYSE and the AMEX are also listed on some regional exchanges to encourage more trading. Smaller firms are also listed. For example, the Pacific Stock Exchange (PSE) requires, in addition to other criteria, net assets of only $1 million for listing. Another advantage of the PSE, due to the difference in time zones, is that it can stay open for trading for a couple of hours later than the New York–based exchanges. Other regional stock exchanges include the Boston, Cincinnati, Intermountain, Midwest, Philadelphia, and Spokane exchanges.

Over-the-counter (OTC) Market All publicly traded securities not sold on an organized exchange are traded on the **over-the-counter (OTC) market.** Securities sold "over the counter" are typically those of small firms that do not have many shares outstanding and/or do not have much trading interest. The OTC has no listing requirements, and about forty thousand securities are available to investors. The price per share for a typical stock is $11.

In the OTC market, buyers and sellers negotiate transaction prices, often using a sophisticated telecommunications network connecting brokers throughout the country. The National Association of Securities Dealers Automated Quotation (NASDAQ) system provides prices on over three thousand securities plus some foreign stocks. There is no central exchange floor for transactions.

An OTC sale occurs when a broker representing a buyer communicates with another broker who has the desired securities. The second broker is more accurately known as a broker/dealer because besides

TABLE 17–1
Securities Listed on Exchanges[a]

Registered Exchanges	Common		Preferred		Bonds		Total Securities	
	Number	Market Value (in millions)	Number	Market Value (in millions)	Number	Market Value (in millions)	Number	Market Value (in millions)
American	772	$ 63,459	117	$ 6,795	336	$ 19,634	1,225	$ 89,888
Boston	97	1,537	0	0	6	148	103	1,685
Cincinnati	4	166	3	59	7	99	14	324
Midwest	9	648	4	24	0	0	13	672
New York	1,477	2,079,195	717	49,316	3,513	1,447,023	5,707	$ 3,575,534
Pacific	54	1,204	30	716	98	4,111	182	6,031
Philadelphia	20	383	23	1,794	42	2	85	2,179
Intermountain	N/A	N/A	N/A	N/A	N/A	N/A	N/A	N/A
Spokane	33	11	0	0	0	0	33	11
Total	2,466	$2,146,603	894	$58,704	4,002	$1,471,017	7,362	$3,676,324

Source: Securities and Exchange Commission, *SEC Monthly Statistical Review,* May 1987.

[a] Excludes securities that were suspended from trading at the end of the year, and securities that, because of inactivity, had no available quotes.

offering the usual brokerage services the firm can also "make a market" for one or more securities. ***Market making*** occurs in an effort to provide a continuous market as a broker/dealer maintains an inventory of specific securities to sell to other brokers and stands ready to buy reasonable quantities of the same securities at market prices. When a broker sells securities in which the firm has made a market, the buying investor must be informed that the firm made the market.

The transaction price is negotiated because there are two prices involved. The ***bid price*** is the amount a broker is willing to pay for a particular security, and the ***asked price*** is the amount a broker is willing to sell a particular security for. The investor pays the broker a nominal sales commission, in addition to the negotiated price, except when the transaction is for securities for which the broker makes a market. In that event, the spread is the profit earned by the broker.

Newspaper Stock and Bond Quotations
The daily buying and selling transactions of stocks and bonds are summarized in the nation's most widely read financial newspaper, *The Wall Street Journal.* Additional detailed information on each company and trading transactions can be found in the weekly newspaper *Barron's,* which is available at many newsstands. Since a number of stocks and bonds will be traded on more than one exchange, the details are reported most often under the listings for the larger exchanges. Abbreviated information is also published in most daily newspapers but generally is confined to activities on the New York Stock Exchange, the American Stock Exchange, and selected OTC stocks of local interest. The remainder of this section shows you how to read newspaper quotations for listed stocks, over-the-counter stocks, and bonds.

Figure 17–3 gives quotations for listed stocks on the New York Stock Exchange on one particular day. The companies listed have an abbreviated trading symbol. Let's examine the listing for Rockwell Corporation, indicated by the "Rockwl" symbol. The listing is for Rockwell Corporation common stock. We will follow the quotations column by column.

1. **Columns 1 and 2: 52 Weeks, High/Low** The first two columns show that Rockwell traded stock at a high price of 30⅞ and a low of 18½ during the past 52 weeks, not including the current trading day (June 1, 1987). Stock transactions are reported in eighths, with each eighth representing 12½ cents. Thus, during the past 12 months Rockwell stock ranged in price from $30.88 to $18.50.

2. **Column 3: Stock** This column gives the name of the stock, in this example, Rockwell.

3. **Column 4: Div.** This dividend amount is based on the last quarterly declaration by the company. For example, Rockwell last paid a 16½ cents quarterly dividend, which would be multiplied by 4 (quarters in a year) to obtain the estimate of 66 cents as an annual dividend.

1	2	3	4	5	6	7	8	9	10	11
52 Weeks				Yld	P-E	Sales				Net
High	Low	Stock	Div.	%	Ratio	100s	High	Low	Close	Chg.
50³/₈	20¹/₂	Rebok s	.40	1.0	15	2790	41¹/₈	39¹/₂	41	+ 1¹/₂
12³/₄	9	Reece	...		39	45	12⁵/₈	12³/₈	12⁵/₈+	¹/₈
1⁵/₈	³/₈	Regal	...	...		504	1³/₈	1¹/₄	1³/₈+	¹/₈
9⁷/₈	6³/₄	ReglFn n	...	...		65	7¹/₄	7	7¹/₈+	¹/₈
17	15	ReichT n	...	...		548u	17³/₈	17	17³/₈+	³/₈
48¹/₂	28³/₈	ReichC	.80	2.2	16	185	36⁵/₈	36¹/₄	36¹/₄ -	¹/₄
11¹/₄	7¹/₂	RelGp n.12e	1.2	11	1664	10³/₈	9³/₄	10¹/₈+	¹/₈	
13⁵/₈	7⁵/₈	RepGyp	.36	4.4	13	75	8³/₈	8¹/₈	8¹/₈	...
57³/₄	44	RepNY	1.16	2.4	9	98	48¹/₄	47³/₄	48¹/₄	...
29³/₈	17¹/₂	RepBk	1.00	4.2	20	359	23⁷/₈	23¹/₂	23³/₄	...
29	25	RepBk pf	2.12	7.7	...	17	26¹/₈	25⁷/₈	26¹/₈	...
93	64	RepBk adj	5.61e	8.4	...	12	67	67	67	+ ¹/₂
37⁷/₈	25	RshCot	.32	.8	18	1478u	39¹/₂	37¹/₂	38¹/₂+	1¹/₄
21³/₈	10¹/₄	Revlon	...	...		99	19³/₄	19³/₄	19³/₄	...
47¹/₈	26³/₈	Rexhm	.80	2.1	13	129	39⁷/₈	38⁵/₈	38³/₄ -	1¹/₈
74³/₄	38¹/₂	ReyMtl	1.20	1.9	13	756	64¹/₄	63¹/₂	64¹/₄+	⁷/₈
32	15³/₄	Rhodes	.36	2.3	11	148	15⁷/₈	15³/₄	15⁷/₈-	¹/₈
39³/₄	26³/₄	RiteAid	.66	2.0	18	904	33³/₄	32³/₄	33³/₈+	³/₈
2¹/₂	¹/₄	RvrOak				141	¹⁵/₁₆	⁷/₈	⁷/₈	...
18¹/₄	10⁷/₈	Robtsn 1.20j	...	...		10	13⁵/₈	13⁵/₈	13⁵/₈+	¹/₈
25³/₈	7¹/₂	vjRobins	...		7	862	23⁷/₈	23	23¹/₄	...
29⁷/₈	15⁵/₈	RochG	2.20	13.5	5	579	16¹/₂	16¹/₈	16¹/₄	...
52	39¹/₂	RochTl	2.64	6.1	12	63	43³/₄	43¹/₄	43³/₈-	¹/₈
22¹/₂	18¹/₂	RckCtr	1.80	9.5	15	432	19³/₈	19	19 -	¹/₄
30⁷/₈	18¹/₂	Rockwl	.66	2.5	12	3155	26¹/₂	25³/₄	26 +	¹/₈
13	9	RodRn n.07e	.8	9	4	9¹/₈	9¹/₈	9¹/₈+	¹/₈	
47³/₈	28¹/₂	RoHaas	80	1.8	19	699	44¹/₄	43¹/₂	43³/₄+	¹/₈
33¹/₄	24³/₄	Rohr		...	14	1012	26	25³/₈	25⁷/₈+	⁵/₈
34⁷/₈	17³/₈	RolinE s	.08	.2	42	1355	32¹/₂	31³/₄	32¹/₄+	¹/₈
23¹/₄	10¹/₄	RolE wi		...		44	22¹/₄	21⁷/₈	21⁷/₈+	¹/₈
19⁵/₈	14⁵/₈	Rollins	.50	2.8	23	664	17³/₄	17³/₈	17³/₄+	¹/₄
29⁷/₈	14⁷/₈	Roper s	.48	1.8	11	132	26¹/₄	26	26¹/₄	...
52¹/₂	35¹/₄	Rorer	1.16	2.5	42	1368	46	42¹/₄	45¹/₂+	3
25⁵/₈	12¹/₈	Rothch n	...	...		1447	13¹/₄	12³/₄	13¹/₈+	⁵/₈
8¹/₄	3³/₈	Rowan	...	...		1259	7	6⁷/₈	7	...
36¹/₄	22	Rown pf2.12	6.5	...	18	32³/₄	32³/₈	32¹/₂+	¹/₄	
134³/₄	74¹/₈	RoylD	6.04e	4.8	15	2310	125³/₈	124⁷/₈	125³/₈-	¹/₈
11⁵/₈	5	RoyInt	...		75	85	6³/₄	6¹/₂	6³/₄+	¹/₈
11³/₈	8³/₈	Royce n	...	...		637	9¹/₂	9¹/₄	9¹/₂+	¹/₈
30	18¹/₈	Rubmd	.28	1.0	29	598	29⁵/₈	28⁷/₈	29³/₈-	¹/₈
43⁵/₈	25¹/₈	RussBr	.60	1.6	17	758	37	36	36⁷/₈+	1⁷/₈
36¹/₄	25³/₄	RusTog	.90	2.8	12	14	31⁵/₈	31³/₈	31⁵/₈+	¹/₂
20¹/₂	13³/₈	Rusel s	.20	1.2	15	226	16⁷/₈	16¹/₄	16¹/₂-	¹/₈
50³/₄	30¹/₂	RyanH	1.20	2.5	13	214	47⁵/₈	47¹/₂	47¹/₂-	¹/₈
43	24¹/₂	Ryder	.52	1.4	17	559	37⁷/₈	37	37¹/₈-	³/₄
32³/₈	22¹/₄	Rykoff	.60	2.5	23	90	24	23⁵/₈	24 +	⁵/₈
33	15	RyInd s	.40	1.8	10	149	22⁷/₈	22	22¹/₈-	¹/₂
24¹/₈	15³/₈	Rymer	...	...		16	18⁵/₈	18³/₈	18¹/₂	...
14	11³/₈	Rymer pf 1.17	10.0	...	66	12	11³/₄	11³/₄	...	

EXPLANATORY NOTES
(For New York and American Exchange listed issues)

Sales figures are unofficial.

PE ratios are based on primary per share earnings as reported by the companies for the most recent four quarters. Extraordinary items generally are excluded.

The 52-week High and Low columns show the highest and the lowest price of the stock in consolidated trading during the preceding 52 weeks plus the current week, but not the current trading day. The 52-week high and low columns are adjusted to reflect stock payouts of 10 percent or more.

u—Indicates a new 52-week high. d—Indicates a new 52-week low.

g—Dividend or earnings in Canadian money. Stock trades in U.S. dollars. No yield or PE shown unless stated in U.S. money. n—New issue in the past 52 weeks. The high-low range begins with the start of trading and does not cover the entire 52 week period. pp—Two installments. s—Split or stock dividend of 25 per cent or more in the past 52 weeks. The high-low range is adjusted from the old stock. Dividend begins with the date of split or stock dividend. v—Trading halted on primary market.

Unless otherwise noted, rates of dividends in the foregoing table are annual disbursements based on the last quarterly or semi-annual declaration. Special or extra dividends or payments not designated as regular are identified in the following footnotes.

a—Also extra or extras. b—Annual rate plus stock dividend. c—Liquidating dividend. e—Declared or paid in preceding 12 months. i—Declared or paid after stock dividend or split up. j—Paid this year, dividend omitted, deferred or no action taken at last dividend meeting. k—Declared or paid this year, an accumulative issue with dividends in arrears. r—Declared or paid in preceding 12 months plus stock dividend. t—Paid in stock in preceding 12 months, estimated cash value on ex-dividend or ex-distribution date.

x—Ex-dividend or ex-rights. y—Ex-dividend and sales in full. z—Sales in full.

pf—Preferred. rt—Rights. un—Units. wd—When distributed. wi—When issued. wt—Warrants. ww—With warrants. xw—Without warrants.

vj—In bankruptcy or receivership or being reorganized under the Bankruptcy Act, or securities assumed by such companies.

FIGURE 17–3
How Listed Stocks Are Quoted

Source: Wall Street Journal, June 1, 1987. Reprinted by permission of the *Wall Street Journal*, © Dow Jones & Company, Inc., 1987. All Rights Reserved.

4. **Column 5: Yld%** The figure in this column is the yield calculated by dividing the current price of the stock by the dividend. The current price of the stock ($26) is in column 10, thus $.66 ÷ $26 = 2.5 percent.
5. **Column 6: P-E Ratio** This figure is the price earnings ratio based on the current price. The earnings figure used to calculate the P/E ratio is not published in the daily newspaper but is the latest available 12-month earnings amount published by the company.
6. **Column 7: Sales 100s** This figure indicates the trading activity of the stock in hundreds. Thus, 315,500 shares of Rockwell were traded on this day.
7. **Columns 8, 9, and 10: High/Low/Close** These three figures indicate the range of prices at which the stock traded on this day. "High" is the highest price at which it traded, "low" is the lowest price, and "close" is the last trade of the day before the market closed.
8. **Column 11: Net Chg.** The net change represents the difference between the closing price on this day and the closing price on the previous trading day. The Rockwell closing price of $26 was down ⅛ from the previous closing price, which thus must have been 26⅛.

Figure 17–4 shows recent over-the-counter stock quotations. We can see that Food Lion A stock paid a recent dividend of 13 cents. On

FIGURE 17–4
How Over-the-counter Stocks Are Quoted

Source: Wall Street Journal, June 1, 1987. Reprinted by permission of the *Wall Street Journal*, © Dow Jones & Company, Inc. 1987. All Rights Reserved.

365-day High	Low			Yld	P-E	Sales (hds)	High	Low	Last	Net Chg.
9⅛	3¾	Flow System		..	257	220	5⅜	4⅞	5⅛	+ ⅛
15⅛	10⅜	Fluorocrbn	.28	1.9	14	542	14¾	14½	14¾	+ ⅛
14⅛	5¼	FMI Fncl	.10d	.8	5	148	13	12⅞	13	+ ⅛
49½	34	FNW Bncp	.72	1.5	..	9	48	47	48	+2
9⅝	4½	Fonar Corptn		..	77	311	6⅜	6	6⅛	...
15¼	9¾	FoodLionA	.13	.9	36	1078	15⅛	14⅞	15⅛	+ ⅛
17	11¾	FoodLionB	.12	.8	38	243	15¾	15½	15¾	+ ¼
43	28¾	FrmostAm	.96	2.9	20	15	33¾	33¼	33¼	...
19	6⅜	Forest Oil	2k	..	..	78	12⅝	12¼	12½	+ ⅜
22¼	9¾	Forschner Gr		..	..	2	21½	21½	21½	+ ½
28	14¾	FortuneF	.10b	.4	8	609	26½	23½	26½	+3⅜
2¾	1	Fortune Syst		..	..	383	2⅛	2 1-16	2 1-16	−1-16
9⅞	5⅛	ForumGrp	.06	1.1	17	1921	5½	5¼	5¼	− ¼
6¼	2⅛	FosterLB	.02h	..	..	13	3⅜	3¼	3¼	− ⅛
27	19¼	FourthFin	.92	4.4	9	87	21	20½	21	+ ¾
18⅜	12	Framingham		..	..	66	12¾	12½	12¾	...
6⅛	1½	Frnkln Cmptr		..	..	40	5	4¾	5	+ ½
21½	16¼	FranklinEl	.56	2.7	13	26	21	20½	21	+1
15⅞	10¼	Franklin S&L		..	..	35	10½	10¼	10¼	...
21¼	11¼	Freedom FSB		..	18	479	20¼	19½	20¼	+ ¾
26⅞	14¾	Frem Genl	.60	3.9	..	285	15¾	15½	15½	− ¼
16½	5	Fretter Inc		..	19	109	5¼	5⅛	5⅛	− ⅛
13¾	9¾	Freymiller Tr		..	..	132	11¼	10½	11¼	+ ¾
11	7¼	Frontier Insur		..	8	110	9	8¾	9	+ ¼
9⅝	3¼	Frost Sull	.14	1.7	22	111	8¼	8	8¼	...
13	10	FrozenFd	.14b	1.2	9	15	11¾	11¾	11¾	...
4⅛	1⅜	Fuddruckers		..	..	237	2⅛	2	2	...
36	14½	Fuller HB	.42	1.2	17	73	35¼	34¾	34¾	− ¼
9½	7⅛	FultnFSL	At	..	..	132	7⅝	7⅜	7⅝	...
31¾	21½	FultonFin	.72g	2.9	12	3	24½	24½	24½	...

Bonds	Cur Yld	Vol	High	Low	Close	Net Chg.
Ens 10s01	cv	6	106¾	106¾	106¾	+ ¼
EnvSys 6¾11	cv	20	98	98	98	+ 1
EqutR 9½06	cv	50	249	248	249	+ 1
Equitc 10s04	cv	4	97½	97½	97½	...
Exxon 6s97	7.5	66	81¼	80½	80½	+ ½
Exxon 6½98	7.7	10	83⅞	83⅞	83⅞	+ ⅞
ExonFn 10½89	10.3	40	101¾	101½	101¾	...
Frch 9¾98	11.2	4	87	87	87	− 1
Feddr 5s96	cv	1	63	63	63	+ 2
FedCo 6s17	cv	29	93½	91½	92½	− 1
FedN 4⅜s96	cv	10	204	204	204	+ 8
Fldcst 6s12	cv	1	97	97	97	+ ½
FinCpA 11⅞98	13.6	29	87	82½	87	+ 5
FinCp dc11½02	cv	97	78½	78	78½	...
FleetFn 8½10	cv	7	141	139½	141	+ 5½
FrdC 4½96	cv	10	350	350	350	...
FrdC 8⅜01	9.1	14	91⅞	91½	91⅞	...
FrdC 7⅞89	7.9	38	99½	99⅜	99½	...
FrdC 8½02	9.2	10	92	92	92	...
FreptM 10½14	cv	74	108	106¾	108	+ 1
FreptM 10⅞01	11.1	7	98	98	98	...
Fruf 13½96	13.7	33	98¼	98¼	98¼	+ ¼
Fuqua 7s88	7.1	1	99	99	99	...
Fuqua 9½98	9.9	14	95¾	94⅜	95¾	+ 1½
GAF 11⅜95	11.2	34	101¼	101¼	101¼	+ ¼
GATX 11½96	11.2	11	103	102⅜	102⅜	− ⅝
GTE 10⅝95	9.4	2	112⅞	112⅞	112⅞	− 2⅛
Gelco 14⅝99	13.9	10	104⅞	104⅞	104⅞	...
Gelco 14¼87	13.7	5	104¼	104¼	104¼	+ 2¼
GCinem 10s08	cv	10	220	220	220	+ 1
GCinem 10s09	cv	10	184	184	184	...
GnDev 12⅝05	12.7	3	99⅝	99⅝	99⅝	− ⅛
GnEl 5.3s92	6.0	25	88⅜	88	88	− ½
GnEl 7½96	8.1	130	93	93	93	+ 1
GnEl 8½04	9.1	3	93	93	93	...
GElCr 8¼97	8.8	50	94⅜	94¼	94¼	− ⅛
GElCr 13⅝91	13.0	36	105⅛	102¾	105⅛	− ⅞
GnHme 12¾98	13.6	25	94	94	94	+ ½
GMills zr88s	...	45	96	95 25/32	95 25/32	+ 9/32
GMA 8s93M	8.4	54	95½	95⅛	95½	− ⅛
GMA 7¾94	8.2	30	94⅞	93⅜	94⅞	+ 2⅝
GMA 7⅛92	7.7	25	92⅝	92⅜	92⅝	+ ⅜

FIGURE 17–5
How Corporate Bonds Are Quoted

Source: Wall Street Journal, June 1, 1987. Reprinted by permission of the *Wall Street Journal*, © Dow Jones & Company, Inc. 1987. All Rights Reserved.

June 1, 1987, 107,800 shares were traded at prices between 14⅞ and 15⅛, and the price of the closing sale was up ⅛ from the last sale (bid) of the previous day.

Figure 17–5 shows corporate bond quotations for the Exxon Company for June 1, 1987. The second line shows that 1,000 Exxon bonds, due in the year 1998, with a coupon yield of 6½ percent, were sold. In bond quotations, the number quoted is the sales price expressed as a percentage of the bond's face value. Thus, these Exxon bonds were sold at $838.88. The closing sale of the day also was $838.88, representing a ⅞ increase from the last sale of the previous day. Each bond pays 6½ percent interest, or $65 annually; thus the current yield (Cur Yld) is rounded to 7.7 percent ($65 ÷ $838.88 = 7.74).

Regulation of Securities Markets

Self-regulation is important in the securities industry because the public must trust the market before it will invest. Accordingly, organized exchanges have rules and regulations for listing and for trading. Similarly, the over-the-counter market is self-regulated by its trade association, the National Association of Securities Dealers. The primary aims are to provide investors with accurate and reliable information about securities, maintain ethical standards, and prevent fraud against investors.

State regulation of securities began in Kansas in 1911 with the passage of "blue sky laws." These were intended to prevent investors from being defrauded by companies selling securities about as valuable as "a piece of the blue sky." All states now require that securities to be sold within the state be registered and that brokers and salespersons be licensed.

Federal regulation of securities began in 1934 with the formation of the Securities and Exchange Commission (SEC). It has focused on requiring disclosure of information about securities to the investing public and on approving the rules and regulations of the larger organized securities exchanges. The SEC requires registration of listed securities with appropriate and updated information. It also regulates all exchange members and prohibits manipulative practices, such as using insider information for personal gain or illegally causing the price of a security to appear to rise or fall. The SEC regulates the advertising of securities and requires that proxies and proxy statements be mailed in a timely manner to all stockholders. The SEC possesses investigative police powers and has been characterized as a government agency that "strictly regulates the honesty and practices of the securities industry."

Investors' insurance is available to further protect the investing public. The Security Investors Protection Corporation (SIPC) is a government agency that safeguards the funds investors entrust to a brokerage firm in case the firm fails (providing the firm is registered with the Securities and Exchange Commission). As a matter of convenience, many investors prefer to leave titles to securities in the name of their broker rather than to take physical possession themselves. Each of an investor's accounts is protected against financial loss as a result of unreturned securities and cash up to a total of $500,000, but no more than $100,000 cash. This coverage insures the return of the value of your securities when the SIPC audits the bankrupt broker's accounts. Since this audit could take a few weeks, it might permit an uninsured decline in the value of your portfolio.

Sources of Investment Information

To reduce investment risks and increase returns, the wise financial manager seeks out and utilizes investment information. This section takes a how-to approach to gathering investment information about general economic conditions, securities markets indexes, industry data, and company news.

Information about General Economic Conditions

Knowing when to buy or sell securities requires an overview of the general economic conditions. You need to know where the economy is in the business cycle (recession or prosperity) and what are the current interest and inflation rates. Also, you should know what economic conditions are to be expected in the next twelve to eighteen months.

By reading a local daily newspaper, you can gain insights into the economic conditions of the local community, the state, region, country, and world. This is especially true for readers of cosmopolitan newspapers such as the *Los Angeles Times, Miami Herald,* and *Washington Post.* Many of these big city newspapers are available in community libraries or by mail subscription.

You can obtain specific economic news from the *Wall Street Journal* (published each weekday) and the weekly issues of *Barron's.* The two most popular financial newspapers in the country, they are also usually available at large public and university libraries as well as at brokers' offices. Select a few publications to read regularly to keep abreast of general economic conditions.

Securities Market Indexes

Securities market indexes measure the value of a number of securities chosen as a sample to reflect the behavior of a general market of investments. Investors use the indexes to determine trends that might help guide them in investment decisions. Short-run price movements may or may not be important compared to longer term situations. Ideally, for example, an investor would want to buy securities at low prices during the depths of a bear market and sell at high prices during the height of a bull market. Popular indexes are the Dow Jones Industrial Average, Standard & Poor's 500, the New York Stock Exchange Common Stock Index, and the American Stock Exchange Market Value Composite. A NASDAQ index is reported on about 2,000 OTC stocks by the National Association of Securities Dealers automated quotation system. Indexes on bonds, commodities, and other types of investments are also published. The most popular indexes are described below.

Dow Jones Industrial Average (DJIA) The DJIA is the most widely reported of all indexes. When the evening newscaster reports that "the Dow rose three points today in heavy trading," realize that these "points" are changes in the index, not actual dollar changes in the value of stocks. Figure 17–6 provides yearly highs and lows of the DJIA. The prices of only thirty stocks are followed in determining the DJIA. For many years, however, the index has been respected as a good barometer of daily activity of securities traded on the New York Stock Exchange, as the stocks chosen broadly represent the interests of the investing public. The Dow Jones Company also reports separate averages for transportation (twenty stocks in the index) and utilities (fifteen stocks) to provide investors with information in these industries.

Standard & Poor's 500 S & P's 500 is an index that reports price movements of 500 NYSE-listed stocks. It includes stocks of four hun-

FIGURE 17–6
Dow Jones Industrial Average

Source: Adapted from Standard & Poor's Corporation, *The Outlook*, Vol. 59, No. 1 (January 7, 1987). Used with permission.

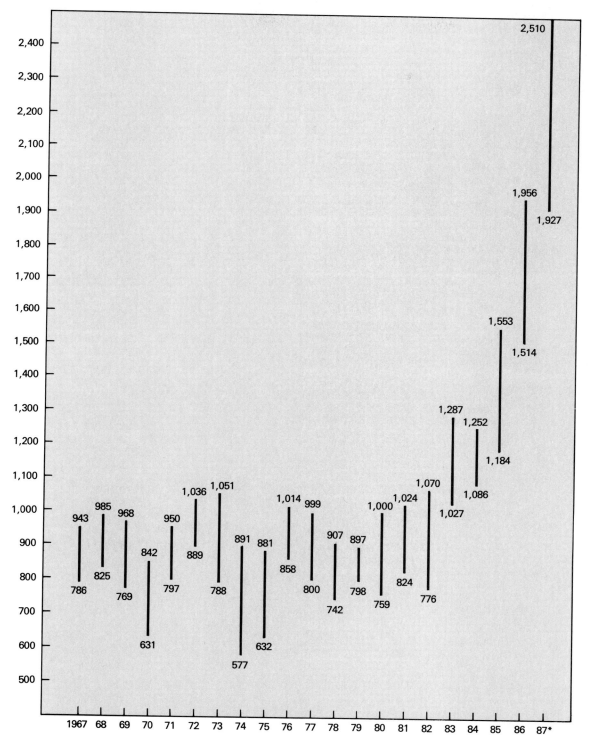

* As of September 8, 1987, the high was 2,722.

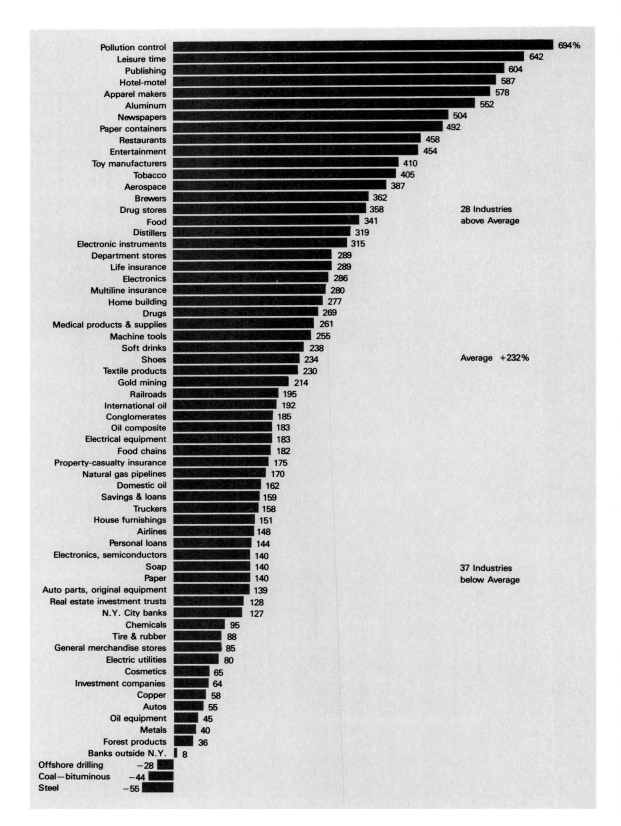

Industry	Percent
Pollution control	694%
Leisure time	642
Publishing	604
Hotel-motel	587
Apparel makers	578
Aluminum	552
Newspapers	504
Paper containers	492
Restaurants	458
Entertainment	454
Toy manufacturers	410
Tobacco	405
Aerospace	387
Brewers	362
Drug stores	358
Food	341
Distillers	319
Electronic instruments	315
Department stores	289
Life insurance	289
Electronics	286
Multiline insurance	280
Home building	277
Drugs	269
Medical products & supplies	261
Machine tools	255
Soft drinks	238
Shoes	234
Textile products	230
Gold mining	214
Railroads	195
International oil	192
Conglomerates	185
Oil composite	183
Electrical equipment	183
Food chains	182
Property-casualty insurance	175
Natural gas pipelines	170
Domestic oil	162
Savings & loans	159
Truckers	158
House furnishings	151
Airlines	148
Personal loans	144
Electronics, semiconductors	140
Soap	140
Paper	140
Auto parts, original equipment	139
Real estate investment trusts	128
N.Y. City banks	127
Chemicals	95
Tire & rubber	88
General merchandise stores	85
Electric utilities	80
Cosmetics	65
Investment companies	64
Copper	58
Autos	55
Oil equipment	45
Metals	40
Forest products	36
Banks outside N.Y.	8
Offshore drilling	−28
Coal—bituminous	−44
Steel	−55

28 Industries above Average

Average +232%

37 Industries below Average

dred industrial firms, forty financial institutions, forty public utilities, and twenty transportation companies. In addition, S & P's 500 is weighted for the proportional market value of each stock and the number of shares outstanding. Thus, the index is adjusted daily to eliminate the effects of capitalization changes, new listings, and delistings. Although not as popularly reported as the DJIA, S & P's 500 is a more accurate index of daily transactions on the New York Stock Exchange.

New York Stock Exchange Common Stock Index As the title suggests, this index includes all stocks traded on the NYSE. Consequently, it provides a comprehensive measure of the general price movements and value changes of those stocks.

American Stock Exchange Market Value Composite This index is based on the market value of all stocks traded on the American Stock Exchange. Although it genuinely reflects trading activity, its relative newness makes it less popular.

Information about Industries

There are many types of industries in which to invest, such as aerospace, apparel, automotive, beverages, chemicals, construction, drugs, electronics, financial, foods, machinery, and metal industries. The current price of the securities of individual companies is often affected by the performance of the industry as a whole. General economic events can have considerable impact on an entire industry and depress the stock of even a very profitable company. For example, J. C. Penney could be having a most profitable year, but if a recession is anticipated and general retail sales are expected to drop, the value of its stock is held down even if Penney's is enjoying a good year. Studying industries of interest to you will help you make intelligent buying and selling decisions. Industry information is often reported in several publications, particularly *Business Week* and *Forbes* (one issue of the latter per year analyzes the performance of all major industries). Figure 17–7 illustrates profitability data for selected industries. Specific information about industries is also available from trade associations and investment publications.

Trade Associations A *trade association* is an organization representing the interests of companies in the same industry. For example, the American Council of Life Insurance is composed of representatives of life insurance companies, and the American Bankers Association represents the interests of the banking industry. Besides lobbying to

---

FIGURE 17–7
Percentage Increase of Stocks of Sixty-five Industries over Ten Years (January 1977–January 1987)

Source: Standard & Poor's Statistical Service, *Security Price Index Record*, 1986 edition; Standard & Poor's Statistical Service, *Current Statistics*, March 1987.

present the views of the members, trade associations also have available a tremendous amount of detailed information on the history, current activities, and future prospects of the industry. Although the projections for the future are often optimistic, it is useful to know an industry's view of its prospects.

To contact the trade associations of interest to you, look up names and addresses in the *Encyclopedia of Associations*, published by Gale Research Company, and the *National Trade and Professional Associations*, published by the U.S. Department of Commerce. Both are available in larger libraries.

Industry Investment Publications   You can spend a lot of money subscribing to investment publications and advisory services. The publications include *Industry Surveys* and *The Outlook* (published by Standard & Poor's), *Value Line Investment Survey* (Arnold Bernhard & Company), the *Monthly Economic Letter* (Citibank), and *Industrial Manual* (Moody's). Fortunately, many of these publications can be found in large libraries (especially at universities) and in brokers' offices.

Information about Companies

Of course, before buying any securities, you should learn about the company that is offering them. You can obtain this information from corporate annual reports, prospectuses, 10-K reports, and investment ratings publications.

Annual Reports   Every public corporation publishes an annual report that summarizes its financial activities for the year. Investors use these reports to compare results from recent years and to find out about management's views of the immediate future. Keep in mind that the tone of these reports is generally optimistic, as the company wants investors to think highly of the firm. Interesting information, sometimes negative, is often found in the footnotes. To receive an annual report, ask a broker or write directly to the corporation.

Prospectuses   When a company issues any new security, it must file a *prospectus* with the Securities and Exchange Commission. This is a disclosure of facts about a corporation, including the experience of its management, its financial status, any anticipated legal matters that could affect the company, and potential risks of investing in the corporation. The language is legalese, but the details are there for the interested investor. Note that a company must issue a prospectus and make it public to any potential investor only when it issues a *new* security. Although many prospectuses are out of date, they might provide some needed background information.

10-K Reports   Companies registered with the Securities and Exchange Commission must regularly report many financial particulars to the SEC using a *10-K report*. This is a comprehensive document containing much of the same type of information as a prospectus or annual report and provides additional updated financial details on corporate activities. You can obtain these reports from the SEC or find them in university libraries.

Investment Ratings Publications You can also read about specific public corporations in this country in the following investment ratings publications: *Stock Reports* and *Stock Guide* (Standard & Poor's),

FIGURE 17–8
Sample Stock Report from Value Line

Source: Value Line Investment Survey. Reprinted by permission of Value Line, Inc., 711 Third Avenue, New York, NY 10051.

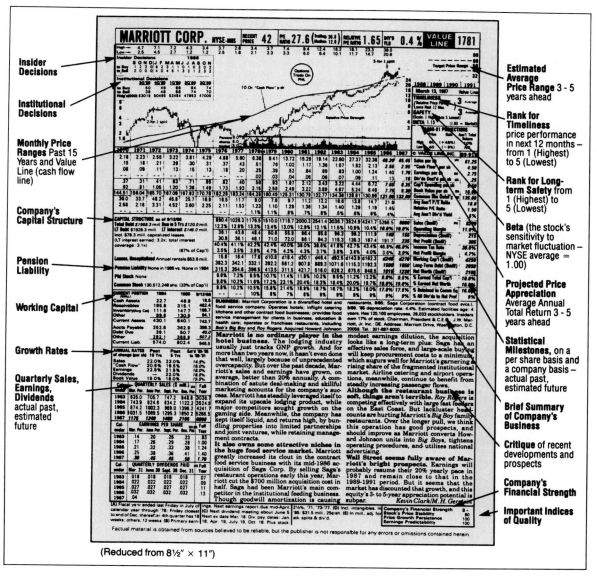

(Reduced from 8½″ × 11″)

Moody's Manuals (Moody's Investor Services), *Value Line*, *Stock Picture* (M. C. Horsey & Company), *Trendline's Current Market Perspective* (Trendline), and the *Blue Book of 3-Trend Cycligraphs* (Securities Research Company). These publications all rank and rate corporations on performance.

A stock report for a corporation in an investment ratings publication typically contains a summary description and current outlook, important developments, comparisons with competitors, and tables with financial data going back ten years. Figure 17–8 illustrates a sample stock report from *Value Line*. You can find these publications in larger libraries and in brokers' offices.

Calculating a Stock's Potential Total Return

All individual investors who consider alternative investments are interested in earning a return somewhat greater than the rate of inflation. Otherwise, the investor loses money because of inflation and the payment of income taxes. For example, assume that inflation is 4 percent and Jefferson Schwertly of Norfolk, Nebraska, has invested $3,000 in a stock paying a cash dividend of $130 per year. Just to stay even with a 4 percent inflation rate, Jefferson needs an annual return of $120 ($3,000 × .04). Since he is in the 28 percent tax bracket he also needs a return of $34 ($120 × .28) to stay even with the federal Internal Revenue Service, which gets 28 percent of his earnings. Because he needs $154 ($120 + $34) to break even with inflation and taxes, and his actual return is only $130, he is losing. Jefferson will continue to lose unless the market price of the stock rises and he sells to realize a capital gain of $24 ($154 − 130) as well.

Desired Rate of Return

The return on the virtually risk-free U.S. Treasury bills historically has been just about the same as the rate of inflation. For this reason, investors often use the yield on Treasury bills as a base number that provides a zero real rate of return. In addition, since there is some risk in quality long-term corporate bonds the rate of return on corporate securities is a little higher than that for Treasury securities. If Treasury bills were yielding 7.5 percent, high-quality, long-term bonds might be yielding 10 percent. Moreover, many investors figure that to earn a positive real return in stocks they must have a desired rate of return at least three percentage points above that available on quality long-term corporate bonds to compensate for the additional risks taken by investing in stocks.

Procedure

A stock's *potential total return* is determined by adding anticipated dividend income and price appreciation over a period of perhaps five years or more. As an investor, your task begins by applying an estimated five-year growth rate to the latest twelve-month earnings per

TABLE 17–2
One Investor's Projections of the Potential Total Return for Running Paws Catfood Company

End of Year	EPS	Dividend
1	$2.20	$ .66
2	2.53	.76
3	2.91	.88
4	3.35	1.01
5	3.85	1.16
Total dividends		$4.47

share. Then multiply the fifth-year earnings by a projected price/earnings ratio for the same year. Estimate dividends by applying an estimated growth rate to the current cash dividend. Finally, sum up the projected dividends and price appreciation. Table 17–2 illustrates the process.

Illustration: Running Paws Catfood Company

For Running Paws, Jefferson determined the following information: current price was $30 per share, its latest twelve-month earnings per share (EPS) was $2 and the current cash dividend was $.60 per share. He calculated the price/earnings ratio to be 15 ($30 ÷ $2).

Last year's annual report for Running Paws suggested an estimated earnings per share this year of $2.40 and a cash dividend of $.72. After discussions with a stock broker and reviewing published stock reports by Standard & Poor's and Value Line, Jefferson lowered *his* personal estimate of this year's earnings for Running Paws to $2.20. Things look good for Running Paws this year, Jefferson thought, but $2.20 was more likely. As shown in Table 17–1, he then estimated a 15 percent rate of growth for the earnings per share for each year ($2.20 × 1.15 = $2.53 × 1.15, and so forth). Since the dividend payout ratio had been .30, he continued that assumption ($2.20 × .30 = $.66, and so forth). This represents a 15 percent growth rate in the cash dividend.

Using the same P/E multiple of 15, Jefferson estimated the market price at the end of the fifth year to be $57.75 (15 × $3.85). This gives a projected appreciation of stock price over five years of $27.75 ($57.75 minus the current price of $30). The *annual average dividend* computes to $.89 by dividing the $4.47 in dividends by five years. Combined with the sum of the estimated cash dividends of $4.47, the total return is $32.22 ($27.75 + $4.47).

The *approximate compound yield (ACY)* is a measure of the annualized compound growth of a long-term investment. You can determine this by using formula 17–1. If you substitute the data from Table 17–1, being certain to use the average annual dividend and not the specific projected dividends, you will obtain an approximate compound yield of 15 percent.

$$ACY = \cfrac{\text{average} + \cfrac{\cfrac{\text{projected price}}{\text{of stock}} - \cfrac{\text{current price}}{\text{of stock}}}{\text{numbers of years projected}}}{\cfrac{\cfrac{\text{projected price}}{\text{of stock}} + \cfrac{\text{current price}}{\text{of stock}}}{2}} \qquad (17\text{--}1)$$

$$= \cfrac{\$.89 + \cfrac{\$57.75 - \$30}{5}}{\cfrac{\$57.75 + \$30}{2}}$$

$$= \cfrac{\$.89 + \$5.55}{\$43.88}$$

$$= 14.7\%$$

The total five-year return of $32.22 on a cost of $30 works out to an approximate compound yield of 15 percent (14.7 percent rounded). This compares favorably to high-quality, long-term bonds, which yield about 10 percent. Jefferson Schwertly estimated that total projected return advantage for Running Paws would be 5 percentage points (15 percent − 10 percent), and this would make it a good buy at its price of $30.

Using a Brokerage Firm

Almost all securities transactions in the primary and secondary markets are executed with the assistance of a brokerage firm that owns seats on the various organized exchanges. You can use a general brokerage firm or a discount broker; both will charge a commission for any trading they do for you.

General Brokerage Firm

The traditional general brokerage firm typically offers full services to customers. These services include a house investment newsletter that discusses general economic trends and offers investment recommendations, periodic reports that cover particular market trends and industries, capsule written research analyses on thousands of individual companies (available to customers just for the asking), and the personal advice and attention of a stockbroker. These firms maintain up-to-the-minute contact with the investment world through electronic equipment (usually a quotation board, which is an electronic display of all security transactions on the major exchanges reported as they occur) and subscribe to an expensive but valuable newswire service that can keep customers apprised of world news affecting particular investments. Brokerage firms also maintain a reference library and provide custodial services for customers, since it is generally safer and more convenient for most investors to have a broker hold securities for them.

Customers receive monthly statements summarizing all transactions and commissions, dividends, and interest. Of course, price quotations on securities are available over the telephone to the interested investor.

Discount Broker

In recent years, a growing number of investors have chosen to use a *discount broker*. This is a brokerage firm that features especially low commission charges because it provides limited services to customers. It focuses on one function: efficiently executing orders to buy and sell securities. Discount brokers do not normally conduct house research or provide specific investment advice to customers. Transactions usually are initiated by an investor who calls the discount broker at a toll-free telephone number.

As Table 17–3 shows, you can save considerably by using the services of a discount broker. Reductions in actual commissions of up to 75 percent are possible. Many investors, however, may prefer to pay more for the full services of a general brokerage firm.

Commissions and Fees

Brokerage firms receive a commission on each securities transaction in order to cover the direct expenses of executing the transaction and other overhead expenses. At one time commissions were fixed by the SEC, but now the SEC permits negotiation of commissions between brokers and investors. In actuality, most brokers have an established fee schedule that they use when dealing with any but the largest investors. These fees represent a declining commission rate as the total value of the transaction increases. For example, in addition to a minimum commission charge of $25, a broker might charge 2.8 percent more on a transaction amounting to less than $800, 1.8 percent on transactions between $800 and $2,500, 1.6 percent on amounts between $2,500 and $5,000, and 1.2 percent on amounts over $5,000.

These transaction costs are based on sales of *round lots,* which are blocks of stock in units of one hundred shares. *Odd lots* are in units of more or less than one hundred shares. When brokers buy or sell shares in odd lots, they often charge a fee of 12.5 cents (called an *eighth*) per

TABLE 17–3
Broker's Typical Commission Charges

Size of Transaction	Type of Broker	Price per Share						
		$10	$20	$30	$40	$50	$70	$100
100 shares	Full-service	$50	$ 67	$ 91	$111	$135	$150	$180
	Discount	30	42	54	60	66	78	94
200 shares	Full-service	70	93	128	155	189	210	252
	Discount	42	60	66	82	90	99	115
300 shares	Full-service	90	120	165	200	240	270	320
	Discount	50	60	75	90	100	120	150

share on the odd-lot portion of the transaction. For example, an order for 140 shares at $25 each (total value $3,500) could carry a round-lot commission fee of $40 (100 shares × $25 = $2,500 × .016) plus an odd-lot fee of $12.50 (40 shares × $25 = $1,000 × .125) and a minimum commission charge of $25 for a total of $77.50.

The payment of commissions can quickly reduce the return on an investment. A purchase commission of 2 percent added to a sales commission of another 2 percent means that the investor must earn a 4 percent yield just to pay the transaction costs. Although abuses in the securities industry are kept to a minimum, a small minority of unethical stockbrokers practice *churning* of investor's accounts by encouraging investors to frequently buy and sell securities in an effort to earn large commissions for themselves. You should carefully consider transaction costs when making securities investments.

Opening an Account with a Stockbroker

If you decide not to buy and sell securities through a discount broker, you must select a suitable general brokerage firm and a specific account executive at that firm to best represent your interests. Make these decisions with care. The brokerage firm should be *exchange registered,* meaning that it must comply with the rules and regulations of the exchange. The New York Stock Exchange has the highest standards of conduct; about five hundred firms are registered with it. Most brokerage firms emphasize fundamental analysis in their approach to investments (see Chapter 15). As a result, investors should be very interested in the quality of the firm's research analysis. Since not all firms carefully research each industry, you need to obtain research reports from various brokerage firms and compare them. The firm you select should be responsive to the needs of both large and small investors and should have a policy of automatically investing customers' idle monies in a money market account, where it will earn interest before being reinvested. And certainly, the reputation of the firm for fairness and honesty is paramount. Avoid brokerage firms with even a slightly suspect reputation.

All individual stockbrokers at each brokerage firm must go through an extensive training program before taking licensing examinations. Ask for the recommendations of your banker, lawyer, and knowledgeable friends and choose an account executive with an investment philosophy similar to yours. Your account executive should be willing to discuss your finances thoroughly and follow your particular investment objectives. If the broker seems interested in short-term profits when you are a long-term investor, seek help elsewhere. Similarily, make sure your broker has a lengthy record of success in your areas of interest and will be available to you when you want advice. If after a while the account executive or brokerage firm no longer suits your needs, by all means change. A new broker can have your account transferred almost immediately.

When you open an account with a general brokerage firm or a discount broker, or both, you must supply them with your Social Security number and fill out a statement of personal financial worth. Though interested in earning commissions, the broker is required by the SEC to refuse orders that exceed a customer's financial capability. Often brokers will review investment limits with new customers. If you submit a buy or sell order over the limit, your broker will likely telephone you to discuss and confirm it.

You can open two kinds of accounts with a brokerage firm, a cash account and a margin account. A **cash account** requires an initial deposit (perhaps as little as $50) and specifies that full settlement is due the broker within five business days (or seven calendar days) after a buy or sell order has been given. After sale transactions, your account is quickly credited with the proceeds. You can place uninvested monies in the broker's money market account with interest credited to you.

A **margin account** requires a deposit of substantial cash or securities ($2,000 or more) and permits you to buy other securities on credit using additional funds borrowed from the firm. The Federal Reserve Board and the brokerage firm establish rules on the maximum amount of credit that can be used to purchase other securities. Buying on margin is discussed later in this chapter.

Stock and Bond Certificates

A certificate is a document that serves as evidence. **Bond certificates** are evidences of debt that are issued to investors who purchase them from corporations and governments. Corporations issue **stock certificates** to common and preferred shareholders as evidence of ownership.

A bond certificate must be presented for payment when the bond is sold or when it reaches maturity and is redeemed. Similarly, when stocks are sold the certificates must be transferred to the new owners. Holders of stocks and bonds might find it convenient to keep certificates in a safe-deposit box, but many investors who do a considerable amount of trading prefer to keep their certificates in the name of the brokerage firm. The securities are quite safe this way and signatures are not needed when ownership is transferred upon sale.

Investors must pay a penalty for lost stock and bond certificates, generally a fee of 3 percent of the value of the securities. This money pays for an indemnification bond in the event that another person tries to make a wrongful financial claim with the certificates. It is wise to keep a list of the certificate numbers apart from the certificates.

Securities Transactions

It is not unusual to have 50 million shares of stocks traded daily on the over-the-counter market and another 200 million shares traded on the New York Stock Exchange. For every trade there must be a buyer and a seller to conclude the transaction at a given price.

| The Trading Process | Figure 17–9 illustrates the process of trading securities. Say you instruct broker A to purchase a certain number of shares of Running Paws Catfood Company at a specific price. Broker A relays the buy order to representative A, who coordinates the trading of company A brokers around the country. Since company A has a seat on the exchange, the buy order is then given to floor broker A, who in turn contacts a specialist. This is a person on the floor of the exchange who specializes in handling trades of the particular stock ordered. The buy order is filled with shares, from the specialist's own inventory and/or by matching another trader's sell order. In Figure 17–9, your stock is purchased from the seller who contacted broker B. |

The Trading Process

Figure 17–9 illustrates the process of trading securities. Say you instruct broker A to purchase a certain number of shares of Running Paws Catfood Company at a specific price. Broker A relays the buy order to representative A, who coordinates the trading of company A brokers around the country. Since company A has a seat on the exchange, the buy order is then given to floor broker A, who in turn contacts a specialist. This is a person on the floor of the exchange who specializes in handling trades of the particular stock ordered. The buy order is filled with shares, from the specialist's own inventory and/or by matching another trader's sell order. In Figure 17–9, your stock is purchased from the seller who contacted broker B.

Matching or Negotiating Prices

On the organized exchanges, there must be a *match* between the buyer's price and the seller's price for a sale to take place. Therefore a specialist could hold a specific order for a few minutes, a couple of hours, or even a week before a match is made. With actively traded issues, a transaction normally is completed in just a few minutes. A slower-selling security can be traded more quickly if an investor is willing to accept the current market price (discussed below under "Types of Orders").

On the over-the-counter market, the bid and asked prices represent *negotiation* of a final price. If a buyer does not want to pay the asking price, he or she instructs the broker to offer a lower bid price, which may or may not be accepted. If it is not, the buyer might want to cancel the first order and raise the bid slightly in a second order in the hope that the seller will let the shares go at that price. Otherwise, the buyer may have to pay the full asked price. Generally, OTC trades occur at prices between the bid and asked figures.

Types of Orders

There are actually only two types of orders, buy and sell. When a broker buys or sells securities according to prescribed instructions, it is called executing an order. The constraints that can be placed on the price of those orders are called market, limit, and stop orders.

Market Order A *market order* instructs the broker to execute an order at the best possible price. The best price to a seller, of course, is a high one; the buyer desires the lowest possible price. The broker can generally secure a transaction within a few minutes at the *prevailing market price,* which is the current selling price of a security. In reality, the floor broker tries to match the instructions (getting the best price) within the narrow range of prices available from the specialist. The behavior of traders on the floor of the stock market shouting back and forth is this effort to obtain the best price.

Limit Order A *limit order* instructs the broker to buy at the best possible price but not above a specified limit or to sell at the best possible price but not below a specified limit. It provides some protection against buying a security at a price higher than wanted or selling at too

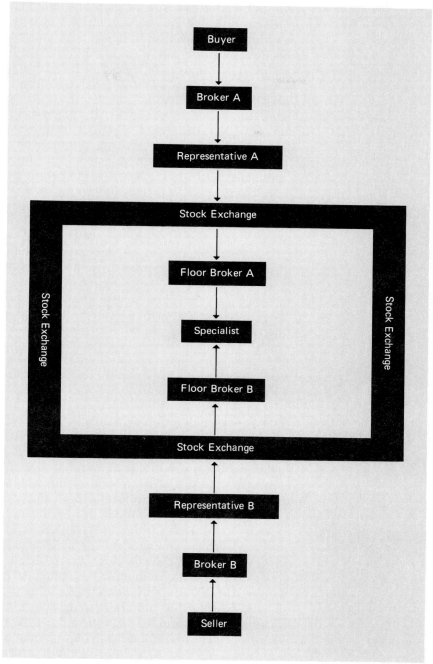

FIGURE 17-9
The Process of Trading Securities

low a price. The broker transmits the limit order to the specialist. The order is executed if and when the specified price or better is reached and all other previously received orders on the specialist's book have been considered.

A disadvantage for a buyer who places a limit order is that the investor might miss an excellent opportunity. Assume that you put a limit order in with your broker to buy 100 shares of Running Paws common stock at 60½, since you've seen in the newspaper that it has recently been selling at 61 and 61¼. You hope to save $.50 to $1.00 on each share. That same day the company announces publicly that it plans to expand into the dog food area for the first time. Investor confidence in the new sales effort pushes the price up to 70. If you had given your broker a market order instead, you would have gotten 100 shares of Running Paws at perhaps 61¼ or 61½, which would have given you an immediate profit of about $850 (70 − 61½ = 8½ × 100 shares) on an initial investment of $6,150 (61½ × 100).

A disadvantage for a seller placing a limit order is that it could result in no sale if the price drops because of some news. Assume that you bought stock at 50 that is currently selling at 58 and that you have placed a limit order at a price of 60. You hope to take your profit if and when it sells at that price. However, the price could creep up to 59 and then fall back to 48. In this event, you own securities that you did not sell because the limit order was priced too high. Now they are worth less than what you originally paid for them. A limit order is best used when you expect great fluctuations in the price of a stock and when you buy or sell infrequently traded securities on the over-the-counter market.

Stop Order   A *stop order* instructs the broker to sell at the next available opportunity when a stock reaches or drops below a specified price. It is often called a *stop-loss order* because the investor uses it to protect against a sharp drop in price and thus stop a loss. The specialist executes the recorded order as soon as the stop-order price is reached and a buyer is matched at the next market price.

Let's consider an example of how to stop a loss. Assume that you bought 100 shares of Running Paws stock at 70. You are nervous about its entry into the competitive dog food business and feel the company might lose money. So you place a stop order to sell your shares if the price drops to 56, thus limiting your potential loss to 20 percent ($70 − $56 = $14 ÷ $70). Sure enough, some months later you read in the financial section of your newspaper that even after six months the newest competitor in the dog food industry, Running Paws, still has less than 1 percent of the market. You call your broker, who informs you that Running Paws stock dropped in price drastically in response to the article, which was published the previous day in *The Wall Street Journal*. He reports that all your shares were sold at 55 and that the current price is 49. The sales transaction notice is already in the mail to your home. The stop order cut your losses to a little over 20 percent ($70 − $55 = $15 ÷ $70 = 21.4 percent) and saved an additional loss of $6 ($55 − $49) a share. Thus, the stop order reduced your loss to $1,500

$[(100 \times \$70 = \$7,000) - (100 \times \$55 = \$5,500)]$ instead of $2,100 $[(100 \times \$70 = \$7,000) - (100 \times \$49 = \$4,900)]$.

You can use a stop order to protect profits, too. Assume that you bought 100 shares of Alpo Dog Food Company at $60 per share and the current selling price is $75. This gives you a paper profit of $1,500 ($75 − $60 = $15 × 100 shares) less commissions. To protect part of that profit you place a stop order with your broker to sell at $65 should the price drop that low. If your stock is sold you still have a real profit of $500 ($65 − $60 = $5 × 100 shares). If Alpo Dog Food stock climbs in price instead, perhaps in response to the bad news about Running Paws, the stop order would have cost you nothing. If the price does climb, you might replace the stop order with one priced a bit higher to try and lock in an even greater amount of profit.

Time of Orders

Investors have several ways to place time limits on their orders. A *fill-or-kill order* instructs the broker to buy or sell at the market price immediately or else the order is canceled. A *day order* is valid only for the remainder of the trading day during which it was given to the broker. Unless otherwise indicated, any order received by a broker is assumed to be a day order. A *week order* is valid until the close of trading on Friday of the current week. A *month order* is good until the close of trading on the last business day of the current month. An *open order* (also called a *good-till-canceled order*) is good until executed by the broker or canceled by the investor. If you give a broker an order longer than a week in duration, you must carefully monitor events to be sure you can alter the order if situations change substantially.

Special Factors Affecting the Price of Securities

One factor that affects the market price of a stock is whether or not it is selling *ex dividend*. One factor that affects the selling price of a bond is how the interest is calculated. Both topics are discussed below.

Ex Dividend If stock is selling *ex dividend,* it means that investors buying the stock will not receive the next dividend that has been recently declared by the company. Since it usually takes four or five business days to record a new buyer's name on the list of registered stockholders, stock exchanges list stocks as "ex div" for four to five days before the *record date.* This is the day companies take note of what shareholders deserve dividends. Since the company's declared dividend has been anticipated by investors, the price of the stock should drop accordingly when the stock is listed as ex dividend.

Calculation of Bond Interest If you purchase an interest-paying bond in the secondary market, remember that it has been paying interest since the day it was issued. Specifically, it has been earning interest since the last payment was made to the previous owner. For example, an 8 percent, $1,000 bond that pays interest semiannually paid the original owner $40 on the first day of January and July. If you purchase it on September 1, the original owner deserves the amount of interest earned between July 1 and August 31, and so this interest is added to the sales price you pay for the bond. You later receive the full interest payment.

How to Invest: A Six-step Process

The following six-step process will help you attain your investment goals.

1. **Identify your personal investment philosophy**   Before you make any investment, you must ascertain whether you are a speculative, moderate, or conservative investor. (This is discussed in Chapter 15.) All three types of investors can buy stocks, mutual funds (see Chapter 18), and real estate (see Chapter 19) to match their interest. For example, some mutual funds specialize in commodities, an investment medium characterized by volatile price swings (commodities are discussed in Chapter 20).

2. **Identify your desired total return**   It is also important to identify the range of total return you desire, given the amount of risk you accept. For example, a conservative investor might be quite pleased with safe investments yielding 7 to 8 percent annually. A moderate investor might prefer a return of 9 to 12 percent, and a speculative investor could aim for a total annual return of 13 to 30 percent. (Recall that the returns are relative and they are better compared on a real return basis, after inflation and taxes.)

3. **Choose an investment for its components of total return**   Your task is to choose an investment that will provide the desired potential total return through income and/or price appreciation in the proportions that you desire. For example, Willis Phillips of Nashville, Tennessee, has narrowed his investment selections to two rather comparable choices. The first is a well-known growth stock with an anticipated cash dividend of 3.5 percent and a projected annual price appreciation of 7 percent for an anticipated total return of 10.5 percent. Willis' second choice is a lesser-known growth stock with an annual hoped-for cash dividend of 1.5 percent and capital gains of 10 percent for a projected total return of 11.5 percent.

4. **Choose your preferred investment medium**   Study carefully and decide on the kind of investment you prefer to earn the desired total return. Some people love stocks and hate bonds, and others prefer real estate to either. Still others want to earn good yields using both mutual funds and selected common stocks.

5. **Study available alternatives**   Study your specific investment alternatives. If you decide on stocks, examine the suggestions on investment approaches for long-term and short-term investors given later in this chapter. If you decide on mutual funds, real

estate, or some particular high-risk investment, Chapters 18, 19, and 20 will help you.

6. **Make a list of probable actions** The last step of the investment process requires you to carefully establish and write down a list of probable strategies, tactics, and actions you can take given certain investment conditions. For example, Willis Phillips has determined that he wants to hold a new stock investment for five years or a little longer. If the price appreciates more than 20 percent during any given year he will sell to take his profits. Alternatively, if it loses more than 15 percent of its value in any twelve months he will sell and invest his proceeds elsewhere. Also, Willis has decided that if the economy seems to be peaking out, with a possible recession forecast, he will immediately sell out and put the proceeds in bonds or a money market account.

Unfortunately, most investors do not determine a list of strategic and tactical actions to take to obtain maximum gain. Rather, they do one of two things. They might follow their own speculative, moderate, or conservative nature and buy and sell investments as events occur; the resulting transaction costs eat substantially into potential profits. Or they may simply invest their money and forget about it, hoping that when the time comes to sell the investment the return (and current market values) will be positive. The wise investor decides in advance what investment strategies and tactics to follow.

Short- and Long-term Investment Approaches

Whether speculative, moderate, or conservative, investors have many choices available. The sequence of investment success is (1) select investment approaches that are compatible with your investment philosophy, (2) become highly knowledgeable about the approaches you choose, and (3) maintain the necessary discipline to follow through on the decisions you make. Investment approaches can be classified as long term (used by investors who buy and hold securities) or short term (used by investors who frequently trade securities).

Long-term Investors: Buy-and-hold Approaches

A *long-term investor* is generally moderate or conservative in investment philosophy and wants to hold a security as long as it provides a return commensurate with its risk, usually for a number of years. Investment approaches for long-term investors are as follows: dividend reinvestment plans; business-cycle approach; portfolio diversification; dollar-cost averaging; monthly investment plans; rules, charts, and formulas; investment clubs; and employee stock purchase plans and stock options.

Dividend Reinvestment Plans *Dividend reinvestment plans (DRIPs)* permit stockholders to reinvest dividends by purchasing additional shares directly from the corporation at no commission, and sometimes at discounts of up to 5 percent. Many firms also allow additional cash purchases of stock free of commissions. More than one thousand companies now can credit you with whole and fractional shares of stock instead of sending dividend checks. About one-third of AT & T's 3 million investors buy extra stock with their quarterly dividends. Obviously, you should not participate in such a plan if you need the cash dividends for living expenses.

DRIPs allow the long-term investor to purchase a small number of extra shares in the company in a convenient, systematic, and inexpensive way. Some corporations allow an extra cash addition of perhaps no more than $3,000 a quarter.

The Internal Revenue Service has ruled that the value of administrative costs, fees, and brokerage commissions avoided through DRIPs is considered a taxable dividend to investors. Thus, an investor with 200 shares receiving DRIP of 1.7 shares may have a taxable dividend of about $1. Note also that you must pay income tax on DRIPs each year just as if you had taken cash. Still, dividend reinvestment plans are a bargain way to purchase shares of stock.

Business-cycle Approach Investors are frequently successful if they follow the business-cycle approach. Figure 17–10 illustrates various phases of the business cycle. This approach requires investing in securities when the general economy is in a *recession* (when reduced economic activity results in increasing unemployment, lower industrial production, and fewer retail sales) and prices of investment securities may have been declining over several months (a bear market). Then,

FIGURE 17–10
Phases of the Business Cycle

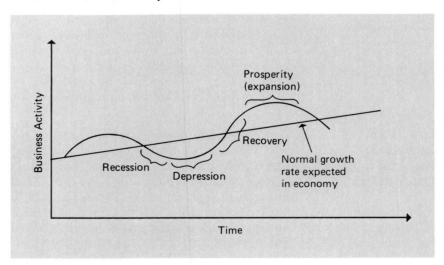

the investor must sell securities when the general economy is prospering and a bull market characterizes the investments scene. The difficulty confronting the investor is to have the courage to buy during times of economic recession or depression when most other investors are thinking about selling for fear that prices will drop even further. Similarly, it is difficult to sell during the peaks of prosperity when most investors are considering buying in the hope that prices will continue to climb.

The challenge to the investor using the business-cycle approach is to know when to buy or sell. For example, an investor does not want to be buying stocks during the high points just before prices begin to fall, and thus must be able to estimate the length and depth of each business cycle. Most important, an investor must choose securities that will appreciate in price along with generally rising markets. If you want to be a successful business-cycle investor, you probably will have six to eight full business cycles occur during your lifetime in which to act. During shifts in cycles there definitely will be clear opportunities for profit.

Portfolio Diversification   With every market cycle, different investment alternatives become relatively attractive. For example, if the economy is growing and inflation is low (early months of recovery), common stock prices could be underpriced. Farther along in the cycle, during times of economic prosperity, increasing inflation could have pushed interest rates up, making bonds more attractive than stocks. As an investor, you can either spend time trying to figure out how and when to move your money or have a diversified portfolio.

Diversified Portfolios of Selected Investors

Tommy Jacobson, age 26
Santa Monica, California
Annual income: $36,000
Current income needs: minimal
Objectives: 15–17% annual growth
Investment philosophy: moderate
Net worth: $40,000
Value of investments: $14,000

Money market fund	10%
Mutual fund (aggressive growth)	20
Mutual fund (income and equity)	30
Growth stock (lesser known)	20
Growth stock (lesser known)	20

Ronda and Ricardo Garcia,
   ages 41 and 43
Baltimore, Maryland
Annual income: $64,000
Current income needs: minimal
Objectives: 12–14% annual return
Investment philosophy: moderate
Net worth: $130,000
Value of investments: $48,000

Money market fund	5%
Mutual fund (growth and income)	5
Mutual fund (growth and income)	10
Mutual fund (growth and income)	20
Bonds (high-quality corporate)	20
Growth stock (well known)	5
Growth stock (well known)	10
Growth stock (lesser known)	10
Limited partnership	10
Gold	5

Portfolio diversification is the process of selecting alternatives that have dissimilar risk–return characteristics; this process provides a lower but acceptable overall potential return. Portfolio diversification offsets the riskiness of individual investments and it smooths out the ups and downs of individual investment returns. Investors in securities, for example, can diversify within an investment medium (such as in stocks) or across alternatives (such as in stocks and bonds).

Securities investors can diversify according to industry. Placing all your funds in a portfolio of transportation securities is riskier than diversifying into three economic industries, such as transportation, chemicals, and electronics. If transportation securities decline in value, your chemicals and electronics holdings may retain their values or even increase.

Common stock investors can diversify by type of stock. The moderate investor, instead of placing all funds into growth stocks (a prolonged recession would hold down values), might buy some growth stocks and some income stocks. The conservative investor could purchase some countercyclical income stocks.

Investors in bonds can diversify by maturity. By purchasing bonds with maturities spaced out over several years, you minimize the risk that they would all come due at a time when interest rates were low. Of course, you should realize that an increasing diversification not only minimizes risk but is also likely to increase your brokerage costs. The extent of diversification you choose depends on your personal investment philosophy and the amount you have to invest. Table 17–4 shows guidelines for diversified investment portfolios.

TABLE 17–4
Guidelines for Model Portfolios for Moderate-philosophy Investors

Investment Alternatives	Types of Investors					
	Average Investor	Single, Starting Out	Single, More Affluent	Working Couple, Childless	One-income Couple with Two Young Children	One-income Couple Nearing Retirement
Fixed-dollar savings/ investments	5–15%	20–30%	10–20%	5–10%	10–20%	15–20%
Bonds	10–20	—	10–20	5–15	5–15	15–40
Common stock	10–20	10–20	10–30	10–30	10–20	10–15
Mutual funds	15–30	20–50	20–30	20–40	20–50	10–15
High-risk investments	0–10	5–20	0–5	5–10	5–10	0–5
Real estate (excluding private residence)	15–40	—	15–20	20–30	10–20	10–30

Dollar-cost Averaging *Dollar-cost averaging* requires investing the same fixed dollar amount in the same stock, at regular intervals over a long time with the result that you purchase more shares when the price is down and fewer shares when the price is high, therefore, most of the shares are accumulated at below-average costs. This approach avoids the element of investment timing, since the stock purchases are made regularly regardless of the price.

Table 17–5 shows the results of systematic investments in a stock under varying market conditions. Commissions are excluded. Let's say that you put $300 into a stock every three months. To illustrate dollar-cost averaging, assume first that the funds were invested during the fluctuating market shown in Table 17–5. As the initial price is $15 a share, you receive 20 shares. Then the market drops—an extreme but easy-to-follow example—and the price goes down to $10 a share. Still you buy $300 worth and receive 30 shares. The market price rebounds to $15 three months later and you invest another $300, receiving twenty shares. Then it drops and rises again.

You now own 120 shares, with a total investment of $1,500. The **average share price** is a simple calculation of the amounts paid for the investment and it is calculated by dividing the total share price total by the number of regular investments. It is $13.00 ($65 ÷ 5) in this example. The **average share cost** is a more meaningful figure to the investor. This is the actual cost basis of the investment used for income tax purposes; it is calculated by dividing the total dollars invested by the total shares purchased. It is $12.50 ($1,500 ÷ 120) in this example. Note that since the recent price is $15 a share, your 120 shares are worth $300 more than you paid for them ($15 × 120 = $1,800 − $1,500).

Markets can decline for quite a long time period, as well as rise, and this affects dollar-cost averaging also. The "declining market" portion of Table 17–5 shows purchases of 190 shares for lower and lower prices, eventually reaching $5 a share at the bottom of that declining market. In a declining market, if you keep investing using dollar-cost averaging, you will purchase a lot of shares. Should you have to sell when the market is way down, you will not profit. In this example, you have purchased 190 shares at an average cost of $7.89 and they have a depressed recent price of $5. Selling now would result in a substantial loss of $550 [$1,500 − (190 × $5)]. Dollar-cost averaging requires that you continue to invest should you believe the longer-term prospects suggest an eventual increase in price.

During a "rising market," as illustrated in Table 17–5, you continue to invest but buy fewer shares. The $1,500 investment bought only 140 shares for an average cost of $10.71. In this rising market, you profit because your 140 shares have a recent market price of $20 a share for a total value of $2,800 (140 × $20).

Almost anyone can profit in a rising market. If you use dollar-cost averaging over the long term, you will continue to buy in rising, falling, and fluctuating markets. The overall result is that you buy more shares when the cost is down, which lowers the average share cost to below-

TABLE 17–5
Dollar-cost Averaging for a Stock Purchase

	Fluctuating Market			Declining Market			Rising Market		
	Regular Investment	Share Price	Shares Acquired	Regular Investment	Share Price	Shares Acquired	Regular Investment	Share Price	Shares Acquired
	$ 300	$15	20	$ 300	$15	20	$ 300	$ 6	50
	300	10	30	300	10	30	300	10	30
	300	15	20	300	10	30	300	12	25
	300	10	30	300	6	50	300	15	20
	300	15	20	300	5	60	300	20	15
Total	$1,500	$65	120	$1,500	$46	190	$1,500	$63	140

Average share price: $13.00
($65 ÷ 5)

Average share cost: $12.50
($1,500 ÷ 120)

Average share price: $9.20
($46 ÷ 5)

Average share cost: $7.89
($1,500 ÷ 190)

Average share price: $12.60
($63 ÷ 5)

Average share cost: $10.71
($1,500 ÷ 140)

average prices. To illustrate, totaling in Table 17–5 reveals an overall investment of $4,500 ($1,500 + $1,500 + $1,500) used to purchase 450 shares (120 + 190 + 140) for an average cost of $10 a share ($4,500 ÷ 450). With the recent market price at $20, you will have a long-term gain of $4,500 ($20 current market price × 450 shares = $9,000 − $4,500 amount invested.) Note that the dollar-cost averaging method would still be valid if the time interval for investing was monthly, quarterly, or even semiannually; it is the regularity of investing that counts.

It should be clear that dollar-cost averaging reduces the average cost of shares of stock purchased over a relatively long period. Profits are made when stock market prices fluctuate and eventually go up. Although the possibility of loss is not eliminated, losses are limited during times of declining market prices. What is very important, profits are accelerated during rising market prices. This approach to investments is not particularly glamorous, but it is the only approach that is *almost guaranteed* to make a profit for the investor. It takes neither brilliance nor luck, just discipline.

Monthly Investment Plans   A *monthly investment plan (MIP)* is an arrangement you make with a brokerage firm to invest regularly (perhaps monthly or quarterly) a specified amount of funds ($40 to $1,000) in a common stock listed on a major stock exchange. This plan provides you with the advantages of dollar-cost averaging. Additional features of MIPs offered by brokerage firms include the purchase of fractional shares, special low commission rates, automatic reinvestment of dividends, noncontractual agreements featuring no penalty should an investment payment be missed, and monthly statements evidencing ownership. Conservative or moderate investors are often quite satisfied with the results of a monthly investment plan. The primary drawbacks are the effect of commission charges on return rates and the lack of diversification.

Rules, Charts, and Formulas   Many investors set their own investment rules. "Sell whenever prices drop 15 percent or more" might be a good rule for the conservative investor. "Sell only when the loss exceeds 40 percent" could be a speculator's rule. "When the price drops sharply, double the investment" also could be used by the speculator. This latter rule is called *averaging down;* its merit is that the price need not rise to its original level to regain the investor's losses. For example, assume you have 1,000 shares at $10 per share for an investment of $10,000. The price drops to $5 and you buy an additional 2,000 shares for another investment of $10,000. Thus, your total of $20,000 is invested in stock worth $15,000 (3,000 shares at $5 each). Because of averaging down, the stock price need only reach 6¾ before you recoup losses and have a profit (3,000 × 6¾ = $20,250). If the price rises to $8 before you sell, the gain is $4,000, or 20 percent (3,000 × 8 = $24,000 − $20,000 = $4,000 ÷ $20,000).

Charts of different types help serious investors decide when to buy or sell securities. Investors can do their own daily charting of stock activities (high, low, close, volume, etc.) and/or subscribe to advisory services that provide charting for a fee. Technical investment analysts or theorists often use complicated mathematical models on which to base their buy-or-sell recommendations.

Many long-term investors follow their own formula-timing guidelines and use a stock's P/E ratio as an indicator of buying low and selling high. For example, perhaps the price/earnings ratio of Running Paws Catfood Company common stock in recent years has ranged between 8 and 24. An investor might decide to buy Running Paws when its P/E ratio is less than 10 and sell when it is greater than 20.

Investors also use formulas to manage their entire portfolio. These formulas are usually predicated on the belief that securities investments should include certain percentages of both an aggressive portfolio and a defensive portfolio. The concept is that securities in the aggressive portfolio should be more volatile (common stocks) than those in the defensive portfolio (usually bonds), and profits are made by varying the percentage of each in bull and bear markets. In a rising market, investors should shift more funds into the aggressive portfolio by selling some from the defensive portfolio; in a declining market, investors should increase funds in the defensive portfolio by selling securities from the aggressive portfolio. Hence, the volatility of common stocks will reap profits in bull markets, and the values of bonds will increase in declining markets.

Investment Clubs   An *investment club* is an organization formed by individuals who want to share their investment knowledge and a limited amount of investment dollars to learn about the securities market and to make a profit. These clubs usually meet monthly, have five to fifteen members, and require a monthly contribution ranging from $10 to $50. The amounts collected are subsequently invested in securities based on decisions made by the entire group. Since trading typically involves substantial funds, commission charges represent a small proportion of each transaction. Generally, different members investigate particular investment alternatives and report their findings to the membership, which then votes on what actions to take according to the club's investment goals. All actions are governed by the bylaws of the club, and a legal partnership agreement protects members.

Brokers are usually happy to assist clubs because members often will open individual accounts as well. The National Association of Investment Clubs (NAIC) provides a complete packet of information to help people establish investment clubs. Included are accounting forms, guidelines for investing, and a sample copy of *Better Investing,* a monthly magazine devoted to investment education that is available on subscription. There are about six thousand NAIC investment clubs in the United States and an estimated twenty thousand unaffiliated clubs. The NAIC sponsors numerous regional and national meetings to improve investors' abilities.

Employee Stock Purchase Plans   Many corporations offer an *employee stock purchase plan (ESPP)* as a fringe benefit for employees. This plan permits employees to buy shares of stock in the company and gives them an extra incentive to do a good job, the hoped-for result being an increase in the profitability of the corporation and in the value of the stock. Generally, the purchase price of the stock is fixed and the amount that may be purchased is limited. In some cases, the employer will make a matching contribution of stock, which greatly accelerates the purchasing efforts of the individual investor-employee. For example, for every $100 of stock the employee purchases (perhaps up to a maximum of $2,000 annually), the company might donate $50 of additional stock.

Short-term Investors: Trading Approaches

A *short-term investor* is speculative or moderately speculative and wants to earn quick profits (over a period of months, weeks, days, or even hours) on small but significant changes in prices of securities. The two widely used investment approaches of short-term investors are buying on margin and selling short. (More speculative investments are discussed in Chapter 20).

Margin Buying   Using a margin account to purchase securities, or *margin buying,* is a method of reducing your equity in an investment in order to magnify returns by borrowing money from a broker. This allows you to buy more stocks and/or bonds than you could with available cash. Use of credit to buy securities is regulated by both brokers and the Federal Reserve Board. The *margin rate* is the percentage amount of the value (or equity) in an investment that is not borrowed.

In recent years, the margin rate has ranged from 30 to 80 percent. Thus, if the margin rate is 40 percent, you can buy stock by putting up only 40 percent of the total price and borrowing the remainder from the broker. The stock purchased, as well as cash or other securities on deposit with the broker, is used as collateral, according to the regulations of the margin account. Interest is charged for the loan at a rate of 1 to 3 percent above the broker's cost of borrowing.

Buying on margin is commonly used to increase return on investment, as Table 17–6 illustrates. For example, let's assume that Running Paws common stock is selling for $80 a share and you wish to buy 100 shares for a total of $8,000. Using your margin account, you will make a cash payment of $3,200 (40 percent × $8,000), with the broker loaning you the difference of $4,800 ($8,000 − $3,200). For the sake of simplicity, omit commissions and assume the broker loans the funds at 10 percent interest. Thus, the equity (market value minus amount borrowed) you have in the investment is $3,200. If Running Paws stock increases in price to $92 by the end of a year, you can sell for proceeds of $9,200, minus the amount invested ($3,200), minus the amount borrowed ($4,800), and minus the cost of borrowing ($4,800 × .10 = $480), for a yield of $720. Since you invested an equity of only $3,200 for a profit of $720, you have earned a return of 22.5 percent ($720 ÷

TABLE 17–6
How Buying on Margin Affects the Return on Investment

	Cash Transaction	40% Margin Transaction
Price of stock rises (from $80 to $92 a share)		
Buy 100 shares @ $80 (amount invested)	−$8,000	−$3,200
Sell 100 shares @ $92 (proceeds)	9,200	9,200
Net proceeds	$1,200	$6,000
Minus amount borrowed	—	− 4,800
Net	$1,200	$1,200
Minus cost of borrowing	—	− 480
Return	$1,200	$ 720
Yield (return ÷ amount invested)	+15.0%	+22.5%
Price of stock declines (from $80 to $70 a share)		
Buy 100 shares @ $80 (amount invested)	−$8,000	−$3,200
Sell 100 shares@ $70 (proceeds)	7,000	7,000
Net proceeds	−$1,000	$3,800
Minus amount borrowed	—	− 4,800
Net	−$1,000	−$1,000
Minus cost of borrowing	—	− 480
Return	−$1,000	−$1,480
Yield (return ÷ amount invested)	−12.5%	−46.25%
Price of stock declines (from $80 to $60 a share)		
Buy 100 shares @ $80 (amount invested)	−$8,000	−$3,200
Sell 100 shares@ $60 (proceeds)	6,000	6,000
Net proceeds	−$2,000	$2,800
Minus amount borrowed	—	− 4,800
Net	−$2,000	−$2,000
Minus cost of borrowing	—	− 480
Return	−$2,000	−$2,480
Yield (return ÷ amount invested)	−25.0%	−77.5%

$3,200). If you had instead put up the entire $8,000 and not bought on margin, your return on investment would have been only 15 percent ($9,200 − $8,000 = $1,200 ÷ $8,000). This illustrates the financial concept of *leverage,* using borrowed money to increase the rate of return on an investment higher than the cost of funds.

Short-term investors like to buy on margin because leverage gives them the potential to make gains over a shorter period. For example, assume the margin rate is 50 percent and you want to purchase 1,000 shares of a $10 stock. Buying on margin, you need only put up $5,000 (50 percent of $10,000). The price of the stock need rise to only $11 over the course of a month for you to make a handsome profit. The $1,000 in proceeds ($11 × 1,000 = $11,000 − $10,000) might be reduced by broker's interest charges of $100, for a yield of $900. That represents a return of 18 percent on the amount invested ($900 ÷ $5,000) in only one month, which is well over 200 percent annually. Note also that the price could have increased in only a week.

By not buying on margin, the short-term investor described above would have had to wait until the price reached 11⅞ (more than a full point higher) to realize a similar return ($11,875 − $10,000 = $1,875 ÷ $10,000 = 18.75 percent). The short-term investor believes that a stock priced at 10 is more likely to rise to 11 than all the way to 11⅞. The percentage growth in price from 10 to 11 is only 10 percent (11 − 10 = 1 ÷ 10), compared with an increase of 18.75 percent if the price moves from 10 to 11⅞ (11⅞ − 10 = 1⅞ ÷ 10).

Realize also that buying on margin can be dangerous as well. Should the price of a security bought on margin decline, leverage can work against you, as Table 17–6 illustrates. If the Running Paws stock bought at $80 dropped to $70 after a year, you would lose $10 a share on the 100 shares for a total of $1,000. Proceeds would be only $7,000. If you bought the stock on margin, against this amount goes the cost of the investment ($3,200), the margin loan from the broker ($4,800), and interest on the loan ($480), for a total of $8,480 and a net loss of $1,480 ($7,000 − $8,480). Thus, a loss of $1,480 on an investment of $3,200 is a negative return of 46.25 percent ($1,480 ÷ $3,200). The same $10 loss per share ($80 to $70) would have been a negative loss of only 12.5 percent if the stocks were not bought on margin ($8,000 − $7,000 = $1,000 ÷ $8,000). When buying stocks on margin, leverage can enhance both profits and losses dramatically.

A *margin call* could also hurt the financial position of the margin buyer. This is a requirement that the margin investor put up more funds if the value of the security declines to the point where the investor's equity is less than the required percentage (such as 25 percent) of the current market value or the broker can legally sell the securities. This protects the broker who has loaned money on securities. For example, the 100 shares of Running Paws at $80 were originally valued at $8,000. You had an equity of $3,200, or 40 percent ($3,200 ÷ $8,000), and borrowed the remaining $4,800 from the broker. Assume that the stock price drops to $60 a share, which makes the current market value $6,000. Since you still owe $4,800 your equity has dropped to $1,200 ($6,000 − $4,800), which is only 20 percent of the value of the securities ($1,200 ÷ $6,000). The broker will immediately make a margin call, demanding that you add funds (perhaps within seventy-two hours) to the account to bring the equity up to a minimum of 25 percent, $300 in this example ($6,000 × 25 percent = $1,500 − $1,200).

To determine at what price a margin call will occur, use formula 17–2. Substituting the figures from the illustration above, the investor will not receive a margin call unless the stock price drops below $64 as his equity at that point is still 25 percent.

$$\text{Margin call price} = \frac{\dfrac{\text{amount owed broker}}{1 - \text{margin call requirement}}}{\text{number of shares bought}} \qquad (17-2)$$

$$= \frac{\dfrac{\$4,800}{1 - .25}}{100} = \frac{\dfrac{\$4,800}{.75}}{100}$$

$$= \$64$$

If you can't meet the margin call, the broker will sell the securities as soon as possible, and you will suffer a sharp financial loss. Table 17–6 illustrates the magnitude of the loss as a negative return of 77.5 percent, compared with a negative 25 percent return if you had not bought on margin.

Selling Short   When you buy a security in the hope that it will go up in value, this is called **buying long**. However, you might suspect that the price of a security is going to go down. You can earn profits when the price of a security drops by selling short. **Selling short** is a trading technique by which investors sell a security they do not own (borrowing it from a broker) and later buy a like amount of the same security at, it is hoped, a lower price (and return it to the broker), thus earning a profit on the transaction. Brokers require a margin account when selling short, as this provides some assurance that you can repay the value of the stock if necessary. Thus the funds in a margin account are effectively tied up during a short sale. Many brokers hold the proceeds of a short sale, without paying interest, until the customer "covers the position" by buying it back for delivery to the broker.

For example, assume that you have concluded that the price of Running Paws stock will drop substantially over the next several months. You have heard that some top managers of the company may resign and that competitors expect to be introducing newer products. Accordingly, you instruct your broker to sell 100 shares of Running Paws at $80 ($80 × 100 = $8,000). In this illustration assume you have a 40 percent margin requirement, which means you have $3,200 (40 percent × $8,000) committed. The shares are actually borrowed by the broker from another investor or another broker. Several months later Running Paws announces lower profits because of strong competition, and the price drops to $70 a share. Now you instruct your broker to buy 100 shares at that price. This gives you a profit of $1,000 ($8,000 − $7,000), less commissions, providing a relatively quick return of 31.3 percent ($1,000 ÷ $3,200).

A very small price drop can provide profits for the short-term investor who sells short and uses the margin. For example, assume you sell 100 shares of a $10 stock with a 40 percent margin requirement. The committed funds amount to $400 (40 percent × $1,000). Even if the price of the stock declines only $1, you still earn a significant profit: 100 shares sold at $10 equals $1,000, minus 100 shares bought at $9 equal $900, for a profit of $100 and a return of 25 percent ($100 ÷ $400).

However, realize that almost unlimited losses can occur should the price rise instead of fall. If the $10 stock rises to $22, the loss will be more than the original investment: 100 shares sold at $10 equal $1,000, minus 100 shares bought at $22 equals $2,200, for a loss of $1,200 and a negative return of 550 percent ($2,200 ÷ $400)! In addition, when the price of a security rises, you are subject to margin calls. Clearly, selling short and buying on margin are techniques to be used only by sophisticated investors.

Knowing When to Sell

Don't you wish we could tell you precisely when to sell your stocks and bonds to make lots of money? Although such certainty of knowledge is not available, following the three guidelines below will help you profit in the securities market.

Take Your Profits

The great financier Bernard Baruch was once asked how he made so much money in the securities market. He replied, "I always sold too soon!" Baruch suggested that one should not be too greedy. When you have earned a satisfactory profit, an amount that only you can determine, sell and take the real profit to avoid the risks of prices dropping later.

Advice for Conservative Stock Investors*

- When the market is retreating and the economy is deteriorating (a bear market), take profits and cut losses on most stocks; consider holding defensive stocks.

- As the bear market continues, plan ahead by being alert for low-priced stocks with high yields or undervalued issues that are likely to surge ahead when the market improves.

- If the market is uncertain, lacks clear direction, and seesaws aimlessly, follow suggestions above.

- When the market is rising, buy on "corrections" if possible. These are brief time periods, a few days at most, when most market prices are depressed because of negative news.

- As the bull market continues, protect some of your profits by placing stop-loss orders with your broker if prices fall back.

- As the bull market matures, consider taking some profits by selling half of your stocks.

* Especially if you have some well-reasoned opinions on the direction of interest rates, inflation, and the economy for the next year or more.

**Cut Losses
Quickly**

Hindsight is sometimes much better than foresight, especially in securities transactions. When you have bought securities due to an error in judgment, sell them. Temporary shifts in prices of 10 to 15 percent happen all the time, but when it is clear that an earlier decision to buy was incorrect, don't wait for a 10 percent loss to develop into a 20 or 30 percent loss some weeks or months later. Accept your error, sell, and make a better investment with the proceeds.

**If You Wouldn't
Buy It Now,
Sell It**

As you review your portfolio of securities investments, don't think about the price you originally paid and the possible capital gains income tax liability. Ask yourself "If I had extra money to invest, would I put it into this security?" and carefully analyze the individual security, the industry, and the prospects for economic growth. If your answer is no, sell the security and don't let a 2 or 3 percent commission stop you.

Summary

1. After securities have been sold in the primary market, organized stock exchanges (such as the New York Stock Exchange) offer a secondary market.

2. Available information on general economic conditions and the securities market indexes, along with industry data and news about corporations, can help reduce investment risks and increase returns.

3. To calculate a stock's total potential return, add the anticipated dividend income and price appreciation over a period of five years or more.

4. To buy and sell securities, you need to open an account at a general brokerage firm or discount broker and pay specific fees on each transaction. A certificate will be provided to you as evidence of stock or bond ownership.

5. The actual transaction to buy or sell securities involves brokers matching or negotiating the final price. Use of stop orders can help you reduce losses as well as protect gains.

6. The six-step investment process includes identifying your desired return as well as making a list of probable actions you can take during certain investment conditions.

7. Investment approaches can be classified as long-term (such as dividend reinvestment plans, business-cycle approach, diversified portfolio, and dollar-cost averaging) and short-term (such as margin buying and selling short).

8. Guidelines on when to sell stocks and bonds include: take your profits, cut losses quickly, and if you wouldn't buy it now, sell it.

Modern Money Management

The Johnsons Compare Investments for the Future

With their incomes increasing and having brought their spending under control, Harry and Belinda have decided to begin investing for the future. They intend to take about $3,000 out of savings and then put an additional $200 to $400 a month into investments. They both have a moderate investment philosophy and seek some cash dividends as well as price appreciation.

1. Calculate the five-year return on the investment choices below. Put your calculations in tabular form like that of Table 17–2.

	Running Paws	Eagle Packaging
Current price	$30	$48
Current earnings per share (EPs)	$2.00	$2.30
Current quarterly cash dividend	$.15	$.18
Current P/E ratio	15	21
Projected earnings annual growth rate	20%	20%
Projected cash dividend	10%	20%

2. Using the appropriate P/E ratios, what are the estimated market prices of Running Paws and Eagle after five years?

3. Show your calculations in determining the projected price appreciations for the two stocks over the five years.

4. Add the projected price appreciation of each stock to its projected cash dividends and show the total five-year percentage returns for the two stocks.

5. Determine the average annual dividend for each stock and use those figures in calculating the approximate compound yields for each alternative.

6. Assume that inflation is about 6 percent and the return on long-term quality bonds is 11 percent. Given the Johnsons' investment philosophy, explain why you would recommend (a) Running Paws, (b) Eagle, or (c) a long-term quality bond as a long-term growth investment.

Key Words and Concepts

Review Questions

1. Explain the difference between primary and secondary markets.
2. What is the role of an investment banking firm in the securities business?
3. Explain the role a stockbroker plays in the process of trading securities in the secondary market.
4. Explain how organized stock exchanges differ.
5. Explain the OTC concepts of market making, bid price and asked price.
6. What is meant by the following stock transaction terms: *stock, div, yld%, sales 100s, P/E ratio, high/low, close, net chg?*
7. What are the components of regulation in the securities market?
8. Why was the Securities Investors Protection Corporation (SIPC) formed?
9. Identify two popular stock indexes used by investors and briefly distinguish between them.
10. Briefly illustrate how to calculate a stock's potential total return.
11. What are the advantages and disadvantages to the investor of using a traditional brokerage firm?
12. Show what the commissions might be at a full-service brokerage firm and a discount brokerage firm on a purchase of 350 shares of a stock priced at $10 a share.
13. Distinguish between a cash account and a margin account and

identify advantages of using each from an investor's point of view.

14. Explain when prices are matched or negotiated.

15. Give reasons why investors would want to use a market order, a limit order, and a stop order.

16. Illustrate what is meant by identifying a desired total return and choosing an investment for its components of total return.

17. Differentiate between long- and short-term investors.

18. Give two examples of what an investor might do, using a business-cycle approach to long-term investing.

19. Explain how portfolio diversification works and tell why some investors use it.

20. What does dollar-cost averaging achieve and how does it work?

21. Give an example of using a formula plan to invest successfully.

22. Describe the effect that buying on margin and leverage can have on securities investments.

23. Differentiate between buying long and selling short.

24. Give an example of one guideline that will help you know when to sell securities.

Case Problems

1. Linda Haag of New Egypt, New Jersey, has operated her own custom packaging business quite successfully for more than five years. She has decided to incorporate her business as Eagle Packaging Incorporated and seeks expansion funds. The total value of authorized stock is to be $450,000, and Linda plans to retain $250,000 of this authorization. Eagle common stock will have a par value of $50 per share. After her own purchase of $5,000 shares, 4,000 shares will be sold to the investing public.
   a. Explain how the shares might be priced and how they will be marketed.
   b. Explain why future trading of the 4,000 shares will occur in the over-the-counter market after they are initially sold to the investing public.
   c. Give an illustration of likely bid and asked prices of Eagle stock.

2. Harold Rubin of Shreveport, Louisiana, is interested in investing in Greenfield Computer Company. He notices that the market price for their common stock has been around $80 in recent months and he wants to buy one hundred shares. Give Harold advice as he ponders the following questions:
   a. Should he use a full-service or discount broker for this purchase? Why?

b. Should he give the broker a market order or a limit order? Why?
c. Should it be a day order or a good-till-cancelled order? Why?
d. What would the discount broker's commission probably be if Harold bought Greenfield Computer for 79½?
e. As Harold is an investor interested in cutting his losses and taking his gains, explain your advice to him to put in stop orders at 67 and 92.

3. Tommy Jacobson of Santa Monica, California, recently received an inheritance of more than $50,000. After paying off some bills and buying a new car, he has decided to invest the balance of $14,000 in the stock market. An investment advisor recommended a portfolio to include a money market fund, some mutual funds and some stocks, as shown in the box, "Diversified Portfolios of Selected Investors." Tommy is hesitant since he has never invested in stocks before and he seeks your advice on selecting growth stocks. He says that cash dividends are of little concern to him since he earns enough money to live comfortably.
a. If inflation is 6 percent and Tommy is in the 35 percent tax bracket (including both federal and state taxes), what would his real return be if he earns 15 percent? Explain how to determine this figure. (Hint: See the box on page 456.)
b. Suggest to Tommy three industries that have had successful earnings in recent years. (See Figure 17–7.)
c. Briefly tell him how and when to obtain information about those industries and particular companies.

Suggested Readings

"Bird-in-Hand Theory." *Forbes,* February 23, 1987, pp. 104–108. Theorists say a stock is worth the present value of all future dividends.

"A Checklist for Stock Market Prognosticators." *Forbes,* May 4, 1987, pp. 110–114. How to tell when the bull market is over.

"The Club That Makes You Rich and Happy." *Working Woman,* June 1987, pp. 72–75+. Success stories and hints on how to start your own investment club.

"Great Investment Portfolios: 9 for the '90s." *Changing Times,* September 1987, pp. 24–34. Suggestions for long-term investments.

"How to Say No (or Yes) to Your Broker." *Changing Times,* March 1987, pp. 77–81. Suggestions on how to deal with your investment broker.

"Managing Your Money Pro." *Working Woman,* February 1987, pp. 36–42. How to evaluate and effectively use a stockbroker.

"Would You Panic if Your Stock Took a Dive?" *U.S. News and World Report,* June 8, 1987, pp. 60–61. Examples to help you assess your goals and investment approach.

CHAPTER 18

Mutual Funds as an Investment

OBJECTIVES

After reading this chapter, the student should be able to

1. describe the various types of investment companies.
2. identify the costs of buying mutual funds.
3. explain the tax status of mutual funds and of investors in mutual funds.
4. distinguish among the four major objectives of mutual funds.
5. classify mutual funds by portfolio.
6. specify the three ways of purchasing mutual funds.
7. list the unique benefits of mutual funds.
8. describe the advantages and disadvantages of investing in mutual funds.
9. discuss the process of selecting a mutual fund.
10. discuss the five factors to consider when determining whether to sell a mutual fund.

The concept of mutual funds began more than one hundred years ago in London with the Foreign and Colonial Government Trust, which was established to provide "the investor of moderate means the same advantages as the large capitalists in diminishing the risk of investing . . . by spreading the investment over a number of different stocks." In essence, the group formed an **investment company,** which is a corporation, trust, or partnership in which investors with similar financial goals pool their funds to utilize professional management and to achieve diversification of their investments.

Mutual funds are the most common form of investment company, and the concept is illustrated in Figure 18–1. A **mutual fund** is an investment company that combines the funds of investors who have purchased shares of ownership in the investment company and invests those monies in a diversified portfolio of securities issued by other corporations or governments.

There are more than 20 million mutual fund shareholders today, and the public is investing in mutual funds more than ever before. Some reasons for this growth are that newer and more attractive types of funds have been recently created, many funds carry little or no sales charges, some have performed much better than an average common stock, and aggressive marketing efforts have been used to promote mutual funds. Many people feel that investing in mutual funds can provide a better return than investing in separate securities.

This chapter examines the appeal and logic of mutual funds as an investment. We first distinguish among the types of investment companies and then cover the costs of buying mutual funds, which are differ-

FIGURE 18–1
How a Mutual Fund Works

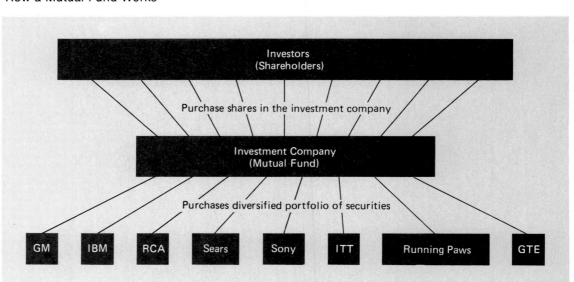

ent from the costs of other securities. Next we discuss returns to the investor in view of the special tax status given mutual funds. We then distinguish among the four major objectives of mutual funds and classify them according to their portfolio holdings. The next section considers the three methods of purchasing mutual funds, and after this are discussed special features of mutual funds that are usually appealing to the average investor. We then offer a summary of the advantages and disadvantages of mutual funds. The final two sections answer key questions about selecting and selling a mutual fund.

Types of Investment Companies

All investment companies operate similarly. They pool funds obtained by selling shares to investors and make investments in particular areas to achieve the financial goal of income, growth, or both. Voting rights are generally retained by management, and investors pay a fee for the management service. Investment companies avoid most federal income taxation as long as they distribute 90 percent of their income to shareholders. These companies are guided by the federal Investment Company Act and SEC regulations. The five types of investment companies are real estate investment trusts, unit investment trusts, small business investment companies, and closed-end and open-end mutual funds.

Real Estate Investment Trusts

A *trust* is a contractual relationship in which one entity (the trustee or fiduciary) manages and holds the title of property for another (the beneficiary). Trustees must act in accordance with the legal doctrine of the "prudent man rule," which suggests that it is legal for trustees to freely invest the money of clients as long as they "conduct themselves faithfully, exercise sound discretion, and pattern themselves after the manner in which prudent men managed their own affairs."

A *real estate investment trust (REIT)* is a type of closed-end investment company in which the proceeds from the sale of the original shares are invested by trust managers in a diversified group of income-producing properties, such as apartments and office buildings. If the REIT is quite profitable, the nonredeemed shares, which are traded like stocks, will rise in value. Chapter 19 details the operations of REITs.

Unit Investment Trusts

A *unit investment trust* is a type of closed-end investment company in which the proceeds from the sale of original shares are invested in a fixed portfolio of taxable or tax-exempt bonds and held until maturity, generally for ten to twenty years. Unit investment trusts are originally sold by large brokerage firms and are essentially unmanaged. After the fund is organized, the investments are made and the brokerage firm receives its commission (generally as low as 1 to 3 percent). No management fee is charged, and the fund itself does not have a precise maturity date. Rather, as the bonds mature (or are paid off early) the proceeds are paid monthly or quarterly to investors on a pro rata basis. The fund self-liquidates when assets drop to about 20 percent of the original holdings and all bonds are then sold on the open market.

Unit investment trusts offer safety of principal and an assured regular income based on yields at the time of purchase. The base yield is fixed at the time of investment, since the interest rates on the portfolio are known. Realize that because shares of unit investment trusts are traded, their price is set by supply and demand. In addition, the market value of these mutual funds declines when interest rates rise because the underlying securities are fixed-rate securities.

Small-business Investment Company

A *small-business investment company* is a corporation licensed by the federal Small Business Administration (SBA) to provide venture capital to small businesses. It helps arrange start-up capital and long-term financing for small businesses in particular geographic areas. Typically, these companies sell shares of stock and bonds through local brokerage firms to private investors. Although these businesses have some affiliation with the federal government through the SBA, the government guarantees them nothing. As such, most small-business investment companies are risky investments.

Closed-end Mutual Funds

A *closed-end mutual fund* issues a limited and fixed number of shares of stock and does not buy them back (*redeem* them), so that after the original issue is sold the price of a share is established by supply and demand in the secondary market. Thus, shares are traded much like the common stock or bonds of a corporation. Standard brokerage commissions must be paid on purchase and sale transactions in the over-the-counter market. Dividends earned by investors cannot be reinvested without paying brokerage firm commissions. Closed-end mutual funds are allowed by law to own stocks, bonds, and preferred stocks. Of the more than sixteen hundred mutual funds, only about 10 percent are closed-end funds.

Open-end Mutual Funds

An *open-end mutual fund* is always ready to sell new shares and to redeem old ones at a price called *net asset value* (the current worth of the underlying securities less company liabilities). Net asset value (NAV) is determined by subtracting the liabilities of the fund from the current market value of all the securities in the fund and dividing the remainder by the total number of outstanding fund shares.

For example, say a fund's liabilities amount to $4 million and the current market value of the fund's securities amounts to $75 million, leaving a remainder of $71 million. If 10 million shares of the open-end fund were outstanding, the net asset value would be $7.10 ($71 million ÷ 10 million). The net asset value is calculated at least twice daily and represents the worth of each share of the open-end mutual fund. About 90 percent of all mutual funds are open-end funds. Shares can be purchased from the mutual fund itself, from a financial planner, or through a brokerage firm; shares can always be redeemed or sold back to the fund.

The Costs of Buying Open-end Mutual Funds

Since most public purchases of mutual funds are of open-end funds, the remainder of the chapter will focus on this type of investment company. The costs of investing in mutual funds may include various charges and fees.

Sales Charges

Open-end mutual funds can be classified as to whether they have a sales charge, also called a *load* (which is a commission earned for selling a mutual fund), collected by mutual fund sales personnel, financial planners, or brokerage firms when a mutual fund is sold to an investor. A mutual fund that does not have a sales charge is generally called a *no-load fund*.

Load Fund A *load fund* is a mutual fund sold to the public that charges a sales commission on the amount invested, usually called a *front-end load*. The charge on a load fund is typically 7.5 to 8.5 percent. The load pays the costs of marketing the mutual fund.

For example, assume that you have discussed the investment potential of the Conglomerate Cat and Dog Food Mutual Fund with a salesperson. After examining the prospectus, you decide to invest $10,000. Since this is a load fund with a commission of 8.5 percent (the maximum permitted by the SEC), you pay $850 to the salesperson. As a result, you have only $9,150 working for you to earn dividends and capital gains. Note that this commission is much higher than stock transaction costs, which are usually about 2 percent.

The sales charge may be shown either as the stated commission or as a percentage of the amount invested. The stated commission (8.5 percent here) is somewhat misleading. The percentage of the amount invested is more accurate, as it is based on the *actual* monies invested and working. A stated commission of 8.5 percent amounts to 9.3 percent of the amount invested: $10,000 − $9,150 = $850 ÷ $9,150). If you want actually to invest $10,000, you would need to pay out $10,930 [$10,930 − ($10,930 × 8.5 percent) = $10,000]. Sales charges are lower on invested amounts of $40,000 or more. Low-load funds have a 2 to 3 percent sales charge. They are often sold by mail, sometimes sold in shopping centers, and are advertised as having small commissions.

No-load Fund   A no-load fund is a mutual fund that historically has charged no sales commission on the amount initially invested and traditionally is bought directly from the fund by the investing public by mail or telephone. Since there generally are no sales intermediaries, interested investors must seek out advertisements for no-load funds in financial newspapers and magazines. Many excellent no-load funds are frequently described and analyzed in publications such as *Forbes, Barron's, Business Week,* and *Money.*

More than half of all no-load mutual funds are charging **hidden loads** of 1 to 1.25 percent *annually,* which pay for marketing and distribution fees on no-load funds as approved by SEC rule 12b–1. Such fees are quite costly for the shareholder over a period of years, and you would be better off with a load fund than paying 12b–1 assessments if you plan to own the fund for more than ten years. A broker or financial planner may claim that a 12b–1 fund is no-load when in fact the fund pays commissions to such sellers.

Other Fees and Charges   Deferred sales charges and exit fees are becoming common on both load and no-load funds. *Deferred sales charges* are commissions of 1 to 6 percent assessed on the mutual fund investor if the shares are redeemed within a certain period after purchase. For example, a fund might charge a 5 percent fee if an investor redeems the shares within one year of purchase. Fees typically decline for every year the investor owns the shares, perhaps reaching zero after six years. *Exit fees* are charges assessed on redemption of mutual fund shares regardless of the length of time the investor has owned the shares. This increasingly common fee is usually 1 percent of the redemption value. The SEC is expected soon to require that funds listed in newspaper financial tables show an *r* after their names if they assess deferred sales charges or exit fees. Clearly it is important to read the fine print in the prospectus on commissions and other fees before investing in a mutual fund, including the heretofore no-load funds.

Newspaper Quotations for Open-end Funds   You can find current prices for load and no-load funds in newspapers (or through a brokerage firm). Figure 18–2 shows how funds are quoted. Fidelity's "Balanced" Fund has a net asset value (NAV) of $10.73, it is a load fund with an offering (offer) price of $10.95, and the NAV has risen $.02 from the closing quotation of the previous day. The NAV is also known as the **bid price,** as it is the amount per share that shareholders receive when they cash in (redeem) their shares. Thus, on this day Balanced is bidding $10.73 to repurchase any shares outstanding. The *asked price,* or *offering price,* is the price at which a mutual fund's share can be purchased by investors; it is the current net asset value per share plus sales charges, if any. Thus, if you wanted to buy Fidelity's Balanced

```
Evergrn      14.03 N.L.+ .08
Evrgrn TR    18.98 N.L.+ .06
Fairmnt      57.61 N.L.+ .05
Farm B Gr    (z)   (z)   ...
Federated Group:
  FBF         9.28 N.L.+ .04
  Fed Flt     9.95 N.L.+ .01
  Fed StkB  x15.73 N.L.− .19
  Cash Tr    10.74 N.L.+ .01
  Exch Fd    55.69 N.L.− .14
  FIMT        9.82 N.L.+ .03
  FT  Intl   24.49 N.L.+ .17
  GNMA       10.88 N.L.+ .04
  Grow Tr    17.67 N.L.+ .04
  Hi  Yld    10.64 N.L.+ .03
  Incm Tr    10.31 N.L.+ .02
  Intrmd      9.75 N.L.+ .01
  SIGT       10.16 N.L.+ .02
  SIMT       10.19 N.L.+ .01
  Stock Tr   24.87 N.L.− .08
  US Govt     9.22 N.L.+ .02
Fidelity Investments:
  Aggr TF    11.05 N.L.+ .07
  Balanc     10.73 10.95+ .02
  Cal HYld   10.72 N.L.+ .13
  Cap App    12.72 12.98+ .04
  Congr St   97.08 N.L.− .30
  Contra     13.64 N.L.+ .02
  Conv Sec   10.54 N.L.+ .03
  CT ARP     10.51 N.L.   ...
  Eq Incm    28.66 29.24+ .04
  Europe     14.09 14.38+ .04
  Exch Fd    73.89 N.L.− .22
  Fidel Fd   17.87 N.L.+ .01
  Flex  B     6.89 N.L.+ .03
```

FIGURE 18–2
How Mutual Funds Are Quoted

Source: Wall Street Journal, June 1, 1987. Reprinted by permission of the *Wall Street Journal*, © Dow Jones & Company, Inc. 1987. All rights reserved.

Fund they would offer to sell it to you for $10.95. The sales commission (load) may be calculated as a factor of the difference between the two prices ($10.95 − $10.73 = .22 ÷ $10.95 = 2.0 percent). By law, this load must be the same whether you purchase shares from a fund or through a brokerage firm.

The newspapers' quotations for no-load mutual funds are easier to comprehend. In Figure 18–2, the Evergreen Fund has a net asset value (NAV) of $14.03, is a no-load fund (N.L.), and had a change in the net asset value (NAV Chg.) of plus $.08 from the closing price of the previous trading day. Thus, if you wanted to buy *or* sell Evergreen on this day, the price would be $14.03 a share. (This does not include the 12b–1 fee, if there is any.)

Management Fees

The professional managers who operate mutual funds are paid with a percentage of the investment company's assets as specified in the articles of incorporation. As the assets of the firm increase, the financial rewards for managers will increase as well. Typically, management fees range from .50 to 1.5 percent of the assets annually (depending on the size of the fund), and the fees are deducted when calculating the net asset value.

Taxes and Mutual Funds

The special tax status of mutual funds and of the returns earned by shareholders is examined below.

Tax Status of Mutual Funds

A diversified investment company (most open-end and closed-end mutual funds) that registers with the SEC qualifies under the Investment Company Act of 1940 and subsequent amendments for special tax status. Like any other registered security, such a regulated investment company must follow specific rules and regulations of the SEC designed to protect investors.

The special tax treatment for mutual funds avoids double taxation on fund earnings of dividends and capital gains. Most of the earnings of mutual funds are not subject to the federal corporate income tax since shareholders must report the same earnings in their own income taxes. The law permits regulated investment companies to exempt 90 percent of their net earnings (excluding long-term capital gains that may be distributed or retained) from corporate taxes if they distribute those profits directly to shareholders. The remaining 10 percent (if any profits are kept) is taxed in the usual way. Thus, tax laws encourage a substantial flow of funds into regulated diversified investment companies.

Tax Status of Mutual Funds for the Investor

Returns to investors in mutual funds take two forms: (1) income and (2) potential price appreciation. Investors in profitable mutual funds receive a quarterly or semiannual dividend check that represents both income from dividends and income from capital gains distributions. An *income dividend* results from the mutual fund's earning dividends and interest on securities (plus some short-term capital gains) after operating expenses are deducted. A *capital gains distribution* is income resulting from net long-term profits realized when portfolio securities are sold at a gain. Mutual fund shareholders pay income taxes on all such income paid to them by the company.

Price appreciation is another form of return on mutual funds. You hope that the market price of the mutual fund will increase in value. If your mutual fund owns common stock in IBM and General Electric and the stocks of those two companies increase in value, the fund will have *capital growth.* This growth is an increase in the market value of a mutual fund's securities and is usually reflected in the net asset value of fund shares. As the value of the underlying securities increases, so does the net asset value of the mutual fund. Of course, price appreciation is only a paper profit until you sell the mutual fund shares and realize the profit.

Objectives of Mutual Funds

A mutual fund states its objectives in its prospectus. There are four major objectives: (1) growth, (2) income, (3) growth and income, and (4) balanced.

Growth Objective

A mutual fund with a growth objective focuses on long-term growth or price appreciation of the value of securities in its portfolio rather than a flow of dividends. The fund buys and holds the common stocks of growing companies, which tend not to declare cash dividends but to reinvest most of their earnings. Stocks of such companies generally increase in value over long periods of time, which pushes up the net asset value of the mutual fund. Such funds strive to provide a very good total return for the investor willing to accept some risk. The return probably will be in the form of small income dividends, some income from capital gains distribution, and a strong potential for price appreciation.

Income Objective

When a mutual fund has income as a primary focus, its almost exclusive aim is to earn a high level of interest and dividends. Capital gains are definitely a secondary consideration. Such a mutual fund would purchase bonds, preferred stocks, and blue-chip income stocks with a history of good earnings and high dividends. These funds provide the investor with a high income dividend, some income from capital gains distributions, and little likelihood of price appreciation.

Growth and Income Objective

A mutual fund with a combination of growth and income as an objective aims for a somewhat aggressive return, not as low as offered by funds with an income objective nor as high as offered by funds with a growth objective. The portfolio of such a fund would include a combination of securities with an emphasis on common stocks. These funds provide the investor with some income dividends, some income through capital gains distributions, and a good chance for price appreciation.

Balanced Objective

Mutual funds with a balanced objective typically emphasize preservation of capital along with moderate growth and income. The objectives of growth and income vary according to economic times, but stability remains paramount. During a bullish economy, the portfolio might include many blue-chip growth stocks. In more bearish times, the fund would purchase more bonds and blue-chip income stocks as a defensive action. These funds provide low financial risk with small income dividends, small income from capital gains distributions, and some opportunity for price appreciation.

Classification of Mutual Funds by Portfolio

With the hundreds of different mutual funds available, there is something for just about every investor's needs. Each mutual fund chooses a variety of investments to achieve its specific investment objectives. The portfolios of mutual funds can concentrate on holdings ranging from risk-free government bonds and blue-chip growth stocks to speculative *letter stocks,* which are securities that have not yet been registered with the SEC for sale to the public. Keep in mind that size is important too, as smaller funds (less than $100 million) have greater flexibility than the perhaps more stable, larger funds. Several classifications of mutual funds are described below, and Table 18–1 presents summary information.

Common Stock Funds

Some mutual funds include only common stocks in their portfolios. The objective of *common stock funds* is growth, evidenced by the six basic types of common stock funds. The first type seeks *maximum capital*

TABLE 18–1
Classification of Mutual Funds by Type and Size

Type of Fund	Number of Funds	Combined Assets (in millions)	Percentage of total
Common stock			
Maximum capital gain	99	32,000	4.5
Growth	268	45,000	6.4
Growth and income	134	51,000	7.3
Specialized			
Canadian international	44	9,000	1.3
Gold and precious metals	18	1,000	a
Industry funds	49	4,000	a
Government securities	113	119,000	17.0
Tax-exempt bonds	270	81,000	11.6
Technology	5	1,000	a
Other specialized	13	3,000	a
Balanced	26	5,000	a
Income	199	61,000	8.7
Bond and preferred stock	45	14,000	2.0
Money market	280	218,000	31.1
Tax-free money market	106	57,000	8.1
Total	1,669	699,000[b]	100.0

Source: Reprinted by permission from the Wiesenberger Investment Companies Service, 47th Edition, Copyright, 1987, Warren Gorham & Lamont, Inc., 110 Plaza, New York, NY 10119.
[a] Less than 1 percent.
[b] Total does not add due to rounding.

gains. This fund places no emphasis on income dividends, relying primarily on price appreciation as the return for the investor. Holdings could be in little-known companies, firms exploring new technology, and other businesses with good long-term profit potential. The fund uses high-risk investment techniques, such as borrowing money for leverage, short shelling, hedging, options, and warrants (see Chapter 20). It is sometimes called a performance fund or a "go-go" fund. A second type is the *growth fund,* the most popular form of common stock fund. It takes a more conventional approach, buying stock in small and moderately well-known companies paying little or no dividends; again, price appreciation is expected. The third type is the *growth and income fund,* also quite popular. Its portfolio generally includes a variety of well-known common stocks paying reasonable dividends, along with stocks from some lesser-known firms with strong growth potential. The fourth type is the *sector fund,* which specializes in common stocks from one particular industry or geographic area. Of course, investing in only one sector increases risks as well as potential returns—even in a diversified portfolio. The fifth type is the *diversified international fund,* which invests in stocks of companies listed on foreign exchanges and often focuses on one country or geographic region. The sixth type is the *index fund,* which is composed of a large number of the best-performing stocks that are part of a particular index, such as S & P's 500. The return is expected to be equal to all the stocks in the index.

Bonds and Preferred Stock Funds

Bonds and preferred stock funds concentrate their holdings on senior securities: bonds and preferred stocks. The emphasis is on safety of principal and income earned through interest and dividends. The bond portion of the portfolio is diversified by maturity date.

Balanced Funds

Balanced funds include various amounts of bonds, preferred stocks, and common stocks in their portfolios. Their investment policy is to maintain a balance of such holdings and vary them according to economic conditions, with the emphasis on conserving the investor's initial principal.

Income Funds

Income funds have a primary objective of current income. They seek a portfolio of bonds, preferred stocks, and some select blue-chip income stocks. Table 18–2 gives a sample portfolio of an income fund.

Municipal Bonds (Tax-exempt) Funds

Investors in *municipal bonds (tax-exempt) funds* seek to earn current tax-exempt income by investing solely in municipal bonds issued by cities, states, and various districts and political subdivisions. The interest income earned on these bonds is exempt from federal personal income taxes.

TABLE 18–2
Sample Portfolio of an Income Fund

	Percentage of Total Holdings
Common stock	13
Preferred stock	35
Municipal bonds (long-term)	25
U.S. government securities (long-term)	10
Corporate bonds	10
U.S. government securities (short-term)	5
Liquid assets	2
Total	100

Specialty Funds

Specialty funds can be created for just about any investment need that requires both concentration and diversification in a field. *Mutual fund funds* earn a return with money invested in the shares of other mutual funds, thereby diversifying extensively. *Socially conscious funds* have investments only in companies that meet their shareholders' ethical or moral standards. Dreyfus Third Century, New Alternative, and Pax World are mutual funds that do not have investments in companies that pollute the environment, have a history of poor labor relations, do business in South Africa, or manufacture weapons.

Money Market Funds

Money market funds are mutual funds that specialize in investments in securities that have very short-term maturities, generally less than one year. These assets include Treasury bills and notes, certificates of deposit, commercial paper, and repurchase agreements. By staggering the maturities of these securities, the money market fund can earn the current cost of money on its investments. Some money market funds have investments only in tax-exempt securities, so the dividends to the investor avoid federal income taxes. Money market funds provide a convenient place to keep money while awaiting alternative investment opportunities. Money market funds are an important part of many investors' cash management plans, as discussed in Chapter 4.

How to Purchase Mutual Funds

There are three ways of buying mutual funds: direct purchase, voluntary accumulation, and contractual accumulation.

Direct Purchase

A *direct purchase* is a method of acquiring shares in an open-end mutual fund where you simply order and pay for the shares, plus any commissions. Anyone can make a direct purchase, and each transaction is considered a one-time purchase. You generally would buy no-load shares directly from the mutual fund company, which would open an account for you and issue you share certificates shortly after it receives your payment.

You may buy load funds through a sales representative of the mutual fund, a financial planner, or a brokerage firm, which will open a regular account in your name to handle the transaction. Note that a minimum commission of perhaps $25 will be charged for each transaction. This means that the occasional mutual fund investor should make purchases of at least $300, since a typical commission rate of 8.5 percent times $300 equals $25.50, an amount just above the minimum fee.

The amount of the commission, of course, reduces the number of shares purchased. For example, if you wanted twenty-five shares of Conglomerate Cat and Dog Food Mutual Fund, which has a net asset value of $16.50 per share, a commission of 8 percent might be charged on the load fund. The twenty-five shares would cost $445.50—$412.50 for the stock (25 × $16.50) plus $33 in commission (.08 × $412.50). The brokerage firm usually keeps the shares in its custody or sends the certificates along to you.

Voluntary Accumulation Plan

The most popular method of investing in open-end mutual funds is through a *voluntary accumulation plan.* Under this plan, you would open an account with a brokerage firm (for load funds) or the investment company itself and voluntarily invest money on a regular basis; periodic notices would be sent to you as reminders. Any commissions are deducted from each investment amount. The amount of your payment (less any sales charge) is invested and your account is credited with ownership of fractional shares measured to three decimal places. The firm mails out a written confirmation for each transaction but does not send share certificates unless you request them.

To open an account, you would fill out an application form and state the amount of the initial investment, which generally must be $100 to $500. Then you would indicate the amount you will invest regularly and the approximate dates of investment. The minimum amount for periodic investment is generally $25 to $50, and larger purchases are encouraged. Investments are generally monthly or quarterly. There is no need for you to stay with the voluntary plan; you may close it and redeem the shares at any time. Because of its flexibility, this plan is also called an *open account.* If your payments become irregular the firm will usually notify you that future transactions will have to be handled through a direct purchase account. This type of mutual fund account is very similar to a monthly investment plan (MIP) account offered by brokerage firms to investors in stocks.

The concept behind a voluntary accumulation plan is twofold: (1) those with enough self-discipline to invest regularly will quickly accumulate holdings in a mutual fund, and (2) those who invest on a regular basis are likely to achieve success because of the principle of dollar-cost averaging. Making regular purchases of shares without regard to price levels will ensure obtaining the maximum number of shares at the lowest average cost. (Dollar-cost averaging was explained in Chapter 17.)

Contractual Accumulation Plan

A *contractual accumulation plan* is a formalized, long-term program to purchase shares in an open-end, load mutual fund. You would sign an agreement to invest a specific dollar amount periodically over a certain number of years, usually ten; commissions are paid as shares are purchased, although they are often accelerated and deducted during the first two years. This plan encourages you to establish a financial goal: a total amount of dollars that will be invested. It permits acquisition of mutual fund shares on a regular, budgeted schedule. To you it represents a type of forced-savings program.

You can open contractual plans with a mutual fund company or a *plan company* (a firm that specializes in selling contractual accumulation plans of load mutual funds to the investing public). You as the buyer/investor should receive a prospectus from such a company. You may complete the plan early by making additional payments. Stock certificates normally are not issued until the plan is completed or discontinued; in the interim they are held by a custodial bank or trust company for a small fee. Contrary to popular belief, a contractual accumulation plan is not a legal agreement. You are not legally bound to make the periodic investments according to the schedule. In fact, you may close the account and liquidate the holdings at any time. Most plans actually permit you to liquidate up to 90 percent of the holdings and later repurchase the same number of shares without having an additional sales commission.

Contractual plans generally sell front-end load funds. In a contractual plan, total commissions and fees on your fund purchases over the entire term of the plan (perhaps covering ten years) are deducted from the amounts you invest on an accelerated basis, usually within two years. For example, assume you have decided to invest $1,000 a year for ten years into Conglomerate Cat and Dog Food Mutual Fund Company, for a total planned investment of $10,000. With an 8 percent load charge for commissions, the entire fee of $800 ($10,000 × .08) might well be deducted from the investments you make during the first two years, or $400 each year. You might be a bit frustrated to realize that only $600 of your first year's investment—$1,000 annual payment, minus $400 commission—is actually working to generate income.

A front-end load motivates mutual fund investors to stay with the investment plan since such a commission schedule has a substantially negative effect on the net amount invested over the short run. Over the long run, the effect of the load will be negligible. SEC figures suggest that nearly half of the investors using contractual plans either complete the plans on schedule or are well advanced toward that goal. Another one-fifth redeem their shares within thirty-six months of beginning the investment.

The Investment Companies Amendments Act of 1970 protects mutual fund investors using contractual accumulation plans who change their minds and decide to liquidate. The law states that any investor is entitled to a full refund within forty-five days. A partial refund, up to 85 percent in some instances depending upon the net asset value of the mutual fund, is available within sixteen and one-half months. Primarily because of the negative effect of the front-end load commission structure, some state legislatures (California, Illinois, and Wisconsin) have prohibited the sale of contractual accumulation plans. Fewer than twenty plans are now being sold to the investing public.

Unique Benefits of Open-end Mutual Funds

The professional management and diversified investments of open-end mutual funds make investing in them different than simply buying common stocks or corporate bonds. The distinct features of mutual funds that make this form of investing unique are discussed below.

Automatic Income Reinvestment

Most mutual funds permit (and some even require) automatic income reinvestment. This is a provision of a mutual fund voluntary or contractual agreement that allows for the automatic reinvestment of earned dividends and capital gains distributions in more shares of the fund. You can elect to have income dividends and/or income from capital gains distributions reinvested in additional shares. Of course, fractional shares are purchased as needed. Over three-fourths of mutual fund shareholders have their income reinvested. The value of automatic income reinvestment is that it compounds share ownership; the number of your shares continues to grow. Figure 18–3 illustrates the concept.

With some funds you may reinvest dividend income at a price that includes a commission charge; with others you may reinvest at the current net asset value. Whether earnings are reinvested or not, you must pay income taxes on dividend income and on income from capital gains distributions in the year earned.

Plan Completion Insurance

Plan completion insurance is declining-value group term life insurance available to investors in contractual accumulation plan mutual funds. The insurance provides proceeds upon the death of the insured in the amount of the unpaid cash balance due on the account, thus awarding the beneficiary the total number of shares applicable in the original plan. This insurance is intended to complete the investment plan so that survivors have a substantial mutual fund holding. The life insurance death benefit pays for the purchase of remaining shares in the plan, plus any applicable sales charges and custodian fees. Insurability must be proven on any policy with a face amount of more than

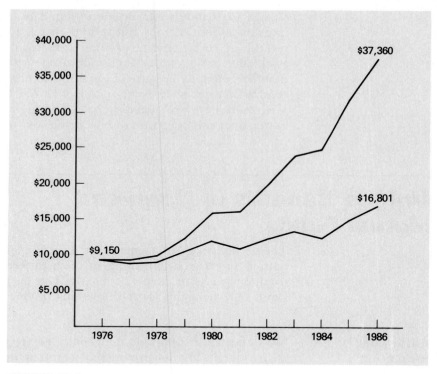

FIGURE 18–3
The Value of Automatic Reinvestment of Income (Dividends and Capital Gains)

An initial investment of $9,150 ($10,000 − $850 commission) grew to $16,801 in ten years while the investor took dividends in cash. If instead the income was left to be reinvested automatically, the amount would have grown to $37,360. Data based on sixty-two growth and income mutual funds in operation over the past ten years.

Source: Investment Company Institute, 1987.

$18,000. Rates charged for the insurance are often higher than premiums for similar coverage available elsewhere.

Insurance Against Loss of Value

Loss of value insurance is available for most mutual funds. This policy covers market value losses from the date of the policy on previously purchased shares (but not on old losses, of course) and newly acquired shares for ten, twelve and one-half, or fifteen years. Any future market value losses are insured at a premium cost of generally 6 percent of the amount invested. For example, should Conglomerate Cat and Dog Food Mutual Fund Company make poor investments resulting in a decline in the fund's net asset value from $16.50 to perhaps $10 per share, the loss would be paid for by the insurance company. If ten years ago you had bought one thousand shares through a direct purchase account for $16,500 and had purchased loss of value insurance, the market value loss of $6,500 ($16,500 − $10,000) would be covered.

The policy covers additional shares for losses when they are sold for less than the original amounts paid. Because of the general trend of rising market prices over the long term, such an insurance purchase is economically unwise. Of course, some people who desire peace of mind buy insurance coverage against the effect of a decline in market value.

Automatic EFT Transfers

Investors in a voluntary or contractual accumulation plan may have their periodic investment payments automatically forwarded to the mutual fund company using electronic funds transfer (EFT) from a checking or savings account. Your financial institution will send you written notification of each withdrawal, and you may stop automatic withdrawals at any time.

Check Writing

Most money market mutual fund companies permit you to withdraw money by writing special checks drawn on your account. This provides you with a high-yielding cash management account.

Note that many other funds also permit check writing. Usually, checks must be written in amounts no smaller than $100 or $500, and only a limited number may be written per year. The effect of writing a check on a mutual fund account is to redeem the number of shares necessary to honor the check. For example, if Conglomerate Cat and Dog Food Mutual Fund shares had a net asset value of $10 and you wrote a check for $500, the fund would redeem fifty shares ($10 × 50 = $500). You may usually repurchase the shares without a sales charge.

Telephone Transactions

You can buy and sell shares by telephone after you have opened an account with a mutual fund company. If you call a toll-free number—where operators record your verbal instructions—the mutual fund company will wire funds to your local bank immediately.

Loan Program

An increasing number of mutual funds permit shareholders to use their investment as collateral for loans. Rules usually require that loans be in excess of $5,000, although this minimum amount is expected to decrease. The interest rate charged is competitive, as it is just a few points higher than the fund company's cost of borrowing. Often there are no repayment terms, which gives you increased flexibility.

Beneficiary Designation

A *beneficiary designation clause* is available from all mutual funds. This clause provides that the shareholder can name a beneficiary in a separate legal trust agreement; in the event of death the proceeds go to the beneficiary without going through probate. (The delays and expenses of probate are discussed in Chapter 22.) Such a clause helps expedite the orderly transfer of assets to the beneficiary. Note, however, that some states prohibit this practice.

Switching (or Exchange) Privileges	A *switching (or exchange) privilege* permits mutual fund shareholders, if their needs or objectives change, to swap shares on a dollar-for-dollar basis for shares in another mutual fund managed by the same corporation. This valuable opportunity exists only for mutual fund shareholders sponsored by the same management team, or in the same "family" of funds. For example, Fidelity offers forty-one stock, twenty-one bond, and six money market funds; Vanguard has twenty-five stock, thirteen bond, and three money market funds. Since your investment objectives could change over time, the switching privilege is valuable. It allows transfer (by telephone or in writing) at no cost or for only a small fee, as little as $5. For example, at age fifty-five a person who has been investing in a growth fund for the past twenty years may want to convert the monies to an income fund to plan for early retirement.

Switching is also valuable for the investor shrewd enough to observe market trends. For example, assume that you have more than $8,000 in your growth fund and have arranged for automatic dividend reinvestment. Fund performance for a couple of years has been around 7 percent and you notice that interest costs are rising in the general economy. You switch to a bond fund yielding 10 percent. Money gets even tighter so you switch again to a money market fund, which increases up to 16 percent for a period of several months. As rates begin to decline you switch back to a bond fund, locking in a yield of 12 percent for almost two years. As yields continue to decline, you move the funds back to a growth and income fund, hoping for significant price appreciation. You can see how being alert to changing market trends can increase your investment returns. Note that if switching results in capital gains, these amounts are taxable events during the year of the exchange.

Systematic Withdrawal Plans	All mutual funds have various types of withdrawal plans available to shareholders. These are used by people who want a periodic income from their mutual fund investments. To be eligible, your investment must have an original net asset value of at least $5,000. Each withdrawal must be no less than $50. The firm mails you checks according to one of the following four plans.

Fixed Dollar Amount   You receive a specified fixed amount per month or quarter until the fund is depleted. Income from dividends and capital gains distributions is used first to make the payments, and then shares are redeemed as needed.

Fixed Number of Shares   You receive varying amounts, as the net asset value of each share changes, until the fund is depleted. This plan always results in eventual liquidation of the fund after a certain number of periodic payments. For example, say you own 500 shares of a mutual fund and request that the proceeds of four shares per month be forwarded to you. Not counting any shares that might be acquired by reinvestment, the fund would run out in just over ten years (500 ÷ 4 =

A Conservative Strategy to Achieve Wealth

Investing $100 a month for the rest of your life will not make you independently wealthy, but it will make you more secure financially. If you invest $100 a month starting at age twenty-two and raise the invested amount by $100 a month each decade, you will be a millionaire at retirement, assuming that the annual return will be only 9 percent. Of course, getting from here to there requires a variety of steps, the most important of which are listed below.

1. *Make decisions, keep records, spend time*   Your investment philosophy will determine whether you aim for a moderate, 10 percent, annual return or a speculative 25 percent and what investments you decide to make. Regardless of your philosophy, it is important to keep good records of the investments you make and to spend time reviewing your portfolio and buying and selling decisions.

2. *Build high-yielding liquid assets*   Since you can't have an investment program without money to invest, your first task is to accumulate sufficient savings to build a cash reserve (amounting to perhaps two or three months' after-tax income), which may take two or three years' time. Be patient. Many investors place funds in money market or sweep accounts (two high-yielding liquid assets). The asset should be quickly convertible to cash.

3. *Invest in mutual funds*   After establishing a cash reserve, start investing other accumulated monies. Mutual funds offer much to a beginning investor: professional management, the opportunity to learn more about investing, and the chance to gain financially. After only three or four years you will have learned a good deal about the market's peaks and valleys. Conservative investors might continue buying shares in a mutual fund for many years.

4. *Select individual stocks*   Conservative investors might consider joining an investment club to learn more about evaluating stocks and stock aspects of market-trend analysis. Members of these clubs attend monthly meetings and are assigned stock research responsibilities. Acting individually, novice investors will probably choose only one or two stocks at first but after a while may accumulate ten stocks to provide needed diversification.

5. *Further diversify holdings*   Conservative investors can further diversify holdings by considering bonds and real estate as additional investments. High-quality corporate and government bonds can assure you of a good return, and well-chosen real estate (discussed in the next chapter) can provide a relatively safe return and potential for steady capital appreciation.

125 months). If the net asset value per share is $40, your beginning monthly check would be $160 ($40 × 4). That value could easily increase to $60 over several years as the mutual fund becomes more profitable and perhaps provide monthly checks of $240 ($60 × 4) during later years.

Dividends and Capital Gains Distribution   You receive periodic payments of varying amounts that represent only the dividends and capital gains distributions of the fund, as the principal remains untouched. For example, if your $20,000 fund declares income dividends of $200 and a capital gains distribution of $300 after three months, you would receive a check for $500. At the same time, the underlying portfolio of the mutual fund could have grown, pushing the net asset value up to perhaps $20,400; of course, the value could also drop. The point is that you can receive dividends and capital gains distributions while the value of your fund continues to increase.

Fixed Percentage of Asset Growth   You receive periodic payments amounting to a percentage of the growth in the value of the mutual fund. For example, you might choose to receive 75 percent of the growth, to be paid quarterly. If your $10,000 fund increases in value to $10,400 during a three-month period, you will receive a check for $300 ($400 × .75). If the assets do not grow, you will not receive a check. Note that this plan permits systematic withdrawals from the mutual fund account without depleting it. In fact, since the withdrawals are always a portion of the growth (less than 100 percent), the value of the fund will likely continue to increase.

Your choice of a withdrawal plan depends on your financial needs and investment goals, and you can change it at any time. For example, you could make withdrawals to help pay for a child's college expenses or to supplement a retirement income.

IRS-qualified Retirement Plans

Most mutual funds have programs that qualify with the IRS as tax-free ways to invest money for retirement. Depending on eligibility qualifications, you can put thousands of dollars a year into a mutual fund, deduct the amount from your income taxes, watch the fund grow tax-free, and pay no income taxes on the profits until retirement. These programs include individual retirement accounts (IRAs) and Keogh retirement plans. (Chapter 21 discusses how to use mutual funds for retirement planning.)

Advantages and Disadvantages of Open-end Mutual Funds

As you consider investing in open-end mutual funds, you should review their advantages and disadvantages. Some of these are described below.

Advantages

1. Dollar-cost averaging permits acquisition of shares at the lowest average cost possible.
2. Accumulation plans motivate continued participation.
3. The variety of funds available makes it fairly easy to choose a fund that matches your investment objectives.
4. The switching privilege permits easy exchange if your investment objectives change.
5. Marketability and liquidity are high, as shares can always be redeemed for the net asset value.
6. The automatic reinvestment of income permits reinvestment of small sums at minimum cost.

7. Systematic withdrawal income plans provide a convenient method of receiving income.

8. Since professional managers run the fund, your supervisory and recordkeeping responsibilities are reduced.

9. No-load funds put all your money to work.

10. Your liability is limited to only the amount invested.

11. You need make only a minimum investment per month or quarter and/or a lump-sum investment.

12. Many funds have the chance to earn returns that beat inflation.

13. You carry less financial risk because the fund is able to diversify investments widely.

14. Estate settlements can be planned to go through smoothly.

Disadvantages

1. Many load funds carry high transaction costs, often above 8 percent; as a result, many people choose no-load funds.

2. Deferred sales charges and exit fees make it difficult to select the better-performing companies.

3. Management costs generally amount to a fraction of 1 percent of the assets of the funds annually. Hidden loads also reduce the annual return to investors.

4. A fund that cannot be switched allows no flexibility should your objectives change.

5. No-load funds are not heavily advertised and thus must be researched carefully.

6. Because load funds are promoted by salespersons who want to earn commissions, they may be represented as promising more than they will deliver.

7. Because of diversification, the return on most mutual funds is 1 to 2 percent less than the total return earned on most common stocks; of course, few individual investors have done as well as the consistently high-performing funds.

How to Select a Mutual Fund

The task of selecting an open-end mutual fund involves examining important sources of information and comparing the performance of various funds.

Sources of Information

You can obtain information about mutual funds from the same sources noted in the previous chapter—for instance, local newspapers, *The Wall Street Journal,* and *Barron's.* The magazines *Business Week, Fortune, Forbes,* and *Money* are also useful. Of particular value are the late August issue of *Forbes*, the October issue of *Money*, and the late February issue of *Business Week*, which feature comprehensive examinations of the performance of numerous mutual funds.

Three popular specialized investment publications that examine mutual funds in considerable detail are often available in large libraries as well as in brokers' offices: *Investment Companies*, an annual publication of Wiesenberger Financial Services; *Johnson's Investment Company Charts*, published by Hugh A. Johnson and Company; and *Fundscope*, published by Fundscope, Inc. Standard & Poor's also rates the safety of some mutual funds using their familiar AAA, AA, A, and B symbols, which gauge a fund's ability to maintain its net asset value and avoid capital losses.

Comparing the Performance of Mutual Funds

As you consider mutual funds, recall the negative impact of inflation. Even if a fund's net asset value increased by 140 percent over a decade, inflation could have pushed prices up 125 percent during the same period. The Dow Jones industrial average may have climbed 160 percent. Thus you should first compare the historical performance of a mutual fund with other broad indicators.

Using Comparative Performance Data

To compare the performance of mutual funds, you can use data from Wiesenberger, Johnson's, Fundscope, *Money, Barron's, Business Week, Forbes,* and other financial services and publications.* They generally rank funds according to one-, five-, and ten-year performance; they also note the risk of each fund relative to performance. Your task is still to match your interpretation of performance data with your own investment philosophy. You might have one of four objectives: maximum appreciation of capital, long-term growth of capital and future income, current income, or relative stability of capital. Or you might have a combination of objectives, as illustrated in Figure 18–4. If you want to realize one specific objective (such as stability of capital), you must usually sacrifice another objective (such as appreciation of capital). *Stability of capital* is akin to freedom from financial risk; it can be defined in terms of relative performance when the value of your shares in a declining market does not decline as much as the values of other shares.

Comparisons among mutual funds by outside firms, such as Wiesenberger, are useful as data are analyzed in a consistent manner. Otherwise, you may become confused as you compare the information from one mutual fund company with that provided by another fund. The SEC is soon expected to issue rules standardizing how mutual

* The following newsletters can be used to compare the performance of mutual funds: *The Exchange Report* (1200 Westlake Ave. North, Seattle, WA 98109), *Donoghue's Mutual Fund Almanac* (Box 540, Holliston, MA 01746), *NoLoad Fund X* (235 Montgomery St., San Francisco, CA 94104), *Professional Tape Reader* (P.O. Box 2407, Hollywood, FL 33022), and *Switch Fund Advisory* (8943 Shady Grove Ct., Gaithersburg, MD 20877). You can obtain complimentary copies by writing to the addresses given.

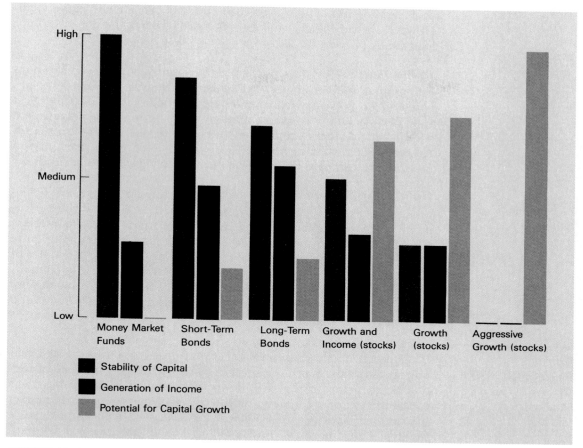

FIGURE 18–4
The Risk/Return Tradeoff

Source: Investment Company Institute, 1600 M Street, N.W., Washington, DC 20036.
Used with permission.

funds calculate current yield, report capital gains, and calculate total
returns. In addition, all advertisements for funds would have to include
the most recent five-year total return.

Another complication in comparing performance arises when you
consider long- and short-term performance. Note that some funds have
been in operation for less than a decade, whereas some older funds may
have changed managers, grown substantially, and adopted a more aggressive investment philosophy. Should you choose a mutual fund that
has done somewhat well over the past ten years or one that has done
very well during the past twelve months? Trading off return for risk, or
vice versa, may be necessary.

There is also the question of choosing a load fund versus a no-load
fund. About one-half of mutual funds are load funds. A load fund with
an 8 percent commission must have an average return of three-quarters

of 1 percent more than a no-load fund to provide the same yield. However, broad evidence indicates that over the long haul load and no-load funds provide the same yield.

Using Mutual Funds Averages Several investment services publish mutual fund averages. Wiesenberger mutual fund indexes are based on a representative group of large mutual funds. Wiesenberger's fund performance is based on total return, assuming a fixed investment with income dividends reinvested and capital gains accepted in shares. Averages such as Wiesenberger's are informative, particularly if you use them to compare the performance of individual mutual funds.

Using Mutual Funds Prospectuses Annual reports provided either by the funds themselves or by brokerage firms detail the performance of individual mutual funds. Specific information can be found in a fund's current prospectus as well. Although the SEC does not require mutual fund prospectuses to be standardized, they do bar the use of false and misleading investment literature. For consistency in comparing funds, you can use the figures of one of the reference investment publications. Figure 18–5 shows a sample description of a mutual fund company from Wiesenberger.

Comparing Performance in Up and Down Markets

It is important to find a fund that has performed well over the past year or past ten years. It is also useful to compare the performance of mutual funds in up (rising) and down (declining) markets. Table 18–3 contains fund data for three recent periods when the general market has declined and three periods when it has risen. For a fund to score highly, it "must perform consistently well in all three up or down periods." If a fund performs poorly, its rating is adjusted downward. The total yield excludes sales charges and assumes reinvestment of all distributions; it is reflected as a compound average annual return rate. Note that the Evergreen Fund is rated A+ in up markets and B in down markets, which illustrates the general difficulty of a growth fund that invests in common stocks during bear markets.

Advice for Conservative Mutual Fund Investors*

- During a bull market, invest in a growth/income fund for long-term growth and current income.
- When interest rates are rising, consider switching to a money market fund until a clear investment opportunity becomes apparent.
- During a bear market, switch to a conservative income fund for high dividend yield.

* Especially if you have some well-reasoned opinions on the direction of interest rates, inflation, and the economy for the next year or more.

THE EVERGREEN FUND, INC.

The Evergreen Fund was incorporated in March 1971, and its shares were initially offered to the public on October 15 in the same year at $10.00 per share. The objective is capital appreciation; income is not a factor in portfolio selections. In pursuit of this objective, investments are made in securities of little known or relatively small companies. From time to time the fund may borrow money to purchase securities, write covered call options, and lend portfolio securities up to 30% of the fund's assets.

At the end of calendar 1986, the fund had 93% of its assets in common stocks of which a major proportion was concentrated in five industry groups: banks (21.4% of assets), thrift institutions (13.8%), consumer products

& services (11.1%), retailing (10.7%), finance & insurance (6.8%). The five principal common stock investments were Eastman Kodak (2.5% of assets), May Dept. Stores (1.9%), Indiana National Corp. (1.5%), and IBM and First of America Bank Corp. (each 1.4%). The rate of portfolio turnover in the latest fiscal year was 48% of average assets. Unrealized appreciation in the portfolio at the calendar year-end was 12.6% of total net assets.

Special Services: An open account provides for accumulation and dividend reinvestment. Minimum initial investment is $2,000; minimum subsequent investment $250. Keogh plans and Individual Retirement Accounts are available.

Statistical History

			Net		― % of Assets in ―								
Year	Total Net Assets ($)	Number of Share-holders	Asset Value Per Share ($)	Yield (%)	Cash & Equiv-alent	Bonds & Pre-ferreds	Com-mon Stocks	Income Div-idends ($)	Capital Gains Distribu-tion ($)	Expense Ratio (%)	Offering Price ($) High	Low
1986	643,814,047	42,011	12.47	1.0	7	―	93	0.14	1.657††	1.04	15.03	12.21
1985	441,404,589	24,240	12.67	4.9	12	―	88	0.659	0.819	1.08	12.69	9.30
1984	242,342,085	17,592	39.75	1.5	8	―	92	0.684	4.792††	1.10	45.58	35.06
1983	221,842,973	12,945	45.12	1.7	5	―	95	0.764	0.211††	1.11	48.20	35.12
1982	147,736,676	9,470	35.66	1.5	18	―	82	0.601	4.305††	1.13	36.08	24.95
1981	99,570,381	7,670	34.78	0.8	10	―	90	0.30	2.76††	1.25	37.44	30.42
1980	83,040,506	5,464	38.36	0.2	7	2†	91	0.069	2.294††	1.34	40.13	22.88
1979	30,051,747	2,143	28.32	0.1	7	―	93	0.042	4.18††	1.61	28.43	20.07
1978	11,909,884	895	23.30		2	―	98			1.62	27.45	15.40
1977	6,897,156	825	16.88	0.3	(1)	―	101	0.05	1.388††	1.72	18.02	14.02
1976	5,183,259	550	14.63	―	(3)	―	103	―		1.83	14.63	9.90

† Includes convertible issues only.
†† Includes short-term gains: 1977, $0.20; 1979, $1.314; 1980, $0.882; 1981, $1.25; 1982, $0.37; 1983, $0.211; 1984, $2.913; 1985, $0.16; 1986, $0.021.

Investment Adviser: Saxon Woods Asset Management Corp. Compensation to the Adviser is at an annual rate of 1% of average net assets.
Custodian and Transfer Agent: The First Jersey National Bank, Jersey City, NJ 07303.
Distributor: None; shares are sold directly by the fund.
Sales Charge: None; shares are offered at net asset value.

Distribution Plan: (12b-1) None.
Dividends: Income dividends and capital gains, if any, are paid annually during the second quarter following each fiscal year in which income and capital gains are realized.
Shareholder Reports: Issued quarterly. Fiscal year ends September 30. The current prospectus was effective in February 1986.
Qualified for Sale: In all states.
Address: 550 Mamaroneck Avenue, Harrison, NY 10528.
Telephone: Toll Free: (800) 235-0064.

	1977	1978	1979	1980	1981	1982	1983	1984	1985	1986			
Value of Shares Initially Acquired Through Investment of $10,000	$11,538	$15,926	$19,357	$26,220	$23,773	$24,375	$30,841	$27,170	$34,641	$34,094			
Value of Shares Resulting From Reinvestment of Capital Gains and Income Dividends (Cumulative)	1,000	1,380	5,957	11,114	12,970	19,604	26,359	30,014	42,804	53,403*			
Total Return	12,538	17,306	25,284	37,334	36,743	43,979	57,200	57,184	77,445	87,497			

Dollar amounts of distributions reinvested:

	Capital Gains	Income Dividends
1977	$ 948	$ 34
1978	―	―
1979	3,105	31
1980	2,051	62
1981	2,686	292
1982	4,548	635
1983	260	942
1984	6,075	867
1985	2,384	948
1986	10,527	856
Total	$32,584	$4,666

Results Taking Capital Gains in SHARES and Income Dividends in CASH

Initial Investment At Offering Price, January 1, 1977	$10,000
Value as of 12/31/86 of Shares Initially Acquired	$34,094
Value of Shares Accepted as Capital Gains Distributions $45,361 ∉	
Total Value, December 31, 1986	$79,454
Total Dividends PAID From Investment Income	$ 4,446

∉ Dollar Amount of these distributions at the time shares were acquired: $31,070

Results Taking All Dividends and Distributions in CASH

Initial Investment At Offering Price, January 1, 1977	$10,000
Total Value, December 31, 1986	$34,094
Distributions From Capital Gains	$19,286
Dividends From Investment Income	$ 2,549

FIGURE 18–5
Wisenberger's Description of a Mutual Fund

Source: Reprinted by permission from the Wiesenberger Investment Companies Service, 47th Edition. Copyright 1987 by Warren Gorham & Lamont, Inc., 110 Plaza, New York, NY 10119.

TABLE 18–3
Comparing Mutual Fund Performance in Up and Down Markets

	In Up Markets[a]	In Down Markets[b]	Average Annual Total Return, 1976–1986[c]	12-month Total Return	Total Assets[c] 6/30/86 (millions)	Total Assets[c] % Change, 1986 vs. 1985	Maximum Sales Charge[c]	Annual Expenses per $100[c]
Acorn Fund	B	A	21.8%	16.7%	$ 425	58%	none	$ .78
Amcap Fund	B	A	22.3	15.6	1,506	25	8.50%	.54
Evergreen Fund	A+	B	27.9	13.2	714	121	none	1.08
Fidelity Magellan Fund	A+	A	35.1	23.6	7,412	158	3.00%	1.08
Nicholas Fund	B	A+	25.1	11.7	1,084	135	none	.86
Partner's Fund	B	A	21.8	17.3	431	94	none	.93[d]
20th Century Select Invest.	A+	B	29.6	20.7	1,987	85	none	1.01

Source: Forbes, February 9, 1987.
[a] Maximum rating A+
[b] Maximum rating A
[c] *Forbes,* September 8, 1986.
[d] Fund has 126-1 plan (hidden load) pending or in force.

When to Sell a Mutual Fund

Since people invest in mutual funds for different reasons and because the objectives of the funds vary widely, it is impossible to generalize about when you should sell a mutual fund. However, we do suggest that you consider the following five factors before selling.

Changes in Net Asset Value

You must remember that all assets fluctuate in value over time. For example, the net asset value of many excellent growth funds can easily vary 25 percent during a one-year period. Learn to determine why a particular holding is falling or rising in value. For example, you needn't panic if all common stock funds are declining, as it is difficult for your funds to grow during bear markets. Keep your investment goals in mind and relate them to the relative performance of the fund. For example, over a year, a growth mutual fund should outperform the Dow Jones Industrial Average and the averages of other similar funds.

Performance in Down Markets

To most mutual fund investors, a down market is not something that lasts only thirty or forty days. (The exceptions are traders in high-performance funds and traders/switchers in families of funds.) A down market could last three months, six months, or longer than a year. An investor in a growth and income fund should expect down-market performance to be not more than 10 percent worse than the decline in the Dow Jones Industrial Average. If the performance is sharply lower than comparable funds, it may be a result of poor fund management. In this instance, you should consider selling.

Performance in Up Markets

An up market is characterized by general market price increases for three months, six months, or longer than a year. If you have invested in a growth mutual fund you should expect superior performance in up markets and generally should not settle for the average of similar funds. Being average for one up market is all right, but if a growth fund shows only mediocre performance during two up markets in succession, you should probably sell it. If you have invested in an income fund, you should expect performance in up markets of at least 2 percent above the current rate that could be earned on a corporate bond. Consider selling when you can realize substantial capital gains. Too many investors believe that an up market will last forever.

Market Trends

Mutual funds investors need to remain alert to general conditions in the business cycle. When it is clear that peaks and valleys are being rounded, selling might be wise. As a bull market begins to peak, the growth fund investor will almost surely see the current high value of the investment begin to drop. Similarly, when the economy begins to pull up from a recession, it may be wise to sell an income fund, as interest rates will probably decline quickly. An advantage of investing in families of funds is that during market shifts you can easily switch from one type of fund to another.

Need for Cash

You will probably not hesitate to sell mutual fund shares when you need money for a down payment on a home, for a child's college education, or to meet an emergency. There are ways to plan for these contingencies so that you can redeem mutual fund shares at the best possible prices. For example, if your child will need money for college two years from now, you should consider the prospects of selling the shares now instead of waiting two years. If your view of the economy over the next couple of years is gloomy, then now is the time to sell shares in a growth fund because they may drop in value and be worth much less in two years. Conversely, you should hold shares in an income fund in a declining economy because interest rates will rise and probably push up the net asset value. Try to anticipate cash needs and consider selling when it is most beneficial.

Summary

1. There are several types of investment companies, and about 90 percent of all mutual funds are open-end funds, where the firm continuously stands ready to sell new shares and to redeem old ones.

2. Investors in mutual funds may be confronted with sales charges (on load funds), deferred sales charges (on no-load funds), management fees, and hidden loads with this form of investment.

3. Most mutual funds are taxed as a diversified investment company, which permits them to exempt 90 percent of their net earnings; returns to investors are in the form of income, as well as potential price appreciation.

4. Mutual funds have one of four broad objectives, which a company must report in the prospectus: growth, income, growth and income, and balanced.

5. Mutual funds can be classified according to their portfolio of investments, such as common stock funds, bonds and preferred stock funds, balanced funds, income funds, municipal bond funds, specialty funds, and money market funds.

6. There are three ways of buying mutual funds: direct purchase, voluntary accumulation plan, and contractual accumulation plan.

7. As a specialized form of securities investment, mutual funds have several unique features, such as automatic dividend reinvestment, plan completion insurance, check writing, and switching privileges.

8. Mutual funds have numerous advantages (such as dollar-cost averaging, professional management, and marketability), as well as disadvantages (such as high transaction costs on load funds and management costs reducing returns).

9. A conservative strategy to achieve wealth includes: making decisions, keeping records, and spending time; building high-yield liquid assets; investing in mutual funds; selecting individual stocks; and further diversifying investment holdings.

10. Selection of a mutual fund involves examining important sources of information as well as comparing performance in both up and down markets.

11. Investors in mutual funds should think about selling when their investment is performing worse than the average of similar funds, as well as when peaks and valleys in the business cycle are being rounded.

Modern Money Management

The Johnsons Decide to Invest in Mutual Funds

After learning about mutual funds, the Johnsons are sold. They really like the concepts of diversification and professional management. Accordingly, they sell their stock and bond investments and now have a nest egg of $9,500 to invest in mutual funds. In addition, they want to invest another $300 a month regularly.

Although not yet completely firm, Harry and Belinda's goals at this point are as follows: (1) they want to continue to build for retirement income, (2) they will need about $10,000 six to eight years from now to use as supplemental income if Belinda has a baby and does not work for six months, and (3) they might buy a super-expensive luxury automobile requiring a $10,000 down payment if they decide not to have a child or to adopt. Knowing that the Johnsons have a moderate investment philosophy, that they live on a reasonable budget, and that they have a well-established cash management plan, advise them on their mutual fund investments by responding to the following questions:

1. Using Table 18–4, if you could recommend two separate funds to meet the Johnsons' goals, what would they be? Why?

2. How would you divide the $9,500 between the funds? Why?

3. How much of the $300 monthly amount would you allocate to each fund? Why?

4. Some comparable mutual fund performance data on stock funds are shown in Table 18–3. Using only that information and assuming that you are recommending a stock fund for their retirement needs, why would you recommend the Evergreen Fund or the 20th Century Select Investors Fund?

5. More detailed information about the Evergreen Fund is presented in Figure 18–5. Assume Evergreen was your first choice. What are four financial reasons why the Johnsons might consider this fund to be a good investment?

6. Assume that the Evergreen Fund performs above average for the next ten years. Then there is a bear market and Evergreen's NAV drops 25 percent from the previous year. What conditions must exist before you would recommend that the Johnsons sell their accumulated shares in the Evergreen Fund?

Key Words and Concepts

asked price, 566
balanced funds, 571
beneficiary designation clause, 577
bid price, 566
bonds and preferred stock fund, 571
capital gains distribution, 568
capital growth, 568
closed-end mutual fund, 564
common stock fund, 570
contractual accumulation plan, 574
deferred sales charges, 566
direct purchase, 572
exit fee, 566
front-end load, 565
hidden load, 566
income dividend, 568
income fund, 571
investment company, 562
letter stock, 570
load (sales charge), 565

load fund, 565
loss of value insurance, 576
money market fund, 572
municipal bonds (tax-exempt) fund, 571
mutual fund, 562
net asset value, 564
no-load fund, 565
offering price, 566
open-end mutual fund, 564
plan company, 574
plan completion insurance, 575
real estate investment trust (REIT), 563
small-business investment company, 564
specialty fund, 572
switching (exchange) privilege, 578
trust, 563
unit investment trust, 563
voluntary accumulation plan, 573

Review Questions

1. Explain how a mutual fund works.
2. Distinguish between a closed-end and open-end mutual fund.
3. Distinguish between a load fund and a no-load mutual fund.
4. How can an 8.5 percent stated commission appear to be misleading?

5. What is the difference between a load fund and a no-load fund with a hidden load?

6. How do investment companies avoid paying income taxes on some of their profits?

7. Distinguish between a mutual fund with a growth and income objective and one with a balanced objective.

8. Identify two types of common stock funds.

9. Briefly distinguish among the different ways of buying mutual funds.

10. Explain the rules pertaining to refunds if you change your mind and want to cancel out of a contractual accumulation mutual fund.

11. Explain how automatic dividend reinvestment works.

12. How could a mutual fund shareholder benefit from switching privileges?

13. Which of the systematic withdraw plans might deplete the total value of the mutual fund the fastest? Which plans allow the values to grow at an increasing rate?

14. Name and briefly explain three advantages of investing in open-end mutual funds.

15. Name and briefly explain two disadvantages of investing in open-end mutual funds.

16. Summarize the process of investing in mutual funds.

17. How would you interpret a mutual fund with an A rating for performance in up markets and a C in down markets?

18. Describe two situations that would cause you to consider selling your mutual fund shares.

Case Problems

1. Marilyn Stephenson of College Park, Maryland, is trying to explain to her friend Charlene Churaman how to read the newspaper financial data on mutual funds. Marilyn turned to the financial section of the newspaper and located the part on mutual funds. Using Figure 18–2, help explain it all by responding to the following questions about the Fidelity Investments group of mutual funds.

    a. How much would it cost to buy 100 shares of Fidelity Capital Appreciation?

    b. What would be the commission charge in dollars and as a percent of the amount invested?

    c. If Charlene already owned 100 shares of Capital Appreciation, how much per share would she receive if she redeemed them?

d. Calculate the commission rates to buy shares in Fidelity Equity Income and Fidelity Europe.

e. How much would it cost to buy 100 shares of Fidelity Exchange Fund?

f. How much would it cost to sell 100 shares of Fidelity Exchange Fund? Explain why.

2. Tina Fortunato works in a marketing firm in Newark, New Jersey, and is willing to invest $2,000 to $3,000 per year in a mutual fund. She wants the investment income to supplement her retirement pension starting in about twenty years. Her investment philosophy is moderate. Advise Tina by responding to the questions below.

a. Would you recommend that Tina invest in a mutual fund with growth as its objective or growth and income? Why?

b. Tina tells you that she wants to invest in a mutual fund that focuses on common stocks. Which two types of common stock funds would you recommend she avoid? Why?

c. Summarize your reasons for recommending that she purchase her mutual fund shares using a voluntary accumulation plan rather than a contracted plan.

d. Explain to Tina your reasons for having her invest in a load fund or a no-load fund.

e. Given Tina's investment objective, select three stock funds listed in Table 18–3 and explain why she should consider investing in each.

Suggested Readings

"The Best Mutual Funds." *Business Week*, February 23, 1987, pp. 64–103. Annual scoreboard of the top-performing mutual funds.

"Building a Worry-free Portfolio of Mutual Funds." *Money,* August 1987, pp. 92–96. How to build a diversified mutual fund portfolio.

"Dispassionate Advice." *Forbes*, March 9, 1987, pp. 160–162. Some things you ought to know before listening to the advice of a mutual fund salesperson.

"Fixed-income Mutual Funds." *Consumer Reports*, September 1987, pp. 570–579. Ratings of fixed-income mutual funds.

"How to Pick the Next Fund Hits." *Money*, May 1987, pp. 34–46. New strategies to help you pick the right fund, including comparing loads and fees.

"Mutual Funds: How to Figure Your Real Return." *Changing Times*, April 1987, pp. 69–70. Suggests that you ignore net asset value and calculate.

"Play Those Sexy Sectors with Care." *Money*, April 1987, pp. 75–88. Suggestions on how to invest in sector mutual funds successfully.

"The Savvy Way to Buy Closed-end Funds." *Money*, September 1987, pp. 153–158. How to avoid overpriced issues and invest at a discount.

CHAPTER 19

Investing in Real Estate

OBJECTIVES

After reading this chapter, the student should be able to

1. identify some of the economic and noneconomic reasons why people invest in real estate.
2. describe the advantages of investing in real estate.
3. describe the disadvantages of investing in real estate.
4. explain ways of determining the price to pay for real estate.
5. distinguish among the types of real estate investments.
6. list the situations in which to consider selling real estate investments.

f you own your home, you know that the money you spend on it does more than just put a roof over your head. Every home also has an investment aspect, since over several years it will probably increase in value. When you sell your home you probably will make a profit on your original investment.

Profits on real estate investments can be fabulous. "John bought his home four years ago for $70,000 and just sold it for $135,000." "Three months after buying her condominium, my cousin Eva got transferred to a new job, and she sold her condo for $6,000 more than she paid." "My friend Kate saw the price of her vacant lot in a subdivision just skyrocket in value because someone is going to put a shopping center next to it." Such alluring stories of big profits have a ring of truth. This encourages average investors to consider real estate as an alternative investment to stocks, bonds, or mutual funds. But should they?

This chapter begins with a discussion of why people invest in real estate, followed by detailed analyses of the advantages and disadvantages of such investments. We then look at how to determine *value,* or the price that might be paid for a particular piece of property. Next we review the types of real estate investments. The chapter closes with a section on determining when to sell real estate.

Why Do People Invest in Real Estate?

Real estate is property consisting of land and all its permanently attached structures and accompanying rights and privileges, such as crops and mineral rights. People invest in real estate for economic and noneconomic reasons. One *noneconomic* reason is that most investors like the feeling of being closely involved with their investments. Some have a sense of pride in being owners of an apartment building or duplex. Others feel satisfaction that they are helping to provide attractive and needed living space for others in their community. In many instances the investor has the opportunity to use a property (perhaps a vacation home) while simultaneously treating it as an investment.

The ultimate *economic* goal of investing in real estate—as well as most other investing—is to maximize after-tax returns. Indeed, real estate offers an investor an average yield of one and one-half to two times that of most common stocks. However, the investor must take the risk of a long-term investment and also give up substantial liquidity. It takes only a few minutes to telephone a brokerage firm to sell shares of stock to raise needed cash; it's a lot harder to sell an apartment building.

All alternative investments offer a total return based on income received and/or price appreciation. The special benefit of real estate to the investor is an enhanced potential total return that comes from two sources: (1) the tax-sheltered benefits of real estate obtained under special income tax provisions (such as depreciation) that often increase current income, and (2) an *entrepreneurial profit,* which is the financial reward for the serious and successful manager of real estate properties and is the result of price appreciation. Investors that are actively and aggressively involved with their real estate holdings can earn substantial entrepreneurial profits.

Advantages of Real Estate Investing

There are four advantages of real estate investing: (1) potential for price appreciation, (2) availability of leverage, (3) positive cash flow, and (4) special tax treatments.

Potential for Price Appreciation

Price appreciation is the amount above cost that an investment is sold for. In real estate, the cost includes the original purchase price as well as expenditures for any capital improvements made to a property prior to sale. *Capital improvements* are costs incurred in making changes in real property that add to the value of the property. Paneling a living room, adding a new roof, and putting up a fence are capital improvements. In contrast, *repairs* are expenses—usually tax-deductible for the investor—that are necessary to maintain the value of the property. Repainting, mending roof leaks, and fixing plumbing are repairs. For example, assume that Keith Martin of Grosse Pointe, Michigan, bought a duplex as an investment three years ago for $100,000. He fixed some roof leaks for $1,000 and then added a new roof and some kitchen cabinets for a cost of $5,000 before selling the property. When Keith sold it this year for $135,000, he happily realized a price appreciation of $30,000 ($135,000 − $100,000 − $5,000).

Availability of Leverage

Lenders normally permit real estate investors to borrow from 75 to 95 percent of the price of an investment property. As a result, leverage can increase the yield on an investment. Consider Keith Martin's property again. Suppose that instead of paying cash for the duplex, he had made a down payment of $30,000 and borrowed the remainder. What effect would this have on his yield? In the first instance he paid $100,000 cash for the building and thus earned a 30 percent return on his investment ($30,000 ÷ $100,000) over the three years. In the second situation, using leverage, he would have an apparent return of 100 percent ($30,000 ÷ $30,000). The true yield would be lower because of mortgage loan payments, interest expenses, and depreciation but still a substantial 60 to 70 percent. These details are illustrated later in this chapter.

The **loan-to-value ratio** measures the amount of leverage in an investment project. It is calculated by dividing the amount of debt by the value of the total original investment. For example, Keith Martin had a loan-to-value ratio of 70 percent (or 70 percent leverage), as his down payment was only $30,000 on the $100,000 property ($70,000 ÷ $100,000).

Positive Cash Flow

For an income-producing real estate investment, you pay operating expenses out of rental income. If the property has a mortgage, as is usual, the mortgage principal and loan interest must also be paid out of rental income. The amount of rental income you have left after paying all operating expenses and mortgage expenses is called *cash flow*. The amount of cash flow depends on the amount of rent received, the amount of expenses paid, and the method you use to repay the mortgage debt. Most investors prefer a positive cash flow to a negative cash flow because any shortages have to be made up by the investors themselves. Many, however, can manage a negative cash flow by taking tax losses for a few years while hoping for profits to come in through substantial price appreciation in the value of the property.

A real estate investment need not generate a large cash flow to be successful. For example, assume that John and Mary Rupé of Draper, Virginia, jointly own a small building that cost them $100,000. After subtracting expenses, they net only $4,000 annually in profits. This appears to be a return of only 4 percent ($4,000 ÷ $100,000). It could be much higher depending on the Rupés' marginal income tax rate and whether they use special tax treatments available to real estate investors. Taxes are discussed in the following section.

Special Tax Treatments

The U.S. Congress, through provisions in the IRS code, encourages real estate investments by permitting investors a variety of special tax treatments. These include depreciation, interest deductions, tax-free exchanges, and rental income tax regulations.

Depreciation Investors in real estate become successful by understanding the "numbers" of real estate investing. For example, assume that Joanne Swiftson of Carbondale, Illinois, invests $115,000 in a residential building ($100,000) and land ($15,000) and rents it for $10,000 a year. The tenant pays all variable costs, such as real estate taxes, insurance, and maintenance. You may think that because the tenant pays all expenses Joanne must pay income taxes on the entire $10,000 in rental income, but the IRS allows her to deduct depreciation from this income amount. *Depreciation* is the decline in value of an asset over time due to normal wear and tear and obsolescence. A depreciated amount can be deducted from the cost of a capital asset over the asset's estimated life. Note that land cannot be depreciated. According to the straight-line method of depreciation, Joanne can deduct an equal part of the building's cost over the estimated life of the property. The IRS has a guideline of 27.5 years for depreciating residential

TABLE 19–1
Effect of Depreciation on Income Taxes and Yield

Cost of rental building		$100,000
Cost of land		15,000
Total amount invested		$115,000
Depreciation permitted for 27.5 years		$ 3,636

	Without depreciation	With depreciation
Gross rental income	$10,000	$10,000
Less annual depreciation expense	—	$ 3,636
Taxable income	$10,000	$ 6,364
Income taxes (33% marginal tax rate)	$ 3,300	$ 2,100
Return after taxes	$ 6,700	$ 7,900
Yield after taxes (divide by $115,000)	5.8%	6.9%

properties, 31.5 years for commercial real estate. Thus, Joanne calculates the amount she can annually deduct from income to be $3,636 ($100,000 ÷ 27.5). Table 19–1 shows the effects of depreciation on income taxes, assuming Joanne is in the 33 percent marginal tax bracket. In this example, the depreciation deduction lowers taxable income from $10,000 to $6,364, and raises the yield on the investment from 6.3 percent to 6.9 percent, a 19 percent increase [(6.9 − 5.8 = 1.1) ÷ 5.8]. Note that this yield is based on an investment of $115,000.

Interest Deductions Real estate investors incur several general business expenses in attempting to earn a profit: real estate taxes, repairs, insurance, utilities, capital improvements, and interest expenses. The largest of these costs is often interest expenses, since most properties are purchased with a substantial amount of borrowed money. Table 19–2 illustrates the effect of interest expenses on income taxes. Joanne borrowed $64,000 to purchase her $100,000 building and $15,000

TABLE 19–2
Additional Effect of Interest on Income Taxes and Yield

Gross rental income	$10,000
Less annual depreciation expense	− 3,636
Subtotal	$ 6,364
Less interest expense ($64,000, 9% mortgage loan)	− 6,179
Taxable income	$ 185
Net cash flow after interest expense	$ 3,821
Minus income taxes (.33 × $185)	− 61
Return after taxes	$ 3,760
Yield after taxes [$3,760 ÷ ($115,000 − $64,000)]	7.4%

land. After she deducts interest expenses, her cash flow is reduced to $3,821, and after she deducts depreciation, her taxable income is reduced to $185. Since she thus has a minor income tax liability (only $61), the after-tax return on her leveraged investment increases to 7.4 percent. Note that this yield is based on an investment of $51,000 ($115,000 − $64,000).

Because the tax laws permit investors to deduct interest expenses, part of the real cost of financing investment property is shifted to the government. The amount of that transfer depends on the investor's marginal tax bracket. Joanne's interest deduction permits her to have an after-tax cash return of $3,760. In essence, the $6,179 in interest is paid with $2,039 (33 percent tax bracket) of the money that was not sent to the government and $4,140 ($6,179 − $2,039) of Joanne's money. Essentially, then, a major reason for using borrowed money to invest is that the government pays part of the loan for the investor.

Tax-free Exchanges Another special tax treatment results when a real estate investor trades equity in one property for equity in another similar property. If none of the people involved in the trade receives any other form of property or money, the transaction is considered a *tax-free exchange.* If one person receives some money and/or other property, only that person must report the extra proceeds as a taxable gain. For example, if you bought a duplex five years ago for $80,000 and now trade it with your friend, giving $5,000 in cash for your friend's $135,000 commercial building, your friend need only report the $5,000 as income this year. You need only report your long-term gains ($135,000 − $5,000 − $80,000 = $50,000 to date) if and when you sell your property.

Rental Income Tax Regulations If the real estate is "business property," all expenses allocable to the rental use of the property are deductible—even if it produces a net loss to shelter other income from taxes. All real estate income and losses are classified for income purposes as "passive income" and "passive losses." Generally, passive losses can be used to offset only passive income.

For high-income people, passive losses cannot be used to shelter salary or other investment income. When personal use of a residence (such as a vacation home) is for fourteen or fewer days and you "actively manage" the property (help make decisions on tenants, rents, and repairs), such passive losses may be valuable for tax purposes. When your adjusted gross income (AGI) is under $100,000, up to $25,000 in passive losses may be used to shelter income from any source, such as salary or other investment income. The limit is gradually phased out as the AGI moves between $100,000 and $150,000. When personal use of a residence is for more than fourteen days, income tax deductions are limited to the amount of rental income from the property. However, excess losses can be carried forward to offset future income generated by the vacation property.

Disadvantages of Real Estate Investing

Since many real estate investments hold the potential for a high total return, they carry high risk. Nine major disadvantages of real estate investments are described below.

Investigation Expenses

Real estate investments require more study and careful investigation than do most other alternative investments. You must be able to analyze the real estate market and anticipate the impact of competition from other investment properties. To invest in commercial real estate, you need to consider location, traffic patterns, and demographics. To buy apartment buildings, you must investigate the income of the tenant population.

High Unit Cost

Investment in real estate generally requires many thousands of dollars, often $10,000 to $25,000 or more. In contrast, the average price of stocks is less than $40 and bonds can be purchased in units of $1,000. For many investors, putting a large sum into real estate reduces the possibility of diversification. This disadvantage can be partially offset through real estate syndicates (limited partnerships) and real estate investment trusts, which are discussed later in the chapter.

Financial Risk

It is quite possible to lose money in real estate investments. Unanticipated events can wreck your best estimates of expected income and expenses for an income-producing property. In times of recession, many investment properties throughout a geographic region just sit empty. Even if the general economy is robust, a large industry fallen on hard times could force local real estate values to plunge. Other unforeseeable problems could be imposition of community rent controls and deterioration of a neighborhood due to population shifts or a change in school-district boundaries. A great influx of college students into an area, for example, usually depresses the values of single-family dwellings and pushes up the prices of multiple-family dwellings.

Amount of Management Required

The level of management your real estate requires depends on the type of investment. You may need the services of both an accountant and an attorney to determine how much to spend for an investment property and when and at what price to sell it. If you are the landlord of your own property, your management time increases sharply. You must know how to advertise for new tenants, issue leases, perform repairs, handle delinquent payments, and legally evict tenants.

Low Current Income

Most of the total return on real estate investments takes the form of price appreciation because income is used for mortgage payments, maintenance costs, occasional capital improvements, and other expenses. During times of relatively high mortgage interest rates, a real estate investor may find that interest expenses cut severely into income. Sometimes these expenses reduce cash-flow return to less than 2 percent or even cause an annual loss.

High Transfer Costs

Substantial transfer costs are incurred when real estate is bought or sold. Real estate brokers charge sales commissions of 6 to 7 percent of the property's sales price. Attorneys' fees usually amount to 1 percent or more. Add to this appraisal fees, title search fees, and accountant fees if special reports are needed to be shown to potential investors. The lender might have a prepayment penalty of 1 or 2 percent. These costs can greatly reduce expected return and force the investor to keep the property for at least three or four years in order to spread out the expenses.

Limited Marketability

Since real estate is expensive, the market for investment property is much smaller than the securities market. Thus, you might receive comparatively few bids for a piece of real estate you want to sell. The nature of real estate is that every investment property is different and must be analyzed separately. Five different buyers might be interested in purchasing an income-producing duplex, but the one you have for sale may not meet their specific requirements. In such an individualized market, a lot of haggling over price occurs.

Limited Liquidity

A real estate investor usually has a substantial amount of money tied up in property. Stocks and bonds are quite liquid, since they can be quickly converted to cash, but real estate is not at all liquid. It may take months to find a buyer, arrange the financing, and legally close the sale. You might have to accept some financial loss if you must convert your real estate into cash in a hurry. The liquidity of real estate investments is even worse during times of high mortgage interest rates since most potential buyers cannot afford steep financing costs.

Difficulty of Accurately Estimating Costs

You estimate the anticipated total return you expect on your real estate investment based upon expected income, expected expenses, and expected price appreciation. If you estimate any of these variables incorrectly, you could lose not only a great deal of money but your investment property as well. There are many dangers in estimating costs. Expenses might be greater because of high tenant turnover. Insurance costs might rise sharply while competition among rental units holds rent increases to a minimum. Rezoning could depress property values. Inaccurate estimates combined with limited reserve funds and unfortunate economic events could force you to sell at a loss and consider bankruptcy.

Determining the Price to Pay for Real Estate

Three methods are commonly used by investors to determine the price to pay for a piece of real estate property: the gross income multiplier, capitalization rate, and discounted cash flow.

Gross Income Multiplier

The *gross income multiplier (GIM)* is a method of determining the price to pay for an income-producing property by dividing the asking price (or market value) of the property by the current gross rental income.

$$\text{GIM} = \frac{\text{asking price of property}}{\text{current gross rental income}} \qquad (19\text{--}1)$$

For example, if the advertised price on a small apartment complex is $240,000 and the gross rental income totals $40,000, the GIM is 6 ($240,000 ÷ $40,000). The GIM is much like a P/E ratio for common stocks. An investment with a GIM of more than 8 probably yields too low a return to be profitable. Real estate publications and local real estate investors can indicate the going GIM rate for various types of properties classed by age and community location. Conversely, if you know the GIM rate for an area, you can rearrange formula 19–1 to estimate the market value or likely asking price of the property as shown below:

$$\text{Asking price} = \text{current gross rental income} \times \text{GIM} \qquad (19\text{--}2)$$

The GIM is limited, as it is only a rough guide to investment property values, since the expenses for properties vary. If the GIM is too high, you might consider offering a lower price to the seller.

Capitalization Rate

The *capitalization rate* is widely used to determine the rate of return on a real estate investment. Also known as *income yield,* it is calculated by dividing the net operating income (first year) by the total investment, or asking price, as shown below:

$$\text{Capitalization rate} = \frac{\text{net operating income (first year)}}{\text{total investment } or \text{ asking price}} \qquad (19\text{--}3)$$

For example, if the *net operating income* (gross income less allowances for vacancies and operating expenses, except depreciation and debt repayments) was $18,000 on a property with a total investment of $240,000, the capitalization rate would be 7.5 percent ($18,000 ÷ $240,000).

Note that this measure of income yield is only a rough measure, since net operating income can be calculated in more than one way among comparable investment properties. It is a popular method of determining the rate of return, however, as comparable data are available on other properties as well as alternative investments. Investors often estimate the market value or asking price of income-producing property by using an assumed capitalization rate and rearranging formula 19–3 as

$$\text{Asking price} = \frac{\text{net operating income (first year)}}{\text{capitalization rate}} \qquad (19\text{–}4)$$

Thus, in this example, the asking price would equal $18,000 ÷ .075 percent (assumed capitalization rate), or $240,000. Alternatively, if you required an income yield of 9 percent you can conclude that the $240,000 asking price for this property is too high ($18,000 ÷ .09 = $200,000). Although valuable, this method has two limitations: (1) it is based on only the first year's return, and (2) it ignores return through price appreciation.

Discounted Cash Flow

The *discounted cash flow* method of estimating the value or asking price of a real estate investment emphasizes after-tax cash flows and the return on the invested dollars discounted over time to reflect a discounted yield. Computer-assisted analyses are willingly calculated through offices of larger real estate brokers and some investment advisers. (You can also use Appendix A2 of this book, as illustrated in Table 19–3.) To illustrate, assume you require a rate of return of 10 percent on a piece of real estate property advertised for sale at $80,000. You estimate that rents can be increased each year for five years. You expect that after all expenses you would have an after-tax cash flow of $4,000, $4,200, $4,400, $4,600, and $4,800 for each year. Assuming some price appreciation, you expect to be able to sell the property for $100,000 after all expenses. How high a price should you pay *now* to buy the property?

TABLE 19–3
Discounted Cash Flow Method Illustration (Asking Price of Property Is $80,000)

Number of Years	After-tax Cash Flow	Present Value of $1 at 10%[a]	Present Value of After-tax Cash Flow
1	$ 4,000	.909	$ 3,636
2	4,200	.826	3,469
3	4,400	.751	3,304
4	4,600	.683	3,142
5	4,800	.621	2,981
Sell property	$100,000	.621	62,100
Present value of property			$78,632

[a] From Appendix A3.

Table 19–3 shows how to answer this question. Multiply the estimated after-tax cash flows, and the expected proceeds of $100,000 to be realized upon the sale of the property, by the present value of a dollar at 10 percent, the required rate of return. Add the present values together to find the total present value of the property, here $78,632. Thus, the asking price of $80,000 is too high for you to earn an after-tax return of 10 percent. Your choices here are to negotiate the price down, accept less than a 10 percent return, or consider another investment. The discounted cash flow method is a superior and widely used way of estimating real estate values because it takes into account the selling price of the property, the effect of income taxes, and the time value of money.

Types of Real Estate Investments

When you invest in real estate, you can choose either *direct ownership,* in which you hold legal title to the property, or *indirect (or group) ownership,* in which you and other investors appoint a trustee to hold legal title on behalf of all in the group. Real estate syndicates (limited partnerships) and real estate investment trusts (REITs) are trustees for indirect ownership.

Joint direct ownership of real estate can take one of two forms, tenancy in common or joint tenancy. In *tenancy in common,* two or more people have control of the property regardless of whether they hold equal shares, and each person retains the right to dispose of (sell or give away) his or her undivided interest. Most unrelated individual investors prefer this kind of ownership. In *joint tenancy,* two or more people have an undivided interest in real estate held in equal or unequal shares; some states require that joint tenants always have a right of survivorship. *Joint tenancy with right of survivorship* requires that upon the death of a joint tenant (one owner) the remaining joint tenant or tenants assume full ownership of the property. Many husbands and wives own property in this kind of joint tenancy. You should decide what forms of ownership you prefer before shopping for real estate investments with others.

Raw Land and Residential Lots

Investing in raw land or residential lots on which you yourself do not intend to build is a speculative affair. No special tax advantages exist for this kind of investment. *Raw land* is undeveloped acreage, typically far from established communities, with no utilities and no improvements except perhaps a substandard access road. A *residential lot* is subdivided acreage with utilities (water, electricity, and sewerage) typically located within or adjacent to established communities. Don't buy acreage unless you believe that (1) you will later build on the property, (2) the price paid today is less than what it might be in the future, (3) comparable acreage will not be available in the future when needed by buyers, and (4) the property will rise substantially in value. Land speculators buy raw land and residential lots to sell to people who "think" they are certain they will build in the future.

"Location, location, and location" are the first three rules of successful real estate investing. A corner lot is better than one in the middle of the block, and a waterfront lot is even better. A lot on the main street of future growth is better than one on a nearby street. Beware the speculative investment of buying unknown land in some distant place as part of a new city retirement village, or resort. You should always see the land, hire an attorney to check out the deal, read the *property report* (a document legally required under the federal Interstate Land Sales Act for properties offered for sale across state lines), and obtain a private property appraisal.

Income-producing Properties

The financial incentives for investing in residential units and commercial properties include deductibility of mortgage interest, real estate property taxes, and depreciation as well as the potential for price appreciation.

Residential Units and Commercial Properties

Residential units are properties designed for residential living, such as houses, duplexes, apartments, mobile homes, and condominiums, with a potential to produce a profit. *Commercial properties* are properties designed for business uses, such as office buildings, medical centers, gasoline stations, and motels, that carry a potential to produce a profit. Making a good investment income from these properties normally requires you to take an active interest in their management.

Of all real estate investments, residential units are probably the easiest to begin with, the easiest to get out of, and the least profitable. One popular way to get a start in real estate investment is to purchase *sweat equity* property. You would seek properties that have good underlying value and attempt to buy at a favorable price, perhaps because the seller is having financial difficulties. Once you acquire the property, you would spend many hours painting, scrubbing, and fixing it up to sell it at a profit or to rent out the units.

Commercial properties carry more risk of remaining unrented than residential units. Further, the services expected by business tenants are usually more extensive and costly, and the buildings have a greater risk of obsolescence. Accordingly, you can charge higher rents on commercial properties to offset the higher risks involved.

You need to consider several criteria in choosing successful, income-producing rental property: good location, the dependability of income, the current value of the property, the condition of the property, the likely impact of future competition of similar real estate, the availability of reasonable financing, moderately priced utilities, stable real estate property taxes, and, of course, return on investment after taxes.

Illustration of a Successful Investment   Table 19–4 shows five-year estimates for hypothetical income-producing property valued at $100,000. The gross income multiplier (GIM) is only 10 ($100,000 ÷ $10,000), so it is likely that the investment may be a poor one from the point of view of current income. The building will be purchased with a $75,000 mortgage loan, so the buyer has to make a $25,000 down payment and also pay $4,000 in closing costs. The gross income is projected to rise at an annual rate of 5 percent, vacancies and unpaid rent at 10 percent, real estate taxes at 7 percent, insurance at 8 percent, and maintenance at 10 percent. Virtually the entire payment for the thirty-year, $75,000, 12 percent fixed rate mortgage loan is assumed to be interest during these early years. For income tax purposes, the land is valued at $10,000 and the building is depreciated over 27.5 years. Thus, the amount of annual straight-line depreciation is calculated to be $3,272 ($100,000 − $10,000 = $90,000 ÷ 27.5). The buyer is in the 28 percent marginal tax bracket.

   Note how difficult it is to earn current income from rental properties when financing costs are relatively high. During the first year the total cash flow loss is projected to be $2,261. Further, because the income tax laws permit depreciation to be recorded as a real estate investment expense, even though it is not an out-of-pocket cost, the total taxable loss is projected to be $5,533. This loss is deductible on the investor's income tax. Since the investor is in the 28 percent tax bracket, the loss of $5,533 results in a first year annual tax savings of $1,549 ($5,533 × .28). Instead of sending the $1,549 to the government in

TABLE 19–4
Estimates for a Successful Real Estate Investment

		Year				
		1	*2*	*3*	*4*	*5*
A.	Gross possible income	$10,000	$10,500	$11,025	$11,576	$12,155
	Less vacancies and unpaid rent	500	550	605	666	733
B.	Projected gross income	$ 9,500	$ 9,950	$10,420	$10,910	$11,422
C.	Less operating expenses					
	Real estate taxes	$ 900	$ 963	$ 1,030	$ 1,103	$ 1,180
	Insurance	400	432	467	504	544
	Maintenance	1,200	1,320	1,452	1,597	1,757
	Interest	9,261	9,261	9,261	9,261	9,261
	Total operating expenses	$11,761	$11,976	$12,210	$12,465	$12,742
D.	Total cash flow (negative)	$ (2,261)	$ (2,026)	$ (1,790)	$ (1,555)	$ (1,320)
E.	Less depreciation expense	3,272	3,272	3,272	3,272	3,272
F.	Taxable income (or loss) (D − E)	$ (5,533)	$ (5,298)	$ (5,062)	$ (4,827)	$ (4,592)
G.	Annual tax savings (28% marginal rate)	1,549	1,483	1,417	1,352	1,286
H.	Net cash flow income (or loss) after taxes (G − D)	$ (712)	$ (543)	$ (373)	$ (203)	$ (34)

taxes, the investor can use it to pay the operating expenses of the investment. Therefore, the cash flow loss of $2,261 can be reduced by $1,549 for a net cash flow loss after taxes of $712 ($2,261 − $1,549). During the first year of ownership the investor will have to come up with the additional $712 (about $60 monthly) to make ends meet.

Assume the property appreciates in value at an annual rate of 6 percent and will be worth $133,823 in five years ($100,000 × 1.06 × 1.06 × 1.06 × 1.06 × 1.06). If it sold at this price, a 6 percent real estate sales commission would reduce the proceeds by $8,029 to $125,794.

Now we can calculate crude annual rates of return on the property, as Table 19–5 shows. A *crude rate of return* is a rough measure of the yield on amounts invested that assumes that equal portions of the gain are earned each year. The total return to the investor was substantial. There were out-of-pocket cash investments of $25,000 for the down payment, $4,000 in closing costs, and $1,865 in net cash flow losses ($712 + $543 + $373 + $203 + $34), for a total investment of $30,865. The investor has a capital gain of $38,154, or a crude before-tax total

TABLE 19–5
Crude Annual Rate of Return on a Successful Real Estate Investment

Amount Invested

Down payment	$ 25,000	
Closing costs	4,000	
Accumulated net cash flow losses	1,865	
Total invested		$30,865

Taxable cost (adjusted basis)

Purchase price	$100,000	
Closing costs	4,000	
Subtotal	$104,000	
Less accumulated depreciation	16,360	
Taxable cost (adjusted basis)		$87,640

Proceeds

Sale price	$133,823	
Less sales commission	8,029	
Net proceeds	$125,794	
Less taxable cost	87,640	
Taxable proceeds (capital gain)	$ 38,154	
Income tax (28% marginal tax bracket)	$ 10,683	
After-tax proceeds		$27,471

Crude annual rate of return

Total invested	$ 30,865	
Taxable proceeds (capital gain)	38,154	
Before-tax total return ($38,154 ÷ $30,865)	124%	
Crude before-tax annual rate of return (124% ÷ 5 years)		25%

return of 124 percent over five years, roughly 25 percent (124 percent ÷ 5) annually.

Second or Vacation Homes

Many people own a second or vacation home, usually a house, condominium, or mobile home located near a lake or a beach, in the mountains, or at some other resort area. The IRS generally considers a second or vacation home as just another piece of property. Thus, owners can deduct only amounts spent for mortgage interest and real estate property taxes. For example, say Alice Skeller of Durham, New Hampshire, buys vacation property with a $600 monthly payment on the west coast of Florida. Interest and taxes amount to $500. Since she is in the 28 percent tax bracket, she realizes tax savings of $140 monthly ($500 × .28). Thus, it still costs Alice $460 ($600 − $140) a month, or $5,520 annually, for the property.

Should she rent out her property, however, she can qualify for additional tax savings if her adjusted gross income is under $150,000. Internal Revenue Service regulations allow you to take losses on part of your vacation home as rental property as long as (1) you "actively participate" in rental operations and (2) your personal use of it does not exceed the greater of fourteen days or 10 percent of the total number of days the home is rented at a "fair rental value." Rental losses for depreciation, repair costs, utility bills, and so forth may be taken as tax deductions. For example, income for Alice could amount to $2,000 for twenty days of rentals. Rental losses might total $3,500 and result in a tax loss of $1,500, but only if she did not personally use the property more than two days herself (10 percent of the twenty rental days). Remember, too, that Alice stands to gain from long-term price appreciation.

A special provision in the tax law pertains to vacation properties that are rented out for fewer than fifteen days during the year. It says that you cannot take any deductions, except for mortgage interest and property taxes, but the rental income you collect is *not* taxable. That might work to your advantage.

Time Sharing and Interval Ownership

Time sharing and interval ownership are relatively new ways of obtaining vacation housing. For from $5,000 to $10,000 buyers can purchase one week's use of luxury vacation housing furnished right down to the salt and pepper shakers. Vacationers also pay an annual maintenance fee for each week of ownership, perhaps $200 per year. The terms *time sharing* and *interval ownership* are not interchangeable. It is important to distinguish between the concepts of right to use and interval ownership. A **right-to-use purchase** of a limited, preplanned time-sharing period of use of a vacation property is actually only a vacation license. It does not grant legal real estate ownership interests to the purchaser, but instead provides a long-term lease permitting use of a hotel, suite, condominium, or other accommodation. This is also known as *non-deeded time sharing*. As in some other situations that involve leasing, should the real owner of the property (the developer) go bankrupt, the purchasers (lessees or renters) have no ownership claim to the property. Many U.S. courts have held that the buyer in a right-to-use time sharing arrangement is nothing more than an unsecured creditor. Therefore, the moment the developer declares bankruptcy, time sharers are locked out of the premises by the creditors. In contrast, an *interval ownership purchase* provides time-sharing buyers with actual titles and deeds to limited, preplanned use of real estate. Purchasers are thus secured creditors who are guaranteed continued use of the property throughout any bankruptcy proceedings. This is also known as *deeded time sharing.*

A variation permits times sharers to "swap" use of their units for housing in exotic resorts around the world. Note that because the organization that arranges swapping generally is not the same legal entity as the firm selling the time sharing, you have no guarantee that you will get a bargain in swapping. Also, trading is a lot easier if you have purchased a week at a ski resort in January rather than in August.

Think hard before getting into time sharing. You have little interest if the property appreciates substantially over several years (one week is only $\frac{1}{52}$ interest in capital gains), and sale of your unit may be difficult, especially when the developer is selling competitive properties. Be leery of gifts and awards often used to promote time sharing units, consider interval ownership rather than right-to-use time sharing, demand a fifteen-day cancellation clause in the contract, and require that your money be placed in escrow until the construction of the time sharing project is completed.

Real Estate Syndicates and Partnerships

A *real estate syndicate* is an indirect form of real property investment often organized as a limited partnership in which a required minimum number of shares (often five) are sold to investors for as little as $500 each to raise capital for local, regional, or national projects. Syndicates finance the building of many office buildings, shopping centers, factories, apartment houses, supermarkets, and motels. Community real estate agents or brokerage firms may form a local real estate syndicate known as a *single property syndicate* to invest in only one property, such as a medical professional building. Once they have purchased shares, investors normally are locked in for the duration of the partnership, often several years. Many of the larger syndicates are registered with the SEC and sell shares through divisions of major brokerage firms. These are often called *blind pool syndicates* because the investors are not notified what specific properties are purchased for investment. A limited secondary market may exist for larger syndicates, and resale of a small number of shares generally can be made only to other participants.

The *limited partnership* form of owning real estate investment property involves two classes of partners: the *general partner* (usually the organizer and initial investor), who operates the syndicate and has unlimited financial liability; and the *limited partners* (the outside investors), who receive part of the profits and the tax-shelter benefits but who are inactive in the management of the business and have no personal liability for the operations of the partnership beyond their initial investment.

Syndicates use leverage and often borrow two to four times the amount of their capital in an effort to enhance profits. Thirty investors might put up $10,000 each, totaling $300,000, for a downpayment on a building costing $1 million. Yields are often 2 to 3 percent above securities investments and are paid monthly. Since the tax laws permit partnership income, losses, depreciation, and capital appreciation to be passed directly through to the investors before being taxed, investors generally receive substantial tax losses to offset passive income and can anticipate long-term capital gains on the value of the properties.

Real Estate Investment Trusts

A *real estate investment trust (REIT)* is an unincorporated business that raises money by selling shares to the public, much like a closed-end investment company does, and owns property or makes mortgage and other loans to developers. REITs (pronounced "reets") were established under the Real Estate Investment Trust Act of 1960, which encourages small investors to place money indirectly into real estate through REITs. These trusts offer the profit potential of property while maintaining the marketability of stock.

REITs are exempt from income taxes if they pay out 90 percent or more of income as cash dividends to shareholders and conform to certain other rules. A real estate investment trust must have at least one hundred shareholders, 70 percent of its income must come from real

---

Mortgage Loans Offer an Alternative Investment

In most communities investors have the opportunity of investing in mortgage loans. To invest in mortgage loans, you would simply buy an IOU with a piece of real estate as security. It is a fixed-income investment much like corporate bonds, government securities, and savings certificates of deposit. Note, however, that if the borrower defaults you may wind up owning the real estate.

Four alternatives are available. First is *seller financing* of a property, in which the buyer makes direct payments to the seller as specified in the mortgage agreement. For example, Sid Margolius might personally finance the sale of his $125,000 home to Nancy Barclay by accepting $25,000 in cash as a down payment and taking back a $100,000 loan on which Nancy will make monthly payments for twenty-five years. A second alternative is a *discount mort-*gage. This is where an investor purchases the above type of mortgage from a seller that needs money now and is willing to let the mortgage go at a discount. For example, after five years Margolius might find he needs cash, so he can sell Nancy's mortgage loan to a private investor, at a slight discount to encourage the sale. A third alternative investment is *buying first mortgages through mortgage pools* offered by a financial institution. These arrangements allow a small number of investors to buy shares of a mortgage, often units of $5,000 each. A fourth alternative is *buying second mortgages*. These are provided through selected financial institutions and are also a place to invest funds. Since in the case of default first mortgages are dominant, the interest rates on "seconds" are generally several points higher.

estate investments, and no more than 30 percent of its income can come from capital appreciation (this discourages investing in highly speculative projects). REITs are not allowed to manage any property owned or to develop land for sale.

There are two types of REITs, mortgage trusts and equity trusts. **Mortgage trusts** do not own property but provide short-term financing for construction loans or for permanent mortgage loans for large projects. (Short-term mortgage trusts are REITs that experienced widespread financial bankruptcies in the 1970s.) **Equity trusts** concentrate on buying or building their own real estate properties, such as apartments, restaurants, nursing homes, condominiums, and office buildings and hire management firms to run the properties.

For the investor, REITs offer the opportunity to invest in real estate without committing a large sum of money. Shares might be sold for between $2 and $80, depending on market forces. REITs are marketable, as they are easily traded through a brokerage firm, but a limited number of potential buyers makes this investment somewhat illiquid.

Real Estate Investment Corporations

The investor who wants some of the allure of real estate along with the advantages of common stock may simply purchase stocks of real estate investment corporations. Like any other public corporation, they are engaged in business to make a profit. Instead of building automobiles or computers, these firms specialize in financing large properties.

Although real estate investment corporations offer no special tax benefits, they can retain some earnings and accordingly grow much faster in size than a trust or syndicate. A variety of stocks are available to investors. Some real estate investment corporations are diversified (such as City Investing), some specialize in hotels and motels (such as Loew's), and some are land development corporations (such as Deltona).

When to Sell Real Estate

Knowing when and how to sell real estate is extremely important because large profits often are made when property is sold rather than while it is owned. Note that investors who decide to sell should avoid doing so in an anxious moment; sellers, like buyers, should carefully analyze the best times to make a transaction. Even though the real estate investment alternatives described in this chapter are quite varied, we can still offer a few selling suggestions. Generally, you should sell in these situations:

1. Your investments are unwise No matter how careful real estate investors are, some investments just do not work out. Perhaps the apartment building is located in the wrong neighborhood or

the vacation property is deteriorating and actually declining in value. When troubles and expenses mount, it is time to consider selling.

2. **You are tired of ownership** There may come a time when you no longer enjoy collecting rents, arranging maintenance, and making capital improvements. Or your vacation spot may lose its attractiveness. Sell the property and find another investment you like.

3. **Alternative investments pay more** Some people buy a piece of real estate and feel they must hold onto it forever. You may have had a vacation property for many years and have paid off the mortgage in full. Or a rental building you bought years ago may still be bringing in a stream of income. Could you make more money by selling or refinancing and investing the proceeds elsewhere? For example, a vacation home valued at $70,000 with no mortgage debt is a $70,000 asset earning no return for the owner. An alternative would be to refinance it, perhaps obtaining $50,000, and to invest that amount.

4. **You need money** Many owners of real estate go through crisis times when they simply need money. In these instances you need not necessarily sell your property. When you refinance property, perhaps at a higher interest rate, you may receive a substantial amount of cash in addition to a new mortgage.

5. **You want to invest "upward"** You can use leverage to enhance profits in real estate. If you sell your own home and invest those proceeds (including price appreciation) into another more expensive property, you can avoid capital gains if you buy a home with the same or a higher value within twenty-four months. You can follow this procedure every few years, investing in increasingly more expensive dwellings, and pay no capital gains tax until you choose not to reinvest. Recall that on a personal dwelling an individual has a one-in-a-lifetime capital gains exclusion of $125,000 beginning at age fifty-five. Thus, $125,000 of these gains can be tax exempt. Investors in real estate properties should consider selling when after-tax gains permit them to expand their real estate holdings.

Summary

1. People invest in real estate to maximize after-tax returns, which could average one and one-half to two times those of most common stocks.

2. There are four advantages to real estate investing: potential for price appreciation, availability of high leverage, a positive cash flow, and special tax treatments that can enhance profits.

3. Disadvantages of real estate investing include extensive investigation expenses, high unit costs, substantial financial risk, low current income, high transfer costs, and the difficulty of estimating costs accurately.

4. You can use three methods to determine the value of, or the price to pay for, a selected piece of real estate property: gross income multiplier, capitalization rate, and discounted cash flow.

5. Examples of types of direct and indirect investment in real estate include raw land and residential lots, income-producing properties, second or vacation homes, time sharing and interval ownership, real estate syndicates, and real estate investment trusts.

6. The investor who wants some of the allure of real estate along with the advantages of common stock can simply purchase the stock of a real estate investment corporation.

7. If you prefer, you can invest in mortgage loans in many local communities, although that is considered a fixed-income investment.

8. Suggestions for when to sell real estate include the following: sell unwise investments, sell when tired of ownership, and sell when an alternative investment will provide a better return.

Modern Money Management

The Johnsons Compare Real Estate Investments

Harry and Belinda are considering some residential income properties as investments. Respond to the following questions, given the financial data presented below on three properties.

	Property A	Property B	Property C
Asking price	$200,000	$220,000	$190,000
Gross rental income	30,000	34,000	27,000
Net operating income (first year)	15,000	16,500	15,000

1. Calculate the GIM for the three options.

2. Give the Johnsons your observations on which properties are the best and worst buys, given that the GIM for comparable residential rental properties in their community is 7.

3. What would the GIMs be if you successfully negotiated the prices downward to $190,000 for property A, $200,000 for property B, and $175,000 for property C?

4. Calculate the capitalization rates on the properties, using the lower negotiated prices. Indicate which properties seem to be the best and the worst in terms of capitalization rate.

5. Recognize that the Johnsons' desire an after-tax total return of 10 percent. Calculate the present value of after-tax cash flow for property C, assuming that the after-tax cash flow numbers are

$8,000 for the first year, $8,400 for the second year, $8,800 for the third year, $9,200 for the fourth year, and $9,600 for the fifth year, and that the selling price of the property will be $220,000 in five years. Prepare your information in a format similar to Table 19-3.

6. Give the Johnsons your advice on whether or not they should invest in property C at its current price of $175,000.

Key Words and Concepts

capital improvements, 595
capitalization rate (income yield), 601
cash flow, 596
commercial properties, 604
crude rate of return, 606
depreciation, 596
discounted cash flow, 602
direct ownership, 603
entrepreneurial profit, 595
equity trust, 610
gross income multiplier (GIM), 601
indirect (group) ownership, 603
interval ownership purchase, 608
joint tenancy, 603
joint tenancy with right of survivorship, 603

limited partnership, 608
loan-to-value ratio, 596
mortgage trust, 610
net operating income, 601
property report, 604
price appreciation, 595
raw land, 603
real estate, 594
real estate investment trust (REIT), 609
real estate syndicate, 608
repairs, 595
residential lot, 603
residential unit, 604
right-to-use purchase, 607
tax-free exchange, 598
tenancy in common, 603

Review Questions

1. List some economic and noneconomic reasons for investing in real estate.

2. Cite and briefly explain two advantages to investing in real estate.

3. Explain the difference between capital improvements and repairs, and give examples.

4. Explain how leverage can help a real estate investor.

5. Give an example of how the loan-to-value ratio is calculated.

6. Describe how a negative cash flow can occur in a real estate investment.

7. Summarize how depreciation and interest costs can help the real estate investor.

8. Describe a circumstance in which a real estate investor might want a tax-free exchange with another real estate investor.

9. Cite five disadvantages to investing in real estate.

10. Describe how you would interpret a gross income multiplier of 7 on a piece of property with an asking price of $120,000.

11. Explain the usefulness of the capitalization rate method of determining the price to pay for real estate.

12. Name the two ways of having joint ownership, and distinguish between them.

13. What are the differences between raw land and residential lots?

14. Why might an investor choose commercial properties rather than residential units for income-producing properties?

15. Explain how a real estate investment can be successful while simultaneously having a negative cash flow.

16. What purposes does calculating a crude rate of return serve?

17. Briefly describe how a vacation home can provide tax benefits.

18. Why should someone considering a time-sharing investment choose internal ownership rather than right-to-use ownership?

19. Explain the difference between limited and general partners in a limited partnership.

20. Cite three reasons to consider selling real estate.

Case Problems

1. Gerald Fitzpatrick of Scranton, Pennsylvania, is interested in the numbers of real estate investments. He reviews the figures in Table 19–2 and is impressed with the potential 7.4 percent yield after taxes. Since Gerald is only in the 15 percent marginal tax bracket, answer the questions below to help guide his investment decisions.
   a. Substitute Gerald's 15 percent marginal tax bracket in Table 19–2 and calculate his taxable income, his return after taxes, and his yield after taxes.
   b. Why does it appear to be a favorable investment for Gerald?
   c. Since the IRS allows only so much for depreciation expense, what other two factors might be changed in Table 19–2 in order to increase the yield for Gerald?
   d. Calculate the yield after taxes for Gerald, who is in the 15 percent tax bracket, assuming he bought the property and financed it with a $64,000, 8 percent mortgage loan with annual interest costs of only $5,500.

2. Linda Berk of Menomonie, Wisconsin, is considering buying a vacation condominium apartment for $65,000 in Park City,

Utah. Linda hopes to rent the condo to others in order to keep costs down. Respond to the questions below to help Linda with her decisions.

a. If Linda's monthly payments are $580 ($500 goes for interest, $30 for principal, $30 for property taxes, and $20 for homeowner's insurance) plus another $40 for the monthly homeowner's association fee, which of these costs will be tax deductions? List the costs and total on an annualized basis.

b. As Linda is in the 28 percent marginal tax bracket, how much less in taxes will she pay if she buys this condo?

c. Given that she would like to personally use the condo for vacations ten to twelve days a year, how many days will she have to rent it out before she would be eligible to deduct rental losses from her taxes?

d. Since Park City is mostly a winter ski resort and few condo renters can be found in the off season, Linda is concerned about qualifying to deduct rental losses. Assuming she could rent the condo for $120 a day, describe the rental IRS-approved alternative she could use to generate income and then calculate the maximum amount of money Linda could obtain using that plan.

e. Figure Linda's annual net out-of-pocket cost to buy the condominium and rent it out minimally for tax-free income. Start with her $7,440 cost for monthly payments ($580) and homeowners's association fees ($40). Then deduct the savings on income taxes as well as the presumed rental for fourteen days.

f. Using the figure derived in part e, how much out-of-pocket cost per day would it be for Linda to use the condo herself if she stayed there ten days a year? Fifteen days a year?

Suggested Readings

"Home-Buying Strategies." *Better Homes and Gardens,* April 1987, pp. 132–137. Three creative moves to make in real estate investing.

"Investing: Any Pay Dirt Left in Real Estate?" *Changing Times,* January 1987, pp. 85–93. Profits can be made in spite of tax reform.

"Low-effort Real Estate Investing." *Changing Times,* August 1987, pp. 22–26. The attraction of REITs, limited partnerships, and land partnerships.

"A New Era for Personal Investing." *Consumer Digest,* January/February 1987, pp. 22–26. How tax reform has changed the rules of investing, especially real estate investing.

"The Party's Over." *Texas Monthly,* June 1987, pp. 110–113+. Chasing real estate fortunes with savings and loan money.

"Tough New Rules for Rental Real Estate." *Money,* April 1987, pp. 193–198. Tax law changes affecting real estate investments.

C H A P T E R 20

High-risk Investments

OBJECTIVES

After reading this chapter, the student should be able to

1. identify the characteristics of high-risk investments.
2. describe diamonds as a form of high-risk investment.
3. describe precious metals as a form of high-risk investment.
4. list and describe the collectibles most often held as high-risk investments.
5. describe stock rights as a form of high-risk investment.
6. describe warrants as a form of high-risk investment.
7. explain how trading in options can be a high-risk, as well as a conservative, investment.
8. describe futures contracts as a form of high-risk investment.
9. identify six suggestions to use when deciding whether to sell high-risk investments.

P eople who invest in stocks, bonds, mutual funds, and real estate instead of in less risky government securities and certificates of deposit do so to obtain higher yields. Most of these people are conservative or moderate-risk investors and avoid highly speculative investments. Speculative investors seek very high returns and are willing to accept a greater degree of risk to achieve them. Some speculative risks are available in all the traditional investment areas of stocks, bonds, mutual funds, and real estate, but certain high-risk investments hold a special allure for many speculative investors. These include diamonds, precious metals (such as gold, silver, and platinum), collectibles (such as stamps, art, and rare coins), rights, warrants, stock options, and futures contracts.

What Are Speculative or High-risk Investments?

Speculative investments are investment transactions that carry considerable risk of loss for the chance of large gains. This means that in addition to the high potential profits there is a clear danger of losing part or all of the dollars that have been invested. Accordingly, investment funds used for speculative purposes should be only those that you can afford to lose.

You can get a start in high-risk investments with a relatively small amount of capital, perhaps only $2,000 or $3,000. Sellers of speculative investments rarely screen customers to be sure that investors can afford to take the risk. The decision as to whether you should become involved in high-risk investments is basically left to you, but the prudent investor limits high-risk investments to a small percentage of his or her total investment portfolio.

The high rewards from many speculative investments frequently come from the profits of short-term market fluctuations. The speculator must act in a matter of hours, days, or weeks rather than years and must have a considerable amount of investment knowledge. To succeed in any area of investing you have to research it carefully and make intelligent decisions. But to succeed in high-risk investments you need to remain constantly alert to developments, become thoroughly familiar with the intricacies of each type of investment, and act decisively to assure profits and cut losses.

In most areas of high-risk investment, losers outnumber winners by three or even four to one. Depending on your own investment philosophy, you may want to rule out high-risk investments entirely, consider speculative risks on an occasional basis, or seek out such opportunities regularly. The remainder of this chapter details the major high-risk investments.

Diamonds

As precious stones, diamonds are more popular than rubies, emeralds, and sapphires. A *diamond* is a pure or nearly pure form of carbon, naturally crystallized in a state of extreme hardness. Investors most often purchase investment-grade diamonds for long-term price appreciation rather than for short-term speculation. Yet possible sharp swings in the diamond market present opportunities for the speculator. For example, in a recent three-year period, the value of diamonds doubled. Then prices dropped 75 percent over the following two years. New diamond mines in the Soviet Union and Australia have created a greater supply than the older South African mines.

For the investor, the best quality diamonds are sold not by local jewelers but by wholesale diamond firms. Your task is to determine how much money you have available and to purchase a stone according to the four C's: color, cut, clarity, and carat weight. The best color for diamonds is pure white or colorless. The best cut for investment purposes is the round-brilliant with fifty-eight facets, or cuts. *Clarity* is the degree of internal perfection of a gemstone or the degree to which a gemstone possesses inclusions (irregularities) that diffuse light and lessen its brilliance. The best diamonds are rated by gemologists as flawless. A *carat* is a unit of weight equal to .2 gram and divided into 100 "points." Thus, a 125-point diamond weighs 1.25 carats. Investment-grade diamonds should be at least one-half carat and preferably more than one carat in weight.

Deal only with reputable firms. Buying over the telephone is clearly unwise. Buying from a firm with a less-than-impeccable reputation could result in problems such as switching of your diamond with a zirconium (very pretty but worth less than $100). A diamond should be graded accurately by a person certified by the Gemological Institute of America (GIA) according to the four C's. Most diamond sellers absorb the cost of having the diamond recertified by an independent laboratory, again using GIA guidelines, when an investor makes a purchase. Since every diamond is unique, these independent firms can also x-ray the stone to obtain a "fingerprint" of its uniqueness. It is best to resell diamonds through the diamond firms, which often accept stones on consignment. Computer listings of diamond brokers have become available in the diamond resale market as interest in gemstones has increased.

Precious Metals

Gold, silver, and platinum are precious metals much in demand worldwide. Silver and platinum, unlike gold, have numerous industrial uses. Many people around the world invest in precious metals as a means of preserving capital in difficult economic times, reasoning that if their national economies experience difficulty they themselves will be able to trade gold instead of devalued paper money. Thus, investing 5 or 10 percent of your investment portfolio in precious metals can be a hedge against political, military, and economic uncertainty.

The prices of precious metals tend to increase in times of economic and political turmoil, especially in times of high inflation. Increased demand for precious metals has also pushed up prices in recent years. For example, over a recent five-year period gold has ranged in price from just over $200 to $600 per ounce. Silver rose from $5 to $50 an ounce in two years. Platinum jumped from $280 to over $800 an ounce in three years.

Price drops are just as rapid. Silver, for example, declined from $50 to $10 an ounce in less than one year. Speculators earn high profits on these sharp price swings over a period of months or weeks.

Note, however, that precious metals pay no dividends. Further, only the wealthy can afford to buy the actual product referred to as bullion. Since gold bullion must be purchased in minimum amounts of one hundred troy ounces, which is just over eight pounds, an investor may need $40,000 or more. Minimums for silver and platinum bullion exist, too. In addition, precious metal bullion has related expenses such as assay fees, shipping charges, insurance, storage fees, sales taxes (states consider these consumer purchases, not investments), and commission charges.

Those interested in smaller investments turn to other ways of owning precious metal investments: coins, certificates, companies that mine metals, and metals futures. Bags of silver coins are sold on the New York Mercantile Exchange. Gold coins are generally available in minimum lots of five, although some banks will sell smaller amounts and, naturally, charge higher commissions. Gold coins that are easy to trade include the American "Eagle," the Canadian "Maple Leaf," and the South African "Krugerrand." Silver coins include the American "Eagle" silver dollar. Some banks sell gold certificates, which evidence ownership of small amounts of gold kept by the institution for safety; of course, these banks charge a commission and storage fee. Stocks of gold-, silver-, and platinum-mining companies have done quite well in recent years, with price changes lagging just behind the general trend of metal prices. Such stocks are risky, but most pay small dividends, whereas the actual metals do not. The stocks also have a daily liquidity by wire or mail. Gold and silver futures, an extremely risky form of speculative investing, are discussed later in the chapter.

Collectibles

Collectibles are cultural artifacts that have value because of beauty, age, scarcity, or simply their popularity. Buying collectibles as assets can become quite a hobby. People collect many types of assets that are not particularly liquid, such as comic books, antique furniture, rare coins, old cars, art, stamps, rare beer cans, and hundreds of other items thought to have value. Stamps, art, and rare coins are collectibles with a sizable resale market.

Collectibles, of course, pay no income dividends; the buyer must rely on price appreciation to earn any return whatsoever. The expectation and hope of the investor is that the value of such assets will increase more rapidly than other investments. Indeed, over some periods the prices of collectibles have risen substantially, but on occasion market values have dropped just as sharply.

Stamps

More than 25 million people in the United States are involved in *philately,* the collection and study of stamps, envelopes, and similar material. You may have heard of the rare and valuable 24-cent 1918 U.S. airmail stamp that was printed upside down, or of the Graf Zeppelin issue, which soared to a value of $10,000 for a very fine mint set of three. Recently, the 1918 stamp was valued above $30,000, but the Graf Zeppelin had slipped to $3,000, reflecting changes in collector demand for each.

The former high school hobbyist needs to approach a high level of expertise before seriously considering stamps as an investment. Forgeries abound among unscrupulous traders. The wise buyer should deal only with the most reputable sellers, diversify stamp holdings, and purchase rare stamps of only the highest quality.

Art

For the patient and knowledgeable investor who does not need current income from an investment, art may be an excellent alternative because prices for many types of works have risen steadily in recent decades. Increases in excess of 10 percent annually are not uncommon in art, and most paintings bought at auctions are purchased for less than $4,000.

Items that have had good values in recent years are oil paintings, watercolors, and vintage prints by nineteenth- and twentieth-century artists. Strong demand exists for old masters (such as Rembrandt) and western art. Works by contemporary artists are generally avoided for investment purposes, excepting those of Warhol, Kline, Rauschenberg, and the like.

Rare Coins

A **numismatist** collects coins, medals, and selected commemoratives. An investor in rare coins is more than just a hobbyist; there are some large profits to be made in this field. An uncirculated, quality 1829 Indian cent bought in 1948 for $11 has increased in value by 3,182 percent, as the price has risen to $350. Many other coins have risen in value by more than 10 or 15 percent a year in the past decade.

Numismatists might collect gold coins issued between 1795 and 1933. Most of the silver coins collected are the Morgan-type dollars minted between 1878 and 1921 and the later Peace dollars issued between 1921 and 1935. "Type" coins are sets of one each of the thirty different designs made over a period of years. A type-coin collection could include Liberty standing quarters, Liberty walking half-dollars, Liberty nickels, Indian cents, and Barber dimes, quarters, and half-dollars. Many numismatists try to obtain a coin of each date and variety, perhaps of Indian cents or Liberty nickels.

In all cases, the rarer the coin and the higher the quality, the better the price and likelihood of appreciation. Investors in rare coins should deal only with reputable sellers, obtain a written guarantee of genuineness from the dealer or auctioneer, and seek another professional opinion to corroborate the grade and value of rare coins.

Rights

Growing corporations frequently need to raise additional capital. They do this by issuing bonds and/or by selling new shares of stock. If additional stock is sold, stockholders of most corporations may experience dilution of their ownership position. For example, assume that Road Runners Shoe Company had one hundred thousand shares of stock outstanding, currently selling for $20 per share. If the company wanted to raise capital it could sell an additional twenty-five thousand shares, perhaps at $18 a share to encourage sales. The bylaws of many corporations and the statutes of most states require a *pre-emptive right* for existing stockholders, which is the right to be given the opportunity to purchase a proportionate share of any new stock issue. This will allow them to maintain their proportionate share in the ownership of the company. If the current stockholders in Road Runners do not purchase the newly offered shares, future company dividends will have to be spread among new and old stockholders. The issuing corporation often prefers selling shares to current stockholders because it is less expensive.

A *right* is a legal instrument to purchase a number of shares of corporate stock at a specific price during a limited time period. Most rights lapse after sixteen days, although some have a one-month limit. Rights have financial value because the shares of the new stock are normally offered to right holders at a price somewhat lower than the current market value of the stock. Consequently, there is a market for the buying and selling of rights, and once again we enter the world of the speculator. An especially attractive speculative investment is using margin to buy rights with the hope that the value will rise.

For example, the right to buy one share of the new Road Runners stock at $18 is worth approximately $2 if the current selling price is $20. (It is actually a little less, since after issuance of the new shares the value of all shares will have been diluted somewhat.) If other investors perceive this new stock offering as an indication that Road Runners will be more profitable in the future, the price of the stock might rise to perhaps $21 or $22 and the price of the right will rise as well. Say you purchase 1,000 rights at $2 each and put up only $500 in cash, using margin for the remaining $1,500. (Special margin rules are permitted for rights transactions.) If the price of the stock jumps to $22, you will have a tremendous profit. The value of each right will have risen to about $4 ($22 − $18), and it may be higher if investor interest has been particularly strong. Selling the right or exercising it to purchase the shares at the specified price will bring you proceeds of $3,500 ($4,000 − $500) on an investment of only $500. This is a return of 700 percent ($500 ÷ $3,500) in just a matter of days or weeks! Note also, however, that the price of the stock could have dropped to below $20, forcing down the value of the right and possibly result in a total loss.

Warrants

A **warrant** is a legal instrument accompanying a security (usually a bond) that gives the holder the opportunity to buy a certain number of shares of another security (usually common stock) at a specified price over a designated period of time (usually five, ten, or twenty years but sometimes in perpetuity). The distinction between a right and a warrant is that rights are issued to current stockholders whereas warrants are issued attached to other securities (such as to bonds or preferred stock). Some of these warrants are detachable and some are not; a trading market exists for detachable warrants.

A company issues warrants along with another security to make the security offer more valuable. For example, a bond sold with a warrant will probably have an interest rate from 1 to 2 percent less than comparable bonds without warrants. Warrants are sometimes called *purchase warrants* and each has a speculative value until the expiration date, at which time it may be worthless. To illustrate, assume that Road Runners common stock is selling for $22 and the company raises capital by selling bonds with detachable warrants. Each warrant provides that the bond purchaser, or later holder of the warrant, can buy one share of common stock at $30 for a period of five years. Five years is a long time, and the warrant could be worth only $.50 at the onset. (Technically, the warrant is worthless; what gives it value is "speculative hope.") If the company continues to be successful and the price of the stock rises, the value of the warrant will also rise. The value of the warrant may continue to increase as long as the common stock price is expected to rise.

Consider two scenarios that might occur. First, the warrant might have a value of $1 while Road Runners common stock is priced at $29. If the common stock price climbs above $30, the warrant value will soar. For every dollar climb in the stock price, the warrant increases a similar amount or more. A warrant bought for $1 will be worth at least $6 if the stock price moves to $35 per share, and the speculator would gain tremendously. If a warrant is actually exercised (which is rare), the company would issue new shares of common stock, which would raise more capital for the firm. In the second scenario, the warrant worth $1 when the price of the stock is $29 could drop in value to $.50 or less if the common stock price declines to $28 or $27. This would cause the speculator to lose half or more of the amount invested. Figure 20–1 shows the *swingers* over a given one-week period. These are stocks and warrants that have gone up and down the most in the past week based on a percentage of change. To estimate the annual rate of return, multiply the percentage by fifty-two weeks. Warrants are truly speculative ventures.

Options

An *option* is a contract that gives the holder the right to buy or sell a specific asset, for example, real estate or common stock, at a specified price. Markets exist for options written for common stocks, debt instruments, foreign currencies, and stock indexes. The most common are stock options, although stock index options have become increasingly popular in recent years. A *stock option* is a contract permitting the holder the right to buy or sell a specific number of shares (normally one hundred) of a certain stock at a particular price (the *striking price*) before a specified date (the *expiration date*). Buying options is a very speculative venture, but selling options is often a conservative investment decision.

Writing Options

Options are created by option writers. Through a stockbrokerage, an *option writer* issues an option contract promising either to buy or to sell a specified asset for a fixed striking price and receives an *option premium* (the price of the option itself) for standing ready to buy or sell the asset at the wishes of the person who has bought the option. Once written and sold, an option may change hands many times before its expiration. The *option holder* is the person who actually owns the option contract. It is always the original writer who is responsible for buying or selling the asset if requested by the holder of the option contract.

There are two types of options: puts and calls. A *call* is an option contract that gives the option holder the right to *buy* the optioned asset from the option writer at the striking price. A *put* is an option contract that gives the option holder the right to *sell* the optioned asset to the option writer at the striking price. The box, "Making Sense of Options," illustrates the relationships between option writers and option holders for both puts and calls.

Most options expire without being exercised by the option holder, and the option writer earns a profit from the premium charged when the option was originally sold. However, an option writer can suffer considerable losses when options are exercised by a holder. The writer of a call may be forced to take a loss when the market price of the optioned asset rises above the striking price. If the writer owned the asset (a *covered option*), he or she might be forced to sell to the option holder at a price lower than the current market value. If the writer does

SWINGERS

The following lists show stocks and warrants on the New York, American and over-the-counter markets that have gone up the most and down the most in the past week based on percent of change regardless of volume. No securities trading below $2 are included. Percentage changes are the difference between the previous week's closing price and last week's close. Footnotes: z-sales in full; x-ex-dividend; s-stock split or stock dividend of 25 percent or more in past 52 weeks; g-dividends or earnings in Canadian money.

New York Stock Exchange

UPS

Name	Sales	High	Low	Close	Chg.	Pct.
Valley Ind	1746	2⅞	1¾	2⅝	+ ⅞	50.0
DayIntl	28605	52⅜	34¾	47⅝	+ 12⅜	35.1
FinCpA flt pf	1692	22	14¾	19¾	+ 4¾	31.7
Kidde pfC	102	144	114⅞	144	+ 32½	29.1
Copwld	796	12¼	9⅝	12¼	+ 2¾	28.9
McDrmInt wt	8263	9⅝	6⅞	9	+ 2	28.6
AudioVid	7776	7⅝	6	7⅝	+ 1⅝	27.1
Kidde 1.64pr	129	96½	91½	95	+ 20¼	27.1
KiddeInc	53451	62¼	48¾	61⅜	+ 12⅞	26.5
Kidde prB	26	144	112¾	142½	+ 29⅝	26.2
PhilVanH s	22589	25¼	19¼	24⅞	+ 4⅞	24.4
RdgBat cv pf	158	12½	9⅞	12¼	+ 2⅜	24.1
KanebSvc	27418	4⅛	2⅞	3⅞	+ ¾	24.0
IntMultifds	22336	38½	29¾	36⅝	+ 7	23.6
vjSmithInt	9374	10	7⅞	9⅞	+ 1⅞	23.4
GalvstHou	3103	4¾	3⅝	4¾	+ ⅞	22.6
vjGlobMr pf	566	6⅞	5⅝	6⅞	+ 1¼	22.2
Northgate g	1406	9⅛	7⅝	9	+ 1⅝	22.0
NII	5642	19¾	15½	19½	+ 3½	21.9
RoyalInt	5226	7⅜	5¼	7¼	+ 1¼	20.8
Tricentrl	970	4½	3¾	4⅜	+ ¾	20.7
vjWhlPitStl	1139	9⅜	7½	8⅞	+ 1½	20.3
vjGlobMar	7810	3	2½	3	+ ½	20.0
KanebEgy	·1448	8⅞	7	8½	+ 1⅜	19.3
Varity	35277	2⅜	2	2⅜	+ ⅜	18.8

DOWNS

Name	Sales	High	Low	Close	Chg.	Pct.
Timeplex	3332	31	27	27	− 3¾	12.2
Lennar	5538	26⅜	22¼	22⅜	− 3	11.8
Airbn Frt	10044	33⅜	28⅛	29¼	− 3⅞	11.7
CannonGp	13322	4⅝	2⅝	3⅞	− ½	11.4
vjCLC Am	451	2⅜	2	2	− ¼	11.1
Hitachi	3190	79⅛	71	74	− 9¼	11.1
Tandem s	59308	31½	27¼	28½	− 3½	10.9
vjAllisChal	7399	2⅜	2	2⅛	− ¼	10.5
Calton	2257	9⅞	8	8½	− 1	10.5
FederalCo s	4435	44½	38¾	40⅛	− 4⅝	10.3
vjAmfesco	354	2⅝	2¼	2¼	− ¼	10.0
CntrCred s	1962	12¾	11⅜	11⅜	− 1¼	9.9
FlowGenl	567	6¼	5⅝	5¾	− ⅝	9.8
ItalyFd n	1211	11½	10⅜	10⅜	− 1⅛	9.8
Sony Corp	4292	28⅜	25⅝	26½	− 2⅞	9.8
OrientExp	257	4	3½	3½	− ⅜	9.7
ConStor	12930	10½	9	9⅜	− 1	9.6
FtCapitHld	12998	10⅜	8½	9⅜	− 1	9.6
MDC Corp	4025	11½	10⅜	10⅝	− 1⅛	9.6
Fisher Fds	270	12¼	10⅝	11	− 1⅛	9.3
GenData	2516	9⅜	8½	8⅝	− ⅞	9.2
FinCpAm pf	42	5¾	5	5	− ½	9.1
FtBcpTex	7686	2⅞	2¼	2½	− ¼	9.1
GreenTree	12556	26¾	22	23⅝	− 2⅜	9.1
PacoPhrm	1738	17⅛	15⅛	15⅜	− 1½	8.9

American Stock Exchange

UPS

Name	Sales	High	Low	Close	Chg.	Pct.
Kidde wt	21448	22⅞	10⅜	22	+ 12⅛	122.8
DI Inds	1277	3⅛	1⅜	3⅛	+ 1⅝	108.3
AdamsRes	1579	3⅞	2⅛	3¾	+ 1½	66.7
TubosMex	4569	6⅞	4½	6¾	+ 2¼	50.0
ESD	140	4½	3⅜	4⅜	+ 1⅛	34.6
PrairieOil s	555	9¾	6¾	8¾	+ 2¼	34.6
vjConsEP	46	2⅞	2¼	2¾	+ ⅝	29.4
UnoRestr n	2489	10¾	8⅛	10⅝	+ 2⅜	28.8
Weathfrd pf	66	11¾	9¼	11¾	+ 2⅝	28.8
LeePharm s	1743	7¼	5⅜	6¾	+ 1½	28.6
KirbyExp	3938	5¾	4½	5¾	+ 1¼	27.8
MountMed	764	5½	3¾	4⅞	+ 1	25.8
ConOil Gas	4435	3¾	2⅞	3¾	+ ¾	25.0
Weathfrd	3065	3⅞	3	3⅞	+ ¾	24.0
MtchlEng	2609	18¾	14⅝	18⅛	+ 3½	23.9
SummittEngy	525	2¼	1⅞	2⅛	+ ⅜	21.4
HersheyOil	912	7¼	5¾	7⅛	+ 1¼	21.3
GalaxyCpt	665	20	16½	19½	+ 3⅛	19.1
PlymRub B	34	2⅜	2	2⅜	+ ⅜	18.8
Armel	817	4¾	3⅞	4⅜	+ ⅝	16.7
FredHolywd	133	11⅜	10	11⅜	+ 1⅝	16.7
CitFst 2.50pf	275	107¾	107	107	+ 14⅝	15.8
WellsAmer	1095	4	3¼	3¾	+ ½	15.4
GECr wtY	1623	4¾	4¼	4¾	+ ⅝	15.2
CrownCrf	141	69½	58	65⅞	+ 8⅜	14.6

DOWNS

Name	Sales	High	Low	Close	Chg.	Pct.
Astrex	1278	4¾	2¼	3¾	− ⅞	18.9
ChampEn wi	632	7⅝	6¼	6¼	− 1⅜	18.0
DeLauFl n	73	7⅞	6⅝	6⅝	− 1⅜	17.2
Ecogen n	969	9⅛	7¾	7¾	− 1⅜	15.1
Commtron	129	6	5⅛	5⅛	− ⅞	14.6
Wedco	162	5	4⅛	4¼	− ⅝	12.8
InstruSys pf	86	3	2⅝	2⅝	− ⅜	12.5
IntegrGeneric	261	4⅞	4⅜	4⅜	− ⅝	12.5
BSN s	365	14¾	12⅞	13	− 1¾	11.9
FriesEnt	381	4¾	3¾	3¾	− ½	11.8
SeamensCp n	3991	7½	6½	6⅝	− ⅞	11.7
MatthWrt n	1230	3¼	2⅜	2⅞	− ⅜	11.5
WstnHlth	139	4⅜	3¾	3⅞	− ½	11.4
ActonCp s	133	18⅛	16⅛	16⅛	− 1⅞	10.4
CompCon	1305	9⅝	8⅜	8⅝	− 1	10.4
IRT Corp	281	5	4⅜	4⅜	− ½	10.3
Greenman s	1484	9⅞	8¾	9	− 1	10.0
EntrMkt s	3120	11½	10	10¼	− 1⅛	9.9
CandgWineA	75	16⅞	15	15¼	− 1⅝	9.6
Int Proteins	222	17	14⅝	15¼	− 1⅝	9.6
CandgaWneB	193	17⅜	14⅞	15½	− 1⅝	9.5
RobtMrk n	55	7¾	7⅛	7⅛	− ¾	9.5
Tofutti	271	5¼	4¾	4¾	− ½	9.5
AlphaInd	1670	11⅛	9½	9⅝	− 1	9.4
OxfordEngy	564	8	7⅛	7¼	− ¾	9.4

Over the Counter

UPS

Name	Sales	High	Low	Close	Chg.	Pct.
HornbckOfsh	326	2	1	2	+ 1	100.0
Radva	1105	3½	2¼	3	+ 1¼	71.4
TiptonCtrs	1315	9½	5¼	9	+ 3¾	71.4
Atcor	31501	22¾	13¾	22½	+ 8¾	63.6
AmNatPtr	1135	2⅝	1¼	2	+ ¾	60.0
Danners Inc	41	4	3	4	+ 1½	60.0
SpecPhar	1224	3¾	2½	3½	+ 1¼	55.6
StringInc	23031	41¼	40¼	40⅜	+ 13⅝	50.9
BartonInd	586	2¼	1⅜	2¼	+ ¾	50.0
BerryPetr	25	24	16	24	+ 8	50.0
TacoVilla	372	3½	2½	3½	+ 1⅛	47.4
FlexblCpt	2704	2 15/16	2 1/16	2 15/16	+ 15/16	46.9
HemisphDev	541	2 9/16	1¾	2 9/16	+ 13/16	46.4
FalconOG	359	4⅜	3	4¼	+ 1¼	41.7
CPAC Inc	492	3	2 1/16	2⅞	+ 13/16	39.4
ConvgtSolu	1137	2 11/16	1 13/16	2 11/16	+ ¾	38.7
WharfResc	1502	5 15/16	4½	5⅞	+ 1⅝	38.2
DiversHumn	45	2¾	2	2¾	+ ¾	37.5
IndBnchInc	50	2¾	2½	2¾	+ ¾	37.5
StanlyInter	1041	11¾	8¼	11¼	+ 3	36.4
DigitalSol	831	2	1½	2	+ ½	33.3
InFerGene	1193	2⅝	1⅞	2½	+ ⅝	33.3
CvgtSolu un	1500	3 9/16	2⅝	3 9/16	+ ⅞	32.6
CademaCp	1775	2⅝	1 15/16	2 9/16	+ ⅝	32.3
NY Test	563	4⅛	3⅛	4⅛	+ 1	32.0

DOWNS

Name	Sales	High	Low	Close	Chg.	Pct.
ZZZZ Best un	955	5	1½	2	− 10	83.3
DataMedC s	8167	5⅞	1¾	2¾	− 3¼	54.2
VM Softw s	13083	24	15	15⅞	− 6⅞	30.2
ElectMissl	1104	3¼	1⅞	2⅛	− ⅞	29.2
Lexitech	440	3	2¼	2¼	− ¾	25.0
SatlAuct wt	79	2⅝	2	2	− ⅝	23.8
AliantCptr	16802	29	20½	22½	− 6¾	23.1
MediRx un	138	21¾	15	15	− 4½	23.1
EnConv 87wt	312	5½	4¼	4¼	− 1¼	22.7
MBI Busin	2642	3¾	2¾	2 13/16	− 13/16	22.4
HE Ventur	361	3⅜	2½	2⅝	− ¾	22.2
RiseTech	613	6¾	4¾	5¼	− 1½	22.2
MediRx	2586	4⅜	2½	3⅛	− ⅞	21.9
Gamogen un	26	2⅞	2¼	2¼	− ⅝	21.7
VideoJukebx un	81	18½	14½	14½	− 4	21.6
WarehseClub	606	4⅝	3⅜	3⅝	− 1	21.6
DecisnSys	115	2½	2	2	− ½	20.0
ElctGas un	110	2½	1⅞	2	− ½	20.0
SatlAuct un	23	13¾	11	11	− 2¾	20.0
SatlAuct	142	5¾	4½	4⅝	− 1⅛	19.6
VideoJuke	1805	3½	2⅝	2 13/16	− 11/16	19.6
BetaPhase	308	5⅛	4⅛	4⅛	− 1	19.5
Telecast	605	5⅜	4¼	4¼	− 1	19.0
DuqusnSy	4217	22¼	17¾	18¼	− 4¼	18.9
MediRx wt	443	4½	3	3¼	− ¾	18.8

FIGURE 20–1
Example of Swingers
Source: Washington Post, May 4, 1987. Used by permission of United Press International.

Making Sense of Options

An option is a contract that gives its holder the right to buy or sell an asset at a specified price. The two principal players in the options game are the option writer and the option holder. Their relationship is summarized below.

Type of Option	Option Writer	Option Holder
Call	If requested by the option holder, the option writer must sell the asset to the option holder at the striking price.	Can force the option writer to sell him/her the asset at the striking price or, may sell the option through an options market or, may let the option expire.
Put	If requested by the option holder, the option writer must buy the asset from the option holder at the striking price.	Can force the option writer to buy the asset from him/her at the striking price or, may sell the option through an options market or, may let the option expire.

not own the asset (a *naked option*), he or she might be forced to go into the market to buy the asset at its current price and then sell it at the lower striking price. Conversely, the writer of a put may be forced to take a loss when the market price of an optioned asset drops below the striking price. The writer probably would be forced to buy the asset from the option holder at a price above the market price. As you can see, writing options is highly speculative. This speculative risk can be offset by writing both puts and calls on an asset at the same striking price; this is called a **straddle**. The writer then simply makes money from the premiums charged for the options.

Options Markets

The actual buying and selling of stock options and other forms of options takes place in five major options markets: the Chicago Board Options Exchange (CBOE)—which is the largest—the American Stock Exchange (AMEX), the New York Stock Exchange (NYSEX), the Philadelphia Exchange, and the Pacific Exchange. Note that these markets are dominated by professionals and that data from the Securities and Exchange Commission reveal that four out of every five options traders lose money.

In reality, option holders rarely buy or sell the underlying asset. They simply buy and sell the options instead. The market price of puts goes down when the market price of the underlying asset goes down; it goes up when the market price of the underlying asset goes up. The market price of calls goes down when the market price of the underlying asset goes up; it goes up when the market price of the underlying asset goes down. As the option nears expiration, its value tends to fall. Actually, more than 90 percent of all options expire worthless. This should not be of grave concern, though, because the speculator-trader profits on rises and declines in the market prices of the options rather than the expiration value of the options. The various classes of options (stock options, stock-index options, and so forth) each have specified expiration dates: usually at the close of the market on the third Friday of specified months. They may last up to nine months.

Buying Options   You might ask why someone would want to buy an option from a writer or holder. Let's first consider calls: options that allow the holder of the contract to buy an asset at a specified price. The lure of calls is that the option holder can control a relatively large asset with a rather small amount of capital for a specified period of time. If the market price of the asset rises to exceed the striking price plus the premium, the holder could make a substantial profit. For example, assume Louise Mohr of St. Petersburg, Florida, buys a March stock option call on Xerox when the stock is selling for $55 per share. The striking price is $60, the expiration date is the third Friday in March, and the price (premium) of the call is $2 per share. Thus, the option contract costs her $200 ($2 × 100 shares under her control). Louise hopes that the price of Xerox will rise. She prefers not to buy the stock outright because 100 shares of Xerox would cost her a great deal more—$5,500 ($55 × 100).

For Louise to break even on the call option deal, the price of Xerox must rise to $62 before expiration, as the following formula shows:

$$\begin{aligned}\text{Break-even price} &= \text{striking price} + (\text{contract cost} \div \\ \text{(for calls)} & \qquad \text{number of shares under control}) \qquad (20\text{--}1)\\ &= \$60 + (\$200 \div 100)\\ &= \$62\end{aligned}$$

If Louise exercises the option, she can obtain the stock at $60 and sell it for the current market price of $62 (ignoring commissions). Thus, she earns $2 per share ($62 − $60), which offsets the $2 per share purchase price of the option. If the price of Xerox stock rises to $65, Louise would make a $3 profit per share on the stock for a total profit of $300. Based on her $200 investment, this amounts to a 150 percent return ($300 ÷ $200) earned over a short period. On the other hand, if the Xerox stock price had failed to reach $60 by late March, Louise's $200 in calls would have expired with no value at all and she would have lost her entire investment.

A similar logic applies when you buy puts, that is, options that allow the holder of the contract to sell an asset at a specified striking price. Puts are a conservative investment and are used to reduce market risk. For example, if you purchase 100 shares of a common stock, you hope that the market price of the stock will go up. If it goes down instead, you may suffer a loss. To reduce this risk, you could buy a put for 100 shares at a striking price close to the purchase price of the stock. The total price of the option contract might be $200 ($2 per share). If the stock price went down, you could sell the stock at the striking price, thereby hedging a loss. If the stock price went up, you could let the option expire. Of course, you would lose the money spent on the option—but you would hope to offset it by the gain from the increased price of the stock. The break-even price on a put option is calculated according to the formula

$$\text{Break-even price} = \text{striking price} - (\text{contract cost} \div \text{number of shares under control}) \qquad (20\text{--}2)$$
(for puts)

Selling Options As mentioned earlier, most option holders never exercise their right to buy or sell the underlying asset. Instead, they simply let the option expire, or they might sell the option to another party. You would want to sell a put or a call when its market price has risen sufficiently (due to changes in the market price of the underlying asset) to ensure you a profit. Or you may want to sell an option if its market price is dropping and you wish to prevent further losses.

Futures Contracts

Investors can profit from increases or decreases in the prices of various commodities (commercial products) by purchasing and selling *futures contracts*. These are marketable contracts that require the delivery of a specific amount of a commodity at a certain future date. The contracts are standardized and traded on organized securities markets, such as the Chicago Mercantile Exchange (trading commodities such as pigs, pork bellies, eggs, potatoes, and cattle); the Chicago Board of Trade (corn, wheat, soybeans, soybean oil, oats, silver, plywood); the New York Coffee and Sugar Exchange; the New York Cocoa Exchange; the International Monetary Market, which is part of the Chicago Mercantile Exchange (foreign currencies and U.S. Treasury bills); the New York Commodity Exchange (gold and silver); and the New York Mercantile Exchange (platinum). Stock futures are also traded on the New York Futures Exchange; in this case the "commodity" is S & P's 500 or the index of another exchange.

An economic need creates futures markets. For example, a farmer planting a ten-thousand-bushel soybean crop might want to sell part of it now to assure a certain price after the crop is harvested. Similarly, a food processing company may desire to purchase corn or wheat now to protect itself against sharp price increases in the future. Or an orange juice manufacturer may want to make sure of a certain supply of oranges at a definite price now rather than take the chance of a winter freeze that could push up prices.

The speculator who buys or sells a commodity contract is hoping not only that the price of the commodity will rise or fall but that it will move in the desired direction before the contract expires. Futures contracts have initial maturities of from three to eighteen months.

The lure is the potential of extremely high profits. Depending upon the commodity, the volatility of the market, and the brokerage house requirements, the speculator can put up as little as 5 to 15 percent of the total value of the contract. Some contracts require a deposit of only $300. Commissions average about $20 for each buying and selling. To illustrate the use of leverage in buying futures contracts, assume that Ronald Edelman of Washington, D.C., purchases one July wheat contract (5,000 bushels) at $3.80 per bushel. The contract value is $19,000 ($3.80 × 5,000), but Ronald puts up only $2,500. Each one-cent increase in the price of wheat represents $50 ($3.81 × 5,000 = $19,050; $3.82 × 5,000 = $19,100, and so forth). If the price rises $.50, to $4.30, by late July, Ronald will make $2,500 and double his investment.

But the potential for loss exists, too. If the price drops 50 cents, Ronald would be out $2,500. As the price declines, the broker will make a margin call and ask Ronald to provide more money to back up the contract. If Ronald doesn't have these funds, the broker can legally sell Ronald's contract and "close out" his position, which results in a true, not a paper, cash loss. Because of the risks involved, most brokerage houses require their futures customers to have a minimum net worth of $50,000 to $75,000 exclusive of home and life insurance.

A speculator can make a large investment—perhaps $50,000 to $100,000—in futures contracts with only a small amount of capital, perhaps only several thousand dollars. The rest is borrowed. Thus, it is a high-leverage game with lots of action. There are no interest charges because the credit is not technically extended until the commodity is actually delivered. Investors do not usually take possession of the commodity, as almost all contracts are just sold to someone else. Investors who have bought contracts normally sell identical contracts to close out their position.

An estimated 85 to 90 percent of investors in the futures market lose money; about 5 percent make good profits (mostly the professionals) and the remaining 5 percent break even. For every winner there is a loser. The buyer of a futures contract benefits if the price of the commodity increases, but the seller suffers. When prices decline, the reverse is true. Thus, mathematicians describe futures trading as a *zero-sum game.* That is, the total wealth of all futures traders remains the same, as the trading simply redistributes the wealth among the traders. Thus, the real rate of return on futures contracts would be zero if there were no transaction costs.

The winning speculators in futures contracts study technical analyses, use the services of a good broker, keep informed, learn to sell short as well as buy long, trade only in active markets, trade only during major market moves, diversify their holdings into several commodities, cut losses short, keep accurate records, and hope. The losing speculators do the same.

Investors who want the glamour and high profit potential of commodities futures but fewer risks can invest in a public commodities

Program Trading

Program trading is the term used to describe the use of computer software programs to generate investment activity. In recent years, software programs have been developed to monitor price fluctuations continuously in the stock, options, and futures markets. The programs have built-in guidelines that instantaneously trigger—and actually place—buy and sell orders when differences in the prices of the various instruments are great enough to provide a profit. Program trading is used by the large institutional investors, who place buy and sell orders in large blocks of ten thousand or more units. Because such large blocks are being traded and many traders are reacting at the same time to the same information, the large number of transactions can have an impact on prices in the markets. This impact can be seen most readily during the so-called triple witching hour. The *triple witching hour* occurs four times per year in the hour prior to the moment (4:15 P.M. EST, on the third Friday of March, June, September, and December) when stock options, stock index options, and stock index futures all expire at once. During this hour the Dow Jones Industrial Average and other indexes have been known to drop by 2 to 5 percent, a steep decline in so short a time period. Program trading has also caused declines at other times when many large traders all move in the same direction at the same time. Fortunately, the market usually recovers within a week or so—but if you wanted to sell during one of these drops you could find yourself taking an unanticipated loss. For the small investor, it might be best to stay out of the market on the days immediately prior to the triple watching hour. On the other hand, the speculative investor might choose this as an opportune time to act.

fund, which operates much like a mutual fund. Losses cannot exceed the amount invested, and most funds close down if assets fall to 50 percent of the original capital. In recent years more than three-fourths of such funds significantly outperformed S & P's 500 stock index.

When to Sell High-risk Investments

To make speculative investments, you need an even temperament and a strong stomach. Since you will probably suffer several sharp short-term losses for every single super-successful investment, you must have sufficient resources to ride out losses and make high-risk investments only with dollars you can afford to lose. It is imperative for you to study a particular area of high-risk investments carefully and develop considerable technical expertise before actually investing; knowledge does not guarantee success but it helps the odds somewhat. In addition, you should choose a brokerage firm that specializes in your particular area of high-risk investments and watch the investments daily to reduce losses and maximize gains. Below are some suggestions on when to sell high-risk investments.

1. **Act when investment targets are reached** You should set investment targets for gains and losses and always take actions to remain within them. For example, a purchaser of warrants might decide to sell when profits reach 30 percent (or when losses reach 20 percent). In a rising stock market, the price of a common stock could be pushing up the value of a warrant sharply, perhaps even 30 percent in a few days. The speculator should wisely avoid the greedy desire to hold the warrant and further increase profits by selling for the profits when the return reaches a preestablished goal. This approach keeps you from holding on too long only to watch the value of your investment drop dramatically.

2. **Cut losses short** You should cut losses short by graciously and faithfully accepting losses when they occur. For example, an option you purchased at 3 that has now declined to 2 has caused you a loss of $33\frac{1}{3}$ percent. If you had earlier decided to sell when losses reach 20 percent, the time to sell is now (or an hour ago). You are ill-served by "leveraging down" in high-risk markets, perhaps by buying another equal amount of options at 2 hoping that a climb in price to $2\frac{1}{2}$ will recoup all losses.

3. **Consider using technical analysis** Technical analysis is a tool that can help you make buying and selling decisions. We are not espousing a particular type of technical analysis or a single advisory service, but we recognize that technical analysis helps some investors make intelligent decisions. Indeed, the recommendations of some prominent technical analysts (such as Joseph Granville) are so closely watched that market swings often occur because of their advice. This approach may also alert you to the thinking of other speculators.

4. **Be patient** You need to be patient before selling tangible assets such as rare coins, stamps, art, and diamonds. The high sales commission costs on these assets can offset most of the paper gain achieved in a year or two. Such assets usually should be held about five years for maximum appreciation.

5. **Use contrarianism** Consider practicing *contrarianism*. This investment philosophy suggests that once the general public has seized upon an idea its usefulness is over and the wise investor should take the opposite action. For example, if after a few days of notable rises in the stock market indexes, the public thinks that the market is in for a sharp increase, then it is already too late to act and take advantage of rising prices. The contrarian would believe that a market correction is about to occur and would sell before the "herd" of other investors sells. The contrarian might also buy some put options, expecting the market

to decline. This approach will help you avoid the peaks and valleys of the market.

6. **Use arbitrage**   You might consider using *arbitrage.* This is the simultaneous purchase and sale of the same security, option, or futures contract in different markets, to profit from unequal prices. For example, assume that silver futures for August delivery sell for $10.67 an ounce, and silver slated for delivery in October of the following year (fourteen months later) sells for $11.67. The $1 spread partially represents the cost of storage and cost of capital for the fourteen months. To profit, you could purchase one thousand ounces of the August silver (taking delivery at that time) and simultaneously sell a contract for October of the next year. Come next October, you would simply deliver the silver purchased and take home a 9.4 percent ($100 ÷ $10.67) profit, less expenses. Arbitrage is used frequently by astute high-risk investors and is a technique often used by program traders.

Summary

1. Speculative investments are investment transactions involving considerable risk for the chance of large gains. Thus funds used for speculative purposes should be only those which one can afford to lose.

2. Investors most often purchase investment-grade diamonds for long-term appreciation rather than for short-term speculation.

3. The price of precious metals, such as gold, silver, and platinum, tends to increase in times of economic, military, and political turmoil, especially if inflation rises quickly.

4. Buying collectibles, such as stamps, art, and rare coins, also provides an additional feeling of personal satisfaction as it can become a hobby.

5. Rights have an intrinsic financial value and if bought on margin can become quite a speculative investment.

6. A warrant has a speculative value until the expiration date, after which it is worthless.

7. The speculative investor can profit in both buying and selling stock options.

8. Profit can be made in the volatile area of futures contracts as increases or decreases in the prices of various commodities occur.

9. Investors should consider selling high-risk investments when they have achieved their target for gains or losses or to cut losses short.

Modern Money Management

Belinda Invests in Commodity Futures

For months, Belinda has been cultivating a new and a very wealthy customer for the stock brokerage firm where she works. Last week, her hard work paid off in the opening of a $500,000 account. In addition to her commission, Belinda was rewarded with a $3,000 bonus by her boss. Since this money was totally unexpected, Harry suggested that Belinda do whatever she wished with the money. She has decided to invest in commodity futures since she can do so through her employer without paying commission fees. For $3,000 she purchased two corn futures contracts (5,000 bushels each) at $2.40 per bushel.

1. What is the total value of Belinda's investment, and what percentage of the total investment is borrowed?
2. If the price of corn goes up $.10 per bushel, what are the return and yield on Belinda's investment?
3. If the price of corn goes down $.05 per bushel, calculate Belinda's paper loss in dollars and as a percentage.
4. Given the loss in number 3 and a margin requirement of 12.5 percent, how much more money would Belinda need to put up to meet the margin call? (See p. 553 in Chapter 17.)

Key Words and Concepts

arbitrage, 631
call, 624
carat, 618
clarity, 618
collectibles, 619
contrarianism, 630
diamond, 618
futures contracts, 627
numismatist, 620
option, 624
option holder, 624
option writer, 624

philately, 620
pre-emptive right, 621
program trading, 629
put, 624
right, 621
speculative investment, 617
stock option, 624
straddle, 625
swinger, 624
triple witching hour, 629
warrant, 622
zero-sum game, 628

Review Questions

1. What distinguishes speculative from other investments?
2. What factors must an investor be concerned with when investing in diamonds?
3. Members of what organization have the responsibility of grading and certifying the authenticity of diamonds?
4. What seems to be the primary reason people invest in precious metals.
5. What type of return may be had from an investment in precious metals?
6. How can investors hope to benefit from buying collectibles?
7. What value is afforded stockholders who take advantage of their pre-emptive rights?
8. What is the distinction between rights and warrants?
9. Of what value are stock options for a holder of stock?
10. What are the rights of option owners?
11. Identify the risks of writing a naked option.
12. What is a futures contract? Identify examples of the types of commodities that are traded with one.
13. How can an investor gain by investing in futures contracts?
14. Why is investing in futures contracts a high-leverage investment?
15. How has program trading affected the volatility of various financial markets?
16. What are the six criteria to use as guidelines when considering selling high-risk investments?

Case Problems

1. Anna Hall of University Park, Pennsylvania, inherited over $100,000 in cash from her deceased husband. She has a house almost paid for, a good life insurance plan for herself and her two children, and several thousand dollars in secure savings accounts. Also, she inherited over $150,000 in stocks and bonds that bring her more than $1,000 a month in extra earnings. In addition, insurance guarantees her a monthly income of $1,800 until her death. Anna talked to an investment counselor about making some high-risk investments. Since she has a steady income, she feels she can absorb any losses without detriment to herself or her children.

a. Considering all the above information, do you feel that Anna is in a position to make high-risk investments?

b. What precautions should Anna take before making high-risk investments?

c. Assuming that Anna knows little about high-risk investments, advise her as to the most important positive and negative features of the major high-risk investments available today.

2. Gail Reichbach of Ypsilanti, Michigan, recently purchased 200 shares of Upjohn Pharmaceuticals common stock at $93 per share. She purchased the stock because the company is testing a new drug that may be a significant medical breakthrough. Already the stock's value has risen $8 in three months, in anticipation of the Food and Drug Administration's approval of the new drug. Many observers feel the price of the stock could reach $100 if the drug is successful. If it is not the breakthrough anticipated, however, the price of the stock could drop back to the $85 range. Gail is optimistic but feels she should hedge her position a bit, so she has decided to purchase two nine-month Upjohn 100-share puts for $3 per share at a striking price of $93 per share. Ignore commissions when answering the following questions.

a. What price would the Upjohn stock need to reach for Gail to break even on her investment?

b. How much would Gail gain if she sold the stock for $102 six months from now?

c. How much would Gail lose if the price of the stock dropped to $85 in six months?

Suggested Readings

"Can You Bank on Bordeaux?" *Esquire,* May 1987, pp. 61–62. The difficulties of investing in wine for future appreciation.

"Collectors Cotton to Texas Bargains." *Forbes,* March 9, 1987, pp. 144–146. Distressed prices of oil have provided bargain-basement prices for collectibles.

"Getting Your Fix from Coins." *U.S. News and World Report,* June 15, 1987, pp. 53–54. Interest in various gold coins increases.

"Gold Is Back." *Changing Times,* September 1987, pp. 95–101. Detailed suggestions on building a portfolio to include gold, gold stocks, and gold mutual funds.

"How to Get the Most from Gold This Year." *Money,* January 1987, pp. 137–142. Suggestions on investing in shares of gold-mining companies, coins, or bullion.

"Mortgage Rates: Catch the Best Deal." *Changing Times,* September 1987, pp. 76–80. How to go about finding the best mortgage deal.

"The Right and Wrong Ways to Buy Gold." *Money,* August 1987, pp. 47–54. How to decide to buy gold and in what form.

"Silk Purses or Sows' Ears?" *Changing Times,* July 1987, pp. 59–63. The difficulties of predicting winners in commodity investing.

"Vintage Investments." *Changing Times,* July 1987, pp. 72–78. Collecting, selling, and trading fine wines.

"A Study in Art Investment." *Consumers' Research,* January 1987, pp. 23–25. Warnings about investing in art.

BROKERAGE SERVICES

Your IRA Custodial

Agreement &

ESTing

ND

PART SIX

Retirement and Estate Planning

CHAPTER 21

Social Security and Other Retirement Plans

OBJECTIVES

After reading this chapter, the student should be able to

1. explain the procedures for estimating retirement expenses and income.

2. describe how to qualify for the Social Security retirement program and the role Social Security plays in retirement planning.

3. calculate the relative benefit of tax-sheltered versus non-tax-sheltered retirement plans.

4. describe the characteristics of company retirement plans.

5. list and describe other supplemental company retirement plans.

6. explain the purposes and benefits of personal retirement plans.

7. discuss how investment strategies change during retirement.

Your retirement may seem to be so far in the future that you needn't worry about it for years. However, you will have financial freedom and security during your retirement years only if you make them happen. This chapter first discusses the whys and hows of retirement planning and then examines the limited retirement benefits of Social Security. Various additional sources of retirement income are explored next: tax-sheltered pension plans, other supplemental corporate retirement plans, and personal pension plans. The final section relates retirement planning and your investment strategy.

Planning for Retirement

Today's retirees are healthier, live longer, are better educated, and have higher expectations than those of earlier generations. When they retire, their goals are much like their preretirement goals—they want the good life. The time to begin planning for retirement is when you are young, although it is not easy. Many young people have enough difficulty balancing their budgets, saving for a down payment on a home, buying furniture, and paying insurance premiums, and must postpone putting away money for their retirement years.

If you plan now, you will avoid the task of having to accumulate retirement money in a hurry, and you will be able to accumulate a larger amount. For example, if you invest $1,000 a year for twenty years compounded at 8 percent, your retirement amount will be $45,760. If you had started ten years earlier (a total of thirty years), the amount would be $113,300 (see Appendix A2).

Estimating Retirement Expenses

Experts estimate that retirees need 65 to 80 percent of their preretirement income to live comfortably. This varies according to retirement lifestyle, of course. Retirement in large cities costs more than in rural areas, and those who want to travel will need more than the average retirement income. Expenses may increase due to growing medical costs as well as financial responsibilities for children, parents, or other relatives and decrease for work-related transportation and clothes. By retirement age, most people will have paid off their home mortgages and will no longer need much, if any, life insurance coverage; in addition, income and Social Security taxes will be either eliminated or significantly reduced.

Table 21–1 shows a sample retirement budget for a couple. Expenditures in the fifth year preceding retirement amounted to $24,300. They might drop to $16,450 during the first year of retirement, or only 68 percent of the preretirement amount ($16,450 ÷ $24,300). Note that some expenditure amounts could increase and others decrease.

People near retirement age can probably estimate expenditures quite accurately and develop a retirement budget with considerable confidence. For proper estimates, the factor of inflation must be in-

TABLE 21–1
Sample Retirement Budget for a Couple

Items	Annual Expenditures in Fifth Year Preceding Retirement	Expenditures in First Year of Retirement (Ignoring Inflation)
Food	$ 3,000	$ 3,000
Housing (including $5,000 in preretirement principal and interest mortgage payments)	7,200	2,200
Clothing	1,200	600
Transportation and related insurance	2,400	2,100
Savings	1,200	900
Life insurance	400	0
Health insurance (out-of-pocket)	1,200	2,800
Medical expenses (out-of-pocket)	1,000	1,850
Leisure and travel	1,200	3,000
Social Security taxes	1,500	0
Income taxes	4,000	0
Totals	$24,300	$16,450

cluded in the calculations. Appendix A1 lists factors that can be used to adjust for inflation when estimating expenses or income. For example, assuming an inflation rate of 5 percent, and five years until retirement, the factor is 1.276. Thus, if the couple in Table 21–1 plans to retire in five years, their $16,450 estimate in current dollars would equal $20,990 after 5 percent annual inflation ($16,450 × 1.276).

People farther away from retirement age have a harder time estimating needed expenditures and accepting the reality of their estimates. For example, if the above couple plans to retire in twenty years, their $16,450 estimate in current dollars would be equal to $43,642 after 5 percent annual inflation ($16,450 × 2.653).

Estimating Retirement Income

Historically, income has risen at a pace just above inflation, although few people receive substantial real income growth during times of high inflation. Many retirees will receive income in the form of Social Security retirement benefits and company pension payments from an employer, totaling perhaps 35 to 60 percent of preretirement income depending on final salary amount. Generally, the larger your final salary amount, the smaller the percentage of retirement income composed of company pension benefits and Social Security payments. Thus, you may need to supplement your retirement income with various personal pension plans.

Social Security Retirement Benefits

In 1935 President Franklin D. Roosevelt signed the Social Security Act and commented that "we have tried to frame a law which will give some measure of protection to the average citizen and to his family . . . against poverty-ridden old age." The Social Security program continues today, with more than 38 million pension and disability checks mailed monthly.

Numerous changes in the program and increases in benefits have occurred through the years, but the focus has remained the same: to provide Americans with a floor of protection against the loss of income from retirement, disability, or death of a family wage earner. Actually, the modern Social Security program is a compilation of eleven social programs, including social insurance, public assistance, welfare services, and children's benefits. In this chapter we will examine Social Security from the perspective of retirement benefits.

Funding for Social Security benefits comes from a payroll tax split equally between employee and employer. It is a mandatory program, and the Social Security taxes withheld from your wages are called FICA taxes (for Federal Insurance Contributions Act). Amounts withheld are deposited in the Social Security trust accounts. Figure 21–1 illustrates how the Social Security system works. Social Security benefits constitute one of the most important assets in the life of a wage earner.

Making Contributions to Social Security

Social Security "contributions," in reality, are taxes. In 1949 the maximum annual contribution by a worker was $30, in 1959 it was $120, in 1969 it was $374.40, and in 1979 it was $1,403.77. Congress frequently raises both the tax rate and the earnings base. Wage earners pay Social Security only on wage income up to the *maximum taxable yearly earnings*. This is the base amount to which the Social Security tax rate is applied and it determines the maximum amount due; taxpayers with

FIGURE 21–1
How Social Security Works

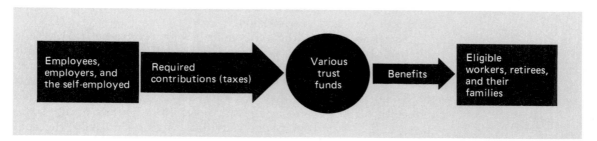

wage income higher than this amount do not have to pay additional Social Security taxes. The maximum taxable yearly earnings figure is adjusted each year for inflation.

For example, the Social Security (SS) tax rate in 1987 was 7.15 percent on the first $43,800 earned. To illustrate, SS law required that a person earning $43,800 pay the maximum Social Security tax of $3,131.70, but a person earning $25,000 paid only $1,787.50 ($25,000 × .0715). Self-employed workers pay a higher tax rate because their contributions are not matched by an employer. In 1987, for example, a self-employed person paid 14.3 percent of net income less a FICA tax credit for a real rate of 12.3 percent. This compares to the employee rate of 7.15 percent. By 1990 self-employed people will be paying 15.3 percent (equal to the 7.65 percent rate for employees plus the 7.65 percent projected for employers for that year), and the special tax credit will no longer be permitted.

Large increases in the amount of the Social Security tax have been made in recent years to ensure that the system remains financially solvent. Increases have been needed because (1) people are living longer and retiring earlier; (2) inflation has pushed up costs since many benefits are legally tied to increases in the consumer price index; (3) greater and more liberal benefits have been granted by Congress to Social Security recipients; and (4) there have been stubborn problems in the economy. In addition, the ratio of people paying in to the system and people receiving benefits has changed dramatically over the years. In 1950, for example, there were sixteen workers for every person receiving benefits; today there are only 3.2 workers. Projections suggest that in 2025 there will be only two workers for every one person receiving benefits.

Who Can Receive Social Security Benefits?

When a worker retires, various members of the family can receive benefits: the retiree; unmarried children under eighteen, or nineteen if still in high school; unmarried children eighteen or over who were severely disabled before age twenty-two and who are still disabled; retiree's spouse if aged sixty-two or over; and retiree's spouse under age sixty-two if caring for a child under sixteen (or over sixteen and disabled) who is receiving benefits. Electing to delay receipt of Social Security benefits beyond age sixty-five results in a monthly benefit increase of 3 percent for each year (one-quarter of 1 percent for each month). Starting in 1990, the credit will be gradually increased until it reaches a total of 8 percent a year in 2008.

Social Security retirement benefits can be received as early as age sixty-two. But if you start receiving benefits before age sixty-five, your benefit rate is permanently reduced to take account of the longer period of likely benefits. The size of the reduction depends on the benefits received before age sixty-five (see Table 21–2). For example, there is a reduction of 20 percent at age sixty-two; 13⅓ percent at age sixty-three; and 6⅔ percent at age sixty-four. Starting in 2000, the full-

TABLE 21–2
Determining Social Security Benefits for Early Retirement

Reduction Months	Reduction Factor	Reduction Months	Reduction Factor
1	.994	19	.894
2	.988	20	.888
3	.983	21	.883
4	.977	22	.877
5	.972	23	.872
6	.966	24	.866
7	.961	25	.861
8	.955	26	.855
9	.950	27	.850
10	.944	28	.844
11	.938	29	.838
12	.933	30	.833
13	.927	31	.827
14	.922	32	.822
15	.916	33	.816
16	.911	34	.811
17	.905	35	.805
18	.900	36	.800

Source: Social Security Administration, "Estimating Your Social Security Retirement Check: Using the Indexing Method," January 1987.
Note: This chart can be used to determine the monthly retirement benefit for Social Security recipients who choose to retire at ages sixty-two to sixty-four. Multiply their basic monthly benefit at age sixty-five by the reduction factor corresponding to the number of months they will be collecting benefits prior to reaching age sixty-five.

benefit age will be gradually increased until it reaches sixty-seven in 2027. This change affects people born after 1937.

Qualifying for Social Security

Nine out of every ten Americans employed in this country are covered by the Social Security program. Some federal, state, and local government employees are exempt because their employers have set up other plans. To qualify for benefits, you need credit for a certain amount of employment (quarters of coverage) in any work covered by Social Security, including part-time and temporary employment, and the employment need not be consecutive. Military service also provides credits. *Quarters of coverage* are calendar quarters accredited by the Social Security Administration (SSA) based on a minimum total earnings in a calendar year. For example, in 1987 workers receive one quarter of credit if they earned $465, and the annual maximum of four quarters of credit if they earned $1,860 (4 × $465). The quarterly dollar figure is raised annually to keep up with inflation.

It is important that your earnings records with the SSA are up to date and accurate. A *statement of earnings,* the SSA's record of your lifetime earnings covered under Social Security regulations, can be requested at any time from the SSA (Box 57, Baltimore, MD 21203). The

TABLE 21–3
Length of Work Requirements for Social Security Benefits

Type of Benefits	Payable to	Minimum Years of Work under Social Security
Retirement	You, your spouse, child, dependent spouse 62 or over	10 years (fully insured status) (If age 62 prior to 1991, you may need only 7¾ to 9¾ years.)
Survivors[a]		
Full	Widow(er) 60 or over Disabled widow(er) 50–59 Widow(er) if caring for child 18 years or younger Dependent children Dependent widow(er) 62 or over Disabled dependent widow(er) 50–61 Dependent parent at 62	10 years (fully insured status)
Current	Widow(er) caring for child 18 years or younger Dependent children	1½ years of last 3 years before death (currently insured status)
Disability	You and your dependents	If under age 24, you need 1½ years of work in the 3 years prior to disablement. If between ages 24 and 31, you need to work half the time between when you turned 21 and your date of disablement. If age 31 or older, you must have 5 years of credit during the 10 years prior to disablement.
Medicare		
Hospitalization (Part A: automatic benefits)	Anyone 65 or over plus some others, such as the disabled	Anyone qualified for the Social Security retirement program is qualified for Medicare Part A at age 65. Others may qualify by paying a monthly premium for Part A.
Medical expense (Part B: voluntary benefits)	Anyone eligible for Part A and anyone else 65 or over. (Payment of monthly premiums required.)	No prior work under Social Security is required.

Source: U.S. Department of Health and Human Services, 1987.
[a] A lump-sum death benefit no greater than $255 is also granted to dependents of those either fully or currently insured.

information will help you calculate an estimate of benefits and enable you to compare it with your personal records for any discrepancies.

The number of quarters of coverage determines your eligibility for benefits. The Social Security Administration has four statuses of eligibility (listed below), and Table 21–3 shows the length of work requirements for benefits.

1. **Fully insured** This status requires forty quarters of coverage for people born after 1929 and provides the worker and/or family with benefits under the retirement, survivors', and disability programs. Once attained, this status cannot be lost even if the person never works again. Fully insured status is required to receive

retirement benefits. Fully insured does not imply that full benefits will be received as the dollar amount of benefits depends on the level of earnings during the working years.

2. **Currently insured** This status requires six quarters (one and one-half years) of coverage of the most recent twelve quarters (three years) and provides for some survivors' or disability benefits but no retirement benefits. To remain eligible for survivors' and disability benefits, workers must continue to earn at least six quarters of the most recent twelve or meet a minimum number of covered years of work established by the Social Security Administration (see Appendix B).

3. **Transitionally insured** This status applies only to workers who reach the age of seventy-two without accumulating forty quarters (ten years) of credit. They are eligible for limited benefits.

4. **Not insured** This status applies to workers who have less than six quarters of credited work experience and are under age seventy-two.

Calculating Social Security Benefits

There are two methods of calculating Social Security benefits, the indexing method and the old method. Since 1984, laws require the use of the *indexing method,* which revalues previous wage earnings in terms of current wage levels by multiplying each year's income by an index factor announced annually by the Social Security Administration. One result of indexing is that it is possible only to "guesstimate" retirement benefits, as the indexing formula for future years is unknown; in 1987 the maximum basic monthly benefit was $789, and this figure increases every year. Social Security benefits are exempted from income tax by the federal government until a recipient has an adjusted gross income plus municipal bond interest and 50 percent of Social Security benefits of $25,000, or of $32,000 for joint returns.

The second approach to determining Social Security benefits is the *old method.* This method, used for persons reaching age sixty-two prior to 1979 and optional for those reaching age sixty-two in 1979–1983, uses current dollars to determine Social Security monthly payments. Because the old method will soon be phased out we will not cover it in detail. Contact your local Social Security office if this method applies to you or someone of interest to you. Appendix B provides a detailed example of the calculation of Social Security retirement benefits using the indexing method.

Receiving Supplemental Security Income

If you do not qualify for Social Security, if you have not been able to plan financially for retirement or have had health problems that wiped out all your assets, the federal *supplemental security income (SSI)* program will provide you with limited monetary benefits. To qualify, you must have no more than $1,500 in cash ($2,250 for a couple), but you can own your home, automobile, and personal belongings of reasonable value. Most states pay a supplemental benefit in addition to the federal SSI payments.

Tax-sheltered Retirement Benefits

A *tax-sheltered (qualified) retirement plan* is approved by the IRS for special tax advantages that reduce taxes and increase retirement benefits. Many employer-sponsored retirement plans—pensions, 401(k) plans, and 403(b) plans—are tax-sheltered plans, as are personal retirement plans such as individual retirement accounts (IRAs), simplified employee pension (SEP) plans, Keogh plans (pronounced "key-oh"), and certain annuity plans. (These terms are defined later in this chapter.) Most contributions to such retirement plans are not taxable until withdrawn and can be used to reduce current taxable income. In addition, taxes on income and capital gains from the retirement plan are deferred until the income and capital gains are paid out as retirement benefits or withdrawn early.

Tax-deductible Contributions

The benefits of tax-sheltered retirement plans are tremendous compared to ordinary savings and investment plans. First, because all or at least a portion of contributions to IRS-approved plans are an adjustment to income, the current year's tax liability is lowered. Second, since income and gains are not taxed until withdrawn, the funds in the plan can grow tax-free.

Table 21–4 illustrates how contributions to an IRA, Keogh, or most other tax-sheltered plans reduce current taxes. As shown, a single person with a taxable income of $17,000 who placed $2,000 into a tax-sheltered retirement plan saved $300 in taxes. In essence, the taxpayer put $1,700 ($2,000 − $300) into the retirement plan, and the government put in the remaining $300. A taxpayer in a higher tax bracket gained even more. A single person with taxable income of $40,000 saved $560 in taxes (based on 1988 tax rates) by making a $2,000 contribution to a tax-sheltered retirement plan.

Taxes Deferred on Earnings

Contributions to tax-sheltered retirement plans also reduce taxes in the future. Because contributions, interest, dividends, and capital gains are not taxed until funds are withdrawn from the plan, the investments have more opportunity to grow and compound in value. When the funds are finally taxed on withdrawal some years later, the taxpayer will probably be in a lower tax bracket.

For example, if a regular savings account had interest income of $1,200, a single person with a $30,000 taxable income would have to

TABLE 21–4
Tax Savings with Tax-sheltered Retirement Plans
(Single Person)

	Person A	Person B
Without tax-sheltered plan		
Taxable income (after deductions and exemptions)	$17,000	$40,000
Final tax liability	2,550	8,879
Marginal tax rate	15%	28%
With tax-sheltered plan		
Taxable income (after deductions and exemptions)	$17,000	$40,000
Less contribution to the plan (an adjustment to income)	− 2,000	− 2,000
Taxable income with plan	15,000	38,000
Tax liability	2,250	8,319
Tax savings		
Tax liability without tax-sheltered plan	$ 2,550	$ 8,879
Tax liability with tax-sheltered plan	− 2,250	− 8,319
Tax savings	$ 300	$ 560

pay $336 in additional taxes (marginal tax rate 28 percent × $1,200); only $864 would be available for earnings the next year ($1,200 − $336). But a tax-sheltered retirement plan permits the full $1,200 to be retained.

Results of Tax-sheltered Investments

If you want to be a millionaire at retirement, you need only invest $3,000 annually for forty years at a 9 percent tax-free return. Figure 21–2 shows the totals earned with this investment plan for ten, twenty, thirty, and forty years (calculations based on figures in Appendix A2).

FIGURE 21–2
How Tax-sheltered Money Grows ($3,000 invested annually at 9 Percent)

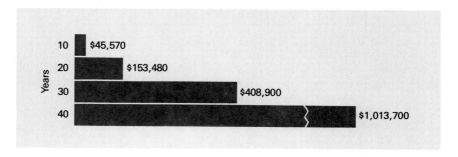

It is important to begin a tax-sheltered retirement plan at an early age. Investing $3,000 a year in tax-sheltered plans for twenty years yields you a total of $153,480, but starting investments ten years earlier (for a total of thirty years) yields $408,900.

Tax-sheltered retirement plans are obviously beneficial, but not all will benefit to the same degree from such plans. By now it should be clear that those in the highest tax bracket will benefit most from any plan that shelters income from taxation. Regardless of your tax bracket, however, there are three things you can do to maximize the benefits you receive from a tax-sheltered retirement plan. First, begin your plan as soon as possible. The value of compounding increases with the length of time the funds are left to earn income. Second, if possible contribute the maximum amount allowed by law. However, do not feel that you should wait to begin a plan until you can contribute the maximum amount annually. Third, choose investments for your plan which pay the highest earnings. The difference between an 8 percent and a 9 percent yield on an annual investment of $3,000 over thirty years is $69,000, and over forty years it is $236,400. A quick look at Appendix A2 will reveal the wisdom of obtaining the highest rates of return.

Company Retirement Plans

Only about half of all workers in private firms are covered by company retirement plans, yet over 85 percent of workers in medium to large firms are covered. According to a report of the White House Conference on Aging, the average retired couple's income comes from Social Security (35 percent), company retirement plans (30 percent), income from owned assets (20 percent), personal pensions and annuities (10 percent), and miscellaneous (10 percent). More than 350,000 companies offer retirement plans regulated by the Pension Reform Act of 1974, also called the Employee Retirement Income Security Act (ERISA). ERISA does not require companies to offer retirement plans but does regulate existing plans.

There are several important elements of company pension plans to consider: benefit participation, vesting, contributory or noncontributory plans, funded or unfunded plans, benefit computation, integration of benefits with Social Security, and distribution of benefits. Each is discussed below.

Benefit Participation

Employees must participate in a retirement plan to be eligible for any benefits. ERISA requires that employers choose one of two approaches in allowing workers to participate in the retirement plan: (1) admitting every employee who has worked for the firm for one year and who is at least age twenty-one, or (2) admitting every employee who has worked three years for the company.

| **Vesting** | ERISA places stringent requirements on **vesting,** a process by which employees obtain during their working years a legal claim to retirement benefits that cannot be taken away in case of dismissal or resignation. Retirement plans must offer government-approved vesting. Two alternatives are available. With the first, an employee is not vested during the first five years but becomes fully vested at the end of the fifth year. The second calls for employees to be 20 percent vested after three years, 40 percent after four years, 60 percent after five years, 80 percent after six years, and 100 percent at the end of seven years of service. All previous time worked for the business since age eighteen must count toward vesting. |

| **Contributory or Noncontributory Plans** | In a *noncontributory retirement plan,* the employer pays all costs. Many private firms offer noncontributory plans for employees. In a *contributory retirement plan,* both employee and employer share in the cost of making contributions. Most government employees (local, state, and federal) are enrolled in contributory plans. A typical contribution is 6 percent of the employee's salary, and the range is 3 to 8 percent. |

Corporations may establish various types of pension and profit-sharing plans. Since corporate contributions to the plans usually are not considered income to employees and are a tax deduction for the company, they may accumulate as tax-sheltered earnings. Contributions by employees to a contributory plan may or may not be taxed, depending on the type of plan. The big benefit comes when both the employer's and the employee's contributions are legally tax-sheltered, permitting all earnings to compound quickly. Taxes are finally due on the funds only as benefits are paid. For example, if an employee with a salary of $30,000 has a company contribution of 6 percent and a personal contribution of 6 percent, $3,600 ($1,800 + $1,800) will be growing tax-free.

Note that with contributory plans employees have rights to their contributions upon job termination. For example, an employee of Running Paws Catfood Company who has contributed $3,500 to a retirement fund and resigns after four years would be entitled to those monies, plus any earnings on the $3,500. Contributions made by the company, unless the employee is vested, usually remain with the firm. Any funds, whether they are employee or employer contributions, which were deposited tax-free, would be taxable upon withdrawal unless transferred into another tax-sheltered plan within specified time limits.

| **Funded or Unfunded** | Pension plans are either funded or unfunded. In a *funded pension plan,* the employer makes full formal payments annually to a trustee, who then places the funds in conservative and relatively safe investments (or annuities) so that full benefits will be available to all employees upon retirement. In an *unfunded pension plan,* retirement expenses are paid out of current earnings rather than from funds set aside to cover cur- |

rent and future liabilities. These are often called "owe-as-you-go" plans and are more risky should the company, nonprofit organization, or government agency operating the plan go bankrupt. Most state and local government retirement plans are unfunded, as is Social Security. However, the "guarantee" of those government programs comes primarily from the political pressure of retirees and current workers who expect similar benefits.

Benefit Computation

Retirement benefits are first based on the benefit computation method utilized, the defined contribution or defined benefit method. With the **defined contribution method,** the amounts contributed to the plan by the employee and employer are clearly specified, but the actual amount of the benefits is unknown until the worker retires, becomes disabled, or dies. This is because the amount available depends greatly on the success of the investments composing the retirement fund.

The **defined benefit method** fixes the level of retirement, survivors', or disability benefits based on the income and/or years of employment of the worker. For example, an employee might have a defined benefit of 2 percent for each year of service multiplied by final average income, which is an average of the last years of service as described in the retirement plan. To illustrate, a worker with thirty years' service and a final average income of $28,000 would have an annual benefit of $16,800 (30 × 2 percent = .60 × $28,000), or $1,400 a month. This amounts to a retirement benefit of 60 percent of preretirement final average income ($16,800 ÷ $28,000), which, when combined with Social Security benefits, might result in a comfortable financial retirement.

There is a growing trend to shift from defined benefit to defined contribution pension plans among the nation's largest corporations. This plan helps the companies by eliminating any unfunded pension liability but presents more uncertainty for workers about the amount of benefits actually due. On the plus side, defined contribution plans generally permit earlier vesting and easy **portability,** which is a contract clause that permits workers to take pension money to another job. Additionally, in a defined contribution plan each employee's contribution is placed in a separate account, out of reach of corporate creditors should the company go bankrupt. The ERISA law established the Pension Benefit Guaranty Corporation, which collects compulsory premiums from all covered programs and pays out benefits to employees of firms that go bankrupt. There are limits to this coverage, however.

Integration of Benefits with Social Security

Benefits from company retirement plans are sometimes integrated with benefits from Social Security. This can be detrimental, as company benefits may be reduced by the amount of Social Security benefits received by the retiree. For example, assume you retire with a company pension of $900 a month and Social Security benefits of $600 a month.

If your Social Security payments rise to $700, the company pension may drop to $800, thus offsetting the $100 increase in Social Security benefits. The net effect is that you lose ground to inflation despite raises in Social Security.

Distribution of Benefits

As indicated earlier, retirement benefits from Social Security come monthly. Three payment methods are used in company pension plans: monthly benefits for the worker's lifetime, regular benefits for a certain number of years, or a lump-sum payment upon retirement. Choosing among these alternatives is an important decision that requires careful analysis of your tax situation and financial condition, your possibilities for earning a good return on a lump-sum investment, and the financial condition of the retirement plan and company. Two important factors affecting the distribution of benefits are your time of retirement and whether you have survivors' and disability benefits.

Early or Normal Retirement?

The earlier you retire, the smaller your monthly retirement benefit will be because you will live more years as a retired person. For example, refer to Table 13–1 on page 400, which lists average life expectancies. On the average, a woman retiring at age sixty-two has nearly seventeen years of life remaining to collect retirement benefits, whereas a male retiring at age sixty-five may collect benefits for only fourteen years. Benefits for the early retiree are calculated to give, in theory, the same total dollar amount of benefits as for the person who retires at age sixty-five. Note that the U.S. Supreme Court has ruled that company retirement benefits must be the same for men and women who contribute equal amounts, even though their average life expectancies differ.

Benefits for early retirement are usually based on actuarial figures (calculations of insurance and pension risks) or a company formula. For example, the full benefit expected at age sixty-five could be reduced by 4 percent for each year a person retires before age sixty-five and an additional 2 percent for every year earlier than sixty. If you retire early—and about three-fourths of all working people do—your monthly benefits could be cut sharply.

Whether early retirement is financially beneficial will depend on life expectancy and the rate at which benefits are reduced. In the case illustrated in Table 21–5, retirement between age sixty and sixty-five appears to have little impact on lifetime benefits received but earlier retirement does have an impact. Of course, the general rule that funds obtained earlier are better than funds obtained later applies here. If you expect to live less than the average expectancy, you may be better off financially by retiring early. The opposite is true if your family history or health status indicates an extremely long life. Most employees are legally allowed to work for as long as they choose, but companies generally do not increase benefits to those who postpone retirement beyond age sixty-five.

TABLE 21–5
Impact of Early Retirement on Monthly and Expected Lifetime Pension Benefits (Woman Retiree with a $1,000 Monthly Benefit at Age 65)

Age at Retirement	Monthly Benefit	Life Expectancy in Months	Projected Lifetime Benefits
65	$1,000	208	$208,000
62	880	236	207,680
60	800	255	204,000
55	500	304	152,000

Survivors' and Disability Benefits The prospect of financial security during retirement is heartening, but survivors' and disability benefits are of even more concern to retirees who are married and/or parents. Survivors' benefits in a company retirement plan must provide for retirement payments to a surviving spouse in the event of the death of a fully vested worker. This can be waived if desired, however. For example, if you cancel your spousal benefit before retirement, your spouse will not receive any benefits upon your death, but during your retirement years your monthly benefit will be higher. This is because when a given benefit is changed to cover two people instead of one the monthly payment must be less. Unless your spouse has his or her own retirement benefits, it is usually wise to keep the spousal benefit. Fur-

Questions to Ask about Company Pension Plans

As you plan for retirement, find out as much as you can about your company's pension plan by asking the following questions:

1. When is an employee eligible to participate in the plan? Is the plan optional or required?

2. Is the plan a defined benefit or defined contribution plan?

3. How do employees become vested?

4. Is the plan contributory or noncontributory? How much does the company contribute?

5. Is the plan insured by the Pension Benefit Guaranty Corporation (PBGC)?

6. Can the plan be discontinued by the company? Can it be changed?

7. Are benefits calculated from final average pay or career earnings? How are they integrated with Social Security benefits?

8. Where are the funds invested? Does the company publish investment reports?

9. What is the earliest retirement age, and what are the reductions for early retirement or increases for late retirement?

10. Are retirement benefits guaranteed for life once you are retired?

11. What are the survivors' and disability benefits?

12. What are the procedures for applying for benefits?

thermore, federal law requires that a spouse agree in writing to a waiver of the spousal benefit.

Disability benefits in a company retirement plan usually provide for payments to employees if they become disabled while still working for the firm. The benefits are normally determined by a worker's present income, life expectancy, contributions to the retirement plan so far, and expected amount of income from Social Security.

Other Supplemental Corporate Retirement Plans

In addition to company retirement plans, many corporations offer other benefits plans to employees that can be used to help with retirement expenses. Two such plans are salary reduction plans and nonqualified deferred compensation plans.

Salary Reduction Plans

A *salary reduction plan,* also known as a *401(k) plan,* is an employer-sponsored retirement savings plan in which employees divert a portion of their salary to a tax-sheltered savings account, where it accumulates tax-free. Some employers proportionately match money saved by employees. With the 401(k) plan (named after that section of the tax code), employees of private corporations may contribute up to $7,000 per year with the combined employee/employer contributions not to exceed $30,000 or 24 percent of income, whichever is less. Employees of nonprofit organizations may contribute up to $9,500 to a similar 403(b) salary reduction plan with the same overall maximums. The funds contributed each year by the employee are in effect a reduction in income subject to tax, and, along with any employer contributions, accumulate tax-free until they are withdrawn at retirement. The funds may be administered directly by the employer or be invested in mutual funds or annuities.

You can accumulate substantial retirement funds by using a salary reduction savings plan. For example, if your contribution of $1,200 per year in such a fund was matched 100 percent by your employer for twenty-five years at an interest rate of 7 percent, it would amount to $151,800 (from Appendix A2, the calculation is $2,400 × 63.25). Because preretirement (age fifty-nine and a half) withdrawals are subject to tax and a 10 percent penalty, you should only place funds that you will not need before retirement in a 401(k) or 403(b) plan. These plans can provide substantial tax benefits when saving for retirement. Nearly one-third of the nation's full-time workers in medium-size and large organizations are enrolled in 401(k) or 403(b) salary reduction plans.

A *nonqualified deferred compensation plan* is an approved process under ERISA regulations that permits an employee and employer to agree to defer large payments for services rendered to a later date when the person is expected to be in a lower tax bracket. Highly paid athletes and executives often prefer such arrangements and frequently request that some funds be paid to them during retirement years. Deferred income is also tax-exempt until received by the taxpayer.

Personal Pension Plans

A personal pension plan can provide you with additional income during retirement years. Most people are permitted to establish one or more of the following personal pension plans: annuities, individual retirement accounts (IRAs), Keogh plans, and simplified employee plans (SEPs). Before reviewing each personal pension plan, let's consider Hobart and Charlotte Jacoby's anticipated retirement income and expenses to determine how much additional retirement income they may need. The process of analyzing their annual retirement income and expenses is shown in Table 21–6 and explained below.

1. Hobart and Charlotte estimate that their monthly Social Security retirement benefits will be $510 and $215, respectively. They assume that they will retire in ten years at age sixty-five and that inflation for those ten years will be 6 percent.

2. Hobart's monthly company pension benefit of $355 is not likely to keep pace with inflation, so he estimates it at an annual increase of 4 percent.

3. Annual income in inflated dollars provided by both Social Security and the company pension is found by adding the totals for steps 1 and 2.

4. The Jacobys estimate that they will live an additional twenty years after retirement. They can estimate the value of their Individual Retirement Account at retirement. Then from Appendix A4 they can determine the annual income from the IRA proceeds for the period of twenty years. The factor they use from Appendix A4 is 14.878 because they assume that they may invest their IRA proceeds at 9 percent and that inflation will be 6 percent, resulting in a real (after-inflation) interest rate of 3 percent. They divide the factor obtained from Appendix A4 into the proceeds of the IRA.

5. They add the totals from steps 3 and 4 to obtain their annual income for the first year of retirement.

6. They estimate annual retirement expenses in current dollars.

7. The Jacobys estimate inflation at 6 percent for the next ten years.

TABLE 21–6

Additional Annual Retirement Income Needed (for Hobart and Charlotte Jacoby) in Ten Years

1. Monthly Social Security retirement benefit

    Hobart $510
    Charlotte + 215
      Total $735
       Multiply by 12 months × 12
        Annual Social Security benefits $ 8,820
        Inflation estimate of 6% (factor from Appendix A1) × 1.791
         Inflated annual Social Security benefits $15,797

2. Monthly company pension benefits

    Hobart $355
    Charlotte + 0
      Total $355
       Multiply by 12 months × 12
        Annual company pension benefit $ 4,260
        Inflation estimate of 4% (factor from Appendix A1) × 1.480
         Inflated annual company pension benefit + 6,305

3. Annual income in inflated Social Security and company pension benefits $22,102

4. Annual income from Individual Retirement Account

    Nine years ago the Jacobys set up an IRA and have contributed $2,000 each year and plan to continue contributing until retirement. The result will be a nest egg of $92,040 (from Appendix A2, assuming a return of 9% for the 19 years; $2,000 × 46.02). This nest egg will give them an annual income of $6,186 for 20 years (their estimated retirement period) at an inflation adjusted 3% rate of return (from Appendix A4; $92,040 ÷ 14,878). + 6,186

5. Total annual income during their first year of retirement 28,288

6. Estimated annual retirement expenses $18,200

7. Inflation estimate of 6% (factor from Appendix A1) × 1.791

8. Annual expenses in inflated dollars at retirement $32,596

9. Excess (shortfall) annual income (line 5 minus line 8) − $4,308

Alternatives to make up the shortfall:

Invest $1,500 per year ($125 a month) for ten years at 9 percent. This would yield $22,789 (from Appendix A2) or $1,531 per year for twenty years (from Appendix A4). This investment could be an IRA in Charlotte's name. If the amount invested is raised to $2,000 per year, the annual benefits at retirement would be $2,042, given the same assumptions as above.

Sell their present home and buy a smaller one or rent. This might yield a lump-sum of $50,000 at retirement, providing an annual income for twenty years of $3,360, given the same assumptions.

Cut back on planned retirement expenses. $2,000 might be reasonably saved per year.

Work a year or two past age sixty-five before retiring. This might yield $16,000 to $34,000, as well as reduce the number of years retirement income is needed from twenty to eighteen, thus increasing the annual yield from investments.

8. Annual expenses in inflated dollars for the first year of retirement total $32,596.

9. The Jacobys find that their income during their first year of retirement is likely to be $4,308 less than their expenses. While this estimate only applies to the first year of retirement, it is a reasonable estimate for future years as well. This is because both their Social Security and company pension benefits will increase with inflation. (Note that an inflation factor was built into their annual benefits from their IRA when a real interest rate was used in the calculation.)

10. To make up this anticipated shortfall, the Jacobys have several alternatives from which to choose. They can (a) invest $1,500 or $2,000 a year for ten years at 9 percent, (b) increase their IRA contributions, (c) sell their present home for ample tax-free gains, (d) cut back on annual planned retirement expenses, and (e) work a year or two past age sixty-five.

Annuities

An *annuity* is a contract that provides for a series of payments to be received at stated intervals (usually monthly) for a fixed or variable time period. Annuities are usually sold by life insurance companies and are often described as being the opposite of life insurance because they provide funds during life, not after death. If you purchase an annuity, you deposit funds with an insurance company, where the funds grow as interest is earned and, possibly, more funds are deposited. Then, at a date specified in the contract, the annuity begins providing a stream of payments while you, the *annuitant* (the person receiving the annuity), are alive, often for the remainder of your life. If at age sixty-five Hobart Jacoby bought a "straight life" annuity, it would pay him a monthly income for the remainder of his life. Such an annuity might cost him $10,000 and might pay him $95 per month for as long as he lives.

Classification of Annuities As with life insurance, there are many different kinds of annuities. Some will pay for the remainder of your life; others pay only for a specified time period. Some are purchased in installments, while others are paid for in a lump sum. With some the proceeds stay fixed, but in others the proceeds vary. There are five ways of classifying annuities: (1) by plan for the payment of proceeds, (2) by number of annuitants, (3) by when benefits begin, (4) by method of purchase, and (5) by variability of annuity payment. Figure 21–3 provides a diagram of these classifications, and the discussion below expands on the diagram.

Payment of Proceeds The simplest kind of annuity is a *straight life (pure) annuity*, which pays a fixed amount per month until the annuitant dies. The example above for Hobart Jacoby illustrates a straight life annuity. Note that if Hobart lived the average number of months (from Table 13–1 we determine that a sixty-five-year-old man has a life

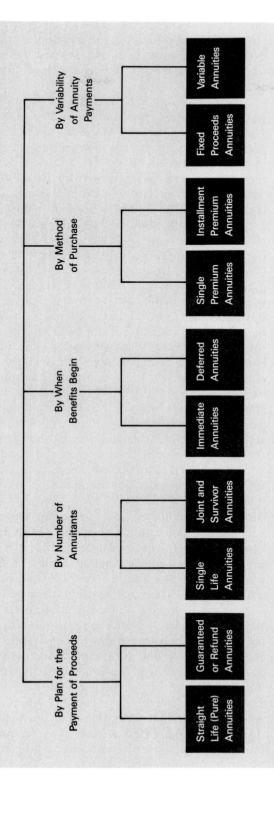

FIGURE 21–3
Classifying Annuities

expectancy of 168 months) past age sixty-five, he would collect $15,960 (168 × $95) in return for the payment of the $10,000 premium. The extra $5,960 results from the interest earned on the premium paid while it is being held by the insurance company, as it pays out only $95 at a time.

With a straight life annuity the annuitant will receive payments until death. If the annuitant dies after only ten months, the contract ends and payments cease. If the annuitant lives well beyond the average life expectancy, payments will continue unaffected. The money the insurance company "saves" from those who die early is used to make the lifetime payments to those who live a long time. You can see, then, that an annuity can serve as insurance against outliving your assets and is therefore an important retirement planning tool.

Straight life annuities are unattractive to many people because payments may cease well before all the money invested has been paid out to the annuitant. In response, several variations of *guaranteed* or *refund annuities* have been developed. An **installments certain annuity** guarantees a minimum number of payments (installments) to the annuitant and/or a beneficiary even if the annuitant dies before the minimum number of installments are paid. A **cash refund annuity** pays the beneficiary a lump sum if the annuitant dies before collecting at least the premium paid. With both types of annuities, the annuitant would continue to receive payments for a lifetime. Because the insurance company must pay some minimum amount under each of these two variations, the monthly proceeds are lower than for an otherwise equivalent straight life annuity. A third variation, the **period certain annuity,** provides payments to the annuitant, or a beneficiary if the annuitant should die early, for a fixed time period. At the end of the time period the payments would cease even if the annuitant survives. If the time period specified is sufficiently short, the payments may be higher than for an equivalent straight life annuity.

Number of Annuitants   Most annuities are **single life annuities,** which cover the life of a single annuitant. Even annuities that provide proceeds to a beneficiary are single life annuities because everything hinges on the life span of the original annuitant. Several annuitants may be covered under one annuity contract, however. Most often, this involves a husband/wife combination and the use of a **joint and survivor annuity,** which pays proceeds until the death of both annuitants. Sometimes the payment is reduced when the first annuitant dies (this allows for higher payments while both are alive), but payments will continue throughout the life of the second annuitant. When there are more than two annuitants, payments will continue until the death of the last surviving annuitant.

When Benefits Begin   Annuities may be classified as either immediate or deferred. An **immediate annuity** provides for payments to begin at the end of the first month or year after final payment of the premium. For example, an immediate annuity providing monthly payments of $400 will generate its first payment thirty days after payment of the $11,000 premium. Immediate annuities are often used as a means of distributing the proceeds of a life insurance policy (see Chapter 13). Most annuities are **deferred annuities,** which do not begin to pay off until a specified time period elapses or an event, such as a sixtieth birthday or retirement, occurs. People often use deferred annuities in retirement planning.

Method of Purchase   Annuities can be purchased with a single payment or with a series of payments. **Single premium annuities** are purchased with a single lump-sum payment. All immediate annuities are single premium annuities. **Installment premium annuities** are purchased with a series of premium payments. Proceeds do not begin until installments cease, and they may be deferred even longer if desired. Some installment premium annuities allow premium payments to vary as the purchaser's ability to pay and desires change. The payment amounts under these annuities will depend on the dollar amount of premiums paid and the amount of time the funds were left to earn interest before being drawn upon. People often use installment premium annuities in retirement planning.

Variability of Annuity Payment   The funds deposited in annuities usually grow at a fixed rate of interest stated in the contract. Similarly, the payments received once the annuitant begins drawing proceeds are fixed. With the volatility in interest rates in recent years, however, new annuity instruments have been developed that reflect changes in interest rates in the economy. These **variable annuities** provide for variable rates of return while the funds are building, and variable payments once proceeds begin. Such annuity contracts usually specify that the current interest rate never fall below some specified minimum (guaranteed) rate, such as 6 percent. Each year, while the funds are accumulating, the annuitant is notified of the rate of return paid during the year and the current balance of the account that results from the year's growth. Some annuity plans permit splitting the funds into various proportions between fixed and variable annuities and even among various investment programs (stocks, bonds, and so forth). Usually you may shift from fixed to variable and among investment plans at your discretion. Once variable annuity payments begin, they will vary upward or downward according to the success of the insurance company's investments. For example, as an annuitant you might receive $125 per month for the first year: this amount might rise to $135 as the company's investments increase in value due to a bull market or drop to $115 in a bear market. Ideally, you would shift your money out of stocks and into bonds before a bear market proceeded too far to keep the payments up to perhaps $120.

Annuities in Retirement Planning   Many people use annuities as a means for saving for retirement. There are some tax advantages to using an annuity as opposed to simply putting money in the bank. For people eligible for 401(k) or 403(b) supplemental retirement plans, *tax-sheltered annuities* can be used to defer income subject to taxation until the funds are withdrawn during retirement. The earnings from annuity accounts are not subject to taxation until they are withdrawn. This feature enhances the compounding aspect of annuities.

Be careful when purchasing annuities. Contract provisions can be complicated due to the many ways of classifying annuities. Further, the tax considerations make it difficult to compare the rate of return you are being promised with that for other investment alternatives. A final warning relates to the fact that many annuities have front and back loads similar to those for some mutual funds. These loads will affect the true rate of return you will receive.

Individual Retirement Accounts

An *individual retirement account (IRA)* allows many people who earn income to make tax-deductible payments (whether they itemize or not on their income tax returns) to their own private investment fund held by a bank, mutual fund, insurance company, or other trustee. It is a special account created by Congress to encourage people to save for retirement, and you may be able to open one even if you participate in a retirement plan at your work place. All employed people not covered by an employer-sponsored, tax-sheltered (qualified) retirement plan (married workers are considered covered if the spouse is covered by such a plan) are eligible to make IRA contributions during any year in which they earn compensation. The maximum tax-deductible contribution is $2,000 or the amount of compensation earned, whichever is less. A married couple may contribute up to $4,000 annually if each of them earns $2,000. The nonworking spouse of a working person can set up a spousal account as long as a combined maximum of $2,250 for both spouses is not exceeded. The $2,250 can be divided in any way as long as one account is not above $2,000.

Even a worker who is considered covered by an employer-sponsored, tax-sheltered retirement plan may be able to deduct IRA contributions. Single workers with incomes below $25,000 and married workers with joint incomes below $40,000 may take the full $2,000 IRA deduction. For those with incomes above these amounts the allowable deductions are reduced $1 for each $5 increase in income until the deduction is entirely phased out at $35,000 for single workers and $50,000 for married workers. For example, a single worker with an adjusted gross income of $30,000 would be able to deduct $1,000 in IRA contributions [$2,000 − ($30,000 − $25,000 ÷ 5 × 1)].

Although there are rules to follow, the IRA regulations are quite flexible. Having an IRA is a tax bargain for two reasons. First, you may use the funds you deposit into the IRA account as a reduction in your taxable income. Second, the income generated by the account over the years is not subject to taxation until it is withdrawn during retirement, thereby enhancing the power of compounding as more money is left to generate income. This sheltering of IRA investment income from taxation exists whether the money deposited in the IRA is used as a tax deduction or not. Figure 21–4 illustrates the difference between taxable and nontaxable returns for equivalent investments. After thirty years, the IRA account totals $297,200 (only $60,000 of which is the worker's contribution). A taxable account would total $183,300, only 61.7 percent of the IRA account. Note that the effects of compounding are small in the early years but quite large in later years, which demonstrates the importance of starting an IRA early. Of course, tax savings is only one of the aspects to use when comparing IRA investments with other investment alternatives.

The law sets no minimum amount for an IRA; you could contribute to an IRA account once and never contribute again. If you withdraw funds before you turn fifty-nine and a half, you must pay a 10 percent tax penalty, and the amount of your withdrawal is considered ordinary income for tax purposes. Transfer of IRA funds from one type of account to another (called a rollover) can be tax-free, but be

FIGURE 21–4

IRA vs. Taxable Returns (assumes 9% annual rate of return and $2,000 annual contribution)

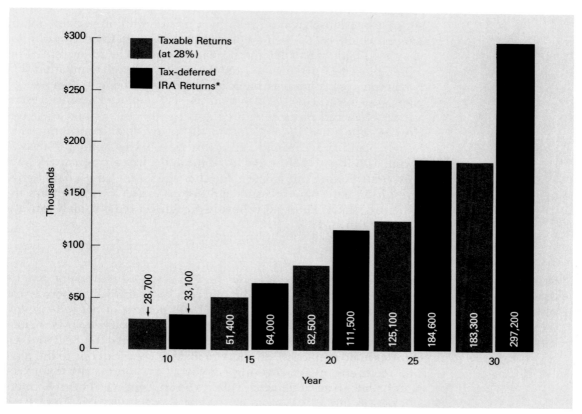

*Upon withdrawal, taxes would still have to be paid on the earnings, as well as on deductible contributions.

sure to find out if your financial institution will charge you a fee for the transfer. Withdrawal of funds from an IRA must begin by age seventy and a half at a rate no less than IRS-approved levels that estimate life expectancies.

You can simply place IRA funds in a savings account at a bank, savings and loan association, or credit union, or you can look for greater return in a money market fund, mutual fund, or insurance company annuity. You can also open a self-directed account with a brokerage firm and invest in stocks. Many experts advocate placing IRA funds in a family of no-load mutual funds, since it allows you to put dollars into a money market fund when interest rates are high and to transfer amounts to growth-focused mutual funds when interest rates decline and the values of stocks begin to go up. (Examples of such family funds are Dreyfus, Fidelity, Scudder, T. Rowe Price, Stein Roe, Neuberger Berman, and Lexington.) This kind of fund shifting does not take a particularly sophisticated investment approach, but it requires an alertness to broad economic events.

Keogh Plans

A *Keogh plan* (also called *HR-10*) allows self-employed people to make large tax-deductible payments for themselves and their eligible employees to a pension-plan fund held by a trustee who, in certain circumstances, could be the self-employed person. A defined contribution plan has a limit of $30,000 (or, if smaller, as much as 25 percent of net self-employed earned income) and this limit is indexed to inflation. The maximum contribution is higher for a defined benefit plan. Keogh plans were instituted in 1962 to motivate self-employed people to establish tax-sheltered retirement programs for themselves and their employees, who must be included in the plans. Both contributions to Keogh plans and earnings on assets are tax-free until withdrawal. Again, withdrawals before age fifty-nine and a half are penalized; however, contributions can still be made after age seventy and a half. Keogh investors face the same investment decisions as IRA owners but can also own real estate. Those who have a Keogh retirement plan can also contribute to an IRA.

Simplified Employee Pension Plans

A *simplified employee pension plan (SEP)* is a special retirement plan for the self-employed and their employees. With an SEP, a person can make tax-sheltered contributions of 13.04 percent of net self-employment income up to a maximum of $30,000. If the self-employed person also has employees, they too will be covered under the SEP and the employer and employee will share in making contributions to the plan. The requirements for covering employees are more strict than for a Keogh plan, so an SEP may not always be appropriate. The investment alternatives for an SEP are more flexible than for a Keogh, however. It is possible for someone to have both an IRA to shelter wages and an SEP to shelter self-employment income.

Investment Strategies for Retirement

Although Social Security and company pension payments may constitute from 50 to 70 percent of preretirement income, those who wish to retire comfortably and maintain their preretirement standard of living will likely need from 70 to 80 percent of their previous income. The difference in income might be made up by a part-time job; but if retirees earn too much, their Social Security benefits can be cut. A personal pension plan, such as an IRA, Keogh, or SEP, can help bridge the income gap. Figure 21–5 shows the sources of retirement income you can begin planning for now.

Investments during your retirement years should focus on a single objective: income generation. No longer can you afford to make speculative investments since you do not have the years left to recoup from poor investment decisions. Retirees would do well to review Table 14–1, which describes eight types of risks of ten different forms of investments. At this stage in their lives, investors need to reduce risks to inflation and to market volatility. Nor will taxes any longer be dominant

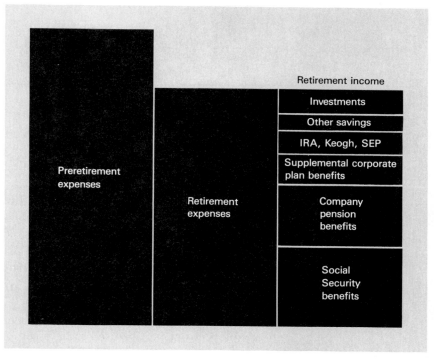

FIGURE 21–5
Planned Sources of Retirement Income

in your investment choices since retirees generally pay low income taxes or none at all.

You can take three specific actions to increase income from investments during retirement: (1) convert non-income-producing or low-income-producing assets into investments with optimum yields (sell a rental property and put the proceeds into high-yielding corporate bonds), (2) convert tax-exempt earnings into higher-yield taxables (sell a municipal bond and put proceeds into a money market fund, assuming interest rates are high), and (3) invade your capital assets to use the funds (cash a $10,000 certificate of deposit to pay living expenses). It would also be wise to own stocks with high dividend payouts and bonds with high coupons and to sell real estate for monthly installment payments.

Summary

1. Planning for retirement early can help you avoid the difficulty of having to accumulate the money needed for retirement in a hurry. The process begins with estimating retirement expenses and income.

2. Social Security retirement benefits are funded by worker- and employer-paid taxes and may provide an initial portion of income needed during retirement years.

3. The advantage of qualified retirement plans is that the contributions are tax-deductible and taxes are deferred on earnings.

4. The Employee Retirement Income Security Act (ERISA) regulates company retirement plans.

5. Other supplemental corporate fringe benefit plans available to employees that can be used to help with retirement expenses include employer-sponsored salary reduction plans and non-qualified deferred compensation plans.

6. Personal pension plans include annuities, individual retirement accounts, Keogh plans, and simplified employee pension plans.

7. Most people who retire find that Social Security and company pensions amount to 50 to 70 percent of their preretirement income, and so other planned retirement income sources need to be available for those who wish to retire comfortably.

Modern Money Management

The Johnsons Consider Retirement Planning

Recently Harry's father, William, was forced into early retirement at age sixty-three because of poor health. In addition to the psychological impact of the unanticipated retirement, William's financial situation is not good because he had not planned for retirement. This has caused Harry and Belinda to take a look at their own retirement planning. They now make about $45,000 a year combined and would like to have a similar level of income when they retire. Harry and Belinda are both now twenty-five years old, and although retirement is a long way off, they know that the sooner they start a retirement plan, the larger their nest egg will be.

1. Belinda feels that they could maintain their current level of living if their retirement income represented 75 percent of their current income after adjusting for inflation. Assuming a 4 percent inflation rate, what would Harry and Belinda's income need to be at retirement at age sixty-five? (Hint: Use Appendix A1.)

2. Both Harry and Belinda are covered by a defined contribution pension plan at work. Harry's employer contributes $1,000 per year and Belinda's $2,000 per year. Assuming a 7 percent rate of return, what would their nest egg be at retirement forty years from now? (Hint: Use Appendix A2.)

3. For how many years would the nest egg provide the amount of income indicated in question 1? Assume a 4 percent after-tax and inflation return. (Hint: Use Appendix A4.)

4. Sometimes Harry likes to dream, and one of his dreams is to retire at age fifty-five. What would the answers to questions 1, 2, and 3 be if he and Belinda were to retire at that age?

5. How would early retirement at age fifty-five affect their Social Security benefits?

6. What would you advise Harry and Belinda to do in order to meet their income needs for retirement?

Key Words and Concepts

Review Questions

1. Explain why it is important for people to begin planning for retirement when they are young.

2. Retirement expenses usually are about what percentage of pre-retirement expenses?

3. What sources of income can retirees expect?

4. Describe how Social Security benefits are financed.

5. Besides the retired worker, which family members can also receive Social Security retirement benefits based on the retired worker's account?

6. How can you qualify to receive Social Security benefits? What are the four statuses of eligibility?

7. How can you get a statement of earnings from the Social Security Administration? Why is such a statement important?

8. What is a tax-sheltered (qualified) retirement plan? In what two ways does such a plan help save on your income tax liability?

9. What federal law regulates company-sponsored retirement plans?

10. What is vesting, and how is it important to a person covered by a company-sponsored retirement plan?

11. Distinguish between the defined contribution method and the defined benefit method as used in pension plans.

12. What disadvantage arises when retirement benefits are integrated with Social Security benefits?

13. How might someone calculate the economic advantage or disadvantage of retiring early?

14. Explain why a salary reduction plan may be an important part of the overall employee benefit program.

15. Describe how an annuity differs from life insurance. What are the five ways of classifying annuities?

16. How can annuities be used to shelter income from taxation?

17. What is an IRA, and how can it be used as a tax-sheltered retirement plan?

18. Who can make tax-deductible contributions to an IRA?

19. Identify the special group of people for whom Keogh plans were devised.

20. What is the most important investment objective during retirement years?

Case Problems

1. Choosing a good job after finishing her formal education is a major objective for Marianna Kinard of Florence, South Carolina. She has many positions from which to select. some are local, some within the state, and a few several hundred miles away. Marianna has been advised to choose a company that offers her not only a good salary but also some good fringe benefits. Most of the companies that interviewed her offered similar salaries, but there was great variety in the type of pension plans available. Marianna was confused by terms such as *vesting, contributory, noncontributory, funded, unfunded,* and *defined benefit,* among others, and needs to spend time sorting them out so that she can decide where to take a job.

   a. Is Marianna overly concerned about the details of pension plans for her first job out of school? Why or why not?

   b. List some questions Marianna can ask to help her sort out the available plans.

   c. What, in your opinion, are some characteristics that would make one pension plan more attractive than another? Justify each characteristic as a positive part of a pension plan.

2. Ben Detrick of St. Louis, Missouri, age thirty-eight, and his wife, Doris, age thirty-five, have a combined adjusted gross income of $45,000. Ben works as a carpenter for a furniture company that provides no pension benefits. Doris, a part-time probation offi-

cer, is not covered by Social Security but is covered by a 403(b) retirement plan through her employer. She has contributed $1,000 per year for the past five years; her employer will match any contributions up to $1,000. Ben has always thought that his Social Security and Doris's pension would be enough for their retirement, but he is no longer so sure. He is exploring the idea of using individual retirement accounts to upgrade his and Doris's retirement plan.

a. Should Ben and Doris be concerned about his Social Security and her pension being sufficient sources of income for retirement? Why or why not?

b. If Ben were to open an IRA for himself and contribute $2,000 per year, what would be the maximum amount he could reduce their taxable income? Would there be any advantage to contributing more than the maximum? Explain.

c. Would an IRA be a wise choice for Doris? Why or why not?

d. What other tax-deductible retirement plan options might be open to Ben or Doris?

Suggested Readings

"Building a Cycle-Proof IRA." *Money*, March 1987, pp. 66–72. Alternative ways to manage your IRA funds.

"Is Your IRA Still a Good Deal?" *Consumer Reports*, January 1987, pp. 12–16. Describes benefits of making tax-deductible and nondeductible contributions to an IRA.

"Last Call for IRAs." *Changing Times*, April 1987, pp. 33–38. Details the value of IRA investment after tax reform.

"Taxes for Young Retirees." *Forbes*, April 27, 1987, pp. 71–73. Options for young retirees on taking a lump sum for early retirement.

"Using Your New Money Freedom." *Working Woman*, February 1987, pp. 31–34. Ideas on how to manage all your retirement plans, such as IRAs, Keoghs, and 401(k)'s.

"Want to Quit Early? It'll Take a Bundle." *U.S. News and World Report*, June 8, 1987, pp. 63–64. Dollar amounts needed to retire early.

CHAPTER 22

Estate Planning

OBJECTIVES

After reading this chapter, the student should be able to

1. explain how an estate transfers to heirs.
2. describe the types and characteristics of wills.
3. calculate estate taxes, given the dollar value of a gross estate.
4. discuss the use of trusts and other mechanisms to avoid estate taxes legally.

P lanning the transfer of your *estate* (wealth you accumulate over your lifetime) while you are young is not being pessimistic. It is simply wise financial behavior. Consider the following story. David, a young attorney, was working hard to establish himself professionally and make a good income for his family. He felt that with hard work his future was rosy, and he didn't see the sense in planning for his estate just yet. Most of his income was going for credit payments on the house, automobile, and furniture. He did have a small insurance policy he had bought just after leaving college, but his mother was the beneficiary since he never bothered to change the designation. David's unexpected death in an auto accident left his family with no income but the proceeds of this small policy, which his mother gave to them. At first, David's wife and child lived on Social Security survivors' benefits. Then his wife worked for several years as a waitress while she finished her bachelor's degree, and after graduating, she finally got a well-paying job with a brokerage firm. David could have spared his family some tough financial times had he faced the facts: a quarter of us will die before reaching retirement age.

This chapter first examines which assets transfer and to whom when a person dies without a will. Details about wills and letters of last instructions are next provided. The chapter ends with a look at how to avoid estate taxes through the use of trusts.

Transfers at Death

After you die, your assets are distributed. A **will** is a written instrument that directs the disposition of your assets at death, but only if the will is executed in accordance with statutory provisions. If you die without leaving a valid will, you have died **intestate**.

Don't Die Without a Will

About 75 percent of the adult population does not have a will. In most states, if you die without a will, an administrator (or conservator) is appointed by the court to liquidate your estate in accordance with the statutes of that state. A commission of perhaps 3 percent of the value of the estate is charged to cover the administrator's fee. If you have minor children, a guardian must be appointed for each, representing another cost to the estate.

The powers given to an administrator by the court are limited, and as a result the administrator must frequently seek the court's permission for specific legal actions, all of which cost money. In most states a court order is required to sell securities and real estate. If the heirs are of legal age, they all must agree upon the sale of real estate or the method of current operation; such agreement is sometimes quite difficult to obtain.

In addition to the extra costs, dying intestate gives the state the complete right to determine how your estate is to be divided, which is rarely how you would want it done. For example, in some states the court gives half the estate to the surviving spouse and half to the children and must appoint a guardian to watch over the children's finances until they reach the age of majority (eighteen in most states). Some states divide the personal property equally but give only one-third interest in any real estate to the spouse.

Generally, when single people die intestate, one-half of their estate goes to each surviving parent, and the entirety when only one parent survives. When such elderly parents die and leave their estate to other children, the first estate is taxed twice: once when it is transferred to the parent(s) and again when it is transferred to the parents' heirs.

In several states the following guidelines apply: if a person with no surviving kin except a spouse dies without a will, the spouse gets the entire estate. If a spouse has children, the spouse takes one half and the other half is divided equally by the children. If the spouse has no children but there are other kin, it becomes more complicated. When the estate is $50,000 or less the spouse gets it all. In estates above $50,000 the spouse gets $50,000, plus one-half of all personal and real property, with the remainder going to the parents of the deceased or to the surviving parent. If parents are dead their portion goes in equal shares to the deceased's brothers and sisters or to their children. If no brothers or sisters exist, the next of kin share the remainder in equal amounts. If there are no next of kin, the share goes to any surviving spouse of next of kin. If there is no such surviving spouse, the share goes to the state by right of *escheat.* This is the reverting of property to the state when there are no persons legally qualified to inherit or make claim to a deceased's property.

What seems least fair in this distribution is that if you have no children and have an estate worth more than $50,000, your spouse may have to share your assets with a distant relative. Since the purpose of intestacy guidelines is solely to distribute assets, make sure the distribution is fair by having a will.

Dower and Curtesy Rights

The *right of dower* is a widow's lifetime right to a portion of her husband's property that he acquires during the marriage. The dower right is usually for one-third of the property. The *right of curtesy* (sometimes called dower) is a widower's lifetime right to a portion of his wife's property that she acquires during the marriage, again one-third. State laws provide that if a spouse leaves a will giving a surviving spouse less than the amount given by the dower or curtesy rights, the survivor has the power to claim the legal amount.

Community property laws, which have been substituted for dower and curtesy rights in some states, distribute the property of deceased persons assuming that property acquired after marriage is jointly owned and equally shared by the spouses, no matter how much was actually contributed by either. (These states include Arizona, California, Idaho, Louisiana, Nevada, New Mexico, Texas, Washington, and Wisconsin.) *Separable property* is property wholly owned by one spouse, even in community property states; it is property that belonged to the spouse before marriage or was received as a gift or an inheritance. States that do not have community property laws, distribute property according to common law, which leaves a variety of options open to the court. For example, in some common law states the husband owns the property entirely even if the wife helped to purchase it. You should learn about the property distribution practices in your state as you begin to acquire property.

Nonprobate Property

Probate is a court procedure for settling and disposing of an estate. Many people decide that portions of their estate will transfer to others without having to go through the sometimes slow process of probate. *Nonprobate property* is an asset transferred by law or by contract without going through probate.

Transferred by Contract Life insurance is a common nonprobated property transferred by contract. The proceeds of the life insurance will be transferred to the beneficiary directly by the life insurance company. The proceeds generally will not be included as part of the probated estate for federal estate tax computations unless the policy is payable to the estate or to a trust created in the will. Money in a corporate profit-sharing or pension plan goes by contract directly to the named beneficiary as nonprobate property. Assets transferred to an established trust are similarly forwarded contractually (the importance of trusts is discussed later in this chapter). Savings bonds may also be contractually assigned, and some business assets of partnerships may be transferred from a deceased to surviving partner without being probated.

Transferred by Law The law provides that some property may be transferred without going through probate, and many people use this to escape federal estate taxes. Property can be owned by two or more persons, such as in joint tenancy or tenancy in common. *Joint tenancy* provides that when two or more persons own property, the survivor(s) get the property. (Some states use other terms to designate similar legal rights, such as joint tenancy with right of survivorship, tenancy by the entirety, or homestead.) Many married couples buy property with a *tenancy in common*, which provides that each spouse retains control over his or her interest in the property and may dispose of it in any manner at any time, thus eliminating any right of survivorship; consequently, the property interest of the deceased may or may not go to heirs without going through probate.

Wills

Mark Twain once said that "nothing is certain but death and taxes." Even after all the years of collecting income taxes from you during your life, the IRS still collects from you after death, in the form of a federal *estate tax*, which is a tax assessed on property owned and/or controlled by a deceased before it is transferred to heirs. (This definition immediately suggests a fundamental loophole in estate taxes—if property is not controlled, it will not be taxed—and we shall examine this subsequently when we discuss trusts.) The major functions of a will are (1) to reduce the tax liability on the estate of the deceased; (2) to transfer assets to particular people; and (3) to choose the executor, trustees, and other fiduciaries who will administer the estate.

The person who makes a will is called a *testator* and upon death is legally referred to as the *decedent*. A person who dies with a valid will has died *testate*, rather than intestate. Anyone at least eighteen years old and of sound mind may make a legally valid will.

An *executor* or *executrix* (female executor) is named in a will to carry out the directions and requests in the will and is provided a certain amount of legal power by the state. In most states an executor (sometimes called a *personal representative*) can dispose of personal property, retain property, make investments, hire professionals, manage real estate, collect debts, borrow, pay debts, marshall and distribute assets, appoint custodians, defend the will against legal contests, and pay taxes. It usually takes from six months to two years to probate a will,

---

Major Provisions of a Will

1. *Identification* of the testator and places of residence

2. *Introductory clause* to provide validity of the will, such as "This is my last will and testament . . ."

3. *Revocation of prior wills clause* if prior wills have been written

4. *Final instructions* for the payment of taxes, debts, funeral, burial, and administrative costs of the estate

5. *Specific bequests* for particular items, such as stamp collections or fur coats

6. *General bequests* out of the general assets of the estate that usually provide for amounts of money to be given to individuals

7. *Charitable gifts* to various organizations

8. *Allocation of residual estate statement* explaining where the remaining portion of the estate goes after the above bequests

9. *Survivorship clause* indicating the guardian(s) for children if both husband and wife die

10. *Trust provisions* to create and/or give directions to trusts

11. *Appointment clauses* to designate the executor of the estate and guardians to represent the interests of children (if any)

12. *Execution clauses* that add to the validity of the will, such as dating, witnessing, and signing

and sometimes longer. You should choose an intelligent relative or friend as executor/executrix or name a financial institution such as a trust company or bank to do the tasks required objectively.

Types of Wills

A *lawyer-prepared will* is a will drafted by an attorney and is least likely to be successfully challenged. A simple lawyer-prepared will can cost $75 to $100, and a more complex one more. A *noncupative will* is an oral will spoken by a dying individual to another person or persons. It is legal in some states but is difficult to verify. A *joint will* (also called mutual will) is a will drawn up by a married couple who have made reciprocal provisions for each other. Experts suggest avoiding a joint will, since the surviving spouse cannot change the provisions of the will years later when circumstances differ.

Some people write their own wills. A *holographic will* is entirely in the handwriting of the person signing the will and is, as some states require, dated with the same hand. For the will to be valid in the decedent's state of residence, two witnesses' signatures may be needed. Since they are not written by an attorney and may be unclear, holographic wills are frequently not honored by courts, and the deceased is assumed to have died intestate.

A *California will* (or do-it-yourself will) is a blank-form document that people can fill out themselves. California was the first state to legally recognize such forms. Note that the form does not provide for tax planning, for people who were previously married and had children, or for people with a complex estate. This extremely simple will was designed for the convenience of married couples with dependent children.

Updating a Will

Some circumstances that often cause people to consider changing a will are moving to another state, getting married or divorced, having children, having a substantial change in assets, or the death of heirs, executors, or guardians named in the will. You update a will either by writing a new will or by adding a *codicil,* which is a legal amendment to a will. A codicil should be drawn up by your attorney, witnessed, and signed.

The original copy of your will should be kept by your attorney in a safe-deposit box, and you should keep copies. Do not put the original of your will in your own safe-deposit box, since upon your death the box will be sealed (even if it is jointly held) until a court order is obtained to open it, which may take several days. Do, however, let your family know the location of your will.

Letter of Last Instructions

Many people prepare a *letter of last instructions* (also called *letter precatory*), which is a written letter in your handwriting, signed, and usually given to the executor that can include transfers of many odds and ends of personal property (both valuable and sentimental) without being made public in the formal will. Often people will put burial instructions and very sentimental items in the letter of last instructions. It is important to include information in it about the location of all your assets, such as various savings accounts and accounts at brokerage firms.

Estate Planning

Estate planning is the process of planning, reviewing, and revising efforts to reduce the tax liability on your estate and to keep probate costs low. Good estate planning will enable you to transfer the greatest amount of assets possible to heirs. We outline some of the important steps in estate planning below, but we recommend that you read further on the subject and consult with a lawyer before taking specific actions. Three major considerations in estate planning are estate taxes, gift taxes, and using trusts to avoid taxes.

Estate Taxes

Making a will gives you confidence that your assets will be divided and transferred as you wish. However, without proper planning a substantial portion of your estate may go for taxes.

Valuation of the Estate The gross value of your estate will be determined during probate. The resulting dollar amount would be your *gross estate,* which includes just about everything you own and amounts owed to you. Any estate taxes due will be paid on the *net taxable estate,* which is the gross estate, minus marital deduction, liabilities, charitable bequests, properties passed by law and contract, and the basic inheritance tax exemption. The latter is the result of 1981 tax revisions that permit a unified tax credit calculated into an exemption equivalent for each state. In 1988 and beyond, the estate of the decedent gets a tax credit of $192,800, which has the effect of reducing the net taxable estate by $600,000.

The estate tax laws also permit an unlimited marital deduction. This provides that everything left to a surviving spouse transfers tax-free. The catch is that the estate may be heavily taxed after the surviving spouse dies.

Estate Taxes To calculate the taxes on a large estate, examine Table 22–1, which lists some estate tax rates and exemptions effective in 1988. Table 22–2 shows the tax calculation given a gross estate of $940,000. The net taxable estate is $760,000, since in this example the surviving spouse was left a marital deduction of only $120,000 in the spouse's will. Applying the tax rate results in a federal estate tax of $59,400. Better estate planning with the use of trusts would have eliminated this liability and permitted more funds to transfer to heirs. State inheritance taxes may also be due. Because of the variability among

TABLE 22–1
Estate Tax Rates (Effective for 1988 and After)

(1) Base	(2) Tax	(3) Rate of Tax on Excess over Amount in Column 1	(4) Unified Tax Credit	(5) Federal Estate Tax
Under $10,000	18% of amount	—	$192,800	—
$ 10,000	$ 1,800	20%	192,800	—
20,000	3,800	22	192,800	—
40,000	8,200	24	192,800	—
60,000	13,000	26	192,800	—
80,000	18,200	28	192,800	—
100,000	23,800	30	192,800	—
150,000	38,800	32	192,800	—
200,000	54,800	32	192,800	—
250,000	70,800	34	192,800	—
300,000	87,800	34	192,800	—
500,000	155,800	37	192,800	—
600,000	192,800	37	192,800	—
700,000	229,800	37	192,800	$ 37,000
750,000	248,300	39	192,800	55,500
900,000	306,800	39	192,800	114,000
1,000,000	345,800	41	192,800	153,000

Source: Internal Revenue Service.

states, the subject is omitted here, but note that such taxes are a credit on the federal estate tax liability. A good tax attorney would be helpful with state inheritance taxes because state exemptions and deductions are much smaller than the federal amounts, which may result in a substantial state inheritance tax on a relatively small estate.

TABLE 22–2
Calculation of Estate Tax Liability (1988 Data)

Gross estate	$940,000
Less deductible expenses and contributions	− 60,000
Adjusted gross estate	$888,000
Less marital deduction	− 120,000
Net taxable estate	$760,000
Estate tax: $248,300 + 39% of $10,000[a]	$252,200
Unified tax credit	− 192,800
Estate tax liability	$ 59,400

[a] From Table 22–1. Net taxable estate of $760,000 is closest to a tentative tax base of $750,000, corresponding to a base tax of $248,300. The difference of $10,000 is multiplied by 39 percent and added to the base amount to equal a total tax of $252,200 ($248,300 + $3,900).

Gift Taxes

The government permits you to give a tax-free gift annually of up to $10,000 each to as many people as you wish. You do, however, need to report these gifts to the IRS. To be eligible for tax-free status, the gift must be considered by the IRS as having *present interest,* meaning that the recipient has an immediate and irrevocable complete right to the property. Such gifts are usually not taxed on the donor. Gifts received are also tax free, but any later income earned from the gift is taxable.

Suppose George Belton of Lenexa, Kansas, wants to give $30,000 to his nephew Jeffrey. The first $10,000 of the gift would be tax exempt. The additional $20,000 goes toward George's basic inheritance tax exemption of $600,000. When George dies, his exemption will be reduced to $580,000, as $20,000 was used earlier during his lifetime.

People may give gifts of up to $10,000 (couples may give $20,000) to reduce the size of their estate, which in turn minimizes estate taxes. People also save by giving gifts in excess of $10,000 because gifts for estate-tax purposes are valued at the time gifts were given, not later, at the death of the donor. For example, a $25,000 gift of a painting in 1988 is valued in 1988 dollars, not at its inflated value when the donor dies perhaps eight years later. Using Appendix A1 and at inflation of 10 percent, this amount of money would be valued at $53,600 (2.144 × $25,000) in 1996 and require higher taxes. Gifts are valuable for estate-tax reduction, but there certainly are limitations on how much should be given away. It should be noted that gifts of income-producing assets to children from parents are given special income tax treatment. Until the child reaches age fourteen, investment income over $1,000 is taxed at the parents' marginal tax rate, just as if it were the parents' income.

Using Trusts to Reduce Estate Taxes

If your estate is large enough to be taxed, probate can be long as well as expensive. An alternative to paying large amounts of estate taxes is to create a *trust,* which is a legal instrument that places the control of some or all of your assets with a trustee. Trusts are an extremely flexible estate-planning tool. For those who do not wish to give their assets directly to heirs, trusts offer an alternative way to provide them with benefits and, at the same time, probably reduce estate taxes. Trusts help avoid estate taxes because the assets held in trust are owned by the trust and are usually not under the control of the person setting up the trust and therefore exempt from estate taxes. Some of the important terms associated with trusts are defined below:

Trustee: person, partnership, or corporation that manages the trust for the use and benefit of the beneficiary or beneficiaries (they normally charge an annual fee of less than one-half of one percent for the services)

Beneficiary: person designated as the recipient of income funds under a trust

Remaindermen: persons named in the trust who are to receive the assets upon termination of the trust agreement

Corpus: principal or capital sum of the trust, as opposed to interest or income

Grantor, settlor, or *trustor:* person who makes a grant to set up a trust

Some grantors avoid having to manage assets by establishing a trust for themselves and receiving benefits from the trustee in the form of monthly income. This is an example of a **living trust** (or *inter vivos*), a trust created by a living grantor for the benefit of self or another. Politicians often establish a form of living trust called a *blind trust,* which prohibits the grantor from influencing the trustee's actions.

There are three forms of living trusts: revocable, irrevocable, and revisionary. A **revocable trust** is subject to change, amendment, modification, or cancellation by the grantor. This means that the assets remain a part of the taxable estate but pass through to the beneficiary without going through probate at the time of the grantor's death. An **irrevocable trust** is not subject to any modification by the grantor during his or her lifetime, thus bypassing probate and estate taxes. A **revisionary trust** is irrevocable or unchangeable for at least ten years (unless the beneficiary and/or remaindermen die), after which time it is revocable. During the irrevocable period, it is not part of the donor's estate.

Trusts used in connection with estate planning can also be **testamentary trusts** rather than living trusts. This form of trust is established and becomes effective upon the death of the grantor according to the terms written in the grantor's will. Such trusts can be designed to provide money or asset management after the grantor's death, to avoid probate, to reduce estate taxes, to provide income for a surviving spouse, to provide income for children, to give assets to grandchildren or great-grandchildren while providing income from the assets to the surviving spouse and/or children, to protect beneficiaries from mismanaging money, to protect assets given to beneficiaries from creditors, and to prevent assets from being lured away from beneficiaries. These laudable objectives can be achieved only with the assistance of an experienced attorney who specializes in trusts.

Totten Trusts A *totten trust* is typically a savings account opened at a financial institution where money is deposited in trust for a beneficiary (usually a loved one) and where the grantor maintains control over the account, including the power of withdrawal. A common purpose in establishing such accounts is for grandparents to help grandchildren pay for college expenses. Upon the death of the grantor, the funds in the account go directly to the beneficiary, thus avoiding probate. However, a totten trust does not avoid estate taxes; when the financial institution forwards the funds to the beneficiary upon the death of the grantor, it must notify the government of the account balance. Income taxes are paid by the grantor.

Short-term Trusts A short-term trust is a revisionary living trust usually established by a parent to benefit a child. The income from the capital of the trust goes to the beneficiary and the corpus is returned to the grantor at the termination of the trust. Such a trust can be a mechanism for providing a stream of income for the child, for use for college expenses or other purposes. Like gifts to children, income from the trust above $1,000 is taxed at the parents' marginal tax rate until the child reaches age fourteen.

Family Trusts   A family trust is a testamentary trust that provides benefits not to the surviving spouse but to children, to other heirs, or to some selected charity. Often a family trust provides for the education expenses of children before turning the corpus over to them at some specified age, such as twenty-five, thirty, or thirty-five.

Sprinkling Trusts   A sprinkling trust is a testamentary family trust that provides the trustee with the power to distribute trust income to the children according to their needs rather than according to a specific formula.

Terminable Marital Trusts   A terminable marital trust is a testamentary trust that gives the surviving spouse full use of the income of the trust, but the assets are untouchable and are given to remaindermen after the death of the surviving spouse.

Life Insurance Trusts   A life insurance trust is a testamentary trust designed to receive the proceeds of a life insurance policy of the decedent and distribute them to beneficiaries in a way that is more flexible than settlement options offered by life insurance companies. For example, the trustee could be instructed to increase the amount of a monthly payment in accordance with inflation or to provide extra amounts if a beneficiary attends college. The testator simply makes a trustee the beneficiary of the policy to effect the agreement.

Summary

1. If a person dies without a will (or intestate), the remaining assets are distributed according to state laws on the subject, including dower and curtesy rights.

2. A lawyer-prepared will is likely to include sections on revocation, final instructions, allocation of residual estate, and execution clauses.

3. Estate planning attempts to reduce the tax liability on an estate and transfer the greatest amount of assets possible to heirs using such techniques as gifts and trusts.

4. Trusts are legal instruments that place the control of assets with a trustee to administer in accordance with the agreement.

Modern Money Management

Belinda Helps Her Uncle Plan His Estate

Belinda has been approached by her uncle, David Lawrence, for some advice about planning his estate. She has been handling some of David's investments and he trusts her judgment on financial matters. David has a net worth of $2,340,000 and at age fifty-four is concerned about preparing his finances in such a way that as much as possible goes to his heirs according to his wishes. David has no will but has set down on paper some of his ideas. He has no wife or children but wants to provide for his mother, four nephews, Belinda, and a disabled sister.

1. What is the first thing David should do in planning his estate? Why?
2. How might David use gifts to help reduce his estate taxes?
3. Why might a revisionary trust be a good idea for David in providing for his mother and sister?
4. What other types of trusts might David use in his estate planning?

Key Words and Concepts

California will, 674
codicil, 674
community property laws, 671
decedent, 673
escheat, 671
estate planning, 675
estate tax, 673
executor/executrix, 673
gross estate, 675
holographic will, 674
intestate, 670
irrevocable trust, 678
joint tenancy, 672
joint will, 674
lawyer-prepared will, 674
letter of last instructions (letter precatory), 674
living trust, 678

net taxable estate, 675
noncupative will, 674
nonprobate property, 672
present interest, 677
probate, 672
revisionary trust, 678
revocable trust, 678
right of curtesy, 671
right of dower, 671
separable property, 672
tenancy in common, 672
testamentary trust, 678
testate, 673
testator, 673
totten trust, 678
trust, 677
will, 670

Review Questions

1. What are the primary purposes of having a will?
2. What is one of the greatest disadvantages to survivors if a person dies intestate?
3. Why should you be careful in appointing an executor or executrix when making a will?
4. Why might you need to update or change a will?
5. What is the purpose of a letter of last instructions?
6. Why is good estate planning important?
7. How can you reduce estate taxes?
8. In what way can paying a gift tax reduce your eventual estate taxes?
9. Give some reasons why people establish trusts.
10. How do a revocable trust, an irrevocable trust, and a revisionary trust differ?
11. Why might a grandparent establish a totten trust?
12. What characteristic of a sprinkling trust makes it unique among trusts?

Case Problems

1. Joe Michael of Sterling Heights, Michigan, is a thirty-four-year-old police detective earning $45,000 per year. He and his wife, Doreen, have two children in elementary school. They jointly own a modestly furnished home and two late-model cars; along with a snowmobile, these are their principal physical assets. Each is covered by a $50,000 term life insurance policy. They have about $5,000 in a joint savings account. Neither Joe nor Doreen has a will.
   a. List four possible negative things that could happen if either Joe or Doreen were to die without a will.
   b. What would be the most important negative consequence of not having a will if both Joe and Doreen were to die in some type of accident?
   c. Joe often mentions the cost of an attorney as a reason for not having a will. How might the problem of not having a will be solved at a lower cost?

2. Robert Alan of Fort Collins, Colorado, has been named executor of the estate of his aunt, a widow, who has recently died. As executor he wishes to determine the estate taxes that will need to be paid. Given the following information, answer the questions below for Robert: gross estate, $1,430,000; deductible expenses, $75,000; totten trusts for the deceased aunt's three grandchildren, $100,000 each; marital deduction, $230,000.
   a. What is the adjusted gross estate?
   b. What is the net taxable estate?
   c. What is the unified estate tax credit for this estate?
   d. How much in estate taxes will be owed?

Suggested Readings

"College Without Clifford." *Forbes,* February 23, 1987, pp. 135–136. Possible investment strategies now that tax reform has eliminated Clifford trusts.

"Keeping a Reign on Your Assets." *U.S. News and World Report,* March 16, 1987, p. 66. Setting up a revocable living trust to pass assets outside a will.

"Lights, Camera, Action!" *Forbes,* February 9, 1987, p. 72. Videotaping and recording wills to discourage contestants.

"Saving for College: One Scheme Has Survived." *Business Week,* January 12, 1987, p. 147. Minor's trusts have escaped some of the effects of tax reform.

APPENDIX A

Present and Future Value Tables

Many problems of personal finance involve decisions involving money values at different points in time. These values can be directly and fairly compared only when they are adjusted to a common point in time.

Four assumptions must be made to eliminate unnecessary complications: (1) each planning period is one year long; (2) only annual interest rates are considered; (3) interest rates are the same during each of the annual periods; and (4) interest is compounded and earns in subsequent periods.

Tables of present and future values can be constructed to make these adjustments. Future values are derived from the principles of compounding the dollar values ahead in time. Present values are derived from discounting (which is the inverse of compounding) the dollar values and transferring them to an earlier point in time.

For most of us it is unnecessary to have the precision of interest at the beginning of a period instead of the end of a period, or if interest compounds daily or quarterly instead of annually. (These require even more tables.) The following tables can be used to compute the mathematics of personal finance with high certainty and to confirm (or reject as inaccurate) what people tell you about financial matters.

The most significant task is to be certain that you are using the correct table. Accordingly, each table is clearly described and illustrations of use appear on the facing page where possible.

Illustrations: Using Appendix A1

1. You invest $500 at 15 percent for twelve years. How much will you have at the end of that twelve-year period?

   The interest factor is 5.350; hence the solution is $500(5.350), or $2,675.

2. Property values in your neighborhood are increasing at a rate of 5 percent per year. If your home is presently worth $90,000, what will its worth be in seven years?

   The inflation factor is 1.407; hence the solution is $90,000(1.407), or $126,630.

3. You need to amass $40,000 in the next ten years to meet a balloon payment on your home mortgage. You have $17,000 available to invest. What annual interest rate must be earned to realize the $40,000? $40,000 ÷ $17,000 = 2.353.

   Read across the "Periods" row to 6 years and across to 2.367 (close enough), which is under the 9% column. Hence the $17,000 invested at 9 percent for ten years will grow to a future value of just over $40,000.

4. An apartment building is currently valued at $160,000, and it has been appreciating at 8 percent per year. If this rate continues, in how many years will it be worth $300,000? $300,000 ÷ $160,000 = 1.875.

   Read down the 8% column until you reach 1.851 (close enough to 1.875). Note that this number corresponds to a period of eight years. Hence the $160,000 property appreciating at 8 percent annually will grow to a future value of $300,000 in just over eight years.

5. You have the choice of receiving $15,000 today as a down payment from someone who wants to purchase your rental property or a personal note for $25,000 payable in six years. If you could expect to earn 8 percent on such funds, which is the better choice?

   The interest factor is 1.587; hence the future value of $15,000 at 8 percent is $15,000(1.587), or $23,805. Thus, it would be better to take the note for $25,000.

6. You want to know how much an automobile now priced at $20,000 will cost in four years, assuming an inflation rate of 5 percent annually.

   Read down the 5% column and across the row for 4 years to locate the factor 1.216. Hence the solution is $20,000(1.216), or $24,320.

7. You want to know how big a lump-sum investment you need now to have $20,000 available in five years assuming a 10 percent annual rate of return.

APPENDIX A1
Future Value of $1 (to Compute the Compounded Future Value of Some Given Present Lump-sum Investment)

Periods	1%	2%	3%	4%	5%	6%	7%	8%	9%	10%	12%	14%	15%
1	1.010	1.020	1.030	1.040	1.050	1.060	1.070	1.080	1.090	1.100	1.120	1.140	1.150
2	1.020	1.040	1.061	1.082	1.103	1.124	1.145	1.166	1.188	1.210	1.254	1.300	1.323
3	1.030	1.061	1.093	1.125	1.158	1.191	1.225	1.260	1.295	1.331	1.405	1.482	1.521
4	1.041	1.082	1.126	1.170	1.216	1.262	1.311	1.360	1.412	1.464	1.574	1.689	1.749
5	1.051	1.104	1.159	1.217	1.276	1.338	1.403	1.469	1.539	1.611	1.762	1.925	2.011
6	1.062	1.126	1.194	1.265	1.340	1.419	1.501	1.587	1.677	1.772	1.974	2.195	2.313
7	1.072	1.149	1.230	1.316	1.407	1.504	1.606	1.714	1.828	1.949	2.211	2.502	2.660
8	1.083	1.172	1.267	1.369	1.477	1.594	1.718	1.851	1.993	2.144	2.476	2.853	3.059
9	1.094	1.195	1.305	1.423	1.551	1.689	1.838	1.999	2.172	2.358	2.773	3.252	3.518
10	1.105	1.219	1.344	1.480	1.629	1.791	1.967	2.159	2.367	2.594	3.106	3.707	4.046
11	1.116	1.243	1.384	1.539	1.710	1.898	2.105	2.332	2.580	2.853	3.479	4.226	4.652
12	1.127	1.268	1.426	1.601	1.796	2.012	2.252	2.518	2.813	3.138	3.896	4.818	5.350
13	1.138	1.294	1.469	1.665	1.886	2.133	2.410	2.720	3.066	3.452	4.363	5.492	6.153
14	1.149	1.319	1.513	1.732	1.980	2.261	2.579	2.937	3.342	3.798	4.887	6.261	7.076
15	1.161	1.346	1.558	1.801	2.079	2.397	2.759	3.172	3.642	4.177	5.474	7.138	8.137
16	1.173	1.373	1.605	1.873	2.183	2.540	2.952	3.426	3.970	4.595	6.130	8.137	9.358
17	1.184	1.400	1.653	1.948	2.292	2.693	3.159	3.700	4.328	5.054	6.866	9.276	10.76
18	1.196	1.428	1.702	2.026	2.407	2.854	3.380	3.996	4.717	5.560	7.690	10.58	12.38
19	1.208	1.457	1.754	2.107	2.527	3.026	3.617	4.316	5.142	6.116	8.613	12.06	14.23
20	1.220	1.486	1.806	2.191	2.653	3.207	3.870	4.661	5.604	6.728	9.646	13.74	16.37
21	1.232	1.516	1.860	2.279	2.786	3.400	4.141	5.034	6.109	7.400	10.80	15.67	18.82
22	1.245	1.546	1.916	2.370	2.925	3.604	4.430	5.437	6.659	8.140	12.10	17.86	21.64
23	1.257	1.577	1.974	2.465	3.072	3.820	4.741	5.871	7.258	8.954	13.55	20.36	24.89
24	1.270	1.608	2.033	2.563	3.225	4.049	5.072	6.341	7.911	9.850	15.18	23.21	28.63
25	1.282	1.641	2.094	2.666	3.386	4.292	5.427	6.848	8.623	10.83	17.00	26.46	32.92
26	1.295	1.673	2.157	2.772	3.556	4.549	5.807	7.396	9.399	11.92	19.04	30.17	37.86
27	1.308	1.707	2.221	2.883	3.733	4.822	6.214	7.988	10.25	13.11	21.32	34.39	43.54
28	1.321	1.741	2.288	2.999	3.920	5.112	6.649	8.627	11.17	14.42	23.88	39.20	50.07
29	1.335	1.776	2.357	3.119	4.116	5.418	7.114	9.317	12.17	15.86	26.75	44.69	57.58
30	1.348	1.811	2.427	3.243	4.322	5.743	7.612	10.06	13.27	17.45	29.96	50.95	66.21
40	1.489	2.208	3.262	4.801	7.040	10.29	14.97	21.72	31.41	45.26	93.05	188.9	267.9
50	1.645	2.692	4.384	7.107	11.47	18.42	29.46	46.90	74.36	117.4	289.0	700.2	1.084

$FV_n = PV \times F$

$FV_n = $ *future value* of interest at some future point in time (n)

$PV = $ *present value* of investment

$F = $ *factor* of future value (given a certain interest rate and n), which is located in the table, or determined by FV_n/PV

The $20,000 future value is divided by 1.611 (10 percent at five years), resulting in a lump-sum investment now of $12,415.

8. You have $5,000 now and need $10,000 in nine years. What rate of return is needed to reach that goal?

Divide the future value of $10,000 by the present value of the lump sum of $5,000 to obtain a future value factor of 2.0. Look along the row for 9 years to locate the factor 1.999 (very close to 2.0). Read up the column to find that an 8 percent return on investment is needed.

9. You want to know how many years it will take your lump-sum investment of $10,000 to grow to $16,000 with an annual rate of return of 7 percent.

Divide the future value of $16,000 by the present value of the $10,000 lump sum to compute a future value factor of 1.6; then look down the 7% column to find 1.606 (close enough). Read across the row to find that an investment period of seven years is needed.

Illustration: Using Appendix A2

1. You want to begin a college fund for your newborn child; you want $30,000 eighteen years from now. If a current investment opportunity yields 7 percent, how much must you invest in a lump sum to realize the $30,000 when needed?

   The interest factor is 0.296; hence the solution is $30,000 × 0.296, or $8,800.

2. You hope to retire in twenty-five years and want to deposit one lump sum that will grow to $250,000 at that time. If you can now invest at 8 percent, how much must you invest to realize the $250,000 when needed?

   The interest factor is 0.146; hence the solution is $250,000 × 0.146, or $36,500. The present value of $250,000 received twenty-five years from now is $36,500 if the interest rate is 8 percent.

3. You have the choice of receiving $15,000 today as a down payment from someone who wants to purchase your rental property or a personal note for $25,000 payable in six years. If you could expect to earn 8 percent on such funds, which is the better choice?

   The interest factor is 0.630; hence the solution is $25,000 × 0.630, or $15,750. Thus, the present value of $25,000 received in six years is greater than $15,000 received now, and is the better choice.

4. You own a $1,000 bond paying 8 percent annually until maturity in five years. You need to sell it now even though the market rate of interest on similar bonds has increased to 10 percent. What will be the lower discounted market price of the bond so that the buyer of your bond will earn a yield of 10 percent?

APPENDIX A2
Present Value of $1 (to Compute the Present Value of Some Known Future Sum)

Periods	1%	2%	3%	4%	5%	6%	7%	8%	9%	10%	12%	14%	15%
1	0.990	0.980	0.971	0.962	0.952	0.943	0.935	0.926	0.917	0.909	0.893	0.877	0.870
2	0.980	0.961	0.943	0.925	0.907	0.890	0.873	0.857	0.842	0.826	0.797	0.769	0.756
3	0.971	0.942	0.915	0.889	0.864	0.840	0.816	0.794	0.772	0.751	0.712	0.675	0.658
4	0.961	0.924	0.888	0.855	0.823	0.792	0.763	0.735	0.708	0.683	0.636	0.592	0.572
5	0.951	0.906	0.883	0.822	0.784	0.747	0.713	0.681	0.650	0.621	0.567	0.519	0.497
6	0.942	0.888	0.837	0.790	0.746	0.705	0.666	0.630	0.596	0.564	0.507	0.456	0.432
7	0.933	0.871	0.813	0.760	0.711	0.665	0.623	0.583	0.547	0.513	0.452	0.400	0.376
8	0.923	0.853	0.789	0.731	0.677	0.627	0.582	0.540	0.502	0.467	0.404	0.351	0.327
9	0.914	0.837	0.766	0.703	0.645	0.592	0.544	0.500	0.460	0.424	0.361	0.308	0.284
10	0.905	0.820	0.744	0.676	0.614	0.558	0.508	0.463	0.422	0.386	0.322	0.270	0.247
11	0.896	0.804	0.722	0.650	0.585	0.527	0.475	0.429	0.388	0.350	0.287	0.237	0.215
12	0.887	0.788	0.701	0.625	0.557	0.497	0.444	0.397	0.356	0.319	0.257	0.208	0.187
13	0.879	0.773	0.681	0.601	0.530	0.469	0.415	0.368	0.326	0.290	0.229	0.182	0.163
14	0.870	0.758	0.661	0.577	0.505	0.442	0.388	0.340	0.299	0.263	0.205	0.160	0.141
15	0.861	0.743	0.642	0.555	0.481	0.417	0.362	0.315	0.275	0.239	0.183	0.140	0.123
16	0.853	0.728	0.623	0.534	0.458	0.394	0.339	0.292	0.252	0.218	0.163	0.123	0.107
17	0.844	0.714	0.605	0.513	0.436	0.371	0.317	0.270	0.231	0.198	0.146	0.108	0.093
18	0.836	0.700	0.587	0.494	0.416	0.350	0.296	0.250	0.212	0.180	0.130	0.095	0.081
19	0.828	0.686	0.570	0.475	0.396	0.331	0.277	0.232	0.194	0.164	0.116	0.083	0.070
20	0.820	0.673	0.554	0.456	0.377	0.312	0.258	0.215	0.178	0.149	0.104	0.073	0.061
21	0.811	0.660	0.538	0.439	0.359	0.294	0.242	0.199	0.164	0.135	0.093	0.064	0.053
22	0.803	0.647	0.522	0.422	0.342	0.278	0.226	0.184	0.150	0.123	0.083	0.056	0.046
23	0.795	0.634	0.507	0.406	0.326	0.262	0.211	0.170	0.138	0.112	0.074	0.049	0.040
24	0.788	0.622	0.492	0.390	0.310	0.247	0.197	0.158	0.126	0.102	0.066	0.043	0.035
25	0.780	0.610	0.478	0.375	0.295	0.233	0.184	0.146	0.116	0.092	0.059	0.038	0.030
26	0.772	0.598	0.464	0.361	0.281	0.220	0.172	0.135	0.106	0.084	0.053	0.033	0.026
27	0.764	0.586	0.450	0.347	0.268	0.207	0.161	0.125	0.098	0.076	0.047	0.029	0.023
28	0.757	0.574	0.437	0.333	0.255	0.196	0.150	0.116	0.090	0.069	0.042	0.026	0.020
29	0.749	0.563	0.424	0.321	0.243	0.185	0.141	0.107	0.082	0.063	0.037	0.022	0.017
30	0.742	0.552	0.412	0.308	0.231	0.174	0.131	0.099	0.075	0.057	0.033	0.020	0.015
40	0.672	0.453	0.307	0.208	0.142	0.097	0.067	0.046	0.032	0.022	0.011	0.005	0.004
50	0.608	0.372	0.228	0.141	0.087	0.054	0.034	0.021	0.013	0.009	0.003	0.001	0.001

$$PV = FV_n \times F$$
$PV = present\ value$
$FV_n = future\ value$ of investment at some future point in time (n)
$F = factor$ of present value (given a certain interest rate and n)

The solution first involves computing the present value of the future interest payments of $80 per year for five years at 10 percent (using Appendix A4), $80 × 3.791, or $303.28. Second, compute the present value of the future principal repayment of $1,000 five years from now at 10 percent: $1,000 × 0.621, or $621.00. Hence the market price is the sum of the two present values ($303.28 + $621.00), or $924.28.

Illustration: Using Appendix A3

1. You plan to retire after sixteen years. To provide for that retirement, you initiate a savings program of $7,000 per year in an investment yielding 8 percent. What will be the value of the retirement fund at the beginning of the seventeenth year?

   Your last payment into the fund will occur at the end of the sixteenth year, so scan down the periods column for period 16, and then across until you reach the 8% column. The interest factor is 30.32. Hence the solution is $7,000(30.32), or $212,240.

2. What will be the value of an investment if you put $2,000 into a retirement plan yielding 7 percent annually for twenty-five years?

   The interest factor is 63.250. Hence the solution is $2,000(63.250), or $126,500.

3. You are trying to decide between putting $3,000 or $4,000 annually for the next twenty years into an investment yielding 7 percent for retirement purposes. What is the difference in the value of investing the extra $1,000 for twenty years?

   The interest factor is 41.0. Hence the solution is $1,000(41.0), or $41,000.

4. You will receive an annuity payment of $1,200 at the end of each year for six years. What will be the total value of this stream of income invested at 7 percent by the time you receive the last payment?

   The appropriate interest factor for six years at 7 percent is 7.153. Hence the solution is $1,200(7.153), or $8,584.

5. You want to know how many years of investing $1,200 annually at 9 percent it will take to reach a goal of $11,000.

   Divide the future value of $11,000 by the lump sum of $1,200 to find a factor of 9.17 and look down the 9 percent column to find 9.200 (close enough). Read across the row to find that an investment period of seven years is needed.

6. You want to know what percent of return is needed if you plan to invest $12,000 annually for nine years to reach a goal of $15,000.

   Divide the future value goal of $15,000 by $1,200 to derive the factor 12.5 and look along the row for 9 years to locate the factor 12.49 (close enough). Read up the column to find that you need an 8 percent return.

APPENDIX A3
Future Value of an Annuity of $1 per Year (to Compute the Future Value of a Stream of Annuity or Income Payments)

Periods	1%	2%	3%	4%	5%	6%	7%	8%	9%	10%	12%	14%	15%
1	1.000	1.000	1.000	1.000	1.000	1.000	1.000	1.000	1.000	1.000	1.000	1.000	1.000
2	2.010	2.020	2.030	2.040	2.050	2.060	2.070	2.080	2.090	2.100	2.120	2.140	2.150
3	3.030	3.060	3.091	3.122	3.153	3.184	3.215	3.246	3.278	3.310	3.374	3.440	3.473
4	4.060	4.122	4.184	4.246	4.310	4.375	4.440	4.506	4.573	4.641	4.779	4.921	4.993
5	5.101	5.204	5.309	5.416	5.526	5.637	5.751	5.867	5.985	6.105	6.353	6.610	6.742
6	6.152	6.308	6.468	6.633	6.802	6.975	7.153	7.336	7.523	7.716	8.115	8.536	8.754
7	7.214	7.434	7.662	7.898	8.142	8.394	8.654	8.923	9.200	9.487	10.09	10.73	11.07
8	8.286	8.583	8.892	9.214	9.549	9.897	10.26	10.64	11.03	11.44	12.30	13.23	13.73
9	9.369	9.755	10.16	10.58	11.03	11.49	11.98	12.49	13.02	13.58	14.78	16.09	16.79
10	10.46	10.95	11.46	12.01	12.58	13.18	13.82	14.49	15.19	15.94	17.55	19.34	20.30
11	11.57	12.17	12.81	13.49	14.21	14.97	15.78	16.65	17.56	18.53	20.65	23.04	24.35
12	12.68	13.41	14.19	15.03	15.92	16.87	17.89	18.98	20.14	21.38	24.13	27.27	29.00
13	13.81	14.68	15.62	16.63	17.71	18.88	20.14	21.50	22.95	24.52	28.03	32.09	34.35
14	14.95	15.97	17.09	18.29	19.60	21.02	22.55	24.21	26.02	27.98	32.39	37.58	40.50
15	16.10	17.29	18.60	20.02	21.58	23.28	25.13	27.15	29.36	31.77	37.28	43.84	47.58
16	17.26	18.64	20.16	21.82	23.66	25.67	27.89	30.32	33.00	35.95	42.75	50.98	55.72
17	18.43	20.01	21.76	23.70	25.84	28.21	30.84	33.75	36.97	40.54	48.88	59.12	65.08
18	19.61	21.41	23.41	25.65	28.13	30.91	34.00	37.45	41.30	45.60	55.75	68.39	75.84
19	20.81	22.84	25.12	27.67	30.54	33.76	37.38	41.45	46.02	51.16	63.44	78.97	88.21
20	22.02	24.30	26.87	29.78	33.07	36.79	41.00	45.76	51.16	57.28	72.05	91.02	102.4
21	23.24	25.78	28.68	31.97	35.72	39.99	44.87	50.42	56.76	64.00	81.70	104.8	118.8
22	24.47	27.30	30.54	34.25	38.51	43.39	49.01	55.46	62.87	71.40	92.50	120.4	137.6
23	25.72	28.85	32.45	36.62	41.43	47.00	53.44	60.89	69.53	79.54	104.6	138.3	159.3
24	26.97	30.42	34.43	39.08	44.50	50.82	58.18	66.76	76.79	88.50	118.2	158.7	184.2
25	28.24	32.03	36.46	41.65	47.73	54.86	63.25	73.11	84.70	98.35	133.3	181.9	212.8
26	29.53	33.67	38.55	44.31	51.11	59.16	68.68	79.95	93.32	109.2	150.3	208.3	245.7
27	30.82	35.34	40.71	47.08	54.67	63.71	74.48	87.35	102.7	121.1	169.4	238.5	283.6
28	32.13	37.05	42.93	49.97	58.40	68.53	80.70	95.34	113.0	134.2	190.7	272.9	327.1
29	33.45	38.79	45.22	52.97	62.32	73.64	87.35	104.04	124.1	148.6	214.6	312.1	377.2
30	34.78	40.57	47.58	56.08	66.44	79.06	94.46	113.34	136.3	164.5	241.3	356.8	434.7
40	48.89	60.40	75.40	95.03	120.8	154.8	199.6	259.1	337.9	442.6	767.1	1,342	1,779
50	64.46	84.58	112.8	152.7	209.3	290.3	406.5	573.8	815.1	1,164	2,400	4,995	7,218

$FV = A_n \times F$
$FV = $ *future value*
$A_n = $ *amount* (periodic payment) of the annuity for n periods
$F = $ *factor* of future value (given a certain interest rate and n)

Illustration: Using Appendix A4

1. You are entering a contract that will provide you an income of $1,000 at the end of the year for the next 10 years. If the annual interest rate is 7 percent, what is the present value of that stream of payments?

   The interest factor is 7.024; hence the solution is $1,000 × 7.024, or $7,024.

2. You expect to have $250,000 available in a retirement plan upon retirement. If the amount invested yields 8 percent and you hope to live an additional twenty years, how much can you withdraw each year so that the fund will just be liquidated after twenty years?

   The interest factor for twenty years at 8 percent is 9.818. Hence the solution is $250,000 ÷ 9.818, or $25,463.

3. You have received an inheritance of $60,000 and invest that sum earning 9 percent. If you withdraw $8,000 annually to supplement your income, in how many years will the fund run out?

   Solving for n, $60,000 ÷ $8,000 = 7.5. Scan down the 9% column until you find the interest factor nearest 7.5, which is 7.487. This is on the row indicating thirteen years; thus the fund will be depleted in approximately thirteen years with $8,000 annual withdrawals.

4. A seller offers to finance the sale of a building to you as an investment. The mortgage loan of $280,000 will be for twenty years and requires annual mortgage payment of $24,000. Should you finance the purchase through the seller or borrow the funds from a financial institution at a current rate of 10 percent?

   $280,000 ÷ $24,000 = 11.667. Scan down the periods column to 20 years and then read across to locate the figure closest to 11.667, which is 11.470. This is in the column indicating 6 percent; thus, seller financing offers a lower interest rate.

5. You have the opportunity to purchase an office building for $750,000 with an expected life of twenty years. Looking over the financial details, you see that the before-tax net rental income is $90,000. Since you want a return of at least 15 percent, how much should you pay for the building?

   The interest factor for twenty years at 15 percent is 6.259, and $90,000 × 6.259 = $563,310. Thus, the price is too high for you to earn a return of 15 percent.

Present Value of an Annuity of $1 per Year (to Compute the Present Value of a Stream of Annuity or Income Payments)

Periods	1%	2%	3%	4%	5%	6%	7%	8%	9%	10%	12%	14%	15%
1	0.990	0.980	0.971	0.962	0.952	0.943	0.935	0.926	0.917	0.909	0.893	0.877	0.870
2	1.970	1.942	1.913	1.886	1.859	1.833	1.808	1.783	1.759	1.736	1.690	1.647	1.626
3	2.941	2.884	2.829	2.775	2.723	2.673	2.624	2.577	2.531	2.487	2.402	2.322	2.283
4	3.902	3.808	3.717	3.630	3.546	3.465	3.387	3.312	3.240	3.170	3.037	2.914	2.855
5	4.853	4.713	4.580	4.452	4.329	4.212	4.100	3.993	3.890	3.791	3.605	3.433	3.352
6	5.795	5.601	5.417	5.242	5.076	4.917	4.767	4.623	4.486	4.355	4.111	3.889	3.784
7	6.728	6.472	6.230	6.002	5.786	5.582	5.389	5.206	5.033	4.868	4.564	4.288	4.160
8	7.652	7.325	7.020	6.733	6.463	6.210	5.971	5.747	5.535	5.335	4.968	4.639	4.487
9	8.566	8.162	7.786	7.435	7.108	6.802	6.515	6.247	5.995	5.759	5.328	4.946	4.772
10	9.471	8.983	8.530	8.111	7.722	7.360	7.024	6.710	6.418	6.145	5.650	5.216	5.019
11	10.368	9.787	9.253	8.760	8.306	7.887	7.499	7.139	6.805	6.495	5.938	5.453	5.234
12	11.255	10.575	9.954	9.385	8.863	8.384	7.943	7.536	7.161	6.814	6.194	5.660	5.421
13	12.134	11.348	10.635	9.986	9.394	8.853	8.358	7.904	7.487	7.103	6.424	5.842	5.583
14	13.004	12.106	11.296	10.563	9.899	9.295	8.745	8.244	7.786	7.367	6.628	6.002	5.724
15	13.865	12.849	11.938	11.118	10.380	9.712	9.108	8.559	8.061	7.606	6.811	6.142	5.847
16	14.718	13.578	12.561	11.652	10.838	10.106	9.447	8.851	8.313	7.824	6.974	6.265	5.954
17	15.562	14.292	13.166	12.166	11.274	10.477	9.763	9.122	8.544	8.022	7.120	6.373	6.047
18	16.398	14.992	13.754	12.659	11.690	10.828	10.059	9.372	8.756	8.201	7.250	6.467	6.128
19	17.226	15.678	14.324	13.134	12.085	11.158	10.336	9.604	8.950	8.365	7.366	6.550	6.198
20	18.046	16.351	14.878	13.590	12.462	11.470	10.594	9.818	9.129	8.514	7.469	6.623	6.259
21	18.857	17.011	15.415	14.029	12.821	11.764	10.836	10.017	9.292	8.649	7.562	6.687	6.312
22	19.660	17.658	15.937	14.451	13.163	12.042	11.061	10.201	9.442	8.772	7.645	6.743	6.359
23	20.456	18.292	16.444	14.857	13.489	12.303	11.272	10.371	9.580	8.883	7.718	6.792	6.399
24	21.243	18.914	16.936	15.247	13.799	12.550	11.469	10.529	9.707	8.985	7.784	6.835	6.434
25	22.023	19.523	17.413	15.622	14.094	12.783	11.654	10.675	9.823	9.077	7.843	6.873	6.464
26	22.795	20.121	17.877	15.983	14.375	13.003	11.826	10.810	9.929	9.161	7.896	6.906	6.491
27	23.560	20.707	18.327	16.330	14.643	13.211	11.987	10.935	10.027	9.237	7.943	6.935	6.514
28	24.316	21.281	18.764	16.663	14.898	13.406	12.137	11.051	10.116	9.307	7.984	6.961	6.534
29	25.066	21.844	19.189	16.984	15.141	13.591	12.278	11.158	10.198	9.370	8.022	6.983	6.551
30	25.808	22.396	19.600	17.292	15.373	13.765	12.409	11.258	10.274	9.427	8.055	7.003	6.566
40	32.835	27.355	23.115	19.793	17.159	15.046	13.332	11.925	10.757	9.779	8.244	7.105	6.642
50	39.196	31.424	25.730	21.482	18.256	15.762	13.801	12.234	10.962	9.915	8.305	7.133	6.661

$PV = A_n \times F$

PV = present value

A_n = amount (periodic payment) of annuity for n periods, or determined by $A_n = PV/F$

F = factor of present value (given a certain interest rate and n)

A P P E N D I X B

Calculating Social Security Benefits

If you qualify based on the number of quarters of coverage you have attained, the Social Security Administration (SSA) has a basic benefit credited to you right now for benefits for your retirement, for a period of disability, or for your survivors if you die. The level of benefits received from Social Security depends on your income in past years that was subject to Federal Insurance Contributions Act (FICA) taxes, commonly known as Social Security taxes. Because income levels in past years were lower than they are now, the SSA adjusts previous years' income using what is called the indexing method. The sections that follow illustrate the calculation of Social Security benefits using the indexing method for hypothetical situations. The calculations are based on 1987 Social Security benefit levels, but you can estimate your own benefits by plugging your personal income data into the steps outlined.

Social Security Retirement Benefits

To illustrate the calculation of monthly retirement benefits from Social Security, using the indexing method, follow the nine steps given below. The example is for a worker, Clyde Johnson, who reached age sixty-two in October 1987 and plans to retire on his sixty-fourth birthday in 1989. An illustration for workers who are older or younger than Clyde will require different figures due to differences in the index factor for each year. Index figures for workers older than Clyde have been published and are available from the SSA in a pamphlet entitled "Estimating Your Social Security Retirement Check: Using the Indexing Method." Index factors for workers younger than Clyde will be available in the update of the same publication published in the year the worker reaches age sixty-two.

Step 1   Retirement benefits are based on earnings over a number of years. From the accompanying chart, select the number of years corresponding to the year Clyde was born. The answer is thirty-one.

Year You Were Born	Number of Years Needed
1925	31
1926	32
1927	33
1928	34
1929 or after	35 (maximum)

Step 2   Clyde filled out the worksheet shown on the next page. Column A shows maximum taxable earnings covered by Social Security. In column C, Clyde listed his earnings starting in 1951. (Write $0 for a year of no earnings.) If he earned more than the maximum in any year, he would list only the maximum. He estimated his earnings for future years. He stopped with the year before he planned to retire, as the SSA instructs.

Step 3   Clyde multiplied his actual earnings for each year by the factor in Column B, writing the result in Column D.

Step 4   He then crossed off his list the years of lowest earnings until the number of years left was the same number as his answer to step 1.

Step 5   Adding the earnings for the years *left* on his list, Clyde wrote the total amount ($730,734) on the total line at the bottom of the worksheet.

Step 6   Dividing the total in step 5 by the number of years he wrote for step 1 resulted in Clyde's average *indexed* yearly earnings covered by Social Security: $23,572.06 ($730,734 ÷ 31).

Step 7   Next, Clyde divided the average indexed yearly earnings by 12. The result was his *average indexed monthly earnings* (AIME). Rounding the result to the next lowest dollar resulted in an AIME of $1,964.

Year	(A)	(B)	(C)	(D)
1951	$ 3,600	6.009	$ 2,800	$ 16,825
1952	3,600	5.657	2,900	~~16,405~~
1953	3,600	5.358	3,100	~~16,609~~
1954	3,600	5.330	3,000	~~15,990~~
1955	4,200	5.095	3,300	~~16,813~~
1956	4,200	4.762	3,450	~~16,428~~
1957	4,200	4.619	3,550	~~16,397~~
1958	4,200	4.579	3,800	17,400
1959	4,800	4.362	4,000	17,448
1960	4,800	4.198	4,800	20,150
1961	4,800	4.116	4,800	19,756
1962	4,800	3.920	4,750	18,620
1963	4,800	3.826	4,800	18,364
1964	4,800	3.676	4,500	~~16,542~~
1965	4,800	3.611	4,800	17,332
1966	6,600	3.406	5,600	19,073
1967	6,600	3.226	6,400	20,646
1968	7,800	3.019	7,200	21,736
1969	7,800	2.854	7,800	22,261
1970	7,800	2.719	7,800	21,208
1971	7,800	2.589	7,800	20,194
1972	9,000	2.358	8,800	20,750
1973	10,800	2.219	10,600	23,521
1974	13,200	2.094	12,500	26,175
1975	14,100	1.949	14,100	27,480
1976	15,300	1.823	15,300	27,891
1977	16,500	1.720	16,500	28,380
1978	17,700	1.593	17,700	28,196
1979	22,900	1.465	20,500	30,032
1980	25,900	1.344	22,300	29,971
1981	29,700	1.221	25,400	31,013
1982	32,400	1.157	24,000	27,768
1983	37,500	1.103	25,600	28,236
1984	37,800	1.042	25,000	26,050
1985	39,600	1.000	24,200	24,200
1986	42,000	1.000	25,630	25,630
1987	43,800	1.000	26,428	26,428
1988	43,800[a]	1.000	28,000	28,000
Total				$730,734

[a] Estimate, as the maximum amount of annual earnings that counts for Social Security rises automatically as earning levels increase.

Step 8 The formula used in this step to calculate the benefit rate applies only to workers who reached age sixty-two in 1987. Clyde multiplied the first $310 of his AIME by 90 percent and obtained $279. He multiplied the next $1,556 of his AIME by 32 percent and obtained $497.92. He multiplied the remaining $98 by 15 percent and obtained the $14.70. Adding these three figures resulted in a basic monthly benefit of $791.62 ($279.00 + $497.92 + $14.70).

This basic monthly benefit is a close estimate of the amount Clyde will receive monthly at age sixty-five. Like all Social Security recipients,

Clyde is eligible for cost-of-living increases starting with the year he turns sixty-two. As a result, his basic monthly benefit will be adjusted upward to reflect the cost-of-living increases. The factors used to make the adjustments were not available when Clyde made his estimate in 1987. Based on past years' adjustments and predictions for inflation, however, Clyde estimated that his basic monthly benefit would be adjusted upward by 4 percent for inflation for both 1988 and 1989. Multiplying his basic monthly benefit by 1.082 (from Appendix A1), he estimates that his basic monthly benefit will be $856 ($791.62 × 1.082 = $856.53, which is rounded to the next lower dollar).

Step 9 Because Clyde wants to retire exactly one year early, his basic monthly benefit will be permanently reduced. The amount of the reduction can be determined from Table 21–4 in the text. Clyde must multiply his basic monthly benefit by the factor in Table 21–4 that corresponds to the number of months he will receive benefits before reaching age sixty-five. The resulting amount, $798 ($856 × .933 = $798.65, rounded to the next lower dollar), is Clyde's estimate of the amount he will receive at early retirement at age sixty-four in 1989.

Social Security Disability Benefits

When a covered worker becomes disabled, Social Security will pay benefits to the worker, dependent children under age nineteen, a spouse caring for dependent children under age sixteen, and a spouse (even if divorced, provided the marriage lasted ten years and the spouse requesting benefits has not remarried) age sixty-two and above. The dollar amount of the benefits will depend on two factors. The first is the eligibility of the disabled worker. All workers who have achieved forty quarters of coverage under Social Security with at least twenty of the quarters attained in the last ten years are eligible for disability benefits. (The quarter in which the disability occurs must also be a quarter of coverage.) A worker under age thirty-one must have attained at least six or one-half of the quarters of coverage possible after age twenty-one, whichever is greater. (For example, a twenty-six-year-old worker would have five years, or twenty calendar quarters, possible and would need ten quarters of coverage.)

The second factor is the level of earnings of the covered worker. To receive full benefits, an eligible worker must have earned the maximum taxable earnings for a specified number of years. Earnings above the maximum taxable earnings in a given year are not taxed and are not included in the calculations. Earnings below the maximum taxable earnings in a given year are included in the calculations. In years past, the maximum taxable earnings were lower than they are today. To adjust for these differences, the taxable earnings for some years are multiplied by the same index factors given in the previous section.

The calculations needed to estimate disability benefits are complex—so much so that Social Security offices will be reluctant to provide an estimate unless the caller is making a claim for benefits. Further, the estimate will change yearly with changes in the worker's income, the index factors, and Social Security regulations. Nevertheless, it is possible to estimate your benefits if you follow certain steps. The steps are outlined below with an example.

John Wilhite, a married father of two small children, turned thirty-two in 1987, when he earned $37,000 and had been employed for ten years. He has paid Social Security taxes for the entire ten years and is therefore eligible for disability benefits. He wants to calculate the annual value of those benefits.

Step 1   Fill out the taxable earnings column (column 4) in the accompanying table for every year since 1951 or the year the covered worker turned twenty-two, whichever is most recent. For years in which the earnings exceed the maximum taxable earnings, write the maximum taxable earnings in column 4.

Step 2   Multiply the amounts in column 4 by the index factor in column 3 and write the answers in column 5. John's figures are included in the table.

Step 3   Workers are allowed to ignore a number of years that have the lowest earnings. The number of years, based on the age of the worker, can be determined from the following chart. John will be able to omit 1977 and 1978, his two years with the lowest earnings, from his calculations. He also excludes the income for the year the disability occurred.

Age of the Worker	Number of Drop-out Years
Under 27	0
27–31	1
32–36	2
37–41	3
42–46	4
47 and above	5

Step 4   Add the remaining earnings in column 5 and divide by the number of years not dropped out. For John Wilhite the answer is $217,915 divided by 8, or $27,239. Dividing this figure by 12 yields the average indexed monthly earnings (AIME). John's AIME is $2,269.

Step 5   Multiply the first $310 of the AIME by .90, the next $1,556 by .32, and the remaining portion of the AIME by .15. Total each of these answers. The result is the disability basic monthly benefit (DBMB). John Wilhite's DBMB is $279 + $497.92 + $60.45 = $837.37.

Calculation of Average Indexes Earnings for Disability Benefits (Indexed for 1987)

(1) Year	(2) Maximum Taxable Earnings	(3) Index Factor	(4) Taxable Earnings	(5) Indexed Earnings
1951	$ 3,600	6.009		
1952	3,600	5.657		
1953	3,600	5.358		
1954	3,600	5.330		
1955	4,200	5.095		
1956	4,200	4.762		
1957	4,200	4.619		
1958	4,200	4.579		
1959	4,800	4.362		
1960	4,800	4.198		
1961	4,800	4.116		
1962	4,800	3.920		
1963	4,800	3.826		
1964	4,800	3.676		
1965	4,800	3.611		
1966	6,600	3.406		
1967	6,600	3.226		
1968	7,800	3.019		
1969	7,800	2.854		
1970	7,800	2.719		
1971	7,800	2.589		
1972	9,000	2.358		
1973	10,800	2.219		
1974	13,200	2.094		
1975	14,100	1.949		
1976	15,300	1.823		
1977	16,500	1.720	$ 0[a]	$ Ø
1978	17,700	1.593	13,100	20,Ø6̶8̶
1979	22,900	1.465	15,300	22,414
1980	25,900	1.344	16,500	22,176
1981	29,700	1.221	17,700	21,611
1982	32,400	1.157	22,900	26,495
1983	37,500	1.103	24,000	26,472
1984	37,800	1.042	29,700	30,947
1985	39,600	1.000	32,400	32,400
1986	42,000	1.000	35,400	35,400
1987	43,800	1.000	37,000	37,Ø0̶0̶[b]
Total				$217,915

[a] John Wilhite's income.
[b] The year the disability occurs is not included in the calculations.

The DBMB is the amount that a totally disabled person would receive in Social Security benefits after the five-month waiting period. It is also used to calculate the benefits for other family members. For example, a dependent child under age nineteen would receive 50 percent of the disabled parent's DBMB. The DBMB can be multiplied by 12 to determine the benefit for one year. In the case of John Wilhite, this results in a basic annual benefit of $10,048.44 (12 × $837.37). Yet this is only an estimate of the actual benefit his family might receive. One more step is needed to determine the maximum family benefit.

Step 6 Multiply the AIME by .85. In John Wilhite's case the result would be $2,269 × .85 = $1,928.65. Then multiply the DBMB by 1.5. The result for John would be $837.37 × 1.5 = $1,265.05. The lesser of these two results is the maximum monthly family disability benefit. For the Wilhite family, the maximum monthly family disability benefit is $1,265.05, or $15,072.66 annually.

Will John's family receive the maximum benefit or something less? To find out, John would need to know the percentage of the DBMB each family member would receive. Dependent children receive 50 percent of the DBMB. Spouses caring for children under age sixteen receive 50 percent, as do spouses age sixty-five or over. Spouses who apply for benefits at age sixty-two will receive 37.5 percent. The Wilhite family will easily exceed the maximum family benefit if all members received the percentage to which they are entitled. Thus, John's family would receive the family maximum for an annual benefit of $15,072.66. Each family member's benefit would be adjusted to keep the total under this limit.

Social Security Survivors' Benefits

When a covered worker dies, Social Security will pay benefits to surviving children under age eighteen (or nineteen if still in high school), to a surviving spouse (even if divorced from the deceased but not remarried) caring for surviving children under age sixteen, to a surviving spouse age sixty or over, and to surviving *dependent* parents over the age of sixty-two. The amount of benefits will depend on two factors. The first is the eligibility of the covered worker. A worker must have paid Social Security taxes for forty quarters in order to be "fully insured." Others may be considered "currently insured" if they have paid Social Security taxes in six of the previous twelve quarters or have paid taxes for a certain minimum number of years. The survivors of currently insured workers receive lower benefits than those of fully insured workers.

The second factor is the covered worker's level of earnings. To receive full benefits, a fully insured worker must have earned and paid Social Security taxes on the maximum taxable earnings for a specified number of years. Because the maximum taxable earnings were lower in the past than they are today, taxable earnings for some years are multiplied by an index factor to adjust for the difference.

The calculations needed to estimate survivors' benefits are performed in a series of steps. The estimate will change yearly with changes in the worker's income, the index factors, and Social Security regulations. As an example, again consider John Wilhite, age thirty-two and the married father of two small children. He has been employed for ten years and in 1987 earned $37,000. He has paid Social Security taxes for forty quarters and is fully insured, although in each year he earned less than the maximum taxable earnings. The calculations estimating his Social Security survivors' benefits if he would have died in 1987 are shown below.

Step 1 Count the number of years after 1950 (or after the year the person reached age twenty-one, if later) and up to (but not including) the year of death, and subtract 5. The number remaining is the number of years of income that must be used in calculating benefits. Since John turned twenty-one in 1976, he must use five years (1977 to 1986 = 10 years; 10 − 5 = 5).

Step 2 Write the earnings subject to Social Security taxes (column 4) in the accompanying table for every year since 1951 or since the year the covered worker turned twenty-two, whichever is most recent. For years in which the earnings exceeded the maximum taxable earnings (column 2), write the maximum taxable earnings in column 4.

Step 3 Multiply each figure in column 4 by the index factor in column 3 and write the product in column 5. John's figures are included in the table.

Step 4 Cross the lowest figures in column 5 until only the number of years determined in step 1 remain (here, five). Add the remaining figures. John's total is $151,714, after 1977–1981 are crossed off. Note that the year of death is also not included in the calculations.

Step 5 Divide the total in column 5 by the number of years used, and then divide that amount by 12. The result is the average indexed monthly earnings (AIME). John's AIME is $2,528.56 [($151,714 ÷ 5) ÷ 12].

Step 6 Multiply the first $310 of the AIME by .90, the next $1,556 by .32, and the remaining portion by .15. Total these three products. The result is the survivor's basic monthly benefit (SBMB). John's SBMB equals $858 ($279.00 + $479.92 + $99.38) rounded down to the nearest dollar. The SBMB can be multiplied by 12 to determine the benefit for one year. John's basic annual benefit equals $10,296 (12 × $858). This is the basic benefit if only one survivor qualifies to receive benefits. One more step is needed to determine the family monthly benefit.

Step 7 Each eligible surviving family member will receive a percentage of the SBMB as shown in the table on page 701. However, there is a family maximum, calculated as follows: Multiply that first $396 of the SBMB by 1.5, the next $175 by 2.72, the next $174 by 1.34, and the

Calculation of Average Indexes Earnings for Survivors' Benefits (Indexed for 1987)				
(1)	(2) Maximum Taxable Earnings	(3) Index Factor	(4) Taxable Earnings	(5) Indexed Earnings
Year				
1951	$ 3,600	6.009		
1952	3,600	5.657		
1953	3,600	5.358		
1954	3,600	5.330		
1955	4,200	5.095		
1956	4,200	4.762		
1957	4,200	4.619		
1958	4,200	4.579		
1959	4,800	4.362		
1960	4,800	4.198		
1961	4,800	4.116		
1962	4,800	3.920		
1963	4,800	3.826		
1964	4,800	3.676		
1965	4,800	3.611		
1966	6,600	3.406		
1967	6,600	3.226		
1968	7,800	3.019		
1969	7,800	2.854		
1970	7,800	2.719		
1971	7,800	2.589		
1972	9,000	2.358		
1973	10,800	2.219		
1974	13,200	2.094		
1975	14,100	1.949		
1976	15,300	1.823		
1977	16,500	1.720	$ 0[a]	$ 0
1978	17,700	1.593	13,100	20,868
1979	22,900	1.465	15,300	22,414
1980	25,900	1.344	16,500	22,176
1981	29,700	1.221	17,700	21,611
1982	32,400	1.157	22,900	26,495
1983	37,500	1.103	24,000	26,472
1984	37,800	1.042	29,700	30,947
1985	39,600	1.000	32,400	32,400
1986	42,000	1.000	35,400	35,400
1987	43,800	1.000	37,000	37,000[b]
Total				$151,714

[a] John Wilhite's income.
[b] The year of death is not included in the calculation of the total, per SSA regulations.

Benefits for Family Members as a Percentage of SBMB	
Each eligible child	75.0%
Widow/widower	
Caring for child under 16 or disabled	75.0
Age 65 at time of application	100.0
Age 60 at time of application	71.5
Parents	
One parent eligible	82.5
Two parents eligible (each)	75.0

remainder by 1.75. The result is the maximum monthly family survivors' benefit (MMFSB). John's MMFSB equals $1,500.91 ($594 + $476 + $233.16 + $197.75). Since John's eligible survivors would be his two children and his spouse, the total of their individual benefits would exceed the family maximum. Each individual's benefit would be reduced proportionately to stay within the family maximum. John's family would receive an estimated $1,500 (benefits are rounded down to the nearest dollar) per month, or $18,000 ($1,500 × 12) per year.

APPENDIX C

Common-sense Principles of Success in Personal Finance

1. Live within your income.
2. Set financial goals.
3. Save regularly.
4. Make realistic budgets.
5. Organize your financial records.
6. Use an interest-bearing checking account.
7. Open a money market account.
8. Comparison shop for more expensive products and services.
9. Do not borrow for the wrong things.
10. Avoid paying too much interest in installment credit purchases.
11. Drive used automobiles instead of buying new vehicles.
12. Avoid paying too much for monthly housing costs.
13. Buy a home for income tax reasons as soon as possible.
14. Reduce your income taxes so you will have more to spend, save, and invest.
15. Avoid paying too much for insurance.
16. Buy inexpensive term life insurance to protect earning power.
17. Open an individual retirement account (IRA) and contribute regularly.

18. Make a will for the security of your heirs.
19. Invest in what you understand and get started early.
20. Make your first investment in mutual funds.
21. Make your second investment in some good readings in personal finance and consider alternative investment opportunities.
22. Begin now to plan for a financially secure retirement.
23. Develop expertise in financial matters and heed your own advice, because ultimately it is you who is responsible for your financial success.
24. Take conservative actions to become more than a millionaire.

APPENDIX D

Personal Computers in Finance

Because personal computers manipulate numbers quickly, reliably, and impartially, they have had a tremendous impact on the field of financial analysis and money management. Either by choice or from competitive necessity, most financial advisors use personal computers to make projections, calculate payment schedules, compare investments, record transactions, write letters, and chart alternatives. Many people use financial programs on their home computers to design personal budgets, enter incomes and expenses into data files, generate cash flow statements, prepare tax returns, print checks, and construct graphs. More and more people are turning the clerical and analytical work of financial planning over to their personal computers; this leaves more time for thinking about alternatives and making decisions.

Software

To use personal computers effectively, you must select the right program, or software. Using the right software package for the job is just as important as using the right tools to build a house. Carpenters spend years learning how and when to use each tool. Many problems beginners have can be traced to using the wrong program. For example, you

This appendix was prepared by David Sullivan, Assistant Professor of Information Systems, Oregon State University.

could maintain a home budget and expense-tracking system with a word processing program, but doing that makes as much sense as cutting a two-by-four in half with a hammer. A home finance management program would make it much easier to enter and update the budget and expense data and would have the added benefit of generating a wide range of reports and graphs from the data almost effortlessly.

You can choose from several general types of programs to help you with personal finance, depending on the kinds of calculations you're doing. After a brief discussion of each type, we'll cover spreadsheet, presentation graphics, and home finance programs in more detail.

Spreadsheet Programs Spreadsheet programs are frequently used for financial modeling and forecasting because they make the power of a computer's numerical processing available to people who have no prior computer experience. One of the most common uses of spreadsheet programs is to construct financial statements and budgets, but any repetitive task that you currently do with a pencil, paper, and calculator can probably be done quicker with a spreadsheet.

Presentation Graphics Programs Sometimes called *business graphics programs,* presentation graphics programs convert numbers into histograms, bar charts, pie charts, and line graphs. Many finance programs can generate presentation-quality graphs from the numbers they manipulate, so for most personal finance needs it is not necessary to buy a separate "stand-alone" program.

Database Management Programs This type of program makes it easy to store, retrieve, and manipulate lists of information. Most database systems have built-in functions for sorting records, printing simple reports, and designing on-screen forms to facilitate the entry of data. The simplest database programs are called "personal filing" programs; they can deal with only one file of information at a time and are ideal for mailing lists, personal inventories, and other light uses. More powerful database systems can merge information from one file into another, generate sophisticated reports, and manage millions of records. At the heart of many accounting and financial recordkeeping systems is a database program.

Telecommunications You can use an ordinary telephone line to link your personal computer to any of thousands of other computers, from the largest scientific supercomputers to a friend's personal computer on the other side of the country. One of the most rapidly growing areas of communications is the linkage of personal computers to information utilities, which are time-shared mainframe computers that offer services ranging from electronic mail to news stories, investment services, biorhythms, and travel guides. Rates for using these services are based mostly on connect time, the time you are logged on to the utility, and go from a low of $5 an hour to well over $100 an hour. Here are some of the things you can do in a few minutes of connect time with an information utility:

> Search the last few months of the *Wall Street Journal* for articles on a particular topic or company.
>
> Order books, cameras, and other items at a substantial discount.
>
> Capture detailed financial information for all the companies on a predetermined list. The information might include stock and bond prices, volumes sold, company revenues, earnings, and financial ratios.
>
> Send letters to be printed and delivered by the post office.
>
> Read any of numerous "on-line" financial newsletters—even transcripts of Louis Rukeyser's *Wall Street Week* from the Public Broadcasting Service.

One unique service provided by information utilities is the ability to search quickly through large volumes of information and find all the items matching criteria you specify. Unfortunately, the commands used by some information utilities are rather hard to master. You can, however, use a communications program, such as Texas Instruments' NaturalLink, on your personal computer that allows you to construct queries that your communications program translates before it sends the queries to the utility.

Home Finance Programs   Also called *personal finance programs,* home finance programs help you monitor your financial health; they vary considerably in their capabilities. The simplest are little more than aids for balancing a checkbook. Most offer the ability to set up a database of income, expense, asset, and liability accounts and provide numerous financial reports along with simple graphs of the data. The high-end home finance programs would satisfy most of the accounting needs of a small business.

Tax-Planning and Preparation Programs   These programs compare alternative tax strategies and help prepare income tax returns. Tax-planning programs allow you to perform "what-if" calculations to explore the tax impact of various tax shelters, changes in income, depreciation methods, individual retirement accounts, estate plans, estimated tax payments, and the like. Tax-preparation programs help you through the maze of filling out your tax return. Often they can print directly on the IRS forms and schedules.

Real Estate Analysis Programs   Real estate analysis programs can provide guidance on real estate transactions that would take hours to calculate by hand. Typically these programs can perform a number of investment comparisons, such as comparing the cost of purchasing with renting, calculating an amortization schedule, making a cash flow projection, or determining if it is possible to qualify a buyer for a particular property. Both real estate analysis and tax preparation are activities that the average person does infrequently, usually no more than once a year. As a result, most of these programs are sold to professionals, who use them in consultation with their clients.

Stock and Bond Analysis Programs   These are tools for screening, evaluating, and selecting investments. Some of these packages focus on technical analysis, an analysis of the security's market price and volume statistics. Other programs stick to analyzing the fundamentals, such as facts from historical financial statements, expected earnings, or subjective evaluations of the company's management and products. Both types of programs allow you to establish a database of information on a list of securities you wish to track. Information can be entered into the database by hand, but most programs are also able to extract the necessary information automatically from an information utility such as the Dow Jones News/Retrieval service. Once the information is in the database, the program's analysis capabilities take over to create reports listing your investments, reports recommending purchase strategies, or charts plotting stock prices, among other things.

Spreadsheet Processing

A spreadsheet program transforms a personal computer into a number-crunching tool capable of solving problems you used to tackle with a pencil, scratch pad, and calculator. It is especially useful for time-consuming tasks, such as performing the same calculations repetitively with different starting assumptions or making decisions among several alternatives. These characteristics make spreadsheet processing ideal for ad hoc financial analysis.

The computer screen is broken into two areas: a program status and help information area, which helps you control the operation of the program much like a car's dashboard helps you drive a car, and a window into the worksheet, which shows you a processed version of the data in the worksheet.

The worksheet can be thought of as an enormous piece of multi-column paper whose size depends on the program. A common size is 64 columns wide by 256 rows deep, although some worksheets have hundreds of columns and thousands of rows. Obviously only a small part of the entire worksheet can be visible on the screen at a time, so the screen acts like a window presenting a tiny part of the entire worksheet. It is possible to move the window through the worksheet by scrolling horizontally and vertically.

The real power of spreadsheet programs lies in their ability to store formulas for calculating numbers as well as storing the numbers themselves. Thus, when critical numbers are changed, the entire model is recalculated, updating any totals or other numbers as necessary to keep everything self-consistent and in balance. For example, if you changed the amount of January's food budget, the total budget for the month would be adjusted automatically.

This instantaneous "what-if" recalculation capability allows people to experiment with the relationships among numbers in a manner that was previously impractical. For example, changing the sales estimate in a business's typical five-year financial plan requires adjustments in manufacturing costs, overhead costs, warranty returns, and many other items. If the forecast is stored on a multicolumn paper worksheet, it can take an accountant hours of error-prone, tedious figuring to predict the implications of a specific set of changes in the forecast's basic assumptions. Such arduous work discourages experimentation and limits how many assumptions about the future are explored.

Presentation Graphics

A graph provides instant meaning to numbers in a manner that no table or paragraph can match. Trends and relationships that lie hidden in a collection of numbers are immediately exposed when the numbers are charted or graphed.

With the right combination of hardware and software, it takes only a few minutes to create graphs that would take hours to prepare by hand. Most programs allow you to preview the graphs on the screen. If you like what you see and have an appropriate output device, you can transfer the image onto paper, an overhead transparency, or 35-mm slides.

In addition to simple bar charts, pie charts, and line graphs, most stand-alone presentation graphics programs have numerous charting options, such as creating stacked bar charts, exploded pie charts, or stock market graphs with tick marks for each day's high, low, close, and open prices. Other features allow you to specify the size and placement of titles or to cross-hatch or color portions of the graph. However, the average person who just wants to graph personal expenses doesn't need the capabilities of a stand-alone graphics program.

Many of the advanced spreadsheet programs include a graphics module capable of generating a limited range of presentation graphics. Once you are familiar with the process, it takes no more than a few seconds to obtain a crude graph. The two major steps are to select the type of graph you want from a menu of options in the control panel and to point out what parts of the worksheet contain the numbers to be graphed.

Many home finance, stock and bond tracking, and other finance programs have very easy-to-use graphing capabilities. For example, a majority of the home finance programs will present a bar chart showing the monthly account balances of any income or expense category that you specify. Requesting one of these charts generally takes no more than a few keystrokes and can provide an immediate insight into your spending habits.

Home Finance Programs

A home finance management program helps record, summarize, print, and graph financial transactions. Basically, it is a miniature accounting system designed to be used by a family or a small business.

Like all accounting systems, a home finance program operates with the help of a chart of accounts. You must tell the program what accounts you want when you set up the system, but it should also be possible to modify the listing later.

Once the chart of accounts has been established, you can begin entering transactions. It is always possible to correct a transaction that you have entered in error. Also, most systems allow you to set up some transactions so that they can be posted automatically. This would make sense for a house payment that is the same amount each month.

A home finance program will record and enter transactions more slowly than you could write them down on paper, but this type of system really pays off when it comes to generating reports. You should be able to preview on the screen or send to the printer a cash flow statement, a personal net worth statement, and various types of transaction listings. In addition, most systems allow you to graph the activity in each account or account category. These graphs can be a real eye-opener and show you trends in your spending habits you hadn't noticed before.

A home finance program will not help you if the only accounting activity you do each month is to balance your checkbook—you can do that more quickly by hand. But if you are already recording your expenses, a home finance program can make the process more reliable and improve the quality of the information you receive from your efforts.

Finding Financial Software

Acquiring good financial software requires research, judgment, money, and luck. Searching for the "best" software package is often impractical because of the tremendous number of packages on the market—over 30,000 programs are available for personal computers.

The price of financial programs varies dramatically. A few excellent programs have been placed in the public domain by their authors; frequently these can be purchased from computer clubs for the cost of duplicating a disk (about $5). Most programs sold for use in the home cost from $30 to $300.

Finding information about financial programs can be difficult. Your local computer retailer is not likely to stock many financial programs; they sell slowly compared to programs like games and word processing. Also, nearly all software outlets are reluctant to lend copies of programs for evaluation because of the rampant software piracy problem in our society. Here are two basic sources to use to begin your search:

> Personal computer magazines can be an excellent source of independent software reviews. You can consult either general personal computer magazines (such as *InfoWorld, Byte,* or *Personal Computing*) or magazines targeted to specific brands of machines (such as *PC World* for IBM PCs or *inCider* for Apple IIs).
>
> *Software catalogues and directories* provide listings of programs organized by category. The boundaries between most categories are unclear; for finance programs you might check investment management, business, real estate, personal or home management, and graphics.

One such financial software program is *Managing Your Money* by Andrew J. Tobias, published by Micro Educational Corporation of America (MECA). This package is designed to allow individuals to organize their personal finances with the help of a microcomputer and to assist in budgeting, bank transactions, investments, taxes, and retirement planning.

Glossary

Acceleration clause A clause that requires that after one loan payment is late (and therefore defaulted) all remaining installments are due and payable at once or at the demand of the lender.

Accident insurance A type of health insurance plan designed to pay a specific amount per day (for example, $100) for a hospital stay that results from an accident, and/or a specific amount for the loss of certain limbs or body parts (for example, $2,000 for the loss of an arm).

Account exceptions The costs and penalties frequently assessed on savings accounts by savings institutions.

Accrual basis budgeting Financial recordkeeping that recognizes earnings and expenditures when money is earned and expenditures are incurred, regardless of when money is actually received or paid.

Actual cash value The purchase price of property less depreciation.

Actuaries People employed to calculate the probability of losses and to establish the rates individuals must pay for insurance.

Add-on loan A second loan taken out for a larger amount before the first loan is repaid. Taking out add-on loans is called *flipping*.

Adjustable life insurance A life insurance policy that allows the policyholder to change the premium, the face amount, or the rate of cash value accumulation.

Adjustable rate mortgage A type of mortgage loan for which the interest rate can fluctuate up or down according to an index of interest rates.

Adjusted gross income (AGI) Total income minus legal adjustments to income when calculating income tax.

Adjustments to income A selected group of legal reductions to gross income, used when determining income taxes, that are generally related to employment.

Agency issues Bonds, notes, and certificates issued by various federal agencies that often pay a yield one-quarter of 1 percent higher than Treasury securities.

Aggregate limits Clauses in health insurance policies that place an *overall* maximum on the total amount of reimbursement that can be made under a policy.

All-risk policy A property insurance or other type of policy that covers all perils except those specifically listed.

Alternative investment A type of investment in which monies are placed in assets that are riskier

For text locations of glossary terms and definitions, see the index.

than savings investments, as neither principal nor earnings are guaranteed.

Amortization   The process of gradually paying off the principal and interest of a mortgage loan through a series of periodic payments to a lender.

Annual percentage rate (APR)   An annualized measure of a finance charge stated as a percentage of the unpaid balance of a debt.

Annuitant   A person who receives an annuity.

Annuity   A contract (generally with a life insurance company) that provides for a series of payments to be received at stated intervals for a fixed or variable time period in return for the payment of a premium or premiums.

Appraisal fee   A fee required for a professionally prepared estimate of the value of property by an independent party.

Appreciation   Increase in value of a home or other property.

Approximate compound yield (ACY)   A mathematical measure of the annualized compound growth of a long-term investment.

Arbitrage   The simultaneous purchase and sale of the same security, option, or futures contract in different markets, to profit from unequal prices.

Asked price   The price at which a broker is willing to sell a particular security; for mutual funds it is the current net asset value per share plus sales charges, if any. Also called *offering price*.

Assessed value   The taxable value of a real estate property.

Assets   Items owned, usually measured in terms of their fair market value.

Automatic funds transfer (AFT)   An agreement with a bank that permits customers to write checks in amounts larger than the funds in their checking account with needed funds automatically transferred from their savings account.

Automatic overdraft loan   An agreement with a bank that permits customers to write checks in amounts larger than the funds in their checking account with needed funds automatically borrowed from their VISA or MasterCard account.

Automatic premium loan   A provision in a life insurance policy that states that any premium not paid by the end of the grace period will be paid automatically with a policy loan, provided sufficient cash value or dividends have accumulated.

Automobile bodily injury liability   Liability that occurs when a driver or car owner is legally re-sponsible for bodily injury losses suffered by others.

Automobile insurance   Insurance that combines liability and property insurance coverage needed by automobile owners and drivers into a single-package policy.

Automobile insurance plan (AIP)   An insurance program that assigns a proportional share of the uninsurable drivers to each company writing auto insurance coverage in a state.

Automobile medical payments insurance   Insurance that will pay for the personal injury losses suffered by the driver of the insured vehicle and any passengers regardless of who is at fault.

Automobile property damage liability   Liability that occurs when a driver or car owner is legally responsible for damages to the property of others.

Average balance account   An account that assesses a service fee only if the average daily balance of funds in the account drops below a certain amount.

Average share cost   The actual cost basis of an investment as used for income tax purposes. It is calculated by dividing the total dollars invested by the total shares purchased.

Average share price   A simple calculation of the amounts paid for an investment, determined by dividing the total of the share prices at each investment by the number of periodic investments made.

Average tax rate   A calculated figure showing a person's tax liability as a percentage of total, gross, adjusted gross, or taxable income.

Balanced fund   A mutual fund that includes various amounts of bonds, preferred stocks, and common stocks in its portfolio.

Balance sheet   A statement describing an individual's or family's financial condition at a particular time, showing assets, liabilities, and net worth.

Balloon auto loan   A loan whereby the buyer takes the title to the car, and the last monthly payment is equal to the projected resale value of the vehicle at the end of the loan period.

Balloon clause   A clause that permits the last payment to be abnormally large in comparison to the other installment payments. Such a payment is called a *balloon payment*.

Bank   A common term for the type of financial institution that offers various forms of both checking and savings accounts.

Bank credit card account   A form of option account in which the user of a credit card (such as

VISA or MasterCard) has the option of paying the bill in full when it arrives or repaying over several months.

Bearer bond A bond whose owner is unknown to the corporation; possession of a series of post-dated coupons attached to the bond represents ownership. Also called a *coupon bond*.

Bear market A market in which stock prices are generally declining.

Beneficiary The person or organization that will receive the life insurance or other benefit payment upon the death of the insured.

Beneficiary designation clause A clause that provides that a mutual fund shareholder can name a beneficiary in a separate legal trust agreement; in the event of death the proceeds go to the beneficiary without going through probate.

Benefit period In a disability income insurance policy, the maximum period of time for which benefits will be paid.

Best buy A product or service that, in one's opinion, represents acceptable quality at a fair or low price for that level of quality.

Beta A statistically determined measure of the relative risk of a common stock compared to the market for all stocks.

Bid price The amount a broker is willing to pay, or "bid," for a particular security; also the amount per share that shareholders receive when they cash in (redeem) their shares.

Billing date The last day of the month for which any transactions will be reported on a credit card statement.

Binder A temporary insurance contract, effective until its expiration or until a permanent policy is issued, whichever occurs first.

Blue-chip stock Stock of a company with a well-regarded reputation and a long history of both good earnings and consistent cash dividends.

Bond An interest-bearing negotiable certificate of long-term debt issued by corporations and governments.

Bond and preferred stock fund A mutual fund that concentrates its holdings on senior securities: bonds and preferred stocks.

Bond certificates Evidence of debt issued to investors who purchase bonds.

Book value The net worth of a company, determined by subtracting the total of a company's liabilities (including preferred stock) from its assets. In automobile insurance, the value of a car based on the average current selling price of cars of the same make, model, and age.

Broker (real estate) A person licensed by a state to provide advice and assistance, usually for a fee, to both buyers and sellers of real estate.

Broker (securities) See *Stockbroker.*

Brokerage firm A licensed financial service institution that specializes in selling and/or buying securities or real estate.

Budget A document or set of documents used to plan and record estimated and actual income and expenditures for a period of time.

Budget account A somewhat limited charge account in which users must repay a specific amount of the charge within thirty days, then pay the remainder over a period of months.

Budget estimates The recorded amounts in a budget that are planned and expected to be received or spent during a certain period of time.

Budget exceptions The difference between budget estimates in various classifications and the actual expenditures.

Budgeting A process of financial planning and controlling that involves using a budget to set and achieve short-term goals that are in harmony with long-term goals.

Bull market A market in which stock prices are generally increasing.

Bunching deductions The process of prepaying some deductible items in order to qualify for the tax advantage of having excess deductions.

Buying long A trading technique in which an investor buys a security in the hope that it will go up in value.

California will A blank-form will that people can fill in themselves; it is legally valid if completed properly on a form that has been codified in state law.

Call An option contract that gives the option holder the right to buy the optioned asset from the option writer at the striking price.

Callable A feature of a bond or preferred stock that permits a company to prematurely redeem its preferred stocks or bonds by paying a slight premium during a certain period if the price reaches a certain amount. If interest rates decline substantially, the issuing agency can pay off the debt before the maturity date.

Capital Funds invested in a business enterprise.

Capital asset Property owned by a taxpayer for pleasure or as an investment.

Capital gain Income received from the sale of a capital asset above the costs incurred to purchase and sell the asset.

Capital gains distribution Income for investors resulting from net long-term profits of a mutual fund realized when portfolio securities are sold at a gain.

Capital growth An increase in the market value of a mutual fund's securities, usually reflected in the net asset value of fund shares.

Capital improvements Costs incurred from making changes in real property that add to the value of the property.

Capitalization rate A widely used method of determining the rate of return on a real estate investment, found by dividing the net operating income (first year) by the total investment. Also known as *income yield*.

Capital loss A financial loss on an investment that occurs when the selling price (plus expenses) is lower than the original amount invested (plus commissions).

Carat A unit of weight equal to 0.2 grams and divided into 100 "points."

Carrying forward balances The noting of residual positive or negative balances from a completed budgeting time period onto the budget of the next budgeting time period.

Cash account An investor account that requires a modest initial deposit with a stockbroker and specifies that full settlement is due the broker within five business days (or seven calendar days) after a buy or sell order has been given.

Cash advance A small loan amount secured by charging the amount to certain debit or credit cards.

Cash basis budgeting Financial recordkeeping that recognizes earnings and expenditures when money is actually received or paid out.

Cash dividends Distributions in cash by a corporation, usually paid out of earnings to holders of preferred and common stock.

Cash flow (real estate) The amount of income available to a real estate investor after subtracting all operating expenses and mortgage payments from rental income.

Cash flow calendar A budgeting device upon which annual estimated income and expenses are recorded for each budgeting time period in an effort to ascertain surplus or deficit situations.

Cashier's check A check made out to a specific payee and drawn on the financial institution itself and thus backed by its finances.

Cash loan A loan that gives a person cash to make purchases or to pay off other debts.

Cash management The task of earning maximum interest on all one's funds, regardless of the type of account in which they are kept, while having sufficient funds available for living expenses, emergencies, and savings and investment opportunities.

Cash management account (CMA) A multipurpose account, offered through brokerage firms and other financial institutions, that combines a checking account, money market fund, stock brokerage account, credit card, and debit card.

Cash refund annuity An annuity that pays the beneficiary a lump sum if the annuitant dies before collecting the original invested money.

Cash value life insurance A type of life insurance contract that pays benefits upon the death of the insured and has a savings element that allows the payment of benefits prior to death.

Certificate of deposit (CD) A form of fixed-time-period savings that pays much greater interest rates because financial institutions can count on having the funds for a fixed period and can make longer-term investments accordingly.

Certificate of insurance A document that outlines the benefits and policy provisions for individuals covered by group insurance.

Certificate of title A legal opinion (not a guarantee) of the status of a title, which is often provided when an abstract is unavailable or lost.

Certified check A personal check written on an account, on which the financial institution imprints the word *certified,* guaranteeing payment of funds in the proper amount to cover the check.

Check clearing The process of transferring funds from the bank, savings and loan association, or credit union upon which the check was drawn to the financial institution that accepted the deposit.

Checking account An account technically known as a *demand deposit;* the bank withdraws funds and makes payment whenever demanded by the depositor, which is typically done in the form of writing a check.

Churning A stockbroker's unethical encouragement of an investor to frequently buy and sell securities in an effort to earn large commissions for the broker.

Civil court A state court where numerous civil and criminal matters are resolved and a written record is made of the happenings; the proceedings are completed with the assistance of attorneys, witnesses, a judge, and often a jury.

Claims adjuster A person designated by an insurance company to assess whether a loss is covered and the dollar amount the company will pay.

Claims ratio The percentage of premiums collected by an insurance company that are subsequently paid out to reimburse the losses of insureds.

Clarity The degree of internal perfection of a gemstone or the degree to which a gemstone possesses inclusions (irregularities) that diffuse light and lessen its brilliance.

Closed-end lease A leasing arrangement in which there is no charge at the end of the lease period.

Closed-end mutual fund A type of investment company that issues a limited and fixed number of shares of stock and does not buy them back (*redeem* them), so that after the original issue is sold the price of a share is established by supply and demand in the secondary market.

Closing The process of financially and legally transferring a home to a new buyer, which usually takes place in the office of the lender or an attorney.

Codicil A legal amendment to a will.

Coinsurance A method by which the insured and insurer share proportionately in the payment for a loss.

Coinsurance cap A stipulation in a health insurance plan that establishes a maximum loss beyond which the coinsurance requirement is not applied.

Collateral An asset a borrower pledges to back up a debt.

Collectibles Cultural artifacts that have value because of beauty, age, scarcity, or popularity.

Collision insurance A type of automobile insurance designed to reimburse the insured for losses to his or her vehicle resulting from a collision with another car or object or from a rollover.

Commercial property Property designed for business uses, such as an office building, medical center, gasoline station, or motel, that carries a potential for profit.

Common stock The most basic form of ownership of a corporation. The owner has a residual claim on the assets of the firm after those made by bondholders and preferred stockholders.

Common stock fund A mutual fund that includes only common stocks among its portfolio of holdings.

Community property Property that is jointly owned and equally shared by spouses.

Community property laws Laws that distribute the property of deceased persons in a manner that assumes that property during marriage is jointly owned and equally shared by the spouses no matter how much each contributed.

Comparison shopping A process of comparing products or services to determine the best buy.

Compound interest The calculation of interest on reinvested interest as well as on the original amount invested.

Comprehensive automobile insurance Insurance that provides payment for property damage losses caused by perils other than collision and rollover.

Comprehensive health insurance A health insurance plan that combines the protection provided by hospital insurance, surgical insurance, medical expense insurance, and major medical expense insurance into one policy.

Comprehensive personal liability insurance Insurance that provides the insured protection from liability losses that might arise out of any activity.

Computer-chip card A plastic card, in which a silicon memory chip is embedded, used for various financial transactions.

Conditional sales contract A credit agreement (also called a *financing lease*) under which the title to the property being financed does not pass to the buyer until the last installment payment has been made.

Conditions Statements in an insurance policy that impose obligations on both the insured and the insurer by establishing the ground rules of the agreement.

Condominium A home ownership arrangement in which the owner holds title to a housing unit within a building or project, and a proportionate interest in the common grounds and facilities.

Consumer credit Nonbusiness debt used by consumers for purposes other than home mortgages.

Consumer price index (CPI) A broad measure of the cost of living for consumers, published monthly by the U.S. Bureau of Labor Statistics.

Contents replacement cost protection An optional feature available in some homeowner's insurance policies that pays the replacement cost of any personal property.

Contingent beneficiary The person or organization that will become the beneficiary if the original beneficiary dies before the insured.

Contract A legally binding agreement between two or more parties.

Contractual accumulation plan A formalized, long-term program to purchase shares in an open-end, load mutual fund.

Contrarianism An investment philosophy suggesting that once the general public has seized upon an idea its usefulness is over and the wise investor should take the opposite action.

Convertible bond A bond that the owner can exchange during a specified time period before maturity for a predetermined number of shares of stock in the same corporation.

Convertible stock A preferred stock that can be exchanged for a certain number of shares of common stock during a specified time period.

Convertible term insurance A type of life insurance policy that allows the policyholder to convert a term policy to a cash value policy.

Cooperative A corporation that owns housing units and whose tenants purchase shares of ownership in the corporation equivalent to the value of their particular housing unit.

Coordination-of-benefits clause A clause in an insurance contract that prevents an insured from collecting more than 100 percent of a loss and designates the order in which policies will pay benefits if multiple policies are applicable to a loss.

Copayment clause A stipulation in a health insurance contract requiring that the insured pay a specific dollar portion of specifically covered expense items.

Corporation A state-chartered legal entity that can conduct business operations in its own name and be totally responsible for its actions as well as its debts.

Cosigner A person who agrees to pay a loan should the borrower fail to do so.

Countercyclical (defensive) stocks Stocks of companies that maintain substantial earnings during a general decline in economic activity because their products are needed.

Coupon The interest rate printed on the bond certificate when it is issued. Also called *coupon yield.*

Coupon bond See *Bearer bond.*

Coupon rate See *Stated interest rate (bonds).*

Coupon yield See *Coupon.*

Court not of record See *Small claims court.*

Credit A form of trust established between a lender and a borrower.

Credit application A form used to record information regarding a credit applicant's ability and willingness to repay debts.

Credit bureau An agency that gathers information on individuals from merchants, creditors, and court records and provides reports of this information to credit grantors for a fee.

Credit card A plastic card identifying the holder as a participant in the credit plan of a lender, such as a department store, oil company, or bank.

Credit card liability A liability for unauthorized use of a credit card that occurs only if the cardholder received notification of potential liability, accepted the card when it was first mailed, the company provided a self-addressed form to be used to notify them if the card disappeared, *and* the card was illegally used before the cardholder notified the company of its loss.

Credit controlsheet A form used to monitor the use of credit, amounts owed, and to whom money is owed.

Credit investigation The process of investigating or checking out an applicant's credit history to compare it with information provided on the credit application.

Credit life insurance A life insurance policy that will pay the remaining balance of a loan if the insured dies before repaying the debt.

Credit limit The maximum outstanding debt on a credit account.

Creditor A person or institution to whom money is owed.

Credit overextension A condition under which excessive personal debts cause extreme difficulty and possible inability to repay.

Credit rating A rating to help the lender determine if a credit applicant should be granted credit.

Credit receipt Written evidence of merchandise returned and the sales price.

Credit union A financial institution developed to serve members/owners that have some common bond, such as the same employer, religion, union, or fraternal association.

Credit union share An investment (savings) in a credit union in minimum amounts of $5 or $10, upon which interest is earned.

Crop insurance Insurance that provides all-risk protection from losses to crops between planting and harvest.

Crude rate of return A rough measure of the yield on amounts invested that assumes that equal portions of the gain were earned each year.

Cumulative A type of preferred stock. Prior dividends must be paid before distributing any future dividends to the common stockholders if the board of directors had voted to skip paying prior cash dividends to preferred stockholders.

Current income Money received from an investment, usually on a regular basis, in the form of interest, dividends, rent, or other such payment.

Current yield A measure of the current annual return expressed as a percentage when divided by its current market price.

Cyclical stock A stock whose price movements typically follow the general state of the economy and the various phases of the business cycle.

Day-of-deposit-to-day-of-withdrawal (DDDW) method A method of determining savings account balance whereby each deposit earns interest for the total number of days it was actually in the institution.

Day order Instructions to a stockbroker that are valid only for the remainder of the trading day during which they were given to the broker.

Death benefit The amount that will be paid under a life insurance policy upon the death of the insured person.

Death rate The term used for the probability that an individual will die at a given age.

Debenture Any unsecured bond.

Debit card A card that permits the holder to make immediate deductions from or additions to accounts through an automatic teller machine.

Debt-consolidation loan A type of credit in which a borrower obtains a new loan to pay off several smaller debts with varying due dates and interest rates and instead has one monthly payment which is usually lower in amount than the payments on the other debts combined.

Decedent A person who has died with a valid will in effect.

Declarations A section of an insurance policy that provides basic descriptive information about the insured person and/or property, the premium to be paid, the time period of the coverage, and the policy limits.

Decreasing term insurance A type of term life insurance contract in which the face amount declines annually and the premiums remain constant.

Deductible Requirement in an insurance policy that an insured pay an initial portion of any loss before receiving insurance benefits.

Deed A written document used to convey real estate ownership.

Default A failure to meet legal financial obligations.

Default risk The likelihood that a bondholder will not receive the promised interest and bond redemption when due.

Defendant In a court of law, the person who allegedly committed a wrong deed and is the subject of litigation.

Deferred annuity An annuity that does not begin to pay off until a specified time period elapses or an event, such as a sixtieth birthday or retirement, occurs.

Deferred sales charges Commissions on load and no-load mutual funds of 1 to 6 percent assessed on the investor if the shares are redeemed within a certain time period after purchase.

Defined benefit method A method of calculating retirement benefits that fixes the level of retirement, survivors', or disability benefits based on the income and/or years of employment of the worker.

Defined contribution method A method of calculating retirement benefits that clearly specifies the amounts contributed to the plan by the employee and employer; the actual amount of the benefits is unknown until the worker retires, becomes disabled, or dies.

Demand deposit An account for which the financial institution must withdraw funds and make payments whenever demanded by the depositor.

Dental expense insurance A type of health insurance plan designed to provide reimbursement for dental care expenses.

Depreciation The decline in value of an asset over time due to normal wear and tear and obsolescence.

Diamond A pure or nearly pure form of carbon, naturally crystallized in a state of extreme hardness.

Direct ownership A type of ownership in which one or more investors have legal title to real estate.

Direct purchase A method of acquiring shares in an open-end mutual fund where the investor simply orders and pays for the shares ordered, plus any commissions.

Direct seller An insurance company that sells its policies directly through salaried employees, mail-order marketing, newspapers, and even vending machines.

Disability income insurance A type of health insurance that replaces a portion of the income lost when the insured cannot work due to illness or injury.

Discount A selling price for a bond that is below its face value.

Discount broker A brokerage firm that features especially low commission charges because it provides limited services to customers.

Discounted cash flow A method of estimating the value or asking price of a real estate investment, which emphasizes after-tax cash flows and the return on the invested dollars discounted over time to reflect a discounted yield.

Discount yield The rate of return on investments that are sold below face value, with the gain at sale or maturity representing the interest for federal income-tax purposes.

Disposable personal income The amount of take-home pay after all deductions are withheld for taxes, insurance, union dues and the like; in other words, gross pay minus payroll deductions.

Diversification The process of reducing risk by spreading investment monies among several alternative investments.

Dividend payout ratio The percentage of the total earnings of a company paid out to stockholders as cash dividends.

Dividend reinvestment plan (DRP) An investment plan that permits stockholders to reinvest stock dividends by purchasing additional shares directly from the corporation.

Dividends Cash profits distributed to shareholders of corporations.

Dividends per share A per-share figure of cash dividends paid out by a company.

Dividend yield The relationship between the current cash dividend and the current market value of a security. It is determined by dividing the dollar amount of a recent annual dividend by the current market value of the stock or by the purchased price if the stock is already owned.

Dollar-cost averaging An investment approach that requires investing the same fixed dollar amount in the same stock at regular intervals over a long time with the result that more shares are purchased when the price is low and fewer shares when the price is high.

Drawee The financial institution at which an account is held and upon which a check is drawn.

Drawer A person who opens a checking account and writes checks. Also called a *payer*.

Dread disease insurance A form of health insurance plan designed to provide reimbursement for medical expenses arising out of the occurrence of a specific disease.

Dual-earner household Two people living together, married or unmarried, with each providing earnings on a regular basis.

Due date The date by which any payment owed must be paid.

Due-on-sale clause A clause that requires that a mortgage loan be paid in full if the home is sold and effectively prohibits a new buyer from assuming the loan.

Dunning letter Notices from creditors that insistently demand repayment of debts.

Earned income Salaries, wages, fringe benefits, and income from sole proprietorships that is taxed in a normal manner.

Earnest money A deposit in advance of the down payment on a real estate purchase.

Earnings per share (EPS) A measure of the profitability of a firm on a per-share basis; it is a dollar figure determined by dividing the corporation's total after-tax annual earnings (before cash dividends) by the total number of shares held by investors.

Effective personal finance management The planning, analyzing, and controlling of financial resources to meet personal financial goals.

Effective rate of interest The actual rate at which deposits earn interest after consideration of all interest calculation variables, costs, and penalties.

Electronic funds transfer (EFT) The use of computers and electronic means to transfer funds from one party to another.

Elimination period (waiting period) In a disability income insurance policy, the time period between the onset of the disability and the date the disability benefits begin.

Employee stock purchase plan (ESPP) A fringe benefit for employees that permits them to buy shares of stock in the company and gives them an extra incentive to do a good job, with the hoped result of an increase in the profitability of the corporation and in the value of the stock.

Endorsement In banking, the process by which checks are transferred from one person to another; when a person signs, or endorses, the back of a check written to him or her, it can then be either cashed or deposited. In insurance, amendments and additions to a basic insurance policy; also known as *riders*.

Endowment life insurance A type of life insurance that provides payment of the face amount at the death of the insured or at some previously agreed-upon date, whichever occurs first.

Entrepreneurial profit The financial reward for the serious and successful manager of real estate properties.

Envelope system A method of strict budgetary control whereby exact amounts of money are placed into envelopes for specific purposes.

Episode limits Clauses in health insurance policies that specify the maximum payment for health-care expenses arising from a single episode of illness or injury.

Equity The dollar value of a home in excess of what is owed on it.

Equity trusts Real estate investment trusts that concentrate on buying or building their own real estate properties, such as apartments, restaurants, nursing homes, condominiums, and office buildings and hire management firms to run the properties.

Escheat The right of the state to take property when no persons are legally qualified to inherit or make claim to a deceased's property.

Escrow account A special reserve account used to pay third parties and often used in conjunction with real estate loans.

Estate planning The process of planning, reviewing, and revising efforts to reduce the tax liability on an estate and to keep probate costs low.

Estate tax A tax assessed on property owned and/or controlled by a deceased before it is transferred to heirs.

Exchange registered An adjective describing a brokerage firm that is a member of an organized stock exchange.

Exclusions (insurance) Clauses in an insurance policy that narrow the focus and eliminate specific coverages broadly stated in the insuring agreements.

Exclusions (tax) Sources of income that are not considered as income for federal tax purposes; such income is tax exempt.

Exclusive insurance agent A person who represents only one insurance company.

Ex dividend A term that means that investors buying a particular stock will not receive the next dividend that the company has recently declared.

Executor A male named in a will (a female is known as an *executrix*) to carry out the directions and requests in the will and provided a certain amount of legal power by the state.

Executrix See **Executor**.

Exemption The legally permitted reduction in the taxpayer's taxable income based on the number of persons supported by that income.

Exit fees Charges assessed upon redemption of mutual fund shares regardless of the length of time the investor has owned the shares.

Expenditure An amount of money that has been spent.

Exposures Items owned and behaviors engaged in that expose one to the risk of financial loss.

Express warranty A written warranty that accompanies many products and is offered by manufacturers on a voluntary basis to induce customers to buy.

Eye care insurance A health insurance plan designed to provide reimbursement for the expenses related to the purchase of glasses and contact lenses.

Face amount In life insurance, the amount of money stated in the policy that will be paid upon the death of the insured party.

Face value The value of a bond as stated on the certificate; also, the amount the investor receives when the bond matures.

Fair market value The price that a willing buyer would pay a willing seller for an asset.

Family automobile policy (FAP) An insurance policy designed for autos owned by families in which there are several persons who might drive the car.

Federal Deposit Insurance Corporation (FDIC) An agency of the federal government that insures bank accounts.

Federal Housing Administration (FHA) A subdivision of the Department of Housing and Urban Development that insures mortgage loans that meet its standards.

Federal Savings and Loan Insurance Corporation (FSLIC) A federal government agency that insures all federally chartered savings and loan associations.

FIFO (first-in, first-out) method A method of determining savings account balances whereby withdrawals are first deducted from the balance at the start of the interest period and then, if the balance is not sufficient, from later deposits.

Fill-or-kill order Instructions to the stockbroker to buy or sell at the market price immediately or else the order is cancelled.

Final expenses Outlays occurring just prior to or after a death.

Final tax liability The resulting tax liability for a taxpayer after deducting the last legally allowable tax credits. It is the amount actually owed the government.

Finance charge The lender's charge for borrowing money.

Financial goals The long-term objectives that one's financial planning and management efforts are intended to attain.

Financial loss Any decline in value of income or assets in the present or future.

Financial planner A person who advises clients about personal finances. He or she has usually undergone training and has met the qualifications for particular professional certifications.

Financial planning The process of developing and implementing plans to achieve financial objectives.

Financial services industry The institutions that offer checking, banking, and/or savings services.

Financial skills The techniques of decision making in personal financial management.

Financial statement A compilation of personal financial data designed to communicate information on money matters.

Financial supermarket A national or regional corporation that offers a great many financial services to consumers.

Financial tools The forms and charts used in making personal financial management decisions.

Fixed-asset investments Investments of a specific amount of funds for a certain amount of time.

Fixed expenses Expenditures that are the same amount each time period.

Fixed income A characteristic of lending investment in which the borrower agrees to pay a specific rate of return for the use of the principal.

Fixed interest rate A constant interest rate on a credit card or any credit arrangement.

Fixed maturity A characteristic of lending investment in which the borrower agrees to repay the principal on a specific date.

Fixed-time deposit A time deposit with a specific time period during which the savings must be left on deposit.

Flat rate income tax An income tax that applies the same tax rate to all levels of income.

Flipping Taking out a second loan for a larger amount before repaying the first loan. This type of additional loan is called an *add-on loan.*

Float The time the check writer actually has the funds in his or her account until the check finally clears.

Floater policy Property insurance that provides all-risk protection for accident and theft losses to movable personal property regardless of where in the world the loss occurs.

Floating-rate bonds Long-term corporate or municipal bond issues, redeemable after two or three years with an interest rate fixed for six to eighteen months, after which it varies according to an index or government interest rate.

Flood insurance Insurance that protects property from losses caused by floods and mud slides provided that the property is located in areas eligible under the National Flood Insurance Act of 1968.

401(k) plan See **Salary reduction plan.**

Fringe benefit Any payment for employment that is not provided in the form of wages or commissions.

Front-end load An arrangement in the purchase of mutual funds specifying that total commissions and other fees will be deducted on an accelerated basis from the amounts invested (usually in the first two years). See also **Load fund.**

Full warranty As defined in the Magnuson-Moss Warranty Act, an express warranty that includes stringent requirements such as free repair or replacement of covered components.

Futures contract A marketable contract that requires the delivery of a specific amount of a commodity at a certain future date.

Future value The valuation of an asset projected to the end of a particular time period in the future.

Garnishment A legal attachment to one's wages directed by a court.

General obligation bond A common type of municipal bond that is backed by the full taxing authority of the issuing agency.

Good-till-canceled order See **Open order.**

Grace period In banking, the time period in days in which savings deposits or withdrawals can be made and still earn interest from a given day of the interest period. In credit, a period after receipt of a credit bill during which no finance charges are assessed. In insurance, a period after the insurance premium due date, usually 31 days, during which late payment may be made without a lapse of the policy.

Gross estate The gross value in dollars of an estate, which includes just about everything owned by and amounts owed to the estate owner.

Gross income All income received in the form of money, property, and services that is not legally exempt from tax.

Gross income multiplier (GIM) A method of determining the price to pay for an income-producing property by dividing the asking price (or market value) of the property by the current gross rental income.

Group insurance Insurance sold collectively to an entire group under one policy.

Group legal insurance plan Insurance that provides reimbursement for legal expenses to eligible members of a group.

Growth stocks (lesser known) Stocks of companies that have had higher-than-average earnings in recent years and have good prospects for the future but may not be the industry giants or industry leaders.

Growth stocks (well known) Stocks of companies that are leaders in their fields and have several consecutive years of above-average earnings.

Guaranteed insurability option An option that allows a cash value life insurance policyholder to buy additional life insurance coverage without proving insurability.

Guaranteed renewability option An option available with term life insurance policies that eliminates the need to prove insurability when the policy is to be renewed.

Hazard Any condition that increases the probability that a peril will occur.

Hazard reduction Action by the insured to reduce the probability of a loss occurring.

Health insurance Insurance that provides protection against financial losses resulting from illness, injury, and disability.

Health maintenance organization (HMO) A group of health-care providers who operate on a prepaid basis.

Hidden load An annual undeclared charge by a mutual fund of 1 to 1.25 percent annually, which pays for marketing and distribution fees.

Holder-in-due-course doctrine Legal protection for a merchant that states that if a merchant sells a product on credit to a consumer and then sells the credit contract to a sales finance company, the legally binding contract exists between the consumer and the finance company and the consumer no longer has the right to withhold payment for faulty merchandise. In 1976 federal law was changed so that today, in the great majority of cases, the ruling does not apply.

Holographic will A will that is entirely in the handwriting of the person signing the will and, as some states require, dated with the same hand.

Home-equity credit line loan A form of second mortgage whereby the lender offers a line of credit up to a maximum loan value of perhaps 75 percent of the home's value minus what is owed on the first mortgage. Money can then be tapped from this account by check, debit card, or credit card.

Homeowner's fee An amount established by the (condominium) homeowner's association that pays for such things as maintenance of common areas and facilities, repairs to the outside of any unit (paid for by all), real estate taxes on the common areas, and fire insurance covering the exterior of the building(s).

Homeowner's general liability protection Insurance that covers situations where the homeowner or renter is legally liable for the losses of another.

Homeowner's insurance Insurance that combines liability and property insurance coverage needed by home owners and renters into a single-package policy.

Homeowner's no-fault medical payments protection Insurance that will pay for injuries to visitors regardless of who was at fault for the loss.

Hospital insurance A health insurance plan designed to protect the insured from the costs arising out of a period of hospitalization (also called *hospitalization insurance*).

Housing ownership record A record that shows the dates and amounts spent to improve, but not maintain, the home.

Human capital The abilities, skills and knowledge people have that permit them to perform work or services.

Immediate annuity An annuity that provides for payments to begin at the end of the first month or year after final payment of the premium.

Implied warranty A legal right based in state law that provides that products sold are warranted to be suitable for sale and will work effectively whether there is an express warranty or not.

Impulsive buying An emotional, almost reckless buying of goods and services with little regard to planning or need.

Income and expense statement A summary of a person's or family's income and expense transactions that have taken place over a specific period of time.

Income dividend Mutual fund earnings of dividends and interest on securities (plus short-term capital gains) after operating expenses are deducted.

Income fund A mutual fund whose primary objective is current income and which seeks a portfolio of bonds, preferred stocks, and some select blue-chip stocks.

Income insurance Insurance that provides protection against the loss of future income.

Income splitting A process that takes place when one person with a high marginal tax rate shifts income to another person who is in a lower tax bracket.

Income stock A stock that pays a cash dividend that is high year after year because the company has fairly high earnings and chooses to declare high cash dividends regularly and retain only a small portion of the earnings.

Income yield See *Capitalization rate.*

Incontestability clause A clause that places a time limit, usually two years, on the right of the life insurance company to deny a claim after the death of the insured.

Indenture A legally written agreement between a group of bondholders and the debtor as to the terms of the debt.

Independent insurance agent A person who represents two or more insurance companies.

Indexing method A technique of calculating Social Security benefits that revalues previous wage earnings in terms of current wage levels by multiplying each year's income by an index factor announced annually by the Social Security Administration.

Indirect (group) ownership A type of ownership in which a group of investors appoint a trustee to hold legal title to a real estate investment on behalf of all in the group.

Individual account An account with one owner who is solely responsible for the account and its activity.

Individual Retirement Account (IRA) An account that allows people earning income to make tax-deductible payments to their own private investment fund held by a bank, mutual fund, insurance company, or other trustee.

Inflation A condition of across-the-board increases in the prices of goods and services.

Insolvent An adjective describing a person with a negative net worth.

Installment credit A type of consumer credit in which the consumer pays the amount owed in equal payments, usually monthly.

Installment premium annuity An annuity purchased with a series of premium payments.

Installment purchase agreement A credit agreement (also called a *collateral installment loan* or *chattel mortgage*) in which the title of the property passes to the buyer as the document is signed.

Installments certain annuity An annuity that guarantees a minimum number of payments (installments) to the annuitant and/or a benefi-ciary even if the annuitant dies before the minimum number of installments are paid.

Insurable interest A situation that exists when a person or organization stands to suffer a financial loss resulting directly from a peril.

Insurance A mechanism for reducing risk by having a large number of individuals share in the financial losses suffered by members of the group.

Insurance agent A person who sells, modifies, and terminates contracts of insurance between the insured and insurers.

Insurance agreement A legal agreement by the borrower to purchase credit and/or disability insurance that would pay the lender the balance of the loan in full should the borrower die or become seriously disabled.

Insurance claim A formal request to an insurance company for reimbursement for a covered loss.

Insurance dividends Payments made by stock insurance companies to their policyholders as partial refunds of premiums.

Insurance policy The written agreement between a person buying insurance and an insurance company.

Insurance rate The cost to the insured for each unit of insurance coverage.

Insured The person buying or covered by insurance.

Insurer Any individual or organization that provides insurance coverage.

Insuring agreements Broadly defined coverages provided under an insurance policy.

Interest The payment one receives for allowing a financial institution (sometimes just an individual) to use and invest one's money.

Interest-adjusted cost index (IACI) A measure of the cost of life insurance that takes into account the interest that would have been earned had the premiums been invested rather than used to buy insurance.

Interest-adjusted net payment index (IANPI) A measure of the cost of cash value life insurance to be held until death.

Interest rate risk The uncertainty of the market value of an asset resulting from possible interest rate changes.

Interval ownership purchase Purchase of vacation property through time sharing, which provides for actual titles and deeds to limited, preplanned use of the real estate and which legally makes the purchaser a secured creditor, thus guaranteeing continued use of property throughout any bankruptcy proceedings.

Intestate Adjective describing someone who dies without leaving a valid will.

Investment assets Tangible and intangible items acquired for generating additional income and/or in anticipation of increases in their value.

Investment banking firm A specialized seller of new securities that serves as middleman between the issuing company and the investing public.

Investment club An organization formed by individuals who want to share their investment knowledge and a limited amount of investment dollars to learn about the securities market and to make a profit.

Investment company A corporation, trust, or partnership in which investors with similar financial goals pool their funds to utilize professional management and to achieve diversification of their investments.

Investment philosophy A personal investment strategy that anticipates specific returns and risks and contains tactics for accomplishing one's investment goals.

Irrevocable trust A trust that is not subject to any modification by the grantor during his or her lifetime and thus bypasses probate and estate taxes.

IRS private letter rulings IRS advisory opinions on individual tax-management proposals, issued annually to several hundred individuals and corporations.

IRS regulations Interpretations of the tax laws passed by Congress and having the force and effect of law.

IRS rulings Decisions based on the IRS interpretation of both the tax laws and their regulations, which provide guidance to how the IRS will act in certain general situations.

Itemized deductions Specific expenses that can be deducted from adjusted gross income.

Item limits Provisions in a health insurance policy that specify the maximum reimbursement for particular health-care expenses.

Joint and survivor annuity An annuity that pays proceeds until the death of both annuitants.

Joint tenancy A type of direct ownership in which two or more people have an undivided interest in real estate held in equal or unequal shares. In the event that an owner dies, the survivor(s) gets the property.

Joint tenancy account An account in which each owner has access to the savings account and both are responsible separately and collectively for deposits and withdrawals.

Joint tenancy with right of survivorship Joint tenancy that requires that upon the death of a joint tenant (one owner) the remaining joint tenant or tenants assume full ownership of the property.

Joint will A will drawn by a married couple who have made reciprocal provisions for each other. Also called a *mutual will*.

Junk bonds Unsecured bonds of low quality with high default risk that pay two to five more interest points than quality bonds.

Keogh plan A pension plan that allows self-employed persons to make large tax-deductible payments for themselves and their eligible employees; the fund is held by a trustee who, in certain circumstances, could be the self-employed person.

Lapsed policy An insurance policy that has been terminated due to the policyholder's failure to pay the required premium.

Law of large numbers A statistical concept stating that as the number of units in a group increases, predictions about the group become increasingly accurate.

Lawyer-prepared will A will drafted by an attorney; the least likely of all wills to be successfully challenged.

Lease A legal contract specifying the responsibilities of both the tenant and the landlord.

Letter of last instructions A letter written in one's own handwriting, signed, and usually given to the executor, which can include transfers of any odds and ends of personal property (both valuable and sentimental) without being made public in the formal will. Also called a *letter precatory*.

Letter precatory See **Letter of last instructions.**

Letter stock A security that has not yet been registered with the Securities and Exchange Commission for sale to the public.

Leverage The use of borrowed money to make an investment that, it is hoped, will earn a rate of return greater than the after-tax costs of borrowing.

Liabilities The dollar value of items owed.

Liability insurance Insurance that provides protection against losses suffered by others for which the insured party is responsible.

Lien A legal right to hold property or to sell it for payment of a claim.

Life cycle A description of the progress of human life along a continuous sequence of family-status periods and stages.

Life insurance Insurance that reduces the risk of financial loss resulting from death.

Lifestyle One's particular way of living.

LIFO (last-in, first-out) method A method of determining savings account balances whereby withdrawals are first deducted from the most recent deposits and then from the less recent ones, and so on.

Limited partnership A form of owning real estate investment property involving two classes of partners, the general partner (usually the organizer), who operates the syndicate and has unlimited financial liability, and the limited partners (the investors), who receive part of the profits and the tax-shelter benefits but who have no voice in the management of the business and have no personal liability for the operations of the partnership beyond their initial investment.

Limited pay life insurance Whole life insurance that allows premium payments to cease sometime prior to the age of one hundred.

Limited warranty A warranty that offers less than a full warranty as defined in the Magnuson-Moss Warranty Act.

Limit order An instruction to the stockbroker to buy at the best possible price but not above a specified limit or to sell at the best possible price but not below a specified limit.

Line of credit The maximum approved amount that a person can borrow without completing a new credit application.

Linton yield A mathematical measure of the true rate of return on cash value insurance.

Liquidity The speed and ease with which an asset can be converted to cash.

Listed securities A security designation given by a stock exchange to securities issued by member companies that meet various criteria regarding number of stockholders, numbers of shares owned by the public, market value of each share, and corporate earnings and assets.

Listing agreement A contract permitting a realtor to list a property exclusively and/or with a multiple listing service and specifying the commission rate and time period of the agreement.

Living trust A trust created by a living grantor for the benefit of self or another. Also called *inter vivos*.

Load (sales charge) A commission earned for selling a mutual fund.

Load fund A mutual fund sold to the public that charges a sales commission, usually called a *front-end load* when purchased.

Loan origination fee The lender's charge to the borrower for doing all the paperwork and setting up the mortgage loan.

Loan-to-value ratio A measure of the amount of leverage in an investment project; determined by dividing the amount of debt by the value of the total of the original investment.

Long-term capital gain or loss A gain or loss occurring after a capital asset has been owned for more than six months at the time of sale.

Long-term goals or objectives Targets or ends that an individual or family desires to achieve using financial resources one or more years in the future.

Long-term investor An investor who is generally moderate or conservative in investment philosophy and wants to hold securities as long as they provide a return commensurate with their risk, usually for a number of years.

Loss of value insurance An insurance policy available for most mutual funds that covers market value losses from the date of the policy on previously and newly acquired shares for ten, twelve and one-half, or fifteen years.

Loss reduction Action by an insured to lessen the severity of loss should a peril occur.

Low-balance method A method of determining savings account balance whereby interest is paid only on the least amount of money that was in the account during the interest period.

Low par A one- or two-dollar par value for a common stock.

Major medical expense insurance A type of health insurance plan designed to provide reimbursement for a broad range of medical expenses (including hospital, surgical, and medical expenses) with policy limits as high as $1 million and deductibles as high as $1,000.

Manufactured housing Partially factory-assembled housing units designed to be transported in portions to the home site, where finishing of the building requires another two to six weeks.

Margin account An investor account with a brokerage firm that requires a deposit of substantial cash or securities ($2,000 or more) and permits the investor to buy other securities on credit using funds borrowed from the firm.

Marginal cost An aid to decision making that compares the additional (marginal) price or cost of something with the additional (marginal) value received.

Marginal tax bracket (MTB) An income range shown in the tax rate schedules for which there is a marginal tax rate.

Marginal tax rate The tax rate at which the last dollar earned is taxed.

Margin buying A method of reducing an investor's equity in an investment in order to magnify returns by borrowing money from a broker.

Margin call A regulation imposed by the broker that requires the margin investor to put up more funds if the value of the security declines to the point where the investor's equity is less than the required percentage of the current market value, or the broker can legally sell the securities.

Margin rate The percentage amount of the value (or equity) in an investment that an investor may not borrow from the stockbroker.

Market interest rates The current interest rates charged on various types of corporate and government debts that have similar risks.

Market making A process designed to provide a continuous market for over-the-counter stocks, in which a broker/dealer maintains an inventory of specific securities to sell to other brokers and stands ready to buy reasonable quantities of the same securities at market prices.

Market order A process that instructs the stockbroker to execute an order immediately at the best possible price.

Market price See **Market value.**

Market rate for savings bonds The rate that series EE and HH savings bonds will pay if held to maturity. The rate is 85 percent of the latest six-month average rate on five-year treasury securities.

Market value The current price that a willing buyer would pay a willing seller for an asset. Also called *market price.*

Marriage tax penalty A result of the progressive tax system that may require married couples to pay more in taxes than couples living together without being married, even though both couples have similar combined taxable incomes.

Maximum taxable yearly earnings The base amount to which the Social Security tax rate is applied and which determines the maximum amount due; taxpayers with wage income higher than this amount do not have to pay additional Social Security taxes.

Medicaid A jointly financed program of the federal government and the states that pays some medical expenses of the poor.

Medical expense insurance A health insurance plan designed to provide reimbursement for physicians' services other than those for surgery.

Medicare A program administered by the Social Security Administration that provides payment for hospital and medical expenses of persons age sixty-five and over and some others.

Medigap insurance A form of health insurance plan designed to supplement the protection provided by Medicare.

Member firm A brokerage firm that has purchased a seat on the exchange (the legal right to buy and sell securities on the exchange) with the approval of the board of directors of the exchange.

Minimum balance account An account that requires the customer to keep a certain amount in the account throughout the month to avoid a flat service charge or fee.

Minor's account An account owned by a minor, who is ultimately responsible for the activity of the account.

Mobile homes Fully factory-assembled housing units built to a certain size and designed to be towed on a frame with a trailer hitch.

Modified life insurance A whole life insurance policy with reduced premiums in the early years and higher premiums thereafter.

Monetary assets Cash or near-cash items that can be readily converted into cash. Primarily used for living expenses, emergencies, and savings.

Money income Income measured in current dollars.

Money market account The generic term for a variety of high-interest earning accounts that have limited checkwriting privileges.

Money market deposit account A government-insured money market account offered through a depository institution, such as a bank, credit union, or savings and loan association.

Money market fund (MMF) A mutual fund that pools the cash of thousands of investors and specializes in earning a relatively safe and high return by buying securities that have very short-term maturities, generally less than one year.

Monitoring unexpended balances A method to control overspending that uses a budget design showing declining balance.

Monthly investment plan (MIP) An arrangement with a brokerage firm that permits regular investment (monthly or quarterly) of a specified amount of funds ($40 to $1,000) in a common stock listed on a major stock exchange.

Month order Instructions to a stockbroker that are good until the close of trading on the last business day of the current month.

Mortgage The legal right of the lender to sell the property purchased (the security) in the event the borrower defaults on the loan.

Mortgage loan An amount loaned to a borrower by a lender for the purchase of a home.

Mortgage trust A real estate investment trust that does not own property but provides short-term financing for construction loans or for permanent mortgage loans for large projects.

Multiple-earnings approach An approach that involves estimating the funds needed to replace the income lost due to a premature death by multiplying the annual income of the person involved by the number of years the income will be needed by dependent survivors.

Multiple indemnity clause A clause in a life insurance contract that provides for a doubling or tripling of the face amount if death results from certain specified causes.

Multiple listing service An information and referral network among real estate brokers allowing properties listed with a particular realtor to be shown by all other realtors as well.

Municipal bonds (munies) Long-term debts issued by local governments and their agencies.

Municipal bonds (tax-exempt) fund A mutual fund that seeks to earn current tax-exempt income by investing solely in municipal bonds issued by cities, states, and various districts and political subdivisions.

Mutual fund An investment company that combines the funds of investors who have purchased shares of ownership in the investment company and invests those monies in a diversified portfolio of securities issued by other corporations or governments.

Mutual insurance company A company that is owned by its policyholders and operates on a nonprofit basis.

Named-perils policy An insurance policy that covers only losses caused by perils specifically listed.

Needs Those items that people find are necessary to have to survive and live in society.

Needs approach An approach for determining life insurance needs that involves estimating the total dollar loss due to a premature death.

Negotiable order of withdrawal (NOW) account An account offered by savings and loan associations, mutual savings banks, and banks, in which money deposited in the account goes to a savings account, where it earns interest income and can be withdrawn by a check.

Negotiating The step in the buying process when the buyer discusses the actual terms of an agreement with the seller.

Net asset value The current worth of the underlying securities in a mutual fund minus company liabilities.

Net gain Total income minus total expenses where income exceeds expenses.

Net loss Total income minus total expenses where expenses exceed income.

Net operating income Gross income of a rental property less allowances for vacancies and operating expenses, except depreciation and debt repayments.

Net surplus The amount of money remaining after all budget classification deficits are subtracted from those with a surplus.

Net taxable estate The gross value of an estate minus marital deductions, liabilities, charitable bequests, properties passed by law and contract, and the basic inheritance tax exemption.

Net worth The dollar value remaining when liabilities are subtracted from assets.

No-fault auto insurance Insurance that allows an insured to collect directly from his or her insurance company for losses resulting from an auto accident without regard to who was at fault.

No-load fund A mutual fund that does not have a sales charge.

Nominal rate See **Stated interest rate.**

Nominal rate of interest The apparent interest rate that is applied to deposits before consideration of the time period. Also called *stated rate of interest.*

Noncupative will An oral will spoken by a dying individual to another person or persons.

Nonforfeiture options Options that prevent the owner of a cash value life insurance policy from losing the accumulated cash value if the policy lapses or is cashed in.

Noninstallment credit A type of consumer credit that includes single-payment loans and open-ended credit.

Nonparticipating policies Insurance policies that do not provide for the payment of dividends to policyholders.

Nonprobate property An asset that is transferred by law or by contract without going through probate.

Nonqualified deferred compensation plan An approved process under ERISA regulations that permits an employee and employer to agree to defer large payments for services rendered to a later date, when the person is expected to be in a lower tax bracket.

No par An adjective describing common stock issued at zero par value.

Note The formal promise of the borrower to repay the lender as detailed in the loan contract.

Numismatist One who collects coins, medals, and selected commemoratives.

Odd lot A block of stock of more or less than one hundred shares.

Offering price See *Asked price.*

Old method A technique of benefits calculation that uses current dollars to determine specific Social Security monthly payments.

Open-ended credit A type of consumer credit whereby the consumer may choose to repay the debt in a single payment or to make a series of equal or unequal payments. Most credit cards operate in this manner. Also called *revolving credit.*

Open-end lease A lease in which one must pay any difference between the projected resale value of a car and its true market value at the end of the lease period.

Open-end mutual fund An investment company that continuously stands ready to sell new shares and to redeem old ones at net asset value.

Open order Instructions to a stockbroker that are good until executed by the broker or canceled by the investor. Also called a *good-till-canceled order.*

Opportunity cost The cost of giving up one financial option for another.

Option A contract that gives the holder the right to buy or sell a specific asset—e.g., real estate or common stock—at a specified price.

Option account A credit account permitting either payment in full when the bill arrives (with no credit costs) or partial payment spread over several months.

Option holder The person who actually owns a stock or other option contract.

Option writer A person who issues an option contract promising either to buy or to sell a specified asset for a fixed striking price and receives an option premium for standing ready to buy or sell.

Organized stock exchange A market where agents of buyers and sellers meet and trade a specified list of securities, which are usually those of larger, well-known companies.

Original source records Formal documents that record personal financial activities.

Over-the-counter (OTC) market A market for trading securities outside the organized stock exchanges, where buyers and sellers negotiate the prices of transactions, often using a sophisticated telecommunications network connecting brokers throughout the country.

Overwithholding The withholding by an employer of more payroll withholding taxes than the actual tax liability due the government.

Package account An account that, for a set fee per month, permits unlimited free checking in addition to a few thousand dollars of accidental death insurance, limited use of a photocopying machine, free traveler's checks, a free safe-deposit box, and perhaps a few more services.

Paid up Adjective describing a life insurance policy for which the time period for premium payment has ended.

Partial disability An injury or illness that prevents a worker from performing one or more functions of his or her regular occupation.

Participating policy An insurance policy that has a provision for the payment of dividends to the policyholder.

Participating preferred stock A stock that allows the preferred stockholder to receive extra dividends above the stated amount after the common stockholders have received a certain amount.

Partnership A business owned by two or more persons operated in the interests of all partners.

Par value The dollar amount assigned to a share of stock by a corporation when issued.

Pawnbroker A specialized business offering single-payment loans to individuals in amounts based on the value of personal property left in possession of the lender.

Payee The persons or firm to which a check is made out.

Payer The person who opens the checking account and writes checks. Also called a *drawer.*

Payroll withholding A method of prepaying income taxes in which an employer withholds a portion of each of an employee's paychecks as an estimate of taxes owed and forwards those funds to the government.

Peril Any event that causes a financial loss.

Period certain annuity An annuity that provides payments to the annuitant—or a beneficiary if the annuitant should die early—for a fixed time period.

Personal automobile policy (PAP) An insurance policy designed for autos owned by an individual driver.

Personal inflation rate The rate of increase in prices of items purchased by a person or household.

Personal spending style An individual's way of spending money, which is influenced by the person's values, attitudes, emotions, and other factors shaped through the experiences of his or her life.

Philately The collection and study of stamps, envelopes, and similar material.

PITI Abbreviation for "principal, interest, taxes, and insurance," the components of many monthly mortgage loan payments.

Plaintiff A person who has filed a small claims or civil court case and is suing the defendant.

Plan company A firm that specializes in selling contractual accumulation plans of loan mutual funds to the investing public.

Plan completion insurance Declining-value group term life insurance available to investors in contractual accumulation plan mutual funds.

Point A fee equal to 1 percent of the amount of the total mortgage loan, which must be paid in full when a home is bought.

Policyholder The person who pays for an insurance policy and retains all rights and privileges granted by the policy, including the right to amend the policy and the right to designate who shall receive the proceeds (also called the *owner*).

Policy limit The maximum dollar amount that will be paid under an insurance policy.

Portability A retirement plan contract clause that permits workers to take pension money to another job.

Portfolio A collection of securities and other investment instruments.

Portfolio diversification In investment practice, the process of selecting alternatives that have dissimilar risk-return characteristics; this process provides a lower but acceptable overall potential return.

Postponing income The process of delaying paycheck(s) to avoid being pushed into a higher marginal tax rate. This method is useful only if the expected income for the following year is lower than usual.

Potential total return A figure estimating the potential value of a stock, determined by adding its anticipated dividend income and price appreciation over a period of five years or more.

Pre-emptive right The right of current common stockholders to purchase additional shares of any new stock issue; this allows them to maintain their proportionate ownership interest.

Pre-existing condition A medical condition that becomes evident and for which treatment is received before the issuance of a health insurance policy.

Preferred provider organization (PPO) A group of medical providers (doctors, hospitals, etc.) who contract with a health insurance company to provide services at a discount to policyholders if the policyholders choose to be served by PPO members.

Preferred stock A fixed-income ownership security of a corporation with the right to assets and earnings before the claims of common stockholders but after those of bondholders.

Premium The fee paid for insurance protection; the difference that results when a bond is sold above its face value; the fee received by an option writer.

Prepayment fee A fee charged by a mortgage lender designed to discourage people from refinancing a mortgage loan every time interest rates drop.

Present interest The immediate, irrevocable, and complete right of a recipient of a tax-free gift to the property or money given.

Present value The current value of an asset that is to be received in the future.

Preshopping research The process of gathering information about products or services before buying them.

Price appreciation Net income received from the sale of capital assets beyond the expenses incurred in the purchase, capital improvements (if any), and sale of those assets.

Price/earnings ratio (P/E ratio, P/E multiple) A ratio of the current market value (price) of a common stock to its earnings per share (EPS) that shows how the market is valuing the stock.

Price-sales ratio (PSR) A ratio obtained by dividing the total current market value of a stock by the total sales over the past year.

Primary market A market that exists when issuers and buyers of new offerings of stocks and bonds are brought together.

Principal The original amount borrowed in a real estate or other loan, or the amount placed in an investment.

Principle of indemnity A philosophy and practice followed by insurance companies, holding that insurance will pay no more than the actual financial loss suffered.

Private mortgage insurance Insurance sold by a company that insures the first 20 percent of a mortgage loan in case of default.

Probate A court procedure for settling and disposing of an estate.

Producer cooperatives Insurance operations owned by individuals or organizations that have come together to provide insurance coverage.

Professional liability insurance Insurance designed to protect individuals and organizations that provide professional services when they are held liable for the losses of their clients.

Program trading The use of computer software programs to generate investment activity.

Progressive tax A tax that demands a higher percentage of a person's income as income increases.

Property insurance Insurance that provides protection against losses resulting from the damage to or destruction of property or possessions.

Property report A document legally required under the federal Interstate Land Sales Act for real estate properties offered for sale across state lines.

Prospectus A corporation's disclosure of facts regarding its operations, including the experience of its management, its financial status, any anticipated legal matters that could affect the company, and potential risks of investing in the corporation.

Proxy A legal procedure used by a common stockholder to assign voting rights to another.

Public debt The national debt.

Purchase contract A formal legal document that conveys the dollar offer and any list of conditions the buyer might want in a real estate or other sale/purchase transaction. Also known as a *sales contract*.

Purchase (sales credit) loan A consumer loan to make a purchase on credit with no cash passing from lender to borrower. Cash passes instead from lender to seller (or the seller may be the lender).

Purchase warrant See *Warrant*.

Purchasing power The dollar amount of goods and services an income can buy after adjusting for inflation.

Pure risk Risk that exists when there is no potential for gain, but a possibility of loss.

Put An option contract that gives the option holder the right to sell an optioned asset to the option writer at the striking price.

Quarters of coverage Calendar quarters accredited by the Social Security Administration that are based on a minimum total earnings in a calendar year.

Rate of return See *Yield*.

Raw land Undeveloped acreage, typically located far from established communities, with no utilities and no improvements except perhaps a substandard access road.

Real estate Property consisting of land and all its permanently attached structures and accompanying rights and privileges, such as crops and mineral rights.

Real estate investment trust (REIT) A type of closed-end investment company in which the proceeds from the sale of the original shares are invested by trust managers in a diversified group of income-producing properties, such as apartments and office buildings.

Real estate property taxes Local (town, city, country, township, parish) taxes based on the assessed value of buildings and land.

Real estate syndicate An indirect form of real property investment often organized as a limited partnership in which a required number of shares (often five) are sold to investors for as little as $500 each to raise capital for local, regional, or national projects.

Real income Income measured in constant prices relative to some base period.

Real return on investment The yield after subtracting the effects of inflation and taxes.

Realtor See *Broker (real estate)*.

Recession A several-month period during which reduced economic activity results in increasing unemployment, lower industrial production, and declining prices of investment securities.

Reciprocal exchanges Self-insurance mechanisms through which the insureds share in the provision of insurance.

Reconciling budget estimates Reconciling conflicting needs and wants as one revises one's budget until total expenses do not exceed income.

Record date The official day when companies take note of which shareholders deserve dividends.

Recordkeeping The process of recording the sources and amounts of dollars earned and spent.

Recurring clause A clause in a health insurance policy that clarifies whether a recurrence of an illness is considered a continuation of the first episode or a separate episode.

Redress To right a wrong.

Registered bond A bond that calls for recording the bondholder's name so that checks for interest and principal can be safely mailed when due.

Regressive tax A tax that demands a decreasing proportion of a person's income as income increases.

Regular passbook savings account A savings account that permits frequent deposit or withdrawal of funds.

Rehabilitation The retraining of disabled persons for their previous, or a new, occupation.

Reissue rate The charge for a title insurance policy that has lower premiums because the property history has been checked in recent years.

Release An insurance document affirming that the insured accepts the dollar amount of the loss settlement as full and complete reimbursement and that no further claims for the loss will be made against the insurance company.

Rent The payment received in return for the use of property (particularly housing space) such as land or a building.

Repairs Expenses, usually tax-deductible for the investor, that are necessary to maintain the value of a property.

Repossession The act of physically seizing the secured property as described in the contract after a loan is defaulted.

Residential lot Subdivided acreage with utilities (including water, electricity, and sewerage) typically located within or adjacent to established communities.

Residential unit A property designed for residential living—such as a house, duplex, apartment, mobile home, or condominium—with a potential to produce a profit.

Retail installment contract A credit agreement used when financing the purchase of a product through the seller or a sales finance company.

Retained earnings Amounts of past and current earnings not paid to shareholders but instead left to accumulate and finance the goals of the company.

Retired bond A bond that has been paid off at the maturity date specified in the indenture.

Revenue bond A type of municipal bond backed by the revenues from the projects built or maintained by the bond's proceeds, such as dormitories, sewers, waterworks, and toll roads.

Revisionary trust A trust that is irrevocable for at least ten years (unless the beneficiary and/or

remaindermen die), after which time it is revocable; during the irrevocable period, it is not part of the donor's estate.

Revocable trust A trust subject to change, amendment, modification, or cancellation by the grantor; the assets remain a part of the donor's taxable estate but pass through to the beneficiary without going through probate at the time of the grantor's death.

Revolving account Any charge account where the user has the option to pay the bill in full or spread repayment over several months.

Revolving savings fund A variable expense classification in budgeting into which funds are allocated; done to create a savings amount that can be used to balance the budget in months when expenses exceed income and prohibit the individual or family from running out of money.

Rider See *Endorsement.*

Right A legal instrument to purchase a number of shares of company stock at a specific price during a limited time period.

Right of curtesy A widower's lifetime right to a portion of his wife's property that she acquires during the marriage, usually one-third.

Right of dower A widow's lifetime right to a portion of her husband's property that he acquires during the marriage, usually one-third.

Right-to-use purchase A purchase of limited, preplanned time to use a vacation property, which is actually a vacation license as it does not grant true legal real estate ownership interests to the purchaser but instead provides a long-term lease or other contract permitting use of a hotel, suite, condominium apartment, or other housing accommodation.

Risk In insurance, the uncertainty about whether a financial loss will occur; in an investment, the uncertainty that the yield will deviate from what is expected.

Risk averse Opposed to risk; efforts are made to avoid it wherever possible.

Risk management A process of identifying and analyzing each risky situation to determine the best means available to manage it.

Risk neutral Adjective describing persons who neither fear nor enjoy risk but view it in an objective rational manner with an eye toward its control when beneficial and feasible.

Risk takers People who are not upset by uncertainty and may even enjoy risky situations.

Round lot A block of stock of one hundred shares.

Rule of 78s A method of calculating rebates of finance charges and the prepayment penalty charged the borrower who pays off an installment loan early.

Safe-deposit boxes Secured lock boxes available for rent in banks and used for keeping valuables.

Salary reduction plan An employer-sponsored retirement savings plan in which employees divert a portion of their salary to a tax-sheltered savings account, where it accumulates interest tax-free.

Sales contract See **Purchase contract.**

Sales finance companies Seller-related lenders who are primarily engaged in financing the sales of their parent companies.

Savings and loan association (S&L) A financial institution whose primary purpose is to accept savings and to provide home loans.

Savings investment A type of investment in which the saver expects virtually no risk for either the principal or the interest.

Secondary market A market where the trading of previously purchased securities occurs.

Second mortgage A loan on a residence in addition to the original mortgage; in case of default, what is owed on the original mortgage is paid first.

Secured bond A bond for which the issuing corporation pledges specific assets as collateral in the indenture or has the principal and interest guaranteed by another corporation or government agency.

Secured loan A loan that requires that certain assets (collateral) be pledged to secure the debt or the assurance of another person (cosigner), who will agree to pay the loan should the borrower fail to do so.

Securities Negotiable instruments of ownership or debt.

Securities market indexes Indexes that measure the value of a number of securities chosen as a sample to reflect the behavior of the general market of investments.

Security agreement The section of a retail installment contract or other credit agreement that gives the lender a legally secure interest in the item being financed.

Security deposit An amount paid in advance to a landlord to pay for refurbishing the unit beyond what would be expected from normal wear and tear; sometimes charged in addition to prepayment of the last month's rent.

Security interest A lender's control over property: when a loan is secured with collateral, security interest gives the creditor the right to go to court to obtain possession of the property in the event the borrower defaults.

Seller financing Arrangements under which the seller of a home agrees to lend the buyer some or all of the purchase price.

Selling short A trading technique by which investors sell a security they do not own (by borrowing it from a broker) and later buy a like amount of the same security at, it is hoped, a lower price (and return it to the broker), thus earning a profit on the transaction.

Senior debenture A type of bond giving all holders a right to all assets not pledged to secured bondholders.

Separable property Property wholly owned by one spouse, even in community property states, which belonged to the spouse before marriage or was received as a gift or an inheritance.

Series EE savings bond A U.S. government bond purchased for 50 percent of its face value. At maturity, it is worth its face value.

Series HH savings bond A U.S. government bond purchased at face value that pays semiannual interest until maturity five years later.

Service contract An agreement between the contract seller and the buyer of a product to provide free or nearly free repair services to covered components of the product for a specified time period.

Service credit Credit extended by professionals such as doctors, dentists, and lawyers, who expect full payment soon after the service is performed.

Settlement options The choices available to the life insurance beneficiary and/or the insured concerning the form of payment of the death benefit of a life insurance policy.

Share draft A document, much like a check, used by credit unions to process withdrawals from an interest-bearing share account.

Shareholder See **Stockholder.**

Short-term capital gain (or loss) A gain or loss occurring when the capital asset has been held for six months or less at the time of sale.

Short-term goals or objectives Needs and wants requiring financial resources that can be satisfied within one year.

Short-term investor An investor who is speculative or moderately speculative and wants to earn quick profits (over a period of months, weeks, days, or even hours) on small but significant changes in prices of securities.

Simple interest Interest earned each period that is withdrawn from an account and not reinvested.

Simplified employee pension plan (SEP) A special retirement plan for the self-employed and their employees that permits contributions from each.

Single-family dwelling A housing unit detached from others.

Single life annuity An annuity that covers the life of a single annuitant.

Single premium annuity An annuity purchased with a single lump-sum payment.

Sinking fund A requirement in a bond indenture that monies be set aside each year to repay the debt.

Small-business investment company A corporation licensed by the federal Small Business Administration to provide venture capital to small businesses.

Small claims court A state court with no written record of testimony, where civil matters are often resolved without the assistance of attorneys, providing that the legal amount claimed is less than a generally low maximum set in each state. Also called *court not of record*.

Social Security disability income insurance Insurance that provides benefits that will help replace the lost income of eligible disabled workers during a period of disability that is expected to last twelve full months or until death.

Social Security survivors' benefits Payments by the Social Security Administration to the family of the deceased; the level of benefits is based on the amount of Social Security taxes paid by the deceased.

Sole proprietorship A business owned by one person who is responsible for and has control over all aspects of the operation.

Specialty fund A mutual fund created for just about any investment need that requires both concentration and diversification in a field.

Speculative investment An investment transaction involving considerable risk of loss for the chance of large gains.

Speculative risk Risk that exists when there is potential for gain as well as loss.

Speculative stock A stock whose earnings record has been spotty but apparently has a potential for substantial earnings sometime in the future, even though such earnings may or may not be realized.

Spread The difference between the purchase price paid by an investment banking firm and expected resale price of a new issue of stock.

Standard deduction The amount all taxpayers, except some dependents, may deduct when filing an income tax return; the government's legally permissible estimate of a person's tax-deductible expenses.

Stated interest rate (bonds) A fixed interest rate printed on the bond certificate. Also called *coupon* or *nominal rate*.

Stated rate (credit) The rate of interest quoted by lenders when asked the rate of interest on a loan or charge account. By law, this rate must be the same as the annual percentage rate (APR).

Stated rate of interest (savings) The apparent interest rate that is applied to savings deposits before consideration of the time period. Also called *nominal rate of interest*.

Statement of earnings The Social Security Administration's record of each individual's lifetime earnings covered under Social Security regulations.

Sticker price The manufacturer's suggested price for a new car and its options as listed on the window sticker.

Stockbroker A person who acts as a middleman in buying and selling securities and who collects a commission on each purchase or sale. (Also known as an *account executive* or a *registered representative*.)

Stock certificate Evidence of a common or preferred shareholder's ownership of a company in which he or she has invested.

Stock dividend An issuance of new stock certificates to existing stockholders on the basis of current proportional ownership.

Stockholder The owner of common stock. Also called a *shareholder*.

Stock insurance companies Companies owned by stockholders that provide insurance coverage in return for the opportunity to earn a profit for their owners.

Stock option A contract giving the holder the right to buy or sell a specific number of shares (normally one hundred) of a certain stock at a particular price (the *striking price*) before a specified date (the *expiration date*).

Stocks Shares of ownership in the assets, earnings, and future direction of a corporate form of business.

Stock split A trade of a given number of old shares of stock for a certain number of newly issued shares.

Stop-loss order See **Stop order**.

Stop order Instructions to the stockbroker to sell at the next available opportunity when a stock reaches or drops below a specified price. Also called a *stop-loss order*.

Stop-payment order A notice assuring that a check will not be honored and cashed when presented to the drawer's financial institution.

Straddle The act of writing both puts and calls on an asset at the same striking price in order to offset speculative risk.

Straight bankruptcy A type of bankruptcy in which all debts are wiped out once the designated bankruptcy trustee has listed the debts and determined that it would be highly unlikely that substantial repayment could be made.

Straight life (pure) annuity An annuity that pays a fixed amount every month until the annuitant's death.

Subleasing Leasing of property by the original tenant to another tenant.

Subordinate budgets A method of budget control that requires explicit details for particular expense categories within the budget.

Subordinated debenture A bond that gives holders a lesser claim to assets perhaps similar to those of the stockholders.

Subrogation rights Rights that allow an insurer to take action against a negligent third party (and that party's insurance company) to obtain reimbursement for payments made to an insured.

Suicide clause A clause that allows the life insurance company to deny coverage if the insured commits suicide within the first few years after issuance of the policy.

Super NOW account A government-insured high-interest NOW account offered through depository institutions. The initial minimum deposit ranges from $1,000 to $2,500, and yields are calculated weekly or monthly.

Supplemental health insurance A form of health insurance designed to fill the gaps in coverage of the standard health insurance plans or provide reimbursement in addition to that provided by the standard plans.

Supplemental security income (SSI) A federal program to provide limited monetary benefits for those of very little financial means.

Surgical insurance A health insurance plan designed to protect the insured from the expenses of surgical procedures.

Sweep account An account that combines a regular NOW account with a money market fund and is offered through various institutions. An investor's money flows between the NOW account and the money market fund, depending on the balance in the account, with a goal of maximizing interest earnings.

Swingers Stocks and warrants that have gone up and down the most in the past week based on a percentage of change.

Switching (exchange) privilege A privilege for mutual fund shareholders that permits them, if their needs or objectives change, to swap shares on a dollar-for-dollar basis for shares in another mutual fund managed by the same corporation.

Tangible assets Physical items that have fairly long life spans and could be sold to raise cash but whose primary purpose is to provide maintenance of a lifestyle.

Taxable income The amount of income upon which taxes are finally assessed after subtracting a variety of adjustments, deductions, and exemptions from a total gross income.

Tax audit A formal examination of a taxpayer's tax forms for accuracy and completeness conducted by the IRS.

Tax avoidance An attempt to avoid paying taxes by reducing tax liability through legal techniques.

Tax credits A group of items that can be deducted dollar for dollar against one's tax liability.

Tax-deductible expenditure record The written record of all income tax-deductible expenditures by date, amount paid and to whom, and tax classification.

Taxes Compulsory charges imposed by a government on citizens and property.

Tax evasion An illegal process that involves deliberately hiding income, falsely claiming deductions, or otherwise cheating the government out of taxes owed.

Tax-free exchange A transaction in which none of the people involved in a trade of property receives any other form of property or money.

Tax liability The actual tax owed on income earned during the previous year.

Tax loss A "paper" loss, created when deductions generated from an investment exceed the income from an investment.

Tax preparation services Companies that help individuals or businesses list appropriate deductions, compute accurately, and determine proper tax liability when preparing tax forms.

Tax-sheltered annuity An annuity used to defer income subject to taxation until the funds in the annuity are withdrawn.

Tax-sheltered (qualified) retirement plan A financial plan approved by the IRS for special tax advantages that reduces taxes and increases retirement benefits.

Tenancy in common A type of direct ownership in which two or more people have control of a property regardless of whether they hold equal shares, and each person retains the right to dispose of his or her undivided interest.

10-K report A comprehensive document filed with the SEC by a corporation; it contains much of the same type of information as a prospectus or annual report and provides additional updated financial details about corporate activities.

Term life insurance A type of life insurance contract that pays benefits only if the insured party dies within the time period of the contract.

Testamentary trust A trust that is established and becomes effective upon the death of the grantor according to the terms written in the grantor's will.

Testate Adjective describing a person who dies with a valid will in effect.

Testator A person who makes a will.

Thirty-day account An account in which debts incurred are expected to be paid in full within thirty days.

Time deposit A savings account deposit in an institution that is expected to remain on deposit for an extended period and is a legal debt upon which the institution must pay interest as specified.

Time period limits Clauses in health insurance policies that specify the maximum payment to be made for covered expenses occurring within a specified time period, usually one year.

Time value of money The concept applied in the comparison and prediction of the present and future values of an asset.

Title The legal right of ownership interest in real property.

Title insurance Insurance required of home buyers by lenders, to protect against the possibility that the title later will be found faulty.

Title search An attorney's examination of the abstract and other documents in order to establish the status of a title of real estate.

Total disability An injury or illness that prevents a worker from performing any of the tasks of his or her previous occupation or any other occupation.

Total return The combination of the dividend yield and the potential capital gains on an investment.

Totten trust A trust that is typically a savings account opened at a financial institution where money is deposited in trust for a beneficiary (usually a loved one) while the grantor maintains control over the account, including the power of withdrawal.

Trade association An organization representing the interests of companies in the same industry.

Transaction costs Fees charged by the broker and the seller to pay for the expenses of transferring ownership of an investment.

Transfer payments Payments by governments and individuals for which no goods or services are expected in return, such as welfare payments.

Travel and entertainment account A special type of charge account used primarily by business people for food and lodging expenses while traveling, generally requiring the entire balance charged to be repaid within thirty days.

Traveler's checks Checks issued as a cash substitute by large financial institutions and sold through smaller institutions such as a local bank or credit union.

Treasury bill (T-bill) A U.S. government security that matures in ninety-one days, six months, nine months, or 360 days. It is sold on a "discount basis," with the gain at maturity representing interest for federal income-tax purposes.

Treasury bond A U.S. government security that is sold in $1,000 and $10,000 denominations, with a maturity of more than ten years and a semiannual fixed interest rate higher than a Treasury note because it is a longer-term issue.

Treasury note A U.S. government security sold in $1,000 and $10,000 denominations, with a maturity of one to ten years, and a semiannual fixed interest rate slightly higher than a Treasury bill.

Triple witching hour The time that occurs four times each year when stock options, stock index options, and stock index futures all expire at once.

Trust A legal instrument that places control of one's assets with a trustee.

Trustee account An account that restricts a child from withdrawing money from the account without a responsible adult's signature.

Underwriting The insurer's process of deciding which insurance applicants to accept.

Unearned income Income from rents, dividends, interest, royalties, and transfer payments.

Uninsured motorist insurance Automobile insurance that protects the insured driver and passengers from bodily injury losses (and, in a few states, property damage losses) resulting from an auto accident caused by an uninsured motorist.

Unit investment trust A closed-end investment company in which the proceeds from the sale of original shares are invested in a fixed portfolio of taxable or tax-exempt bonds and held until maturity.

Universal life insurance A type of life insurance that provides both the pure protection and cash value build-up of whole life insurance but with variability in the face amount, rate of cash value accumulation, premiums, and rate of return.

Unsecured bond A bond that has no collateral named as security for the debt and is backed only by the good faith and reputation of the issuing agency.

Unsecured loan A loan that has the assurance of neither collateral nor a cosigner.

U.S. Treasury note See *Treasury note.*

Usury laws Legal interest-rate maximums that can be charged by lenders.

Variable annuity An annuity for which the payments to an individual vary upward or downward according to the success of the insurance company's investments.

Variable expenses Expenditures over which an individual has considerable control.

Variable interest rate An interest rate on a credit card or other instrument that moves up or down monthly according to changes in an index of the lender's cost of funds.

Variable life insurance A cash value insurance policy that allows policyholders to choose the investments made with their cash value accumulations and to share in the gains and losses of those investments.

Variable-universal life insurance A form of universal life insurance that allows the policyholder to choose the investments made with the cash value accumulated by the policy.

Variance analysis The comparison of actual expenditures with budgeted estimates.

Vesting A process by which employees obtain during their working years a legal claim on retirement benefits that cannot be taken away if they resign or are dismissed.

Veterans Administration (VA) A federal government agency that promotes home ownership

among veterans by providing the lender with a guarantee against buyer default.

Veteran's Administration hospitals Medical care facilities designed exclusively to provide care to veterans.

Voluntary accumulation plan A way of purchasing shares in an open-end mutual fund with a brokerage firm (for load funds) or the investment company itself (for load and no-load funds) by opening an account and investing on a regular basis.

Voting rights The proportionate authority of common stock owners to express an opinion or choice in matters affecting the company.

Wage-earner plan A plan designed for those filing bankruptcy who might be able to pay off their debts given certain protections of the court.

Waiver-of-premium option An option that allows the policyholder to keep a life insurance policy in force without having to pay premiums.

Wants Items people would like to have to improve their comfort and satisfaction.

Warrant A legal option that gives the holder the opportunity to buy a certain number of shares of a bond, preferred stock, or some issues of common stock at a specified price over a designated period. Also called a *purchase warrant.*

Warranty An assurance by a seller to a buyer that goods are as promised.

Warranty insurance Insurance sold through builders and real estate brokers to provide warranty protection for home buyers.

Week order Instructions to a stockbroker that are valid until the close of the trading on Friday of the current week.

Whole life insurance A type of cash value life insurance that provides life insurance protection for the lifetime of the insured and requires the payment of premiums for life.

Will A written instrument that directs the disposition of an individual's assets at death, but only if it is executed in accordance with statutory provisions.

Worker's compensation insurance Insurance that protects employers from liability for any injury or disease suffered by employees and resulting from employment related causes.

Yield (rate of return) The profitability of an investment described as a percentage over a certain time period, usually a year.

Yield to maturity (YTM) The total annual rate of return earned by a bondholder on a bond when it is held to maturity; it reflects both the current income and any difference if the bond was purchased at a price other than face value.

Zero coupon bonds Municipal or corporate bonds issued at prices far lower than their face value; they pay no interest income. The return to the investor comes solely from redeeming them at their face value or selling them for a price higher than what was paid.

Zero-sum game An investment situation in which the total wealth of all traders remains the same, as the trading simply redistributes the wealth among the traders.

Index

Note: Key terms and the numbers of pages on which they are defined are set in boldface type.